Understanding Human Adjustment

Understanding

Human Adjustment

Normal Adaptation
Through the Life Cycle

Douglas H. Powell

Harvard University

Little, Brown and Company   Boston   Toronto

Library of Congress Cataloging in Publication Data

Powell, Douglas H.
    Understanding human adjustment.

    Bibliography: p.
    Includes index.
    1. Adjustment (Psychology) 2. Developmental
psychology. 3. Mental health. I. Title.
BF335.P68 1983   155   82-18029
ISBN 0-316-71549-2

Library of Congress Catalog Card No. 82-18029

ISBN 0-316-71549-2

9   8   7   6   5   4   3   2   1

MV

Published simultaneously in Canada
by Little, Brown & Company (Canada) Limited
Printed in the United States of America

ACKNOWLEDGEMENTS

Picture research by Pembroke Herbert/Picture Research Consultants

The author gratefully acknowledges permission to use material from the following sources.

Photo credits
Chapter 1: Page 7, Sepp Seitz/Woodfin Camp; page 12,

Part I, page 2, copyright © by Walter S. Silver, 19. All rights reserved.
The Schlesinger Library; page 14, Terence Spencer, *Life* Magazine © Time, Inc.; page 15, Keystone-Mast Collection, California Museum of Photography; page 18, Abigail Heyman/Archive Pictures.
Chapter 2: Page 28, Peter Vandermark; page 31, Peter Vandermark; page 48, Jerry H. Gerling/*The Advocates;*
(Acknowledgments continued on page 472.)

To Virginia,
without whom—

Preface

Our lives often seem filled with "one darn thing after another." How we adjust to these daily hassles or cope with more severe problems largely determines how happy we are. Successful adjustment to the stresses we meet throughout our lives is the topic of this introductory text in the psychology of adjustment.

Many excellent texts describe the processes of adjustment and maladjustment. This book emphasizes how people adjust *normally*. It examines the primary characteristics of normality, and how these qualities distinguish normality from other types of adjustment. We learn that normal people are much more diverse and have greater richness in their personalities than those who are maladjusted.

This is an exciting time to study the psychology of normality. Although teachers of courses in human adjustment, mental hygiene, and the life cycle have long been interested in the subject of well-being, little has been published until recently. But now, longitudinal research — some of it begun nearly half a century ago — is bearing fruit in the form of books and articles on normal adaptation through the life cycle. Recent cross-sectional studies of normal men and women supplement this research. With the present explosion of interest in the adult years, we recognize that identity crises, turmoil, and instability are not the special province of youth.

Reflecting the increased interest in the subject of normality is the number of organizations that are turning their attention to this field. The American Psychological Association has established a new division called Health Psychology; a California mental health organization is now issuing *The Wellness Resource Bulletin;* and in 1979, the Surgeon General of the United States published *Healthy People*, a report on how to maintain physical and mental health.

The new information about normal adjustment is an integral part of this book. It does not stand alone, however, but is woven into the topics that comprise older, familiar adjustment texts. An example is the description of high level, healthy self-protective responses to stress, such as anticipation and empathy, which are compared with lower level ego defenses, such as repression and denial.

Six basic themes underlie this book's portrayal of the process of normal adjustment throughout life.

□ *First,* the normal state remains the primary frame of reference throughout the text. Abnormal behavior and conditions are depicted as they contrast with normality.

□ *Second,* the life cycle perspective integrates the activities central to normal adjustment: work, love, and play.

□ *Third,* the text scrutinizes those reactions to stress and mental states that depart from normal but fall well short of mental disorders. One chapter describes temporary overload conditions and another explores crisis reactions.

□ *Fourth,* I draw heavily on more than two decades of experience as a working clinician, and I use case studies and examples liberally to illustrate theory. Though the cases and incidents are wholly fictitious, they are based on real people I have known.

□ *Fifth,* no particular "school" of psychology is espoused — or denied. This text throughout examines contributions from the constitutional, psychoanalytic, behavioral, humanistic, and cognitive traditions.

□ *Sixth,* the ideas central to this book are drawn from three foundations — philosophy, clinical reports, and scientific evidence. When the wisdom of philosophers and clinicians throughout history is validated by up-to-date psychological research, we can have greater confidence in the accuracy of their time-tested wisdom.

Organization

The book is divided into four parts. "Toward a Theory of Normal Adaptation," Part I, begins by defining normality. Chapter 2 discusses the nature of stress and its negative and positive effects on us. How we handle stress and the effectiveness of different adaptive responses is the subject of Chapter 3. This first section ends with Chapter 4, a portrayal of normal personality styles, which are rich in their diversity.

Part II is "Work, Love, and Play in the Life Cycle." Chapter 5 examines three realities of the life cycle: the universal experience of alternating periods of stability and instability, the limited impact of earlier events on later growth, and the differing life cycle experiences of men and women. The remaining chapters look at normal working, loving, and playing activities for each stage of the life span. Typical hazards that can compromise satisfaction from each sphere of life are identified, and consideration is given to how we might avoid or cope with these threats.

"States of Adaptation" is the title of Part III. The chapters in this section portray mental conditions ranging from normal to neurotic disorders. Chapter 9 describes the process of normal adaptation, reviewing the key concepts from the previous sections. Next is examined State 2, the temporary overload conditions that occur when we are under agreeable, time-limited stress. Crisis reactions, State 3, follow — the complex, painful responses to severe trauma or loss. The section ends with Chapter 12, a look into neurotic disorders. These maladjustments feature symptoms without an obvious cause; for example, phobias and continuing oppositional behavior of youngsters. The primary and secondary features associated with each of these states of adjustment are outlined, and ways of helping to maintain or restore normal adaptation are examined.

"Guidelines for Living," Part IV, begins with a look at the road beyond college graduation. Chapter 13 addresses the influence of sex, socioeconomic background, and race on chances of getting ahead. Then it looks at ways of maintaining self-esteem and personal effectiveness. The final chapter presents ten guidelines for living drawn from the wisdom of scholars and clinicians over the ages, to help each of us enhance the quality of our lives.

Each of the book's fourteen chapters offer several learning aids to stimulate interest and thought, as well as to ease comprehension of the material. Every chapter begins with (1) boxed anecdotes, songs, quotations, and case examples, taken from diverse sources, that highlight a central theme; (2) questions to help the reader relate key concepts to personal experience as well as arouse enthusiasm about the subject; and (3) a detailed outline that both anticipates the chapter content and simplifies the process of review. At the close of each chapter a summary and a list of key terms are designed to assist in the understanding of the major points. Finally, suggested readings are presented, organized around particular concepts, such as normality, the life cycle, or stress.

Acknowledgments

Particular groups and individuals have been especially helpful in listening to and criticizing my ideas. Chief among them are my friends and colleagues at the Harvard University Health Services — most especially Warren Wacker, Harry K. Oliver Professor, who has been resolutely supportive and unfailingly encouraging; the faculty of the Northfield Counseling Institute — Stanley King, Graham Blaine, Jr., Jane Leavy, Preston Munter, Janet Sand, and Paul Walters, Jr.; members of Lowell House Senior Common Room; the selection committee and Fellows of the Michael C. Rockefeller Scholarship; the Lawrence University Class of 1956; and the staff at Powell Associates.

Specialized help was gratefully received from Earl Bracker, Concord physician and jogging partner, who has heard much of this text gasped in his ear during our runs; from the remarkable people in the Harvard University and Concord library systems, especially Veronica Cunningham, Assunta Pisani, and Natalie Schatz; from the Mandrake Bookstore of Harvard Square; and from Robert J. Lurtsema of WGBH who soothed my mornings with music and gentle humor.

This text has been greatly enhanced by the thoughtful comments by professors at other universities who have read all or much of this manuscript. They include: Benton E. Allen, Mt. San Antonio College; James J. Berry, Oakland Community College; Barbara Brackney, Eastern Michigan University; Dennis L. Coon, Santa Barbara City College; James Daley, Diablo Valley College; Ronald G. Evans, Washington University of Topeka; Fred S. Fehr, Arizona State University; Bess Fleckman, Miami-Dade Community College; Lawrence C. Grebstein, University of Rhode Island; Harvey A. Katz, Suffolk University; Benjamin B. Lahey, University of Georgia; Connie Mantz, Cerritos College; Robert A. Osterhouse, Prince George's Community College; Joan A. Royce, Riverside City Community College; Alexandra K. Schiller, Western New England College; Thomas L. Weaver, Central Florida Community College; and David G. Weight, Brigham Young University.

Space does not permit the acknowledgment of all of the friends and colleagues, clients and patients, and teachers and students who have shared their ideas or portions of their lives with me, and thus have enriched this book enormously. Mention must be made, however, of Timothy Baehr, Pembroke Herbert, and Laurel Anderson; Ann Bisbee, Winthrop Burr, Randolph Catlin, James Gill, Pamela Hinkson, Robert Tonis, and Raymond Walther; Richard Bauer, Charles Brookes, and Edwin Richards; and John Finley, Peter Gomes, Patricia and Richard Light, Zeph Stewart, and Robert White. Three men who have been mentors to me require special mention: Charles McArthur, Henry Babcock, and George Goethals. Their teaching and encouragement have provided a growing season of more than two decades.

The manuscript would never have appeared in book form had it not been for the valuable help of five especially sturdy individuals. At Little, Brown, developmental editor Janet Beatty assisted in a remarkable salvage operation of several chapters. Book editor Cynthia Chapin smoothly orchestrated the construction of the final project. Much of the quality and finish of this text is due to the ceaseless effort of these estimable women. Jeff McConnell reacquainted me with classical philosophy and compiled much of the glossary. Psychology professor, neighbor, and teaching partner, Robert Furey, wrote most of the teacher's guide. Jo Ann Share prepared the final draft of the manuscript, constructed figures and tables, and alerted me to specific concerns of women.

D. H. P.
September, 1982
Concord, Massachusetts

Contents

Part II
Work, Love, and Play in the Life Cycle   121

Part III
States of Adaptation   273

Chapter 11: State 3: Crisis Reactions   327

Part IV
Implications for the Life Cycle   **399**

Part I
Toward a Theory of Normal Adaptation

Part I, the first of four major divisions of this book, identifies the essentials of normal adaptation. In Chapter 1, we consider the reasons for studying normal adaptation and move on to discuss the inadequacies of several definitions of normality. Then, based on recent studies of normal people, a definition of normal adaptation is presented.

Normality is easily disrupted by stress and restored by effective means of managing stress. Chapter 2 addresses the nature of stress, paying particular attention to its causes. We study the psychological and physical effects of stress, with particular attention to the positive benefits of manageable stress. The major theories of stress are examined. In Chapter 3, we explore the

nature of adaptation. Then we turn our attention to three ways of adapting to stress: (1) self-protective responses, automatic mental processes that diminish our experience of stress; (2) direct control responses, willful means of controlling stress; and (3) direct action responses, behaviors reducing the sources of stress.

Part I ends with a portrayal of normal personality styles. We look at two major ways in which temperament has been classified in the twentieth century. Then we study new developments in thinking about personality style that recognize the importance of constitution and environment. Using this body of work as a background, six normal personality styles are portrayed.

In spite of the vagueness of these concepts and the uncertainty of the fundamental principles upon which judgment is based, we cannot in practical life do without the distinction between normal and pathological.

SOURCE: S. Freud and W. Bullitt, *Thomas Woodrow Wilson: A psychological study*, Boston: Houghton Mifflin, 1967, p. xvi.

Chapter Preview

CHAPTER 1
What Is Normality?

Questions to think about

- ☐ Do you think you're normal?
- ☐ How did you decide?
- ☐ Have you felt sometimes that you were definitely not normal?
- ☐ What is the difference between normal and abnormal?

These are simple questions, but as we all have discovered, they are not so easy to answer. This is a book about normal behavior. In this chapter and in the ones that follow in Part I normality will be defined, and we will see how stresses and reactions to them affect normal adjustment. Then in Part II we will look at how different stages of the life cycle bring surprises or predictable problems that can upset our emotional balance. In Part III various stages of adaptation — ranging from normal to not normal — will be studied. Finally, in Part IV we will consider how what we have learned can contribute to a life of less dissatisfaction, more pleasure, and a better chance of realizing our dreams.

In this chapter we think together about why we should study normal adaptation. Then we turn our attention to three primary ways normality has been described in the past, all of which are unsatisfactory for our present purpose. We then examine the reasons why defining the normal condition has been so hard. Using reports of life cycle research, we arrive at a definition of normal adaptation. This definition emphasizes the importance of satisfaction from a balance of work, love and play, coping effectively with stress, and using resources.

Why Study Normal Adaptation?

Why should you study **normal adaptation?** * Will it help you get a good job? Will it make you more attractive to others? Will it make you happy? No, it won't do any of these. But knowing about the normal condition can help you in some other important ways. First, it can aid you in living a more satisfactory life. You may already know that a good job or being attractive are no guarantee of happiness. Second, knowing about normal adjustment can help you manage stress more effectively. Life tends to be one thing after another. How you cope with stressful events makes a difference in the quality of your life. Third, you can learn the difference between normal and abnormal. Is your little brother who is crazy about punk rock in fact crazy or just going through a phase? And what about your best friend, who is beginning to seem very weird?

Let's examine these reasons for studying normal adaptation in slightly more detail. The first reason to know about normality is to assist us in having a more satisfactory and enjoyable life. If we are aware of the essential ingredients of a normal existence, we can seek these for ourselves. This knowledge also may help us understand the adjustment of those we care about and consider what assistance might be beneficial to them. Those of us who are — or expect to be — parents, or whose intended careers involve caring for children, may find some of the guidelines for living, which come from understanding normal adaptation, useful in directing the generation that follows. If we have a clearer concept of the elements that affect the growth and maintenance of normal adjustment, we can care for ourselves and others with a greater sense of purpose.

The second reason for knowing about normal adaptation is to enable us to learn how to cope more effectively with problems in our lives. Normality is not a snapshot, but rather a moving picture. A critical element in normal behavior is how we respond to stress. We need to be able to reduce the discomfort associated with our immediate reaction to an unpleasant event — for instance, panic at the thought of the first test in this course. But we also need to lower the discomfort without hurting ourselves in other ways — "forgetting" about it or getting drunk instead of studying for the test. In this course we will learn to identify stress and recognize more and less effective ways of dealing with it.

The third reason for learning about normal adjustment is to be able to

---

* For now, the terms normal adaptation, normality, normal adjustment, and the normal condition will be used to mean the same thing. There are minor differences among them that will be explored later.

Differences between one person and another can be hard to identify at first glance. Yet, they may be very important. Can you see differences in these students that might influence how much they will learn in their class?

make more accurate and useful distinctions between normal and abnormal behavior. This is harder than it first appears. Anxiety, depression, conflict, and that feeling that nothing makes sense anymore are typical of people with an emotional disorder. But all of us experience these same emotions from time to time. Your little brother and your best friend both may be intense and moody, dress strangely, be indifferent about school and disagreeable at home, and speak in ways that you have difficulty following. How can you tell that your brother will be fine but your best friend may need help badly?

The differences between normal adjustment and mental disorder often are very subtle. But, as doctor-philosopher William James (1896, pp. 256–257) put it: "There is very little difference between one man and another; but what little difference there is, *is very important.*" Much of this book is devoted to an examination of those "little differences" that alert you to what is normal adaptation and what is madness.

What Is Normal Behavior?

Different opinions exist about what is considered normal. Some informal definitions include notions of "happiness"; others include "maturity." This person calls normality "naturalness," another "following God's will," and someone else "feeling whole." Problems exist with each of these definitions.

Happiness is transient because sorrow invades all of our lives from time to time. Maturity is synonymous with "ripeness," which does not take into account the reality of continuing growth. Though many long for the natural existence of the noble savage, the simple life has its problems too. Many of us have significantly different understandings of God's will. Finally, will those who feel "whole" exempt from normal those of us who are sure we are flawed?

Three more formal ways of thinking about normal behavior are the *mental health*, *statistical* and *ideal* perspectives (Offer and Sabshin, 1974).

The Mental Health Perspective

A synonym for normalcy might be **mental health.** Mental health is usually defined as the absence of illness. This way of looking at mental health is based on a medical model. The patient who comes to the doctor and does not have a diagnosable illness is said to be physically normal. Similarly, someone who does not have a diagnosable mental illness is said to be mentally healthy. This is a little like describing light as the absence of darkness.

The medical model, which has been so successful in identifying signs of physical illness, doesn't work as well for diagnosing emotional disorders. The most recent catalogue of emotional disturbances — the third edition of the *Diagnostic and Statistical Manual*, called the **DSM-III,** published by the American Psychiatric Association (1980) — contains too many conditions that are not clear-cut maladjustments. The difficulty in using it to define normality is that it is too inclusive, diagnosing as evidence of mental disorder too many personal quirks, variations in aptitude, motivation, and ways of handling stress. For example, temper tantrums and stubbornness in a two-year-old, academic underachievement in school-age youngsters, and adult dependence on coffee and tobacco are listed as disorders in the DSM-III. These are widely shared behaviors and are no more likely to be symptoms of emotional maladjustment than acne or being twenty pounds overweight. Because it encompasses so much, it blurs the distinctions between legitimate mental disorders and variations within the normal personality.

The Statistical Perspective

The **statistical perspective** is another way to define normality. It assumes that normal people are those in the middle, at neither one extreme nor the other. Statisticians and psychologists have come to assume that any human characteristic which can be measured (height, weight, reaction time, or intelligence, for example) will be distributed "normally." A **normal distribution** is a statistical concept. In a normal distribution, the greatest number of individual scores or measures cluster around the average score. Relatively few individual scores are very high or very low. The scores, when plotted on a graph, form a **normal curve** with its characteristic bell-like shape. Figure 1.1 shows that I.Q. scores among almost 3000 children fall close to the expectation of a normal distribution. In the top half of Figure 1.1, a bell-shaped curve shows a theoretical

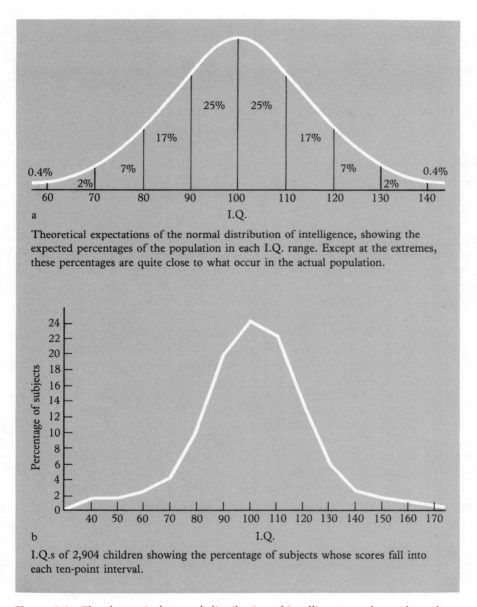

a   I.Q.

Theoretical expectations of the normal distribution of intelligence, showing the expected percentages of the population in each I.Q. range. Except at the extremes, these percentages are quite close to what occur in the actual population.

b   I.Q.

I.Q.s of 2,904 children showing the percentage of subjects whose scores fall into each ten-point interval.

Figure 1.1   The theoretical normal distribution of intelligence and actual results

normal distribution. In the bottom half, the plotting of actual I.Q. scores bears a close resemblance to the theoretical curve.

Is it reasonable to assume that people in the middle are closest to normal, and those toward the ends of these bell-shaped curves abnormal? Probably not. This is because being at one extreme or the other in *some characteristics* can be a great advantage in *some situations*. Consider an ambitious young man who reads rapidly with good comprehension. He has an edge over a roommate with average ambition and reading ability — *provided both are college students*. Should they both be construction workers, the opposite could be true.

The Ideal Perspective

This notion is the opposite of the absence-of-disease conception of normality. Instead of diagnosing us as healthy by ruling out illness, this view lists particular characteristics of someone who is well adjusted. It is a positive statement about what robust mental health is. In most cases, this turns out to be what normality *should be*, which is why it is called the "ideal" view. An example is the list of general features put forward by Marie Jahoda (1958), a pioneer in thinking about positive mental health, to identify well-functioning people. Such people should: (1) understand and accept themselves realistically; (2) view the surrounding world accurately; (3) be free of inner conflicts and be able to manage stress effectively; (4) develop basic physical, intellectual, and social competencies in order to master the environment; (5) possess self-reliance and the awareness of what they want from life; and (6) emphasize the development of potential and move toward self-fulfillment.

Another ideal view of normality is illustrated by Abraham Maslow's description of the self-actualizing person (1962, 1970). Maslow believed that each of us has five basic needs, which follow a developmental sequence, pictured in Figure 1.2. As Figure 1.2 illustrates, human needs are arranged in ascending order from physiological to self-actualizing needs. Maslow thought that the lowest level of unsatisfied need is always dominant. Only when it is fulfilled do we turn our attention to the next higher one.

Each of us has **physiological needs** that must be met to support life itself — oxygen, water, food, shelter, activity, and rest. Only after these basic needs are gratified do **safety needs** become important, such as protection against physical harm. Parents safeguard their youngsters by not allowing them to swallow nails, bleach, or leaded paint, and protect them from playing on fire escapes or inside refrigerators. Gradually, young people are taught to care for themselves — looking both ways before crossing the street, putting a raincoat on when it's raining, eating balanced meals, and locking the door at night.

Love and belonging needs become prominent only when the two needs below them are satisfied. In this category is the desire to be the object of affection of others — parents, relatives, friends, and special loved ones. As we grow we develop to be part of a small group within society. This can be as a family member, in a gang at school, on a bowling team, or as a member of a church or social club.

Esteem needs rest on the base provided when our physiological, safety, and love and belonging requirements are fulfilled. This is the capacity to feel useful and demonstrate competence in various endeavors. It is the ability to do something to please ourselves. This might be learning to read or reading for pleasure, earning a passing grade in Latin, or figuring out how to do square roots. It can be making a lamp that works, dunking a basketball, or receiving a paycheck.

These first four needs are clear, and make common as well as psychological sense. At the peak of this hierarchy of needs is self-actualization. **Self-actualization** is described as:

> . . . ongoing actualization of potentials, capacities and talents, as fulfillment of mission (or a call, fate, destiny, or a vocation), as a fuller knowledge of,

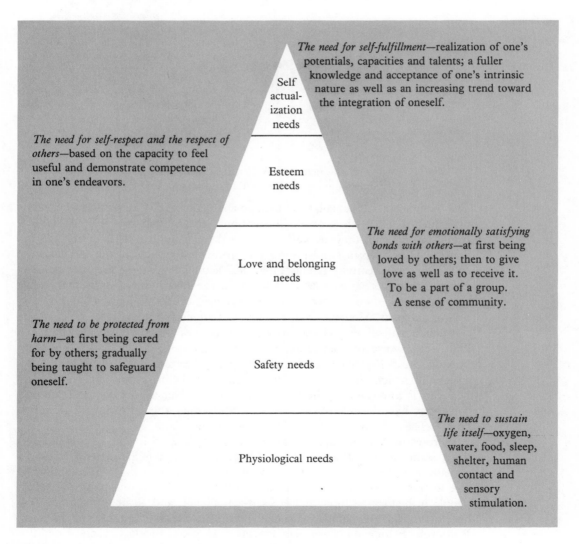

The need for self-fulfillment—realization of one's potentials, capacities and talents; a fuller knowledge and acceptance of one's intrinsic nature as well as an increasing trend toward the integration of oneself.

Self actualization needs

The need for self-respect and the respect of others—based on the capacity to feel useful and demonstrate competence in one's endeavors.

Esteem needs

Love and belonging needs

The need for emotionally satisfying bonds with others—at first being loved by others; then to give love as well as to receive it. To be a part of a group. A sense of community.

The need to be protected from harm—at first being cared for by others; gradually being taught to safeguard oneself.

Safety needs

Physiological needs

The need to sustain life itself—oxygen, water, food, sleep, shelter, human contact and sensory stimulation.

Figure 1.2   Maslow's hierarchy of human needs

A self-actualizing life. Amelia Earhart, first woman to solo the Atlantic, was lost attempting to fly around the world. In a poem published posthumously she wrote, "Courage is the price that life exacts for granting peace."

and acceptance of, the person's own intrinsic nature, as an unceasing trend toward unity, integration or synergy within the person. (Maslow, 1962, p. 25)

The qualities of self-actualization include a superior ability to see reality clearly, undisturbed by wishes or preconceptions. Self-actualizing individuals see problems for what they are and can solve them without disabling anxieties or doubts. They keep in mind the big picture while focusing on the ends as well as the means. Creativity is noticeable. Self-actualizing people are open to new experience and are spontaneous. They have a zest for living. Continuing freshness of appreciation for people and experiences causes their lives to be rarely dull or stagnant. Moments of great joy are frequently found.

Self-actualization is characterized by a sense of kinship with all of humankind. This sense of connection transcends national, racial, class, or ethnic boundaries. Self-actualizing people maintain a certain detachment from the society in which they are a member and resist being propagandized. Their behavior is governed by their own sense of a universal morality and justice. They may have a circle of close friends rather than a wider group of acquaintances. They are independent and can enjoy solitude.

Professor Maslow had an extremely high standard in mind when he defined someone as self-actualizing (White, 1972). Using his criteria for self-actualization, he said that he was able to identify self-actualizing people in only five to thirty percent of the population (1970, p. 44). At one point, he rated people in history he thought were self-actualizing, and all of these were over age forty. His list included Thomas Jefferson, Albert Einstein, and Eleanor Roosevelt. Falling short were Henry David Thoreau, Beethoven, and Franklin Roosevelt.

What is so compelling about the ideal view of normality represented by Maslow and Jahoda is the idealistic, upbeat notion of what human beings can become. The problem with this view is that it suggests what we should be, rather than how most normal people are.

None of these ways of viewing normalcy works particularly well. This is because each was designed for another purpose — diagnosing mental disorders, showing how human traits are distributed, or portraying an ideal state. Though they can be yoked into the task of illuminating some aspects of the normal condition, the light they provide is indirect.

Why Defining Normal Behavior Has Been So Hard

Two problems consistently have made it difficult to define normal behavior: emphasis on children and the effect of culture, race, and social class on expectations for normal behavior.

Little information has been published about normal behavior. What has been written focuses mostly on children. For example, Sigmund Freud was the first person in this century to offer a theory of human growth. His thinking about normal development was concerned primarily with infants and children. The books of his disciples devote most of their pages to infancy and childhood and fewest on the next fifty years of life.

Until recently, research studies of normal behavior have looked at younger people. An example is the work of physician Arnold Gesell. He founded the Yale Clinic of Child Development, which worked with normal youngsters for more than fifty years. The books published by this group include *The First Five Years of Life* (Gesell *et al.*, 1940), *The Child from Five to Ten* (Gesell and Ilg, 1946), and *Youth: The Years from Ten to Sixteen* (Gesell, 1956). As the titles of these books indicate, Gesell's interest was in child development, not growth through the life cycle. It has not been until the last decade that the same vigorous interest has been shown in the years of adulthood. We will turn to these recent studies in the next section.

A large problem in describing normal adjustment is the enormous difference in culture, race, and social class. Even in a single country such as the United States, the variations are huge. What is normal for one subgroup can be deviant for another. For example, desire for achievement — planning for the future, being successful in school and work, being independent, surpassing achievements of parents — is a highly prized value in many communities. Relations with family and loved ones often are sacrificed in these ambition-oriented families for the sake of moving "upward." By contrast, large numbers of other individuals are oriented toward getting along from day to day. They may be indifferent to school and far less willing to break away from friends and family to get ahead.

Differing attitudes about the value of getting ahead exist side by side in the same neighborhood. One investigation looked at two groups of high-school

Two groups of young people — skinheads and hippies — in Picadilly Circus, London, 1969. What is normal dress and behavior for one group is seen as deviant by the other.

boys with similar ability from similar working-class families (Kahl, 1953). The first group was planning to go to college, and the second was not. The difference between the two groups was in values held by their families. The parents of college-bound students were unhappy with their position in life, felt that their lack of education had limited their advancement, and were determined that their sons would not follow in their footsteps. By contrast, the parents of the boys not going to college were not dissatisfied with their attainment in life and saw little need for their children to attend college.

Differences in culture and race create differences in environment and reactions to it that result in different conceptions of normal behavior. For instance, the description of childhood in a Harlem ghetto in Claude Brown's compelling biography, *Manchild in a Promised Land* (1963), would have seemed bizarre to the Jews and Italians in the same generation in Chicago (Strodtbeck, 1958). Yet they were raised less than a thousand miles apart and at the same time.

Recent Life Cycle Research Findings Help Define Normal Adaptation

Until recently, researchers have not been much interested in normal adaptation. Prior to 1960 the number of significant studies of normal people could be counted on one hand. In the ten years before World War II a few hundred Ohio children around Antioch College, youngsters living in Oakland and Berkeley, California, and students at Harvard College were first examined as part of **longitudinal studies.** A longitudinal study follows the same group of individuals for a long period of time — for instance, from childhood or adolescence through the adult years. In the late 1940s, a longitudinal study was started with infants at the Menninger Foundation in Kansas.

In the past decade, these long-term projects have borne fruit. Psychologists have discovered that the personal stability of someone thirty, forty, or fifty has little similarity to that same person's psychological adjustment at six, twelve, or eighteen. Adults with the highest level of adaptation in their lives are often those who balance their working lives with satisfying loving relationships and recreational activities. How people cope with stressful events is a more important factor in determining emotional vitality than adversity itself (Elder, 1979; Vaillant, 1977; Murphy and Moriarty, 1976).

Along with the publication of these data, the first reports have appeared from new longitudinal investigations with students in the midwest and on both coasts. Among other intriguing findings is the observation that adolescence is not usually the period of turmoil and crisis it was once thought to be (Offer, and Offer, 1975; King, 1973; Katz, 1968).

Renewed interest in normal development also resulted in numerous **cross-sectional studies.** Cross-sectional research examines people at one particular stage of their life and compares them with other individuals at different stages. One such project examined men and women at four transitional periods — upon graduation from high school, when newlywed, when the children leave home, and just before retirement — to discover those factors associated with successful ways of coping with stresses accompanying these periods (Lowenthal *et al.*, 1976). In another cross-sectional study, a small number of men were interviewed at mid-life in order to better understand the alternating periods of stability and instability males go through in the adult years (Levinson *et al.*, 1978).

The investigators are the first to admit their results are limited and incomplete. Most are based on small groups of middle-class whites, and females are underrepresented. Also, people in longitudinal studies are influenced by events specific to the era in which the research was carried out — economic depression, wars, or protests are cases in point — which may not affect other gen-

Women smoking in public and wearing revealing bathing suits were thought daring in 1920s, because these actions violated the social code of that era. Today the bathing suits seem modest and smoking, though dangerous, is not daring.

erations. With all their limitations, however, these studies of the normal development of individuals provide information that illuminates the psychology of normality never before. It is largely these findings that enable us to study normal adaptation through the life cycle.

How Do We Adapt Normally?

Normal adaptation is the capacity to find satisfaction from a balance of work, love, and play in the presence of high-level responses to stress.

Finding Satisfaction from Work, Love and Play

Working, loving, and playing were thought by the ancient Greeks to be the primary domains in which a person should be able to function in order to lead a good life. Three twentieth-century physicians verified this thinking in their clinical observations. Sigmund Freud once was asked what a normal person should be able to do. Doubtless the questioner expected a complicated response: "But Freud in the very curt way of his old days is reported to have said, 'Lieben und Arbeiten' (to love and to work)." (Erikson, 1950, p. 229)

Richard Cabot, a Boston physician and professor who lived at about the same time as Freud, wrote a book called *What Men Live By* (1914). In it, he added two domains of activity to Freud's "Leiben und Arbeiten." He said

Table 1.1 Comparison of the best and least well-adjusted men in the spheres of work, love, and play

	BEST-ADJUSTED, %	LEAST-ADJUSTED, %
Job meets ambition for self	92	58
Steady career progress	93	43
Income over $20,000 yearly (1967)	88	48
Rich friendship patterns	64	6
More than twenty years' enjoyable marriage	77	23
Children have emotional/social problems (1975)	23	67
Take full vacation	72	39
Participation in competitive sports (age 40–50)	76	23

NOTE: The differences in percentages are statistically significant (P<.01 and beyond), meaning they would occur by chance at most only one time in one hundred.
SOURCE: From *Adaptation to life* by George E. Vaillant. © 1977 by George E. Vaillant. By permission of Little, Brown and Comapny.

that in order to maintain a normal adjustment, a person should be able to work, love, play — and also pray. Writing nearly fifty years after Freud and Cabot, psychiatrist Karl Menninger saw working, loving, and playing as crucial in recovery from mental illness (Menninger *et al.*, 1967).

Present thinking about normal adaptation supports this theory. The DSM-III states that our level of adjustment is reflected in how effective we are and how much we enjoy our job, social relations, and our leisure time (1980, pp. 28–29). This statement is reinforced by the work of George Vaillant, whose book *Adaptation to Life* (1977) reports on his follow-up work with middle-aged men who entered a longitudinal study at Harvard College just before World War II. The importance of working, loving, and playing is revealed in Table 1.1. This table compares the best and least well-adjusted men in Vaillant's study on behaviors related to work, love, and play. More of the best-adjusted men found their work enjoyable — it met their ambitions for themselves, they were making steady progress, and it generated an above-average income.

In loving, the differences between the best and least well-adjusted men were dramatic. About two-thirds of the best-adjusted reported rich friendship patterns, while only 6 percent of the latter said this was true. The best-adjusted men also had longer, more enjoyable marriages. And finally, evidence that the loving relationships of the least well-adjusted men were impaired comes from the finding that their children were three times as likely to develop emotional and social problems as were the offspring of their better-adjusted classmates.

The best-adjusted men in Vaillant's study play more. Seventy-two percent of them took full vacations and about three-quarters participated in competitive sports when they were between forty and fifty years of age. By contrast, more than half of the least well-adjusted men stinted on their vacations and less than a quarter played competitive sports.

Satisfaction Essential

Satisfaction is the capacity to enjoy life, to be contented, or to be free from displeasure. It is obtaining reasonable gratification from the world in which we live. Satisfaction is not dependent on total fulfillment in any realm of living: expressing ourselves fully in a vocation, enjoying consistent mutuality of orgasm, or experiencing ecstatic arousal in play. These golden moments are not excluded from the definition of satisfaction, but they are not a requirement.

Satisfaction can be a quiet, contented state. Satisfied people can resemble those individuals found by many psychological researchers to be happy and well adjusted. They were not especially growth-oriented, did not search out new challenges, and led relatively circumscribed lives (Besser, 1971; Grinker *et al.*, 1962). Ecstasy is not demanded. Contentment is sufficient.

Finally, satisfaction can be experienced as the absence of displeasure. A developmental fact in the life cycle seems to be that as men and women grow older, they find ways of protecting themselves against displeasure. One way is by decreasing openness to feelings, including sensations of pleasure as well as pain. Older men and women report both fewer positive ("on top of the world" or "pleased") and fewer negative ("depressed" or "very unhappy") emotions than younger individuals (Lowenthal *et al.*, 1976, Chapter 6). Yet they are just as well-adjusted.

Balance

A common thread in the thinking of classical Greek philosophers was the importance of **balance**. In their view, the ideal person should strive for wholeness, to excel in mind, body, and spirit. The Greeks saw no incongruity in combining musical contests with athletic ones. A test of flute playing was an original part of the Olympic games and was conducted alongside chariot racing, hurling the javelin, and sprinting in a full suit of armor.

Because the Greeks considered being versed in several areas essential to the good life, they worried that too great an involvement in one domain would unbalance a person's life. It is this conviction that lies behind the remark that a person ". . . should be able to play the flute . . . but not too well." (Kitto, 1951)

Balance enhances the satisfaction we obtain from life in two ways. First, the domains of working, loving, and playing are interdependent. A man or woman is likely to be more content on the job when relationships with loved ones give purpose to the work as well as providing someone with whom to share the fruits of labor. The usefulness of relaxation and play long have been known to enhance performance at work. William James proposed that every person should have a four-week vacation each year, arguing that overall productivity would be as great in eleven months as in twelve (1873). This anticipated by more than one hundred years the results of modern longitudinal studies confirming his theory (Vaillant, 1977). Also, James believed that the education of American youth should stress the body as well as the mind. He

A sound body is associated with normality. It has been only in the last quarter of the twentieth century that the opportunities for physical fitness and competition for females have begun to equal those for males.

The Balanced Life — A View from the Nineteenth Century

They tell us that in Norway the life of the woman has lately been entirely revolutionized by the new order of muscular feelings with which the use of the *ski*, or long snow-shoes, as a sport for both sexes, has made the women acquainted. Fifteen years ago, the Norwegian women were even more than the women of other lands, votaries of the old-fashioned ideal of femininity, "the domestic angel," the "gentle and refining influence" sort of thing. Now these sedentary, fireside tabby cats of Norway have been trained, they say, by the snow-shoes into lithe and audacious creatures for whom no night is too dark or height too giddy, who are not only saying goodbye to their traditional female pallor and delicacy of constitution, but actually taking the lead in every educational and social reform. I cannot but think that the tennis and tramping and skating habits and the bicycle-craze in this country are going also to lead to a sound and heartier moral tone which will send its tonic breath through all our American life.

SOURCE: The gospel of relaxation (1897), *in* James, W. *Pragmatism and other essays*. New York: Pocket Books, 1975, pp. 238–239.

observed that soundness of the body improved the self-concept of women. Doubtless James would applaud the access young women now have to all sports activities, though he might wonder why it has taken so long.

It is not only that loving and playing support working activities. There are many situations in which a job gives somebody the self-regard to love. Consider Sophie, a married woman whose self-respect had all but vanished because she felt there must be more to life than raising three children and taking care of a house. As her depression grew, it was harder for her to love anyone. Then, when her children were able to manage by themselves, she entered a bank management training program. She found her job satisfying, and appreciated the respect she had from her colleagues. Her self-regard improved, her depression lifted. And she was able to love her family much more fully than before.

The second reason a balance in work, love, and play fosters normality is that each nourishes our spirit in unique ways at different times in our lives. For the child, play is surely most important. In adolescence, loving has high priority. And for the young adult, working is a major source of gratification. Later in life, boredom with work can occur. At this point, play or loving relationships may again become a major source of satisfaction (Lowenthal *et al.*, 1976, Chapter 12). Each of us benefits from having more than one source of satisfaction, no matter what our age.

It is unlikely that a normal person with a normal reality to cope with is able continually to find satisfaction from working, loving, and playing. Things go badly at work, we have a fight with a loved one, our golf game goes to hell. Having more than one area of gratification in our lives enables us to avoid putting all of our eggs in one basket. Take Maria, for example, an adolescent girl whose erupting acne makes her feel she is unattractive. She is able to fight off the frustration of feeling unattractive and maintain her optimism and spirit by doing well in school and by mastering the oboe.

If a primary area of gratification is shut off, we can turn to other spheres for pleasure and so continue to nourish our spirit — that *élan vital* that is essential to human adjustment. Working, loving, and playing all give us pleasure, but they all require practice. As long as Maria knows how to gain satisfaction from working and playing, she can put her energies into these domains if she can't get what she wants from loving relationships with others.

What balance we strike in these areas varies considerably. It changes from age to age and is affected by opportunity and chance and by individual taste. What percentage of time or satisfaction comes from each area is not as important as the need to maintain the continuing capacity to find satisfaction from working, loving, and playing throughout the life cycle.

Coping with Stress Effectively

We might imagine that people become maladjusted because of severe deprivation, crushing life experiences, or perhaps even uniquely bizarre thoughts, terror, or impulses that normal people never deal with. In fact, this is a wrong assumption. Psychiatrists have long observed that the life experiences, thoughts, and feelings of mental patients are no different from those of us who avoid

Table 1.2 Examples of mature and immature or psychotic ways of coping with stress

	MATURE
Anticipation:	Realistic anticipation of or planning for future inner discomfort.
Suppression:	The conscious or semi-conscious decision to postpone paying attention to a conscious impulse of conflict.
Humor:	Overt expression of ideas and feelings without individual discomfort or immobilization and without unpleasant effects on others.

	IMMATURE OR PSYCHOTIC
Denial:	Negating an external reality.
Distortion:	Grossly reshaping external reality to suit inner needs.
Projection:	Attributing one's own unacceptable and unacknowledged feelings to others.

SOURCE: From *Adaptation to life* by George E. Vaillant. © 1977 by George E. Vaillant. By permission of Little, Brown and Company.

mental breakdown (Freud, 1910, p. 50). The distinguishing feature of normal people is how they cope with stress.

Vaillant's work supports this clinical observation. He surveyed psychological mechanisms all of us apply to relieve emotional upset. He described different ways of coping with stress, varying from "mature" to "immature" and "psychotic." Several examples are contained in Table 1.2. The best-adjusted subjects in his study used "mature" ways of managing stress far more often than they used lower-level defenses.

Imagine yourself facing a stress, such as in the final exam of this course. A mature way of responding to this anxiety would be to *anticipate* the discomfort the exam is likely to cause and to try to reduce it by studying; *suppress* other conscious or semi-conscious fears ("I'll never pass!") while studying and use *humor* to vent anxiety about the test. Now think about how the use of denial, distortion, or projection would not be helpful in reacting to exam anxiety.

Rarely does a single event — economic depression, death of parents, or an illness — cause maladjustment. Nor does a pack of problems always damage our mental state. It is how we *react* to these hardships — how we deal with the anxiety and depression coming from these difficulties — that is one of these "little differences" that make much of the difference between normal adaptation and maladjustment.

Using Resources

Until recently, a typical evaluation of someone's mental health consisted in finding out what was wrong with that person. Early trauma, frustrations and conflicts, and failure to resolve developmental tasks would be surveyed along with noting the presence of tension, melancholy, strange thoughts, or bizarre behavior. Nowhere close to the same effort was spent finding out what might be going *right* in that person's life.

Each of us is more than the sum of our minuses. The pluses in our lives contribute greatly to our overall adjustment. On the plus side are satisfactions we derive from work, love, and play, and how we cope with stress. On the plus side, also, are resources. **Resources** are anything we can call upon to cushion the effects of frustrations, bad news, or loss. They provide compensating positive experiences when we may be feeling overwhelmed by life. The presence of — and access to — resources is crucial in normal adaptation.

Of the several resources highly associated with adjustment in life is the capacity to maintain friendly relations with family and others. In Lowenthal's study of high-school graduates, newlyweds, empty-nesters, and pre-retirees, mutually satisfying interpersonal relationships increasingly served as a buffer against preoccupation with past problems and present stress and were correlated with a positive future outlook. These relations with others involved mutual caring and support.

A better than average physical constitution is a significant resource. A common observation about men and women who rise to positions of political, business, and professional leadership is that they seem physically more energetic than those who are not. Vaillant found the healthiest men in his sample were the best-adjusted. The soundest women in the group examined by Lowenthal and her colleagues reported the best health and the most energy. In general, health, energy level, and recuperative powers play a large part in combating emotional stress throughout our lives.

Intelligence is a resource. Superior perception and memory, analysis, reasoning, ingenuity, and verbal skills are associated with success in psychotherapy. These same aptitudes can make the need for professional help unnecessary. Lowenthal and her co-workers discovered that the subjects who managed stress most adaptively had the highest scores on a measure of intelligence. An example of intelligence in action is the case of seven-year-old Phyllis. When her parents told her they were getting a divorce, she thought she would die. Though she was in acute emotional pain, she used her intelligence to recognize that others probably had the same experience. She noticed several of her classmates in school had only one parent at home, and invited three of these girls to her house to play during a weekend. Not only did these classmates help her through the most difficult time in her life, but she also made several new friends.

Resources can be avocational interests. An activity, hobby, or skill can provide both sanctuary and solace. Laid off from his job, Luis found refuge in playing the saxophone. The music he created comforted him, minimized for the moment the distress he felt, and helped him maintain normal adjustment (Horton, 1981). Listening to music, playing sports, collecting stamps, growing things, fishing, or taking long walks can serve the same purpose.

Religious faith is a resource. It enriches the day-to-day life of many. A Jewish family all find strength in their commitment to keeping a kosher home. Born-again Christians feel more joy in living as a result of their recovered faith. Faith sustains many through adversity that otherwise would have broken them. A young man crippled by a tragic car accident after the senior prom maintains a steadfast optimism because of his devout Catholicism. Doubtless some of the appeal of non-traditional religions is that they also respond to the need to have faith in something larger than the self when one is facing day-to-day struggles.

Let us not forget that money is a resource. A larger percentage of children from wealthier backgrounds fare better as adults because they have the money to go to college—in spite of the fact that many are no brighter than poorer youngsters. Money also can pay for the correction of a reading disability that leads to frustration in school or crooked teeth that foster self-consciousness. Money can cushion the effects of a broken relationship with a trip to the sun or the mountains, or mediocrity in work by supporting a comfortable life style and satisfying hobbies, and in times of real trouble it can purchase expert assistance.

Finally, **a dream** is a considerable resource. More than a fantasy, but still short of reality, a dream can be a view of the way the world is, how people are, a sense of self, a specific goal, or a continuity of purpose. Yale professor Daniel Levinson (1978) describes the dream this way:

> . . . the Dream is a vague sense of self-in-the-adult-world. It has the quality of a vision, an imagined possibility that generates excitement and vitality. At the start it is poorly articulated and only tenuously connected to reality, although it may contain concrete images, such as winning the Nobel Prize or making the All-Star team. It may take a dramatic form, as in the myth of the hero: the great artist, business tycoon, athletic or intellectual superstar performing magnificent feats and receiving special honors. It may take the mundane forms that are yet inspiring and sustaining: the excellent craftsman, the husband-father in a certain kind of family, the highly respected member of one's community. (page 91)

A young woman may cope differently with the rigors of studying for exams if her view is that her fate is in her hands, and not that what happens to her is not in her control; if her sense of self is that she is basically capable and not incompetent; if she has her heart set on going to law school as opposed to having no specific goal; and if she sees herself doing something useful and productive after college instead of having no dream at all. Furthermore, when this woman enters the field of law and begins to cope with the long week at work and the inevitable frustrations on the job, one of the major factors that keeps her going may be the sense that she is doing something important for herself, for loved ones, and for the people she serves.

Summary

1. Three reasons make it worthwhile to study normal adaptation: (1) to help us live a more satisfying life; (2) to learn how to handle stress more effectively; and (3) to understand the differences between normal adaptation and maladjustment.

2. Normality is difficult to define. It is not "happiness," "maturity," "naturalness," "following God's will" or "feeling whole." More formal definitions of normal adjustment, based on mental health, statistical, and ideal perspectives, shed only indirect light on this subject.

3. Two stumbling blocks in portraying normal adaptation are the emphasis on children of most theory and research and the effects of culture, race, and social class on expectations for normal behavior.

4. Recent reports of longitudinal and cross-sectional studies of human growth illuminate normal adaptation as never before. They provide data supporting earlier thinking and clinical observations about the ingredients of normalcy.

5. *Normal adaptation is the capacity to find satisfaction from a balance of work, love, and play in the presence of high-level responses to stress.* This definition views satisfaction from the domains of work, love, and play as essential and interdependent, and it recognizes that each of us strikes our individual balance of pleasure from each. Coping effectively with stress and the

use of resources enables us to maintain a normal equilibrium in the face of unpleasant life events.

A Look Ahead

So far, the description of the normal state resembles a still picture. Normal adaptation is a process, more like a movie than a snapshot. Stresses and tensions in living constantly throw us off balance and threaten our ability to obtain satisfaction from work, love, and play. Complex processes that enable all of us to combat upsetting feelings and cope with problems in our world are high-level responses to stress. In the next chapter we will further inspect the nature of stress and consider the hazards and beneficial outcomes of it. We will look at the causes of stress and identify usual stress emotions. Three theories of the reasons for stress emotions will be considered.

Key Terms

normal adaptation
**mental health perspective of
    normality**
DSM-III
statistical perspective (of
    normality)
normal distribution
normal curve
ideal perspective (of normality)
self-actualization
physiological needs

safety needs
love and belonging needs
esteem needs
longitudinal studies
cross-sectional studies
**satisfaction (from work, love, and
    play)**
balance (in work, love, and play)
resources
a dream

Suggested Readings

Normality

Allport, G. *Patterns and growth in personality*. New York: Holt, Rinehart & Winston, 1961. Chapter 7.

Walsh, F. (Ed.), *Normal family process*. New York: Guilford, 1982, Chapters 1 and 2.

   The concept of normality from the perspectives of the individual and the family.

Optimal adjustment

Maslow, A. *Toward a psychology of being*. New York: Van Nostrand, 1968.

   A classic summary of Maslow's thinking on this subject.

Life cycle reports

Vaillant, G. *Adaptation to life*. Boston: Little, Brown, 1977.

Gould, R. *Transformations*. New York: Simon & Schuster, 1978.

Heath, D. *Growing up in college.* San Francisco: Jossey-Bass, 1968.

Levinson, D., with Darrow, C., Klein, E., Levinson, M., and McKee, B. *Seasons of a man's life.* New York: Knopf, 1978.

> Different views on human growth over time.

Balance of work, love and play

Thompson, J. *The Ethics of Aristotle.* (1953) New York: Penguin, 1975. Books I, IX, and X.

Menninger, K., with Mayman, M., and P. Pruser. *The vital balance: The life processes in mental health and illness.* New York: Viking, 1967. Chapter 12.

> An ancient philosopher and a twentieth century clinician agree on the importance of balanced satisfaction from work, love, and play.

Your clammy hands are trembling almost as much as your quaking knees. The pit in your stomach is growing deeper with every breath. Your heart feels as though it's going to burst any second, and you are overwhelmed with a sense of doom. In the midst of this panic, you hear your name called. Your stomach gives a horrendous lurch and you know it's "now or never" time.

Performing on stage, giving a speech, making a presentation in class, interviewing for a job — all of these can trigger the misery known as stage fright. And it's not confined to any age, level of experience, talent, intelligence, or sex. Violinist Isaac Stern is known to make his way to the stage mumbling, "Ah, God, I can't play. Why do I have to play now? *I can't play!*" Interviewing for a first job, Irene has a bad case of stage fright — she fidgets, spills her coffee, and trips over her own dropped pocketbook, certain she has sabotaged her chances for getting the job.

Whether we are Irene or Isaac Stern, all of us know the sometimes painful physical and psychological reactions to stage fright. Would we be better off if we didn't subject ourselves to this stress? Or, is the willingness to bear this initial unpleasantness the price we pay for growing capability and fulfillment in our lives?

CHAPTER 2
The Nature of Stress

Questions to think about

- ☐ What causes stress in you?
- ☐ What are your usual immediate reactions to stress?
- ☐ Have you ever benefited because you had to cope with some adversity?
- ☐ Can you think of how you might handle stress better?

In Chapter 1, we explored definitions of normal adaptation. Then we looked at the first essential element — finding satisfaction in a balance of work, love, and play. But this portrait of normality is easily disrupted by the inescapable stresses that we all respond to. These daily events disrupt our ability to enjoy a job, strain loving relationships, and drive all pleasure from a hobby.

The second part of the definition of normal adaptation — high-level responses to stress — is the topic of this and the next chapter. To make this complex subject easier to understand, it is divided into two parts: the nature of stress, and responses to stress. In this chapter we explore the nature of stress.

What is stress? What are its sources and expressions? How is it measured? What is its impact on us? In the pages ahead, we inspect the nature of stress and assay the factors causing a stress response. The sources of stress common to all of us are inventoried. We look at characteristic stress emotions we all experience. Finally, we examine five theories of the origins and nature of stress emotions.

What Is Stress?

How would you explain what stress is? How would the person who sits next to you in class define it? As you might imagine, many definitions of stress have been offered. The one we will use draws from several that are in use today (Selye, 1974; Hinsie and Campbell, 1970; Weiss and English, 1975). **Stress** is *any event that taxes our emotional and physical balance enough to cause an unpleasant reaction.* The unpleasant reactions can be upsetting feelings or bodily discomfort. Each day brings with it its daily hassles. We have too much to do and become irritable, or not enough and are depressed. Too many people demand our attention and we develop a migraine. Traffic jams, missed buses, and cars that won't start give us high blood pressure, lead to temper tantrums, or push us to the brink.

Ironically, not all stressful events are negative. Even positive events may result in unpleasant sensations of stress. An outstanding personal achievement, a marital reconciliation, or even a vacation can place some strain on any of us. Can you think of any other positive experiences that tax your adjustment?

Hans Selye has devoted his professional life to studying stress. He points to four variations of stress: *overstress* — when we have too much to deal with, *understress* — boredom and lack of self-realization, *bad stress* — unpleasant events, and *good stress* — positive experiences. Selye recommends that we try to strike a balance among these four variations. This requires avoiding too much stress for lengthy periods yet not timidly running away from every unpleasant experience, because conquering difficulties leads to growth and pleasure and, perhaps, less frustration with stress.

A familiar source of stress is an exam. The amount of stress a test causes — and how it affects us — varies greatly from individual to individual.

Sources of Stress

This definition of stress includes both the event and its unpleasant reaction, but the reaction is not inevitably linked to the event. People do react differently to essentially identical events. In order to be stressful, the event must be accompanied by some barrier, or stumbling block, to our action. The barrier may be real or imagined, and it may take the form of *frustration, threat,* or *conflict.*

Frustration

Frustration is the discomfort caused by environmental forces that prevent or delay action. Your boss orders you to work overtime on a hot Friday afternoon just when you were going to ask him if you could leave early to go to the beach. You are a first-grader who can't read, or a teenager too small to make the football team. You can't find a job. You are in a Mexican airport and can't speak enough Spanish to find out where the rest room is.

Frustration is also caused by unacceptable inner impulses. You want to tell off the boss, but you really need the job. You are on a diet, trying to resist a dish of ice cream. You are sexually attracted to someone who is married.

Frustration can be caused by the social structure in which we live. University of Wisconsin Professor David Mechanic (1974) lists three potential sources of frustration rooted in the society at large: (1) inadequate preparation for life's tasks from schools, colleges, or other training; (2) insufficient incentive to sustain motivation; and (3) absence of social supports.

All of us need to be prepared for the work that is rewarded by the society in which we live. This education occurs in schools, apprenticeships, colleges, and military service. If the institutions in the culture do not provide the skills necessary for its graduates to handle the work of the society, then frustration is probable no matter how strong the person's individual strengths.

The incentives a society offers for people's efforts may be frustratingly inadequate. Government manpower programs of the 1960s attempted to relieve the chronically high unemployment rate among minority groups. People were taught to be clerks, telephone operators, welders, or keypunchers. Overall, these programs had an extremely low success rate (Perry *et al.*, 1975). Large numbers of men and women dropped out and went back to being unemployed. The reason was that the individuals were being trained for low-level jobs not especially valued by the society. They were dead-end positions with little possibility for growth. For many, the frustrations of unemployment were easier to manage than the stress of having a job with little value, leading nowhere.

Finally, the experience of frustration is linked to the supports of those in the surrounding society. We depend on relations with others in the culture to maintain and justify our existence. A Mexican-American boy from El Paso wins a scholarship to Harvard. To what extent will he have the support of his friends at home? How many other young people from similar backgrounds will be there in Cambridge to support him? What will it be like when he returns home for Christmas during his freshman year?

Threat

Threat is an expectation of the inability to manage a future situation. A threat differs from frustration because it hasn't happened yet. It causes stress because we imagine future frustration or harm will come.

Consider Bubba. He is a star football player, but he is terrified of speaking in public because he lisps slightly. One requirement for English is to give an oral book report to the class. For him this stress meets all the requirements for a threat — anticipation of frustration because he can't avoid it, and a poor grade in class because he has what seems to him an unalterable problem. So Bubba worries and worries.

Sometimes worrying about worrying constitutes a threat. Bubba may worry that he is thinking so much about his lisping in class that he will be unable to prepare his talk. Insomniacs often report they worry so much about worrying about lying awake that they approach bedtime threatened by the idea they're going to worry about falling asleep.

Conflict

Conflict involves the presence of two competing but mutually exclusive courses of action. Psychologist Kurt Lewin (1935) pointed out three familiar types of conflict: (1) approach-avoidance, (2) approach-approach, and (3) avoidance-avoidance. Stress occurs because only one choice can be made; we often feel we have a rubber band tied to both arms that are anchored to each choice. The closer we move toward making one choice the stronger the pull is toward the other. Sometimes the result is that we make no choice at all and continue to remain in conflict.

The **approach-avoidance conflict** is the most common. We want and don't want something at the same time. Many of us are attracted to occupations that are rich in stimulation but barely pay a living wage. Or we know we should give up smoking but can't imagine the rest of our life without a cigarette.

In **approach-approach conflicts**, we must choose between two agreeable alternatives. The stress comes from the necessity of forsaking the pleasures of the road not taken. The 1977 movie *The Turning Point* tells the story of two middle-aged women who chose different pathways in their twenties. Both were promising dancers who knew that a career would conflict with the pleasures of marriage and family. One elected to go on with her career. The other chose to give up dance. Their touching story centers around what both achieved and missed and their thoughts about what life would have been like had they taken the other career pathway.

Avoidance-avoidance conflicts involve a choice between undesirable options. Instead of the stress coming from the potential satisfactions to be missed, it emanates from a desire to minimize potential pain. Consider a pregnant single woman. She doesn't believe in abortion, but she can't face having a baby. What is she to do? Both choices seem equally unattractive.

These two 30-year old women illustrate an approach-approach conflict. For now, one has chosen a career, the other motherhood. Both are aware of having given up pleasure the other choice would bring.

Stress Emotions

When confronted by stress — an event accompanied by frustration, threat, or conflict — we are likely to react immediately with one or more human emotions. Aggression, depression and anxiety are common.

Aggression

One consequence of stress is **aggression.** An aggressive reaction is an urge to attack the agent of frustration — cussing out the boss who wants us to work overtime, humiliating an attractive person who ignores us, attacking an organization that doesn't offer a job, or kicking the car that won't start.

Many people feel that aggression is a natural instinct, an inborn drive of all species. There is a difference, however, between being angry and behaving aggressively. For many decades it was assumed that everyone has a natural instinct to fight when frustrated (Miller and Dollard, 1941). However, present information indicates that not everyone attacks when angry. Think for a minute about the times something or someone has blocked a desire of yours and you didn't respond angrily. Usually we don't react aggressively when we see the cost as too great (Bandura, 1977). We need the job so we hold back our anger at the boss, or we don't kick the car that won't start because we know it would hurt our foot.

Depression

Depression is actually a complex of feelings that can include helplessness, low self-esteem, and even an inner sense of deserving whatever bad things happen. These emotions may vanish quickly or they may endure for days, turning into months.

Recent studies identify qualities of people who are at high risk to develop depressive feelings (Abramson, Seligman, and Teasdale, 1978):

1. Attributing failure to forces that are internal, global, and stable.
2. Expecting that whatever happens is outside one's personal control.
3. Thinking that positive outcomes are unlikely and negative ones probable.
4. Exaggerating the desirability or undesirability of certain events.

The first characteristic is the tendency to attribute failure or frustration to forces that are internal, global, and stable. That is, people who are likely to be depressed see problems as being caused by something that is *inside* themselves, is likely to occur again and again in *many situations*, and is *unalterable*. Take, for example, a young man who scores poorly on the SATs. If he's vulnerable to a depressive emotional reaction to this event, he may attribute his low scores to his lack of intellectual ability instead of thinking that the test is unfair. He may think he will always do poorly on such tests as opposed to thinking that he had a bad day. He may be convinced that his performance will never improve rather than thinking that his scores could be raised if he worked harder in preparation and received special tutoring.

Individuals with a tendency to become depressed in the face of stress think that their problems are unchangeable. It follows that whatever happens to them, good or bad, is beyond their personal control. Whatever happens, "happens." Men and women with the likelihood of becoming depressed don't feel they can personally affect the world around them. They see themselves blown this way and that by powers greater than their own. This sense of low fate control is the essence of learned helplessness. And it can be a self-fulfilling prophecy. If we believe we can't improve our SATs, we are not likely to worry about the test in advance, which might lead to preparation for it or seeking special help. And as soon as we come to a question we can't answer, we guess quickly rather than try to figure it out. Afterwards, we have no idea of how we've scored because we don't believe our efforts could affect the results anyway.

Finally, one of the most intriguing traits of depressed people is their tendency to exaggerate the desirability or negative impact of a particular event. A specific goal is invested with the power to make everything right, to be the keystone of all happiness. Often the goal itself is unreachable. A depressed young man with a marginal academic record sets his sights on being accepted at Duke University. He files his application, imagining he will be all right if they accept him. When the university rejects him, his mood plummets. He is unresponsive to the suggestion that there are thousands of other colleges in the United States, many of which would be happy to accept him.

Anxiety

Anxiety is uneasiness, apprehension, or tension. We may experience it as an inner physical discomfort—a sick feeling, jitteryness, or a throbbing pulse. Usually it is a reaction to threat or conflict. The source can be external or internal, known or unknown.

Stress causing anxiety is often external, "out there" — an unsympathetic boss, poor school grades, failure to find a job, a bad relationship. Less often it emanates from inside, as when an experienced speaker is nearly overpowered by feelings of inadequacy before giving a simple lecture he or she has delivered capably a dozen times. Anxiety emanates from clear-cut, known origins, but also unknown ones. Many people are tormented by sudden spasms of anxiety that seem to spring out with no warning.

Anxiety is experienced physically. Most of us know the inner sensations: shortness of breath, pumping heart, muscle tightness, sweating, flushing, nausea, and the need to find a toilet in a hurry. Severe anxiety is sometimes like being hit over the head (Sullivan, 1953). We are confused. What we read doesn't make sense. Memory is cloudy and thinking is sluggish.

Suppose you were asked to make up a test to measure anxiety. What questions would you ask? Some possibilities might be "Are you a nervous person?" or "Do you sometimes think you're falling apart?" If you look at these two questions and some others you can think of, you will notice that they report two slightly different ways of looking at anxiety.

A "yes" answer to the first implies an enduring, stable personal quality or **trait**. An affirmative answer to the question "Do you sometimes think you're falling apart?" suggests that a person may have moments of being exceptionally nervous but may not be anxious all the time. This is a temporary **state** of anxiety, which diminishes once the stress is removed.

Examples of the types of questions that measure state and trait anxiety are shown in Table 2.1. The value of distinguishing between *state* and *trait* anxiety is that someone with a high chronic level of tension reacts differently to new stress than a person who is usually not nervous. Imagine twins who are about to take their driving test. Natalie has high trait anxiety and Ellen is low on that scale. Who is going to become more nervous during the examination? The results of several studies find that people who are high on trait anxiety experience a greater increase in nervousness when they confront stress than those with low trait scores (Spielberger, 1966, 1971). Natalie will surely suffer more than Ellen.

Measurement of Stress

What is enough but not too much stress? Where is the borderline between good and bad stress? If we talk among ourselves we might find that each of us has a different idea. Consider graduation from college. You might see this as a highly positive event — a gateway to new challenges. For me, it might be the saddest and most frightening moment of my life; my friends are scattering and I have no idea what I will do with my life. While massive individual variations exist in any stress, two factors influence the impact of these events on all of us: the amount of stress we confront, and the length of time we must deal with it.

Table 2.1   Examples of questions measuring state and trait anxiety

State: How do you feel *at this moment?* Check one answer to each question.

	DEFINITELY NO	MODERATELY	DEFINITELY YES
1. I feel relaxed.	_____(3)	_____(2)	_____(1)
2. My body is shaky.	_____(1)	_____(2)	_____(3)
3. I am at peace.	_____(3)	_____(2)	_____(1)
4. I feel on edge.	_____(1)	_____(2)	_____(3)
5. Nothing is bothering me.	_____(3)	_____(2)	_____(1)

Trait: How do you feel *usually?* Check one answer to each question.

	DEFINITELY NO	MODERATELY	DEFINITELY YES
1. I sleep well.	_____(3)	_____(2)	_____(1)
2. I am restless.	_____(1)	_____(2)	_____(3)
3. I feel calm.	_____(3)	_____(2)	_____(1)
4. I worry a lot.	_____(1)	_____(2)	_____(3)
5. I control my nerves.	_____(3)	_____(2)	_____(1)

It is possible to construct your own measure of state and trait anxiety by using questions such as these. The numbers in parentheses can be totaled to rank order individuals on these two dimensions of anxiety.

Amount of Stress

Have you ever noticed that some people who are under lots of stress start to have other problems too? They seem to be sick more often or may have trouble in school or at work. In the past twenty years psychological researchers have tried to chart the relationship between stressful events and the development of physical and psychological problems.

Holmes and Rahe (1967) developed the first way of measuring the magnitude of stressful experiences. They made a list of forty-three life events and ranked them according to how much adjustment is required to cope with them. They called their list the **Social Readjustment Rating Scale** (SRRS), shown in Table 2.2. This scale shows the rank order of forty-three events on the SRRS ranging from the death of a spouse to minor legal violations. Because some life stresses have greater impact on us than others, each is given a different weight according to how much readjustment is required.

After this scale was developed it was given to a large number of people. They were asked to mark how many times each of these life events had occurred in the past six months. Then the total amount of stress for each person was calculated by adding up all of the items. The total is the number of **Life**

Table 2.2   Social Readjustment Rating Scale

LIFE EVENT	IMPACT IN LIFE CHANGE UNITS (LCU'S)*	LIFE EVENT	IMPACT IN LIFE CHANGE UNITS (LCU'S)*
Death of spouse	100	Trouble with in-laws	29
Divorce	73	Outstanding personal achievement	28
Marital separation	65		
Jail term	63	Spouse begins or stops work	26
Death of close family member	63	Begin or end school	26
Personal injury or illness	53	Change in living conditions	25
Marriage	50	Revision of personal habits	24
Fired at work	47		
Marital reconciliation	45	Trouble with boss	23
Retirement	45	Change in work hours or conditions	20
Change in health of family member	44	Change in residence	20
Pregnancy	40	Change in schools	20
Sex difficulties	39	Change in recreation	19
Gain of new family member	39	Change in church activities	19
Business readjustment	39	Change in social activities	18
Change in financial state	38	Mortgage or loan of less than $10,000	17
Death of close friend	37		
Change to different line of work	36	Change in sleeping habits	16
Change in number of arguments with spouse	35	Change in number of family get-togethers	15
Mortgage over $10,000	31	Change in eating habits	15
Foreclosure of mortgage and loan	31	Vacation	13
		Christmas	12
Change in responsibilities at work	29	Minor violations of the law	11
Son or daughter leaving home	29		

SOURCE: Reprinted with permission from T. H. Holmes and R. H. Rahe, The social readjustment rating scale, *Journal of Psychosomatic Research*, Vol. 11, 1967, pp. 213–218. Copyright 1967, Permagon Press, Ltd.

*Impact in Life Change Units (LCUs) is the measure of relative readjustment required to manage the stress.

Change Units (LCUs) the individual has experienced. Getting married might involve the following stresses:

EVENT	IMPACT IN LIFE CHANGE UNITS
marriage	50
change in financial state	30
change in living conditions	25
revision of personal habits	24
change in residence	20
change in social activities	18
change in number of family get-togethers	15
change in eating habits	15
Number of Life Change Units	197

The SRRS has enabled psychological researchers to compare the amount of life stress — expressed in the total number of Life Change Units — with other types of problems. We will look at these findings shortly.

Useful as the SRRS has been, the device can be criticized because each of us has a different way of rank ordering life events. For me, getting married might cause far more than 197 Life Change Units of readjustment, while your wedding might add up to far less. A related criticism is that the SRRS combines positive and negative stresses. A personal achievement and having in-law trouble probably have different effects on us even though they have close to the same rated impact on the SRRS.

An effort to improve the measurement of stress is the **Life Experience Inventory,** shown in Table 2.3. We can see that this new stress-measuring scale is an improvement because it asks for a personal rating of the extent that the event has had a negative or positive impact.

Duration of Stress

Each of us has a limited tolerance for stress. When these boundaries are exceeded, we break down. Physician Hans Selye (1956) developed a three-stage theory of the way the body responds to stress. It is called the **general adaptation syndrome,** shown in Figure 2.1. This model applies to people who have been subjected to stress for a long period of time. Though originally he intended it to describe physiological reaction patterns to stress, Selye later noted that it fits psychological responses as well (1974).

The three phases of the General Adaptation Syndrome are *alarm, resistance,* and *exhaustion.* At the first exposure to a sudden or unfamiliar stressful event, the adaptive level is diminished. This is caused by disrupting anxiety, fear, depression, or mental disorganization. Health declines. If the person has the adaptive tools to combat this stress, a phase of resistance follows the alarm. In this period, the individual rises well above the usual level of coping. Earlier stress reactions — anxiety, fear, or disorganization — disappear as higher-order functioning takes over. Health improves. With continued exposure to the stress, however, the individual moves into the third phase. Resistance is worn down and exhaustion sets in. Feelings of hopelessness and apathy are apparent. Inaction is common. Health declines again, and the psychological signs of wear and tear appear.

Hazardous Effects of Stress

Too heavy a burden of stress, either in amount or duration, so taxes the adaptive efforts of an individual that a breakdown can occur in a number of areas. Physical disorders and emotional maladjustment, decreased effectiveness at work and in relations with others, and reduced adaptive energies are all hazardous effects of stress.

Physical Disorders and Emotional Maladjustment

Physical disorders and emotional maladjustment are the clearest hazards of stress. Studies of people under severe stress bear this out. An example comes from the studies of flight crews during World War II. The bomber crews reporting the most physical disorders and emotional maladjustment were those just beginning to fly in combat (28 percent) and those who had flown more than thirty missions (nearly 50 percent). Those who had flown between eleven and twenty-five missions had the lowest rate of reported illness. The relationship between illness and the number of missions flown upholds Selye's theory.

Figure 2.1
Selye's general adaptation syndrome in response to stress

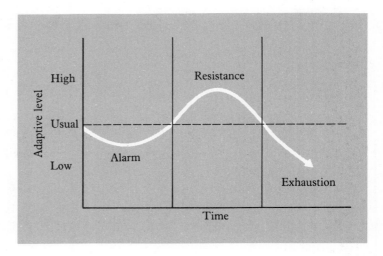

Table 2.3 The life experience survey*

	0 TO 6 MO.	7 MO. TO 1 YR.	EXTREMELY NEGATIVE	MODERATELY NEGATIVE	SOMEWHAT NEGATIVE	NO IMPACT	SLIGHTLY POSITIVE	MODERATELY POSITIVE	EXTREMELY POSITIVE
1. Marriage			−3	−2	−1	0	+1	+2	+3
2. Detention in jail or comparable institution			−3	−2	−1	0	+1	+2	+3
3. Death of spouse			−3	−2	−1	0	+1	+2	+3
4. Death of close family member			−3	−2	−1	0	+1	+2	+3
5. Foreclosure on mortgage or loan			−3	−2	−1	0	+1	+2	+3
6. Death of close friend			−3	−2	−1	0	+1	+2	+3
7. Outstanding personal achievement			−3	−2	−1	0	+1	+2	+3
8. Minor law violations (traffic tickets, disturbing the peace, etc.)			−3	−2	−1	0	+1	+2	+3
9. *Male:* Wife/girlfriend's pregnancy			−3	−2	−1	0	+1	+2	+3
10. *Female:* Pregnancy			−3	−2	−1	0	+1	+2	+3
11. New job			−3	−2	−1	0	+1	+2	+3
12. Serious illness or injury of close family member			−3	−2	−1	0	+1	+2	+3
13. Sexual difficulties			−3	−2	−1	0	+1	+2	+3
14. Trouble with employer (in danger of losing job, being suspended, demoted, etc.)									
15. Trouble with in-laws			−3	−2	−1	0	+1	+2	+3

39

	−3	−2	−1	0	+1	+2	+3
16. Major change in financial status (a lot better off or a lot worse off)	−3	−2	−1	0	+1	+2	+3
17. Major change in closeness of family members (increased or decreased closeness)	−3	−2	−1	0	+1	+2	+3
18. Gaining a new family member	−3	−2	−1	0	+1	+2	+3
19. Change of residence	−3	−2	−1	0	+1	+2	+3
20. Marital separation or divorce	−3	−2	−1	0	+1	+2	+3
21. Marital reconciliation with mate	−3	−2	−1	0	+1	+2	+3
22. *Married male:* Change in wife's work outside the home	−3	−2	−1	0	+1	+2	+3
23. *Married female:* Change in husband's work	−3	−2	−1	0	+1	+2	+3
24. Major change in usual type and/or amount of recreation	−3	−2	−1	0	+1	+2	+3
25. Borrowing more than $10,000	−3	−2	−1	0	+1	+2	+3
26. Borrowing less than $10,000	−3	−2	−1	0	+1	+2	+3
27. Being fired from job	−3	−2	−1	0	+1	+2	+3
28. *Male:* Wife/girlfriend having abortion	−3	−2	−1	0	+1	+2	+3
29. *Female:* Having abortion	−3	−2	−1	0	+1	+2	+3
30. Major personal illness or injury	−3	−2	−1	0	+1	+2	+3

(*Table continued on following page*)

Table 2.3 Continued

	0 TO 6 MO.	7 MO. TO 1 YR.	EXTREMELY NEGATIVE	MODERATELY NEGATIVE	SOMEWHAT NEGATIVE	NO IMPACT	SLIGHTLY POSITIVE	MODERATELY POSITIVE	EXTREMELY POSITIVE
31. Major change in social activities			−3	−2	−1	0	+1	+2	+3
32. Major change in living conditions of family			−3	−2	−1	0	+1	+2	+3
33. Serious injury or illness of close friend			−3	−2	−1	0	+1	+2	+3
34. Retirement from work			−3	−2	−1	0	+1	+2	+3
35. Son or daughter leaving home			−3	−2	−1	0	+1	+2	+3
36. Ending of formal schooling			−3	−2	−1	0	+1	+2	+3
37. Engagement			−3	−2	−1	0	+1	+2	+3
38. Breaking up with boyfriend/girlfriend			−3	−2	−1	0	+1	+2	+3
39. Leaving home for the first time			−3	−2	−1	0	+1	+2	+3
40. Reconciliation with boyfriend/girlfriend			−3	−2	−1	0	+1	+2	+3
Other recent experiences which have had an impact on your life. List and rate.									
41. _____			−3	−2	−1	0	+1	+2	+3
42. _____			−3	−2	−1	0	+1	+2	+3
43. _____			−3	−2	−1	0	+1	+2	+3

Section 2: Student only

	-3	-2	-1	0	+1	+2	+3
44. Beginning a new school experience at a higher academic level	-3	-2	-1	0	+1	+2	+3
45. Changing to a new school	-3	-2	-1	0	+1	+2	+3
46. Academic probation	-3	-2	-1	0	+1	+2	+3
47. Being dismissed from dormitory or other residence	-3	-2	-1	0	+1	+2	+3
48. Failing an important exam	-3	-2	-1	0	+1	+2	+3
49. Changing a major	-3	-2	-1	0	+1	+2	+3
50. Failing a course	-3	-2	-1	0	+1	+2	+3
51. Joining a social organization	-3	-2	-1	0	+1	+2	+3
52. Financial problems about school	-3	-2	-1	0	+1	+2	+3

SOURCE: From I. Sarason, J. Johnson, and J. Siegel, Assessing the impact of life changes: Development of the life experience survey, *Journal of Consulting and Clinical Psychology* 46 (1979), 932–46. Copyright 1979 by the American Psychological Association. Adapted by permission of the publisher and authors.

*Please check those events that you have experienced in the recent past and indicate the time period during which you have experienced each event. Also, for each item checked, indicate the extent to which you viewed the event as having a positive or negative impact on your life. A rating of −3 would be extremely negative; a +3 would be extremely positive.

Note the U-shaped curve in Figure 2.2, which roughly corresponds to the three phases of the General Adaptation Syndrome.

Are people who have experienced a high total of Life Change Units within a period of a few months more likely to develop a physical or psychological problem than those who have faced a lower total of LCUs? The answer appears to be yes. In a series of studies, investigators found a direct association: the higher the number of LCUs, the greater the health hazard (Holmes and Masuda, 1974). The results are presented in Table 2.4.

If the total of LCUs was between 150 and 199, then just over a third of the men and women had physical or psychological problems. At 300 or above, the percentage was nearly eighty.

It is a rare college student who does not experience periods of relatively high stress in which the number of LCUs may approximate 200. Think about exam periods. We should recognize, however, that experiencing a great deal of stress for a short period of time does not invariably result in physical or emotional changes. As Table 2.4 shows, fewer than half the individuals experiencing less than 300 LCUs showed significant health changes.

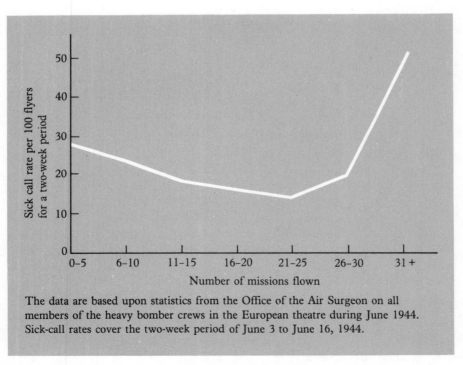

The data are based upon statistics from the Office of the Air Surgeon on all members of the heavy bomber crews in the European theatre during June 1944. Sick-call rates cover the two-week period of June 3 to June 16, 1944.

Figure 2.2 Sick-call rate and number of missions flown by bomber crews

Table 2.4 Relationship of impact measure to stress

IMPACT MEASURE	PERCENTAGE OF INDIVIDUALS SHOWING HEALTH CHANGES, %
150–199	37
200–299	51
Over 300	79

SOURCE: Adapted by permission from T. Holmes and M. Masuda, Life change and illness susceptibility, in B. Dohrenwend and B. Dohrenwend, eds., *Stressful life events: Their nature and effect* (New York: Wiley, 1974).

Type A Behavior: Self-Induced Stress

Not all stress comes from the outside. Some individuals put themselves under continuing pressure, inducing a condition of chronic strain that may be linked to physical problems.

California physicians Meyer Friedman and Ray Rosenman (1974) noted that many of their coronary patients possessed similar personal qualities, which they called **Type A behavior:** insecurity of status, time urgency, and excessive hostility.

Type A behavior is exhibited by men and women who are insecure in their appraisal of their own status. This absence of self-esteem results in an anxious searching for validation from others, especially those in a superior role.

The insecurity gives rise to two other features of the Type A picture, time urgency and excessive hostility. Type A people constantly strive to achieve more and more in less and less time. A striking characteristic of Type A people is their ceaseless struggle with the clock. Time is the enemy. Type A's search for ways to stretch the day so they can do more faster: they do two or three things at once; they finish other people's sentences for them. They constantly look for time-saving gadgets.

To some extent, the time urgency of Type A people is based on the conviction that if they can use the time efficiently, they can get more done. And more is better. In this assumption they are mistaken. The quality of their work is no better, and often worse, than that of those who work more deliberately.

Type A people live by schedules that must be met no matter what. These deadlines have a tyranny to them. Often there is a plan for accomplishments to be achieved in particular sequence. For one student it is a B average at the end of freshman year; on the varsity as a sophomore; member of the right social group as a junior; and senior year being crowned by being president of a political organization and several good job offers. For another, it is the schedule of steady advancement in an occupation, being a perfect mother and homemaker, being an exciting wife, and running the Sunday School program at church. Failure to meet these self-imposed expectations occasions serious distress.

Type A individuals show many signs of inner tensions — restlessness, twitching, jiggling, impatience, and facial tension. They have great trouble having nothing to do. Partly this is because if they are not accomplishing something they begin to feel inadequate. Even vacations are planned for maximum benefit — seeing all the old ruins, the tour in the glass-bottomed boat, and fishing and scuba diving. No idling at the beach in the sun for them.

Type A people are excessively aggressive; they are often found competing against or challenging others. Easily aggravated, they express anger by talking loudly, pounding a table, and grimacing. The remembrance of past events that caused anger frequently will trigger an outburst of rage. No discussion is too relaxed nor game too casual to escape becoming a test of competence into which all aggressive energies are mobilized.

Individuals with Type A behavior patterns have increased risk of coronary heart disease. As a factor in heart disease, it is of the same order of magnitude as age, blood pressure, cholesterol, or smoking (Friedman, 1979). Efforts to modify Type A behavior in patients who have had heart attacks by teaching them to lower the amount of stress they inflict on themselves — examining the reasons they feel insecure in their status, being more relaxed about time, and monitoring their hostility level — have yielded promising results in lowering the chance for future heart problems (Friedman, 1980).

Decreased Effectiveness at Work and in Relations with Others

Stress can reduce effectiveness at work and in relations with others. The exam grades of some students are always well below their classroom performance. This is because anxiety causes them to have trouble studying beforehand, interrupting their sleeping and eating habits. During a test it may narrow their attention so they misread questions, disorganize their thinking, and block memory. Making a guess as to whether an answer is true or false can be agonizing and seem to take forever. These students have lost their "gut feeling" for the right answer.

Stress taxes relationships with others. Frequently this is because a person is so caught up in combating the moment-to-moment pressures of the work day, little energy is left over to maintain loving relationships. A man who has had a hard day at work comes home, grabs his beer, plops down in front of the TV (where he has his dinner), and falls asleep afterwards. Relationships with his wife, children, and dog, to say nothing of the pleasure he obtains from his hobby of refinishing a car, are postponed temporarily.

Reduced Adaptive Energies

One of Selye's most controversial observations is the effect of continuing stress. Contrary to the belief of many that stress is good for you and makes you better able to handle later problems in life, Selye takes the position that chronic stress uses up adaptive energies (1974). He does not believe in the full regeneration of adaptive strengths, and likens adaptive powers to an inherited fortune. We can spend this resource but the redeposits are always less than the original withdrawal. The best we can anticipate is to use our energy wisely and consider how to avoid or reduce stresses that burden our lives and lower our adaptive strength.

Indirect support for this theory comes from observations of people over time. We noted in the first chapter the absence of displeasure is a characteristic of some groups of normally adjusted older people. Research shows that most people in their twenties experience a great deal more stress than in their later years (Lowenthal *et al.*, 1976; Holmes and Masuda, 1974). These findings could be explained by the theory that the wear and tear common to the twenties results in a decreased power to deal with stressful situations later in life. On the other hand, perhaps these older men and women recognize the emotional toll these struggles entail and have learned greater skill at avoiding or reducing stress so as to conserve their adaptive energies.

Beneficial Aspects of Stress

Striving for goals, seeking relationships, and pursuing pleasures in living require the willingness to endure frustration, conflict, anxiety, and disappointment. Without these satisfactions life would be poor indeed. Three clear benefits to be derived from confronting a manageable level of stress are (1) satisfying an innate need, (2) developing a carry-over skill for new situations, and (3) stress inoculation.

Satisfying an Innate Need

Selye (1974) says the absence of stress is death. He argues that all of us need to confront an optimal level of stress in order to get what we want from life. Others wonder whether human beings have an innate need to escape boredom by seeking stimulation that activates our physical and mental systems (Ellis, 1973).

On the basis of experiments with people who have been deprived of sensory stimulation, psychologist Marvin Zuckerman agrees. He developed a theory that all human beings have an inborn need to seek stimulation. He developed a **sensation-seeking scale** (Zuckerman, Eysenck, and Eysenck, 1978). This combines four types of desire for sensory input: thrill and adventure seeking; experience seeking; disinhibition; and boredom susceptibility. Items that measure these qualities are shown in Table 2.5. We can see from this table that *thrill and adventure seeking* is associated with such items as wanting to be a mountain climber or trying parachute jumping. Liking earthy smells or trying new foods are items measuring *experience seeking*. Associated with *disinhibition* are liking wild parties or getting high. *Boredom susceptibility* has to do with a dislike for seeing familiar movies or faces.

Would you think that sensation seeking is greater among young people or that males and females might differ on this characteristic? Zuckerman found that sensation seeking does indeed decline over age and that women score

Table 2.5   Four Components of Sensation Seeking

Thrill and adventure seeking

I sometimes like to do things that are a little frightening.

I would like to take up the sport of water skiing.

I would like to go scuba diving.

I would like to try parachute jumping.

I like to dive off the high board.

I think I would enjoy the sensations of skiing very fast down a high mountain slope.

Experience seeking

I like some of the earthy body smells.

I like to explore a strange city or section of town myself, even if it means getting lost.

I would like to try some of the new drugs that produce hallucinations.

I like to try new foods that I have never tasted before.

I would like to take off on a trip with no pre-planned or definite routes or timetables.

Disinhibition

I like wild "uninhibited" parties.

I enjoy the company of real "swingers."

I often like to get high (drinking liquor or smoking marijuana).

I enjoy watching many of the "sexy" scenes in movies.

Boredom susceptibility

I can't stand watching a movie that I've seen before.

I get bored seeing the same old faces.

I usually don't enjoy a movie or a play where I can predict what will happen in advance.

I get very restless if I have to stay around home for any length of time.

I like people who are sharp and witty even if they do sometimes insult others.

SOURCE: Sample items from M. Zuckerman, S. Eysenck, and H. Eysenck, Sensation seeking in England and America: Cross-cultural, age, and sex comparisons. *Journal of Consulting and Clinical Psychology,* 46 (1978), 139–149. Copyright 1978 by the American Psychological Association. Adapted by permission of the publisher and authors.

slightly lower than men. Figure 2.3 shows these differences by age and sex. The aspects of sensation seeking that decline most over age are thrill and adventure seeking and disinhibition. Apparently we become more cautious as we grow older. These two also are the categories that separate men and women the most.

From Zuckerman's research it appears that each of us does have an innate need for stimulation throughout our lifetime. Some of the sensations we seek are potentially stressful. Each of us has our own taste in pursuing these life experiences, and we are less likely to look for thrills at 60 than at 16. But the desire to enrich our life by inviting stress into it remains with us to the end of our days.

A Carry-Over Skill

In their studies of Kansas children, Murphy and Moriarty (1976) found that psychological growth was enhanced by the experience of coping successfully with developmental difficulties. As long as the stress was manageable, it challenged the youngsters, bringing out added energies to master difficulties. This resulted in a **carry-over skill,** a growing capacity for coping, as the child developed.

Why might facing stress successfully help us in a totally different situation? Some reasons are the confidence that comes from having managed successfully in the past, knowing that our initial reactions to stress — being upset and disorganized — will pass and will not undermine our ability to handle the problem, having tried-and-true ways of dealing with both our emotions and the external source of stress, and the anticipation of the event itself. Have any of these ever helped you combat a difficult event in your life? For example, is someone able to manage the breakup of a second romantic relationship more easily than the first?

Stress Inoculation

The third benefit from confronting and managing stress is **stress inoculation** — the reduction of the psychological impact of future difficulties. Put yourself in the place of a woman waiting for surgery to have her gallbladder removed. Nothing she can do short of avoiding the operation altogether is going to eliminate the anxiety she feels about the surgical procedure. What will the surgeon be doing to her? How much and what kind of pain will she experience? How long will the discomfort last?

What might help her manage the stress of this operation? Would she handle it better if she knew what the operation entailed, and what the pain would

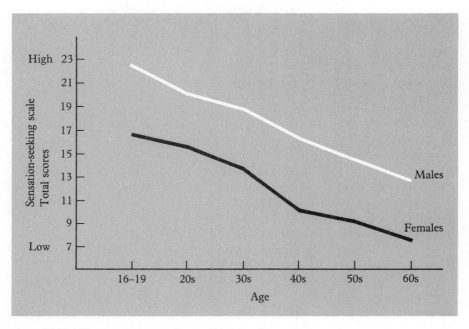

Figure 2.3   Changes in sensation seeking by age and sex

Stress-seeking seems to run in the Knievel family. Here is Robbie, son of famed motorcycle jumper Evel, hurtling over two vans and fifteen cars.

be like? Or would she recover with less difficulty if she put the whole thing out of her mind until the last moment?

Psychologist Irving Janis (1958, 1977) investigated these very questions. He discovered that patients who are mildly fearful prior to the operation are more likely to have a satisfactory postoperative adjustment than those who are either relatively placid or very worried beforehand. Janis maintains that **anticipatory fear** — the work of worrying about a stress in advance — is essential to adaptively dealing with a potential threat. Looking at it squarely and anticipating what it will be like, what the hazards are as well as what support will be available, help in coping with difficult situations.

Not everyone benefits from anticipatory fear. Expecting to confirm Janis's findings, Cohen and Lazarus (1973) studied a group of preoperative surgery patients. The researchers were slightly surprised to discover that some patients didn't want to know about the surgery and didn't worry in advance about the postoperative pain. Yet they showed a smooth and rapid recovery after the operation. Why might that be?

The answer seems to be personality style. In another study, patients about to experience a painful diagnostic medical procedure were shown a film of the stressful event three times, once, or not at all (Shipley, Butt, Horowitz, and Farbry, 1978). As expected, those who saw the film three times were less anxious before, during, and after the procedure; but if the patients were divided into **sensitizors** (being open to feelings) and **repressors** (avoiding and denying feelings) the results were very different.

Figure 2.4 shows the increase in anxiety as measured by the number of heartbeats during the first five minutes of the diagnostic procedure. Among the sensitizors, more exposure to the film resulted in greater decrease in anxiety as expressed in heart beat. Among repressors, however, an unusual thing happened. Those who had not seen the film at all and those who viewed it three times both had small increases in pulse rate. For those in this group, seeing the film once was clearly worse than never being exposed to it. If you were waiting for an operation, what would be your preference?

Theories of Stress Emotions

Why does one of us react with anxiety when frustrated, while another becomes depressed and a third lashes out? Where do these emotions come from? How do these reactions affect overall adjustment? Nearly every major theory for understanding human nature addresses these questions. Each attempts to explain how these emotions come about and affect our mental balance. Five schools of thought are the constitutional, psychoanalytic, behavioral, humanistic, and cognitive theories of personality. They are listed in rough chronological order from oldest to youngest. As we survey each of these, we will focus

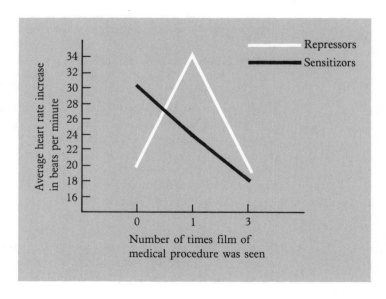

Figure 2.4
Increase in heart rate among sensitizors and repressors during the first five minutes of a medical procedure

on some of their basic principles as well as their explanations of why we react as we do to stress.

Constitutional

Could it be that our physical makeup disposes us to particular stress reactions to life events? Long ago, doctors thought that an imbalance of certain bodily chemicals caused abnormal behavior. In ancient Greece, Hippocrates, the father of modern medicine, believed that irritability was brought on by too much yellow bile in the liver and depression by an excess of black bile in the spleen. Doctors in eighteenth-century America thought that agitation resulted from veins and arteries being overcharged with blood, and treated these conditions by frequent bleeding (Rush, 1962).

These specific theories were discredited by later discoveries, but the idea of a physical vulnerability to specific emotional maladjustments is experiencing a rebirth today. We will examine three bodies of evidence that suggest that normal stress emotions may be partially a function of constitutional makeup: a small tendency for mental disorders to be inherited, emotional changes resulting from a brain injury or chemical imbalance, and the association of physical factors with personality style.

Inheritance. The first body of evidence is that children of people who have had mental disorders have a slightly higher risk of developing these same problems than individuals from similar backgrounds whose parents were normal. Less severe problems also show a small tendency to run in families. For example, one hyperactive child in five has at least one parent who had been unusually restless as a child. Among normal children only one in twenty has a parent with a history of hyperactivity (Gross and Wilson, 1974).

Brain Injury or Chemical Imbalance. A second body of evidence partially supporting a constitutional theory of emotional reactions comes from studies of how people act when they experience brain injury or have an imbalance of certain bodily chemicals. Individuals whose brains have been damaged usually become moody afterward, showing symptoms of depression as well as angry outbursts. Explosive rage is sometimes associated with a certain type of epilepsy called temporal lobe epilepsy. Although their brains may be normal, and appear to be undamaged in currently used testing, some people suffering from this epilepsy become violently aggressive with little provocation (Hare, 1970). The similarity of the angry outbursts of brain-damaged patients to the seizures of epileptic patients has caused some doctors to treat these conditions with anticonvulsive medication; this often controls the emotional explosions.

Hyperactivity in youngsters is thought by some to be the result of diet (Feingold, 1973). They speculate that ingesting too much sugar, food additives, or aspirin throws the body's chemical balance off. Extreme restlessness results. While the jury is still out on this theory, the hyperactivity of some children is reduced by dietary changes. Evidence is accumulating that the more serious mental disturbances are associated with too much or not enough of certain chemicals in the bloodstream, which disturbs the normal functioning of the brain.

Personality Style. The third body of evidence giving support for a constitutional contribution to emotions comes from the studies of personality types. Imagine we are observing two children from the same family, less than a year apart in age. We might find that the girl is energetic and aggressive and her brother cautious and quick to tears. These traits tend to persist over time. Specialists in child development at the Menninger Foundation in Kansas, who studied infants growing into children, commented on the continuity of the personalities of these youngsters:

> As one notes behavioral alterations from infancy to . . . later pre-school ages, one knows that not a single behavior has remained the same, yet one is struck by the inherent continuity of behavioral styles. . . . (Escalona and Heider, 1959, p. 9)

These experts think that the differences in the behavioral style of infants is caused by variation in constitutional factors, especially activity level and sensitivity to outside events. These innate differences might explain why a sister and brother react very differently to the same surroundings.

Because some individuals with mental disorders have parents with similar conditions, because emotional changes seem to be related to brain damage or chemical imbalance, and because physical makeup is associated with personality style, it appears that constitution plays a part in how people react to stress. Though the role of constitution is detectable, it is not large. Other factors contribute more significantly.

Psychoanalytic

Sigmund Freud was the creator of psychoanalysis. From his work with disturbed patients in the later part of the nineteenth century, he developed the theory that the cause of their problems lay buried in the past. Psychoanalysis was the treatment he devised to correct these disorders. Though Freud was mostly interested in the reasons for and the treatment of emotional disturbances, his ideas gradually came together to form a psychoanalytic theory of personality. We will examine Freud's three-part organization of personality, his notion of layers of awareness, and his ideas about the origins of anxiety and depression.

The Three-Part Organization of Personality. Psychoanalytic theory divides the personality into three parts: id, superego, and ego. The **id** houses the impulses for gratification, which are the major source of emotional energy. The id is driven by a single purpose, to satisfy the pleasure principle. If tension develops within the person — the need for food or buildup of sexual drive or anger — the id functions to gratify these impulses. It does so without concern for laws or reason or society. It contains neither values nor morals. The

Psychoanalysis

Psychoanalysis assumes that present emotional problems are caused by repressing unbearable emotions or thoughts of the past, usually childhood. The job of the psychoanalyst is to help the patient reexperience these long-ago repressed emotions and ideas. The treatment as it was originally employed was lengthy, complex, and expensive. Psychoanalysis takes three to five years of treatment, typically four to five days a week. During the sessions the patient lies on a couch, with the doctor sitting out of sight. One of the techniques is free association. The patient is instructed to say whatever comes to mind without regard to how upsetting or bizarre. The therapist analyzes the stream of associations for clues to what has been repressed. Then the patient is helped to feel these old, upsetting emotions again, gain insight into their origins, and learn new ways of dealing with them. Because psychoanalysis is so expensive and results have been questioned, this treatment procedure is practiced infrequently today. However, many of the techniques of psychoanalysis are used in other forms of modern therapy.

id ". . . is demanding, impulsive, irrational, asocial, selfish, and pleasure loving. It is the spoiled child of the personality." (Hall, 1954, pp. 26–27).

By contrast, the **superego** is the personality's judge. The superego is the standard-setter, the moralist, the rewarder of good thoughts or behavior and the punisher of the bad. Its purpose is to regulate the desires whose unbridled expression would destroy the society in which the person lives or lead to intolerable punishment.

The **ego** mediates between the competing forces of the id and the superego, organizing the personality to meet the requirements of the outer world. The ego carries out the executive functions of the mind. This involves seeing the outer reality clearly, thinking, deciding, following a plan of action, and making corrections as needed. As the id is driven by the *pleasure principle*, the ego is driven by the *reality principle*, which reconciles inner desires to the demands of the environment. Gratification of needs is delayed until an appropriate time when it would not be costly to the individual.

Layers of Awareness. One of Freud's most intriguing conceptions is that awareness can be separated into three layers: conscious, preconscious and unconscious. Those behaviors, thoughts, desires, and recollections we are presently aware of are said to be **conscious.** Those which are **preconscious** are in the twilight zone just short of awareness, but can be brought into consciousness if our attention is directed to them. Ingrained habits and superstitions are preconscious, such as always putting the sock on the right foot first in the morning or knocking on wood after talking about good fortune. Disquieting thoughts or emotions are often put out of mind, suppressed to the preconscious while we go about our business. For instance, we don't think about a party we are missing this weekend while we are studying for a Monday-morning exam.

Far deeper than the preconscious layer is the **unconscious.** Here are instinctive, aggressive, and sexual urges that are part of everyone's makeup. Also present are impulses, thoughts, and memories that have been repressed, banished from consciousness because continuing awareness of them causes stress. The case of Miss Lucy illustrates the repression of painful thoughts and feelings to the unconscious. The thought Miss Lucy could not bear was that her desire to marry the wealthy widower could never be fulfilled, so she repressed the entire thought that she was ever in love with him in the first place.

Freud's Discovery of Repression in the Case of Miss Lucy

Toward the end of the nineteenth century, another doctor referred to Sigmund Freud a patient with most puzzling symptoms. The patient was Miss Lucy, an English governess who worked for a wealthy Viennese widower. Just before his wife died, Miss Lucy, a distant relative of the woman, made a deathbed promise to her that she would always look after the children. Miss Lucy's problem was that she constantly smelled burning pudding. Everywhere she went this odor pursued her. She also had chronic fatigue, diminished appetite, and low spirits.

As he talked with her, Freud discovered the moment that Miss Lucy had first remembered smelling the disagreeable odor. It was two months earlier, a few days before her birthday. She had received a letter from her mother in Scotland. The children playfully took the letter, saying that she couldn't open it until her birthday. As she tried to retrieve the letter, a strong odor assailed her nostrils. Miss Lucy had forgotten that she had put pudding on the stove to cook, and now it was burning.

Instinctively, Freud homed in on the letter. What was in it? In the letter, her mother said how pleased she was that Miss Lucy would be leaving her employer and coming back to Scotland to live. "Leaving your employer?" Freud inquired. "What about the deathbed promise? Has something happened between you?"

Indeed something had happened. Miss Lucy had fallen in love with her employer after a tender moment between them. She had begun to imagine herself as his wife, mother to his children and mistress of his estate. Then one day he reproached Miss Lucy severely for allowing an elderly family friend to kiss the children, which was just *not done* in Victorian Vienna. Miss Lucy was devastated. The cold and impersonal manner with which her employer chastised her dashed Miss Lucy's hopes of marriage.

Freud found that Miss Lucy could not bear the anxiety triggered by her employer's outburst because she could not tolerate the thought that he regarded her merely as a governess. Her dream of marrying him was shattered. Unable to cope with this overpowering reality, Miss Lucy banished these unwelcome thoughts from her mind.

Why did the odor of burning pudding haunt Miss Lucy? She associated this burning pudding smell with the time that her mother's letter arrived. This letter reminded Miss Lucy momentarily of her unfulfilled love and broken dreams. These poignant thoughts were quickly repressed, or banished, from her awareness. The smell of the burning pudding remained as a trace left in the consciousness, which symbolized the repressed feelings.

SOURCE: Adapted from Freud, S. and Breuer, J. (1895) Studies on hysteria. *The standard edition of the complete psychological works of Sigmund Freud.* (Edited and translated by James Strachey, in collaboration with Anna Freud.) London: Hogarth Press, 1974, vol. 2.

When a ship suddenly sinks, a floating spar or oil slick marks the spot where the craft went down. Similarly, when unacceptable desires are repressed, their former presence is marked by a symbol that remains in the conscious mind. In Miss Lucy's case, the smell of burning pudding remained to symbolize the broken dream she had banished from her awareness.

Origins of Anxiety and Depression. Anxiety is a centerpiece of Freud's understanding of personality. He thought the function of anxiety is to signal us that danger may be imminent. In his view, there are three kinds of anxiety: reality, neurotic, and moral anxiety (Freud, 1926). *Reality anxiety* is what has already been discussed as a reaction to stress out there in the real world — a boss who gives us a hard time, a loved one who leaves us, an unexpected bill for the car. *Neurotic anxiety* comes from within us, arising from apprehensions that an impulse will slip its controls, resulting in undesirable consequences. Take, for example, a boy who was raised in a Quaker family in which aggression was deeply frowned upon. As a child he was punished for any manifestation of anger toward siblings, or even competition in the classroom or on the basketball court. As an adult, anxiety is triggered every time someone makes him angry, or even when he thinks he might win a game of handball. This neurotic anxiety does not stem from the stress itself but from leftover childhood remembrances.

Moral anxiety is a first cousin of neurotic anxiety. Similar to neurotic anxiety, it stems largely from feelings and thoughts we have that violate our inner standards. Moral anxiety can be identified by the sense of anxious guilt that we are likely to be punished or humiliated if we act on an inner desire. Consider a little girl who loved to go around naked in the summertime. She was punished for this by her mother, who calls this "lewd and lascivious" behavior. Throughout her childhood and adolescence, the girl avoided being seen with no clothes on to avoid guilty feelings coming from associating nakedness with promiscuous thoughts and deeds. As an adult, the woman forgets that her mother had shamed her for her nakedness, but she experiences anxiety and guilt at being seen undressed by her husband.

From Freud's thinking also came an understanding of why some people become depressed under stress (Freud, 1917). He noted the tendency for some people to view any frustration or setback as evidence that they are no good. Also, some individuals become depressed because they stake their entire self-esteem on an outside event. If my view of whether I am a worthwhile person depends on my boss's permitting me to leave early, or on some other equally trivial event, I am set up to become depressed. One of Freud's most perceptive understandings about the depressive reaction was its connection with aggression. He saw depression as hostility turned inward. Instead of getting mad at my boss because he's a tyrant, I turn this anger on myself, feeling worthless and deserving of abuse.

Many of today's scholars and clinicians take exception to major aspects of psychoanalytic theory and treatment. A large number of Freud's basic ideas, however, remain helpful in understanding normal adaptation. Especially useful are his ideas about the layers of awareness and how people handle stress emotions.

Behavioral

The central assumption of behavioral theory is that reactions to stress are learned in the same way as other knowledge and behavior. That is, we respond with aggression, depression, and anxiety to unpleasant events because we have been taught to do so. The "teaching" has not been in the classroom but rather by how others react to our behavior and by our copying of what others do. Three concepts describing how emotions are learned are the conditioned reflex, reinforcement, and modeling.

Conditioned Reflex. The fathers of behavioral theory were Russian physician Ivan Pavlov and American psychologist John Watson. During the period of his greatest work — the same time that Freud was in his prime — Pavlov discovered the **conditioned reflex** (1927). He was able to cause dogs to drool with anticipation as though they were about to be fed, even though no food was present, just by ringing a bell.

Watson was the founder of the behavioral school in America. He applied Pavlov's understanding of conditioning to the learning of fears. The initial phase of his career was spent trying to demonstrate that human emotions to stress could be conditioned by unpleasant experiences. He tried to prove that stress emotions develop because each of us learns to become anxious when something unpleasant happens to us. For example, we are almost hit by a car while jaywalking as a child and are frightened. If we carry this fear into adulthood and become extremely nervous every time we cross the street — even though there are no cars coming — that might prove Watson's point. The conditioned response occurs in the presence of an event similar to the original one.

In an effort to prove his theory, Watson ran an experiment with Little Albert, a healthy eleven-month-old boy. Those were the days before researchers worried much about ethics in experimentation. Such treatment of a human being is neither justified nor permissible today in psychological research. Still, his work with Little Albert convinced Watson that a fearful response to a rat could be conditioned. Moreover, this reaction transferred from the rat to similar objects — other small animals, furry objects, a Santa Claus mask, and even Professor Watson's own hair.

A later study found that existing fears could be eliminated by pairing desirable events with the cause of the apprehension. Mary Cover Jones (1924) eradicated the fear of a rabbit in a little boy by showing him the animal at a distance when he was doing something he enjoyed — in his case, eating. Gradually, the rabbit was brought closer and closer while the youngster had the positive experience of eating. Eventually, he showed no fear of rabbits or other small furry beasts. Today a variation of this same technique is used successfully to treat phobias such as the fear of flying.

Little Albert and the Rat

Professor Watson attempted to condition fear to a white rabbit in little Albert by showing him a white rat and striking a heavy steel bar behind him as soon as he reached to touch it. Here is his report:

". . . We first showed by repeated tests that Albert feared nothing except loud sounds.

". . . Everything coming within twelve inches of him was reached for and manipulated. . . . His reaction, however, to the sound of the steel bar was characteristic and what we had been led to believe is true of most if not all infants . . . a sudden intake of the breath and an upward fling of the arms. On the second stimulus (the bar being struck), the lips began to pucker and tremble, on the

third he broke into a crying fit, turned to one side and began to crawl away as rapidly as possible. . . .

"*Eleven months, three days old.* (1) White rat suddenly taken from basket and presented to Albert. He began to reach for the rat with left hand. Just as hand touched the animal the bar was struck immediately behind his head. The infant jumped violently and fell forward, burying his face in the mattress. . . . (2) Just as his right hand touched the rat, the bar was struck again. The infant jumped violently, fell forward and began to whimper.

"In order not to disturb the child too seriously, no further tests were given for one week.

"*Eleven months, ten days old.* (1) Rat presented suddenly without sound. There was a steady fixation but no tendency at first to reach for it. The rat was then placed nearer, whereupon tentative reaching movements

Reinforcement. Reinforcement is the shaping of behavior by responding to some actions and ignoring others. Have you ever trained a puppy? Usually we watch until the little fellow does his business on the paper and then praise him lavishly. This is **positive reinforcement. Negative reinforcement** is removing an aversive stimulus when the desired response is achieved: when our parents stop nagging us about doing our homework as we start to study. In both cases learning takes place in response to some reaction to behavior.

Unlike conditioning, which sets out to create a reaction in advance — causing little Albert to become anxious around furry things — reinforcement waits until a person makes a desirable response and then rewards it. Pioneer behaviorist B. F. Skinner (1938, 1974) found he could shape behavior in animals and people without their being aware of it by positive and negative reinforcement.

A story is told about a Yale psychology professor, lecturing his class on principles of reinforcement. The class was given in a large lecture hall with a podium resting in the middle of the stage. Normally, the professor stood behind the podium as he talked. Taking seriously the principles of reinforcement, the students got together and decided to look at the teacher only when he moved to his right. Otherwise, they would ignore him. Gradually, the professor kept moving to his right until he was giving his lecture from the wings on that side of the stage.

Emotional reactions to stress can be learned by reinforcement. An aggressive response to stress is reinforced by the mother who nods her head and began with the right hand. When the rat nosed the infant's left hand the hand was immediately withdrawn. . . ."

Combined stimulation with rat and sound:
Then the rat was presented to Albert B. five times while the bar was struck. Then the rat was presented alone. The instant the rat was shown to the baby he began to cry. He raised himself on all fours and began to crawl away as rapidly as possible. It was then agreed that little Albert B. had been conditioned to fear white rats.

The experimental question became whether he would be afraid henceforth only of rats or whether the fear would be transferred to other animals and possibly other objects.

Five days later Albert was first tested with blocks. He reached readily for them, playing with them as usual. First he was shown a rat and Albert exhibited the same fear reaction as before. Then a rabbit was suddenly placed in front of him. The reaction was pronounced. He leaned as far away from the animal as possible, whimpered and then burst into tears. A dog was placed in front of him. It did not produce as violent a reaction as the rabbit, but Albert shrank back as the animal came nearer, and he attempted to crawl away. A fur coat was shown. Albert B. withdrew immediately and began to fret. The coat was put close to him and he turned immediately, began to cry and tried to crawl away. A Santa Claus mask was then brought and presented to him. Albert B. was again very negative toward it. Just in play, professor Watson put his head down to see if Albert B. would play with his hair. Albert was completely negative.

SOURCE: Adapted from Watson, J. *Psychology: From the standpoint of the behaviorist.* second edition. Philadelphia: Lippincott, 1924.

smiles when her son says he wants to punch the bully who stole his lunch money. Anxiety or helplessness is instilled when a father encourages his boy's worry that he will be pulverized if he tries.

Modeling. A three-year-old girl catches a garden snake in the backyard and brings it to her mother, who screams. One nine-year-old boy watches his father become depressed when he is laid off. Another youngster observes her father raging at the system where a good man can't find work. The parents of these three youngsters are **modeling** reactions to stress. A growing number of psychologists believe that stress emotions are learned by imitating the response of others. Thus we react with panic, depression, or rage to a stressful situation because it has been demonstrated and we imitate it.

The linchpin of modeling theory is that we learn emotional reactions by observational learning. Social workers and police consistently observe that antisocial, aggressive youngsters were raised in homes with much physical abuse. The battered become the batterers. On the other hand, children raised in environments in which overt aggression is not the characteristic response to frustration by adults and others they observe are less likely to express anger outwardly. In the past two decades, Stanford University Professor Albert Bandura and others have conducted various experiments with children to determine the extent to which watching people express particular emotions influences them to behave similarly. In one study, investigators found that a group of children who watched adults assault a large, inflatable doll — verbally abusing

A father's aggressive response to a stressful situation may influence his children to behave similarly when frustrated.

it, kicking it, throwing it into the air, and hammering it with a mallet — behaved more aggressively in the playroom afterwards than did youngsters who did not see the demonstration (Bandura, Ross, and Ross, 1961). Research shows that watching others cope with stress without fear or helplessness enables people to cope with situations that usually occasion stress emotions. Bandura, Blanchard, and Ritter (1969) reported ninety-two percent of a group of people who had snake phobias were able to overcome their fear by watching someone handle vipers without anxiety.

From the vantage point of understanding reactions to stress, behavioral theory has many attractive features. It is less complicated, is free of abstraction, and applies principles that can be demonstrated in a laboratory. However, it is yet to be demonstrated that an individual's stress emotions are unfailingly a product of conditioning, reinforcement, or modeling. Other factors surely complicate the picture.

Humanistic

Another factor that contributes to how we react to stress is our picture of ourselves. Do you think of yourself as usually a nervous person or given to rages or bouts of depression? This self-perception, or self-concept, influences our responses to life's difficulties.

During the heyday of psychoanalysis and behaviorism it was not fashionable to speak of the self. But since World War II, far more interest has been shown by psychologists in the effect we have on ourselves. Newer theories take the position that we all have within us the potential to govern our own emotions.

This idea is one of the foundations of the humanistic school of psychology.

The ideas of William James and Abraham Maslow, together with the theory of Carl Rogers, form the foundation of humanistic theory. Humanists emphasize a positive view of human nature: that men and women naturally strive for maintenance, enhancement, and self-actualization; and that our inner tendencies are for healthy growth (Rogers, 1951). We will explore their ideas about the development of self-concept, self-esteem, and the purpose of stress emotions.

The Self-concept. How would you define yourself? Is it what you possess? What you do? Or your feelings about yourself? Throughout history human beings have always thought that we possess some inner essence, a core that has been called the soul, psyche, mind, organism, ego, or, more recently, identity. Though the terms have somewhat different meanings they share the notion of an "I" or "me," a central point of reference from which we experience the outer world.

Many years ago William James set the stage for current definitions of the **self-concept,** what he called the Empirical-Me, when he identified three components: (1) what we possess, (2) what we do, and (3) how we feel (1890). The first part of the self is what we can call our own — clothes, house, car, children, and bank account, as well as our reputation. The second part of the self is the actions for bodily preservation, for social recognition, and for personal development. The third part is all the feelings we have about ourselves — happiness, complacency, or dissatisfaction. Modern psychologists use two of James's three meanings of the concept of self: *the self as an object* — what we think of ourselves — and the *self as a doer* — our activities (Hall and Lindsay, 1957, Chapter 12).

Most of the time we behave in ways that are consistent with our self-concept. If you see yourself as attractive, nice to others, and likable, you probably will present yourself in that way when you meet someone new in class. If I consider myself not particularly bright but basically honest, I am not likely to cheat on the next exam even though I may be given the opportunity to do so without being caught. We are not always true to our self-concept. And sometimes when we behave in keeping with our view of ourselves there is a cost — such as having to be nice to people we can't stand, or coping with growing panic as we face exams we may fail.

Self-esteem. **Self-esteem** is the way we see ourselves, and in addition, how favorably or unfavorably we react to this picture of ourselves (Allport, 1937, Chapter 6). You may be pleased with your picture of yourself and, in that event, you can be said to have high self-esteem. Your sister's self-esteem may be low because what she sees in herself is displeasing.

Suppose we had to measure our own self-esteem. How would we do it? One way is to compare the degree of similarity between how we see ourselves and how we would like to be (Butler and Haigh, 1954). Carl Rogers and his co-workers found that they could judge the effectiveness of their counseling with students by comparing the students' self-esteem — the difference be-

Do we see our real self when we look into the mirror? Picasso's 1932 painting, *Girl before a Mirror*, illustrates the ancient myth that a mirror possesses magical qualities that reveal the inner self. (*Girl before a Mirror*, collection, The Museum of Modern Art, New York, gift of Mrs. Simon Guggenheim.)

tween their "actual" and "ideal" selves — before and after counseling. A group of young men and women coming for counseling were asked to rate themselves as they saw themselves and as they would like to be. Prior to therapy little relationship existed between the two ratings. At the end of counseling, the students' actual and ideal views were closer together, indicating an improvement in self-esteem.

We can't care about everything. Usually our self-esteem rests on a small number of things we care most about. For you these may be being intelligent and witty; I may stake my self-esteem on being a boxer and a leader. I may not care in the slightest whether I am two from the bottom in a class of a hundred as long as I pass this course. You may die a little if your grades surpass all but two. On the other hand, you may be totally indifferent to the fact that everyone you know is a better boxer, and I may live in shame if I am only the second-best fighter in school (James, 1890, Chapter 12).

The Purpose of Stress Emotions. In contrast to psychoanalytic and other theories of personality, Rogers does not see stress emotions as disruptive or damaging. Rather he views anger, fear, and anxiety as essential to continued growth (1951). Anger at a teacher who gives us a poor grade can fuel our desire to work harder next time to prove we are capable. Fear may be helpful to our survival if it causes us to jump out of the way of a speeding automobile. Anxiety several nights before an exam can propel us into studying for it.

For Rogers, human beings don't just naturally grow up to be fulfilled. Rather, life is a struggle. We strive to maintain ourselves — to meet our basic needs for food and shelter, safety, acceptance of others, and self-esteem. Throughout our lives we move toward greater independence and responsibility and, for some, self-actualization.

In seeking a richer life, we grow away from a secure balance of satisfactions to fresh challenges and a new adjustment. Like bruises and cuts, broken bones, and blisters, anger, depression, and anxiety are the price of a full and adventurous life (Vaillant, 1977, Chapter 16).

The perspective that the self-concept theory has on stress emotions is unique. Moreover, it is in keeping with current thinking, which sees emotional distress as associated with periods of transition to new stages of development (Levinson, 1978). We should remind ourselves, however, that anger, depression, and anxiety can be extremely painful and disrupt growth. Whether stress emotions are tied to personal maturation or are part of what retards our development is determined by how we handle these feelings.

Cognitive

The uniqueness of cognitive theory is in its emphasis on thinking. Practitioners of this approach believe it is the *interpretation* we give to our immediate physical or emotional discomfort in the face of stress that determines whether these responses will continue. If we *think* that our initial feelings are not merely momentary and will disappear in a moment, but will in fact worsen, they will surely persist: my burning cheeks and reflexive anger always become a temper tantrum when my mother says "No!"; your momentary feeling of inadequacy always makes you feel helpless when your boss criticizes you; the churning stomach always turns to panic in my friend when he has to speak. If, on the other hand, we believe we can control our responses to a difficult situation — I can count to ten to hold my temper in check or my friend can learn to relax in order to stop the physical symptoms of anxiety — we have a good chance to manage these emotions and continue to function reasonably well.

Cognitive theory makes three assumptions about reactions to stress: (1) emotions grow from thoughts about the self in the surrounding world; (2) behavior results from the appraisal of the stress, the immediate reaction to it, and the expectation of coping; and (3) we can learn to control thoughts that influence emotion and action.

Emotion and Thoughts. The first assumption — that emotions develop from internal ways of thinking about the self and the surrounding world — is set forth most clearly by University of Pennsylvania psychiatrist Aaron Beck and by New York psychologist Albert Ellis. In his work with depressed and anxious mental patients, Beck (1976) was struck by the tenacity with which patients held on to particular irrational thoughts. He identified distinctive cognitive patterns for several types of emotional problems. In anxious people, thoughts of danger predominate. A salesman who has to fly to the West Coast to call on a client reads of an airplane crash in Europe and begins to feel anxiety welling up. He knows such accidents always occur in threes. Before long, he is near panic. He doesn't know how he will ever be able to get to that airplane feeling the way he does.

Beck also found that men and women who are prone to depression consistently devalue themselves, put the worst interpretation on life events, have a low expectation of their capacity to cope, and are pessimistic about the future. We might imagine our salesman reacting to this fear by being critical of himself for feeling apprehensive; thinking that his initial discomfort will lead to great difficulty in getting on the plane, resulting in his arriving on the West Coast too wrung out to make the sale; being convinced that he will not be able to do anything to help himself; and being certain the overall outlook is bleak.

Ellis (1973) believes that thinking precedes our emotional reaction. He puts forward an **A-B-C model of faulty thinking,** which he holds is responsible for continuing distress: A is a stress in our lives; B is how we think about the event; and C is our resulting emotions and behavior. A boy's girl friend leaves him (A). The boy tells himself that he can't live without her (B). His depression results from his believing what he tells himself — that he can't face life without her (C). Ellis mentions certain other core irrational thoughts that he feels are the basis for most emotional disturbances (Ellis, 1962). These are shown in Table 2.6.

Table 2.6 Irrational assumptions at the core of many emotional disturbances

1. That it is a dire necessity for an adult to be loved by everyone for everything he or she does.
2. That certain acts are awful or wicked, and that people who perform such acts should be severely punished.
3. That it is horrible when things are not the way one would like them to be.
4. That human misery is externally caused, and is forced on one by outside people and events.
5. That if something is or may be dangerous or fearsome one should be terribly upset about doing it.
6. That it is easier to avoid than to face life's difficulties.
7. That one needs something greater than oneself on which to rely.
8. That one should be thoroughly competent, intelligent, and achieving in all possible respects.
9. That because something once strongly affected one's life, it should indefinitely affect it.
10. That one must have certain and perfect control over things.
11. That human happiness can be achieved by inertia and inaction.
12. That one has virtually no control over one's emotions and that one cannot help feeling certain things.

SOURCE: From Albert Ellis, *Reason and emotion in psychotherapy.* Secaucus, N.J.: Citadel Press, 1962. Reprinted by permission.

Appraisal of Stress, Immediate Reaction, and Expectation of Coping. A second assumption is that stress emotions arise as part of a sequence of adaptations to stress. Essentially our feelings are stimulated by three elements: how threatening the external cause is, the evaluation of physical feedback we get from our body, and the estimate of our ability to cope with it (Murray and Jacobson, 1978).

A young man in college may react differently to being called on in a class in which he sees the teacher as friendly and supportive, if he has had the experience of successfully answering questions before, and if he interprets the queasiness in his stomach as natural butterflies that will go away once he begins speaking. Imagine how the same student might react if he saw the classroom environment as hostile, if he had little experience speaking in class, and was sure that the uneasiness in his stomach was going to result in his throwing up at any moment.

Control of Emotion and Action Can Be Learned. Beck (1976) and Ellis (1970) have put forward ideas about how to recognize unwanted thought patterns that influence emotional reactions, see their harmful effects, and replace them with more positive thoughts and actions. Recall Ellen, going for the road test for her driver's license. She is aware she has a tendency to become nervous in test situations, and her driving deteriorates. Ellen can improve her chances of passing the exam by finding out what tasks the test involves and practicing them with a friend who pretends to be a particularly critical licensing officer. During this role play, she can practice controlling her anxiety and blocking this feeling by concentrating on the driving itself.

At this moment, cognitive theories of the origins of stress emotions and ideas for modifying maladaptive responses are intriguing to scholars and clinicians alike. Part of the promise is the promise of youth. The cognitive perspective has many new, exciting ideas, but they have not yet withstood the test of time, patient follow-up, critique, and competition from new ideas. Perhaps the most exciting aspect of the cognitive theories is that they combine an appreciation of inner experience, the effect of external determinants of behavior, and — most important — recognition of the interaction between the two (Mahoney and Arnkoff, 1978).

Summary

1. Stress is any event that taxes our physical and emotional balance enough to cause an unpleasant reaction.
2. Stress is caused by frustration, threat, and conflict. *Frustration* is discomfort caused by environmental forces that delay the expression of desired behavior. *Threat* is an expectation of discomfort or the inability to manage future situations. *Conflict* involves the presence of two competing but mutually exclusive courses of action.
3. Three common stress emotions are aggression, depression, and anxiety.

     Aggression is the urge to attack the agent of frustration. *Depression* is a complex of feelings including helplessness, low self-esteem, and an inner sense of being deserving of bad events. *Anxiety* is uneasiness, apprehension, or tension, usually in response to threat or conflict.

4. Stress can be measured by totaling the amount of stress we confront or the length of time we combat it. The *Social Readjustment Rating Scale* is an example of the former. Selye's *General Adaptation Syndrome* with its phases of alarm, resistance, and exhaustion is an illustration of the impact of stress over time.

5. *Stress has negative and positive effects.* Stress can result in physical disorder and emotional maladjustment, in decreased effectiveness at work and in relations to others, and in reduced adaptive capacities. Beneficial results of manageable stress are satisfaction of innate needs, development of a carry-over skill, and stress inoculation.

6. Five theories of stress emotions are the constitutional, psychoanalytic, behavioral, humanistic, and cognitive.

7. The evidence for a *constitutional* origin of distressing feelings is indirect, but suggests that physical makeup has a small though detectable influence on how we react to stress.

8. Freud's theory of anxiety is the centerpiece of the *psychoanalytic* theory. He saw three types of anxiety: reality, neurotic, and moral.

9. The *behavioral* theories assume that we develop stress emotions by conditioned reflex, reinforcement, and modeling. Conditioning theory sets out in advance to cause a response in the presence of an event by pairing it with a stimulus. Reinforcement theory waits until the subject makes a desired response and then rewards it. Modeling theories assume that stress emotions are developed through observational learning.

10. *Humanistic* theories emphasize a positive view of human nature. Self-concept and self-esteem are essential elements of this theory. Stress emotions are seen as normal reactions to human growth.

11. *Cognitive* theorists believe that how we think about the immediate physical and emotional responses to a stress determines whether we will continue to feel this way. This theory maintains that emotions grow from thoughts about the self in the world; that behavior results from the appraisal of stress, immediate reactions, and expectations of coping; and that control of emotions and actions can be learned.

A Look Ahead

Our understanding of how people manage stress so far has emphasized knowing about stressful agents and understanding reactions to them. In the next chapter we will look at the nature of the adaptive response and its levels of effectiveness, and at ways of combating problems in living. We will identify the ingredients of the concept of adaptation and learn that adaptation is a continuum ranging from highly effective means of controlling distress to less helpful ways of responding. Three ways of managing stress will be studied.

Key Terms

stress	stress inoculation
frustration	anticipatory fear
threat	sensitizor
conflict	repressor
approach-avoidance conflict	id
approach-approach conflict	superego
avoidance-avoidance conflict	ego
aggression	conscious
depression	preconscious
anxiety	unconscious
trait (anxiety)	conditioned reflex
state (anxiety)	reinforcement
Social Readjustment Rating Scale	positive reinforcement
Life Change Unit	negative reinforcement
Life Experience Inventory	modeling
general adaptation syndrome	self-concept
Type A behavior	self-esteem
sensation-seeking scale	A-B-C model of faulty thinking
carry-over skill	

Suggested Readings

Stress

Selye, H. *The stress of life*. New York: McGraw-Hill, 1956.

———— *Stress without distress*. New York: Signet, 1974.

> The nature of stress and the general adaptation syndrome.

Stress reactions

Seligman, M. *Helplessness*. San Francisco: Freeman, 1975.

Spielberger, C. (Ed.), *Anxiety: Current trends in theory and research*, vols 1 and 2. New York: Academic Press, 1972.

Bandura, A. *Aggression: A social learning analysis*. Englewood Cliffs, N.J.: Prentice-Hall, 1973.

> A full description of the nature of responses to stress.

Effects of stress

Kutash, I., Schlesinger, L., and associates (Eds.), *Handbook on stress and anxiety: Contemporary knowledge, theory, and treatment*. San Francisco: Jossey-Bass, 1980, chaps 10, 11, 16, 17, and 19.

Monat, A., and Lazarus, R. (Eds.), *Stress and coping: An anthology*. New York: Columbia Press, 1977, chaps 2, 3, 9, 15, 19, 21, and 23.

> These bring together the diverse negative effects of chronic and overpowering stress.

Eddie was . . . a ten year old boy . . . [who] had been referred to the clinic by his school because of truancy. In spite of frequent absences, his school achievement was at least average, his attitude toward teachers and classmates was friendly, and his conduct was irreproachable. Why did he skip school? He told us. Every now and then when his father was drunk Eddie needed to stay home to take care of him. And then, because there was no money for food, he had to find odd jobs in the neighborhood for a little while until his father could go back to work. When his father was able to get work again, Eddie would go back to school.

His father was a brutal drunkard. His mother had been committed two years earlier to a state institution for mental defectives.

Two older brothers and one sister were also in institutions for the feeble-minded. The four oldest children in the family, now old enough to be out on their own, all had police records dating back to childhood. Eddie was the youngest. He was the only one still living at home. His intelligence was at least normal. He had a good scholastic record. He had never been involved in delinquent acts. He had no neurotic symptoms, but he was slightly obese.

How did this child survive? It is not remarkable that the others in this diseased home should have succumbed one by one, but how do you explain an Eddie?

SOURCE: Fraiberg, S.: *The magic years*. New York: Scribner Lyceum, 1959, pages 289–290.

CHAPTER 3
Adaptation to Stress

Questions to think about

□   Have you handled stress pretty well sometimes and not so well on other occasions? What was the difference?

□   To what extent does the way you adjust to problems affect the rest of your life?

□   Do you know people whose dress, speech, or other behavior has changed since they began college? Why might that be?

□   When real problems that can't be avoided cause distress, how might we find relief?

What is it that enabled Eddie to maintain his emotional balance while living with the same conditions that caused his brothers and sisters to become casualties? He faced the same deprivation and brutality that would have placed him high on anyone's scale of distress. He must have shared many of the initial reactions of his siblings to these stresses — frustration, confusion, helplessness, anxiety, despair. What kept him going?

In contrast to Eddie, youngsters from stable families with financial advantages sometimes break down in response to comparatively minor stress. A ten-year-old boy, the son of wealthy and loving parents, becomes depressed and stops going to school when a teacher makes fun of his artwork in front of the

A sudden shadow behind us can be threatening when we are alone. Our adjustment is taxed when we face a potential outer menace as well as when we feel the threat of a strong but unacceptable inner desire.

class. Other children feel their lives collapsing around them because they don't make a team, have a falling out with a friend, get a C-plus on a test, don't get a summer camp award, or have a disagreement with parents. Adults also may bear up under extreme stress and fall apart in the face of minor incidents. Why do some cope with stress exceedingly well and others fail?

In the years since Eddie was treated in a community clinic, new understandings have emerged about the processes we use to maintain a normal state as we manage problems in our lives. These processes embrace many activities, ranging from highly effective means of managing stressful emotions to responses that are inefficient and have undesirable effects on the quality of our life.

The term we will use to describe this process of adjusting to stress is *adaptation*. In this chapter we study the essential features of adaptive responses. We look at three ways of responding to stress: (1) Self-protective responses are automatic mental processes that go to work to reduce emotional discomfort before we are even aware of it. While they diminish inner upset, self-protective responses do nothing to remove the cause. (2) Direct control responses are based on the clear recognition of the inner psychological discomfort. They work on the inner responses to reduce the distress. Like self-protective responses, however, they do nothing to affect the cause. (3) Direct action responses recognize the source of the problem and operate to remove it.

What Is Adaptation?

Of all the words fashioned to characterize ways of managing stress, **adaptation** is the best suited (White, 1974). As we will see later in the chapter, other types of responses are part of this adaptive process — accommodation, ego defenses, coping — but have more limited meanings. Austrian psychiatrist

Heinz Hartmann spent much of his career thinking about the essentials of adaptation. The following definition is distilled from his considerable writing (Hartmann, 1958, pp. 23–27, 40–42; 1964, pp. 15–17) on the subject:

> Adaptation is a continuing process of maintaining inner harmony while fitting into an average, expectable environment without undue compromise.

Let us look at each feature of this process.

Hartmann's Definition of Adaptation

Continuing Process. Adaptation is not an adjustment, but the continuing activity of adjusting (Devereux, 1956). It is a continuing day-to-day, sometimes hour-to-hour practice. Dealing with problems as they arise results in less buildup of anxiety and other upsetting emotions, as well as less erosion of the pleasures of living.

A fluid appraisal and reappraisal of the causes of stress, our immediate reaction to it, and ways of lessening it are hallmarks of normal adaptation (Lazarus, Averill, and Opton, 1974). Imagine Hillary reacting to the thought of final exams in her first year at the university. She panics, sure that she'll never pass, and has the impulse to drop out of school immediately. Then Hillary gathers herself. Is this panic reaction justified? Gradually she reevaluates the cause of the stress. Up until now her grades have been pretty good; in the past she's always been nervous before her finals, but she has always done pretty well. She begins to think of the exams in less catastrophic terms. Hillary realizes her initial intense anxiety was far out of line. As she recognizes this, Hillary identifies options other than leaving the university. Maybe she can cope with the exams after all.

This continuing fluid process of appraisal and reappraisal is a little like piloting a boat or plane. As most pilots quickly discover, it's impossible to steer a craft straight toward a point. Because the bow or nose has a tendency to hunt from side to side, the pilot must make small corrections to remain on course. If the small, continuous corrections are not made, the ship or plane will veer off course. When this happens, the corrections needed are substantial. In human adjustment, the quicker the potential stresses are anticipated, the less dramatic the corrective response needs to be. This makes for smoother adaptation to the stresses we encounter in everyday life.

Maintaining Inner Harmony. Inner harmony is a sufficiently comfortable condition to permit us to find satisfaction from a balance of work, love, and play. Because no one lives in a hermetically sealed stress-free capsule, internal comfort is continually rocked by disturbing events. Each of us can act on ourselves to preserve our inner stability. We have within us the power to tolerate flurries of anger, helplessness, or fear without becoming violent or disorganized or locking into paralysis. We can understand the origins of distress, can scale down the terror of a fearful reality, control inappropriate impulses, and can convert unrealistic fantasies into obtainable objectives.

Think about Eddie. Surely he did not keep his emotional balance by pretending he didn't feel angry because his father was drinking, depressed because his mother was in a hospital, or anxious because he felt abandoned and alone. Just as shivering tells us something is making our body cold, psychological distress signals something is disturbing our emotional adjustment. Being aware we are upset enables us to find the cause. In Eddie's case, the origin was obvious. In other cases, the source of the distress is sometimes obscure and counseling is needed to uncover it.

In successful adaptation, insight is not enough. Action must follow. Knowing that he was upset permitted Eddie to take action to reduce the stress. Perhaps his working or taking responsibility for his father and other family members reduced his distress. Perhaps eating a little more than he needed also comforted him and helped maintain an inner peace.

Fitting into an Average, Expectable Environment. Adaptation involves fitting into an average, expectable environment. What is an average, expectable environment? It's easy to imagine what it is not: jail, concentration camp, or combat. It probably isn't growing up with psychotic parents or alone. Jam-packed living conditions, serious physical limitations, or continual unemployment are neither average nor expectable. These are unusual, brutal and alien realities, requiring survival behaviors that would challenge most conceptions of normal.

An average, expectable environment is a setting in which outer realities are usual for the segment of society in which the individual is a member. An average, expectable environment also refers to the self. It is a physical constitution within normal limits and inner impulses in keeping with what we have come to expect, as well as what others experience. An average, expectable environment leads to anticipation of reality requirements — demands of work, desires of loved ones, when a vacation is possible, and when our own needs that we have put off can be gratified. The more accurately we can forecast what the environment has in store for us, what it demands, and what it gives, the greater likelihood we can meet our own needs and those of outer reality.

For example, Hillary knows in advance that relations with her closest friends will be strained when she takes her final exams. She tells them about it beforehand and makes plans to spend time with them afterward. Because she can anticipate her own frazzled mental state, Hillary plans to take some time off when her tests are finished, which will help her regenerate her energy and spirit.

Fitting into an environment doesn't mean passive submission. Some stresses are brief or lead to desirable consequences, and so they are bearable. If a reality is chronically or acutely unacceptable — it consistently fractures inner comfort, episodically causes great distress, and doesn't give enough pleasure in return — then the price may be too high to pay. A person always has a choice: accommodation, alteration, or change. Consider Hillary, who is pre-med. She may experience the constant demands and competition as worth the

anxiety and acid stomach she lives with. She accommodates by yoga and an-
tacids. She might also try to alter her environment by reducing the pressure —
taking only the minimum pre-med requirements, spacing difficult courses, or
seeking a tutor. Finally, Hillary may conclude that she doesn't want to live
with the pressure being a pre-med student brings with it, so she gives up her
dream of being a doctor and plans instead to go into business.

Without Undue Compromise. Every medication has some side effects. Similarly, each adaptation to stress has its cost. One cost is the extent to which
enjoyment in areas of living unconnected to the problem is undermined. Another cost is how much the future is mortgaged in dealing with today's difficulties. In normal adaptation, the response to lessen the stressful event does
not unduly compromise other parts of life or future freedom of action.

Consider Hillary again. She decides to put up with the competitive pressure and hard work of being a pre-med student because the anticipated future
rewards are great. She chooses to live with her tension, moderating it as she
can with relaxation techniques and medication. She worries from time to time
that she may be doing permanent damage to her mental or physical health
because she's treating the symptoms and not the cause. So far, however, the
anxiety and discomfort go away when she takes a vacation. If they persist she
plans to lighten her course load.

How much does the rigorous self-discipline Hillary must apply to herself
compromise her relationships with others? Does she have time to be in friendly
contact with people she cares about? How much do built-up tensions express
themselves in temporary outbursts or self-pitying depressions, which alienate
those close to her? Knowing that relationships with others can be threatened
by the amount of time she works and by outbursts of anger or depression,
Hillary can plan to improve the quality of the time she spends with her friends
and do nice things to compensate them for putting up with her occasional
flare-ups.

Types of Adaptive Responses

Adaptive responses are efforts to maintain our psychological balance. These
range from high-quality ways of managing stress, which conform to the definition of adaptation in the last section, to those which fall far short of these
high standards. Three types of adaptive responses are self-protective responses, direct control responses, and direct action responses. These are shown
in Figure 3.1.

Generally, **self-protective responses** (SPRs) work by blocking out full
awareness of distressing feelings along with knowledge of what is causing them.
Miss Lucy's repression of her sadness at not being able to marry the widower
(see page 53) is an illustration.

University of California psychologist Richard Lazarus (1976) has made
distinctions between direct control and direct action responses. **Direct control**

Figure 3.1
Three classes of adaptive responses

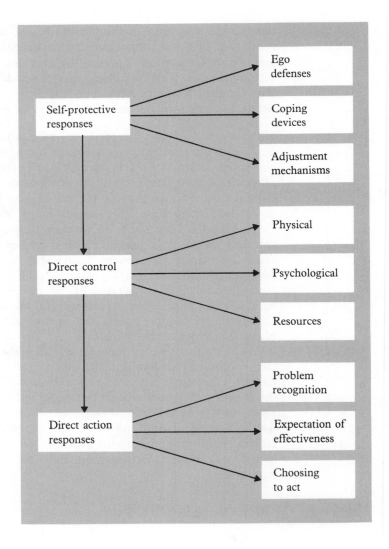

responses (DCR) operate to relieve the symptom of the distress. An example is taking a tranquilizer to relax. As the name implies, **direct action responses** (DAR) go right to the source of the problem. Having a talk to straighten out a misunderstanding with a friend is an illustration of a direct action response.

The dotted lines and arrow connecting the self-protective responses and direct control responses to direct action responses in Figure 3.1 show a connection between them. Many times, especially when the origin of the upset is known, a self-protective response or direct control response may be a link in a chain of responses that eventually leads to the elimination of the stressful event itself by direct action.

Self-Protective Responses

Self-protective responses are personal, mental practices that diminish the awareness of a painful emotion or the cause of it. They are self-initiated acts to help sustain inner harmony by masking unacceptable inner urges or external realities. They can restrain a violent impulse by shutting it out of awareness, soften the effect of a depressing situation by filtering out its most unpleasant elements or alleviate sexual frustration by converting it into constructive energy. As these examples show, SPR's guard internal stability by altering the subjective experience of a stress emotion. Instead of feeling angry, helpless or frustrated, we are more in control and tranquil. At first, all SPRs are automatic. They are not well-thought-out, strategic maneuvers applied after deliberation. Some of these resemble more closely the psychological equivalent of a knee-jerk reflex. Others are more like a prepackaged balm we habitually apply to soothe jangled nerves. But all SPRs are self-acting. They are in place before we know it — reducing anger, assuaging depression, and relieving anxiety.

Psychologists have advanced the theory that the difference between SPRs that normal people use to manage stress and those that individuals with emotional disorders use is a matter of degree, not of type (Haan, 1977; Kroeber, 1963). Adaptive reactions are on a continuum extending from high-grade ways of managing upsetting events to far less effective means of reducing emotional upset.

Said differently, the repression, denial, and other maladaptive ways of coping with distress that Vaillant noted in his less well-adjusted men (see Table 1.2 on page 20) were examples of a normal process gone bad. These mechanisms were not brand-new behavior patterns, but a distorted version of normally effective SPRs. For the moment, imagine walking out of a store with a record you did not pay for. Outside, a security guard stops you. "Do you have a sales receipt for that record? Come with me to the manager's office!" As you confront the manager, you find yourself breathing rapidly, a normal physical reaction that pumps more oxygen into the blood, and exhaling the waste product carbon dioxide. This enables you to think and act at an optimum level. Your mind works rapidly, enabling you to explain why you forgot to pay for the record. However, if you breathe in and out too rapidly, you may upset the delicate acid level of the blood because too much carbon dioxide is exhaled. Instead of feeling more alert you may find yourself becoming dizzy, tingly, numb, and close to fainting. This condition is called *hyperventilation*, a natural physical process of coping with stress gone awry. In the psychological realm, many low-level SPRs bear this same connection to high-level means of managing stress.

It is possible to identify three levels of SPRs. They are — from lowest to highest — ego defenses, coping devices, and adjustment mechanisms. Their primary features are summarized in Table 3.1.

Table 3.1   Characteristics of three levels of self-protective responses

| | ADAPTATION LEVEL | | |
| | LOW— — — — — — — — — — —HIGH | | |
CHARACTERISTIC	EGO DEFENSES	COPING DEVICES	ADJUSTMENT MECHANISMS
Trigger	unacceptable impulses or urges	greater-than-usual but manageable stress	mild clash with environment
Knowledge of stress	Unaware	Aware	Aware
Appraisal/reappraisal of reaction	Fixed	Compartmentalized	Fluid
Orientation	Past and present	Present and near future	Future and present
Freedom of action	Little	Limited	Considerable
Compromise	Significant	Some	Minimal

Ego Defenses

Ego defenses are mental mechanisms that protect us from disconcerting stress emotions by automatically blocking out of our awareness the cause of these feelings (Hinsie and Campbell, 1970). They mask inner impulses and outer stresses. The lust for our neighbor's spouse is not acted upon because the desire is shut out of consciousness by an ego defense. Because an ego defense shuts out the conscious feeling of anger, we do not lash out at a waiter who adds an extra ten dollars to our bill.

Ego defenses are triggered without our awareness or volition by a small amount of anxiety called **signal anxiety.** This tiny degree of emotional discomfort calls into operation the ego defense that maintains the state of inner harmony. Though ego defenses are effective in restoring mental quiet, the cost is considerable. Recall Miss Lucy, who used the ego defense of repression. For her, the price of relief from discomfort was the blocking out of awareness of the problem and her reaction to it. Because she was blind to her own distress, she couldn't do anything to try to improve the relationship with the man she loved. No appraisal and reappraisal of the stress and her reaction to it were possible. All she could do was plan to leave him for reasons that were opaque to her. The orientation of her SPR was in the past, and she achieved inner harmony without being aware that she might have alternatives other than leaving. Finally, the repression surely compromised many other areas of her life.

Four examples of ego defenses are repression, denial, projection, and reaction formation. Their characteristics and examples follow.

Repression. **Repression** is the forcing of an anxiety-arousing perception out of consciousness (Hall, 1954). Repression is *the* primary ego defense. Most other ego defenses have repression as a part. Often the other defenses operate to sustain repression.

We have seen repression in action with Miss Lucy. A modern-day example might be Luis, an engineer. His problem is that his boss is an aggravating petty tyrant who makes him angry. Because he was raised to abhor violence, Luis represses his rage toward the boss. But repression isn't a once-and-for-all event. Repressed feelings are restless, constantly looking for avenues for expression. Repressed urges often express themselves indirectly: in humor, dreams, and slips of the tongue (Menninger, 1967, Chapter 7).

Though he may feel no conscious antagonism, Luis may make malicious jokes about his boss's dress or mannerisms. Another indirect route by which hostile feelings express themselves is in dreams. Though Luis is unaware of any hostility toward him, he is made uncomfortable by a recurring nightmare of his boss being maimed in a bloody car accident.

Slips of the tongue may also convey unconscious feelings or thoughts. The Reverend Paul Buttrick, former Preacher to the University at Harvard, told the story of listening carefully to what parishioners said to him after his sermons. One parishioner shook his hand and said enthusiastically, "I loved your sermon. It was like a glass of water to a drowning man!" Later, a faculty member exclaimed, "Each of your sermons is better than the next!"

Denial. **Denial** has two meanings. The first is *complete denial*, the rejection of the existence of an unmistakable, threatening reality. Complete denial is seen in people confronting serious danger. In her book *On Death and Dying* (1969), which broke open the subject of death for clinical study and research, Dr. Elisabeth Kübler-Ross pointed out that denial is a typical response of patients who have just been told that they have a terminal illness. "Oh, no, it can't be true!" is a common human reaction.

Imagine Chantal, who is obese and has high blood pressure. She knows she should lose weight, but can't seem to stay with any diet. To relieve her anxiety about what she's doing to her health, and her frustration because she can't lose weight, Chantal says that she simply doesn't believe that being seriously overweight will harm her, no matter what anyone says.

Admitting a threatening reality but negating its consequences is a second type of denial. This also might be observed in Chantal, who notices an increasing difficulty breathing. She tires more easily and is bothered by bouts of dizziness and headaches. She acknowledges that these are possible signs of hypertension, but affirms with unfounded certainty that she is "sure" she is all right.

Projection. **Projection** is the assigning of an unacceptable urge to others. Projection works by converting an inner impulse to an outer threat. It relieves anxiety by blocking the acknowledgement of the feeling in the self and projecting it outward onto someone or something else.

We can see two types of projection in action. The first is *seeing in others those desires that can't be faced in the self.* Imagine Angus who is obsessed with the impulse to cheat on his income tax and becomes upset because the thought violates his moral code. He might control his moral anxiety by suspecting a co-worker is not reporting all of his income and that his expenses are just another way of obtaining tax-free enjoyment.

The second version of this SPR is *seeing others as being critical of feelings that cannot be acknowledged.* Bothered by the desire to cheat, Angus unconsciously assigns his own self-critical feelings to others. Thus he may become greatly bothered because he thinks his brother is silently accusing him of defrauding the government when he innocently asks Angus if he has filled out his tax return yet.

Reaction Formation. Reaction formation is behaving in a manner directly opposite to a strong, undesirable feeling. This ego defense blocks stress by expressing the antithesis of it. Think about Bubba. He plays on his high-school football team. In a big game he knows he will have to block an All-State defensive end who is bigger, faster, stronger, and overall a better player than Bubba. But the coach thinks Bubba is the best player for the job. His first impulse is to feel terrified: How will he be able to block out this player? He'll never be able to do it. He'll let his team and his coach down. Quickly he blocks this fear. Instead, Bubba assumes a swaggering bravado. That All-State defensive end isn't so tough, he tells his teammates and himself. Bubba will stop him. No problem.

Often **counterphobic behavior** can be detected as part of a reaction formation. This is when someone does what is most disliked. Imagine a six-year-old boy who is deeply bothered by intense feelings of helplessness. Left unchecked, they would keep him at home with his mother, suffering the humiliation that would surely come at the hands of classmates and teachers. The counterphobic behavior results in the boy's thrusting himself boldly out of the house, leaving early, staying later than his other classmates, and refusing to stay home when ill. He becomes fiercely independent. If a teacher tries to help him get his raincoat buttoned he will stoutly refuse, stamping his feet and saying, "I want to do it myself!"

Coping Devices

As Table 3.1 shows, **coping devices** fall in the middle of the range of automatic means of lowering discomfort. They are usually reactions to what is experienced as a more-than-usual stress. What is seen as "more than usual" varies for each of us. For you, it may be the death of your mother, while for me it might be a term paper. The essential point is that coping devices are not the common, everyday adjustment mechanisms that we each use for small-scale problems or events, which require only minor alterations to continue to function normally, but either entirely new behaviors or modifications of familiar ones.

Looking at Table 3.1 we can see the differences between coping devices and ego defenses. Unlike ego defenses, which block out disruptive feelings or thoughts from our awareness, coping devices permit greater recognition of unsettling emotions and the events causing them. Moreover, coping devices allow us to be aware of our first response to the source of the stress and are often part of larger-scale actions to manage the problem. For example, if I have a long term paper to write, which will be a big part of my grade in a course, the coping device I use to deal with this stress enables me to see both my anxiety and the reason for it. Unlike Miss Lucy, I know I am upset, and I know why.

Coping devices help maintain inner harmony not only by lowering discomfort but by being part of large-scale actions to relieve the problem. I resolve to begin the reading for my paper this afternoon, and put everything else out of my mind until it is done. Immediately, I feel better.

The problem with coping devices, however, is that they don't allow for much reappraisal. I might become so involved with my reading, for example, that I don't leave enough time for writing. Or if I put everything else out of my mind while I'm working on the paper, I may ignore worsening problems in my personal life.

The orientation of coping devices is in the present and the near future. As such, they are useful in combating the stress surrounding current problems. However, the cost of the relative freedom from emotional discomfort is the failure to anticipate the future.

Coping devices also may cause us to be unaware of the effect of our behavior on friends, family, or colleagues, or on other domains of our life. As we will see shortly, this can lead to minor and sometimes major undesirable consequences.

Coping devices, then, are usually seen as temporary measures to handle unusual difficulties. Often we feel there is something special about them. They are like band uniforms: distinctive, trotted out for significant occasions, and used in earnest. When the event is over, they are put away until the next special stressful event. Let us examine four coping devices: suppression, rationalization, sublimation, and undoing.

Suppression. Suppression is the deliberately pushing of an unsettling reality or emotion out of direct awareness, all the while being aware that we have done it. Whereas repression happens without our awareness, suppression is a conscious or semiconscious plan to compartmentalize — to worry about one thing at a time (Vaillant, 1977). Suppression allows us to pay attention to pressing current matters while keeping a mental inventory of other difficulties that need to be resolved.

Walter is a man who uses suppression. His architect's job keeps him going seventy hours a week on two projects — a building he is overseeing that is nearly finished, and a new contract to submit a bid for the redesign of the waterfront. Then there is his boss, who never has a kind word to say to him. And, because he's been working long hours, Walter has been separated from his family a good deal, and his wife is starting to seem distant. Finally, he's feeling run-down physically. If Walter worried about all of these stresses at the same time he might become so upset that he wouldn't be able to do anything. Instead, he uses suppression to hold back his confusion about the waterfront project while he checks the building that is almost finished. He makes a conscious decision not to think about how nervous his boss makes him, and he works out his tensions on the racquetball court. When he works on the plan for the waterfront, Walter shuts out his fears about his marriage and whether his health is all right. As soon as the project is finished, Walter tells himself, he and his wife will get away to Barbados. As soon as he returns, he'll have a medical checkup.

Rationalization. Rationalization permits someone to be aware of part of a distressing reality but to avoid confronting important unpleasant truths. This is because acknowledging these would be too upsetting at the time. Rationalization protects us from an unpleasant reality, giving momentary respite, while we regroup to attack the problem later on. The tenacity with which some people can avoid looking at crucial aspects of a distasteful event is sometimes astonishing.

Rationalization comes in many guises. Consider Don, a college senior caught cheating on his LSAT tests. All of a sudden, his college degree is in jeopardy, as well as the future. He is flooded with panic and despair. While he tries to sort out what is likely to happen and what he should do, he may instinctively use rationalization to cope with his stress reactions. He offers "reasons" for cheating. He might say that his cheating was motivated by forces beyond his control. These external forces might be *situational* ("With all I have

Is this rationalization at work? What reasons do these pregnant women find to explain their smoking when they know it may be harmful to themselves and their children?

to do there is just not enough time to do all the preparation for the exams"), *interpersonal* ("Everyone does it"), or *cultural* ("This society puts so much pressure on you that cheating is necessary to get ahead").

Two special forms of rationalization are sour grapes and sweet lemon. **Sour grapes** is named after Aesop's story of a fox who wanted to eat a cluster of what appeared to be delectable grapes. Unable to jump high enough to reach them, the fox coped with the disappointment by deciding the grapes were sour anyway. Don may decide that the benefits of going to law school are overrated. Lots of people who didn't go into law are rich and happy. The **sweet lemon** rationalization is adopting the conviction that everything happens for the best. "Maybe getting caught cheating is a signal that I shouldn't go into law. I probably will be happier in another field," Don rationalizes.

Sublimation. **Sublimation** transforms an unwelcome feeling or thought into a more acceptable form. The key to understanding how sublimation works is to be aware of the process of *transformation* — as when water is converted into steam. The transformation causes stress emotions to change from alien to agreeable. Usually the result is a change from behavior that has potentially disagreeable consequences to actions that do not.

Imagine Benjy, a small-town boy, transplanted suddenly into the suburbs. He feels a great deal of antagonism toward his classmates because they make jokes at his expense about his clothes and mannerisms and his accent. He knows that directly venting his anger toward them would lead to rejection and a further sense of not belonging. Instead, he unconsciously transforms his hostility into a "healthy competitiveness." Benjy works prodigiously to beat out his classmates, especially on the athletic field. The energy he puts into this competition and the satisfaction he derives from besting them is out of proportion to the realistic merits of the task or the achievements.

The transformation of hostility to an acceptable level of competitiveness is evidence of sublimation in action. Also characteristic is the fact that Benjy doesn't feel the same intense need to be victorious when he visits friends in the small town he used to live in. No anger fuels his competition with them.

Undoing. **Undoing** annuls an undesirable, initial action by behaving in a manner directly opposite to it. Undoing behaviors are usually motivated by anxiety or fear that the first behavior will result in an unacceptable response on the part of the person to whom it was addressed. While reaction formation is acting in the opposite way to what we feel, undoing is the counterbalancing of a previous behavior. The intended effect is to wipe the slate clean. In class, Darlene says something nasty to a teacher. Then she laughs, attempting to cover over her aggressive action, implying that she was just kidding. The teacher replies that Darlene had better smile when she says things like that to him.

Sometimes the undoing behavior is aimed more at the strength of the feeling than the manifest expression. On these occasions, the undoing behavior can seem inappropriate to the outside observer. Darlene strongly dislikes her teacher but can't deal with these feelings. In spite of her best efforts, she has fantasies of humiliating the teacher and showing him up in front of others. One day in class, her teacher is discussing how to calculate percentages. On the blackboard he writes 41%. Darlene raises her hand and says in a quiet voice, "I believe that percentage figure is 14%, not 41%." After class, Darlene remains quite upset. She apologizes profusely to the teacher for "embarrassing him" in front of the others. The teacher doesn't feel embarrassed at all and thanks Darlene for the correction. He doesn't realize what Darlene imagines she has done.

Coping devices have the value of allowing us to be aware of both the distress and the cause of it. They permit a flexible response, an ability to choose, and the environment in which to operate. A major limitation of coping devices, however, is that they control stress by putting it to the side or otherwise masking it. It is handled after an initial appraisal, rather than being monitored more or less on a continual basis. This is fine as long as the stress doesn't change. But what happens if it does? What if the problems with Walter's marriage can't wait until he and his wife go to Barbados?

Another problem with coping devices is that they often work so well in obliterating discomfort that they make it difficult for us to recognize its cause. After realizing that undoing had been a primary way of coping with anger for most of her life, one woman put it this way: "I feel I've spent my life on my knees making amends without ever asking myself how I got into those situations anyway."

Coping devices may work well in the short run. They can help us deal with our distress until we can begin to work out what we're going to do. But if these techniques for reducing stress become habitual, they work against a smooth adaptation to stress and a fulfilling life.

Adjustment Mechanisms

In Table 3.1 **adjustment mechanisms** are shown to be at the highest point on the scale of adaptation. They meet most of the high standards for relieving distress (Loevinger, 1976; Hartmann, 1964, 1958). They permit awareness of the cause of the stress. They allow for a continuing, fluid process for appraising the stress and our reaction to it, which in turn enables us to modify our responses as needed. The orientation is future and present. By our own choice we can accommodate, alter, or change our environment to lower inner tension without seriously compromising other areas of living.

Though she uses other words to describe adjustment mechanisms, Haan (1977) makes several useful observations about the nature of these SPRs. She points out that they are mobilized at moments of developmental disequilibrium — as when we enter college, don't get what we want, or are required to deal with a boring, trying, unpredictable, or complicated stress. These are trying but usually nontraumatic mild clashes between ourselves and the environment.

We have seen that ego defenses handle alien thoughts and feelings. Coping devices are brought out to manage what we experience as major stress coming from trying events. With ego defenses, considerable energy can go into holding disquieting urges from our awareness. When coping devices are in action, we are not "ourselves." When we employ adjustment mechanisms, however, the resulting behavior is more in keeping with our usual personality style and manner of relating to the world. Let us examine four adjustment mechanisms: identification, fantasy, empathy, and anticipation.

Identification. **Identification** is the process of assuming characteristics of those seen as admirable in a mildly stressful setting. The qualities can be values, attitudes, goals, or mannerisms that are taken on as one's own, gradually blending smoothly into the existing personality. Eventually these characteristics may become part of what is an ongoing identity, or they may be discarded when their usefulness comes to an end.

Identification is not obvious as a response to the anxiety generated by transition periods in human development. Consider the nervous but not terrified Hillary during her first week as a freshman in college. She appears wearing clothes that were the "uniform" of her high school — jeans, work shirt, and waffle-soled hiking boots. Her sentences are sprinkled with the idioms, phrases, and even the epithets that were in everyone's vocabulary back home. Hillary carries her books and notebook in a pack on her back.

If she responds with the adjustment mechanism of identification to her anxiety about college, the first evidence is likely to be in her apparel. The jeans, work shirt and boots are traded for the uniform of the college — painter's pants, blouses, and sneakers with no socks. The pack is retired to the attic because Hillary now carries her books in her arms like the upperclassmen. By November, the idioms and phrases she used in high school have dropped out of Hillary's vocabulary. In their place are those common to the college. By Thanksgiving vacation Hillary's change will be noticeable to her hometown friends.

Identification is not a thought-out strategy to mute the anxiety Hillary feels about her first year at college. It is an automatic effort to diminish apprehension and restore mental tranquility. Moreover, Hillary may not be aware of exactly what she's doing, though she will acknowledge it when one of her former high-school teachers points out the changes.

Fantasy. **Fantasy** is a means of obtaining satisfaction or venting stress emotions when the usual ways are closed off. The fantasies can be erotic, aggressive, or playful. One illustration is the frightened Marine recruit being chewed out by a drill instructor for a small infraction. The hapless grunt stands there and takes the abuse as he silently imagines the sadistic ways he will exact revenge once boot camp is over. Doubtless these thoughts have sustained countless recruits as well as others of us who have been in the same fix.

At another level, Maria has found a way to tolerate a boring committee meeting she must attend. She tunes out, thinking about lying on a sunny

Have you ever had these feelings toward a loved one right after a fight? This Charles Addams cartoon shows how fantasy can discharge violent emotions, enabling us to control them better in real life.

beach. The others have no idea what is behind Maria's benign smile during the meeting.

Fantasies have the advantage of occurring largely without guilt, because they are accompanied by no requirement for achievement. In the privacy of our daydreams, we can imagine a variety of wicked activities without enduring much shame or anxiety (Schafer, 1968).

Empathy. Empathy is the ability to sense how others feel or think without being aware of our effort to do so. It is automatically putting ourselves in someone else's shoes while remaining in our own. Freud (1921) pointed out the self-protective application of empathy. He saw it as an attempt to render someone else's anxiety-provoking behavior "safe" by sharing the anxiety or even mimicking it. As one woman said, "I can tell if my friends are happy or upset when I am around them because I feel the same way."

An example of empathy in action is Phyllis, a little girl who can tell that her father has had a tiring day at work by the way he walks in the house, how he holds his body, and how he looks. She is in a far better position to master the anxiety his irritability will cause her and tailor her behavior to cope with him than her brother, who may not be as empathetic.

Anticipation. Anticipation is the ability to predict the influence of current choices on the future. It involves seeing the relationship of desired future outcomes to present behavior (Vaillant, 1977).

Anticipation is not always a smooth or conflict-free act of volition. As a high-level adaptive response, it nearly always engages competing impulses for action. Frequently it involves fending off anxiety or other stress emotions that come about when a choice is made.

Consider how Grace, a single parent, uses anticipation. She is lonely and would like to meet eligible men. A friend suggests attending a meeting of Parents Without Partners. On one hand, Grace is attracted to the possibility of making new friends. But on the other she is nervous about going to the meeting. Will the men be interested in a widow with two kids? Suppose no one finds her attractive? Suppose someone does: what then? As a means of combating these worries, Grace can utilize anticipation to focus on the potential benefits of the meeting. She enumerates the benefits, perhaps even writing them down or fantasizing about them.

These are but a few of a much larger list of highest-level SPRs. In spite of their estimable virtues, adjustment mechanisms have the same basic characteristics of other SPRs — they are inner, mental mechanisms to restore peace, and they are initially reflexive. Often they operate without our being aware of them.

Useful as SPRs are in containing many emotional responses to stress, not everyone can get along solely with these mental mechanisms. Many of us deal with a reality that overpowers whatever SPRs we bring into play. We are furious with a demeaning but necessary job. We feel helpless as we fall further behind in our race with inflation. We can't shake out despondency after a divorce or the death of a friend. Our children worry us constantly. Our blood pressure and cholesterol are up.

Adjustment mechanisms and coping devices may be the first link in a chain of action to relieve stress by allowing us to recognize a problem, look at how we are reacting to it, and consider how our life is being affected by these events. The next links in the chain of activities to reduce stress are direct control responses and direct action responses.

As their names suggest, direct control responses primarily reduce inner upset, while direct action responses focus on the cause of the distress. The primary difference between these direct responses and the self-protective responses we have just discussed is that the direct responses do not begin automatically. They require conscious effort do to something to diminish distress. Another difference is that direct control responses and direct action responses are large-scale, holistic activities, rather than mental mechanisms.

Direct Control Responses to Stress

Two ways of adjusting to stress are fight or flight. We can see these responses in our pets — the dog snarling and ready to attack and the cat standing with arched back, hissing, ready to run counterattack. We can feel it welling up in ourselves on a dark night in a strange neighborhood when we turn a corner and come face to face with a gang of unfriendly locals.

The fight-flight instinct is inherent in both human and beast. However, each of us has to cope with realities of daily living when neither response is possible: we must continue to live with parents from whom we have become alienated; we have to take a class we're sure we can't pass; we have kids who are driving us mad; and on and on. We are stuck, and have to put up with our stress reactions.

Direct control responses (DCRs) address the reaction to stress, seeking to lessen it and make us feel better. For the most part they do nothing intentionally to alter the stressful agent. If we watch people attempt to handle their emotions, we can observe three types of direct control responses — physical, psychological, and the use of resources.

Obtaining Physical Relief

More than in any other country, citizens of the United States count on drugs to relieve emotional upset. Tranquilizers outsell all other prescription drugs. Hard on their heels are potions for sleep. Coming up fast are megavitamin tablets promising stress relief. Prescriptions for antidepressant medication are at an all-time high. The shelves of drug stores and supermarkets bulge with headache powders, stomach relaxers, and other potions, beckoning the troubled shopper, assuring deliverance from migraine, acid stomach, and that tired-all-over feeling.

Various self-medications are physical ways of controlling the emotional ravages of stress. Many people feel they cannot survive without alcohol, marijuana, or other drugs. But there are less obvious stress self-medications. Without coffee to get them going in the morning, cigarettes to sustain them during work and school, and tea to calm their nerves in the afternoon, many people feel they could not make it through the day.

Another physical DCR is overeating. Eating too much or ingesting junk food with little nutritional value are examples. Just how common these avenues of relief are is evidenced by the fact that obesity is a problem for more than thirty million Americans (Craddock, 1973).

Finally, some physical forms of stress relief don't involve taking any substance at all. A growing body of research indicates that regular exercise — jogging, aerobic dancing, weight-lifting — relieves anxiety and improves mood (Greist, et al., 1979; Folkins, 1976).

Seeking Psychological Relief

Some DCRs are psychological strategies. When fight or flight is impossible, the emotional and physical stress reactions can be greatly reduced by regular psychological activities such as meditation. These are practiced by many for this purpose. Four types of meditation are shown in Table 3.2.

One of the most popular psychological techniques to cope with stress is the **relaxation response,** popularized by Herbert Benson (1975). A physician

Table 3.2 Four types of meditation

1. *Mental repetition:*	A word or phrase repeated over and over again — called a "mantra." Examples are "one" or "Lord Jesus Christ, have mercy on me."
2. *Physical repetition:*	Focusing attention on a physical act. An example is the meditative posture characteristic of Hatha yoga.
3. *Problem contemplation:*	Focusing on a paradoxical problem — called a "koan." An example is "What is the sound of one hand clapping?"
4. *Visual concentration:*	Focusing on an image. Examples are a leaf, flame, or a "mandala" — featuring a square within a circle.

SOURCE: From George S. Everly and Robert Rosenfeld, *The nature and treatment of the stress response: A practical guide for clinicians.* New York: Plenum Press, 1981, pp. 72, 73, 75. Reprinted by permission.

concerned about the relationship between stress reactions and high blood pressure, heart disease, and stroke, Benson drew from modern psychological medical data as well as the wisdom of Eastern religions. The technique is summarized in the box following.

This procedure requires four steps to bring forth the relaxation response: (1) a *quiet environment*, one that is calm and with as few distractions as possible; (2) a *constant stimulus*, to shift the mind from external thought by the

The Relaxation Response

1. Sit quietly in a comfortable position.

2. Close your eyes.

3. Deeply relax all your muscles, beginning at your feet and progressing up to your face. Keep them relaxed.

4. Breathe through your nose. Become aware of your breathing. As you breathe out, say the word "ONE" silently to yourself. For example, breathe IN . . . OUT, "ONE"; IN . . . OUT, "ONE"; etc. Breathe easily and naturally.

5. Continue for 10 to 20 minutes. You may open your eyes to check the time, but do not use an alarm. When you finish, sit quietly for several minutes, at first with your eyes closed and later with your eyes open. Do not stand up for a few minutes.

6. Do not worry about whether you are successful in achieving a deep level of relaxation. Maintain a passive attitude and permit relaxation to occur at its own pace. When distracting thoughts occur, try to ignore them by not dwelling upon them and return to repeating "ONE." With practice, the response should come with little effort. Practice the technique once or twice daily, but not within two hours after any meal, since the digestive processes seem to interfere with the elicitation of the relaxation response.

SOURCE: From Benson, H. *The Relaxation response.* New York: Morrow, 1975.

repetition of a sound, word, or phrase; (3) a *passive attitude,* letting distracting thoughts pass through without worrying about them and returning to the repetitive sound; and (4) a *comfortable position* in which there is no undue muscular tension.

Some who practice the relaxation response are able to lower blood pressure and minimize other physical reactions to stress. It also works well in the psychological realm. One man found he could deal more effectively with the nervousness and depression he felt when his wife left him by learning the relaxation response and practicing it once a day.

Not everyone benefits from this direct control response. Benson's optimistic claims for the relaxation response have been tempered by the failure of other clinicians to replicate his results (Everly and Rosenfeld, 1981). It does appear, however, that each of us has the capacity to use relaxation to lower overall tension. Is it possible that some of us could benefit from a "relaxation break" rather than a coffee or cigarette break?

Another psychological DCR is to be found in how Ellen coped with her fear that she might pass out at the sight of blood. Ellen visited her grandfather when he was dying and passed out when she saw him in the intensive care unit. Since then, Ellen fainted two other times — once when having a tooth

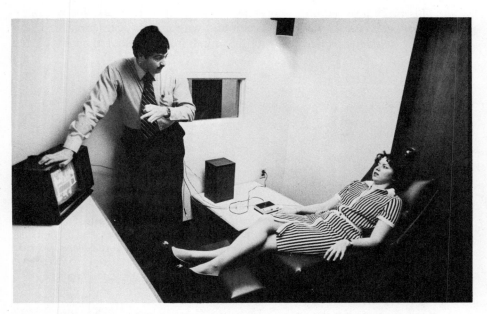

Biofeedback aids people with stress-produced physical problems. By monitoring visual or auditory displays of their muscle tension, hand warmth, perspiration, or other bodily states, individuals can learn to lessen their symptoms.

filled and another when she came suddenly upon a car accident. Afterwards, she avoided any movie or TV show that might have gory scenes. Soon she began to avoid most movies and TV programs altogether, because she was afraid she might see an unexpected bloody event and faint. This severely restricted her social life.

Through the help of a professional counselor, Ellen learned to combat her stress reaction by mobilizing within herself an adrenalin response. She taught herself to imagine, whenever she felt faint, a scene in which she was angry. The surge of adrenalin opposed the feeling of weakness, to the extent that Ellen was able to watch a horror movie, go to the dentist, and even give blood.

Biofeedback is another major means of alleviating stress reactions. It has been especially useful in controlling a large number of bodily states affected by stress, including high blood pressure, hyperacidity, heart rate, and other physical responses (Turin and Johnson, 1976). Biofeedback operates by hooking the patient up to a sensitive recording device that measures a specific physical function, such as blood pressure, and then displaying the information to the patient. Some people can use this information actively to control a body state when the information is constantly displayed. For example, when information about a man's high blood pressure is fed back to him he is often able to reduce it on his own. As yet we don't know how this mechanism of direct self-control operates, but the potential of this process seems considerable.

Learning to Use Resources

Closely related to the psychological DCR is the use of resources to divert attention from or cushion the impact of the stressor. Murphy and Moriarty (1976) were impressed by the usefulness of people and activities in helping children who were under stress. They also noted that the supportive presence of loved ones made a difference in how the children handled difficult situations.

As he thought about the findings that as adults the men he studied seemed to cope better with stress than they did as adolescents, Vaillant (1977) speculated that the primary factor was the continuing relationship with loved ones. The greater the number of resources, the higher the life satisfactions in the group he studied.

With resources, more is better. A man waiting to hear if he's going to be offered a job he wants can cope with the anxiety better if he can share his worries with people who care about him. And when he's all talked out, he can further lower his internal distress by playing the saxophone or pounding a tennis ball. Temporary though they may be, these resources bring welcome respite.

The advantages of DCRs are obvious. There are times when we can't or don't wish to mobilize ourselves to rid ourselves of a problem distressing us: told that he has a chronic but not terminal physical disease, one man overeats because it helps a little. Another woman cannot say no to her aging mother who asks to live with her, but she develops high blood pressure for which she takes medication.

Effective as many DCRs are in restoring mental harmony, they have one glaring disadvantage: DCRs do nothing to relieve the agent at the root of the discomfort, and in fact they may even perpetuate a stress reaction. This is because DCRs control the maintenance of the coping devices and ego defenses. Tranquilizers assist Walter's suppression, which helps him handle his massive work load and the repression of anger toward his boss, by lessening his overall level of tension. If Walter continues to do nothing to reduce his work load or to resolve the conflicts with his boss, he may even acquire two more problems: suppression of all feeling and a drug dependency.

On the other hand, our recognition that we must use DCRs sometimes enables us to gather ourselves to attack the cause of the distress. One day Walter may come to the bottom of his bottle of tranquilizers and realize that for several months he has been taking them without asking why. At this point he might reopen the question with himself and his family about whether he wants to remain at his job.

DCRs can be the second step in a chain of events that leads to direct action to eliminate or sharply reduce the reason for the stress reaction. For example, a young man may feel helpless in the presence of a dominating father. As a result, he never seems to measure up to his father's demands to stay out of trouble, work harder, do well in school, and make something of himself. Talking to an older sister, he learns to react more assertively when confronting his father, telling him that his overbearing manner makes him so upset that he can't react to the father's directions, no matter how valid they may be. As a result, the father, who really didn't know that he was affecting his son so strongly, begins to act in a more tactful, humane manner and even begins to see some of his son's better qualities. The pressure lessens. The boy feels less helpless and more competent. Soon he begins to do things that please himself and, incidentally, his father, too.

Direct Action Responses to Stress

Earlier in this chapter we saw that one of the characteristics of high-level adaptation is the ability to accommodate, alter, or change an environment. SPRs and DCRs are more effective in enabling us to accommodate to an environment we can't or do not wish to change. Suppose, however, that we do want to change a part of the world in which we live that's adversely affecting us — making us angry, depressed, or anxious; giving us headaches, high blood pressure, or dyspepsia. The boy's more assertive behavior with his father to alter his environment is an example. If Walter quits and finds a less stressful job, that is another.

Direct action responses (DARs) are activities intended to improve environmental accommodation or change it. They depend on problem recognition, expectation of one's own effectiveness, and choosing to act.

Problem Recognition

The greatest hazard to effective adaptation is being unaware of the emotional or physical reaction to stress. DARs are dependent upon this awareness. If we can recognize a problem, we have a good chance of solving it. Most of the time we have a clear view of both the cause of the stress and our reaction to it: we have an exam on Friday, and that's why we are upset. Occasionally, however, we are not exactly sure of what is wrong but can use our emotional reaction to the stress and work backward to find the cause. Imagine when a relationship with a best friend begins to change. We can point to no reason, but we do know that instead of feeling good when we're together, conversation is wary and strained. We can use this sign that things are not well between us to sit down with our friend and try to find out what is wrong.

Ego defenses get in the way of understanding our feelings. Coping devices and DCRs also inhibit direct action because they mask stress effects. Walter's suppression and Chantal's overeating limit their distress. Their partial solutions work against their taking action to adapt more effectively to the problems in their lives.

Expectation of Effectiveness

The second requirement for a DAR is the expectation of personal effectiveness. If we anticipate that our actions will have a beneficial impact, we are more likely to work harder and stay with the struggle longer than we will if we have little hope.

The capacity to affect the environment around us, rather than merely be affected by it, is the heart of DARs. University of Chicago psychologists Suzanne Kobasa (1980) and Salvatore Maddi (1980) identified three elements in individuals who respond to stress by direct action: *commitment* (versus alienation), *control* (versus helplessness), and *challenge* (versus threat).

Commitment is a disposition to involve ourselves in whatever it is we deal with rather than disengaging. Control is a tendency to believe we can influence what happens to us, instead of being a passive victim. Challenge is a way of seeing stress as normal and necessary for growth, rather than viewing any change as frightening.

Kobasa and Maddi studied groups of executives, lawyers, and military officers over several years. They found that if the amount of stress each group faced was held constant, those individuals who showed strong commitment, control, and challenge exhibited fewer medical and psychiatric illnesses than those who did not.

Choosing to Act

Insight and the expectation of effectiveness are not enough. No direct action is possible without the willingness to choose to act, to confront the problem that is the source of the distressing reactions. Direct action is also encouraged by having effective behaviors available to use. Many of us have seen friends or relatives tolerate continuing mental anguish caused by a condition that they seemingly could change. What we overlook is that this action requires making a choice, a choice between two possible but mutually exclusive alternatives. It may be the choice between attractive possibilities or selecting the least worst alternative — does the wife of workaholic Walter, increasingly unhappy in her marriage, continue to settle for an unsatisfying relationship, or does she separate from her husband and live alone with the children?

The willingness to take direct action is assisted by previous success, modeling (watching others do it), and being encouraged and supported by others (Bandura, 1977). If we find ourselves in a situation in which a DAR is needed, but we have no previous success and no one to show us how it is done, we might still use friends, relatives, or a professional counselor to encourage and support us in our effort to find a way.

Recall Bubba and his problems with the All-State defensive end in the big game. Imagine that a coach could help Bubba to recognize that his bravado and his mean, smiling comments were actually a cover-up for what he really felt. Stripped of the SPRs of reaction formation and undoing, Bubba becomes aware of his real emotions — helplessness, lack of confidence in his ability to block a much better player, depression at the certainty that his teammates will blame him for losing the game, and anger at being put in the situation in the first place.

Once these thoughts and emotions behind the feelings are understood, they set the stage for DARs. He recognizes the problem — how to block the All-State defensive end. In the past Bubba has been an effective blocker, so there is reason to imagine that he still is. Bubba realizes that he has a choice: he can refuse to play against the All-State or he can try his best. He decides to try his best. But how? He has had no experience trying to block anyone this good before.

He and his coach might borrow a page from the cognitive learning approach outlined by Mahoney, called personal SCIENCE (Mahoney, 1977). The word **SCIENCE** is made up of the first letters of the seven steps in this process of adjustment: *S*pecify the general problem; *C*ollect information; *I*dentify causes or patterns; *E*xamine options; *N*arrow options and experiment; *C*ompare data; *E*xtend, revise, or replace.

Talking with the coach, Bubba agrees that the general problem is to limit the All-State defensive end to around his usual number of tackles. Then Bubba collects information from game films and watches others play against the awesome All-Star end. Several patterns come to light. The end prefers to fake inside on his defensive rush and then use his superior speed to go around the blocker; when he does go inside, he is overpowering. Bubba examines his options: he could anticipate that the defensive end will always go to the outside and be ready to block him that way, but the end will eventually figure out what Bubba is doing and will change his game to beat Bubba inside; or, Bubba could try to guess what the All-Star will do on each play, but no opponent has been successful at that. Bubba and his coach decide to anticipate the All-Star

To avoid having to choose between the satisfactions of a profession and a homelife, these women doctors have taken direct action. They have formed a group practice that allows them to schedule patient and family time flexibly.

end will take an outside rush on certain crucial plays. Bubba will use his speed to try to neutralize him on these occasions. The rest of the time, he will try to react to what the defensive end does and accept that Bubba may be unable to block him some of the time. They realize this decision is a gamble, but the odds are in their favor. Bubba experiments, asking some of his speedier defensive teammates to try to go around him on their rush. He compares data on the best way to block defensive ends who charge to the outside. As the game comes nearer, Bubba extends, revises, and replaces components of his plan to block the All-Star end. By game time, Bubba feels ready with a strategy that will allow him to do his best.

Adaptation in Living

All of these ways of managing emotional and physical reactions to stress exist in everyone's personality. None of us relies exclusively on adjustment mechanisms and direct action. There are moments when we cannot look at another unpleasant reality so we turn our backs, pretending for a while that it doesn't exist. We tolerate a dead-end job, bad marriage, or correctable physical limitation — drinking to forget or taking tranquilizers to deaden the psychic pain, knowing the relief is temporary. Why? Because temporary and ineffective as these maneuvers are, they enable us to survive even at the cost of continued suffering (Menninger, 1967). Perhaps sometime later we can gather our strength to work out more adaptive ways of handling these life problems.

The mixture of adaptive responses within each of us is the cornerstone of our personal adjustment. As we will see in the coming chapters, being able to cope with stress reactions by using high-level SPRs, being able to control anxiety when it is appropriate and relieve it by direct action when it is not are all highly correlated with normal functioning. By the same token, low-level responses to stress, responses that perpetuate maladaptive behavior, and the unwillingness to make a choice to act to relieve manageable stress are correlated with emotional disorder.

Summary

1. Adaptation is a continuing process of maintaining inner harmony while fitting into a reasonable environment without undue compromise.
2. Three types of adaptive responses can be catalogued: self-protective responses, direct control responses, and direct action responses.
3. *Self-protective responses* are automatic mental practices that diminish the awareness of a painful stress reaction or the cause of it. In ascending order of effectiveness, three classes of SPRs are ego defenses, coping devices, and adjustment mechanisms.
4. Depression, denial, projection, and reaction formation are four examples of *ego defenses*, which hold back alien thoughts and impulses.
5. Mobilized to meet unusual stress, middle-level means of regulating discomfort are *coping devices*. Four coping devices are suppression, rationalization, sublimation, and undoing.
6. *Adjustment mechanisms* are the highest-level SPRs, meeting most of the standards for the highest level of responses to stressful events. Examples of adjustment mechanisms are identification, fantasy, empathy, and anticipation.
7. *Direct control responses* address the reaction to the stress, seeking to moderate its effects. Three types of direct control responses are physical, psychological, and the use of resources. They do not alter the stressful agent, yet can be a link in a chain of direct action.
8. *Direct action responses* aim to improve accommodation to environmental distress or to change it. DARs depend on problem recognition, expectations of effectiveness in dealing with it, and choosing to act.
9. All three levels of managing stress reactions exist within everyone's personality. Each of us employs a mixture of responses at all levels. There is a correlation between the level of adaptive responses and emotional adjustment.

A Look Ahead

In the next chapter, normal personality styles are described. We look at some of the characteristics of human beings that drew the attention of people watchers beginning thousands of years ago. Some of the more interesting of these personality types are examined in detail. We then study six personality styles commonly seen today.

Key Terms

adaptation	rationalization
self-protective responses	sour grapes
direct control responses	sweet lemon
direct action responses	sublimation
ego defenses	undoing
signal anxiety	adjustment mechanisms
repression	identification
denial	fantasy
projection	empathy
reaction formation	anticipation
counterphobic behavior	relaxation response
coping devices	biofeedback
suppression	SCIENCE

Suggested Readings

Adaptation

White, R. Strategies of adaptation: An attempt at systematic description. In G. Coelho, D. Hamburg, and J. Adams (Eds.), *Coping and adaptation*. New York: Basic Books, 1974.

A highly readable definition of the procss of adaptation.

Self-protective responses

Freud, A. *The ego and the mechanisms of defense.* (1937) New York: International Universities Press, 1966.

Vaillant, G. *Adaptation to life.* Boston: Little, Brown, 1977, Chapters 5, 6, 7, 8, and 9.

Numerous self-protective responses viewed from clinical and research standpoint.

Direct control responses

Walker, C., Hedberg, A., Clement, P., and Wright, L. *Clinical procedures for behavior therapy.* Englewood Cliffs, N.J.: Prentice-Hall, 1981. Chapters 3, 4, 5, 10, 13, and 15.

Schwartz, G., and Shapiro, D. (Eds.), *Consciousness and self-regulation: Advances in research.* Vols. I and II. New York: Plenum, 1976 and 1978.

Descriptions of a range of behavioral techniques for controlling stress emotions.

Direct action responses

Lazarus, R. *Patterns of adjustment.* Third edition. New York: McGraw-Hill, 1976. Chapter 4.

Mahoney, M. *Self-change strategies for solving personal problems.* New York: Norton, 1979.

Reasoned and systematic approaches to self-help.

Theophrastus (372–287 B.C.) was a philosopher of ancient Greece. One of his most famous books was *Characters*, which sketched 32 personality styles commonly found in his day. Below are descriptions of several of these types.

□ The *Boor:* exhibits behavior that offends propriety; drinks too much and offends others.

□ The *Loquacious Person:* is a know-it-all; has an opinion about everything and always assumes that opinion is the correct one.

□ The *Newsmaker:* is a gossiping rumor spreader; spreads stories having no verifiable truth for the sake of impressing others.

□ The *Grumbler:* complains about what is received; after being praised will complain that the speaker left out several important achievements.

□ The *Avaricious Person:* has an excessive desire for base gain; sells watered wine to friends.

□ The *Patron of Rascals:* keeps company with dishonorable people or causes; consorts with those guilty of criminal causes, championing worthless issues or people because of a similarity to them.

□ The *Coward:* a shrinking of the soul through fear shows excessive fear on a voyage.

SOURCE: Jebb, R. *The Characters of Theophrastus.* London: MacMillan, 1909.

Chapter Preview

CHAPTER 4
Normal Personality Styles

Questions to think about
- How many different personality types can you think of?
- Which type best describes you?
- Can anything change your personality?
- Are some types of personality styles "better" than others?

It is hard to sit for long in a bus station or airport and resist people-watching. Over there are three men sitting together: one is flashily attired; a second is in wrinkle-free shades of gray; the last is rumpled and unmatched. A couple hurries by — he red-faced and shouting that they can make it if they hurry and she pale, tense, with a look of smiling resignation. In the corner a young man does magic tricks for a little girl placidly eating an ice cream cone and for her brother, who can't sit still. A man in the ticket line is complaining because he was assigned to a nonsmoking section, while someone with a cigarette behind him accepts the same treatment without comment. Sitting on our left is a woman reading, whose face invites conversation. Next to her is a woman embroidering, whose countenance invites combat. Directly across from us is someone watching us watch everyone else.

This scene illustrates the enormous variety among normal people. Normal people differ among themselves far more than those who are emotionally dis-

The many variations in personality style show that there are more ways of behaving normally than abnormally.

turbed. In this chapter we begin by thinking about what personality style means. Then we look at two major ways in which temperament has been classified in the twentieth century. Following that is a look at new developments in thinking that recognize the importance of physical constitution and environment. Using this body of work as a background, six normal personality styles are portrayed. Finally, we explore the interaction between personality type and adjustment as they are affected by environment and constitution.

What Is Personality Style?

People-watching has been developed to a high art by those whose vocations require knowing how to instantly size up others — waitresses, panhandlers, salesmen, receptionists, police officers, or evangelists. They quickly learn that body posture, choice of clothes, physical mannerisms, or way of speaking often reveal much about the individual's temperament. They know the signs that indicate the size of tip, readiness to buy, probability of being given a hard time, or likelihood of being born again.

Without formal learning, these students of human nature have come to recognize the two major ingredients of personality style — *consistency* and *stability*. Indeed, psychologist David Shapiro (1965) defines personality style as consistency of behavior that is slow to change. **Personality style** includes traits, interests, inclinations, quirks, and prejudices. Usually personality style results in habitual ways of emoting, thinking, and looking at outside events as well as our responses to them.

In contrast to many aspects of ourselves that change throughout the life cycle — for example, body shape and personal values — personality style remains relatively stable. You can probably find examples of consistency among friends or family. If you know your sister's personality style, you can predict with reasonable accuracy how she will react to classical music, criticism, new people at a party, a beggar on the street, final exams, political candidates, and your request to borrow her tennis racquet. You might know, without ever having catalogued these elements, that she generally likes classical music, has trouble seeing that she could possibly make a mistake, is uncomfortable with people she doesn't know, ignores the downtrodden, systematically prepares for final exams, favors the law-and-order stance of one of the candidates running for office, and will lend you her tennis racquet only on the term that you return it in exactly the same condition it was in when you borrowed it. That is what is meant by consistency in many areas of behavior.

Youngsters with very different personality styles can be produced by the same parents, as can be seen in the faces of these two children.

Historical Description of Normal Personality Styles

One of the first to record his observations about different personality types was the ancient Greek physician Hippocrates. The personality types he identified are shown at the beginning of the chapter. He described four basic *humors,* or temperaments, he found in the patients he treated in his medical practice: (1) the **phlegmatic** or placid and cool, (2) the **melancholic** or serious and gloomy, (3) the **choleric** or irascible and easily annoyed, and (4) the **sanguine** or cheerful and hopeful. About a hundred years later Theophrastus, a philosophy student of Aristotle, categorized Greeks he met on the streets of Athens into thirty different groups on the basis of their behavior. His groupings included the Flatterer, the Late Learner, the Grumbler, and the Patron of Rascals (Jebb, 1909).

People haven't changed much. If Hippocrates and Theophrastus returned to earth today, most likely they would find most of the same characters they described, here in the twentieth century.

Like these ancient Greeks, twentieth-century scholars have made numerous attempts to portray personality types. Two especially useful theories are Carl Jung's model of extravert-introvert, and Eduard Spranger's system of value orientations. These fertile theories have had a powerful impact on modern psychology.

Extraverts-Introverts

Probably the most widely known and useful division of personality styles is Jung's extravert-introvert model (Jung, 1923). The characteristics of the extraverted and introverted personalities are summarized in Table 4.1. **Extraverts** and **introverts** differ on two central qualities that affect their thinking, feelings, and social relations: the degree of objectivity or subjectivity with which they deal with the world around them.

Extraverts are objective in orientation. Hard facts and measurable reality are what guide their intellect, feelings, and relations with others. Personal reactions or intuitions are shut out in favor of logical analysis. Once a plan is devised or principle agreed upon, all doubt is cast aside. These plans are positive, forward-looking, and thought to be of personal or general benefit. Those of us who are extraverts are pragmatic at heart, however, and we change quickly to new plans or principles if our expectations aren't fulfilled.

Introverts are subjective in orientation. By "subjective" Jung means the emotional reaction we have to outside experiences. Those of us who are introverts see the world not merely as a set of objective facts, figures, measurable events, and concrete data, but instead pay attention to the responses these trigger in ourselves. For introverts, this personal response *is* reality. They may reject ideals or principles that don't agree with their intuitive sense. Among introverts, the issue is never "How many people believe it?" but rather "Does it feel right to me?" They can be negative, critical, and difficult to convince.

Table 4.1 Primary characteristics of extraverts and introverts

EXTRAVERT	INTROVERT
Objectively oriented, values external reality	Subjectively oriented, values personal reaction to external reality
Seeks plans or principles to govern life	Difficulty in finding ideals to guide living
Positive, pragmatic	Negative, stubborn
Lives life to the fullest	Seeks inner intensity
Conventional	Unconventional
Team players	Individualistic
Dominant	Aloof
Inspiring mentors so long as interests coincide	Empathic, strong commitment when bond formed

SOURCE: Adapted from *The collected works of C. G. Jung*, trans. R. F. C. Hull, Bollingen Series 20, vol. 6: *Psychological types*. Copyright © 1971 by Princeton University Press. Reprinted by permission of Princeton University Press.

Extraverts need a diet of fresh experiences. While they may attack a new problem with extraordinary vigor, as soon as the end is in sight their interest flags. They seek exposure to new things that will excite their senses; they want to live life to the fullest. They may appear to "collect" experiences — hang gliding, opening night at the opera, hot tubs, jogging, group therapy, or wine making. The extravert is up on the latest thing.

In contrast, introverts pursue interests that arouse an inner intensity without regard to whether they are currently fashionable. They will pursue the type of work or hobbies that excite a personal sensual reaction — stamp collecting, raising dogs, growing roses, or white-water canoeing. These interests may continue over a lifetime. Some introverts possess an unusually fine ability to discriminate among sensations. They may have a dozen recordings of the same piece of music because each one stimulates a slightly different response.

In relations with others, extraverts are conventional, team players, and drawn to power. Their dress is likely to be guided by the tastes of others they respect. Their mannerisms, habits, and conversational topics are not unusual. Instinctively team players, extraverts have the same expectations of others. With members of their team they are generous, but with people they regard as opponents, they are remorseless competitors. Extraverts like to dominate and be in charge, or near people in power.

Extraverts make good mentors because they are inspirational. Rewards await protégés who follow their lead. One liability, however, of having an extravert for a mentor is that the protégé must believe what the mentor believes in order to retain status. Also, because these extraverted leaders are continually searching for new challenges, the protégé may be left behind when the mentor moves on to a new opportunity.

In relationships with others, introverts can seem initially aloof. According to Jung, introverts are empathetic, but they frequently stop short of using their sensitivity to give assistance unless directly asked. Once a bond is formed with a friend or a protégé, it is often maintained lifelong.

None of us is a "pure" extravert or introvert. There is a continuum between the two extremes. You may fall more toward the extraverted side with some introverted features, while I might be largely introverted with a sprinkling of extraversion. An **ambivert** has an exact balance of extraversion and introversion.

Today Jung's characterization of temperament may seem relatively coarse. A real test of the usefulness of a theory is the refinements that have grown from it. In the past half-century since Jung first presented his ideas, more than a dozen tests have been developed to measure traits associated with extraversion or introversion.

Value Orientations

Another way of looking at personality types is by dominant value orientations. These values are what we believe to be important in life. Eduard Spranger (1928), a philosophy professor at the University of Berlin, thought that everyone has six basic value orientations: theoretical, economic, aesthetic, social, political, and religious. The degree to which each of these values is prominent shapes our personality. The primary characteristics of these six basic values are shown in Table 4.2.

Individuals with high **theoretical** orientations value reason, objectivity, and skepticism above all else. They are truth-seekers. Their method is to apply

Table 4.2   Characteristics of six basic value orientations

BASIC VALUE ORIENTATION	PRIMARY CHARACTERISTICS
Theoretical	Values reason, objectivity, and skepticism.
Economic	Values activities and ideas that contribute to self-preservation and the accumulation of wealth and comfort.
Aesthetic	Values the subjective response and anything enriching personal experience.
Social	Values love of others, individually and in groups.
Political	Values power, domination, influence, control, and respect of others.
Religious	Values quest for unity and God's grace.

SOURCE: From Spranger, E. *Types of men: The psychology and ethics of personality.* Translation of the German 5th ed. by P. Pigors. New York: Hafner, 1928.

This woman might be classified by Spranger as someone with an aesthetic value orientation.

reason that is not influenced by personal feelings to discover what is objectively true. The "truth" these theoretical people cherish is provable reality — data, theorems, or principles. For people with a theoretical orientation there is no good or bad, ugly or beautiful, just true or false. Any presumption is subjected to merciless skepticism until it is proven. Theoretical individuals seek predictability and consistency in their daily lives and in the universe.

People with strong **economic** values see wealth as essential to self-preservation and basic to what makes life pleasant. Men and women with this orientation are drawn to activities or ideas which contribute to the enterprise of accumulating wealth. Any behavior is judged on the basis of its usefulness in furthering these ends. All things are good or bad, ugly or beautiful, true or false according to whether they contribute to economic gain.

People with a dominant **aesthetic** orientation value experiences or objects that enrich subjective experiences. Art, music, pomp, and things beautiful or sublime are appreciated because they arouse internally pleasing sensations. What is beautiful is judged by a personal, intuitive standard and is not affected by the reactions of others. People with aesthetic values hunger for self-development. They want to be in touch with all aspects of their individuality and pack as much sensual experience into their lives as possible.

For those with a **social** orientation the greatest pleasure is giving love to others. The "others" can be a single person, a group, or all of humankind. Men and women with social values view every human being as being worthy of being loved. No one is too ugly, corrupt, demented, or vicious to be unlovable. Everything that lives, including plants and animals, is bathed in the love of the person with extremely high social values.

Persons with a strong **political** orientation seek power. Power is the ability to influence, control, or dominate others. Binding the will and destiny of others to one's own is the primary concern for the political individual. The desire to be admired by those who are dominated is strong. Like individuals with aesthetic or social values, the political person lives through others.

People with a powerful **religious** orientation strive for unity with an absolute immortal, all-embracing God. This is an individual, subjective, peak experience of being in harmony with a deity; it has been called a sense of salvation or being "born again."

It is hard to imagine anyone who is motivated solely by any single value orientation. The personality styles of most of us are a blend of different proportions of several types of values and attitudes. In fact, psychologists have devised a personality inventory called *A Study of Values* that measures the relative strength of each value orientation (Allport, Vernon, and Lindzey, 1960). A profile of an imaginary minister with dominant theoretical and religious value orientations is shown in Figure 4.1.

Not surprisingly, Figure 4.1 shows a man with high religious and low economic values. What else might we suspect about this minister's personality

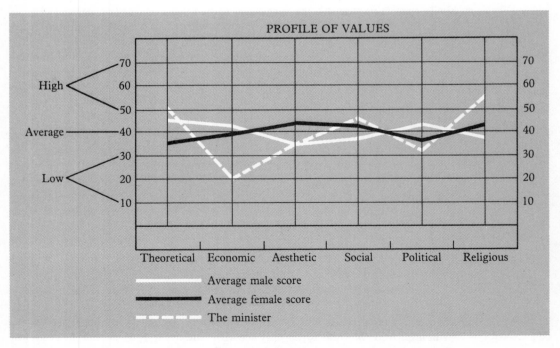

Figure 4.1　A profile of a minister with dominant theoretical and religious value orientations

on the basis of this test? The high theoretical orientation along with lower-than-average political leanings suggests that he might be more attracted by the teaching aspects of his work than by community action. The middling score on social values — slightly above that of the typical man but lower than that of the average woman — may indicate that calling on the aged or ill is not his favorite activity.

Single-Trait Measurement of Personality

Another way of looking at personality style is to rank people on the strength of a particular personality trait. Instead of pigeonholing individuals as this or that "type," this approach sees everyone as having a more or less specific quality. An example is sensation-seeking, which we looked at in Chapter 2. Other single-personality dimensions that have been studied in depth are dominance, authoritarianism, and need for achievement.

Some investigators have combined the measurement of several single traits into a paper-and-pencil device that assesses a number of personality dimensions at the same time. An example is the *16PF Test* (for the sixteen personal factors it measures). The traits assessed are contained in Table 4.3.

We can see from Table 4.3 that this device allows us to chart simultaneously someone's relative ranking on several personality qualities.

Given a test asking a large number of questions about a large number of human characteristics, it's possible to imagine an instrument that could give everyone a slightly different profile of scores. In other words, the more we learn about someone the more different from everyone else that individual becomes. Each person is his or her own personality type.

This method is useful for understanding the unique qualities of each of us. But it moves us away from the quest for a smaller number of personality types that have stable features in different life situations. Let us return to a consideration of contemporary ways of viewing personality style.

Other Ways of Classifying Personality

In the more than fifty years since Jung and Spranger's works, others have come forward with their own breakdown of personality styles. Table 4.4 shows five of these typologies.

Table 4.4 presents two kinds of information. The first kind is the basis upon which the personality styles are divided. Two of the theories claim that physical constitution is important. For Gesell it is infant activity patterns (Gesell and Ilg, 1946). Sheldon thinks physique is the key to understanding personality (Sheldon and Steven, 1942). Psychoanalyst Roy Shafer (1970) represents a psychological viewpoint. He believes that personality type is determined by what we look at in the world around us and how we make sense of it. David Reisman and Florence Kluckhohn are convinced that the society in which we are reared affects our personality type. Reisman (1950) thinks soci-

Table 4.3   Scales for the 16PF test

Cool	Warm
Concrete thinking	Abstract thinking
Affected by feelings	Emotionally stable
Submissive	Dominant
Sober	Enthusiastic
Expedient	Conscientious
Shy	Bold
Tough-minded	Tender-minded
Trusting	Suspicious
Practical	Imaginative
Forthright	Shrewd
Self-assured	Apprehensive
Conservative	Experimenting
Group-oriented	Self-sufficient
Undisciplined self-conflict	Controlled
Relaxed	Tense

SOURCE: From the *16PF Test Profile*. Copyright 1956, 1973, 1982 by the Institute for Personality and Ability Testing, Inc., Champaign, Ill. Adapted and reproduced by permission of the copyright owner.

ety shapes temperament. Kluckhohn's opinion (1956) is that the dominant value orientation of the part of the culture in which we are raised controls much of personality.

The second type of information in Table 4.4 concerns the different personality types and their characteristics. If we glance through them we can find considerable overlap: Gesell's Rapid and Facile have a lot in common with Sheldon's Mesomorphic and Shafer's Romantic; Reisman's Tradition-Directed and Kluckhohn's Being-Oriented have many similarities. In addition, some of the other types share some specific traits, for instance, the slow and stolid and the Endomorphic; the Comic and the Being-in-Becoming.

A Look at Contemporary Personality Styles

We have now studied more than two dozen personality styles, which is an unwieldy number. People who observe human behavior often find it difficult to resist forming their own typologies. The author is no exception. Here is a description of six contemporary personality styles — controlled, pessimistic,

Table 4.4 Classification of personality styles on the basis of physical constitution, psychological viewpoint, and society

RESEARCHER	BASIS FOR CLASSIFICATION	PERSONALITY TYPES	PRIMARY CHARACTERISTICS
Gesell	Infant activity level	Slow and stolid	Matures slowly; cautious in new situations; assimilates gradually; depends on self.
		Rapid and facile	Matures rapidly; not cautious in new situations; adapts easily; clear about demands of others.
		Irregular and uneven	Matures irregularly; can be over or under cautious; overreacts; uneven demands on environment.
Sheldon	Physique	Endomorphic (soft and round)	Relaxed; likes comfort; slow reactor; friendly; tolerant; complacent.
		Mesomorphic (athletic)	Assertive posture; adventuresome; energetic; risk-taker; competitive.
		Ectomorphic (slender)	Restrained; quick reactor; enjoys privacy; intense; self-conscious; inhibited.
Schafer	Psychological vision of reality	Comic	Optimistic; improvement-oriented; social concerns; difficulty planning; fickle.
		Romantic	Life is a quest; success against great odds; rugged individualist; nostalgia for the "good old days."
		Tragic	Heroic struggle against overwhelming odds; awareness of defeat in victory and victory in defeat; skeptical.
		Ironic	Detached; subjective; satirical; minimizes differences in values.
Reisman	Society in which a person is raised	Tradition-directed	Bound by cultural heritage; behavior controlled by elaborate rituals; deviance punished by shame.
		Inner-directed	Guided by traditions but not bound by them; awareness of competing values; follows own lights; deviance punished by guilt.
		Other-directed	Look to contemporaries to guide; approval-seeking; changeable; diffuse anxiety when no external values to direct.
Kluckhohn	Valued personality type in culture	Being-oriented	Oriented by ancestors and traditions; comfort with status quo; fatalistic; controlled by nature; restrained.
		Being-in-becoming-oriented	Oriented by friends and present relatives; eager for self-realization; sees humanity and nature as harmonious whole; controlled.
		Doing-oriented	Oriented by future goals; values accomplishment; nature is to be dominated and harnessed; individualistic; energetic.

prickly, theatrical, active, and optimistic — each illustrated by a fictitious character. A summary of the qualities of each is shown in Table 4.5.

Looking at the main features of each personality style shown in Table 4.5, we can see that it may be more right than wrong to imagine that personality styles are arranged along a continuum rather than specific categories. If we imagine a single dimension ranging from introversion to extraversion, we can see that the qualities associated with the controlled and pessimistic personality styles are close to the introverted side, active people and optimists are near the extraverted end, and the prickly and theatrical men and women are in the middle.

The Controlled Personality

Mainly concerned with keeping things regulated and predictable, the **controlled personality** prizes neatness and precision. Sharply focused attention and a strong affinity for detail are qualities shown by individuals with a controlled temperament. Controlled people worry. They fret about minor flaws or unexpected events and are intensely vigilant waiting for something to go wrong.

Temperance is their central trait. People with controlled personalities try to manage their emotions by "understanding" them. Like Jung's thinking-oriented people, they tend to search for explanations and theories for anything unexplained or surprising. In part this is a purely pleasurable, intellectual exercise. To some degree, however, it is an effort to avoid disorganizing feelings.

Controlled people tend to be introverted, restrained, and intense. Routine and rituals are important to them. They are punctual. They are wary of new experiences and move into them slowly. Once involved they enjoy them fully. Controlled individuals do not like taking risks unless probability is heavily weighted in their favor. If asked to make a prediction about an outcome, they may feel that the evidence is insufficient to make a judgment.

Men and women with controlled personality styles worry about mistakes others make. They are frequently found delegating responsibility but not authority. This may cause inaction or a tendency to "play it safe" among those who work under their jurisdiction, in order to avoid making errors. Controlled individuals are not without a sense of humor, though it is usually dry and infrequent.

Hillary. Hillary is a student at a state university in Ohio. Hillary exhibits many traits of the controlled personality. Well-groomed, slightly understated in her dress, Hillary carries her personal neatness into most areas of her life. She always arrives early for classes. "I don't want to be rushed," she says. "I prefer to have time to organize myself before the professor starts."

Hillary is a good student, and part of the reason is that she faithfully does her homework, completes her assigned labs, and studies for tests. She has an excellent eye for detail, a good memory, and seldom makes a mistake. While her lab partner admires Hillary's work, she gets frustrated because Hillary

Table 4.5   Characteristics of six normal personality styles

Controlled
keeps things regulated
orderly, precise, neat
detail-oriented
worries about flaws
relies on rituals
temperate, wary of impulses
wary of new experiences
low risk-taker
delegates anxiously
dry wit

Pessimistic
prepared for disappointment
tragic vision
moody
looks for flaws
congenial rituals
enjoys new experiences
examines instincts
resigned risk-taker
delegates critically
gallows humor

Prickly
devil's advocate
oppositional, feisty, charming
cynical, looks for flaws with zest
surprised to be taken seriously
idealistic
subjective, thin-skinned
guided by instincts
enthusiastic risk-taker
disorganized
delegates erratically
undoes hostility with intimidating wit

Theatrical
dramatic and impressionistic
reacts strongly
romantic
intuitive
changeable
disorderly
expresses feelings
blandness, low accountability
delegates poorly
humor through mimicry

Active
on the move
drawn to challenges
uses instincts
efficient
accepts flaws, missing information
risk-taker, resilient, pragmatic
shifts attention smoothly
future-minded
delegates easily
raucous wit

Optimistic
hopeful
idealistic
selective attention, rationalizes problems
concern with beginning, regeneration
infectious enthusiasm attracts others
apparently guileless
values social cohesion
righteous indignation but forgiveness
benign neglect
egalitarian humor

seems to take forever to do an experiment. "It's irritating sometimes to work with Hillary," her lab partner comments. "But it's good, too, because she hardly ever makes a stupid mistake."

Hillary's roommate says that Hillary is even-tempered. "Hillary must have been born a prim old lady," is how she puts it. "She never acts like a college student. It's like having a parent in our room." The roommate remarks that the only time Hillary ever seems to get upset is during exams — "She always worries and always gets A's and B's." Hillary also gets upset when people borrow things and don't return them in exactly the condition they were when they were lent.

When she goes shopping, Hillary always has a list. She knows what she wants and which stores she will go to, in which order. Hillary almost always keeps to her schedule.

For the past three years, Hillary has had an affair with her former high school guidance counselor. He is married. Though her roommate knows about this relationship, they don't talk about it. "It's a funny kind of thing between them," her roommate observes. "They get together for a couple days every two or three months but that's all." Neither Hillary nor the man has any plans to alter this relationship.

The Pessimistic Personality

Always prepared for disappointment, the **pessimistic personality** "knows" that flaws exist in the best solutions to problems and that unexpected events will ruin grand schemes. Pessimists focus on the uncertainties, sufferings, limitations, and paradoxes that seem to infest everyone's life. For individuals with pessimistic personalities, life resembles a Greek tragedy with moments of success and enthusiasm followed by failure and heartbreak just around the corner. Schafer (1970, p. 285) believes that pessimists, like people with tragic vision, may simply see accurately what the rest of us fail to acknowledge:

> . . . the inescapable changes, terrors, mysteries, and absurdities of existence
> . . . the elements of defeat in victory and victory in defeat; the pain in plea-
> sure and the pleasure in pain; the guilt in apparently justified action; the loss
> of opportunities entailed by every choice and by growth in any direction; the
> inevitable clashes between passion and duty; the reversible fortune that hovers
> over those who are proud and happy.

Because they are reacting to a subjective inner sense of potential tragedy, pessimists may from time to time seem withdrawn, introverted, and melancholy without apparent cause.

Prepared for the worst, these men and women are pleasantly surprised when things work out well. This doesn't result in their being less gloomy the next time someone hatches a new plan. Any optimism is likely to be subjected to intense scrutiny and criticism.

Pessimists don't mind confronting a new experience or problems. They will appraise novel situations, slowly examine their own subjective reactions, and decide how to respond. They trust their own judgment. Though usually temperate, pessimists don't mind loosening controls, feelings, or thoughts in an appropriate setting. As with Spranger's aesthetics, they enjoy examining the depth and range of their inner experience. This is not so much for self-improvement or realization as for the sensation itself.

Many pessimistic personalities show a perfectionistic attention to detail. They organize their lives around congenial rituals — exactly the same breakfast each morning, a day organized into manageable blocks and a predictable behavior pattern on arriving home. Like being-oriented individuals, they are comfortable with the status quo and are unsure that change is likely to result in improvement.

They don't avoid risks but take them with a sense of possible failure. When a child, a friend, or colleague fails, they are tolerant rather than surprised or upset. Since they are prepared for and respect failure, pessimists often find pleasure in examining what went wrong. Their discussions may be lightened by gallows humor.

Luis. Many of the traits of a pessimistic personality can be seen in Luis, a 53-year-old electronics engineer in Hartford. Dubbed "Knight of the Woeful Countenance" by a fellow engineer, Luis is well known at work for his tendency to see the hole and not the doughnut. Aside from the four years he spent in the Navy, Luis has lived all his life in Hartford. Tall and gaunt, he dresses conservatively and walks with a limp from a childhood motorcycle accident. All but one of his four children are out of the house, and recently his wife began part-time work in a bank.

Cigarette smoking — two packs a day — is Luis's only intemperance. Occasionally he likes to stay up late and drink wine, smoke marijuana, and listen to his excellent jazz collection with some friends. He plays the saxophone and lifts weights. He still rides a motorcycle.

When the company decided to spend a great deal of money trying to develop the high-altitude performance of a missile guidance system, Luis said little; but when asked by his boss what he thought of the program, he said he didn't think it would work because it was too complex. In spite of his forecast of failure, no one worked harder than Luis to make the program work.

Young engineers who come to Luis for help find him a little cool at first but then extremely receptive and sensitive. "He doesn't give you a lot of advice. He just sits and listens." Some note his moodiness and sense that he withdraws into himself from time to time. He has surprising empathy, especially for depressed feelings. At one point a colleague became depressed because of a separation from his wife and told Luis that he was thinking of killing himself. Luis's reported response was, "In many ways, the only question is why everyone doesn't commit suicide." At first the man was startled, but then he realized Luis could empathize with his desperate feelings of depression, and he began to feel better.

People who work with Luis are dazzled by his capacity to untangle complicated problems. However, Luis will also talk for hours about missile guidance systems they planned to produce but which never worked or were obsolete by the time they were deployed. Luis sometimes amuses his friends by wondering if somewhere in Russia he doesn't have an exact twin doing precisely the same thing as himself, and that their efforts cancel each other out.

The Prickly Personality

The professional devil's advocate, the **prickly personality** is very predictable; others automatically anticipate nay-saying and negativism from this personality. Remorseless truth-seekers, prickly personalities call facts as they see them. Highly subjective, these men and women are frequently sensitive to subtle cues that others overlook. From these perceptions they may generate ideas others may think are unusual, creative, or bizarre. More sensitive than most, the feelings of prickly personalities are more easily bruised by negative reactions than are others. At this point they may withdraw for a while.

Prickly people are irrepressible. They bounce back with enthusiasm the next time an idea or cause excites their interest. They are at heart romantic, individualistic, and inner-directed. Not temperate, they are willing risk-takers. They follow their enthusiasms. They may stay up too late, eat and drink too much, take a vacation on a whim to visit a friend a thousand miles away. Organization is not their long suit. They are often seen rumpled, unmatched, and in need of grooming. Their desks overflow, they are late for appointments, and not infrequently they take on too much: either they finish late or don't complete the project at all.

Prickly persons can be inspirational mentors. They attract unusual loyalty from subordinates. Protégés are given lots of responsibility along with authority and the enthusiastic support of their prickly teachers and bosses. Sometimes, however, what is delegated is greater than the protégé's capacity to cope with it.

The wit of prickly people may be the best of all personality styles — provided one finds humor in irreverence and the lampooning of commonly held ideas and stereotypes.

Angus. Angus illustrates the primary features of the prickly personality style. Angus is a 39-year-old reporter for a large newspaper in New York City. He was invited to join the paper after his small paper published his investigative report about officials siphoning money from the lottery in another state. Shortly after Angus arrived in New York, the metropolitan editor wondered if they had made a mistake. "Angus told me we were a bunch of gutless wonders," the editor recounted. "He said he thought we were too close to the politicians we were supposed to be covering. Then he made hash out of an idea I had about investigating the police force. Is he good enough to be this bad?"

Eventually, the editor and others became accustomed to Angus's tirades and rather began to expect him to oppose ideas everyone else agreed with. His colleagues and supervisors, however, occasionally became irritated with what seemed to be Angus's instinctive opposition and the chain-saw ferocity with which he could dismember the ideas of others. When they retaliate, Angus is usually surprised and hurt. "I wasn't attacking them personally," he will typically say, "just their ideas."

His wife observes that Angus can dish it out better than he can take it. She acknowledges that Angus is sometimes moody, irascible, and unpredictable. "We all walk on eggshells around him sometimes," she says, "yet he is one of the warmest, most loving people you'll ever meet."

Her sentiments are echoed by young reporters working for Angus. In contrast to his prickly behavior toward colleagues and bosses, Angus is usually a warm, supportive mentor. He talks to them for hours, telling funny stories about the newspaper business; he gives them leads, and even edits their copy.

"He's the best teacher I ever had in anything" is the way one journalist summed up his feelings.

Angus is not especially concerned about appearance, organization, or the clock. One cub reporter remembers the day Angus came to work in a three-piece suit but no socks. His desk is a chaos of notes, half-filled coffee cups and overflowing ashtrays, phone call slips, letters, and books. People complain that he forgets to return phone calls, doesn't answer letters, and rarely appears on time. A publisher gave him an advance to write a book about the lottery scandal. The deadline is well past and Angus hasn't written more than an outline. The publisher doesn't press him too hard, however, because he thinks if Angus ever writes the book, it will be a best-seller.

The Theatrical Personality

Dramatic and impressionable, the **theatrical personality** often reacts strongly to events. Romantics at heart, anything which they are involved with is the *most* — the most lovely, grand, exciting, meaningful, and spectacular; or the most despicable, obscene, calamitous, or disastrous. Because they are so intuitive, theatrical people have trouble citing details or facts in support of their impressions. They are capable of great enthusiasm and will make a major commitment to an idea, often one that is currently popular. Easily influenced by other people and experience, they are changeable and will lose interest in jobs, individuals, and hobbies rather quickly. Organization is not their long suit.

People with theatrical personality styles express emotions easily. Outgoing and extraverted, they like face-to-face contact, and will walk half a mile to talk to someone rather than using either the phone or the mail. Should they offend someone with their emotional displays, these men and women may react blandly or with rapid retreats, saying they didn't mean it.

Theatrical people often take on more than they can handle and show poor judgment in their perception of what others can do. They can vacillate between being overly critical of others and extraordinarily tolerant. They can be hilariously funny — especially when they tell stories mimicking others.

Darlene. The primary qualities of the theatrical temperament are exhibited in Darlene. She is a dental hygienist in Ft. Lauderdale, Florida. She is 28 years old, single, and lives with her cat and boyfriend. Though she is thirty pounds overweight, Darlene manages to radiate considerable appeal because she behaves as though she is attractive. Occasionally patients ask her for a date, but Darlene always declines politely, saying it is against office policy.

Her patients are generally treated to a recital of the dramatic events in Darlene's life: how wonderful and divine her new diet is, which is *guaranteed* to take off thirty pounds in a month; her *beautiful*, adorable pussycat who can be a little *devil;* a new lounge, which is simply *fantastic;* her new shoes, which are *killing* her feet; and the last patient, who was the most *brilliant* person she'd ever met. If she is asked whose diet she is following, what about the cat is beautiful or devilish, or how to get to the new lounge, Darlene is not likely to provide the details easily. She focuses on the "big picture" of her intuitive feelings rather than the details of what, who, why, when, where, or how.

The young man with whom Darlene is living occasionally complains that he has to do all the shopping: "Otherwise we'd be eating goldfish crackers and drinking piña coladas for breakfast." Her boyfriend doesn't mind because "She has a knack for making the apartment look terrific with things you buy in a yard sale for a dollar and a half." Her friends are always drawn to Darlene's ideas about entertainment or vacation. They note they never know exactly where they're going to wind up. "She is also one of the funniest people you'll ever meet," her boyfriend laughs, "especially when she pretends she's the landlord!"

Once Darlene heard someone speak of the plight of the Cuban refugees in Miami and signed up to be a tutor on Saturday afternoons. She convinced several of her friends to join her. She accused one reluctant acquaintance of being a racist because she wouldn't sign up to be a tutor. Then Darlene couldn't understand why the women became upset at her remark. "I didn't mean to offend her," she said. Later, when her friends were tutoring, they noted Darlene had stopped. She had decided to take a CPR course instead.

Sometime later, an elderly patient had a heart attack in the dentist's office while a filling was being put in. The dentist panicked. Darlene told him to call for an ambulance and administered cardiopulmonary resuscitation, saving the man's life.

The Active Personality

Always energetic and on the move, **active personalities** are doing-oriented. They value accomplishment above all else. They judge themselves and others by what they accomplish or plan to achieve. Active people are drawn to challenges. If one doesn't exist naturally, they will create one.

They are positive in their outlook. Saying that something can't be done just excites their interest more. These are the people who create more electricity or reliable sources of irrigation by damming rivers, or create rivers on hotel roofs for aesthetic purposes. The mysteries of nature are scrutinized through scientific research that splices genes, creates synthetic materials, or sends astronauts to the moon.

People with active temperaments are in touch with their impulses and draw power from the primitive, baser parts of their nature. They are attentive to objective facts and the practical use of theory, but they are comfortable with the knowledge that there is never enough information to make a decision. They accept risks and flaws and the possibility of failure every time they undertake an enterprise. Successful or not, active people don't look back and second-guess their plans or decisions. Efficiency and time-saving are prized. Type A behavior is common among these men and women.

Active women and men delegate responsibility smoothly. As long as students, assistants, and others who work with them are attracted to the same goals, people with active personality styles are excellent mentors. They take considerable pain in bringing their protégés along. Like Jung's extraverts, however, if their protégés do not follow the same path, active personality types quickly lose interest in them. Their wit can be entertaining, occasionally raucous, but not especially sensitive to the feelings of others.

Walter. Walter is close to the pure type of the active personality. He is 35 years of age, an architect for a large firm in Philadelphia. He is mostly black, but notes with pride he is one-sixteenth Comanche Indian. Walter is the prototypical self-made man. An only child of a single-parent mother who worked all her life as a telephone operator in an exclusive club in Philadelphia, Walter knew early that he had to excel in school in order to get ahead. He held part-time jobs as a student at the University of Pennsylvania and graduate school, but still managed honors grades. "It took me two years longer," Walter says with a slight smile, "but it was worth it."

After he finished architectural training, Walter went to work for his present firm. Though his architectural skills are not remarkable, he moved ahead faster than his contemporaries because he worked harder and was especially good at dealing with clients. Walter himself says that what he likes most about the work is convincing prospective clients to buy his firm's proposals: "Everyone needs a challenge, and I guess I need one more than most."

He attracted the notice of top management when he put together a plan for redeveloping a portion of the waterfront in Philadelphia before anyone else had the idea. Walter then prepared the way for his firm to make a proposal to the city by obtaining the support of several influential people who were members of the club where his mother worked. Walter made the presentation and the proposal was accepted. At that point, Walter knew he had a chance to become a partner with the firm. "If you don't take risks you don't accomplish anything," Walter said. The report was accepted, and it was a turning point in his career. Afterward, instead of being elated, Walter felt curiously depressed. Shortly thereafter he found a new project and his spirits lifted again.

Walter works seventy hours a week. He has a traditional marriage and doesn't want his wife to work. As he puts it, "After the kids are raised she can get a job if she wants, but there is room for only one career in this family." His children don't see much of him, but say he's fun to be with because when he is with them he takes them places — sports events, the symphony, fishing. Walter believes that it's the quality, not the quantity, of the time you spend with kids that counts.

He is obsessed with using his time productively. One Sunday night in the fall, his wife noticed that he was watching the Philadelphia Eagles on TV, listening to the 76ers basketball team on the radio, and paging through a magazine all at the same time. He is thinking about installing a telephone in his car.

For his own recreation, Walter likes ocean fishing. "It's quiet," he says. "No phones ringing, people running into your office, or letters to be answered. I just like being off by myself sometimes."

The type A personality in action: this man is using every minute by making business calls while waiting for the commuter train to his New York City office.

His secretaries are a little in awe of Walter, but they acknowledge that his enthusiasm for new projects means lots more work for them. The architects who work with him feel a little the same way, but they're happy to have been assigned to a "winner."

The Optimistic Personality

Hopefulness is the major identifying feature of the **optimistic personality.** These people share the same interest in overcoming obstacles as active types, but — as with Spranger's socially oriented individuals — they are more often attracted to programs for human welfare. They can be found soliciting money for the heart fund, volunteering to help the poor, or trying to rehabilitate mental patients. Schafer (1970, p. 281) portrays their optimism this way:

> No dilemma is too great to be resolved, no obstacle too firm to stand against effort and good intentions, no evil so unmitigated and entrenched that it is irremedial, no suffering so intense it cannot be relieved, and no loss so final that it cannot be undone and made up for. The program is reform, progress, and the tidings of joy.

The positive thinking of these personalities results in highly selective attention. They are far more responsive to information corresponding with their hopeful view and tend to ignore or put in the most favorable light negative findings or flaws.

Optimists are doers. They are most enthusiastic when they are planning something entirely new or contemplating a fresh phase of a project. Extraverted in their orientation, they radiate an upbeat, expansive, hopeful view of things. Their enthusiasm is infectious. Partly this is because optimistic people are often open, enthusiastic, friendly, and apparently guileless.

Though they value closeness to others, optimists may relate to subordinates with benign neglect. Though they know they have the goodwill of their optimistic bosses, underlings often wish they had more personal contact with them. The guidelines optimistic people draw for others to follow are vague. Optimistic people don't usually have much humor. When it is expressed, it is typically egalitarian or self-effacing.

Maria. Maria is an optimistic person. She is 36 years old and lives in Denver, Colorado. She has been married nineteen years to a 40-year-old policeman, like her of Mexican-American descent. Their children are aged 17, 15, and 8. Maria is an assistant manager of a nutrition store.

For the past three years she has been the director of a privately supported program to encourage white families in affluent suburbs to act as foster parents for inner-city youngsters during the school week. Maria's work involves convincing inner-city and suburban people that the program is a good idea, mediating when difficulties arise, and seeking political and financial support.

Everyone who knows her is impressed by Maria's honesty, openness, and commitment to the cause. A lot of Maria's work involves solving problems that come up every day: inner-city youngsters accused of stealing from a foster family; a foster family said to be racist; a suburban high-school principal who claims inner-city boys and girls demand to be treated differently from the other students; and parents who worry about their children being beaten up. Maria always seems to be in the thick of these skirmishes. Someone close to her said, "These problems are so 'daily' they just wear you down, but she just keeps going, saying 'It'll be all right.' "

Maria's forte is convincing suburban families to act as foster parents. She's an excellent money raiser, too. "I would hire her any time in our sales department," one company president said after he authorized a six-figure contribution to the program. "That woman could convince people to buy anything."

Maria likes to have everyone agreeable. She can reason with dissenters, trying to convince them of the virtue of her ideas. If people continue to oppose her, she's been accused of being ruthless. "Maria just cuts them free of the raft," a friend says. Maria puts it differently. "I don't understand how people can oppose what we are doing. If they do, I plain don't have time for them." Should they decide to support the cause, Maria would welcome them back into the group.

She uses her sense of humor to make a point without offending anyone. Once when several members of the committee thought of splitting off because they disagreed with the way Maria was running things, she said with a tired smile, "If we spent half the energy we use fighting among ourselves in finding foster families for these kids, we'd have it made."

Personality Style and Adjustment

Can you see yourself as closer to one of these six personality styles than others? Or do you think your temperament better corresponds to one of the types portrayed by some other researcher? Most of us fit into one or another personality category, but no one exactly matches a particular type. Some may be closer to a pure strain than others, but none is a perfect fit. Furthermore, we all have qualities that are not included in a list of characteristics associated with a prevailing temperament.

No ideal personality style exists. Normally adjusted people come in all types. Each temperament has its particularly effective ways of understanding and dealing with the world, and each has its limitations. Consider how members of a class might prepare for the final exam. Some may discipline themselves to do their assignments regularly so the final represents no significant added pressure. Others may have done very little reading but have paid close attention to the teacher and have an intuitive feel for what might be on the exam. And a third group will cram a semester's worth of studying into a forty-eight-hour period.

In the years since Jung and Spranger, thinking about personality styles has changed. It used to be believed that our temperament was shaped largely by psychological self-protective responses to stress (Reich, 1949). In the years following World War II, the power of the culture in which we live to influence our temperament has become increasingly apparent, and, more recently, biological makeup is recognized as a significant contributor to personality.

Anyone who has been in the military service knows about the impact of environment on behavior. Otherwise timid, tranquil, rebellious, and disorganized men can be trained into ferocious, disciplined combat soldiers. Similarly, every family, school, organization, and occupation has preferred value orientations and behavior patterns. This family reinforces controlled style by rewarding exactitude and punishing sloppiness. The faculty of that school models an optimistic attitude toward the future. If an organization is a frantic, rushing place, with people shouting at each other irritably all of the time, it may not be long before a new employee is behaving in a like manner. And the daily experiences of some occupations may result in the development of particular attitudes and values. The nature of your work may encourage a pessimistic style if you are a police officer and a prickly style if you drive a cab.

The question is, of course, to what extent do these socially reinforced qualities remain when our environment changes. How long after discharge does it take for a Marine to revert to his former tranquil or disorganized self? Does the pessimistic style of a police officer or the prickly temperament of a cabbie persist if they move into different occupations? The answer is both yes and no. Yes, the central features of our core personality style are likely to reappear when the environment stops reinforcing natural tendencies. But the answer is no, too, because a former environment will leave its mark on us. Even though it may be decades since we were in the service, many of us still make our beds with hospital corners, have particular ways of saying things, or move in a special manner. Some former police officers and cabbies retain a residue of their work experience in their attitudes toward people and society.

Powerful as the effects of the world around us are, there remains in each of us an unalterable element of personality that is hard to change. Moreover, these core ingredients of our personality do seem to have a biological origin. Recent thinking has it that our biological makeup gives us a long leash, a freedom to develop a range of personality qualities within a limited scope (Lumsden and Wilson, 1981; Wilson, 1978). The temperament of each of us is constrained by our inheritance.

Our underlying temperament can influence long-term adjustment. For example, over one hundred medical students were classified according to Gesell's types, described in Table 4.4: slow and stolid, rapid and facile, and irregular and uneven. The medical students were contacted fifteen to thirty years after they received their M.D. This study found that the irregular and uneven personality types had a higher incidence of physical and emotional problems than the other two groups (Betz and Thomas, 1979).

Unfortunately, studies such as this one do not pay attention to the fit between personality style and environment. If the surrounding world rewards the type of personality we are, we are more likely to be better adjusted than if it does not. An active, restless baby girl may have a more frustrating experience living with highly controlled parents than her more placid brother, who is not bothered by their anxious efforts to manage his behavior. A teacher who encourages accuracy may be harder on someone who is theatrical than on a pessimistic person, yet the theatrical individual may be far better in sales. As long as the environment enables us to find some satisfaction in our work, in loving relationships, and in play, within the limits of our personality style, our adjustment is not likely to be affected. If, however, our needs are continually frustrated because the outer world cannot accommodate our personality style, then maladjustment may occur unless changes are made.

The adaptation of young people can be helped by parents and teachers

Does this driver's aggressive reaction identify him as someone who could be a cab driver? To what extent do basic temperament and environment shape personality?

who take into account personality style. Gesell noted that irregular and uneven children may have difficulty in school. He suggested that if teachers aided these children by helping them plan and anticipate and by directing, restraining, prodding, and channeling their efforts, they can help the children cope more effectively with the world around them (Gesell and Ilg, 1946).

Counselors who advise high-school and college students about fields of concentration or potential work are likely to be more effective if they pay attention to how dominant traits of the personality will connect with the requirements of particular course work or occupation. Would Maria be as satisfied in a laboratory science as Luis? How happy would Darlene be in Walter's job and vice versa? In the end, however, we have to rely on ourselves. There is value in understanding the type of person we are and trying to predict our behavior in various situations. These insights can be useful in helping us to anticipate whether a particular school situation, job, or relationship will be challenging and growth-enhancing or stressful. They can help us adjust more effectively now and in the future.

Summary

1. Personality style is consistency and stability in many areas of behavior that are slow to change. It can include traits and interests, quirks and prejudices, as well as habitual ways of experiencing emotions, thoughts, and outside events.

2. The twentieth century has been highlighted by numerous efforts to portray personality styles. Two of the most influential are Jung's extravert-introvert and Spranger's system of value orientations.

3. Another way of looking at personality style is to rank people on the strength of a particular personality trait. Some paper-and-pencil tests combine the measurement of several traits at one time.

4. Contemporary ways of categorizing personality have been based on physical constitution and the influence of environment, as well as on psychological perspectives.

5. Six normal personality styles evident today are the controlled, pessimistic, prickly, theatrical, active, and optimistic personalities. They fall on a rough continuum between introvert and extravert.

6. The dominant traits of most people fit into one or another personality style. However, none of us is a pure type, and we will have many characteristics that are not included in a categorization of our temperament. No ideal personality style exists.

7. The power of culture and biological makeup to influence personality style has been recognized. Our experiences in a family, school, organization, or occupation leave their mark. Biological makeup limits the range of our personality style.

8. Some personality styles blend better with some environments. Parents, teachers, and others can assist in adaptation by helping individuals find

environments suited for particular personality styles. We can all, however, assist ourselves by recognizing particular traits that are adaptable in particular environmental settings.

A Look Ahead

In the next section we will examine normal behavior through the life cycle. A chapter will be devoted to normal working, loving, and playing behaviors throughout life. Attention will be given to satisfactions from each of these domains as well as to threats to pleasure. This section will begin with a description of the life cycle. We will begin with a definition of the concept, and then look at factors that influence change during a lifetime. We will consider differences between the life span experiences of men and women, discuss the extent to which our lives have periods of stability and instability, and consider how much of our present behavior is controlled by early experience.

Key Terms

personality style
phlegmatic temperament
melancholic temperament
choleric temperament
sanguine temperament
extravert
introvert
ambivert
theoretical orientation
economic orientation

aesthetic orientation
social orientation
political orientation
religious orientation
controlled personality
pessimistic personality
prickly personality
theatrical personality
active personality
optimistic personality

Suggested Readings

Extraverts-introverts

Eysenck, H. *The biological basis of personality*. Springfield, Ill.: Thomas, 1967.

Discussion of these two personality types, and an empirical definition.

Personality styles

White, R. *The enterprise of living: Growth and organization of personality*. New York: Holt, Rinehart & Winston, 1972. Chapter 15.

————.*Lives in progress*. Third edition. New York: Holt, Rinehart & Winston, 1975.

Clinical portrayals of how different personality styles.

Temperament-environment interaction

Thomas, A., and Chess, S. *Temperament and development*. New York: Brunner/Mazel, 1977.

Survey of the complex relationship among personality style, environment, and adjustment.

Part II
Work, Love, and Play in the Life Cycle

In Part II we focus on normal behavior through the life cycle. Chapter 5 presents current thinking about the life cycle itself. We look at a scheme for understanding human growth based on traditional thinking and on newer concepts. We study three questions about development through the life span: (1) Are we all likely to have periods of stability and instability in our lives? (2) How does early experience affect later adjustment? (3) How do the experiences of males and females differ? Chapter 5 ends with a description of a seven-stage life cycle model within which distinctive working, loving, and playing behaviors are later described.

In the remaining three chapters of Part II, we look at normal working, loving, and playing activities for each phase of life. Each of these chapters begins with a definition of work, love, or play. Human needs satisfied by each sphere are considered. The relationship between adjustment and satisfaction from work, love, and play is explored. We explore types of working, loving, and playing that are found in almost all phases of the life cycle, and we identify typical working, loving, and playing behaviors that are characteristic of, or begin at, each stage of the life cycle.

Typical hazards that may compromise our satisfaction from work, love, and play at each developmental stage are considered. We try to discover ways to avoid or cope with these predictable threats to satisfaction in each phase of the life cycle.

All the world's a stage,
And all the men and women merely players.
They have their exits and their entrances;
And one man in his time plays many parts,
His acts being seven ages. At first the infant,
Mewling and puking in the nurse's arms.
And then the whining school-boy, with his
        satchel
And shining morning face, creeping like snail
Unwillingly to school. And then the lover,
Sighing like furnace, with a woeful ballad
Made to his mistress' eyebrow. Then a soldier,
Full of strange oaths, and bearded like the
        pard;
Jealous in honour, sudden and quick in
        quarrel,
Seeking the bubble reputation
Even in the cannon's mouth. And then the
        justice,

In fair round belly with good capon lined,
With eyes severe and beard of formal cut,
Full of wise saws and modern instances;
And so he plays his part. The sixth age shifts
Into the lean and slipper'd pantaloon,
With spectacles on nose and pouch on side;
His youthful hose, well saved, a world too
        wide
For his shrunk shank, and his big manly voice,
Turning again toward childish treble, pipes,
And whistles in his sound. Last scene of all,
That ends this strange eventful history,
Is second childishness, and mere oblivion,
Sans teeth, sans eyes, sans taste, sans every-
        thing.

SOURCE: William Shakespeare, *As You Like It*, act 2, scene 6.

Chapter Preview

CHAPTER 5
The Life Cycle

Questions to think about

- [ ] What portion of the life cycle are you in now? What comes next?
- [ ] Have you had periods in your life when everything was fine and when, for no obvious reason, you began to feel confused and depressed?
- [ ] In what ways might the life cycle experiences of men and women differ?
- [ ] How do early experiences affect the rest of our lives?

At no time has interest in questions like these been greater than now. More and more professors and clinicians, as well as popular writers, are being drawn to the subject of the life cycle. In part this is because psychological specialists are turning their attention away from childhood and adolescence to the following fifty years of life. Gail Sheehy's best-selling book *Passages* (1976), describes the predictable crises of adulthood, drawing much popular attention to this period. The appearance of this book and others like it led the editor of at least one scholarly journal to wonder if we are now entering the "century of the adult" (Graubard, 1976).

Along with greater interest in adulthood has come a surge of interest in the life cycle itself. This enthusiasm is not only for learning about how people change or remain constant over time, but also for thinking about the life span in new ways. Previously, psychological growth was imagined to follow a biological model: each of us passes from infancy to old age in a uniform series of irreversible stages. Current thinking broadens the biological model to include social and historical events as well as unpredictable critical instances, all of which cause change throughout our lives.

In this chapter we define the term "life cycle," look at ways it has been viewed since ancient times, and study three models for understanding how changes occur in our lives. These are the biological, Eriksonian, and pluralistic models. Then we examine three issues about the life cycle: (1) Are we all likely to have periods of stability and instability in our lives? (2) How does early experience influence later adjustment? (3) How do the experiences of men and women differ through the life span? At the chapter's end we separate the life cycle into seven overlapping stages. This model is to be used for discussing distinctive working, loving, and playing behaviors for each period of life in the remaining chapters of Part II.

How Do We Grow?
Three Models of Life Cycle Development

The words **life cycle** refer to a way of looking at a lifetime.* Essentially, it means that each of our lives is broken up into periods of time of a specific length. For example, the years from 13 to 19 might be called the stage of adolescence. Within each time period, particular events usually occur, which may be physical, social, or psychological. For example, a physical event usually occurring in adolescence is the growth of secondary sexual characteristics, a beard or breasts, and so on. A social event is high-school graduation. Establishing a clearer sense of identity is a psychological happening.

Three models of looking at how we grow through the life cycle are the biological model, Erikson's eight stages of development, and the pluralistic theory.

The Biological Model

The **biological model** of life cycle development assumes that psychological growth proceeds the same way as physical development — a baby first turns over; then it crawls, stands up, walks, and eventually rides a bicycle. In the psychological domain every stage has characteristics and tasks specific to that time of life and no other. In the verse at the beginning of the chapter, Shakespeare's eye sees particular behaviors unfolding in a sequence — the lovesick, sighing adolescent and the reputation-seeking young adult.

These descriptions of life span development have an element of truth in

---

*The definition of the life cycle is taken from two of the meanings of the term "cycle" from the compact edition of the Oxford English Dictionary (New York: Oxford University Press, 1971), p. 365.

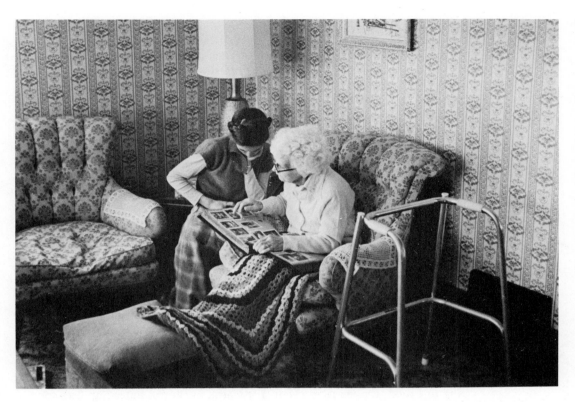

An elderly woman remembers her past as she and her granddaughter look at the family photo album — a record of her life cycle.

them. Also, they make five assumptions about human growth that are characteristic of the biological model (Baltes, Reese, and Lipsett, 1980).

1. Psychological development through life can be divided into stages that unfold in a predictable sequence, for example, childhood, adolescence, and adulthood.
2. Stages begin and end at approximate ages. For instance, adolescence starts around 13 and finishes about 19.
3. Each stage contains growth tasks essential to that era and no other. For example, the primary issue for a young adult is finding an occupation to pursue.
4. The stages of emotional growth are irreversible. Once a teenage boy begins to sprout a beard, he doesn't revert to being smooth-faced. In the psychological domain, once the trying issues of adolescence have been worked out, we don't have to face them later on.
5. The phases of growth apply to everyone, no matter what sex, social class background, or race.

Some of the most influential twentieth-century doctors and psychologists organized their theories around the biological model. The primary example is Sigmund Freud. He believed that everyone passes through four stages of development depending on which zone of the body pleasure primarily comes from: oral, anal, phallic, and genital (Hall and Lindzey, 1957, Chapter 2).

The first year of life is referred to by Freud as the **oral stage** because he believed that most of the infant's pleasure comes from the mouth. Examples are sucking and eating, biting, and spitting unpleasant things out. The **anal stage** occurs during the second and third years. The focus is on the pleasure which comes from bowel control in reaction to parental pressure for toilet training. Most learn to enjoy postponing the desire to have a bowel movement in their pants in order to go in the toilet and please their mother.

The **phallic stage** covers the years from about 3 to 5. During this phase the child gradually recognizes the pleasure coming from his or her sexual organs. Masturbation often occurs. Freud believed that these erotic feelings resulted in the boy or girl's wishing to sexually possess the parent of the opposite sex. In boys this is called the **Oedipus complex,** named for the ancient King of Thebes who unwittingly killed his father and married his mother. In girls this is called the **Electra complex** (Freud, 1940). Freudian theory has it that eventually boys and girls give up the idea of possessing the loved mother or father and develop a desire to be like the same-sex parent.

After the phallic stage the child goes into a state of sexual hibernation called latency. During this quiet period of five to six years, sexual impulses are held in check. Puberty marks the beginning of the **genital stage.** According to Freud, the teenager eventually learns to control inner impulses for sexual satisfaction, to love others, and to begin to think about getting a job, settling down and raising a family.

The Freudian explanation of human growth has been criticized on many grounds. Two of the most telling are that Freud's scheme is not a theory of life cycle development but of childhood and that it lacks research verification. Surprisingly, Freud never studied children directly but relied on childhood memories of his adult patients. Yet many of Freud's basic ideas have served as a launching pad for much of the life cycle thinking of today.

The biological model has limited application to human development. For example, some issues crucial to psychological development occur and recur throughout a lifetime. Consider occupational identity. At 20, a young man decides to be a policeman. At 30 — having worked as a policeman for seven years, now married with three children, and feeling ground down by the work — he decides to change careers. He returns to school part-time to train as a computer programmer. Sometimes we have more than one task of development to deal with at the same time — a woman at 37 may be dealing simultaneously with the needs to get ahead in a career, have a satisfying relationship with her spouse, and be a competent mother. Many of us do not pass through the stations of psychological growth in the same order. While one woman may marry, have children, and not begin work until her early 30s, another may work in an occupation for many years before getting married. Finally, most thinking about the life cycle applies to male, middle-class development. Shortly we will study evidence suggesting that a woman's experience in living is very different from a man's.

Erikson's Eight Stages of Development

Among psychologists in the final half of the twentieth century, the man whose thinking about the life cycle has been the most influential has been Erik Erikson. His eight stages of human development are shown in Table 5.1. Erikson's basic idea is that every one of us passes through eight stages of growth from infancy to old age. Within each period are central conflicts that we must settle and growth tasks we have to master. Successful resolution of these conflicts and mastery of the tasks results in special adaptive strengths (Erikson, 1976).

Erikson believes that in infancy we all have to resolve the conflict of *trust vs. mistrust*. Developing a feeling that we can have trust in others results in a feeling of *hope*, which is a highly adaptive asset in coping with most stress. In early childhood the central issue is *autonomy vs. shame, doubt*. Successful negotiation of this conflict in favor of autonomy results in the determination to

Table 5.1 Eight stages of human development of Erik Erikson

STAGE OF DEVELOPMENT	CENTRAL CONFLICT	PRIMARY TASK TO BE MASTERED	RESULTING ADAPTIVE STRENGTH
Infancy	Trust vs. mistrust	Trust	HOPE
Early childhood	Autonomy vs. shame, doubt	Autonomy	WILL
Play age	Initiative vs. guilt	Initiative	PURPOSE
School age	Industry vs. inferiority	Industry	COMPETENCE
Adolescence	Identity vs. identity confusion	Identity	FIDELITY
Young adulthood	Intimacy vs. isolation	Intimacy	LOVE
Maturity	Generativity vs. self-absorption	Generativity	CARE
Old age	Integrity vs. despair, disgust	Integrity	WISDOM

SOURCE: From Erikson, E. Reflections on Dr. Borg's life cycle, p. 22, by permission of *Daedalus*, Journal of the American Academy of Arts and Sciences, Vol. 105, no. 2, spring 1976, Boston, Mass.

exercise *will*, the ability to make free choices as well as use self-control. In Erikson's third age, play, the conflict is *initiative vs. guilt.* Resolution of this struggle on the side of initiative yields a sense of *purpose*, the capacity to pursue valued goals energetically. The tension caused by *industry vs. inferiority* is the main focus of the school age. Mastery of this conflict results in a feeling of *competence.*

The primary problem of adolescence is *identity vs. identity confusion.* Coming to know who we are produces the adaptive strength of *fidelity*, the power to sustain loyalties in spite of inevitable contradictions and confusions of competing value systems. The opposition of *intimacy vs. isolation* is the primary problem of young adulthood. The outcome, maintaining an intimate relationship with someone, is *love*, the mutuality of devotion. Maturity features the task of dealing with *generativity vs. self-absorption.* Developing generativity, which Erikson (1981) sees as blending procreation, productivity, and creativity, leads to *care.* This is a concern for others and things, which widens as we grow older. The final stage is old age. Here the central conflict is *integrity vs. despair, disgust.* Winning this internal battle opens the way to *wisdom*, an active yet detached concern with life even while confronting death itself.

Erikson's stages of development build on Freud's basic theory, extending it through the life span. As we can see, however, most of Erikson's elaboration of Freud is centered in the interval between about age 5 (school age) and young adulthood. In the years after age 30 or so, Erikson visualizes only two stages. Since Erikson advanced his eight stages of growth, others have attempted to "fill in" the adult era. We will look at some of their thinking at the chapter's end.

The Pluralistic Model of Human Development

Like the biological model, Erikson's vision of growth through the life cycle has a basic truth to it. Some changes occur in our lives because we are a teenager or middle-aged. However, it also has many of the same limitations as the biological model. New perspectives on growth and change over a lifetime suggest that Erikson's theory of the life span is too restrictive and in some respects incorrect.

Attempting to account for the several forces that influence psychological change in people's lives, Pennsylvania State University Professor Paul Baltes and his colleagues have developed a **pluralistic model** of human growth, which adds other influences to the developmental tasks associated with age. They distinguish three influences — age-related, historical, and critical incidents — that can affect the course of our lives (Baltes, 1979). Table 5.2 shows examples of these influences.

Age-Related Influences. Age-related events are physical and social, happening at about the same time to everyone in the same way. Entering the first grade at about age 6, getting a driver's license at about 16, and retiring between age 55 and 65 are events most of us can expect. Each of these happen-

Table 5.2 Examples of three influences on human development

AGE-RELATED	HISTORICAL	CRITICAL INCIDENTS
First walking and talking	Epidemics	Serious injury or illness
Entering school	Wars	School failure or success
Puberty	Genocide	Opportunity for action
Driver's license	Resettlement	Mentor
Starting work	Political unrest	Marital separation
Marriage	Economic depression	Winning the lottery
Birth of first child		
Retirement		

SOURCE: From Baltes, P. Life span developmental psychology: Some converging observations on history and theory. In P. Baltes and O. Brim (Eds.), *Life span development and behavior*. Vol. II. New York: Academic Press, 1979; and Goethals, G. *Stage theory and critical events: A reconsideration of critical events*. Paper presented at the Eastern Psychological Association, Boston, Mass., May, 1978.

ings is highly associated with chronological age, and the effect on each of our lives of these age-related events is substantial. Can you recall how your life changed when you entered school? Can you imagine what the impact of retirement will be on your personality?

Human development proceeds very differently after adolescence than before. In the first twenty or so years of life, specific events are closely tied to age and powerfully affect us. Obtaining a driver's license is an illustration. Think about how possessing a driver's license, or not having one, influences what a 16-year-old boy thinks about and does with his friends, how it affects his relationships with the opposite sex, and how it may even control where and how much he works part-time.

After the teenage years, however, the stages of development are far less predictable and more elastic. Events are only weakly associated with a particular time of life, and the resulting human attitudes, values, and behavior patterns are poorly correlated with chronological age.

Consider the twentieth reunion of a high-school class. At the same table will be 38-year-old grandparents, couples who have been married less than ten years, and other couples still trying to decide whether to have children. At the bar is a man who has worked for General Motors twenty years already and is looking ahead to retirement. Next to him is a neurosurgeon who completed his training only four years ago and is just beginning his career. In the corner is the former star of the high-school football team, who went on to become an All-American at State and played for three years in the pros. He's been washed up for a decade now and hasn't been able to catch on to anything. With him are two women. One is divorced with three children and is about to go back to work; the other never married and is an executive in a life insurance company. Watching all of this is another classmate — a wretchedly poor, briefly married "writer," who has yet to sell anything and wonders if he'll ever make it.

We can see from this brief look at these individuals that the stages of the life cycle do not unfold in a predictable manner in the adult years. The former football star's career was finished at a time when most were still preparing to settle into an occupation. In his mid-twenties, he may have had more in common with those in a mid-life crisis or facing retirement than his contemporaries. At 38, he and the divorced woman are both finding that stages of the life cycle are to some degree reversible. They may feel like youths who are trying to find an occupation they might enjoy and someone to love.

The length of time spent in each phase of adult growth is far more elastic than earlier in life. Consider the very brief period of relatively carefree youth of the grandmother or the General Motors factory worker. Contrast this with the exceptionally long period of youthful status of the doctor and the writer. As they approach 40, they are dealing with maturational issues more typical of those ten to fifteen years their junior.

In the adult years, specific events have a lower probability of being associated with a particular time of life. The single woman confides to her former best friend, the grandmother, that she is head over heels in love with a man she wants to marry and have children with. The grandmother can't remember what those feelings are like. It has been two decades for her. By the same token, the man who has worked for the same company for twenty years is reminded of his own younger days of questioning himself when he listens to the writer, divorced woman, and former football star wondering out loud about what line of work they will follow.

Age is not a primary factor in determining what adults feel, think, or do. University of Chicago human development specialist Bernice Neugarten notes (1979):

> . . . our society is becoming accustomed to the 28-year-old mayor, the 30-year-old college president, the 35-year-old grandmother, the 50-year-old retiree, the 65-year-old father of a preschooler, and the 70-year-old student, and even the 85-year-old mother caring for a 65-year-old son.

She goes on to wonder if we are becoming an "age irrelevant" society. This is clearly the case for those of us beyond adolescence and short of advanced age.

Historical Influences. Historical influences are general events that affect everyone within a specific culture and may trigger significant changes in us. Some examples that were cited in Table 5.2 are epidemics, wars, organized massacre, and resettlement. The parents and grandparents of today's students have no trouble recalling the terrible effect of losing loved ones through epidemics and war. For many who survived it, the genocide of the Holocaust remains a vivid, brutal memory. Resettlement has a very large effect on the

After the attack on Pearl Harbor opened World War II, Japanese-Americans were resettled in camps because the government believed that some might be spies. Their lives were permanently changed by the uprooting and confinement brought about by this historical event.

personalities of those who must move into a new culture. And those living in the culture into which others immigrate often experience considerable stress as well: witness the hostile reactions of Americans living in the communities into which refugees from Cuba and Southeast Asia have moved in recent years.

Political unrest can change our lives. Note what happens in any country when a government is overthrown. Even in bloodless coups, the impact on the psychological growth of those within the country is staggering. Students from these nations, temporarily studying abroad — for example, Iranians in the United States — have encountered enormous pressure as they try to piece together their futures. In the United States the political unrest in the 1960s caused many students, faculty, and families massive distress. Today, some of these individuals say they have not been the same since these events.

Not all historical events have a negative influence. Many people have benefited from war, resettlement, and political unrest. Even economic depression can bring unexpected benefits. Sociologist Glenn Elder (1974) looked at the children of the Great Depression whose families lost their money. Elder had access to the records of longitudinal studies begun in Oakland and Berkeley, California, in the 1930s. These subjects had been followed into their adult years. Elder recognized he had a golden opportunity to look at one of the major historical events of this century and its impact on human development.

The effect of the Depression was a little like a tornado. It went down a block destroying this house and that one, leaving the ones next door intact. Among the families of the Oakland/Berkeley youngsters were those whose parents lost much of their money as well as those whose family income remained the same. How do you think keeping and losing their money during the Depression influenced the development of those children over the next thirty or forty years?

One result may surprise you. The youngsters from financially ruined families achieved greater success educationally and vocationally, as well as having fewer psychiatric problems, than the children whose families kept their money. Also, the deprived men were more family-centered and viewed their children as a major source of gratification in their lives.

Why did this happen? Elder has two explanations. The first is that boys and girls were forced into adult work roles — paid work or regular domestic chores — and so had more equal relationships with adults and were more comfortable with them. They felt greater control over their lives, and were able to engage in and manage real-life problems as an apprenticeship for adult life. The second contributing factor to the better adjustment of the deprived group is that later historical events had a positive impact on development. In the words of Elder and a colleague:

> Our analysis underscores the value of military service, a rewarding work life, and possibly the emotional support and gratifications of marriage and family life. (Elder and Rockwell, 1978)

Before we assume that severe economic hardship is good for all of us, we should be aware of some of Elder's other findings, which cast a less positive light on the psychological effects of the Depression. For one, youngsters from working-class backgrounds had a much harder time if they did not go to college. For another, relationships between sons and fathers were strained as the paternal role was devalued when the father lost his money. Interestingly, mother-daughter relationships were strengthened. Finally, most of the deprived boys had stormy teenage years, though the girls emerged as competent, resourceful adolescents (Elder, 1979).

Critical Incidents. **Critical incidents** are environmental or physical events such as tornadoes, floods, fires, earthquakes, and other "acts of God" as well as accidents and man-made disasters. Critical incidents occur unpredictably but profoundly shape our growth from that moment onward. Unintended and unexpected, they do not happen to everyone, are not related to chronological age, and follow no expectable sequence. Critical incidents dramatically influence the quality and direction of our lives, having as great, and sometimes even greater, impact on us than age-related or historical influences (Goethals, 1978).

A principal characteristic of a critical incident is that it stimulates a fresh view of ourself in the world. For example, a college senior was greatly upset when he was rejected by each of the sixteen medical schools he applied to. At that point he sat down with his friend and tried to decide what to do. Should he spend the next year working in a research lab and apply to several more medical schools next year? The more he talked, the clearer it became that he didn't really want to be a doctor after all. As he looked back on his life he began to realize that he had always enjoyed working with youngsters. He had worked at a summer camp for four years, taught Sunday School, and volunteered on Saturdays at a community center. He became more excited about the idea of a career in education, which seemed to him to be consistent with his past interests and enthusiasms. He gave up the idea of medicine and decided to spend another semester in college to earn the education credits needed for teaching credentials.

Not all critical incidents are so dramatic. It can be as simple an incident as having a characteristic attributed to us by someone else. A boy tries out for the parish CYO basketball team and the coach tells him he has promise. Noting a nasty argument between her niece and nephew, an aunt tells the girl she would make a good lawyer. Casual comments can be critical instances, sticking with us, becoming a central part of our identity, and governing our behavior for a major portion of our lifetime.

Many critical incidents involve people: teachers, pastors, scout leaders, coaches, neighbors, and best friends. They can change our lives by affirming us, serving as role models, pointing the way, helping sort out something that is blocking our chances for growth, or supplying love and care at a time when our life seems not worth continuing one step further. Levinson (1978) vividly describes the importance of a mentor in the personal and career development of young men and women.

A critical incident can be an action. What we do during childhood and adolescence can have a powerful impact on what is pursued in later life. For example, a pollster began his interest in the subject as a project for a statistics course in high school. Would he have developed the same interest in the subject had the teacher required a theoretical paper instead? How many newspaper carriers develop an interest in writing? How many people in the food business find their way there because of a first job in a restaurant?

Critical incidents are not limited to childhood and adolescence. A physician began medical school in her late thirties after raising a family. She had always wanted to be a doctor, but had given up the idea for marriage. It wasn't until she started to work at a hospital as a volunteer that her initial dream of becoming a physician was revived. What might have occurred had she volunteered with the neighborhood garden club instead, or done nothing at all?

Sometimes critical incidents occur within historical influences. At his retirement, a man who devoted his career to classifying fish was asked how he came to be interested in such work. "It was an accident, actually," he replied. "I was on a destroyer in the South Pacific in World War II, dropping depth charges. After the explosions, all sorts of fish would float to the surface. I began to wonder how many kinds of fish there are."

Generally, age-related events are the most influential in childhood, adolescence, and advanced age. Historical events and critical incidents are most potent agents of change in the adult years (Baltes, 1979). It is also true that *when* an event happens is almost as important as whether it occurs at all. This is brought home by Elder's work on the families who went through the Great Depression. He found that the youngest children among those families who lost money were much more adversely affected than the older youngsters. And among their fathers, it was the younger men, who were just beginning their careers, whom the Depression struck hardest. The older men had a less difficult time because their careers were already established (Elder, 1974).

But in the end, it is how we react to the age-related or historical influence or the critical incident and what resources we have at our disposal to cushion its effect, that make the difference in whether our growth and joy of living are stunted or are enhanced.

Periods of Stability and Instability

Our lifetimes are marked by periods of stability and instability. During long spans of time, things are quiet and go reasonably well. We are doing things we are comfortable with, and we have people around us we can count on. Values and dreams direct us toward goals that seem worthwhile. Changes and new demands are handled smoothly. We begin school, have a first menstrual cycle, fall in love, finish our education, find a job, cope with the death of parents, and watch our children leave home, all without disruption.

But these long plateaus of tranquility can be interrupted without warning. Suddenly confusion and turmoil abound. Certainties about our abilities, identity, even what makes us happy, are in question. Relationships that were comfortable and supportive are now strained because loved ones can't understand what has come over us. Goals that seemed worthwhile a few months ago now appear worthless and are abandoned. External beacons, values that guided us, wink out one after another, and we are lost. Dreams are laid waste. We feel cut off from the past. As we are beset by anxiety, depression, and moments of fury, the stresses of day-to-day living seem more than we can handle. For long moments, we doubt our sanity.

All of us have had or will have moments of instability that contain some or all of these elements. They are universal experiences and not necessarily tied to a special period of life or connected to particular events. Moreover, these emotional storms are the basis for continuing growth.

Associations with Age

Periods of stability and instability are not always associated with a particular time of life. Some maintain that specific ages are more often linked with turmoil than others.

Adolescence is an example of a time when instability is thought by many to be a universal experience. Erikson (1968) linked the identity crisis to adolescence. Freud's daughter, Anna, a famous child therapist, called adolescence a normal developmental disturbance in which ". . . the upholding of a steady equilibrium during the adolescent process is in itself abnormal." (1956)

This book is intended for people who have been through or are currently experiencing adolescence. You might therefore take a moment to consider whether your personal adjustment changed markedly during this period. If it hasn't, does this mean your psychological growth is retarded because you've not been through a crisis? Probably not. Contrary to what many might think, most of us do not change dramatically during adolescence.

Two psychiatrists in the Chicago area carried out careful interviews with high-school and college students. To their surprise, they discovered few signs of emotional turbulence (Grinker, Grinker, and Timberlake, 1962; Offer, 1969). In another study the development of several thousand students at Berkeley and Stanford was analyzed beginning in their freshman year (Katz *et al.*, 1968). One of the expectations was that a third of the subjects would have an identity crisis during their college years. Instead, it was discovered that during these four years of college, these young people grew to have a more adequate self-concept and increased their ability to control their time, make decisions, and handle money. Students were more open about their own feelings and in their ability to express them. They showed an emerging capacity for relationships with the opposite sex.

Clinical researcher Stanley King scrutinized approximately six hundred Harvard college students in four consecutive freshman classes in the early 1960s. His conclusions are shown in the accompanying box.

Like the others, King found that crisis and turmoil were not usual. Instead, most students were typified by what he called "progressive maturation." During their four years, these men had pleasant relationships with their parents and peers, maintained feelings of self-worth, had greater comfort with their impulses, exhibited stable and deepening interests, and were involved in goal-directed activities.

The adult years are now pictured by some as having not one but many intervals of instability alternating with longer times of relative tranquility. Levinson maintains that stormy periods occur every seven to ten years. Figure 5.1 shows Levinson's model of growth in the adult years. Basically, he divides this time into three major stages of early, middle, and later adulthood. In his view, each of us is vulnerable to episodes of instability and crisis at five specific ages. He identifies them by calling them times of transition.

At the age 30 transition, most of the men Levinson studied experienced considerable stress. The anxieties of many were aroused as they reassessed their lives and looked ahead: What have I done with my life so far? What do I want to make of it? What things are missing? How do I get them before it's too late? What do I have to resign myself to? In one way or another, these questions and others like them come up at many transition points and are the basis for both periods of instability and further growth.

Levinson believes that specific ages are more likely than others to trigger an unstable period. The often described "mid-life crisis" is an illustration: Shortly after turning 40, a minister buys a luminescent Porsche with the Mission Fund, abandons his family and congregation, and heads south with a precocious 16-year-old from the confirmation class.

Characteristics of College Students Studied over a Four-Year Period

1. The identity crisis is not a common occurrence, and the amount of turmoil and conflict is limited. . . .

2. Relationships between the adolescent and his parents are generally good. Little evidence exists for a generation gap, and the adolescent in many ways follows the parental value system and life style. There is some rebellion, typically in early adolescence, in the service of growing autonomy, but generally it is limited to small issues and does not involve delinquency or acting out.

3. Relations with peers are good. Healthy adolescents have many friends and are able to share feelings with them.

4. The sense of competence and self-esteem is high. Adolescents at times have doubts about themselves, but these are balanced by the feeling that they can learn. Depression and guilt are limited in scope . . . and when they occur most adolescents have ways of working them out.

5. Capacity for coping is high. . . . Adolescents can deal with painful feelings, confront them and share them, rather than having to block or turn inward their fear, depression, or anger. Healthy adolescents deal also with such feelings by shifting focus to some other topic, most often involvement with physical activity. Such activity also serves to sublimate aggressive and sexual energy, especially through competitive sports, which also gives a sense of competence, kinesthetic satisfaction, and release of tension. A sense of humor is used to blunt feelings of anxiety, keep perspective on their problems, and limit self-doubt and guilt by the ability to laugh at themselves. They are able to use anticipatory planning and role rehearsal as an adaptive strategy for new and unusual situations, and anxiety motivates them to seek out information about new situations and integrate this with previous experience.

SOURCE: From King, S. Coping mechanisms in adolescence. *Psychiatric Annals*, 1971, *1*, 4–29.

Others think that periods of instability are not linked to a specific chronological age. Vaillant's (1977) long investigation of men now in their 60s revealed evidences of confusion, despair, and disruption, as well as disenchantment with career, marriage, and self. These conditions were found to arise at any time from the early 30s onward.

Associations with Events

Just as instability is not bound by age, neither is it tied to a particular event. Have you ever weathered a difficult situation successfully only to find yourself on some other occasion thrown into a crisis by an apparently far less stressful occurrence? What is the difference? Two types of experiences have a high probability of triggering significant distress: major changes that affect large segments of our life, and "off time" events.

Some occurrences seem to throw us into maximum psychological disarray. Colin Murray Parkes, a British psychiatrist, specified four ingredients that these events have in common (1971). They are: the feeling of a *major change*, occurring in a *short period of time*, which has *undesirable, lasting future impact*, and affects *large areas of life*. Consider Benjy, a 10-year-old living comfortably with his family in a rural Virginia town. One morning his father tells Benjy that he is being transferred to suburban Washington. Benjy is badly shaken. This certainly is a massive change and for him it has occurred suddenly. As he contemplates an existence in a new town without his best friends, the fields and streams he loves, and the school he's doing well in, it is clear to Benjy that large areas of happiness in his life will be taken away. He is sure that he will never be happy in another town, and maybe never again.

Another factor affecting our reaction to stress is whether it occurs "on time" or "off time" (Neugarten and Hagestad, 1976). Researchers believe that we seem to bear difficult events without falling into a crisis state when they

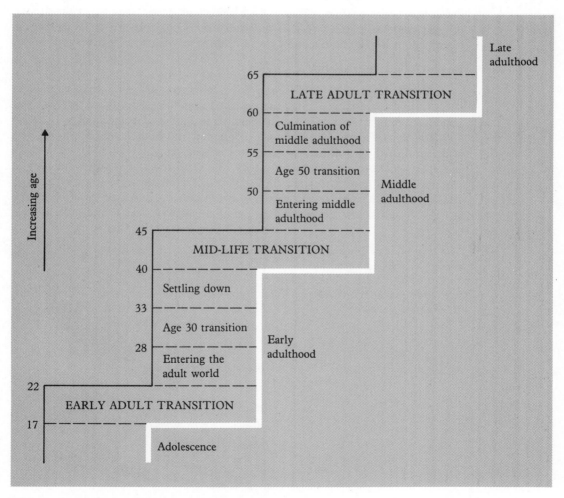

Figure 5.1 Developmental periods of adulthood.

happen at an expectable time, that is, at about the same time as when others in our group have similar experiences. However, when we have these stressful events at a time different from that of our contemporaries, they are more likely to trigger psychological upset. For example, the beginning of menstruation would not be likely to be as difficult for a 13-year-old girl as it would be if she were 9 or 17. The death of a mother affects us one way when we are 50 but quite differently if we are 12. Most parents can more easily cope with their youthful offspring leaving than continuing to stay at home.

It may be that the reason off-time stresses are more often associated with severe emotional upset is that they lower our self-esteem and disrupt social relationships (Neugarten, 1979). People have a tendency to base their self-worth on a comparison between themselves and others of the same age. They judge how they are doing by how their gains and losses stack up against those of their contemporaries. Also, out-of-time events can fracture social networks. Think about Benjy. Think about young widows or men who have retired early.

Benefits of Instability

Periodically rattling the structure of our lives seems to be a human characteristic. Dramatic, disorganizing, painful, and sometimes costly as this can be, instability often results in clear-cut benefits to human development.

The first benefit is that periods of turmoil and questioning are associated with continued growth and satisfaction in living. Imagine a single woman living as a "ski bum" in Colorado. At 23, she can't imagine a better life. If the woman is still doing the same thing five years later, however, she's likely to feel increasing anxiety as she becomes aware that the average age of ski bums is still 23 and she is getting older. Another stage of life beckons. In it, she

The instability of times of transition is represented by this cartoon — a scary looking ladder bridging two solid developmental stages.

knows her current capabilities, styles of relationships to people, and attitudes will not fit as well as before. If she chooses to enjoy the fruits of the early adulthood era — forming a primary bond, thinking about a career and children — it will be necessary for her to give up some things and take on new ones.

Second, the willingness to question the value of previous certainties or successes, to resist being defined by outside expectations, is insurance against a lifetime of frustration, desperation, or cynicism. When he was 70, reminiscing with Erik Erikson (1968, p. 143) about a painful period of his life at 20, the famous writer George Bernard Shaw said his turmoil was brought about by feeling trapped in an occupation:

> I made good in spite of myself, and found, to my dismay, that Business, instead of expelling me as the worthless imposter I was, was fastening upon me with no intention of letting me go. Behold me, therefore, in my twentieth year, with a business training, in an occupation I detested as cordially as any sane person lets himself detest anything he cannot escape from. In March, 1876, I broke loose.

Shaw's dissatisfaction fermented an unstable transitional period. During it, he broke free of his job, family, friends, and his native country, and began to find himself as a writer.

A third benefit from these turbulent times is that they stimulate us to carry forward those values, interests, competencies, and relationships that enable us to fit comfortably into a changing world. Passing from one stage to another through an unstable transitional period is a little like moving from one residence to another. Whenever we move, we look around to see what we will take and what we will leave behind. So, too, these periods give us an opportunity to reevaluate ourselves and our lives. We may decide to cast off old treasured behaviors that don't work so well anymore, leave behind a relationship to make room for new ones, and abandon dreams that are no longer reliable. Some things we take with us: perhaps a familiar personal quirk that we should really rid ourselves of but can't seem to part with; illusions that give life meaning; a career, lover, or hobby because they continue to give pleasure; or old values that still point us in the right direction.

Beneficial as it is for us to pass through these times of transition in order to continue to grow, it is not easy. Just as when we move into a new apartment, when we open the door of a fresh stage of our life, we feel the characteristic hollowness of new beginnings.

Early Experiences and Later Development

How much do you think that what happens to you early in life molds your adult adjustment? To what extent is the direction of your future growth shaped by good or bad mothering, a traumatic or tranquil childhood, or a culturally deprived or enriched home life? If you resolve developmental tasks in the first five years of life in favor of trust and hope, autonomy and will, and initiative and purpose, while I have learned mistrust, shame and doubt, and guilt, does this promise you happiness and me misery in the later years? Are there particular periods of the life span, especially in the first few years, when we are unusually receptive to experiences that will drastically alter the course of our lives?

Theories of Early Deprivation

In the past, the answers to these questions have been a resounding Yes! Psychological theorists have mostly agreed that poor mothering, traumatic experiences, and cultural deprivation were associated with poor adult adaptation. Freud felt that failure to resolve developmental tasks in a favorable direction forecasted major problems later on. As he put it (1940, p. 141):

> [T]he child is psychological father to the adult and . . . the events of his first few years are of paramount importance for his whole later life.

Others have thought that infancy and childhood is the time when positive or negative experiences exert an immense influence on later character adjustment and happiness. Psychologist Burton White (1975, p. 257) summarized his convictions when he said, ". . . *to some extent*, I really believe it *is* too late after age three."

These and similar pronouncements have led many to feel that little can be done to help someone whose first few years have been marked by bad handling, deprivation, or trauma. Another result has been the certainty that somewhere in childhood is a "critical period" within which early experiences have permanent effects on the remainder of life. According to this reasoning, if help can be given to children in these first years, then the odds are greatly improved that they will be well-adjusted adults. This is part of the rationale behind the Head Start programs, Upward Bound, and camps for children. It is also the basis for the shelves of books hectoring parents about the "necessity" for natural childbirth, breast-feeding, quality parenting, and an enriched educational environment.

Early Experience and Later Adjustment

Facts coming from current research and clinical observation tell a different, if somewhat more complicated, story. While being beaten, rejected, undernourished, buried in an avalanche, losing both parents in a war, or growing up in extreme poverty are mildly associated with later emotional disorder, early difficulties do not unfailingly result in disorder later on.

In their book *Early Experience: Myth and Evidence*, English psychologists Anne Clarke and A. B. D. Clarke (1976), have raised some serious questions about this view of human growth. Their research on deprived adolescents — those who have experienced severe emotional and physical deprivation, extreme suffering, sudden death of both parents, isolation, and other difficult experiences — failed to find consistent support for early deprivation theories.

Childhood events are much less potent, and human beings are far more resilient to stress, than previously thought (Kagan, Kearsley, and Zalaso, 1978). Also, the healing effects of a loving relationship and a caring environment are often strong enough to compensate for early bad experiences, especially if they occur prior to adolescence (Clarke and Clarke, 1976).

It is probably true that responsiveness to a healing environment becomes progressively smaller as we grow older. Clarke and Clarke (1976) call this their **wedge theory.** Figure 5.2 indicates a greater positive reaction to a loving and supportive environment in early life — at the thick end of the wedge — gradually tapering off to far less response in adulthood.

Even Freud, who believed that early emotional problems usually result in later personality disorder, acknowledged that this is not always the case:

> Signs of childhood neurosis can be detected in *all* adult neurotics without exception; but by no means all children who show these signs become neurotic in later life. It must be, therefore, that certain determinants of anxiety are relinquished and certain danger situations lose their significance as the individual becomes more mature. (1926, p. 77)

Freud's clinical observations are confirmed by Vaillant's men who were much better able to cope with stress as adults than during their adolescence. Vaillant speculated that unaided improvement was a function of greater familiarity with stress, greater familiarity with the ways of coping with anxiety, and the presence of a network of interpersonal support and biological maturation (1977).

We cannot deny the impact of negative childhood events for some people.

Figure 5.2
The wedge theory of positive responsiveness to a healing environment.

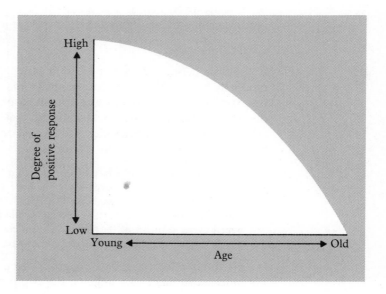

To what extent is adult behavior determined by the web of past events? Current evidence suggests that early experience plays a less critical role than previously thought.

Clinicians regularly see adults whose present emotional disturbance is a direct result of early deprivation, trauma, or failure to resolve a crucial developmental task. Moreover, there is a limit to the psychological damage that can be repaired by a healing environment. The point is that early difficulties have been vastly overrated as the origin of later psychological problems and the positive effects of later compensating experiences underappreciated.

Critical Period

A "critical period" does not exist in human development in which we are especially ripe to benefit from exemplary mothering, the right food, intellectual stimulation, or country air. No single phase of the life span, even if all the ideal experiences are packed into it that we can think of, can program future growth. Edward Ziegler (1975), Yale professor and former director of the Head Start program, says it well:

> I, for one, am tired of the past decade's scramble to discover some magical period during which interventions will have particularly great pay-offs. My own predilection is that we cease this pointless search for magic periods and adopt instead the view that the developmental process is a continuous one, in which every segment of the life cycle from conception through maturity is of critical importance and requires certain environmental nutrients.

No doubt efforts to assist youngsters through programs such as Head Start, hot lunches, summer enrichments, Big Brothers, Scouts, Outward Bound, and

Upward Bound, and special education are all worthwhile on their own merits. But they are not all decisive molders of adult adaptation.

Moreover, we are beginning to be aware of mounting evidence that older people are far more receptive to programs to help them than previously imagined. It has been found that adults benefit greatly from many types of experiences — parent training, continuing education, job enrichment, and family counseling. The growth and change of adults as a result of these opportunities further undermines the idea of a critical period and that efforts to assist grown-ups are wasted (Brim and Kagan, 1980). More and more we are beginning to look at adult and aging populations as resources that are undervalued and underutilized, whose adjustment and contribution to society may be enhanced by special programs and opportunities for continuing growth.

Differences in the Life Cycles of Men and Women

Are women's experiences during the stages of life similar to men's? Is one woman's development more similar to the next woman's than to men in general? Observations of parents, brothers and sisters, friends, and other relatives might suggest to us that somehow men and women grow up differently, have dissimilar developmental hurdles to cope with at particular phases of their lifetimes, and relate to each other distinctively. Even when talking about politics or the world series, women seem at first to come at the subject from different directions.

From our observations, we can see that the female's experience in living differs from the male's experience. For generations, however, the most influential thinkers about adult development have based their schemes of the life cycle on the lives of men only. The result is that theories of normal human growth generally fail to account for life as women know it. In her book *In a Different Voice*, Carol Gilligan (1982) documents the male bias of life cycle theories. She found that the most widely accepted schemes overemphasized growth issues characteristic of men: independence, competition, achievement, and definition of principles to guide behavior. Significant concerns for women are overlooked: empathy, attachment, and care. Because women's progress through the life cycle doesn't follow the same pathway as that of men, male theorists often consider women as deviant.

Gilligan scanned the writing of the most famous life cycle thinkers and discovered that they barely considered females at all. Jean Piaget (1932), the prominent Swiss child psychologist, based his writing about intellectual growth on the observations of boys. Erikson (1976) oriented his eight stages of man to male growth. Kohlberg's theory of moral development (1981), which is said to apply to everyone, is rooted in the study of eighty-four boys. As useful as their insights are about male growth, these psychologists are probably wrong, Gilligan notes, in their claim that their theories of development apply equally to women.

Generally, insufficient attention has been paid to important concerns in the lives of females. Consider again Erikson's developmental scheme shown in Table 5.1, especially the five stages through adolescence. The task of the first stage of life, developing trust resulting in hope, applies equally to baby girls and baby boys. From then on, however, Erikson clearly is speaking of male maturation. The young child is supposed to develop will power, the "determination to exercise free choice as well as self-control" (Erikson, 1976) out of a growing feeling of *separateness* and *independence* from parents. The next two growth tasks center around learning *initiative*, which results in a sense of *purpose* and a feeling of *competence*. The forging of an identity in adolescence is possible because of separateness and independence, initiative, purpose, and competence. Only *after* identity forms does a young man turn to intimacy —a loving attachment to others.

Erikson deals with women only as they relate to men. According to him, the task for a young woman is different. For her, the capacity for intimacy precedes the sense of self in the world that identity brings. Moreover, the teenage female never has the same experience of an independent identity as a young man has. The adolescent girl bases her identity on the man to whom she becomes attracted and by whom she will be defined. Indeed, all of her life, a woman defines herself and is defined by her relationships with others.

Having theorized that a woman's identity centers around caring for others, most life cycle thinkers assign females the role of supporting male growth. As Gilligan (1982) puts it:

> Woman's place in man's life cycle has been that of nurturer, caretaker, and helpmate, the weaver of those networks of relationships on which she in turn relies.

A concrete example of the validity of this point is Levinson's notion (1978) that for a young adult man to get ahead, he needs a relationship with a "special woman."

The woman's functions of nurturer and caretaker are largely ignored by researchers in human development. Instead, the emphasis is on independence, competition, and achievement — rarely on empathy, attachment, and caring. Yet concern for intimate relationships conditions much of the behavior of women and results in a distinctive pattern of normal growth. Three differences in the development of females and males in contemporary western society are (1) less concern with independence from parents, (2) more concern about competition, (3) and a morality that centers on caring more than on principles.

Concern with Independence

The poet Dinah Craik (Bartlett's, 1980) tells us one mother's view about sex differences in separation from parents:

> Oh, my son's my son till he gets him a wife,
> But my daughter's my daughter all her life.

Kent State, 1973. A young woman responds to someone she does not know who has been shot. Might this illustrate male-female differences in caring?

Is it true that females and males differ in their need to become independent of parents? The life cycle theories of men, such as that of Erikson, point to separation from mother — no longer being a "mama's boy" — as a developmental milestone in normal male growth. Masculinity is tied to this independence. Research suggests little girls grow up differently. Femininity is less linked to severing intimate contact with mother. On the whole girls stay physically closer to parents, are less venturesome, and seek help more often than boys (Whiting and Pope, 1973).

Does this mean that females are more likely than males to grow up to be more dependent, compliant, and focused on relationships with others? For the most part this is not the case (Basow, 1980, Chapter 4). In adolescence, boys are just as dependent on their friends as girls are. As adults, men have a tendency to form groups more readily and more often have difficulty living alone. In most situations, women are not more compliant than men. Studies have indicated that an exception is when pressure exists to conform to opinion in a strange group. Women are less willing to express open disagreement than men. One study asked a group of adolescents to list in order their personal concerns. Girls and boys put identity and sexuality in the top two spots. In third place a difference occurred. Girls rated interpersonal relations as their third greatest concern, while boys worried more about independence.

Concern with Competition

While girls seem to worry less about becoming independent, they are more anxious about competition. Two lines of evidence support this observation. Janet Lever (1976) watched 10- and 11-year-old children during free times at school. She noted that boys played competitive games much more than their female classmates. Boys' games also lasted longer. The reason, Lever discovered, was that boys stopped the game more often to quarrel about a disputed play. In fact, boys seemed to enjoy the legalistic debates about whether someone was safe or out, or whether the player was out of bounds, as much as they enjoyed the game itself. In no case did a dispute terminate the game.

The girls argued much less. Squabbles between the girls, however, usually ended the game. Lever speculated that this was because the girls were extremely sensitive to the feelings of others and were reluctant to enter into debates that would threaten their relationships. Girls took hurt feelings more seriously than the question of who was right.

A second line of investigation centered on the so-called fear of success motive in women. Matina Horner (1970, 1972) raised the question of whether young women have anxiety about achievement by asking college students to write stories in response to this test question: "At the end of first term finals, Anne (John) finds herself (himself) at the top of her (his) medical school class." Horner found that about two-thirds of the college women wrote stories containing fear of success imagery, as opposed to less than ten percent of the males. Anne lost all her friends or would never marry; she doubted her femininity or wondered if she were normal; or a mistake had been made and Anne was not really at the top of her class. From her work, Horner (1978) concluded that the fear of success motive can arise when the need for achievement is accompanied by the expectation of a negative outcome.

Horner's work attracted considerable attention. It has been criticized from many vantage points (Rohrbaugh, 1979, Chapter 10). It has become clear that fear of success is neither a particularly female nor an especially stable trait. A 1974 summary of studies of fear of success found that the percentage of fear of success found in women ranged from eleven percent to eighty-eight percent and in men from twenty-two percent to eighty-six percent (Tresemer, 1977). Recent thinking is that fear of success is probably not a stable trait but is affected by the situation in which someone finds herself or himself (Basow, 1980, Chapter 9). It is possible that the females in Horner's research were more anxious about attaining success because of the awareness that one person's achievement is often at the cost of someone else's failure. Could it be that females worry more about this than do males? The evidence so far is mixed (Sassen, 1980; Saad, Lenauer, Shaver, and Dunivant, 1978).

Morality

Psychologist Lawrence Kohlberg (1981) constructed a scale of **moral reasoning** — the ethical standards we use to justify our behavior. In summary, the rationale guiding an action when a moral choice must be made progresses this way:

Stage 1: avoid punishment
Stage 2: exchange favors
Stage 3: follow the Golden Rule
Stage 4: uphold social order
Stage 5: do what's best for the community
Stage 6: conform to universal ethical principles

According to Kohlberg, the level of moral reasoning advances with age. His view is that this is a natural unfolding rather than a result of social learning (Kohlberg and Gilligan, 1971). Though confirmation of this assertion remains to be produced, it is an intriguing notion.

Studies of women consistently find that women justify their moral choices of the basis of Stage 3 logic — the right action is that which exhibits concern for and preserves relationships with others. As men grow older, they increasingly see morality as defined by principles of social order, community, and universal justice. Females retain their commitment to human relationships as a basis for their actions.

Gilligan (1982) maintains that the problem is not that females are stuck in mid-range of Kohlberg's theory of development, but that his theory doesn't fit the feminine gender. Basically, female concerns always include understanding and caring for others. Early on, a girl knows life comes from her body. As she grows to womanhood, she gradually develops a greater understanding of her role as caretaker and with it a greater interest in knowing the feelings of others. For a woman far more than a man, inflicting hurt is immoral whether it is in the service of social order or universal justice.

Six Stages of Moral Judgment

Psychologist Lawrence Kohlberg has devoted most of his career to studying moral development. What interests him is why we decide an action is right or wrong. Suppose a man's wife will die without a specific drug, but, unfortunately, he doesn't have the money to buy it. The man becomes desperate and breaks into a drugstore to steal it. Should he have done it? Why was the action right or wrong?

Kohlberg devised a test consisting of moral dilemmas similar to this one. From his analysis of the reasons his subjects gave to justify their action, Kohlberg constructed a six-stage sequence of increasingly more mature moral judgment.

Stage 1: Behavior guided by the expectation of a reward or punishment at the hands of a superior power. The man shouldn't steal because he is sure to be caught and put in jail.

Stage 2: Behavior is guided by the anticipation of favors returned — I'll scratch your back if you'll scratch mine. The man will steal the drug for his wife because he may need her to do something similar for him some day.

Stage 3: Behavior is guided by the Golden Rule — putting yourself in the place of the less fortunate. The right behavior is that which exhibits loyalty and sensitivity to our feelings of others. The man steals the drug because he wants to relieve his wife's distress.

Stage 4: Behavior is guided by obedience to laws that maintain social order. The man decides not to steal the drug because it is against the law. If he did it, everyone would do it, and society would disintegrate into an "every man for himself" free-for-all.

Stage 5: Behavior is guided by a judgment of doing the greatest good for the greatest number in the community. The man steals the drug because the community is better served by a person's living rather than dying.

Stage 6: Behavior is guided by universal ethical principles. The man steals the drug — even though it is against the law — because human life is sacred.

SOURCE: Kohlberg, L. *Essays on moral development,* vol. 1. *The Philosophy of moral development.* San Francisco: Harper & Row, 1981.

Why is there a difference between men and women? Is it all cultural? Do we train females from birth to be caretakers? Or could it be biological? Are women instinctively drawn to the nurturing, empathic role because without their caring life could not be sustained? Currently, fragmentary evidence favors a biological difference between the sexes in empathy, on which caring and attachment rest (Wilson, 1978; Whiting and Whiting, 1975). Beyond biology are powerful social forces that reinforce behavior according to male or female stereotypes (Basow, 1980). Parents are more tolerant of aggression in boys and encourage doll playing in girls. Adults expect women to smile and be polite and men to look people in the eye and be aggressive. But much remains to be learned.

A major failing of traditional life span thinking is to try to fit female development around a male form. The growth of women requires the same attention that has been paid to men. Another failing is to overlook the importance of empathy, attachment, and caretaking. These dimensions may be just as critical in the development of men as women. It is not hard to imagine that young women may suffer less inner conflict and have fewer emotional problems if they are trained to be more assertive and comfortable with competitiveness. Is it possible that the adjustment of men could be enhanced by understanding that empathy, expressions of affection, caring for others, and even crying are legitimate? Gilligan (1982, p. 23) puts it well when she suggests

> . . . only when life cycle theorists equally divide their attention and begin to live with women as they have lived with men, will their visions encompass the experience of both sexes and their theories become increasingly fertile.

The Lifeline: Stages of the Life Cycle

When we go about separating the life cycle into developmental stages, the operation is a little like carving a roast beef. There are differences between young and middle-aged and old, just as there are differences between rare, medium, and well-done. But where we put the knife that divides one portion from another is entirely arbitrary, and the "slices" can be thick or thin. We can carve a lifetime into three, eight, ten, or twenty separate pieces if we choose.

In the next three chapters, we look at normal working, loving, and playing behaviors through the life cycle. To make it easier to study them systematically, the lifeline is divided into the seven stages shown in Figure 5.3. Most of us anticipate that specific events will happen at particular times of life (Neugarten, 1979). People will tell us when a person should marry, should settle down, is too old to have more children, must give up heavy exercise, or retire. In the chapters that follow we will examine distinctive work, love, and play associated with each of these stages of life.

As Figure 5.3 shows, the age divisions are elastic. The overlap is least at the beginning and end of life and greatest in the three stages following adolescence. Note that the first stage in this model is *childhood*, the span of years

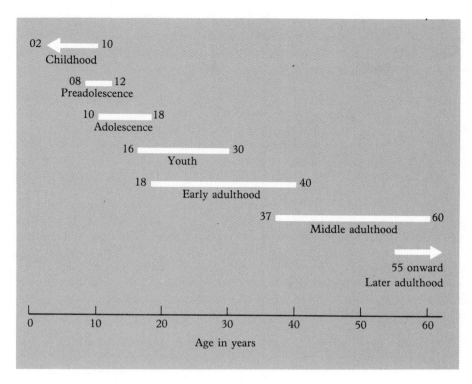

Figure 5.3 The lifeline: stages of the life cycle.

from 2 to 10. We do not begin with infancy — the first two years of life — because normal working, loving, and playing behaviors are not established until after that period. The second stage is *preadolescence*, from as early as 8 to about 12, bridging the years between childhood and adolescence. Here a notable event is the appearance of the best friend.

Adolescence encompasses most of the teenage years, from the onset of puberty to high-school graduation. During this phase, part-time work and involvement with a group of agemates is usual. The fourth stage is *youth*. For some it begins as early as 16 (Coleman, 1974), and may not end until about 30 for others (Kenniston, 1971). This is a time in which openness to new experiences is the greatest and the widest exploration occurs. In youth, the distance traveled from home and family — both emotionally and in actual miles — is usually maximal.

The remaining stages — early, middle, and later adulthood — follow Levinson's model shown in Figure 5.1. The time spans for each era differ slightly from his conception, but each is consistent with other views, which see considerable variation in the time in which stages of adulthood begin and end (Baltes, 1979; Vaillant, 1977).

Early adulthood starts as early as 18 for some men and women, but not until a dozen years later for others, extending through most of the fourth decade. Markedly dissimilar from youth, its primary identifying features are settling down, forming a primary relationship, and beginning to advance in an occupation.

Middle adulthood (37 to 40 through 55 to 60) brings a changing perspective (Neugarten, 1979). Time is recast in terms of years to live rather than years since birth. The changing time perspective is a two-edged sword. It causes anxiety but also acts as a prod to see how much pleasure still can be obtained, how many new projects can be started, in the years remaining. The distinguishing features are trying to get ahead while caring for younger children and older parents, and a serious reappraisal of occupation and primary relations.

The stage of *later adulthood* embraces the years from approximately 55 onward, as long as physical and mental faculties remain intact and opportunities for satisfaction from working, loving, and playing are accessible. Some observers distinguish between "young-old" and "old-old," separating the still vigorous, healthy, and active group from those who are not (Neugarten, 1979). Some of the normal identifying features of this period include greater avocational interests, concern about leaving behind something of ourselves, and planning for retirement.

Summary

1. The words "life cycle" refer to a way of looking at a lifetime. It involves dividing our lives into specific spans of years, with particular events and developmental growth tasks assigned to each era.
2. Three models of the life cycle were discussed: biological, Eriksonian, and pluralistic. Early thinking followed a biological model. This assumes development is divided into stages that (1) occur in the same order, (2) start and stop at a specific time, (3) contain activities typical of that phase and no other, (4) are irreversible, and (5) apply to everyone.
3. The most influential model of human growth in the last half of the twentieth century has been Erikson's eight stages of development. He identifies for each stage central conflicts to be mastered, which result in particular adaptive strengths.
4. A pluralistic conception of growth and change during the life span includes age-related and historical events and critical incidents. Age-related events are both physical and social, happening at about the same time for everyone. Historical events have impact upon everyone within a specific culture — for example, an economic depression. Critical incidents are those events, often unexpected, that have substantial effects.
5. Three major issues about the life cycle were examined. The first concerned the expectation of alternating periods of stability and instability throughout the life span. One type of experience that causes change can be recognized by the feeling of a major alteration occurring in a short

period of time, which is perceived as having undesirable lasting future effects on major areas of life. Another is an "off time" event or experience.

6. The second issue involved the limited effect of early experience on later adjustment. We are not prisoners of the past, nor does there exist any magic time in which special help is especially beneficial.

7. The final issue involved significant differences between the life cycle experience of men and women. Three differences in the growth of young women when compared to men are: (1) less concern with independence from parents, (2) more concern about competition, and (3) a morality centering more on caring than on principles.

8. A seven-stage working model of the life cycle was presented. It is divided into overlapping stages of childhood, preadolescence, adolescence, youth, early adulthood, middle adulthood, and later adulthood. Within this framework, distinctive normal working, loving, and playing behaviors will be identified and discussed in the three remaining chapters of this section.

A Look Ahead

In the following three chapters we examine normal working, loving, and playing behaviors characteristic of each stage of life. We also focus on those which seem to extend over a lifetime. In the next chapter we begin by defining working. We look at different types of work, consider the specific human needs gratified by work, and examine the relationship between pleasure from working and adjustment. Issues such as whether we are basically lazy or self-motivated and the factors that supply satisfaction from work are looked at more closely. Then we move to a consideration of typical working behaviors, beginning with childhood and moving through the life cycle.

Key Terms

life cycle   genital stage
biological model   pluralistic model
oral stage   age-related events
anal stage   historical influences
phallic stage   critical incidents
Oedipus complex   wedge theory
Electra complex   moral reasoning

Suggested Readings

Life cycle theory

Baltes, P., and Brim, O., Jr. (Eds.), *Life-span development and behavior*. Vols. I and II. New York: Academic Press, 1979 and 1980.

A compendium of thinking about life through time.

Instability

Erickson, E. *Identity: Youth and crisis*. New York: Norton, 1968.

Sheehy, G. *Passages: Predictable crises of adult life*. New York: Dutton, 1976.

Crises in adolescence and the adult years.

Positive factors in later adjustment

Vaillant, G. *Adaptation to life*. Boston: Little, Brown, 1977.

Bronfenbrenner. U. *The ecology of human development: Experiments by nature and design*. Cambridge, Mass.: Harvard University Press, 1979.

Exploration of the complex factors that positively influence adaptation in the adult years.

Sex differences

Maccoby, E., and Jacklin, C. *The psychology of sex differences*. Stanford, Calif.: Stanford University Press, 1974.

A comprehensive review of research on sex differences and similarities.

The blue-collar blues is no more bitterly sung than the white-collar moan. "I'm a machine," says the spotwelder, "I'm caged," says the bank teller, and echoes the hotel clerk. "I'm a mule," says the steelworker. . . . "I'm an object," says the high-fashion model. Blue collar and white collar call upon the identical phrase: "I'm a robot." . . . It was some time ago that John Henry sang, "A man ain't nothin' but a man." The hard, unromantic fact is: he died with his hammer in his hand, while the machine pumped on. Nonetheless, he found immortality. . . .

SOURCE: From Terkel, S. *Working*. New York: Pantheon, 1974, p. xiv.

Chapter Preview

CHAPTER 6
Working Through the Life Cycle

Questions to think about
- □ Why do you work?
- □ What is the normal work of a child? Of an adolescent? Of a retired person?
- □ What is the difference between a job, an occupation, and a career?
- □ How do you know if you've made it? What happens then?

Earlier we took a brief look at a definition of working. In this chapter we amplify this definition and examine types of work. We look at the reasons people work. We explore human nature in relation to working, looking at whether we are basically lazy — needing to be motivated by the carrot and the stick — or essentially energetic, responsible, and self-starting. Then we study the relationship between satisfaction from working and adjustment.

In the remainder of this chapter we turn our attention to those behaviors that are the work of each of the seven stages of life from childhood onward. We discover that even a child has "work" to do. At the other end of the life cycle we consider the usual work of men and women in the later years and retirement. In the course of the chapter we see differences in how men and women experience work.

155

As the quotation opening this chapter informs us, the possibility of becoming bored, apathetic, and frustrated at work is very real. In each segment of the life span we note those factors that threaten the satisfaction we gain from working, and consider what might be done to anticipate and avoid these potential pitfalls.

What Is Working?

An activity is **work** when it contains four elements: the feeling of obligation, the expenditure of energy, the experience of making something happen, and approval by society.

In his book *The Adventures of Tom Sawyer,* author Mark Twain has Tom fool two other boys into whitewashing his fence for him. He does it by pretending it's a game that's lots of fun rather than a dreary chore. Afterward, Tom concludes, "Work is whatever a body is obliged to do." (Twain, 1876, p. 14) This commonsensical statement underscores one way of telling whether we are at work: the fact that it involves the *feeling of obligation.* The sense of obligation can come from the necessity of having to support a family or to cook meals for them. It can come from not wanting to let down co-workers at the plant: a woman drags herself out of bed, even though she has the flu, to get to her place on the English muffin line at the bakery, because "they won't turn out right without me." Or it can come from an obligation to an abstract idea: a doctor sees himself as a healer, staying in his office late at night to care for the patients who need him.

The remaining components of our definition come from the thinking of historian Paul Schrecker (1948). The second element is an *expenditure of energy* intended to overcome some resistance an object offers to change. The "object" we must change can be anything that requires putting forth some effort: groceries to be bagged, ideas on a page to be learned, an airplane to be flown, children to be cared for, or a plan to be executed. The "resistance" to be overcome can be exhaustion, incomprehensibility of the author's writing, gravity, frustration, or the will of others.

The third characteristic of work is that it is designed to *make something happen.* Expending energy alone is not enough. To qualify, an action should contribute to the society in which we live. The change might be substantial, as when a manufacturer of wood-burning stoves opens up a company in a depressed region of New Hampshire and employs several hundred men and women. Or the effect on the culture can be small. A man who welds legs on the stove the company produces might not think that his job has much effect on society, yet surely it does. He's building a product that contributes to the company's continued existence when they are sold for a profit. The wages from this low-level job, when spent by the man and his family in the community, improve its economy.

Finally, working *gains society's approval* by producing something of value. The society of which we are a part views the endeavor as something that should be done and provides benefit for others (Special Task Force, 1972). Most kinds of work fit this definition — schoolwork, child rearing, and paid employment. Safecracking, dealing drugs, gambling, panhandling, and prostitution are probably not work by these criteria.

Types of Work

"Job," "occupation," "vocation," and "career" are words related to working — all similar but with slightly different meanings. Let's distinguish among them before proceeding further.

A **job** is a task or a responsibility performed by one person within an organization (Super *et al.*, 1957, p. 131). A job can be operating a jackhammer or a computer. People who do not work in positions in companies and who do not receive money for their efforts can also have jobs. A student in school has the job of going to class and doing homework, and a preschool child may be required to empty the trash and feed the dog. A housewife has many responsibilities and tasks that constitute her job.

An **occupation** is a classification of work. Usually this classification is based on an economic or psychological perspective (Super *et al.*, 1957, p. 131). An economic classification would place jobs together that pay about the same amount of money. Doctors, lawyers, and executives might be a high group; college professors, newspaper reporters, and military officers in the middle; and file clerks, grocery baggers, and salespeople in a department store at the bottom.

Another way of looking at occupations is psychological: lumping together occupations that have a similar focus and tend to attract people of similar personality types, interests, and values. Psychologist John Holland (1973) divided all work into six broad groups that he called *general occupational themes*. Table 6.1 shows these general occupational themes and particular jobs associated with each.

Occupations associated with the *realistic* theme are foresters, veterinarians, highway patrolmen, and farmers. Typically, they attract people who are rugged, practical, and have good physical skills. They like to work outdoors and often prefer to work by themselves because they have difficulty communicating with others.

Engineers, dieticians, meteorologists, and computer programmers are lumped with the *investigative* occupations. People in these lines of work are thought to have interests centering around scientific activities. They are task-oriented and not especially drawn to work with other people.

Men and women in *artistic* occupations are aesthetically motivated and are inclined toward work in which their sensitivity can be expressed. They are independent and unconventional. Artists, cartoonists, interior decorators, and English teachers fall into this category.

Counselors of all kinds, speech therapists, playground leaders, and ministers are some of the occupations represented by the *social* group. These positions attract people who are humanistic and concerned about the welfare of others. They prefer working with people rather than things.

Enterprising occupations consist of work which involves management, sales, and adventurousness. Examples are most positions in business management, commission sales, sports promotions, TV producing, and small business owners. Individuals in these fields enjoy persuading others, and like power, status, and wealth.

Secretaries, bankers and bank tellers, bookkeepers, and traffic managers illustrate the *conventional* occupations. This type of work has in common orderliness, working within a chain of command, and dealing with specific, clearcut problems. People in these jobs like to know exactly what is expected of them.

A **vocation** is, strictly speaking, a calling to an occupation. One man feels called to the ministry, another to the sea. People in vocations pursue them with enthusiasm and purpose. The calling can involve apparent occupational change, though a close look tells us that the vocation remains the same. A woman with a call to public service may express this in a faculty position in the government department of a university, when she is appointed to the State Department, or when she moves to a position within a foundation that advises government agencies.

Finally, a **career** is a sequence of jobs, positions, or occupations throughout a working life (Super *et al.*, 1957, p. 131). Sometimes a career and a vocation are identical, as with the woman noted above. Many times, however,

Table 6.1   Six general occupational themes

OCCUPATIONAL THEMES	EXAMPLES OF OCCUPATIONS
Realistic	Forester, veterinarian, army officer, physical education teacher, highway patrolman, farmer, conservationist
Investigative	Engineer, medical technician, dietician, dental hygienist, meteorologist, computer programmer, technical writer
Artistic	Artist, actor, cartoonist, photographer, interior decorator, entertainer, English teacher
Social	Counselor, personnel director, speech therapist, playground leader, minister, social worker, director of Christian education
Enterprising	Business executive, buyer, realtor, sports promoter, TV producer, funeral director, life insurance salesman
Conventional	Secretary, banker, bank teller, accountant, traffic manager, bookkeeper, executive housekeeper

SOURCE: From Holland, J. *Making vocational choices: A theory of careers.* © 1973. Englewood Cliffs, N.J.: Prentice-Hall. Adapted by permission.

Work is the sense of obligation to exert effort to make something happen that is approved by the society in which we live.

a career pattern has far less logic to it. A woman may work as a waitress, secretary, nurse, airline cabin attendant, homemaker, and teacher, without a sense of calling to any of them.

Needs Gratified by Work

Four basic human needs are gratified, or frustrated, by working. They are self-preservation, social bonding, appreciation, and competence. They are not limited to any special stage of life. To some extent, these follow Maslow's hierarchy of needs (Figure 1.2, page 11). The world of work is not the only sphere of life in which these needs are fulfilled, for most also find gratification in loving and playing.

Self-Preservation

Each person has a need for self-preservation, which must be met before any other. The way most adults take care of this is by working for money to pay for food and shelter. Mental health workers studied people who did not have to work, or who wanted to work but couldn't, and found that even though the basic needs were met through unemployment compensation, welfare, or the support of others, there were signs of significant emotional disturbance (Powell and Driscoll, 1973; Lantos, 1943). When our job provides enough money so that we don't have to worry abut our next meal or putting a roof over our head, then it is possible to think about other sources of satisfaction from the world of work.

Social Bonding

Do you remember how you felt the first day back in high school in the fall of your junior year? Now think back to when you were sick or on a vacation that caused you to be out of school for a week or more. How much did you miss being there? One of the pleasures for many of us in returning to school and remaining there is the feeling of belonging, being part of a group. This is called social bonding: feeling connected to a larger whole, such as our school, club, team, or friends.

More than any other activity, working attaches us to society (Freud, 1930). Being able to work at school or on the job enables each of us to feel the acceptance of others that comes from membership in a social group: it assigns us a function to carry out in the culture, and it can be the basis for self-definition. Maslow makes the point that everyone has a fundamental need to be accepted by others. In school, much of this acceptance will come from classmates and teachers. Much later it comes from co-workers and bosses.

This 1891 barn raising around Kenosha, Wisconsin, illustrates one of the needs gratified by work — social bonding.

Without working, we are cut off from others. It is this need for acceptance from others that keeps students in class who hate schoolwork, causes sick workers to stay on the job, and even drives wounded soldiers back to their buddies in combat.

Working gives everyone a function to carry out. One woman may be a mother and another a lawyer. A third may be both. Each one's job reinforces her sense of having a useful place in society.

A large chunk of our self-definition is tied to our work. Imagine being a 24-year-old at a party. Someone you don't know asks you about yourself. Your self-description may be very different if you are a college student, laboring on an electronics assembly line, or in the Navy; or, if you are not working, are married, and seven months pregnant. Moreover, our job strongly influences how we dress, what we talk about, what we read or watch on TV, and whom we vote for or against.

Appreciation

How many times in the last month have you felt that your work was not appreciated? You were not alone. Doctors, postal carriers, housewives, teachers, students, all agree on one point: their efforts are not sufficiently appreciated. As Maslow pointed out in Chapter 1, appreciation — having our efforts acknowledged in a positive way — is a need we all have. Work is the primary arena in which this need can be satisfied.

Many qualities of a job that satisfies us can be grouped under the category of appreciation. Among them are having our efforts recognized by others, being promoted, and being given greater responsibility and compensation. These are ways every school or industry has to show its appreciation. To a large extent, these same factors are used to motivate pupils to study and workers to function more productively.

Competence

Remember how good you felt when you were able to ride a two-wheeler without falling? That was an experience of feeling competent, an inner pleasure at being able to make something happen. This feeling of competence at whatever we do radiates without the need for a parent saying, "Oh, how wonderful!" Psychology professor Robert White first suggested that all of us have an instinctive urge to make things happen. Everyone possesses the capacity to feel joy and to be a cause of it (White, 1972). We see the same striving to gratify the need to express competence in every portion of the life cycle. The pleasure a girl finds in knowing her times tables, how to find a square root, or make a computer program work is real, whether or not a teacher grades her. A man feels good when he looks at a gleaming house he has finished painting, or perhaps when the barbecued ribs he cooked turned out well. In both cases, he is pleased with having an impact.

The sense of competence comes from *knowing* we can do something as well as actually doing it. A pianist finds satisfaction both from playing the instrument and from knowing she can practice it when she wishes in the future. This awareness is part of self-esteem and identity.

Human Nature and Working

Are you basically lazy, avoiding work whenever you can? Or do you have a need to work? Would you stay at it even though no one rewarded you? These are questions about human nature that have attracted the interest of many generations of psychologists.

A man who captured the essence of these two views of human nature was Douglas McGregor. Studying the ways in which organizations manage their employees, he concluded that they operate on the basis of two theories of human nature. He called these two approaches to the management of people Theory X and Theory Y (McGregor, 1960).

Theory X assumes that, on the average, people are inherently lazy, dislike working, and will avoid it every chance they have. Security is the only thing that motivates them. Because they are not ambitious and shun responsibilities, workers want to be directed. Therefore, to drive them to produce on the job, they have to be coerced, threatened, and manipulated by the carrot and the stick. Good work is rewarded and inadequate results are punished. Critics of Theory X say it operates on the "Jackass Fallacy" (Levinson, H., 1973): it assumes that people are like jackasses — dumb, stubborn, and unwilling to budge unless prodded by the threat of being fired or tempted by a raise.

Theory Y assumes that an expenditure of effort in working is as natural as resting. Individuals are ambitious, have an inborn desire to be challenged, and seek responsibility. If encouraged, men and women can be self-directed and motivated to exercise their own initiative and creativity to solve their problems at work.

Some companies have used Theory Y in management strategies to increase worker satisfaction, which resulted in improved production: they gave open houses for workers and their families, assigned greater decision-making responsibility to the employees, and encouraged teamwork, rewarding the best group performance. As a result of the changes, the employees felt their work was more interesting. Also, the quality of the work output improved (Frank, 1973).

Not all efforts to implement Theory Y strategies turn out so well. An ardent enthusiast of Theory Y, Maslow spent a year in California observing a small company that tried to practice these management techniques. It was not a success. The demand for initiative, responsibility, and achievement was more than many workers could handle. Maslow concluded that Theory Y companies are far more demanding than Theory X companies. Some workers function more productively and are happier if they are merely expected to do what they are told (Drucker, 1973).

Working and Adjustment

In the first chapter we scanned evidence showing that people who are happy and successful in their work are better adjusted than those who are not. Table 1.2 on page 20 shows that the best-adjusted of Vaillant's men more often made steady career progress, had higher incomes, and had a job that met their personal ambition.

Other evidence across a broad spectrum of people has found that most men and women feel a need to work, whether they are successful or not. In the early 1950s, four hundred men from ages 21 to 65, in occupations ranging from unskilled to professional and managerial, were asked: "If by some chance you inherited enough money to live comfortably without working, do you think you would work anyway or not?" Eighty percent said they would continue to work (Morse and Weiss, 1955). Twenty-five years later, the number was seventy-two percent (Vecchio, 1980). The reasons a quarter of the men in the earlier study gave for continuing to work supports the idea that employment provides a channel for energies that otherwise might be disruptive. They said that if they didn't work, they might feel lost, bored, wouldn't know what to do with their time, would have difficulty staying out of trouble, or go crazy (Morse and Weiss, 1955).

Working Through the Life Cycle

Normal working activities specific to each stage of the life cycle often begin at one period and carry on through several phases of the life span. For example, schoolwork starts in childhood and is a central working activity for some until the fourth decade of life. These working activities will be discussed under the heading of the point at which they first appear. While there are typical types of work for each age, their first occurrence varies because of differing circumstances, opportunities, and individual psychological characteristics. As you read, notice also some of the usual hazards to finding pleasure from these working activities and think about ways these problems can be avoided or remedied.

Childhood and Preadolescence

What we are obliged to do begins early in life. Until the twentieth century, children were pressed into productive work very early. They played a vital role in the hard and hazardous work of settling America. Even after life was relatively stable and secure, the Puritans required that every child work at a job. When the parents failed to keep their children working, the selectmen intervened to find suitable employment. At the beginning of the Civil War, only four states had minimum age laws. In Connecticut, a child had to be all of 9 years old to work in a manufacturing plant (Abbot, 1968). As late as 1900, twelve percent of the youngsters aged 10 to 13 were in the labor force. Today, only a tiny fraction of children are not in school.

Today we view the work of youngsters very differently. We recognize the need for compulsory education of the young to provide the skills necessary for a growing society and to protect children from the health hazards of premature employment. Instead of paid employment, the typical working activities now include developing good habits, learning self-care, carrying out chores, performing satisfactorily in school, and imagining adult work.

Developing Good Habits. The first work of the child is learning to develop good habits. **Habits** are automatic repetitive behavior patterns. They do not require new learning or acts of will to carry out. They are energy-efficient. If we are in the habit of getting up in the morning, sitting still to study, and finishing what we start, our life is much easier than if we have to wrestle ourselves out of bed, bind ourselves to the chair to study, or fight to maintain our enthusiasm before we complete a project.

Good habits are the foundation upon which dreams become reality. No one is born with habits already formed or ready to unfold like a leaf in spring. As Maslow (1968) tells us, even the "born doctor" spends a great deal of effort developing the ability to force himself or herself to do things that are hard, putting off pleasures and molding habits to fit an arduous occupation. Good habits lead to freedom of action. If we don't have the habit of being able to study and have an exam Monday morning, our weekend is likely to be one in which we are never free. We have to study whenever the mood strikes us, because we don't know how long it will last.

By contrast, those who have developed habits of working when they choose can go out Friday night and enjoy Saturday, because they know they can tear themselves away from the Sunday football game and prepare for the exam. George Bernard Shaw (1903) summed it up well when he said habits allow us to seize the line of greatest advantage, rather than following the course of least resistance.

Each of us learns to develop habits by modeling and reinforcement. Children learn habits subconsciously by mimicking the behavior of older children and parents. A little girl will copy how her older sister combs her hair and sits at the dinner table, or how her mother organizes the dresser drawers. Children also learn from the negative reactions of parents and teachers. Based on adult reactions, they learn to eat peas with a fork instead of a knife and chew with their mouths closed rather than open. Habit formation gradually improves into adolescence. Many teenagers are paragons of self-control and discipline, putting their parents and others to shame.

For some, however, there is a continuing struggle to get to places on time, to remember where a book or sweater is, to concentrate for more than a few minutes at a time, and to sit still. This internal struggle can remain a problem through adolescence. The failure or unusually slow growth of habit formation causes some young people a great deal of stress, because their messiness, inability to be punctual, forgetfulness, or wiggliness irritates parents and teachers. Their plight is not eased by the adult expectation that they should improve each year. They just seem to fall further behind. As all of us who have had one or more of these problems can attest, we eventually "grow out" of them. Also, as we grow older, there are fewer new habits to learn. We have more practice at mastery.

Self-Care. The ability to care for ourselves grows through childhood. Self-care is the work of keeping free from harm — crossing the street properly and not ingesting bleach. It also involves minimal health maintenance, such as brushing teeth, washing hands before eating, and knowing what to do to avoid infection from cuts and scrapes.

Self-care improves greatly in adolescence (Gesell, Ilg, and Ames, 1974). At all ages, girls are usually neater than boys. And 10-year-olds of either sex bathe infrequently and then only under protest. Indifferent to style, they put on clothes without a great deal of thought and could wear the same outfit several days in a row.

By age 15, boys and girls usually bathe every day and brush their teeth and comb their hair without being reminded. They are interested in clothes that are currently fashionable and go together. Some 15-year-olds keep their room immaculate, while others don't mind living amidst a mess.

In adolescence self-care is harder. In addition to the fact that it relies on the ability to form habits, personal grooming requires continuing adjustment. It requires greater effort for a youngster to care for teeth when there is a greater intake of sweets and junk food in adolescence. The bathing that kept an 8-year-old body clean and free of offensive odors is insufficient for a 14-year-old.

Inadequate self-care nets nagging hostility from adults; it also compromises interpersonal relations. Old friendships can be corroded by bad breath or new ones put off by offensive odors.

Chores. Responsibilities that adults assign to children are chores. They can be relatively simple — making the bed, emptying the trash, or cutting the lawn. They can sometimes be unusually taxing, as in the case of a 10-year-old girl, the daughter of a single-parent mother. Every day her chores consist of taking care of her 2- and 4-year-old brothers after school, cooking dinner, and cleaning up afterward. On weekends, she does the grocery shopping and helps her mother clean up the apartment.

During the first part of adolescence, the ability and willingness to do household chores gradually improves. Though a 10-year-old rarely carries out a chore without groaning first, by 13 he or she is able to do housework without resisting too much or becoming angry. By mid-adolescence, however, boys and girls begin to invest a considerable amount of time in academic work, school-related activities, and part-time jobs. (Gesell, Ilg, and Ames, 1974). The 16-year-old with college preparatory courses, and who sings in the choir, may also work at a gas station or at a regular baby-sitting job 15 hours a week. The chores of such a person may drop off significantly, and the parents seem to accept this reality.

Schoolwork. The primary vocational activity from kindergarten through the high-school years and, for many, well beyond, is schoolwork. We all know what the work of these years involves: going to class, studying homework, writing up projects, performing in class. Compensation comes in the form of grades and teacher comments: not like a weekly paycheck but more often four times a year, like stock dividends. Toward the end of childhood, the ability to derive pleasure from learning itself increases — from reading, understanding how decimals work, watching water change from a solid to a liquid to a gas, making a map of Africa.

School can be enjoyable if we are doing well enough. For some, however, it is a nightmare. A large number of grade-school children — some estimate the figure to be as high as 5 million — have learning disabilities of one sort or another (Garmezy, 1978). For them, learning anything that requires the orderly or sequential processing of information or techniques — reading, spelling rules, punctuation, or arithmetic calculation — can be extraordinarily difficult. These learning disabilities can lead to poor school performance and the inner conviction of being stupid.

Fortunately, special education programs have been set up for many of these children. The programs emphasize early diagnosis and treatment. Special tutoring methods and emotional support can improve the learning of many students and thereby restore their self-confidence.

A limited relationship exists between grades in school and how much we enjoy it. "A" students are usually more satisfied than those of us with marginal grades, but the correlation is far from perfect. For example, one girl's "A's" bring her only a sense of disaster averted. She holds her breath every time a test or paper is returned, praying it will not be graded with a "B." The "A," however, produces only temporary relief at having survived again — not real pleasure.

Many students with average marks are perfectly satisfied with their academic performance. Their problem is coping with parents and teachers who consider them to be underachievers because they are not using their potential to the fullest. As long as students' grades generally meet their own expectations, do not result in chronic hassles from adults, and do not close off future options, marks are not especially associated with adjustment.

Imagining Adult Work. Imagining adult work begins early in life (Ginzberg, Ginsburg, Axelrod, and Herma, 1951). At first, children play the roles of adults they see around them and doing exciting things on TV: firefighters, nurses, doctors, teachers, detectives, astronauts, mothers, or professional athletes. Gradually, young people begin to think more about jobs and fields they like because of exposure or talent. As youngsters move into preadolescence and adolescence, they begin to give up hobbies, interests, and other pursuits. To some extent this is because they are greatly influenced by their friends and are extraordinarily cautious about venturing into activities that will result in the disapproval of their peer group or show them to be less than competent. The coin collecting that gave pleasure to a 7-year-old boy does not meet his needs at 11 because his best friend likes to build rockets. Another boy with talent and enthusiasm for the flute as a middle-schooler abandons it at 14 because everyone else in the high-school flute section is female.

To some extent, young people give up interests to make room for new ones or to spend time with friends. However, since early activity is often the basis for later vocational interests, parents and teachers need to be aware of the youngster who gives up things and replaces them with nothing. Encouraging these young people to take up new enterprises can be taxing and frustrating for parents, teachers, and others who work with young people.

Adolescence

During adolescence, reality is given greater weight than fantasy. The working activities of many adolescents are continuations of the work begun in childhood and preadolescence. Some teenagers are still learning to develop habits and carry out self-care and chores reliably. Nearly all are enmeshed in schoolwork and increasingly trying to imagine themselves in adult work. Beginning in adolescence, teens begin to think about finding paid part-time work and acquiring the skills needed to manage personal affairs, go further in education, or enter into an occupation. One young boy decided to pursue business because he enjoyed making his own spending money as a child and later began a pool-cleaning and lawncare business. A female classmate had a talent for sewing her own clothes and imagined herself as a dress designer. The young man prospered, hired some friends to help him, and became increasingly certain that business was for him. The young woman's interest in sewing faded. As she came to the end of her teenage years she didn't know what she wanted to pursue, except that apparel design wasn't it. As adolescence ends many, though not all, young people develop a sense of the general direction of their occupational interests.

Part-Time Jobs. The percentage of young people in school who also work grows steadily through adolescence. Table 6.2 shows that at age 14 to 15 less than twenty percent of boys and girls in school also work part-time. By 16 to 17, the proportions have more than doubled. Until age 21, the percentage of students who have full- or part-time jobs grows only slightly.

In addition to providing money, after-school work is useful in other ways: it reinforces the development of habits, it shows the value of education, and it provides a clearer view of a particular career.

Luis had a job Saturdays and three afternoons a week at a gas station. At first he pumped gas, but eventually he began to help with minor and then more complicated car repairs. From this experience he learned that he was fascinated by how machines work. This was one of the reasons he decided to be an engineer.

It is always striking to watch an apparently indifferent, unmotivated student in school turn into a dynamo of energy, initiative, persistence, and re-

Table 6.2 Percentages of young people enrolled in school who also work (1978)

AGE	PERCENTAGE ENROLLED IN SCHOOL		PERCENTAGE WHO ALSO WORK	
	MALE	FEMALE	MALE	FEMALE
14–15	98	98	19	18
16–17	89	88	47	43
18–19	48	43	48	46
20–24	24	19	55	58

SOURCE: U.S. Department of Labor. *Handbook of Labor Statistics*. Washington, D.C.: U.S. Government Printing Office, 1980.

sponsibility when he or she reports to a part-time job in a gas station or restaurant. Clearly, these young people are able to enjoy experiencing their competence on a job in a way that is closed to them in school.

As noted earlier, the early teenage years are often marked by boys and girls giving up things and being reluctant to take on new interests. Boredom leading to apathy and antisocial behavior is a problem for many adolescents. Working is one way to stimulate interest and direct energies into more productive channels. The overall effect of part-time work on young people is beneficial. Studies of adolescents who work part time show them to be more self-reliant, have greater social understanding, and exhibit fewer physical and psychological symptoms than young people who do not work (Steinberg et al., 1981a; Steinberg et al., 1981b; Greenberger, Steinberg, and Vaux, 1981). Also, the capacity for young people to work is positively connected with later success in life (Vaillant and Vaillant, 1981).

Acquiring Skills. Learning skills needed to manage personal affairs competently and prepare for future education or entry into a specific occupation is another working activity for the adolescent. A good deal of concern has been voiced that high-school graduates do not have the skills to take care of themselves. Presently, several states demand that every graduating high-school senior be competent in several "personal survival" areas. In Oregon, for example, the high-school graduates must be able to balance a checkbook, rank in order the effectiveness of birth control devices, use a road map, explain what pay check deductions are for, plan a nutritious diet, work a calculator, and fill out a short-form 1040 tax return (*Newsweek*, January 20, 1975, p. 69).

The acquisition of information and techniques for solving problems is essential to the forty percent of those teenagers who plan to continue their education directly after high school. Verbal facility, especially in reading, has deteriorated among high-school students. One result is considerable academic difficulty for adolescents who move into competitive colleges. Many institutions of higher learning accommodate to the lower level of skills possessed by their entering freshmen by offering courses in reading, writing, and elementary math. Other colleges and universities design courses to teach and motivate students with serious learning disabilities.

A change has occurred in the career goals of college freshmen in the past ten years. A recent study found today's women to be far more ambitious and materially oriented than females ten years ago. As Figure 6.1 shows, college women are considerably more interested in going into business and the professions, and less drawn to majoring in the traditionally female-dominated occupations such as teaching. Moreover, this study showed that seventy-two percent more women want to be well-off financially than in 1969. A far higher proportion of the females in this study want to make a contribution to their field, become an authority, and earn recognition from peers (Magarrel, 1980).

Adolescents entering the job market directly from high school are often in for some rough sledding. Compared to other groups of young people, a larger proportion of 16- to 19-year-olds who want work cannot find jobs. These figures are presented in Table 6.3.

The reasons for the relatively high unemployment rate among adolescents, especially minority group members, are several. Former Commissioner of Ed-

Fast-food restaurants such as these employ the growing numbers of young people. Working part-time can influence adjustment and adult career choice.

ucation Sidney Marland (1974) has said that one of the biggest problems for young men and women entering the labor force is that they are occupationally illiterate, knowing little about what sorts of jobs are available and what sort of preparation they require. Many have had little training or experience in high school to prepare them for useful and interesting jobs.

The solution to this problem has been to alter the educational experience of adolescents to include practical experience along with academic learning. Marland points to efforts in the state of Georgia to include vocational training for all students in grades seven through twelve. In junior high school, students were placed in business, industrial, or agricultural settings to observe the workers and the work. The boys and girls were then asked to talk about what they saw and felt to help them clarify what they might be interested in. Later they took mini-vocational courses and used tools or processes specific to a work setting. From then on, the students were given gradually more exposure to hands-on occupational experience through work-study programs, apprenticeships in the summer, and in some cases vocational training. The result of this educational experience was far less unemployment among these high-school graduates.

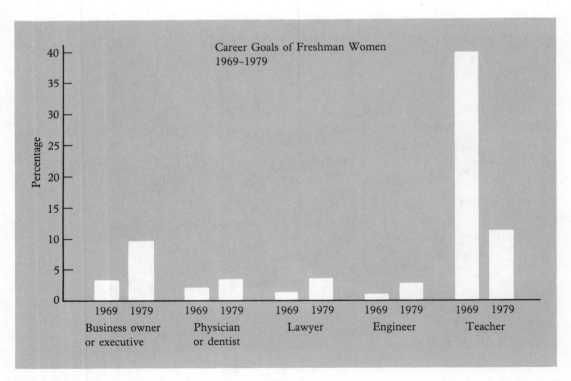

Figure 6.1   Career goals of freshman women, 1969– 1979

Table 6.3 Unemployment by sex, age, and race in the labor force (1979)

	MALE		FEMALE	
AGE	WHITE, %	BLACK AND OTHER, %	WHITE, %	BLACK AND OTHER, %
16–19	14.2	32	14.2	36.4
20–24	7.4	17	7.8	20.8
25–34	3.6	8.6	5.6	11

SOURCE: From U.S. Department of Commerce, Bureau of the Census. *Current Population Reports*, Series P-20, No. 365. Washington, D.C.: U.S. Government Printing Office, 1981.

Criteria for unemployment: people who say they are available for work and have made efforts to find a job in the past four weeks.

Another approach is to blend vocational and academic training in community colleges. The programs described in the box are but a few of many programs in hundreds of community colleges across the United States. Indeed, it is the community colleges that currently most effectively bring together occupational and academic learning at a pace that can be controlled by the student.

Youth

Youth is a transitional period, one of noncommitment to occupation or school. Instability in work, as well as in relationships and geography, is a quality of this period. Instability can be expressed in multiple job changes or dropping out of college before settling down. For some, this is a brief and fleeting moment; for others, the instability may last a decade or more.

A man or woman who has been at a job five years or less is seven times more likely to change than someone who has been working twenty years or more (Troll, 1975). Largely this is because jobs for young people are low-level, low-paying, and boring. Another reason is that many young people don't want to be hemmed in; they want to see what other positions, companies, or parts of the country have in store for them.

A story is told about a company representative who consistently was unable to attract top graduates of a business school. By accident, he discovered that half of them moved on to a different company from the one that first hired them in the first three years after graduation. He decided to alter his strategy. Instead of trying to hire the business-school graduates in their senior year, he merely introduced himself and listened attentively to their ideas of what they wanted from their first job. Two years later he contacted those he liked and asked them if they would be interested in talking about a job with his firm. He had no trouble hiring the people he wanted because they were ready for a change.

Dropping out of college is as common as completing a degree on time. Figure 6.2 shows the percentage of students entering college who are still enrolled four years later.

Occupational-Academic Education in Four Community Colleges

Pasadena City College (California) offers sixty-four career-oriented courses — from commercial airline pilot training to metal processes technology — which engage about half of its 14,000 student body. Stressing interdisciplinary cooperation between academic and occupational skills, each year a major event consists of having the students — with the cooperation of interested professionals, laborers and area businesses — build and sell a model home. . . .

New York City Community College serves a student body of 15,000 in thirty-four career-education and college-transfer day and evening courses. About eighty percent of the students elect to take at least one of the occupational offerings. The overall career program has three components — general education, orientation, and training in specific skills. The curriculum for the last is determined largely by the entry-level requirements of industry or by the state's licensing boards. . . .

Of the students participating in cooperative education programs in engineering technologies, data processing, and accounting, better than eighty percent were offered permanent jobs.

Central Piedmont Community College (Charlotte, North Carolina) never closes its doors to its 8,000 students, offering thirty-four occupational programs round the clock, including an automobile mechanics course that gets under way at midnight and runs until 7:00 A.M. This is not only to make full use of expensive facilities and handle heavy class loads but also to accommodate those students who work during the day. . . .

One of the most recent additions to the curriculum is a Human Services Degree program geared to employment in day-care centers, nursing homes, orphanages, and other welfare-related service agencies.

Lane Community College (Eugene, Oregon) serves nearly 20,000 full- or part-time students each year, offering some forty-two separate career-oriented courses, each designed to lead directly to employment. Courses are added or deleted to reflect the shift in the job market, and the emphasis of instruction concentrates on the personal needs of the individual. A key step there has been the development of more than 850 Vocational Instructional Packages designed by the faculty with assistance from experts in business, industry, labor, and the professions.

An open-entry/open-exit instructional strategy allows the student to enter a program at any time, accomplish the desired objectives, and leave when the requirements of the job sought are completed. . . . All students receive on-the-job experience before completing their program.

SOURCE: Adapted from Marland, S. *Career Education: A Proposal for Reform.* New York: McGraw-Hill, 1974, pp. 224–227.

Men are slightly more likely to remain in college than women, and minority women have the highest attrition rate. These statistics have not changed much in twenty-five years.

What Figure 6.2 does not tell us is how many of those who leave college return at a later time. A survey in the midwest followed college student dropouts for a ten-year period. Seventy percent of those who left college returned, and about half of those eventually graduated (Eckland, 1964). We do not know how many of those who dropped out again returned to school in the following decade.

Erikson (1968) called this instability of youth a **psychosocial moratorium.**

This means taking time out — one to four years — to do something entirely different while trying to piece together what we wish to do with our life. Career decisions are put off. Enlistment in the armed forces, a tour in the Peace Corps or VISTA, or picking grapefruit on a kibbutz in Israel can be of enormous value as a transitional experience. This "time out" frequently results in returning to a job or to colleges and other training with a more coherent view of ourselves and a clearer understanding of what we want in the next phase of life.

In 1980, the average age for males to marry was 24.6 and for females 22.1. About half of people under age 25 are married, and most of them have at least one baby. The point of bringing up these statistics is to show that the youthful instability of young men and women comes to an end before the decade of the 30s as they face the realities associated with starting and supporting a family. A smaller number of married couples put off having children until their late 20s or early 30s, while they move from an unstable to a stable life style, complete their training, or establish themselves in an occupation.

For many women, married or not, the question of having children becomes more and more a pressing issue as the third decade of the life cycle closes. They know that bearing a child is a piece of work that remains for them to make a decision about. They must grapple with extremely compli-

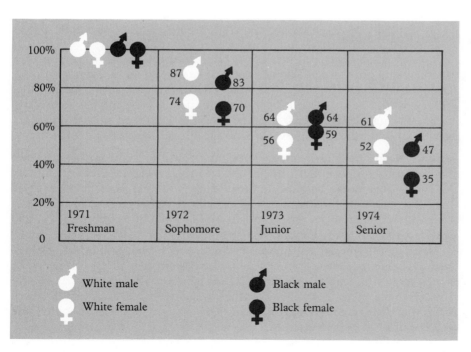

Figure 6.2 College dropout rates, 1971–1974

cated questions about motherhood: yes or no; now, later, or never; what will having a baby do to my relationship with my mate; can I have a baby and a successful career too; does day care work? Books such as *Up Against the Clock* (Fabe and Wikler, 1979) and *Sooner or Later: The Timing of Parenthood in Adult Lives* (Daniels and Weingarten, 1982) clearly address these specific issues. They do not conclude that the satisfactions of having a child outweigh those of not having one, but they point out the pleasures associated with each and the importance of making a decision.

Toward the end of youth, the domains of work and love become far more closely entwined. The satisfactions from one become dependent upon satisfactions from the other. For some, it is almost as though working and loving areas become fused because of how closely pleasures from both are tied together (Smelser, 1980). We can see how much those two spheres are blended by seeing the anxiety, depression, and other stress emotions which develop when one exists without the other. A single policeman in his early 30s wondered why his work and life itself seemed meaningless until he figured out it was because he didn't have someone he loved with whom to share his life. A married 28-year-old female high-school teacher became increasingly upset without knowing why. Finally, in a talk with her best friend, she realized that her husband's inability to settle down and stay with a job was blocking her increasingly strong desire to establish roots, plan for children, and begin to move more fully into her occupation.

Young Adulthood

Young adulthood is signaled by the end of preparation for an occupation. The apprenticeship or formal education is over. The moving around and job-changing of youth come to an end, and the individual finds a place in the world of work in which he or she can be reasonably comfortable for the foreseeable future. Working activities characteristic of young adulthood are settling down, forming an occupational identity, getting ahead, and adjusting to dual careers.

Settling Down. For the young adult, settling down — forming a life structure in which youthful aspirations can be realized — is a central focus (Levinson, D., 1978). This means building and maintaining a stable basis for the support of the self and others. Within this framework, we make the first major choices of adulthood: what to do, where to live, style of living, whom to marry, and whether or not to have children.

Separation from parents, begun in adolescence, is now established. Though close attachments remain, young adults have their own place and generally enough money to begin to sustain their own families. The future starts to have as much meaning as the present. Savings accounts begin. Couples talk about how to pay for the college education of their children. Health, disability, and life insurance ads attract interest.

The inability to settle down and make a commitment to the future can cause much dissatisfaction during this phase. As Levinson tells us (Levinson,

D., 1978), the dissatisfaction grows when someone can't resolve the questions that bedevil youth: "Is this what I want to do?" "Is this occupation too narrow?" "Do I want to marry this person?" "Is this where I want to live?" "Can I stand to give up all the other possibilities I could have chosen?" The sorrow experienced at this period can be exquisite, but it is only by answering each question that the commitment and the growing of deeper roots necessary to work and love is possible for the young adult.

Forming an Occupational Identity. In this stage of the life span, men and women find those jobs at which they are sufficiently competent and with interests deep enough to form an occupational identity. A young man who becomes an apprentice at a printing plant finds that he is skillful at the work and begins to think of himself as a printer. A woman who entered law school in her mid-20s after several false starts in other jobs that didn't hold her interest finds herself drawn to the subject of tax law. With increasing clarity, she sees herself as an attorney specializing in tax work.

In Chapter 1 we examined Levinson's notion of the dream (Levinson, D., 1978). More than a fantasy, yet still short of a carefully thought-out plan, a dream is a central organizing core of the occupational identity for young adults. Children, adolescents, and youths have visions of themselves in the adult world that are gradually tempered by experience. In young adulthood, the dream is connected to an occupation.

Whatever the dream's nature, its function is to organize us toward goals at work. It sustains each one of us through the years of struggle and frustration that might be necessary to realize our dream. As long as the apprentice and the law student have their dreams, the long hours and difficult or boring work have meaning and can be satisfying. Without a dream, work is endless, purposeless drudgery.

Getting Ahead. Ambition to succeed in the chosen occupation takes a central place in the lives of young adults. The quest is earnest, serious business, and most satisfaction from working comes from making forward progress. Hard work, generally without conflict or complaint, is the price willingly paid. The journeyman tolerates hours of overtime because he makes good money, which in turn tells him he is getting ahead.

"Gold stars" are important again. The young woman takes particular pride in receiving a job offer from a prestigious law firm at a starting salary above the class average. This lets her know she is progressing. After a few months with the firm, a senior partner asks her to help her with a big case. This also is forward movement. Pleasure in new learning at work is considerable. Frequently this is because knowing a new procedure provides an opportunity for advancement.

Not getting ahead, when all of our other contemporaries talk about nothing but how successful they are, can be extraordinarily frustrating and depressing. The man who is not asked to fill in for a sick assistant foreman over the weekend may feel a setback. The woman who has put off having children while establishing herself in a law career may become uncomfortable around her college classmates with good jobs *and* 1.5 darling, intelligent children.

A **mentor** especially enhances the prospects of getting ahead. Psychologically a mixture of parent and peer, the mentor is usually an older man or woman at the work place. The mentor

> . . . may act as a *teacher* to enhance the young man's skills and intellectual development. Serving as a *sponsor*, he may use his influence to facilitate the young man's entry and advancement. He may be a *host* and *guide*, welcoming the initiate into a new occupational and social world, acquainting him with its values, customs, resources and cast of characters. Through his own virtues, achievements and way of living, the mentor may be an *exemplar* that the protégé can admire and seek to emulate. He may provide *counsel* and moral support in times of stress.
>
> The mentor has another function . . . to support and facilitate the *realization of the Dream*. (Levinson, D., 1978, p. 98)

Though Levinson says that mentors are usually the same sex as the protégé, this is not always true. Levinson himself was greatly influenced by a female mentor.

Like all intense, loving contacts, the relationship with a mentor becomes strained as the young adult moves into greater competence and responsibility. Many times the young man or woman feels criticized, smothered, and restricted by what yesterday seemed to be the mentor's useful criticism, care, and advice. On their part, mentors usually see the protégé as touchy, unreceptive, and irrational in the face of expert advice. By the time the relationship comes to an end, there is truth on both sides.

Though mentor relationships do come to an end — some rather stormily — the young adult carries his or her mentor within for the rest of life. Invariably, the acknowledgments in books such as this one express gratitude to a mentor.

Dual Careers. In this stage most people are married and more than half of the time both spouses are employed. Initially this presents no problem, as most young couples enjoy the fact that both are employed. The money is nice, the housework usually is shared, both careers are advancing nicely, and no one has to give up anything yet. Just how sweet this life might be was summed up in an article in *Fortune* magazine, reprinted in the box.

Just as with other aspects of living, however, things change as new problems are presented to the married couple. The biggest change involves having children. We can discern five distinct "stations" in a dual-career marriage, which center on the issue of having children: (1) no children, (2) first child, (3) more than one child, (4) youngest child in school, (5) youngest child's leaving home. From station two onward, a distinct adaptation to offspring is required.

Let us imagine Laurie and Hal of the *Fortune* article five years from now, when they have their first child. They are at the second station. Laurie has

On the Fast Track
to the Good Life

Twenty-five-year-old Laurie, an engineer, and her husband, Hal, make $60,000 a year. They expect to have a family in five years or so, once "we're financially secure enough to afford good child care so I can continue to work. . . . We want to make sure my career is well established, that we have all the material things we want, that our bills are caught up so we don't have to fight over what little money we'll have to raise a family on. With our life-style, we can't afford good child care now and all the things we like."

SOURCE: Adapted from Kinkhead, G. On the Fast Track to the Good Life. *Fortune*, April 7, 1980, p. 82.

established herself as an engineer. She takes time out for maternity leave, and before returning to work she finds an excellent live-in housekeeper. Her life may be slightly more hectic but she can manage.

Let us now imagine the stresses involved when their second child is born, which puts them at the third station. With two youngsters to care for, the life of Laurie and Hal becomes much more complicated. Which one of them is going to take the kids for checkups, respond to emergencies, and scout day-care centers and nursery schools? What happens if the housekeeper leaves and new applicants have to be interviewed? Since both of them invest long hours in their work, who will take time out for these necessary tasks?

The answer is generally the mother. With two children, it is far more often that it is she who reduces her commitment to her career to manage the household. With the birth of the second child, women often look for reduced work loads or less demanding jobs, or they take time out from their careers entirely while caring for their children. If they continue to work, they are aware of the costs. As one mother who stopped working after her second child was born put it, "I miss my job, but I missed seeing my first child learning to ride her tricycle and I don't want to miss it next time."

Companies with built-in day-care centers are a great advantage for women and men who work in these organizations. Being able to have preschool children cared for in the same company means more time together with one parent, shared experience, greater understanding between the parent and children of what the other is doing, and availability for emergencies.

Station four, when the youngest child goes to school, brings a little relief. But still the tasks to be done by two working parents are significant. More often than not, women pay the price in physical exhaustion. Staines and O'Connor (1979) surveyed a representative sample of workers in America. They examined the number of hours worked by dual-career couples who had children under 18 and those who did not. The results are shown in Table 6.4. The average married woman with children labors about thirteen and a half hours on a workday and about fourteen hours on a non-workday. These figures compare to about twelve hours on a workday and nine hours on a non-workday for her spouse. Exhaustion menaces satisfaction from working, as well as from loving and playing.

To some degree, a working mother never escapes from the guilt she feels about not being a full-time mother. This is reinforced in direct ways by children who are reluctant to be sent to baby-sitters or to go to bed, or who demand their mother's time just at the point she needs to relax. To some extent, this is also reinforced by increasing conflict in the marriage. Table 6.5 shows the percentage of workers in a recent survey who reported conflict between work and family life. We can see that when both parents are employed, more conflict occurs between work and family — especially from the woman's vantage point. Among working women with no children, twenty-nine percent reported some or a lot of conflict between job and family life. With children, the percentage jumped to forty-four percent. Table 6.5 also indicates that from

Table 6.4 Time spent in work, child care, home chores, and leisure among working parents and non-parents

ACTIVITY	HOURS SPENT ON WORKDAY BY:			
	FEMALE PARENT	MALE PARENT	FEMALE NON-PARENT	MALE NON-PARENT
Work	7.52	8.93	7.96	8.54
Child care★	3.50	1.76	—	—
Home chores	3.51	1.16	2.40	1.21
Leisure	1.77	2.03	2.23	2.46

ACTIVITY	HOURS SPENT ON NON-WORKDAY BY:			
	FEMALE PARENT	MALE PARENT	FEMALE NON-PARENT	MALE NON-PARENT
Work	—	—	—	—
Child care★	7.48	5.15	—	—
Home chores	6.56	4.00	5.39	3.38
Leisure	3.56	5.05	4.84	6.16

Adapted from Staines, G. and O'Connor, P. *The relationship between work and leisure.* (Ann Arbor, Michigan. Survey Research Center, 1979.) Paper presented at the American Psychological Association, New York City, 1979. Reprinted by permission.

★Indicates only parents of children under eighteen.

Table 6.5   Extent to which job and family care interfere with each other

Approximately 1000 workers were asked the following question: "How much do your job and family life interfere with each other: a lot, somewhat, not too much, or not at all?"

| | PERCENTAGE REPORTING WORK-FAMILY CONFLICT | | | |
| | MEN | | WOMEN | |
	LITTLE OR NONE	SOME OR A LOT	LITTLE OR NONE	SOME OR A LOT
Spouse works, no children	72	28	71	29
Spouse works, children	66	34	56	44
Spouse doesn't work, no children	74	26	No data	
Spouse doesn't work, children	60	40	No data	

SOURCE: Adapted from Pleck, J., Staines, G., and Lang, L. Conflicts between work and family life. *Monthly Labor Review*, 1980, 103(3), 29–31.

the male point of view, however, it is not the wife's work that increases conflict between work and family — it's having children. Forty percent of men with non-working wives reported job and family conflict.

Some types of occupations and organizations lower the stress level for mothers who have a career outside the home. For instance, positions that allow women to set their own hours, be at home when their children return home from school, or permit work at home are very helpful. Going to work for companies that have day-care centers, that do not penalize women for taking time off to have children or that permit job splitting with another working mother, are also examples. These organizations are often repaid with greater productivity and loyalty, as well as lower turnover.

Station five — when the youngest child leaves home — can be a rebirth of the first phase. Conflict between work and family diminishes, and considerable pleasure comes from being able to devote full time to an occupation without wondering what is happening with the kids. Women who have continued to work during the child-rearing years have several advantages over their contemporaries who have taken a good deal of time out: they are further along in their career and don't have to deal with the loss of confidence associated with being out of work for a long period.

Middle Adulthood

At mid-life, many women and men are potentially in the most productive years of their lives. With apprenticeship, child-rearing, and often years of experience behind them in their occupations, yet with relatively full vigor, most middle-aged workers achieve their greatest successes. They are making it. In this phase, they also begin to worry about how much time they have left until retirement.

Coping with the simultaneous demands of a career and family is a reality that affects an increasing number of adult women.

For many, this results in reappraisal of whether they want to remain in their line of work or try something else. Let us examine the two central working activities in this stage — making it and reappraisal — paying close attention to the hazards and conflicts associated with each.

Making It. In mid-life, the most gratifying satisfaction comes from "making it" — being successful in one's occupation. For many in this phase of the life cycle, there is a strong sense of being in full stride, in total command of their powers, reaping both internal satisfaction and external reward from working. By this time, some have found a career in which they feel able to express themselves. An example is Carl Bates, the stonemason in Studs Terkel's book *Working* (1974). As Bates puts it:

> . . . it's a pretty good day layin' stone or brick. Not tiring. Anything you like to do isn't tiresome. It's hard work; stone is heavy. At the same time, you get interested in what you're doing and you usually fight the clock the other way. You're not lookin' for quittin' . . . I take a lot of pride in it and I do get, oh, I'd say, a lot of praise or whatever you want to call it. . . . I think I'm pretty well recognized.

Not everyone is able to find the same pleasure from working as Carl Bates. Studies of people who say they are satisfied with their job give conflicting pictures (Mortimer, 1979). Job satisfaction remained high after World War II and through the early 1970s — over ninety percent of the men and women over 30 said they were at least moderately satisfied with their occupations. More recent surveys of worker satisfaction find a greater range of dissatisfaction at all levels of employment.

The primary reason that is offered to explain this decline in satisfaction is that men and women have higher expectations from their occupations. Partly this is because the educational level of workers is higher than before. Those with the most education are the least content. Even with reasonably adequate job security and economic benefits, modern workers feel disenchantment — voiced in the quotes beginning this chapter — because of monotony, lack of control over what they do, and absence of recognition (Mortimer, 1979).

These observations are supported by recent studies of *job complexity*. A survey of over 3000 men in occupations at all levels found that those in the most complex jobs had greater respect for their own capacities, were more open to experience, and felt a greater control over their lives (Kohn, 1980). Those whose work was complex, that is, requiring independent thought, judgment, and self-direction, also had more interesting hobbies. They were more adventurous and intellectually demanding. Moreover, those with the more complex occupations felt a greater sense of continuing personal and intellectual growth than those in less complicated ones.

Unfortunately, job complexity is one of those factors contributing to two major hazards to satisfaction from work at mid-life: workaholism and burnout. **Workaholism** is a passion for satisfaction from an occupation, which results in chronic overwork and severely lessened gratification from other spheres of life. Though the work of many at mid-life is extremely satisfying, there is always more to do than can possibly be accomplished. Few people can work over sixty hours a week without other areas of satisfaction being compromised. Some of the symptoms of workaholism are shown in Table 6.6.

A primary danger of workaholism is **burnout**. Burnout has been described as depleting oneself, exhausting physical and mental resources, wearing oneself out by excessive striving to secure some unrealistic expectation imposed by

Table 6.6   A test for workaholism

- Do you get up early, no matter how late you go to bed?
- If you are eating lunch alone, do you read or work while you eat?
- Do you make up daily lists of things to do?
- Do you find it difficult to do nothing?
- Are you energetic and competitive?
- Do you work on weekends and holidays?
- Can you work anytime and anywhere?
- Do you find vacations "hard to take"?
- Do you dread retirement?
- Do you really enjoy your work?

Eight or more yes answers to these questions suggests the possibility of being a workaholic.

SOURCE: Reprinted from *Workaholics: Living with them, working with them* by Marilyn Machlowitz, Ph.D., copyright © 1980, by permission of Addison-Wesley Publishing Co., Reading, MA.

Are You Burning Out?

Look back over the past six months. Have you been noticing changes in yourself or in the world around you? Think of [your work] . . . the family . . . social situations. Allow about thirty seconds for each answer. Then assign a number from 1 (for no or little change) to 5 (for a great deal of change) to designate the degree of change you perceive.

1. Do you tire more easily? Feel fatigued rather than energetic?

2. Are people annoying you by telling you, "You don't look so good lately"?

3. Are you working harder and harder and accomplishing less and less?

4. Are you increasingly cynical and disenchanted?

5. Are you often invaded by a sadness you can't explain?

6. Are you forgetting? (appointments, deadlines, personal possessions)

7. Are you increasingly irritable? More short-tempered? More disappointed in the people around you?

8. Are you seeing close friends and family members less frequently?

9. Are you too busy to do even routine things like make phone calls or read reports, or send out your Christmas cards?

10. Are you suffering from physical complaints? (aches, pains, headaches, a lingering cold)

11. Do you feel disoriented when the activity of the day comes to a halt?

12. Is joy elusive?

13. Are you unable to laugh at a joke about yourself?

14. Does sex seem like more trouble than it's worth?

15. Do you have very little to say to people?

The Burn-Out Scale

0–25	You're doing fine.
26–35	There are things you should be watching.
36–50	You're a candidate.
51–65	You are burning out.
over 65	You're in a dangerous place, threatening to your physical and mental well-being.

SOURCE: From Freudenberger, H., with Richelson, G. *Burn-out: The high cost of high achievement.* New York: Anchor Doubleday, 1980, pp. 17–18.

oneself or the larger society (Freudenberger and Richelson, 1980). A test for burnout was developed by psychologist Herbert Freudenberger.

As we can see from Freudenberger's test, burnout is workaholism carried to the extreme: we are working harder and getting less satisfaction; relationships with others are compromised; and we are receiving clear signals that things are not well with us via anxiety, anger, depression, and physical symptoms. Unchecked overwork can lead to even more severe consequences. Writer Ellen Goodman sketches one tragic outcome.

Workaholism and burnout can be combated (Freudenberger and Richelson, 1980). Scrutinizing attitudes toward work is a good place to start. Do you have it or does it have you? Take some time off or delegate some of your responsibilities. It's amazing how everything always seems to get done when we are sick or on vacation. No one is irreplaceable. Renewal of relations with others is a cushion against overwork. Determine what you might be doing to strain contacts with those you care about. Do you have time for people you love? To what extent can you listen? Concentrate on redeveloping loving skills. Finally, it is important to inject more joy into life. Try new things at play that will add fun to your life. Have a good time. For many of us, this may be harder than it seems, but we can all make progress toward these goals.

The Company Man

He worked himself to death finally and precisely at 3 A.M. Sunday morning. The obituary didn't say that, of course. It said that he died of a coronary thrombosis, . . . but every one of his acquaintances knew it instantly. He was . . . a workaholic, a classic, they said to each other and shook their heads, and thought for five or ten minutes about the ways they lived.

This man who worked himself to death finally and precisely at 3 A.M. Sunday morning — on his day off — was 51 years old and he was a vice-president. He was, however, one of six vice-presidents and one of three who might conceivably — if the president died or retired soon enough — have moved to the top spot. Phil knew that.

He worked six days a week, five of them until 8 or 9 at night. . . . He had no outside "extracurricular" interests, unless, of course, you think about a monthly golf game that way. To Phil, it was work. He always ate egg salad sandwiches at his desk. He was, of course, overweight by about twenty or twenty-five pounds. He thought it was okay though, because he didn't smoke. On Saturdays Phil wore a sports jacket to the office instead of a suit, because it was the weekend. . . .

The obituary . . . list[ed] his "survivors." . . . He is survived by his wife, Helen, 48 years old, a good woman of no particular marketable skills who worked in an office before marrying and mothering. She had, according to her daughter, given up trying to compete with his work years ago when the children were small. A company friend said, "I know how much you will miss him," and she answered to no one in particular, "I already have."

His "dearly beloved" eldest of the "dearly beloved" children was a hard-working young executive in a manufacturing firm down South. In the day and a half before the funeral he went around the neighborhood researching his father, asking the neighbors what he was like. They were embarrassed.

Phil's second child was a girl who is now 24 and newly married. She lives near her mother and they are close but whenever she was alone with her father, in a car driving somewhere, they had nothing to say. . . .

The youngest is 20, a boy, a high school graduate who has spent the last couple of years, like a lot of his friends, doing odd jobs to stay in grass and food. He was the one who tried to grab at his father and tried to mean enough to him to keep the man at home. He was his father's favorite and over the last two years Phil stayed up nights worrying about the boy. The boy once said, "My father and I only board here."

At the funeral, the 60-year-old company president told the . . . widow that the . . . deceased meant much to the company and would be missed and would be hard to replace.

By 5 P.M. on the afternoon of his funeral, the company president had begun, discreetly, of course, with care and tact, to make inquiries about his replacement. One of three men. He asked around: "Who's been working the hardest?"

SOURCE: Excerpted from Goodman, E. *Close to home.* New York: Simon and Schuster, 1979, pp. 18–19.

At the other extreme, unemployment is a reality for a large number of individuals in middle adulthood. Worry about not being able to find a job often keeps people at work they find unsatisfying. Prolonged unemployment leads to progressive personality deterioration. An investigation of unemployed engineers and scientists noted four declining stages of adjustment in reaction to being out of a job. The authors of this study conclude:

> The image of competent and energetic men reduced to listless discouragement highlights the personal tragedy and loss of valuable resources when there is substantial unemployment. It presses us to seek more thorough and intensive methods of remotivation and more dignified avenues of return to the world of work. Perhaps more significantly, the situation of these middle-class unemployed further dramatizes the plight of the larger number of unemployed non-skilled workers whose fate is to deal with unemployment often during their lifetime. (Powell and Driscoll, 1973, p. 26)

At the other extreme are those who have achieved just the goals they sought, but now face a life of no further challenge. It has been said: "In this world there are only two tragedies. One is not getting what one wants, and the other is getting it. The last is much the worst, the last is a real tragedy!" (Wilde, 1905)

In middle age, we begin to see the end of the line of our careers. Some are lucky enough to visualize continued advancement and challenge through the remainder of their lives. Others, however, have a feeling of **topping out** in middle adulthood, going about as far as they will go. Sure, there may be cost of living increases and compensation or another title, but the days of the big gains are finished. For some who have found climbing the mountain more enjoyable than being at the top, this can be distressing. Job changes, retraining, and having a flexible work week all help a little. But the relief is often temporary. Men and women at mid-life have to begin to find other satisfactions from the work place or other areas of working. We will look at these as we examine later adulthood.

Reappraisal. Reappraisal of our occupation, along with almost all other aspects of life, has been called the "mid-life crisis" (Sheehy, 1976), "middlescence" (Leshan, 1975), or a "midlife transition" (Levinson, D., 1978). Though far from a universal phenomenon, this process does take on crisis proportions for some. According to Levinson (1978), the thinking associated with this reappraisal involves (1) inspecting the direction our career has taken, (2) considering how much of the young adult dream was an illusion and what is left that is solid to go forward with, and (3) thinking about the possibilities of a better or worse life in the future.

Coming to terms with all the interesting careers and experiences they will never know is a major task men and women face during this stage of life. Grieving for the unrealized satisfactions and happiness that might have been known in another occupation is the normal work of middle adulthood. For the biology teacher who always wondered what kind of doctor she would have

Stages of Declining Adjustment Of Unemployed Engineers and Scientists

Stage 1: **Period of Relief and Relaxation**

Most have seen it coming, were increasingly anxious about whether or not they would be let go, and so were relieved for a while when they were finally laid off. They relaxed, read, pursued hobbies, and caught up on things that needed doing around the house and took a vacation. Initially they did not worry much about finding another job.

Stage 2: **Period of Concerted Effort**

After about three weeks, the men began to feel bored and edgy. At this point they began to go about trying to find work, using ways which had been successful in the past — calling friends, sending out résumés, contacting the college placement center. They worked hard at finding work, were well organized, optimistic and resilient in the face of rejection.

Stage 3: **Period of Vacillation and Doubt**

By now the men have been out of work longer than ever before. They have realized that

their ways of finding employment were not effective. Their efforts to look for a job become sporadic — periods of furious activity interlaced with times of growing length of lying fallow. Their organization, planning and optimism deteriorated. Extreme moodiness characterized these men. Relationships with loved ones became very strained.

Stage 4: **Period of Malaise and Cynicism**

After three to nine weeks, job seeking virtually stopped. On the infrequent occasions they did look for work, it was more with the intent of protecting themselves against rejection than aggressively pursuing likely prospects. There was a growing tendency to look for the perfect match. Feelings of powerlessness and apathy abounded. Cynicism in the face of efforts to help them back to work were common. Many of them had given up hope.

SOURCE: From Powell, D. and Driscoll, P. How middle-class unemployed men feel and act: Four progressive stages. *Society*. January/February, 1973.

made, for the professional baseball player who quit the minor leagues after four years to buy a laundromat and wonders if he would have ever made the big leagues had he stuck it out, this can be a sad time. Neither can ever know what joys awaited down the road not taken.

Reappraisal of a job sometimes results in recommitment to the same occupational pathway or moving to a similar interest area. A smaller number make a major change. But problems attend these readjustments. A stockbroker who decided to become a priest at 45 cited one: "My dues at the Southampton Country Club are more than I made in my first year in the parish." Those who make changes usually attack their careers with renewed zest. Those who remain seem content enough to continue with their occupation, which is now routine, while redirecting energies toward relationships with others and leisure activities.

In his book *Holding On or Letting Go*, Osherson (1980) points out the reciprocal relationship between work, personal growth, love, and play, which are reawakened by mid-life reappraisal. Though often a painful process, questions of personal identity and commitments to others, submerged by work in early adulthood, can be reconsidered with profit at this time. If a man's identity or sense of self-worth is tied up in being a successful businessman, or a woman's in being a traditional wife of a respected executive and mother of well-behaved, accomplished children, these individuals may be in for a stormy time when they wonder in middle age whether this is what they really want to be doing. Relationships with others, which may have been pushed aside in the striving to get ahead, take on greater importance as the need to have most of one's satisfaction from work diminishes. For some, this means more intense loving relationships with spouse, family, and friends. Others find these relationships lacking and look for this needed pleasure from others. Joy from leisure activities, which may have been postponed in the 30s, becomes an active pursuit in the 40s and beyond.

Later Adulthood

At no time in history has interest in older workers been greater. Partly this is due to the growing interest of life cycle researchers in adulthood and aging. There are many other reasons that are even more compelling:

1. Because of the declining birth rate, the nation is growing older — about 24 million 65 years old or older in 1978, 27 million by 1985, and 32 million projected for the year 2000.
2. Older people are physically hardier and more capable than ever; the health of the 55-year-old today compares with a 40- or 45-year-old in 1970.
3. Because of the declining birth rate, older workers are more important than in the past.
4. Federal laws against age discrimination and raising the mandatory retirement age to 70 have allowed many who wish to continue working to do so. (Rosow and Zager, 1980)

Just when we cross over the barrier into later adulthood varies enormously. According to federal law designed to protect the rights of older workers, organizations are forbidden to reject applicants over 40 on the basis of their age. For most, later adulthood on the job is experienced around 50 or 55 (Rosow and Zager, 1980). The primary incentives to work remain strong motivators in later adulthood: economic survival, social relations, competence, and having something to do. In addition, three other work activities are frequently found in this age group — continuing to feel useful, generativity, and anticipating and planning for retirement.

Continuing to Feel Useful. Feeling useful is a satisfaction gained from working at all ages, but its importance seems intensified for many men and women in later life. This may be because the anxieties of earlier periods have been relieved by experience: we have settled into our occupation, made some progress, and survived the reappraisals of mid-life. The last child has left home, educational bills are paid, and life is less stressful. Finally, pleasures coming from work are taken less for granted. We can see the end of our working days. Almost all have been unemployed, have had close friends out of work, or have

One aspect of Erikson's concept of generativity is the passing on of our skills and knowledge to younger people.

been worried about being laid off. These factors may partially explain why older people have fewer absences, are more satisfied with their work, feel less stress on the job, and even have fewer accidents than younger employees (Rosow and Zager, 1980).

Little relationship exists between chronological age and ability to work competently in later adulthood. Hard facts indicate that the intelligence of people remains relatively constant until at least age 70. Memory remains largely clear, and work-related abilities are unimpaired (U.S. Department of Health, Education, and Welfare, 1978).

Generativity. One meaning of Erickson's term **generativity** (1950) is the establishment and guidance the generation to follow. At home, this is fostering the growth of our children. At work, it may be being mentor to a younger colleague. Even though mentor relationships can be painful, the pleasure in feeling that some part of ourselves is being carried forward into the generation that follows is considerable. Rare are the senior professors who do not have the Ph.D. dissertations of their students in their bookcases. Through them professors feel connected to their protégés. Also, they may sense the continuity with the tradition of scholarship beginning thousands of years before and continuing into the future.

Generativity is sometimes experienced through a nonfinancial legacy left at work. A secretary finds gratification in knowing that a procedure that she established for getting the bills out on time will continue after she is gone. The professor facing mandatory retirement at the university is pleased to donate his books to the library, which will leave a trace of him behind.

Few men or women in late adulthood have not felt that their ideas have been ignored or worried that their knowledge or skill is antiquated. Few have not struggled to contain the green monster of envy that wells up when a younger man or woman moves up faster than they did, or when they are sidetracked to allow these hotshots to move past them. These experiences can lead to bitterness and withdrawal, the sense of being no longer valued. Taking an interest in younger colleagues, who have eyes only for making it and may not be especially sensitive, can be difficult. Yet persons in later adulthood have much to teach younger people from their more mature perspective.

Anticipation and Planning for Retirement. Gradually for some, suddenly for others, deceleration occurs at work in later years. When it happens gradually, it comes as a reduced taste for overtime, late hours, weekend work, shortened vacations, or breaking new ground. Some people, however, never slacken their pace, and they work as hard as they can until their health fails. A story is told about the famous heart specialist Dr. Paul Dudley White when he himself was terminally ill. Upon hearing that a patient of his was in the same hospital, he rose out of his own bed to see the patient. At the time, Dr. White was 87 years old.

Even if we do not feel ourselves slowing down, an essential part of working in this era is anticipation and planning for retirement. Present thinking is that this should be a gradual process, beginning at any time after age 50. Some of this anticipatory work involves considering probable financial requirements at retirement and reviewing potential income. It involves considering physical needs and the availability of medical care. Finally, it involves thinking about the question of social relations — if we want to move to Arizona and give up our present friends and family, maybe we should begin to spend some time there making friends before we retire.

The hazards of not thinking about retirement beforehand are exemplified by the case of Clara, a woman who suffered a serious emotional breakdown when forced to retire. Clara had a highly productive career as a professor at a state university. However, even in her 69th year, she never planned for her own retirement. When asked by her colleagues what she planned to do afterward, she said that she "knew" the university policy required faculty members to retire at 70, but that she hadn't made any plans yet. When her 70th birthday came, Clara continued to work, ignoring calls and letters from the dean ordering her to vacate her office. Shortly thereafter, when Clara came to work, her office had been cleaned out and the dean stood in the doorway and asked Clara for her keys. At that point, Clara broke down and was hospitalized briefly for a mental disorder. She recovered her emotional resiliency before long.

Eventually she found her way back into teaching on a part-time basis, but later she remembered ruefully that the transition would have been much easier had she faced retirement directly and been able to make her own plans.

A great deal of thinking is presently going into imagining new programs for older adults when their primary careers come to an end (Jacobson, 1980). These include new working environments. Companies are hiring retired individuals part-time at all levels of skills. Some are flirting with the idea of phased retirement, gradually reducing working hours without decreasing pension benefits. Opportunities for retraining and redeployment to areas in need also improve the possibility for older people to remain partially in the work force if they desire.

It is not imperative that everyone continue to work after mandatory retirement. For many, the pleasure of a new life style without working — the freedom to nourish relationships with kin and friends, to engage in playing wholeheartedly — can be pleasant indeed.

Summary

1. Working is an activity that involves a feeling of obligation, an expenditure of energy, making something happen, and producing something of value.
2. Words describing different types of work are "job," "occupation," "vocation," and "career." A job is a task or responsibility performed by one person. An occupation is a classification of jobs, often based on their economic similarities or on the nature of their demands. A vocation is a calling. A career is a sequence of jobs or occupations.
3. Human needs that are gratified through the life cycle by working include self-preservation, social bonding, appreciation, and competence.
4. The relationship between obtaining satisfaction from working and emotional adjustment is shown by Vaillant's work. Other evidence across a broader spectrum has found that most people would plan to continue to work in the absence of financial necessity.
5. Theories of human nature in relation to work are Theory X and Theory Y. Theory X assumes that people are inherently lazy, dislike working, and will avoid it every chance they get. Theory Y assumes individuals are naturally drawn to work and that they are ambitious, with an inborn desire to be challenged and to seek responsibility.
6. Specific activities may be associated with or begun in particular phases of the life cycle. In childhood and preadolescence, the typical working activities include learning good habits, learning self-care and the capacity to carry out chores, performing satisfactorily in school, and imagining adult occupations.
7. Two types of working endeavors characteristically beginning in adolescence are part-time paid jobs and the acquisition of skills needed for self-management or to prepare for future learning and/or entry into an occupation.

8. In youth, instability at work is notable. This is a transition period of non-commitment to occupation or school.
9. Those working activities characteristic of young adulthood include settling down, forming an occupational identity, getting ahead, and, if necessary, coping with the problems of being a dual-career family.
10. At mid-life, making it and reappraisal are the two primary areas of work. Each of these is laced with numerous hazards and conflicts, which threaten satisfaction from working as well as loving and playing.
11. The American population, which is growing older, is physically hardier, is more important to the job market, and, because of federal legislation, is now legally able to work until at least age 70. The specific issues related to later adulthood are continuing to feel useful, generativity, and anticipating and planning for retirement.

A Look Ahead

It is probably true that working consumes more overall time and energy during the life cycle than any other sphere of activity. Next in line is loving. In the next chapter, we will consider a modern definition of love and examine typical loving behaviors at each phase of the life cycle. We will pay particular attention to the differences in loving activities of males and females from adolescence onward. We will look at some of the changes in loving relationships among adolescents and youth, especially with reference to such issues as living together, marriage, and children. We will consider some of the realities in adulthood, such as how to cope with the necessity of going it alone.

Key Terms

work	habit
job	psychosocial moratorium
occupation	mentor
vocation	workaholism
career	burnout
Theory X	topping out
Theory Y	generativity

Suggested Readings

Study skills

James, W. *Principles of Psychology.* (1890) Vols. I and II. New York: Dover, 1953, chapters 4 and 26.

Higbee, K. *Your memory: How it works and how to improve it.* Englewood Cliffs, N.J.: Prentice-Hall, 1977.

Armstrong, W. *Study tips: How to study effectively and get better grades.* Woodbury, N.Y.: Barrons, 1975.

> James's ideas about willpower and habits lay the groundwork for learning effective study skills.

Tradeoffs

Greiff, B., and Munter, P. *Tradeoffs: Executive, family, and organizational life.* New York: New American Library, 1981.

Levinson, H. *Executive stress.* New York: New American Library, 1975.

> Balancing work demands with responsibilities to family, community, and self.

Burnout

Veninga, R., and Spradley, J. *The work-stress connection: How to cope with job burnout.* Boston: Little, Brown, 1981.

Pines, A., and Aronson, E., with D. Kafry. *Burnout: From tedium to personal growth.* New York: Free Press, 1981.

> Identifying signs of burnout and how to cope with it.

Unemployment

Bolles, R. *What color is your parachute?* Berkeley, Calif.: Ten Speed Press, 1982.

> Useful, lively guide for job hunters and job-changers.

Ask Agatha

Dear Agatha:

I'm a Scorpio girl who is obsessed with sex. Since the age of 12 I've had many close brushes, but never finished making love (I'm 14 now). But I really want to. My boyfriend calls me a nympho and says we're too young to have sex. I can't talk to my mother. Do you think there is something wrong with me?

— Sexy Scorpio

Dear Agatha:

My wife has had a heart condition for fourteen years. At 71, I am as healthy and vigorous as a man half my age. A widow about 50 moved into our condominium and sometimes we like to go for walks and play cards. Yesterday, she asked me to kiss her after lunch, and I think she's making a play for me. I still love my wife, and I don't want to have an affair with this other woman. What should I do?

— Ft. Lauderdale Frank

Dear Agatha:

Ken and I are best friends. We like to take long walks, play sports, camp, and do everything else together. We have a lot of fun just by ourselves. My mother is beginning to bug me. She says he and I are seeing too much of each other and it's unnatural that two 19-year-olds should like to be with each other so much. I think she thinks we're queer but we're not. What do you think?

— Questioning in Riverside

Chapter Preview

CHAPTER 7
Loving Through the Life Cycle

Questions to think about

- How can you tell if you are in love?
- How many different types of loving can you think of?
- If you want to show affection to a friend of the same sex does this mean you have homosexual leanings?
- What are the characteristics of a successful marriage?

In the first chapter a short description of loving was offered. This chapter extends that portrayal to embrace a wider range of loving actions. These will include tender attachment to family, friendship, idealistic love, sexual desire, and romantic love. Each of these five kinds of love can provide pleasure at most stages of the life cycle. Some of these are illustrated by the letters to "Agatha" opening this chapter.

After defining love broadly, we look briefly at different types of love. Several basic needs are gratified through loving. Then we look at normal loving activities associated with phases of the life span from childhood through later adulthood. Differences in males' and females' experience of love are highlighted as they appear.

We then scrutinize factors that endanger satisfaction from loving. These include dealing with forces in the society that run counter to forming a pri-

The *Kiss* by sculptor Constan-
tine Brancusi. There are many
different types of love. Do
you think Brancusi meant to
portray romantic love, friendship, love between parent
and child, love between siblings, sexual love, or all of
these?

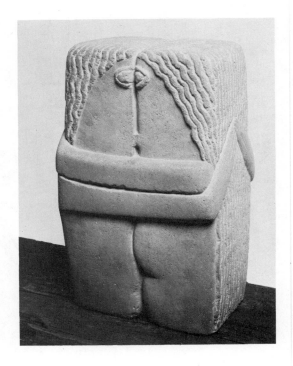

mary loving relationship. We also look at hazards to pleasure from loving that occur at specific periods of life. As we examine these hazards, we consider what can be done to anticipate and reduce their effect on our lives.

What Is Loving?

Love is a special type of relationship with another person. It is characterized by a feeling of warm affection and desire for attachment. It can include caring within family, friendship, idealistic love, and romantic love.

Loving is an active process. In his book *The Art of Loving*, Erich Fromm (1956) stresses the point that love is an act of giving, not receiving. Three false assumptions about love often interfere with our developing skill at loving. These are (1) loving means being loved; (2) loving is a function of who the object of our love is; and (3) loving is falling in love (Fromm, 1956). In fact, loving is not being loved but being able to express it toward someone else. Being able to love is not dependent upon being "turned on" by someone else tall, dark, and handsome; or blonde, buxom, and blue-eyed. Rather, it is an inner faculty for loving, which is within our power to express when we choose. Finally, we should not confuse the exhilarating experience of falling in love with staying in love. Being able to love means continuing to express warmth and affection, along with care, responsibility, and respect for the other, long after the excitement has passed (Fromm, 1947).

Types of Love

The study of love has a long past but a short history. Systematic study about types of love has only recently begun, so most of our insights come from philosophers, novelists, poets, and playwrights (Cunningham and Antil, 1981). Present thinking identifies five types of love: caring with family, friendship, idealistic love, sexual desire, and romance. Through most of our lives we obtain satisfaction from expressing love in one or more of these ways. We will look at each type of love in this chapter.

Caring Within Family

The first experience of loving someone else is within the family. Throughout our lives the family into which we are born and the family most of us create through marriage remain primary centers to express affection and caring.

Reciprocity in Infant-Parent Relationships at Three Weeks Old

In our lab at Children's Hospital in Boston, we . . . have been studying these patterns of interaction between small babies and their parents. . . . Clear differences show up as early as three to four weeks in the baby's response to his mother versus those to his father. For instance, with mother in sight, the baby is likely to set the pace of their interaction. His face will brighten, his hands and legs "reach" out toward her gently, curling back in a rhythmic smooth fashion. If we watch his face and eyes, we see that they brighten with an intensely interested look as his mother attempts to engage him, alternating with a dull look as he withdraws into himself. Often he rolls his limbs or averts his gaze in order to recover from the intense looks he gives her. . . . These cycles of intense looks alternating with withdrawal are going on at the rate of four per minute.

The mother, too, looks gentle and smooth as she softly plays vocal or facial games with her baby. These are rhythmic, too, and are directly tied with baby's rhythmic behaviors, following his alertness and withdrawal. As the infant becomes alert, the mother may vocalize softly or give a bright look or even a gentle gesture. . . . [O]ne sees that she is playing the infant's game, tuning in and out,

with her advances and withdrawals timed exquisitely to his. . . . My colleagues and I see this as the basis for baby's earliest ability to communicate socially. As the mother and baby respond to each other's rhythms, they are saying to each other that they are really in touch, locked in to each other at several levels.

[A] father is likely to set up a different pattern with his baby. . . . Fathers are much more likely . . . to excite the baby by heightening the rhythm of their interaction. A father is more likely to use rhythmic games of tickling or tapping on parts of the baby's body, often tapping right up the body to the face, in order to produce a heightened response from the baby. Exaggerated gestures or expressions seem to say, "Now let's play." At first the baby will watch the father's antics as if he were trying to adjust to them and take them in. His shoulders will hunch, and his eyebrows will become raised in eager anticipation. As he gets older, he will laugh out loud, bouncing up and down in his eagerness to continue this kind of playful interaction with his father.

SOURCE: Excerpted from the book *On becoming a family: The growth of attachment* by T. Berry Brazelton, M.D. Copyright © 1981 by T. Berry Brazelton. Reprinted by permission of Delacorte Press/Seymour Lawrence. A Merloyd Lawrence Book.

At what point does a child begin to express affection back toward the parents? Pediatrician T. Berry Brazelton (1981) provides some interesting observations about the responsiveness of one-month-old infants and their parents. Even at this age, the infant is able to distinguish between mother and father and respond differently to each. The infant's reactions to the parents were so distinctive that Dr. Brazelton and his colleagues could look only at a baby's toe or finger on a videotape, blocking out the rest of the picture, and accurately predict whether the baby was with the mother or father (Brazelton, 1981). This early response to each parent may be the first time we interact affectionately with others.

One of the experiences many of us have is the sense of returning to a rhythm of parent-child loving interaction when we see our parents after an absence; we invariably do or say something that triggers a response in our parents and is attended by a special sense of caring. In some families, these same special loving physical relationships exist with grandparents, aunts, uncles, and cousins, occurring throughout our lives.

As we grow into our own adulthood, most of our loving energy is directed toward the family we create through marriage and children. Until relatively recently, the need to care for aging parents had not been a significant problem for many adults. But as the population of people in their 70s, 80s, and 90s increases, so does the need to provide continuing emotional care for these older relatives (Figure 7.1).

As we grow older we become closer to our relatives. Sociologist Norman Shulman asked men and women who lived in Toronto, Canada, to name six people they were closest to. Overall, forty percent of the individuals named were kin (reported in Dickens and Perlman, 1981). Looking more closely at these data, Shulman found a connection between age and the number of relatives in the friendship network. We can see that among Shulman's subjects the proportion of relatives increased and nonrelatives decreased as these men and women grew older.

Table 7.1 Relatives among closest relationships ages 18– 65

AGE	PERCENTAGE REPORTING ONE OR MORE RELATIVES AMONG CLOSEST RELATIONSHIPS
18–30	60%
31–44	66%
45–65	77%

SOURCE: Adapted with permission from W. Dickens and D. Perlman, Friendship over the life-cycle, in S. Duck and R. Gilmore, eds., *Personal relationships, 2: Developing personal relationships*, p. 113. Copyright: 1981 Academic Press, Inc. (London) Ltd.

Friendship

Can you remember your first friend? What was special about that relationship? When two or more people who are neither lovers nor relatives are joined together in a benevolent bond, that is called **friendship.** We express friendship in many ways: through warm affection; providing understanding, sympathy, or support; reciprocal sharing of secrets; sometimes discussing thoughts, feelings, and fantasies; and finding pleasure in another's success and achievement.

Many of us marvel at the ability of a person we know to attract friends. If we go to a camp, party, or club where neither of us is known, within a few minutes that individual will be surrounded by people while we sit glumly by ourselves. Is it that these men and women emit a special aroma, or a homing signal that draws others to them? The answer is that the individuals who appear to be making friends effortlessly are, in fact, working hard at it. They have taken Fromm's principles to heart. Also, they are doing things that make them attractive to others. What might these be?

The ancient Greek philosopher Aristotle had an idea about why people are drawn to be friends with someone (Thomson, 1953). He said that friendships were based on pleasure, utility, or virtue. Things have not changed much in the 2500 years since. If someone gives pleasure — is informative, amusing, good company, or otherwise pleasant — we find ourselves drawn to that person. I might be attractive to you as a friend because of my utility — if I am an especially good listener, am willing to let you lead, play cards with you regularly, or can transport you in my car. The problem, of course, with friendships based on pleasure or utility is that after a while we become bored with someone who is merely pleasant or useful (we may no longer need the useful person's car). At this point, the friendships dissolve unless something else sustains them.

The "something else" is virtue, Aristotle's third condition for friendship. The mutual attraction in this type of friendship is based on the view of the other person as admirable rather than what he or she may contribute to our pleasure or ease of living. Affectionate bonds are built upon each one's thinking that the other is a good person who also seeks their mutual welfare.

Why do we make friends with this person instead of that one, who is equally pleasant, useful, or good? Dickens and Perlman (1981) list some of the reasons for picking specific friends. We like those who: (1) live near us, (2) are approximately the same age, (3) are of the same sex, (4) are physically attractive, (5) have personalities similar to our own, (6) have attitudes similar to our own, (7) like us. These reasons were given by groups ranging from children to senior citizens.

Idealistic Love

Menninger has said, "The world's greatest lovers have not been Don Juans and Casanovas but Schweitzers, Gandhis, Helen Kellers, and such Saints as Francis of Assisi." (1967 p. 365) The loving these people have expressed is altruistic, or idealistic, love. **Idealistic love** is a passionate concern with an abstract concept: adoration of God, celebration and protection of all life, fervent desire to help the needy, or love of nature. This type of loving has two primary features: altruism and passion.

Altruism is the renouncing of our own desires and replacing them with someone else's needs or the demands of a higher calling. This selflessness usually springs from the golden rule of doing for others what we wish would be done for us. This is part of the motive for giving ourselves to others. The other part typically has to do with the conviction that if we all behaved likewise, the world would be a far better place. At the extreme of altruistic love for others are doctors living and working in leper colonies, soldiers sacrificing themselves to save their buddies' lives, or missionaries who seek to convert cannibals to Christianity. A more domestic equivalent of this altruistic spirit might be found in religious men and women who work, and sometimes die, trying to calm the rage in the asphalt jungles of large cities, inspire nonviolent civil rights demonstrations, and establish sanctuaries for youngsters, battered wives, alcoholics, and the down-and-out.

On a less dramatic level, many of us express altruistic love in a variety of ways. I give directions to a blind woman who is lost, and you might stop at the side of the road at night to help an elderly couple change a tire. Also, altruistic love is exhibited by giving to charity. Among the men he studied, Vaillant (1977) found that better-adjusted men gave more to charity than those who were less well adapted.

Anyone who has heard a religious man tell of his love of God, seen a student teaching retarded children, talked to a Sierra Club member picketing a hearing about the damming up of another river in Colorado, or has read the latest antivivisection ads cannot help being impressed by the passion of idealistic love. Its fervor is as strong as the most intense feelings of romantic affection. To some extent this zealous love is a fuel that gives life meaning and purpose, just as caring within family and romantic love.

Sexual Desire

Sexual desire is a physical urge to stimulate our bodies to the point of orgasm. When we reach orgasm with another person, it can produce considerable pleasure.

Sexual urges are caused by both hormones — chemical agents in the bloodstream — and external stimulation (Sullivan, 1953). At puberty, certain hormones are secreted for the first time, or become present in greater amounts than before, and our sexual urges intensify (Tanner, 1971). These chemicals result in a buildup of seminal fluid in men, which presses for release through ejaculation. In females hormones cause a sexual restlessness just before and after the menstrual cycle. Hormones also are responsible for physical changes in all of us. For a young woman, the hormone is **estrogen,** which is secreted by the ovaries. This causes and maintains the development of secondary sexual features in females — breasts, pubic hair, widening of the hips, and beginning of the menstrual cycle. In boys, **androgen** is the agent of change. Produced by the testes in large amounts at puberty, androgen triggers the development of typical male secondary sexual characteristics — accelerated penis and scrotum growth, pubic hair, the beginnings of a beard, and deepening of the voice.

Sexual desire is more than chemistry. In order for sexual urges to be felt clearly, an external agent is usually needed to stimulate them. For one person it may be a picture in a magazine or a story, movie, or song; for another it may be a look, a touch, a thought, or a smell. For each of us, distinctive things trigger sexual excitement and the desire for release.

According to sex researchers and therapists William Masters and Virginia Johnson (1966), sexual drive toward release in fact consists of four distinguishable phases: (1) excitement, (2) plateau, (3) orgasm, and (4) resolution. In the excitement phase, nipples become erect, a flush spreads across the face and body, blood pressure increases, and muscles tense for both males and females. For a man, his penis becomes erect, and his testicles pull closer to the body. For a woman, her breasts enlarge, and the lips of her vagina engorge with blood to open the vaginal passage, and vaginal lubrication begins.

In the plateau phase, muscle tension increases, as do heart rate, blood pressure, and breathing. During this second stage, neither men nor women are likely to respond to any stimuli other than sexual ones. Both are moving toward release of the physical and psychic tension that has been building.

The orgasm is the shortest but the most intensely pleasurable of all the phases. It is experienced differently by males and females. For men, their ejaculation is a spasm felt in the penis; seminal fluid is propelled through the urethra and discharged — all in only a few seconds. For women, orgasm involves contraction of the muscles of the uterus and the orgasmic platform of the vagina. Figure 7.1 shows the usual pattern of sexual responses in males and females. While men tend to follow the same pattern and have only one orgasm, women vary. Masters and Johnson found three patterns of orgasm in women they studied. Pattern A is two orgasms, separated by a brief plateau phase in between. Pattern B is a number of orgasms of lower intensity. Women with Pattern C spend very little time in the plateau phase and move quickly toward a rapid, single orgasm.

The final phase of the sexual response cycle is resolution. Heavy perspiration is common. At this time, men return to their usual unaroused sexual state. Most men have difficulty becoming stimulated again without a period of relief. Most women, however, are capable of multiple orgasms and can easily be restimulated.

Sexual intercourse is a biological, not a loving, action when it is nothing more than orgasm with a casual partner. It becomes an expression of romantic love when sexual attraction draws two people together so other forms of love can grow.

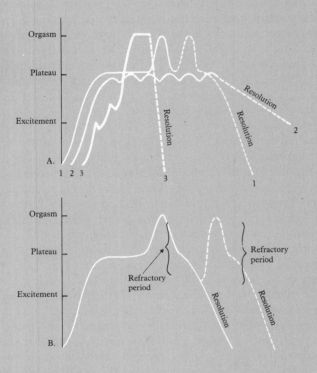

The Sexual Response Cycle

A. Three representative variations of female sexual response. Pattern 1 shows multiple orgasm; pattern 2 shows arousal that reaches the plateau level without going on to orgasm (note that resolution occurs very slowly); and pattern 3 shows several brief drops in the excitement phase followed by an even more rapid resolution phase.

B. The most typical pattern of male sexual response. The dotted lines shows one possible variation: a second orgasm and ejaculation occuring after the refractory period is over. Numerous other variations are possible, including patterns that would match 2 and 3 of the response cycle.

1. *Excitement* results from sexual stimulation which may be physical, psychological, or a combination of the two. It can be triggered not only by direct physical contact but by vision, smell, thought, or emotion.

2. In the *plateau* phase, high levels of sexual arousal are maintained and intensified, potentially setting the stage for orgasm.

3. *Orgasm* is the point where the body suddenly discharges its accumulated sexual tension, usually lasting for only a few seconds during which rhythmic muscular contractions produce intense physical sensations followed by rapid relaxation.

4. The period of return to the unaroused state is called the *resolution* phase. For females, the possibility exists for multiple orgasms, having additional orgasms without dropping below the plateau level. For males, the resolution phase includes a *refractory period* immediately after ejaculation, during which further orgasm or ejaculation is physically impossible.

Figure 7.1   Sexual response cycles in males and females

Romantic Love

Romantic love blends sexual desire with intimacy. Intimacy is a link between two people, which is characterized by "close and confidential communication . . . through nonverbal as well as verbal channels" (Rubin, Z., 1973, p. 214). Two people intimately involved with each other can communicate volumes with a touch, a glance, or a change in posture. While sexual desire refers to our individual feelings, intimacy describes a relationship between a loving couple rather than the two parties individually.

Intimacy does not preclude a unique existence separate from the loved one. As Fromm puts it, "In love the paradox is that two beings become one and yet remain two" (1956, p. 17). We can think of the notion of two people becoming one but remaining separate in mathematical terms. A fact in multiplication is that $1 \times 1 = 1$. Here we have two wholes, joined together to make another whole. Each is a whole, something already complete, and the greater whole they make constitutes their relationship. Neither is simply "half," but a whole thing in himself or herself, and each contributes a wholeness to the greater entity.

We should make a distinction between psychological intimacy and sexual intimacy. Two people may be deeply involved with each other, totally attuned to one another's needs, convictions, desires and frustrations, sharing dreams and experiences that no one else is a part of, and yet have no significant sexual contact.

We should distinguish also between sexual desire and romance. In his book *Love and Will*, psychologist Rollo May (1969) describes the difference between sexual passion and romantic love, which he calls "eros," this way:

> [T]he aim of the sex act . . . is indeed the orgasm. But the aim of eros is not: eros seeks union with the other person in delight and passion, and the procreating of new dimensions of experience which broaden and deepen the being of both persons. It is a common experience, backed up by folklore as well as the testimony of Freud and others, that after sexual release we tend to go to sleep — or, as the joke puts it, to get dressed to go home and *then* to sleep. But in eros, we want just the opposite: to stay awake thinking of the beloved, remembering, savoring, discovering ever-new facets of the prism of what the Chinese call "many-splendored" experience. (pp. 74–75)

Romantic love is an experience we wish to cling to, bask in, and desire to increase.

Like all descriptions of anything as complex as loving, this one may make distinctions that are hard to separate in real life. Moreover, a single instance of loving might include many types. In the act of sexual intercourse a couple may be gratifying sexual desires and also expressing caring within family, friendship, idealistic love, and romance.

According to the definition and description of love in this chapter, most affectionate behaviors expressed through the life span are nonsexual. If we wish to determine whether we are gaining sufficient pleasure from the loving sphere of our lives, we must look at our affection toward family members, toward contacts with friends, to romantic but celibate relationships, and even to our ability to care about an abstract ideal. These are far more reliable indicators of loving behavior than coitus.

Needs Gratified by Love

Throughout the life cycle three human needs are fulfilled through loving: preservation, social bonding, and competence. In every stage of life satisfaction comes from gratifying one or more of these basic urges.

Preservation

Loving relationships provide the basis for the biological preservation of the species and the social preservation of the larger community. At the level of biological preservation, loving between males and females results in sexual contact, leading to reproduction of their kind.

But if it were not for affectionate feelings between men and women and their offspring, the human species would not survive for long. Unlike other mammals, human babies need years of being cared for before they can live on their own. Scientists tell us that this caring, which preserves the species, goes back at least three-and-a-half million years (Johanson and Edey, 1981). When the first humans began to walk erect, the first nuclear family was possible. Roles could be specialized: females could remain in one place, creating a home, nurturing the young, and gathering; males could hunt more efficiently and successfully in groups to secure the food necessary for survival. The bonds of love that grow between pairs and among those in families eventually became a building block of society. Knit together, these loving units create a larger community.

Social Bonding

Did you ever go to a new neighborhood, town, school, or camp and find yourself temporarily without friends? How did you feel? You may have felt disconnected, lonely, unappreciated, and diminished in self-esteem. All forms of loving are a basis for social bonding, which diminishes these feelings. When our basic needs for food, shelter, and safety are taken care of, we recall what Maslow told us (see Figure 1.2 on page 11), that the next level is the need for love and belonging.

Love bonds us to society. It gives us a place and a function just as surely as a paid job. We locate ourselves in our world by whom we love. As a middle-aged man, I love my parents, spouse, children, and friends. To a large extent my life is anchored in this purpose. Without it I would feel less a part of my world.

Competence

To be able to love others is a source of competence. For some, self-confidence is rooted in having someone to love on a regular and intense basis. These individuals have taken to heart Fromm's advice (1956) that it is worthwhile to master the art of loving have mobilized the necessary discipline, patience, concentration, and concern for excellence to do it well. For these individuals, a home full of children, a club or church packed with friends, or a party with a few intimates gives them a chance to do something they do very well — love. When children, friends, and loved ones leave, a large part of the reason they feel upset is that there is no one for them to express caring for.

Loving and Adjustment

It has been said that behind every successful man stands a "good woman," or that "love cures all." These sayings reflect the conviction of the poet and philosopher that our loving relationships directly affect adjustment. Some research evidence and clinical observations support this thinking.

In Chapter 1, we cited some of Vaillant's work (1977) supporting the notion that the ability to love is tied in to adaptation level. Table 1.1 on page 16 shows that the best-adjusted of Vaillant's men had rich friendship patterns, had been married enjoyably for more than twenty years, and less often had youngsters with emotional and social problems. Looking more closely at his information, we see that there are dramatic differences in the psychological and physical adjustment of those with friends, stable marriages, and normal children, and those without them. Some of the dissimilarities in their adaptation are shown in Table 7.2.

The more loving men were close to their families but were not dominated by their mothers, coped with stress at a higher level, and evidenced less physical and mental disorder. From a psychiatrist's perspective, Karl Menninger

Table 7.2 Adjustment of more and less loving men

	MORE LOVING	LESS LOVING
Distant from family of origin	15%	39%
Distant from own children	13%	50%
Mother dominant in adult life	0%	54%
Immoderate use of drugs/alcohol	11%	39%
Chronically ill by age 52	4%	46%
Ever labeled psychiatrically ill	11%	54%
Immature defensive style	11%	85%

SOURCE: From *Adaptation from life* by George E. Vaillant. © 1977 by George E. Vaillant. By permission of Little, Brown and Company.

(1967) sees the importance of love in recovering from mental illness. He believes that "the establishment . . . of relationships with fellow human beings is the basic architecture of normal life." It is love that lays the groundwork for the ability to work and play.

Loving Through the Life Cycle

In the following sections we study normal loving activities that are specific to, or first appear at, each stage of the life cycle. Also, we note problems that interfere with gratification from loving and consider what we might do to minimize their effect.

Childhood

Surprisingly little interest has been shown by psychologists in the friendships and other loving relationships of children, though infancy and adolescence have otherwise received considerable attention (Giapa, 1981). In fact, at least three loving activities in this stage can be distinguished. These are (1) being the object of love, (2) developing friendships with peers, and (3) maintaining close relationships with parents.

Objects of Love. Being loved by parents is one of the most important, necessary experiences in human development. This is the origin of self-love, upon which the capacity to express affection toward others rests (Erikson, 1976; Fromm, 1956).

The mother-child relationship is central to the experience of being loved. Freud (1924) and others (Erikson, 1950) have argued that the way a mother expresses her love for a child is through breast-feeding. Reliable data indicate, however, that breast-feeding is not the essential element in an infant's adjustment and later capacity to love. Of far greater importance is the warmth of the mother-child relationship. In their extensive study of the effect of child-rearing patterns, Sears, Maccoby, and Levin (1957) found the warmer the mother's feelings for the infant, the better adjusted the child was later. This was true whether the child was breast-fed or not.

Clinical evidence supports the thinking that adult disturbances are directly related to being unloved during childhood. Loving relationships at every stage are important, however, for within each period lies the potential for healing previous maladaptations (Sullivan, 1953). If the absence of loving bonds persists into adolescence, the development of trust and self-love grows with much greater difficulty.

Developing Friendships with Peers. In childhood other youngsters increasingly become the focus of interpersonal activity. Friendships begin to develop at age 2, starting as parallel activity; for example, two 3-year-olds playing in the same room while their mothers talk. The final stage, mature friendship, is represented by a collaboration to satisfy mutual interests.

Selman and his colleagues (Selman and Jaquette, 1977) isolated five progressive stages of children's friendships, based on reasons youngsters give for why they want to play with another child.

Table 7.3 shows that as youngsters move through childhood their awareness of other boys and girls changes. At the first stage of development, about age 3 to 7, friends are seen as Momentary Playmates. They are valued for what they have and what they can do. At the second stage of development, from about age 4 to 9, the child thinks of friendship as One-Way Assistance. A friend is someone who does something good for the youngster.

Beginning about age 6 is the Fair-Weather Companion. Here for the first time friendship is understood in terms of cooperative behavior: "I'll be the sheriff and you be the outlaw" (Gesell *et al.*, 1940). By now children know they have to give to others to receive from them, but they see the purpose of the relationship as self-interest, not mutual sharing. At Selman's higher levels, friendship is seen as something based on intimate mutual sharing and moves toward more complex interdependence. These relationships will be discussed in the section on preadolescence.

In order for friendships with peers to continue to develop, the child needs to be able to cooperate with other children. This means managing to work amiably in spite of conflicting needs, competitiveness, and the occasional cruelty youngsters express toward each other. A 7-year-old boy learns to tolerate the disappointment of having to play soccer, at which he is not skilled, instead of football, where he usually stars, so everyone can participate. Important to getting along with one's peers is the ability to compete congenially, a willingness to compromise, and an understanding that when one wins others sometimes lose.

Close Contact with Parents. While youngsters continue to be largely the receptors of love, spontaneous affection toward parents and other adults begins

Table 7.3   Reasons for children's friendships: Four stages of growth

STAGE	AGE	REASON FOR FRIENDSHIP
0	(3–7)	Momentary physical playmate
1	(4–9)	One-way assistance
2	(6–12)	Fair-weather cooperation
3	(9–15)	Intimate mutual understanding
4	(12+)	Autonomous interdependence

SOURCE: Adapted by permission from Selman, R. and Jaquette, D., Stability and oscillation in interpersonal awareness: A clinical-development analysis. In E. Keasey, ed., *Nebraska symposium on motivation. 1977* Copyright © 1978 by the University of Nebraska Press.

to be apparent in later childhood. Crushes on teachers, who are seen as extensions of parents, develop. Childhood brings increasing closeness between children eager to please their parents and parents particularly responsive to them. During this time they identify uncritically with parental attitudes, affect their manners and dress, and share their activities (Gesell and Ilg, 1946). Perhaps this is why parents think back on the time prior to puberty as the golden years of child-rearing.

Widening experience with the world outside the family enables the child to perceive differences between the values and standards expressed at home and those maintained elsewhere. This perception leads to a good deal of questioning: "Our apartment is bigger than the Thompsons'; does this mean we're rich?" "Why aren't you thin like Carmen's mother?" "The Woodwards are Democrats but Jack says they aren't Communists; why does Daddy say all Democrats are Communists?" Questions like these make it plain to the parents that their days of controlling their children's experiences and opinions are over.

Preadolescence

Did you ever have a best friend in the years from 8 to 12? Do you remember what it was like? One of the two distinctive loving activities of preadolescence, a critical interpersonal event for this stage, is finding a best friend. The second loving activity is remaining connected to adult-controlled groups.

Finding a Best Friend. Toward the end of childhood, a youngster moves from friendships based on cooperation to a far more intense involvement with an individual. Selman shows this as stage 3: intimate mutual understanding (see Table 7.3). Friendship for the first time becomes truly mutual. Typically this friendship is with **a best friend** of the same sex. The quality of this experience is described by psychiatrist Harry Stack Sullivan:

> . . . A new type of sentiment is developed, and there is a new development within the sentiment of self. It is no longer enough that the other one contributes reflections favorable to one's self-esteem. It becomes more important to contribute to the self-esteem of the other, and one's own pleasure becomes secondary to the satisfaction at causing pleasure to the friend (1972, p. 163).

The best friend provides the first experience of collaboration, of sensitivity and concern for the welfare of someone else, and a willingness to help that person do things to make him or her happy without the thought of personal gain.

Best friends are happiest when they're together. No one can possibly replace that special individual. A mother notes that her 10-year-old's birthday party consists of six best-friend duos, who come and leave together, sit in the same chair, hold hands, and generally seem only to have eyes for each other.

Youngsters often find their best friends in Little League sports, recreational programs, camp, Scouts, Sunday School, and so forth. A best friend is invaluable at this age because the intimate sharing between these preadolescents is the basis of the ability to express appropriate loving behavior later on. Without a chum, the learning of loving skills is delayed. A best friend can help relieve loneliness and isolation, which first appear at this stage of life (Sullivan, 1953). The sense of "we-ness" emerging from the preadolescent friendship greatly diminishes the feeling of being alone. Also, this friend makes it easier to become part of a large group because it is easier to join a gang as part of a best-friend duo.

Suppose you are 10 and do not have a best friend and want one badly. What are the qualities which might attract other children to you? Four have been identified among children, preadolescents and adolescents: conventional morality; mutual activities; empathic understanding; and loyalty and commitment (Giapa, 1981). As the name implies, the quality *conventional morality* refers to friends playing fairly, avoiding trouble with adults, not being "phony," and not liking someone else. The second quality, *mutual activities*, is based on a friend's enjoying the same games, sports or other interests. *Empathic understanding* is the feeling that a friend is someone who can be trusted with secrets and will give help to make the other person feel better. *Loyalty and commitment* is a willingness to stand by the other person in time of need and not share this exclusive intimacy with anyone else. These qualities are not much different from those that bind friends of any age.

Having a best friend is the most important new loving activity for the preadolescent. For the first time the happiness and welfare of an equal is as important as the youngster's own.

Remaining Connected to Adult-Controlled Groups. Just as young people have to develop the ability to collaborate with their peers, they also must learn to cooperate so as to function comfortably within adult-controlled groups. They need to learn to behave according to the prescriptions of teachers, church leaders, playground directors, coaches, camp counselors, and later on, employers. This doesn't necessarily mean that youngsters have to love these grown-ups — though this occurs regularly. What is crucial is that a girl or boy does not alienate adults who then retaliate by banishing them from a group where their friends are.

Problems begin between preadolescents and adults when the youngsters behave provocatively. Older Boy Scouts bedevil their leaders by bringing fireworks and cigarettes on camping trips. Seventh-graders mutter unintelligible things to each other, just out of the hearing of a teacher to cause irritation. Park league basketball players smirk at something a coach tells them, to drive him into a rage.

The questions of these young people seem increasingly aimed at revealing inconsistency, inaccuracy, hypocriticalness, or irritability in adults they know. This provocative behavior usually is intended to demonstrate the emerging competence and separateness of the young person, rather than to hurt the feelings of or to enrage adults. However, harm is often done. Some adults can become so upset they banish the youngsters from the group. This hurts the development of youngsters in two ways. First, it cuts them off from their peers; second, it is in the best interests of the young to stay in contact — even acrimonious contact — with grown-ups. A 14-year-old is not the best guide of another 14-year-old. As difficult as it sometimes can be, having an older person to knock around with — even knock up against — helps adolescents clarify values and attitudes that affect lifelong behavior patterns.

Adolescence

The loving actions that usually make their first appearance in the teenage years are involvement in a gang, altruism, and the first big romance.

Involvement with a Gang. Gang membership is important in adolescence. These young people band together for collaboration, mutual support, protection from isolation, exchange of information, assistance in being independent, and a sense of identity. Younger adolescents will say that their friends mean almost as much to them as their parents do. They can tell the members of their gang "everything," and it will be understood. Moreover, the group members will do *anything* for each other. A lot of what young people learn about the world they learn from each other in gangs (for example, much information and misinformation about sex is exchanged).

The gang reinforces the individual's increasingly strong quest for independence from parents. "But everyone's doing it!" is the usual argument parents hear from their teenagers to justify the clothes they wear, consuming instant breakfasts, staying out late, cutting school on Friday afternoon, or smoking dope.

Gangs have been classified with names that give a one-dimensional view of their members' identity: "jocks," "brains," "greasers," or "heads." In high-school gangs, the boys and girls will dress similarly and use phrases and gestures intelligible only to the inner circle of the gang. They share the same interests, prejudices, and activities.

Though gangs work well enough in helping adolescents feel connected to others, they often obscure or make difficult real variations among individuals. Anything that causes a young person to stand out as different from other group members may be a threat to his or her continuing membership in the gang. An example is getting good grades in school. Unless a student is in a clique in which high marks are acceptable, a gang member may minimize his or her accomplishments rather than stand out and risk being ostracized (Coleman, 1961). Another alternative is to perform at the level of the peer group. This may be one reason grades of many students drop so dramatically in the middle school years.

Being without friends at any time in life is a serious problem. In adolescence, however, not belonging to a group of friends can be devastating. Suppose you move to a new place where you don't know anyone. How can you go about making friends? Some psychologists suggest that one set specific goals to improve one's relationships with others and then monitor the progress toward these goals (Royce and Arkowitz, 1978). This approach involves graded steps moving week by week from practicing interpersonal relationships to eventually inviting acquaintances over to one's own place (Table 7.4). Obviously, each person might have slightly different goals for each week, and the order might be dissimilar. What is important to remember in setting and monitoring goals for making friends is that one must be willing to take risks in order to achieve the desired outcome: making friends.

Altruism. Altruism typically appears first in adolescence. Teens manifest this selfless concern for principles or others in fervent church-going, in commitment to being a missionary, in volunteer work at a nursing home, or in crusades to save baby seals from pelt-hunters. These activities are a form of idealistic love characterized by both selflessness and passion. Young people who become involved in these altruistic expressions will tell us that they love God, old people, or all living things. The gleam in their eye and the intensity with which they speak tells us they mean it.

It is probably no accident that books such as Dickens's *Tale of Two Cities* (1859) has such appeal to adolescents. The selflessness demonstrated by Sidney Carton going to the guillotine in the place of Charles Darnay for the sake of the woman he loved resonates with the desire of many young people to give themselves completely out of idealistic love.

Finding Outlets for Sexual Desire. An undeniable reality of adolescence is the growth in the intensity of sexual desires that press increasingly for release (Sullivan, 1953). Finding suitable outlets for these urges can be a difficult task for the adolescent.

The main hindrance is that primary emotional ties are with the gang of

Table 7.4   Making friends: A systematic approach of setting and monitoring goals

WEEKLY GOAL	OVERALL GOAL
	TO MAKE TWO FRIENDS
Week 1:	□ Purchase a book on how to make friends
	□ Practice in the mirror talking to others, recording and playing back imaginary conversations
Week 2:	□ Join folk dancing group
	□ Go to church and stay afterward for coffee
Week 3:	□ Continue with folk dancing and join another comparable activity
	□ Go to a young people's church picnic
	□ Engage in casual conversation with at least three people, expressing what I feel and think
	□ Make a phone call to two people for information
Week 4:	□ Invite one person every other day to do something on the spur of the moment — attend a game, go to a movie, have a cup of coffee, go for a ride
	□ Make an effort to be pleasant, useful, or interested in another's welfare
	□ Call four people for casual conversation
Week 5:	□ Invite several members from the folk dance and church group to my place afterwards for a snack
	□ Plan a party

Inspired by Royce, W. and Aukowitz, H. "Multi-modal evaluation of practice interaction as treatment for social isolation." *Journal of Consulting and Clinical Psychology*, 1978, *46*, 239–245.

same-sex adolescents. Increasingly, however, the young person would like to experience sexual gratification with the risk of being cast out of the group. This means that he or she approaches other packs of boys or girls as a gang member. This works against one-to-one contact, except at a superficial, generally unsatisfying level. As a result, masturbation is a regular outlet for sexual urges through adolescence.

Homosexual exploration is another avenue of sexual release for one teenager in ten (Sorenson, 1971). Little reliable information exists, though, on the number of adolescents who then go on to an exclusively gay sexual orientation; clinical experience suggests most do not. Presently, about five percent of adults report being gay (Butler, 1979). One study of homosexuals in the San Francisco Bay area found that the average age of the first homosexual experience was 22, with less than forty percent of the individuals reporting their

initial affair at 19 or younger (Bell and Weinberg, 1978). This research confirmed the findings of other reports, noting that about half the individuals who
say they are gay also had sexual relations with the opposite sex.

Some adolescents react with guilt to growing sexual desires. Psychoanalyst
Karen Horney (1935) noted four types of personality changes among teenage
girls in reaction to the guilt they feel about sexual feelings:

1. Developing an aversion to the erotic sphere; instead becoming intensely
   absorbed in religion, ethical, artistic, or scientific pursuits.
2. Becoming intensely absorbed in the opposite sex; interest in and capacity
   for schoolwork declines rapidly.
3. Becoming detached and aloof; nothing matters much.
4. Turning away from heterosexual relations and developing intense friendships with the same sex.

Horney's observations seem just as appropriate for boys as for girls trying to
cope with their sexual urges.

An enormous variation exists in rate, tempo, and sequence with which
physical development happens in adolescence (Tanner, 1971). Girls mature
more rapidly than boys, typically one to two years earlier. Striking differences
occur among 13-year-old girls and 15-year-old boys. One girl may be completely mature physically, while her best friend is not yet in a training bra. On
a ninth-grade basketball team we might have one player 6 feet, 4 inches tall —
who has been shaving for a year — playing with a prepubescent lad a foot
shorter and seemingly light-years behind him developmentally. This physical
diversity can be correlated with differing sexual drives, which tend to cause
the more mature adolescents to feel guilty and uncomfortable, and the less
advanced to feel left out and envious.

The First Big Romance. Most young people have their first big romance during their teens. It meets all the criteria for a loving relationship, blending
sexual sharing, attachment, caring, and intimacy. The two date each other,
plan events for a lengthening future, grow increasingly closer emotionally and
physically, feel bereft without the actual presence of the other. For these two,
their romance features powerful emotions they have not experienced before.
Because of the freshness of it, and to some degree because of the anxiety associated with these emotions, they may never feel the same powerful sensations again.

Many adolescents ask themselves, "How will I know I'm in love?" Others
wonder if they can tell the difference between love and a relationship based on
friendship, mutual interests, sex, or just liking someone. Psychologist Zick
Rubin (1973) developed a series of questions which discriminate "liking" from
"loving." The sample questions Rubin uses to measure liking and loving shown
in Table 7.5 indicate the differences. Liking is based on respect and admiration. Love, on the other hand, is made up of attachment, caring, and intimacy.

Most loving relationships begin as friendships between a man and a woman. At some point the two cross over the threshold and they tell each other, "I love you." Where is that point? British psychologists John Cunningham and John Antill (1981) identified five areas in which feelings change as a couple moves from like to love. As Table 7.6 tells us, feelings in four areas undergo a shift: *equity* — less monitoring of who owes or is owed; *equality* — seeing each other as equals and interdependent, despite any objective assessment that they are unequal; *shared identity* — a "we-feeling" and a sharing of the other's pain and pleasure; and *selflessness* — pleasure in giving to the other no matter how costly.

The first romance brings the possibility of a unique understanding of the self, which comes from being together. Erikson (1950) has said that a romantic attachment enables adolescent lovers to arrive at a clearer definition of their own identity by using the other person to understand themselves. "This is why," he says, "many a youth would rather converse and settle matters of mutual identity than embrace." This is not to say that adolescents prefer talking to embracing. A survey of sexual behavior of teenagers reported that seventy-two percent of the boys and fifty-two percent of the girls reported having experienced sexual intercourse (Sorenson, 1973).

A recent survey comparing sexual behaviors of adolescents now with earlier periods reveals several patterns (Wagner, 1980). First, teenagers vary tremendously in their sexual activity. For instance, the percentage of 14- and 15-year-old adolescents reporting having had premarital intercourse ranged from five to twenty-six percent for females and eight to ninety-four percent for males. Among 16- to 17-year-olds the figures are twenty to forty percent for females and twenty-one to one hundred percent for males. Generally, teenagers who are closer to their parents, are religious, and experience later puberty are more likely to remain virgins longer than those who are more influenced by peers, are less religious, and place a higher value on independence.

The second pattern is that physical sexual expressions — light petting, heavy petting, and intercourse — are occurring at an earlier age than a decade

Table 7.5 Am I in like or love? Sample questions measuring differences between liking and loving

LIKING SCALE	LOVING SCALE
1. I would highly recommend ——— for a responsible job.	1. I feel that I can confide in ——— about virtually anything.
2. I have great confidence in ——— 's good judgment.	2. I would do almost anything for ———.
3. ——— is one of the most likable people I know.	3. If I could never be with ———, I would feel miserable.

SOURCE: From Z. Rubin, Measurement of romantic love, *Journal of Personality and Social Psychology* 16 (1970), 265–273. Copyright 1970 by the American Psychological Association. Reprinted by permission.

The first big romance —
where anything and every-
thing is enjoyed because it is
shared with a loved one —
often occurs in adolescence.

ago. Increase in coitus among teenagers is confirmed by evidence showing five times as many of them seeking contraceptive advice from clinics and doctors in 1975 as in 1969. In spite of this, pregnancy among adolescent girls is on the increase and venereal disease among 15- to 19-year-olds is at an all-time high.

A third pattern is that changes in sexual activity have been greater among females than males. The percentage of 15- to 19-year-old males who are sexually active has not changed in a quarter of a century. But the percentage of females who report having had intercourse has just about doubled in this same period. The reasons given for greater sexual activity among teenage women are more equality between the sexes and the adoption of the standard that permits sexual relations when an affectionate bond exists between an adolescent couple.

In many ways, these teenage intimacies resemble the best-friend relationship except that sex is now part of it. The same intense affection, idealization, selfless concern, and pleasure in collaboration characterize this bond. There is exquisite joy in sharing experiences together — the beauty of the sun setting on a lake, the smell of freshly cut grass, the taste of an ice cream cone. Everything shared with the loved one is enriched. On the other hand, being apart is often painful. When the girl accompanies her parents on a two-week summer vacation, she feels as though part of her body has been severed.

Table 7.6   Moving from like to love: Five change points

	LIKING	LOVING
1. Feelings about equity	Keeping score, assessing continually, who has over- or under-benefited and restoring equity.	Far less keeping tabs on who gave and who took.
2. Feelings about equality	Status and ability differences clearly perceived, a sense of partners being of unequal worth.	Greater respect for each other as equals and as interdependent.
3. Feelings about shared identity	Sense of separate identities and responses to own successes or failures far greater than to same events in other's life.	Strong "we-feelings," pleasure and pain in response to events in lover's life nearly as strong as reactions to happenings in our own.
4. Feelings of selflessness	Acts benefiting the other are acceptable, so long as they are reciprocated.	Acts benefiting the loved one are rewarding in themselves.

SOURCE: From Cunningham, J. and Antill, J. Love in developing relationships. In S. Duck and R. Gilmore (Eds.), *Personal relationships. 2: Developing personal relationships.* London: Academic Press Inc. (London) Ltd., 1981, pp. 31–33. Adapted by permission.

A hazard of this romantic attachment is to become so dependent upon the lover that the sense of self is dissolved. In *Love and Addiction*, Peele and Brodsky (1975) speculate that some individuals need to be involved romantically the way drug-dependent people need a fix in order to cope with the stresses in their life. These individuals require the loved one's attention at all times in order to make their lives bearable. Threat of withdrawal of this love creates a constant craving. Peele and Brodsky propose six criteria that distinguish a romantic relationship from an addictive one.

Youth

The loving activities unique to this bridging period, between adolescence and early adulthood, are moving a maximum distance from parents, acquiring a widening circle of diverse friends, living together, and forming a primary bond.

Maximum Distance from Parents. The ability to distance oneself from parents or other key adults sets the stage for other growth in loving. The distance traveled between the self and parents, in both psychological and physical terms, is greatest in youth. Ties with parents continue the process of loosening begun in earlier eras. The questioning and provocative behavior gives way to a more finely tuned perception of adults as individuals. Instead of seeing them as wonderful or demonic, young people begin to see grown-ups as three-dimensional figures with neither flaws that undermine the young person's developing sense of identity nor capabilities that overpower or stunt the young person's growth.

Sometimes the distance is physical, as young people go away to college in other parts of the country, join the Navy to see the world, take jobs in far-flung outposts, or backpack through China. Parents often feel the lengthening distance more than their offspring do. They struggle with competing inner arguments to let go and hold on.

Without this separation, normal maturation is impeded. After graduation, Walter found that his take-home pay made it impossible for him financially to live on his own. While he was happy with his work, his relationship with his mother began to deteriorate. She didn't like his coming and going at all hours, his new friends stopping by for a few beers after work, and what appeared to her to be a breakdown in his morals and values. If these same activities were going on in college, the Army, or a job somewhere else, his mother probably wouldn't have minded so much.

Widening Circle of Friends. The kinds of friends that young people make during this time of life are somewhat different from the kinds they made in adolescence. Adolescents tend to make friends of people who share their values and attitudes. Young people now choose their friends differently: "[T]he individual can relate warmly to others that are different from him, valuing them for their dissimilarities from himself." (Keniston, 1971)

A fact of life for every youth is losing old friends. This happens when too much time and distance come between people. It happens when old friends don't fit with new ones, or old friends drift away because they can't accept one's own changes in attitude, behavior, or even success. Since old friends connect us with our past, the breakdown of these affiliations can result in moments of depression and apathy. This can be especially difficult for upwardly mobile individuals who move away from their geographical and interpersonal roots as they achieve success.

Criteria for Love vs. Addiction

1. Does each lover have a secure belief in his or her own value?

2. Are the lovers improved by the relationship? By some outside measure, are they better, stronger, more attractive, accomplished, or sensitive individuals?

3. Do the lovers maintain serious interests outside the relationship, including other meaningful personal relations?

4. Is the relationship integrated into, rather than set off from, the totality of the lovers' lives?

5. Are the lovers beyond being possessive or jealous of each other's growth and expressions of interests?

6. Are the lovers also friends? Would they seek each other out if they ceased to become primary partners?

SOURCE: Adapted from Peele, S. and Brodsky, A. *Love and Addiction.* New York: New American Library, 1975, pp. 83–84.

Living Together. A growing number of young people choose to live together without being married. In a summary of the numerous studies about living together, Butler (1979) reported that twenty to fifty percent of young people living in large cities were cohabiting. The incidence of college students sharing a bedroom regularly with someone of the opposite sex varies from five to fifty percent but appears to be increasing (Middleton and Roarke, 1981). Some male and female friends prefer to room with each other instead of strangers. This may be in pairs or in a communal setting. In some cases the cohabitation is not romantic, each member of the couple going elsewhere for that. Many young people, however, begin as friends and become lovers.

The advantages of living together often cited are (1) the security of a predictable friend and sexual partner; (2) convenience, efficiency, and cost-effectiveness; and (3) trying out a relationship without the legal problems of marriage. Several minor and major problems are associated with living together. Two minor difficulties are anxiety about telling parents and what to call the person with whom one is living. After several years of living together many young people still have not told their parents about the arrangement because they don't want to upset them.

Some devise complex deceptions. A student at a large southwestern university advertises her service as a "roommate" for college women who are reluctant to tell their parents they are living with a man. For twenty-five dollars a month she supplies an address, forwards letters, and answers parental telephone calls — explaining that their daughter is "out" and will return the call as soon as she returns. For an additional fee, the young entrepreneur allows her clients to move in with her when their parents visit (Middleton and Roarke, 1981).

Eventually, live-in lovers are introduced to parents, professors, and bosses. This brings up a second minor question — what to call them. One solution is contained in the acronym **POSSLQ.**

More serious problems exist with nonmarital unions. Living together is not a trial marriage. Aside from the problems of leases, money management, and dealing with relatives, anxiety about the future is usually present but not discussed. Typically it is the female who begins to wonder when the male will want to marry her. However, she feels too constrained by their living arrangements to bring the topic up directly. Rarely is there a verbalized joint commitment to a future beyond a college term or the expiration of the lease.

In living together there is less often a sense of shared ownership of resources. This can result in compulsive record keeping about who owes how much for what or obsessive thoughts of splitting everything down the middle. It can also result in hurt feelings when one partner spends money from a tax refund on a new stereo without consulting the other.

It may be that some of these pressures are responsible for the decrease in romantic feelings among unmarried couples living together. A study of young men and women who were dating, living together, or married, showed slight differences in measures of romance, loving, and liking (Table 7.7). Overall,

There's Nothing That I Wouldn't Do If You Would Be My POSSLQ

Rich as the English language is, it does not have a word for everything. For years it has been evident that no term exists to describe — much less introduce — the person of the opposite sex with whom we are living. Do we say, "Mom, meet Julia, my roommate"? That doesn't quite do justice to the complexity of the relationship, but if we say to our boss, "I'd like to introduce my lover, Brian" that might go too far. We are left with a group of verbal alternatives which are equally unsatisfactory: "fiancé" goes too far, "boyfriend" not far enough, and "affiliate" sounds like part of an industrial conglomerate. A word has been invented to describe this relationship by — of all organizations — the United States Bureau of the Census. The word is POSSLQ — an acronym the Census Bureau uses to stand for "*P*erson of the *O*pposite *S*ex *S*haring *L*iving *Q*uarters." Precise, business-like, and non-judgmental, this is the word many have been looking for. Now we can say to our mother, "Meet Joanne, my posslq," or to our boss, "This is Bill. We're posslqs."

SOURCE: Adapted from Osgood, C. *There's nothing that I wouldn't do if you would be my POSSLQ.* New York: Holt, Rinehart and Winston, 1981, p. 179.

the daters were more romantic than married couples but both had higher romance scores than cohabitors. The married pairs scored highest on measures of liking and loving, with the daters second and couples living together finishing last. While the magnitude of these differences is small, they are significant in reflecting the strain that living together places on romantic feelings. It is interesting to note that for both daters and cohabitors the probability of marriage increases the love in the relationship.

Forming a Primary Bond. The loving activity of greatest significance for young people — and signaling the beginning of the end of youth — is forming a primary bond. This is the establishment of an exclusive relationship with a loved one that results in a mutual commitment of affection, interdependence, and the sharing of future plans. Typically these begin as romantic relationships — with a difference. The difference is that by this time most young men and women have been in love before, have had a number of brief encounters, and, for some, have been involved in long-term liaisons. They know now that love is a two-edged sword (Goethals, 1973). On one hand they know the ecstasy being in love can bring. On the other, they have emotional scars to show how much pain breaking up with a lover can bring. For many young people a wariness to put themselves in "harm's way" — to fall in love again — remains. But most do. And the romantic feelings can be as strong or stronger than ever before.

While the primary bond between youthful men and women eventually blends sexual satisfaction with pleasure from other forms of love, some evidence suggests that a "go slow" attitude about intercourse is associated with greater romantic feelings and progress towards marriage. To those who applauded the growing freedom of sexual expression between men and women

Table 7.7 Romance among daters, cohabitors, and married young men and women

	DATERS	COHABITORS	MARRIEDS
Number of couples	70	96	117
Male's age	23.8	29.4	32.3
Female's age	22.6	25.6	29.5
Male's romanticism score	19.5	18.0	18.7
Female's romanticism score	19.6	17.1	18.2
Male's liking score	52.7	51.0	54.1
Female's liking score	55.3	51.7	54.2
Male's love score	56.7	55.7	58.9
Female's love score	58.8	55.9	59.3

SOURCE: From Cunningham, J. and Antill, J. Love in developing relationships. In S. Duck and R. Gilmore (Eds.), *Personal relationships. 2: Developing personal relationships.* London: Academic Press Inc. (London) Ltd., 1981, p. 44. Adapted by permission.

in the decades of the sixties and seventies, this may seem like heresy. The facts do indicate, however, that at this time of life a more conservative attitude towards sex before marriage, or at least before commitment to the possibility of marriage, is associated with stronger ties between the partners and greater interdependence (Cunningham and Antill, 1981).

Indeed, a counter-wave has been forming recently opposing the notion that free and easy sexual relations make for better, healthier, loving relationships. More and more people, many of them in their 20s, are choosing to be celibate. In her book *The New Celibacy*, Gabrielle Brown (1980) notes that while virginity was an embarrassment a decade ago for many women, it is now staging a revival. Both males and females are less willing to be pressed into sexual affairs when no other forms of caring exist. Other women and men who "put sex first" in a relationship report increasing disillusionment. They thought they were starved for sex and found they were starved for love. After a period of sexual activity they then become scrupulously chaste, saving further sex for marriage or for a stable, primary bond with someone.

During the period in which the primary bond is forming — some call this "courtship" — the relationship can take on several remarkable features. Goethals (1980) described some of them this way:

1. The relationship generates continued change — in the individuals themselves and in the couple.
2. Empathy grows — nothing has to be worked on.
3. There is a lower amount of sexual or social stereotyping and far greater role sharing.
4. The sexual relationship becomes exclusive by fact rather than by agreement and develops great power and scope.

When the couple feel themselves growing as a result of this bond, experience powerful empathy for each other, and desire to collaborate for a shared future, the resulting sexual passion between them can be intense. This is because the sexual act is a way of expressing the intellectual and emotional contact that already exists (Goethals, 1980).

Major factors working against settling down with one person and forming a primary bond are the prevailing myths about love in the American culture. These myths espouse independence, flexibility, and personal fulfillment and oppose commitment, intimacy, and settling down. Ann Swidler (1980) distinguishes four sources of tension in loving relationships that cause difficulty in forming a primary bond in the American culture. They are shown in Table 7.8.

Forsaking an intimate loving relationship because of the fear of limiting our growth or experience overlooks some of the creative possibilities in a pri-

---

How to Be Celibate: Taking a Vacation from Sex

□ It's not a diet or an exercise. It's a vacation from sex. So think of it as a vacation.

□ During a vacation, you can expect to feel more rested, more relaxed, less pressured, more open to new experiences. You can expect the same from celibacy.

□ During a vacation, you try new activities that you don't ordinarily try at home. During a period of celibacy, there are some things you can do that you can't when you're involved sexually:

— You can express all your *other* feelings.

— You can plunge into your work or your other interests without distraction or guilt.

— You can forget about birth control and still miss a period.

— You can dine with a friend and (1) eat as much as you want, (2) meet someone else afterward, (3) go home alone.

— You can become intimate friends with your intimates without negotiations.

— You can fall in love all over again, enjoy romance, court and be courted.

— While you are celibate, you can play with sexually active people.

□ Don't tell everyone you are celibate. The resulting onslaught of sexual advances, no matter how subtle, will knock you out. The challenge is just too much for most sexually active people.

□ Don't tell your parents that you are celibate if they are just getting used to your having sex. It's not fair.

□ Celibacy by choice versus celibacy by default: It's best to decide that you want to take a vacation. Getting fired from work is not the same thing.

□ Enjoy yourself. You'll probably have a lot of energy for a lot of things you've been thinking about doing.

□ If sexual thoughts come up, don't attend to them. There's no sense being celibate if you make it a big strain on yourself. Thinking about sex constantly can be just as sexual as having sex. And not as rewarding.

□ You can be celibate for as long a time as you want to be — for a week, a month, a year, or more. When you do return from vacation, everything will look fresh and new again.

SOURCE: From Gabrielle Brown, *The new celibacy: Why more men and women are abstaining from sex — and enjoying it.* Copyright © 1980 by Gabrielle Brown. Reprinted by permission of McGraw-Hill Book Company.

Table 7.8   Prevailing myths that impede the formation of a loving bond

1. *The tension between choice and commitment:* We can't remain faithful to one partner and continue to grow as individuals. A choice to make a commitment to one person may mean stagnation, not living happily ever after.
2. *The tension between rebellion and attachment:* A loving bond may make it easier to be independent of family, background, and constraints of the past. But using love to support the quest for autonomy may be trading one form of dependence for another.
3. *The tension between self-realization and self-sacrifice:* Marriage involves willingness to put aside personal desires to give to loved ones. Self-realization, however, requires more than finding personal satisfaction in giving to others.
4. *The tension between sexual expression and sexual restraint:* A primary bond requires sexual expression be limited to the loved one, but many believe that sex should be shared with others for whom affection is felt.

SOURCE: From Ann Swidler, Love and adulthood in American culture in *Themes of work and love in adulthood*, Neil J. Smelser and Erik H. Erikson. © 1980 by The President and Fellows of Harvard College. Reprinted by permission of Harvard University Press.

mary loving bond. Swidler (1980) observes that love provides a crucible in which our identities continue to develop, partially through continuing choice to remain with the loved one. The loving relationship can support a shared rebellious streak and open us to new people, jobs, and experience. It is easier to be adventuresome with a loved one. Giving to others, as long as it is not exploitive, can be a basis for enormous satisfaction. And sexual restraint deepens and intensifies loving contacts.

As the primary bond strengthens, each person develops greater respect for the autonomy of the other and feels less need to share everything and intrude into every corner of the other's experience. Loving endures in the physical absence of the loved one. The primary bond provides both with security, esteem, and a stable pattern of sexual satisfaction. This is a prerequisite for moving into early adulthood.

Early Adulthood

The loving activities that appear first in early adulthood are sharing a dream, getting married or finding an acceptable alternative, and caring for children.

Sharing a Dream. An outcome of a loving bond in early adulthood is having someone with whom to share a dream. A young adult couple can find enormous pleasure in imagining a life in the future together, especially when this is blended with an already existing romantic, tender, sexual affection. The dream can have a specific shape — the young man will finish college and go to law school while the young woman works; when he has a job with a particular type of firm, in a specific town, she will finish her education, get pregnant, have three children, and return to work when the last child enters third grade.

Or a dream can be a more general agreement — both decide to postpone discussions of vocation, location, and children until a later date. This shared dream based on a loving relationship organizes the activities and affects the choices, attitudes, and values of the young adult more than any other single element.

The dream shared by both partners cushions the hardships of early adulthood. The absence of such a vision of a future, or disagreement about future goals and life style toward which a couple is working, makes present sacrifices difficult to bear. The lack of a shared dream, or a unilateral change by one of the partners, fractures many loving relationships.

Marriage. Most loving behaviors occur within the context of marriage. In spite of the rising divorce rate and tendency for men and women to live together without being married, ninety-six percent of Americans eventually marry. This is a larger percentage than at any other time in history (Bane, 1975).

More and more men and women are waiting until they are in their thirties before they have children. Yet producing and caring for children remains a key loving event for young adult men and women.

How long does it usually take for a relationship to progress from the first casual date to marriage? What are the different patterns? A group of psychologists interviewed individually men and women from a hundred couples and asked them to graph their courtship (Houston, Surra, Fitzgerald, and Cate, 1981). Strong agreement was found between members of each couple as to how their relationship progressed. Four patterns are shown in Figure 7.2. From Figure 7.2 we can see that there are two types of accelerated courtships. The *accelerated – arrested* pattern starts fast, moves quickly to a high probability of marriage, at about two and a half months loses momentum, and then proceeds to a marital commitment at about fourteen months. *Accelerated* courtship ac-

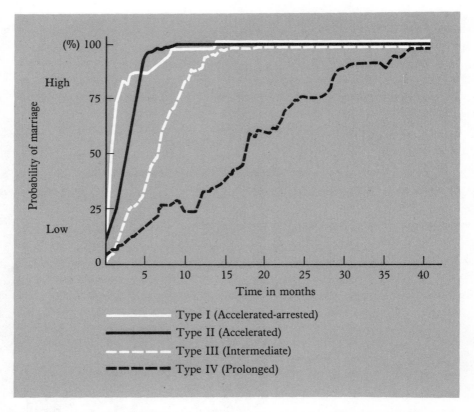

Figure 7.2 Time and pattern of courtship. *Each member of 100 couples was interviewed to construct a graph describing their courtship. The average age for the women was 22 and for the men 24. The individuals were asked to estimate their perception of the probability that they would marry their spouse from the first meeting onward. For example, on the first date, they might estimate the chance of marrying that person at zero, and just before their wedding at 100 percent. The individuals were asked to indicate on a graph when they were dating casually, were seriously involved with each other, and were certain of marriage. Four patterns emerged.*

Table 7.9 Median age of women and men at
first marriage

YEAR	MEN	WOMEN
1930	24.3	21.3
1940	24.3	21.5
1950	22.8	20.3
1960	22.8	20.3
1970	23.6	20.8
1980	24.6	22.1

SOURCE: From U.S. Bureau of the Census. *Current
Population Reports*, Series P-20, No. 349, 1977, and
No. 365, 1981. Washington, D.C.: U.S. Government
Printing Office.

celerates more slowly, reaching a high probability of marriage at about three
and a half months but then moving to a certainty of marriage in less than a
year. *Intermediate* courtship is slower than the first two. It reaches a high probability of marriage at about nine and a half months and then goes through a
rocky period before climbing to a commitment at about nineteen months. *Prolonged* courtship has a long and difficult path to marriage, taking on the average over three years.

In spite of the slight trend in the direction of later marriages, there is little
difference in the average age of marriage in the past fifty years. Table 7.9
shows the average age of the first marriage since 1930. A growing number of
men and women are choosing to remain single during their twenties. We can
see from Table 7.10 that the percentage of individuals 20 to 24 who choose to
remain single has increased 14 percent between 1970 and 1980. The percentage in the 25 to 29 age bracket has doubled. Individuals from poorer families
marry earlier, have children sooner, and have more of them than those from
wealthier backgrounds (Neugarten and Hagestad, 1976).

Whom are we likely to marry? The answer is people like ourselves. Men
and women tend to marry people with similar social class backgrounds, race,
religion, education, age, and even neighborhoods, to their own. Moreover,
people who are most alike are most apt to be happy in marriage and those least
similar most often to have trouble in the marriage (Veroff and Feld, 1970).

Most couples who marry in North America say they are in love with each
other. Young couples who are married or engaged are likely to see the most
important ingredient in love to be sharing, understanding, companionship,
and mutual support (Baum, 1972). The flames of passion diminish somewhat
after marriage, and in their place grows an increasing sense of shared purpose,
interdependence, and affection. Though being in love is the most important
factor in the decision, liking the prospective spouse also is an important element. Liking each other — the degree of respect, admiration, and identifica-

Table 7.10 Percentage of never-married men and women, 1970 and 1980 comparisons

AGE	NEVER-MARRIED FEMALES		NEVER-MARRIED MALES	
	1970	1980	1970	1980
20–24	36	50	55	69
25–29	11	21	19	32
30–34	6	10	9	16

SOURCE: U.S. Department of Commerce, Bureau of the Census. *Current Population Reports*, Series P-20, No. 365. Washington, D.C.: U.S. Government Printing Office, 1981.

tion between members of a couple — is almost as strongly associated with a permanent bond as love (Rubin, 1973, Chapter 10).

After marriage, the problems must be confronted regarding the ideal of two becoming one yet remaining two. Differences that were obscured during the courtship — competing needs; differences in abilities and opportunities; and limited time, energy, and money — threaten to split the couple's unity (Cunningham and Antill, 1981). No marriage maintains daily a fifty-fifty split

Sometimes I Hate My Husband

There's a secret that a lot of us women rarely tell each other, and often find it hard to tell ourselves: that no matter how deeply and dearly we love our husbands most of the time, there are also those times when we do not love them at all. When what we feel, at best, is a vast indifference. When what we feel, at worst, we would have to call hate. . . .

We hate our husband, some of the time, for qualities that we, most of the time, will tolerate. Not *like* or *accept* or *approve of*, God knows, but *tolerate*. So if, like Rachel's husband, he's super-critical; or if, like Julie's husband, he's always working late; or if, like Ellen's husband, he never praises us; or if, like Betty's husband, he's too bossy; we grumble and put up with him — to a point.

But just to a point. . . .

Once a wife starts hating her husband, tolerance disappears and everything about him gets on her nerves. Has he always chewed his food so noisily? Does he really think that

stupid joke is funny? How can a woman have any respect for a man who thinks that stupid joke is funny? Furthermore, the small, nervous habits a husband may happen to have — like clearing his throat a lot or scratching his head — may start to be experienced as unbearable. And even those things about him that in our nonhating days we actually think are cute will now enrage us.

During these days or seasons of hate a wife may see her husband as the enemy — no longer her ally against the world but a person who belongs to Them, not Us. . . .

These seasons of hate are terrible times, for all the connections are broken and a silence or an icy politeness prevails, while up in the bedroom we may turn our back — how can he want to make love to a person who hates him? . . .

And yet, though we feel bitter or cold or violent or vengeful or seething or alienated, we will — if we don't kill or divorce — actually come to the end of hating our husband. Impossible and incredible as it may seem to us of resources, of support for further education and training, of doing chores, of child care, and of managing emergencies at home. One way of coping with these problems are to agree in advance on guidelines governing allocation of roles and resources.

This involves developing working assumptions about who will be primarily in charge of which areas of responsibility. For instance, rarely does a couple have enough money and energy to allow each to prepare for a career simultaneously. Therefore, joint decisions need to be made about whose education is primary for the moment. If it is the woman who gives up the most in the early part of marriage, they must agree on what plans will be made for her future development when the husband is established. If both are going to work, who will do the shopping, laundry, cooking and cleaning? How about child care? If the wife contributes the larger share of furnishings or financial resources to the household, what will the husband do in return?

These and numerous other potential conflicts can be avoided by openly discussing problems in advance and agreeing on general guidelines. Some couples do this quite casually, trusting the other to do the right thing. Other couples are far more scrupulous in detailing who is responsible for what.

Many couples react strongly against traditional marriage contracts which stipulate that the husband is head of the household and is responsible for the

at the time, we will begin to love our husband again.

Ah, but how?

Hate passes, it seems, for as many different reasons as it starts. "Time helps," says Betty. "Comparisons help too." Comparisons with David, who pouts, or Eddie, who plays around, or the husbands of Rachel and Julie and Millie and Ellen. She also compares the life she has with the life of Marianne, divorced and exhausted and raising three children alone. "I know that isn't for me," she says. "I know I couldn't stand it. And I start feeling very thankful for what I've got."

The flow of daily living also helps to make hate pass, by sweeping us into involvement with each other. "He asks, 'Did you do the wash today?' Or I say, 'Should we give the kid his allowance?' And suddenly we're back in the marriage."

Shared pleasures are another help in dissipating hate — a night at a Mel Brooks movie can sometimes work wonders. And even though a Julie feels that sex won't work unless

it's done in love, some wives say that what can start as sex can end in love. "Great sex," one woman says, "brings me back to my husband."

Sometimes hate will go away because we'll come to see that he isn't quite the villain that we paint him. He'll do something nice or he'll say something right, and we'll suddenly recall the very excellent reasons why we married him.

"Well, what do you know!" we'll say to ourselves in amazement. "He's not bad at all."

Finally, hate vanishes because, for some of us, hate is seasonal — a phase in this complex whole we call marriage, a phase in the natural rhythms of married life.

Where seasons of love give way to seasons of hate.

Where seasons of hate give way (if we can only hang on and hold out) to seasons of love.

SOURCE: Excerpted from Judith Viorst, Sometimes I hate my husband, *Redbook*, November 1976, pp. 73–74. Copyright © 1976 by Judith Viorst. Reprinted by permission.

support of the family, while the wife is responsible for domestic services and child care. Consistent with greater equality between men and women, many couples marrying today prepare their own contracts stating how leadership is to be shared — all major decisions to be agreed on by both parties, both to contribute financially to the support of the household, domestic and child care to be equally shared, and so on. More and more women do not take their husband's name and keep their own driver's license, credit cards, and bank account in their maiden name (Weitzman, 1977). Because everyone's life takes unpredictable turns, informal or formal agreements need to be reexamined and altered from time to time.

As the article by Judith Viorst (1976) indicates, not all of the problems in a marriage can be anticipated. All of us have moments of hating those we love most. Usually these periods pass quickly.

Alternative Loving Styles. According to government statistics, the traditional family with father working and mother at home with one or two children accounts for only seventeen percent of American households today. The remaining households include:

- 28 percent with father and mother working and with one or more children at home
- 32 percent married couples with no children or none living at home
- 7 percent headed by single parents, mostly women, with one or more children at home
- 5.3 percent headed by a single parent, mostly women, with one or more children and other relatives
- 3 percent unrelated persons living together

These data (U.S. Bureau of the Census, 1977) do not record how many of those in nontraditional households were originally in traditional families at one point or another. However, the data do point out the number of alternatives to traditional marriage.

Disenchantment with traditional marriage and high divorce rates have led many to speculate that the traditional marriage will never again be in style. Some suggest the majority of adults will live in other family structures by the year 2000. Some of the alternative living arrangements are shown in Table 7.11. These five alternative living styles for expressing love are most common in early adulthood. These nontraditional affiliations work very well and endure for some people. Interesting and attractive as these options are, they are far less stable than marriage. Most reports show the average duration of these alternatives to be less than two years (Butler, 1979).

Caring for Children. Producing and caring for children is a usual event for this stage of life. We noted in previous chapters that childless women begin to feel an increasingly strong urge to bear children as they move into their late 20s or early 30s. Whether this is a biological drive, a result of societal pressure, or related to something else entirely different is not clear. But bearing chil-

Table 7.11 Alternatives to traditional marriage

Open or core marriage

Two partners are committed to their own and each other's growth through openness to growth-enhancing opportunities. The need for privacy is recognized and possessiveness is discouraged. Other relationships, including sexual ones, which may contribute to the development of one or both are permitted. Though trust in each other is stressed, written or verbal contracts specify rules and boundaries that are shaped to fit each partner.

Expanded families

These are households of related and unrelated adults, children, and families who make a voluntary commitment to each other. Expanded families take many forms, but share specific characteristics: (1) three to four adults living together with children seeing all adults as kin; (2) frequent sexual intimacy and feelings shared openly; (3) family functions and services shared.

Group marriage

Three or more adults living together who see themselves are being married to each other, though no legal bond exists. Children of adults are included. Sexual contact occurs on a fixed rotation and can combine group sex. Regular meetings are held to facilitate communication.

Communes

A loose confederation of adults living together with or without children. Communes are usually organized around an ideology — agricultural subsistence, crafts, spiritual-mystical beliefs, drug taking, or political beliefs. Some do not have a central focus, and these tend to be disorganized, often with a rapidly changing membership.

Homosexual unions

Two partners of the same sex are committed to one another. These unions make the same assumptions about fidelity, sharing of roles, and commitment to the growth of the other as heterosexual marriage. Children from a previous marriage are raised by both serving as parents.

SOURCE: From *Traditional marriage and emerging alternatives* by Edgar W. Butler. Copyright © 1979 by Edgar W. Butler. Reprinted by permission of Harper & Row, Publishers, Inc.

dren is an issue that must be contended with from time to time during this phase of life. In fact, Erik Erikson has wondered whether the advances in birth control techniques — which allow sexual satisfaction without worrying about pregnancy — do not cause unconscious conflicts in young adults because they are holding their procreative drives in check (Erikson and Erikson, 1981).

The satisfaction derived from loving bonds with children is not restricted to the mother. Fathers who are active in the care of children form strong attachments. Research suggests that fathers over 30 remain in closer contact with their children longer and seem more comfortable in the role than do younger men. Greater role sharing among today's young adults may free men to remain in more satisfying relationship with their children longer than in the past, when fathers' interest turned away from their children after the first year (Troll, 1975).

While it is true that children are a source of pleasure, we recall from the last chapter that the presence of youngsters also increases the degree of husband-wife conflict. Females seem to experience substantially greater stress than males. This may be because of the increasing feeling of females of being more and more in charge of the infant as the husband increasingly turns his attention back toward his occupation. This can result in feelings of bitterness and isolation. Women who work or wish to begin an occupation sometimes feel they are falling behind and start to lose confidence in their capabilities. Both partners have a stake in striving to maintain the wife and mother's self-esteem during this period, when she is the prime nurturer.

Do dual-career parents or single parents produce a larger number of maladjusted children or adults than traditional families? For that matter, what is the impact on young people of being raised in alternative family structures, such as by lesbian mothers? Overall, the differences are modest. Children of working mothers do not appear to experience serious problems in their adjustment to life. A study conducted by University of Michigan researchers found no significant differences among children of working and nonworking mothers in the dimensions of physical health, depression, anxiety or a range of psychological symptoms (Douvan and Inglehart, 1979). However, many youngsters of working mothers don't like it and do what they can to instill guilt.

The notion that parental divorce in childhood is an important contributor to adjustment problems in later life receives little support from studies of adults who were raised in broken homes (Weingarten and Kulka, 1979). While divorce is a crisis at the time and may cause severe unhappiness in childhood and adolescence, its effects wane over time. Adult men are more likely to be affected than women by divorce. A slightly larger percentage of males than females make less of an investment in being a parent and report dissatisfaction at work. But the differences are not large.

Studies of children raised by divorced homosexual and heterosexual mothers consistently show more similarities than differences (Kirkpatrick, Smith, and Roy, 1979; Mandel, Hotvedt, Green, and Smith, 1979). While the children of both groups had significant stress reactions to the divorce, these upsets were no more common among the youngsters of lesbian mothers. No differences in later sexual identity were found in the boys and girls of gay or straight mothers. Homosexual mothers, however, tend to worry more about the sexual orientation of their offspring than heterosexual ones.

Of all the alternatives to marriage, the most common is singlehood: a conscious choice to remain single. The majority stay single because they haven't met the right mate or are responsible for invalid or aging parents. An increasing number shy away from traditional marriage for fear that it will restrict personal freedom and growth. Single men and women value freedom to have control over their working, social, loving, or sexual relationships without having to worry about restrictive expectations or legal ties. There is a desire to remain open to new people and experiences.

Maintaining affiliative bonds with others as a single person is hard work, probably more difficult than if one is married. As they move into middle age, men especially have a hard time with singlehood, exhibiting a higher rate of alcoholism, emotional difficulties, and suicide than married males.

Middle Adulthood

In the middle years, from about 37 to 60, the loving activities center around developing a satisfying marital style, coping with marital stress, caring for two generations, and maintaining friendships.

Marital Styles. Developing a satisfying and workable marital style is a central issue of men and women in their middle years. John Cuber and Peggy Haroff (1965) studied the marriages of more than 200 affluent men and women who had been married 10 years or more to the same person, and who said they had never seriously considered splitting up. From their interviews, Cuber and Haroff identified five stable marriage styles on the basis of their most distinguishing features. The prominent features of each are as follows.

In the *conflict-habituated* marriage, much of the interaction between the couple is characterized by fighting. At best, the conflict is discreet and controlled. At worst, it is loud and vicious. Both partners acknowledge that their conflicts are basic and extensive, and that the likelihood of fighting is always strong. Their friends and children, accustomed to their fighting, may comment with a shrug and a smile, "There they go again," and wonder whether the couple needs to fight in order to stay together.

The key feature of the *devitalized* marriage is the discrepancy between the middle-age reality and the remembrance of the exciting, vital first years together. Both partners recall the early phase of their relationship with fondness — they were deeply in love, spent lots of time together, enjoyed sex, and were closely identified. But presently, little time is spent with (as opposed to "around") each other. Interests, activities, thoughts, and feelings are not shared. Sex is dull, far less satisfying than before. These couples continue to function effectively as a team, are good parents, and have a circle of friends. If asked why they stay together, the partners say there is still something between them, if only memories.

In the *passive-congenial* marriage, no contrasting memories of being deeply in love pain the couple — primarily because there never was much romance in the relationship. No disillusionment has occurred. The relationship between the couple is comfortable, calm, and moderate. They either share interests and values or resolve differences without significant conflict. These marriages work especially well in permitting both partners freedom to pursue individual interests, and some accomplish a great deal.

For the partners in a *vital* marriage, the relationship with each other is central. There is excitement in being together, whether it be for a vacation, tennis, or a quiet dinner, watching children perform in a high-school play, or simply sitting around a breakfast table over coffee. Though the partners usually agree on essential matters, they have separate identities and values. They may disagree on significant matters — accepting a promotion that means moving or where a child should attend college — but they confront disagreements directly and solve them.

In the *total* marriage, almost everything is shared. One partner tends to see the other as an extension of the self, so that neither has a private existence. The partners want to be together as much as possible and will make considerable sacrifices to do so. Little tension or conflict exists in this marriage because other matters are put aside until a problem is resolved.

Cuber and Haroff point out that these types of marriages are stable and all produce satisfaction. Among the five types, no subjective differences in the degree of happiness are reported by the married couples. Moreover, with the exception of the infrequent total marriage, hostility, disenchantment, infidelity, and separation or divorce do occur.

Coping with Marital Stress. Marriage at mid-life comes under considerable stress. Three sources of difficulty are the tradeoffs made earlier, a shift in the work-love balance, and sexual dysfunction. The CPA at 32 may say to his wife and family, "You won't be seeing much of me for the next decade because I want to spend as much time as possible working to become a partner." Then he proceeds to ignore his family for this next decade. When he achieves his goal of becoming a partner, he may discover that his family has given up trying to love him. Once withered, this affection does not flourish easily again.

The other side of the coin is seen with the women who have willingly made substantial adjustments to their husbands' needs, as well as their children's. The result may have been a stable marriage during the young adult years, but if these women forsake their own needs for growth and continuing development of competence for the role of nurturer, bitterness toward their husbands can become a major issue at mid-life (Bernard, 1973).

Another source of marital discord is a shift in the work-love balance among men and women. It appears that at midlife, men and women may be moving in opposite directions (Fiske, 1980). In middle age, men who until this time have been largely career-oriented begin to show far greater interest in loving relationships with others. They are more and more comfortable with passivity, caring, and the intimacy they put off while getting ahead. Women, on the other hand, who suppressed their achievement ambitions while being the primary caretaker, are now far more focused on moving forward in their work, and are far less interested in loving.

Problems of sexual dysfunction are a third cause of stress at mid-life. These can be caused by waning sexual desire, male anxiety about sexual aptitude at 40 or so — when the female feels greater sexual vitality — boredom, or other reasons. The problems are usually expressed in primary and secondary impotence, premature ejaculation, and orgasmic dysfunction. *Primary impotence* is the inability to achieve an erection. *Secondary impotence* is difficulty maintaining it during sexual intercourse. When a man reaches a climax just before or after penetration, that is called *premature ejaculation*. A woman's inability to achieve a climax is *orgasmic dysfunction* (Masters, Johnson, and Kolodny, 1982). It should be understood that these are problems when they become chronic conditions, not occasional happenings.

Masters, Johnson, and Kolodny speculate that half of the marriages in the United States have one or more of these sexual problems. They pioneered the development of therapies that are successful in overcoming these problems when applied by trained therapists. Overall, four out of five men and women with sexual problems are generally improved by sex therapy (Masters, Johnson, and Kolodny, 1982). While sexual adjustment is rarely ideal in mid-life, little erosion of loving relationships occurs as long as there is reasonable expression of love that is neither unpleasant nor feared (Vaillant, 1977).

Boredom threatens sexual satisfaction. If we look at reports of frequency of intercourse by age we will discover that a normal healthy couple may have sexual relations 5000 times or more during their marriage. It is not hard to imagine a man or woman at mid-life losing interest in any activity they have done thousands of times with the same person.

On the other hand, think of other things we do hundreds or even thousands of times. We bowl or fish or play golf, tennis, or cards year after year with the same people. We never feel we are in a rut. Usually this is because we enjoy doing something we like with people who care about us and vice versa; we schedule sufficient time for it; we do it regularly; feelings are expressed and accommodated; and there is variety — we bowl at different lanes, fish for bass, trout, and bluegills; and play a dozen different types of poker.

Recommendations about how to improve sex usually recognize these same principles. A fulfilling sexual experience is more often with someone we express loving feelings toward and who makes us feel loved. Just as players set aside an hour or two for a tennis game, the best sexual loving is that in which both partners take their time. It is hard to enjoy any physical activity with another person if we do not practice regularly, and sexual behavior is no exception. Open communication of what brings pleasure, what is unpleasant, and suggestions for mutual satisfaction are essential to stable sexual loving just as in other physical activities with someone else. Finally, as with any form of repetitive physical acts shared with others, imagination and creativity can be put to use in sexual matters. A story is told about a man who came home for his 40th birthday and was greeted by his wife with a suitcase and a picnic basket packed with wine, cheese, and bread. A baby-sitter was playing with the children and had been scheduled for the evening. His wife had made reservations at a local motel. This event shows the importance to this marriage both placed in a high-quality sexual relationship (Kreitler and Bruns, 1981, Chapter 12).

As we grow older, our bodies secrete hormones at lower levels, which results in menopause in women and lower sexual drive in men. However, regular sexual activity is possible well into the older adult years. One study found seventy percent of men over 65 had sexual intercourse one to four times a month (Rubin, I., 1976). The continuation of sexual expression is a function of health as well as the willingness of both partners to help each other maintain their sexuality.

Sexual problems, boredom, and other stresses on marriage at mid-life can lead to extramarital affairs, separation, and divorce. More than a quarter-century ago, Kinsey (1953) found that half of the men and a quarter of the women he had interviewed reported sexual contact outside of marriage. Accurate information on infidelity today is sparse, but there is general agreement that the percentage of married people having outside affairs is increasing, especially among females (Gordon, 1978).

The context in which adultery occurs varies considerably. Cuber (1969), who earlier studied types of marriages, examined over 400 normal individuals between 30 and 55 who were having or had had in the past an extramarital affair. He identified three types of adulterous behavior: (1) *compensatory affairs*, a long-term relationship with another person that fills in something missing in the marriage: a woman has an affair because of her husband's impotence; (2) *separation affairs*, adultery as a result of lengthy periods of time apart due to military service or occupational requirements; and (3) *"Bohemian" affairs*, in which people willingly commit to marriage but never to monogamy.

Though marriage counselors point to the destructive impact of adultery on marriage, Cuber reaches a different conclusion. He found many of the people he studied who were having affairs were able to maintain their marriages, some even with the knowledge of their spouse. It is also true, however, that extramarital affairs cause stress. At least as many men and women believe adultery is morally wrong as think that it is right. This means that individuals carrying on sexual liaisons will have to deal with their own guilt or someone else's disapproval. Also, adultery usually places the "other woman" or "other man" in a position of second-class status. More often than not they are seen at the convenience of their adulterous lovers. Finally, most affairs end painfully and, because of their clandestine nature, it is difficult to find someone to share the distress with.

Since about 1960, the rate of separation and divorce in America has been rising sharply. In 1980 there were 2,413,000 marriages in the United States and 1,182,000 divorces (U.S. Public Health Service, 1981). Three reasons for the greater number of couples splitting up have been summarized by sociologist Robert Weiss (1975):

1. the lowering of legal barriers and more permissive attitudes on the part of organized religions;
2. the opportunities for women to be self-supporting;
3. the ethic of self-realization, resulting in less willingness to tolerate a marriage which is not satisfactory.

Whatever the cause, many loving relationships do dissolve. Learning to rebuild loving relationships is difficult, as Weiss (1979) notes in his book *Going It Alone*. Loneliness — including feelings of hollowness, inadequacy, and anxiety — is common among newly separated people. This is often complicated by a yearning for the attachment to a lost spouse even though no love remains. Loneliness is made even more unbearable by a feeling of being cut off from former friends whom one knew as a couple. Combating this loneliness is a major task confronting every newly single person. In spite of the very real problems of meeting people, about four men in five and three out of four women eventually remarry. This rate has been rising steadily. Some who remarry report far greater happiness because they work much harder at creating a successful marriage the second time.

Most people remarry someone with children. Today one million youngsters and five hundred thousand adults become members of step-families each year (Vishner and Vishner, 1979). At present one out of every six American children is a stepchild. These new family structures put added stress on children and the parents — divided loyalties, jealousy, relationships with new in-laws, unrealistic expectations. Do children raised by "step" or "blended" families have more adjustment problems than those brought up in other circumstances? As with other special situations in which children are raised, the answer seems to be "no." Generally, boys and girls with stepparents are as well adjusted and grow up to be normal adults in the same proportion as those reared by natural parents. Some data indicate that stepfathers get along better with children of the mother than stepmothers get along with their stepchildren.

Not everyone who is disenchanted with their marriage splits up. As Weiss points out (1975), many people stay in loveless marriages because a bond of attachment persists. This presents individuals in a barren marriage with a difficult choice: either to split up and face the certain loneliness, anxiety and depression, and money problems, or to remain in a marriage that provides little satisfaction. No ideal solution exists, only tradeoffs.

Others reappraise the reasons for their marital disenchantment and try to resolve long-standing or emergent problems in order to reestablish a loving bond. Books, workshops, seminars, and counselors abound, all with ideas about how couples can resuscitate a failing marriage. The ways to combat sexual boredom are high on everyone's list. Other suggestions for normal men and women who are experiencing disenchantment at middle age include the following (Kreitler and Bruns, 1981):

1. *Spouse is number one:* Be sure that your spouse knows you think he or she is number one in spite of conflicting demands to care for others.
2. *Conserve energy to love:* Take a break at work to have enough energy "left over" for the partner at the day's end.
3. *Add romance:* A small gift remembering an important shared event, candlelight and wine, a crackling fire and music, and a well-chosen restaurant can refresh a marriage.
4. *Recognize the value of shared humor:* Taking opportunities to laugh together at events that occur regularly in a marriage foster open communication, intimacy and problem solving.

5. *Have fun together:* Playfulness in marriage can rejuvenate old feelings which were so appealing in younger days.

Sometimes when a couple wonders if they have "grown apart," this is a time for a marital checkup. Talking with a third party — a minister, priest, or rabbi; a family doctor or other physician; or a psychologist or marriage counselor — can be helpful in appraising the present status of the marriage, identify trouble spots, and take corrective action.

How can we tell if our marriage is reasonably healthy? Psychologist Carl Rogers identified five qualities that characterize a strong loving bond. Though he was describing slightly different types of loving encounters, the qualities shown in the box are often found in revitalized marriages at mid-life and beyond.

Caring for Two Generations. One definition of middle age may be "to be midway between the ages," that is, having caring responsibilities for both children and parents. Caring for two generations, children and parents, is a normative loving activity at this stage.

One woman put it this way: "Right now, I don't have much to say to my middle-aged friends who aren't caring for their children, parents, or usually both, because that is what takes up most of my day." She went on to describe her previous week: Monday the 14-year-old son needed to talk to her about

---

Characteristics of Loving Relationships

1. *Sensitivity:* Continuing close relationships depend on the willingness of both parties to understand the other's emotions and experiences. This takes time, energy, and, most important, the desire to care how a loved one feels and understand that person's day-to-day experience.

2. *Open communication:* Persistent feelings, especially negative ones, should be expressed, so that they do not block closeness, and also so that the loved one has an opportunity to decide whether he or she wishes to change.

3. *Transparency:* Even though it's difficult to achieve, the strongest bond between lovers has a large component of self-disclosure. We are able to say, with more or less honesty, where we hurt, and those things we fear, as well as what we cherish and aspire to. We are able to express joy, despair, fury, and irreverence without worrying about the impression we are making. We are willing to be vulnerable.

4. *Respect for autonomy:* While a marriage is characterized by openness on both sides, there is acceptance of the rights of the loved one to believe and behave according to his or her own standards. We do not require that the person, in order to be our lover, meet our conditions for values, attitudes, and actions.

5. *Rhythm:* Marriages have a rhythmic variation to them. There is openness and sharing of feelings, and then a period of assimilation of these experiences. Intense confrontation with anxiety and change are followed by a secure time of no change and quiet. A marriage is not a continuous encounter group.

SOURCE: Adapted from Rogers, C. *A way of being.* Boston: Houghton Mifflin, 1980; and Rogers, C. The necessary and sufficient conditions of therapeutic personality change. *Journal of Consulting Psychology,* 1957, *21,* 95–103.

why he didn't have any friends, and her mother-in-law called about whether she should have a hip operation; Tuesday, her 17-year-old daughter wanted to talk about whether she should go to college or get a job, and her widowed father wondered if she could do some shopping for him; Wednesday, her 24-year-old daughter, who had been out of the house for three years, called from North Carolina wondering if she could come home for a while to "get my head together," and her father came over to tell her that a widow at church is beginning to pursue him; Thursday, her middle child needed to talk about whether she should join the Army just at the time she was leaving for the hospital to see her mother-in-law; Friday, her father-in-law confided he was not happy with his wife of forty-five years and was thinking of leaving her, just as her daughter from North Carolina came in the driveway.

Not every week is like this one. But this anecdote brings home the essential truth of Erikson's theory that in middle age a primary task is caring for others to whom we have an obligation that has "been generated by love, necessity, or accident; it overcomes ambivalence arising from irreversible obligation." (Erikson, 1976)

Many middle-aged men and women feel considerable ambivalence about their loving obligations. Sociologist Leon Sheleff (1981) observes that children bring exquisite pain as well as pleasure. Young parents can be worn down and come to resent the sleepless nights and the expense and unending demands of children. Though adolescents and youthful offspring are better able to care for themselves, the parents are rare who do not envy the growing physical and intellectual power of their children as their own powers are noticeably waning, who do not find it sometimes difficult to listen to their children's shining dreams as their own have been frustrated, and who often do not resent the fact that parental sacrifice is neither acknowledged nor thanked.

One myth is that middle-aged couples are afflicted by the "empty-nest syndrome" — depression and anxiety when the last child leaves home. In fact, the reverse usually is true. Once children are launched on their own, the freedom from parental responsibility results in far better relationships between husband and wife. For a few it's a second honeymoon. The couples have more time just for themselves, they go out when they wish, see old friends, and travel.

Another popular myth is that American families are isolated from one another. In fact, the opposite is true. Sixty percent of older people live within walking distance of one child, and the percentage is no different in the United States, Denmark, or England (Shanas, Townsend, Wedderburn, Friis, Milhoj, and Stehower, 1968). Though middle-class couples tend to live farther away from their parents than working-class families, the telephone has done much to shrink distances. Indeed, in many families, failure to communicate regularly by phone is considered a serious breach of family obligations (Azubike, 1979).

Older parents do need to be able to count on their progeny or other relatives for physical help as well as friendship. In their book, *The Other Generation Gap,* Cohen and Gans (1978) suggest that children who are first-line resources for their older parents beware of being motivated by guilt or aspirations for martyrdom. They point to the value of setting reasonable limits to the amount of attention they give their parents and encourage them to take advantage of others who could give care — friends, neighbors, and social agencies.

Maintaining Friendships. On the wall of a small out-of-the-way restaurant overlooking a lake in Wisconsin is a series of pictures of four men. Each one shows the men standing in fishing gear holding up their catch to the camera. If we look at the dates on these pictures, we can see they were taken over a thirty-year period. These men have been friends for a long time.

This graphic demonstration of maintained friendships points to the significance of this loving activity in middle adulthood. Like these men, many of us have friends of long standing at this time of life, with whom we have accumulated experiences over the years and who bring considerable pleasure when we are with them.

At mid-life most of us can name ten people or so who we would call friends. As the example of the fishermen illustrates, males typically have friends who share mutually enjoyable activities. Females, on the other hand, value their friends as confidantes (Reisman, 1981). Cross-sex friendships are rare. Because of the freedom from day-to-day child-rearing, middle-age has been described as second only to adolescence as a time for forming new friendships or refurbishing old ones (Reisman, 1981). This may be especially true for those who experience severe disruption in their personal life, such as a career change, relocation, or separation from a spouse.

As Vaillant (1977) observes, "The seeds of love must be eternally resown." Having friends is increasingly associated with better emotional adjustment as we grow older. New friends need to be acquired to replace continuing shrinkage through moving away, death, or alienation.

As part of maintaining a network of friends, forgiveness is essential. By mid-life, most people have experienced the treachery of valued colleagues and the deceit of intimates, been savaged by loved ones in moments of greatest need, and been repaid with indifference for generous acts of loving. Almost everyone has grounds to conclude that "people are no damn good" and could feel justified in withdrawing affection from friends who are closest. This narrow, legalistic, adversary thinking does not do justice to the complexities of human relations. For example, it ignores the fact that we ourselves might have caused friends and loved ones pain through overweening ambition, insensitivity, or momentary meanness. To continue to love and be loved, these assaults to caring must be forgiven and forgotten.

Age brings a growing tolerance for diversity. Our ability to love our friends seems to grow. Older men and women are more competent and practiced at being sensitive, open, honest, and caring than they were when they were younger. This may be because they know the value of loving relationships and are willing to invest the time and patience and energy to do it well.

Success in maintaining friendships is an important loving
activity in the adult years.
These men have enjoyed participating in different activities together for many years.

Later Adulthood

From about age 55 onward the loving activities include grandparenting, living alone, and accepting the care of others.

Grandparents. One of the pleasures of life is being a grandparent. To a large extent, this is because older adults can enjoy grandchildren on their own terms without feeling responsible for them. They can play with youngsters, have them over to visit, spoil them, and then return them to their mothers and fathers.

Five different types of grandparenting styles have been described (Neugarten and Weinstein, 1964):

1. *Formal:* Clear demarcations between parents and grandparents and their roles; grandparents provide special treats only, and occasional minor services.
2. *Fun-seeker:* Grandparenting is a leisure activity or a self-indulgence.
3. *Surrogate parent:* Mostly characteristic of grandmothers when mothers work or are incapacitated.

4. *Reservoir of family wisdom:* Mostly true of grandfathers who are seen as dispensers of special skills.
5. *Distant figure:* A benevolent but infrequent visitor who emerges from the shadows on holidays and ritual occasions.

To some extent, these may depend on particular cultures or on the personality of the grandparent.

Today, grandparents are more likely to be vigorous, youth-oriented, and working than were their predecessors (Troll, 1975). Because of this, they may not be as receptive to baby-sit the grandchildren while the parents have a night out. Again, grandparents differ a good deal among themselves, but a large number experience requests to take care of the grandchildren, not as an opportunity to interact with the youngsters, but as a case of "dumping the kids with us."

Finding and maintaining the proper psychological distance between daughters and themselves seems to be a problem for many grandmothers. On the whole, women with children feel the wish to move closer to their mothers in adulthood. The grandmothers, however, often feel discomfort with their daughter's desire for closeness (Cohler and Grunebaum, 1981). This can be a problem unless it is discussed and the right degree of intimacy worked out.

Life Alone. At some point or another, most of us face life alone. For an increasing number, this occurs in young and middle adulthood through separation and divorce. For others, it comes in later adulthood, most often because of death of the spouse. We recall from p. 35 in Chapter 2 that death of a husband or wife ranks highest of all sources of stress. Men and women who lose their spouse are more likely to become physically ill or die than their contemporaries who do not (Parkes, 1972).

A spouse's death brings numerous losses in addition to that of the physical presence of the loved one (Cohen and Gans, 1978): someone who knows them well, is tolerant of personal quirks, has shared thousands of experiences and memories, and is a reliable companion to do things with. It also brings with it an increasing isolation from other couples who have known the survivor as part of a marital pair. This can intensify the normal depression, anxiety, and anger of the grieving process.

After the grief process is over, older adults need to rebuild their social network and fill the void left by the spouse. Golden Age and senior citizens' groups, the Gray Panthers, church activities, neighborhood centers, and other community agencies are places where other older people can make new friends.

The social world of older adults is distinct from that of younger people because far fewer men inhabit it. Today, the life span of women is nearly 10 years longer than that of men (U.S. National Center for Health Statistics, 1977). This reverses the usual pattern of men initiating contact with women. Often, older men find themselves being vigorously pursued by ardent widows.

Perhaps the greatest danger in confronting life alone is the inability — or the unwillingness — to discontinue grieving for the lost loved one and get on with the business of living. Nothing interferes with making new friends or being open to fresh relationships; nothing guarantees loneliness, more than failure to let go of memories of past love. Assistance for prolonged mourning is obtainable through church and medical specialists as well as through volunteer and community organizations.

Accepting the Care of Others. Later adulthood brings with it the inevitable necessity of accepting the care and support of others. An older person must learn to walk a very difficult tightrope between independence and dependence upon friends, family, and other caretakers. Generally, this includes working hard at avoiding being a burden to those we love, and at the same time accepting with grace the inevitable dependency upon the younger generation.

In their book on the care of older parents, Cohen and Gans (1978) set out several principles which can serve as guidelines for the loving care of older adults. These include:

1. *The fact that older adults have survived in the later years means they have retained many physical and emotional strengths:* take advantage of them.
2. *Physical health is going to deteriorate, not improve, over time:* do not deny the undeniable and set realistic expectations.
3. *Old habits will become more pronounced:* personal quirks which could be overlooked at a younger age are less attractive as they become magnified in older age.
4. *Change affects older people greatly:* routine should be preserved as much as possible.
5. *The independent functioning of adults should be prolonged as long as possible:* nursing homes are a last resort.
6. *Limit the extent of expectations from relatives and friends:* there is a limit to what can be asked from loved ones and a time to use other resources.

While these guidelines are intended to help the adult children of aging parents, they work very well for men and women who are themselves in later adulthood.

It is useful to focus on what we can do as older people rather than lamenting what is impossible. If a stroke has made fishing very difficult, a person can still play bridge, attend lectures, or go to movies with friends. Looking at our health realistically as we age is important in order to know what we can and cannot do. If arthritis causes pain and limits movement, we have to learn to take appropriate medication and find things that we can manage to do with friends. We should know that a penchant for malodorous cigars or beer may gradually grow as we get older. The smoke may offend those we care about, and alcohol intake needs to be monitored, as it is a major problem among the aging.

Because change is harder for older people, familiar routines and surroundings enhance adjustment. We should continue operating out of our own place, taking care of ourselves for as long as we can manage it, difficult as it may be.

Nursing homes present a whole new range of problems and should be used only when no other alternative exists. Finally, we need to be sure that our children and those who care for us are helping without being motivated by excessive guilt, obligation, or martyrdom. Other resources need to be used as much as possible.

Summary

1. Love is a special kind of relationship with another, characterized by warm affection and desire for attachment.
2. Five types of loving behavior can be identified: caring within family, friendship, idealistic love, sexual desire, and romantic love.
3. Human needs gratified by loving during the life cycle are preservation, social bonding, and competence.
4. Research shows that the best-adjusted individuals are able to love friends, a spouse, and their offspring. Love is important in the recovery from mental disorders and lays the groundwork for work and play.
5. Specific normal loving activities are associated with, or initiated during, particular ages of the life span. In childhood, these are being the objects of love, developing friendships with peers, and maintaining close contact with parents.
6. In preadolescence, the most significant loving events are finding a best friend and remaining connected to adult-controlled groups.
7. The central loving activities in adolescence are involvement with a gang, altruism, coping with sexual desire, and the first big romance.
8. Young people generally move a maximum distance from parents, acquire a widening circle of diverse friends, live together with a loved one, and eventually form a primary bond.
9. In early adulthood, the normal loving activities usually include sharing a dream, getting married or finding an acceptable alternative, and caring for children.
10. In middle adulthood, the major loving activities are developing a satisfying marital style, coping with marital stress, caring for two generations, and maintaining friendships.
11. In later adulthood, grandparenting, life alone, and accepting the care of others are all major events associated with loving behavior.

A Look Ahead

The next chapter is about playing. This is one activity that we can enjoy without the feeling of obligation or the need to do well at it; we can fit it to our changing whim. No other sphere of life is quite like this. In Chapter 8 we will define playing, look at the relationship between playing and adjustment, see how play has been seen as supportive of other life events, and consider what human needs are met through play during the life cycle. Then we will survey playing actions of normal individuals at each phase of the life cycle. In every stage, we will consider hazards to satisfaction from playing and think about what can be done to reduce or eliminate them.

Key Terms

love
friendship
idealistic love
altruism
sexual desire

estrogen
best friend
androgen
romantic love
POSSLQ

Suggested Readings

Types of love

Lewis, C. *The four loves.* New York: Harcourt Brace Jovanovich, 1960.

May, R. *Love and will.* New York: Norton, 1969.

    Many faces of love from literary and philosophical perspectives.

Love through the life cycle

Pope, K., et al. *On love and loving: Psychological perspectives on the nature and experience of romantic love.* San Francisco: Jossey-Bass, 1980.

    Fresh portrayal of romantic love among children, adolescents, and adults.

Shyness

Zimbardo, P. *Shyness.* Reading, Mass.: Addison-Wesley, 1977.

    Self-help for people who are shy or unassertive.

Parenting

Gordon, T. *P.E.T. — Parent effectiveness training.* New York: Wyden, 1970.

Ginott, H. *Between parent and child: New solutions to old problems.* New York: Macmillan, 1965.

    ———— *Between parent and teenager.* New York: Macmillan, 1969.

Salk, L. *What every child would like his parents to know.* New York: Warner, 1973.

    Practical advice for raising children and teenagers

Today's short working hours present a problem that our ancestors never had to concern themselves with — how to spend leisure time. The creation of leisure activities and products is now a multi-million dollar industry in the United States. Despite all the offerings, some Americans still do not know what to do with the time on their hands. Leisure guidance organizations have grown to help people enjoy themselves. Here are some of the activities offered by such companies:

Leisure Guidance offers a personalized counseling service for individuals seeking to improve the quality of their leisure experience, to explore new interests, and to rejuvenate their feelings for life.

Our programs are specifically tailored to your problems, wants, and needs. Together with a trained leisurologist, you will draw up a program which might include any of the following:

□ Development of a comprehensive leisure profile to examine your present leisure picture in full.

□ Leisure facilitation experiences. Immersion experiences in leisure options, sessions in bodily movement and social skills.

□ Assessment of your completed leisure profile and recommendation of leisure area best suited to your needs.

□ Assess to our Leisure Data Bank, containing over 1000 leisure activity listings.

□ Follow-up. Group workshops and/or individual counseling on interest maintenance, and on disciplinary and motivational problems.

How do you spend your leisure time? Can you imagine ever needing assistance to enjoy life?

Brochure from Leisure Guidance, The Center for Leisure Guidance, P.O. Box 1980, Cambridge, MA 02138.

Chapter Preview

What Is Play?
Types of Play
Needs Gratified by Playing
    Arousal
    Catharsis
    Social Bonding
    Competence

Playing and Adjustment
Playing Through the Life Cycle
    Childhood and Preadolescence
    Adolescence and Youth
    Adulthood
Summary
A Look Ahead

CHAPTER 8

Playing Through the Life Cycle

Questions to think about

☐ What is play?

☐ How is play satisfying to you?

☐ Can you think of types of play that continue through life?

☐ What are the threats to pleasure from play?

Right now, Americans spend more money on play than they have at any other time in history. Of every eight dollars we earn in this country, we spend almost one dollar for leisure — a larger share than we allot for national defense or housing construction (*U.S. News and World Report*, 1980). As Figure 8.1 shows, we spent an estimated $218 billion on recreation in 1980, almost four times the amount spent 15 years ago.

In this chapter we look at play more closely and identify features that distinguish play from work and and love. Next we look at four lifelong types of play. Then we turn our attention to how play affects our overall adjustment — specifically, how play enhances mood, self-concept, and physical fitness. Finally, we identify playing activities associated with each stage of the life span.

Factors that undermine pleasure from playing are discussed. These include the time and energy leeched away by the pursuit of work and love, when

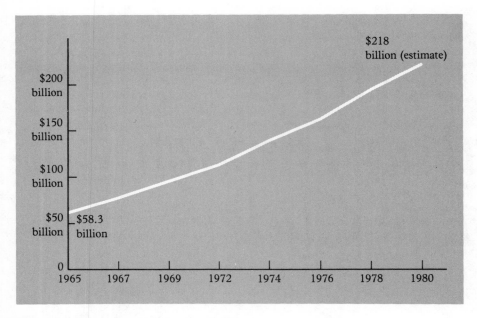

Figure 8.1   Spending on leisure activities

play is compromised by being converted to work or manipulated in the service of other ends, or when it has lost its freshness. As we look at these hazards to satisfaction from playing, we consider ways to anticipate and so minimize their impact on the pleasure that play gives us all.

What Is Play?

"Leisure activity," "recreation," and "having fun" are some of the nearly one hundred meanings of the word **play**. Three characteristics that distinguish play from work or love are lack of obligation, freedom from necessity of high achievement, and malleability.

Work is what we are obliged to do, Mark Twain (1876) tells us, and play is what we are *not* obliged to do. Twain's character Tom Sawyer persuaded his friends to whitewash his fence by presenting the task as a volunteer activity that he pretended to enjoy, not as the chore it was. In this example, Twain put his finger on the first significant feature of playing: *lack of obligation*. The activity is voluntary, motivated primarily by inner desire rather than economic necessity or responsibility to others. For example, bass fishing down a river in Arkansas is recreation for the vacationing couple from Los Angeles but not for the guide. A woman who chooses to be a member of her church's choir may be having fun; but her neighbor, who was pressured into joining by her friends because they needed another soprano, may not consider this recreation at all.

Freedom from the necessity of high achievement is the second characteristic of play. Perfection, winning, or providing goods and services for others is not essential to enjoyment. A woman enjoys singing even when she misses a few notes here and there. A man still has fun playing tennis, even though he hardly ever wins. For a gifted amateur photographer, the fun is in taking and developing the pictures rather than selling them.

This does not mean that doing a leisure-time activity well or winning isn't important to many individuals. Some of us need to do everything as well as we can, whether it's playing cards or the piano. Others love to compete with others to make the highest score in a game of darts or the lowest in a round of golf. Still others enjoy competing with themselves. As one woman jogger put it after finishing among stragglers in a weekend road race, "I feel terrific! I beat my best time by thirty seconds!"

The third feature of play is that it is *malleable*. In no other sphere of living is there as much freedom to mold an activity to individual choice as play. Moreover, recreational activities provide a continuing activity for having fun now rather than putting it off, for having a feeling of freedom rather than restraint, for pursuing pleasure without guilt, and for expressing individuality in freely seeking fresh experiences rather than being locked into routine (Dangott and Kalish, 1979).

For the most part, schools and jobs require us to adapt to their systems,

A raft trip may seem like play to these youngsters, but it is also a way of learning to work together as well as share the enjoyment.

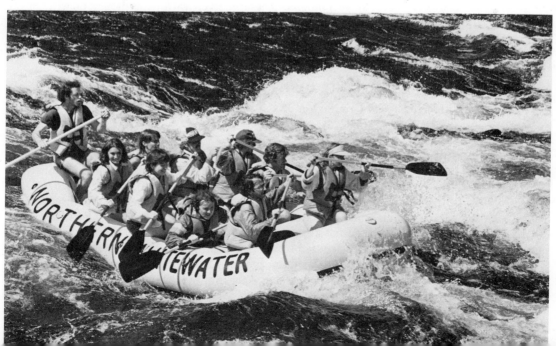

demanding that we restrain our desire to enjoy ourselves in the present. Philosopher Herbert Marcuse (1966) makes the point that civilization requires labor that is often mechanical and repetitive. At the workplace, individuality is not considered a value, and a person is in danger of becoming "the mere imprint of his occupation." Marcuse sees play as the only area in which we can realize our individuality.

"What about loving?" we might ask ourselves. Surely there are times when expressing love is as playful, and a lot more satisfying, than a game of bowling. Loving requires a sensitivity to someone else, however, and a willingness to please that person. By contrast, play offers us a unique opportunity to pursue pleasure without feeling guilty that we are not pleasing someone else.

In play we can seek pleasure, choosing from a range of possibilities, and are constrained only by law, opportunity, and talent. Play can be active or passive, useful or useless, done with others or alone, organized or not. Unlike working and loving, we can easily engage in different types of play as our interests change. Over a ten-year period, a man remained in the same job and in the same family. Yet during this decade his playing interests moved from photography, to mountain climbing, to flying, to sailing. His wife named their sailboat *What Next?*

Types of Play

What kinds of play do you enjoy? How many other types can you think of? Psychologists Lillian Dangott and Richard Kalish (1979) compiled an exhaustive list. Nine types of play, excerpted from their much larger number, are shown in Table 8.1. Looking at Table 8.1, it is clear that dozens of activities can be a source of recreational pleasure. Even with little money or with physical limitations, we can find numerous opportunities for pleasure in play.

Needs Gratified by Playing

Four needs that can be gratified through play during most of life are arousal, catharsis, social bonding, and competence.

Arousal

In Chapter 2 we studied Zuckerman's theory that each of us has a need to seek sensations — to pursue thrill and adventure, to become less inhibited, to seek fresh experiences, and to reduce boredom (Zuckerman, 1979). Psychologist Michael Ellis reached the same conclusion. He set out to discover the reasons human beings play. His book *Why People Play* (1973) lists more than a dozen motives. What he saw as being the most powerful motive was **arousal**. Each of us seeks to arouse ourselves to an optimal level of excitement or interest that is not provided by loving or working. Stimulating experiences that excite our interest are likely to be *new* (our first Frisbee), *complex* (understanding

Table 8.1   Types of play

Self expression	Self-pleasuring-activities	Contemplative
Growing houseplants	Going barefoot	Listening to music
Redecorating	Sunbathing	Reading scriptures
Gardening	Napping	Meditating
Needlework	Shopping	*Being with nature*
Performing	Taking a hot bath	Looking at a sunset
Photography	Receiving a massage	Driving in the country
Art or craft	*Educational*	Walking in the woods
Collecting	Going to a museum	*Games*
Cooking	Learning another language	Crossword puzzles
Carpentry	Taking a class	Cards
Writing	*Sports*	Board games
	Water (swimming)	TV games
	Earth (hiking)	*General pleasure*
Spectator	Animal (raising fish)	Traveling
TV watching	Individual (billiards)	Going to garage sales
Seeing sporting event	Team (volleyball)	People watching
Going to movies	Air (parachuting)	Planning trips
Attending a concert	Snow (snowmobiling)	Reading

SOURCE: From the book *A time to enjoy: The pleasures of aging* by Lillian R. Dangott and Richard A. Kalish. © 1979 by Prentice-Hall, Inc. Published by Prentice-Hall, Inc., Englewood Cliffs, New Jersey 07632. Reprinted by permission.

how a carburetor works), or *dissonant* (tomatoes we set out that keep wilting and dying in our garden).

This theory maintains that experiences are not likely to excite us as much when they are no longer new, when we solve their complexity, and when we make them work our way. Thus, to maintain a level of excitement, many of us trade our Frisbee for a pair of roller skates, turn from carburetors to transmissions, or begin growing roses when we figure out how to keep tomatoes healthy.

Catharsis

Catharsis is the purging of built-up tensions and stress emotions, restoring ourselves to a placid and relaxed state. Nowhere is catharsis more obvious than watching children at play during recess. Some youngsters are yelling and screaming, others are running and kicking a ball. In one corner of the playground, a group seems determined to get as messy as possible, while in another corner children are talking a mile a minute. Adults find the same relief as youngsters in venting their aggressive urges by swatting a tennis ball or knocking tenpins down with a bowling ball. A woman who has kept her feelings in check all week while working and taking care of her family unwinds at a long lunch on Saturday with a good friend. "I just dump," she says, "letting out everything I've held in all week and usually feel better."

While it seems clear that activity brings release from built-up tensions, can we have a cathartic experience by watching an emotionally stimulating drama or game? Here the opinions are mixed. The Greeks originally used the term *catharsis* to describe the effect of certain music and theatre to expel the emotions of the audience. Aristotle (McKeon, 1947, p. 631) thought that people who watched a Greek tragedy would leave the theatre purged of fear or other disabling feelings. Many of us have had the experience of emotional release while watching powerful drama on the stage or screen — the *Iliad* or *Hamlet* or, more recently, *One Flew Over the Cuckoo's Nest*, *The Poseidon Adventure*, or *Rocky*.

Another opinion, however, is that excessive viewing of movies or television or of games containing significant violence has the opposite effect of catharsis. Studies of young people and adults who watch a higher percentage of TV shows containing violence indicate that these people are more likely to behave aggressively than those who watch television programs with a lower amount of violence (Eron, Huesmann, Lefkowitz, and Walder, 1977). This is not particularly surprising; we learned in Chapter 2 about the role of modeling in encouraging aggressive behavior.

Does being a spectator at a football game serve as catharsis, allowing us to drain away aggressive urges, or do we become more aggressive as a result? Certainly in many stadiums in the United States, the violence in the stands rivals the aggression on the field. Homeowners near stadiums complain of postgame violence: fans tearing down fences, trampling shrubs, or generally running amok. Nearby emergency wards treat aasorted cuts, bruises, and breaks of spectator combatants.

On the other hand, to say that greater overt hostility among Americans is due to watching violent TV shows or athletic combat does not do justice to other factors in society that encourage violence. Liquor and drug consumption, unemployment, and even world political tensions cannot be lightly dismissed as contributing factors. Also, it's hard to know whether people who are more aggressive to begin with are drawn to watching violent shows and games. In thinking about this issue, we need to keep in mind that the great majority of people who watch violence on TV or are season ticket-holders to local football games do not become aggressive. Many of them enjoy a thriller on television or love to express bottled-up feelings while cheering their favorite team to victory or despairing over its defeat. They come out of the experience more tranquil than before.

Social Bonding

As with working and loving, playing serves as a vehicle for creating and maintaining social relationships. This use of play for social contact begins in childhood. Most of the loving contacts between family members have a playful element to them — playing "peek-a-boo" with Mom and Pop, hide-and-go-seek with brothers and sisters, and checkers with grandfather. Without others to play with, many youngsters complain they have "nothing to do" while sitting amidst a pile of attractive toys and games (Millar, 1974).

In adolescence, play is a way of being with friends after school or work. This can range from being a "tennis bum" or "rink rat" to hanging around a street corner, doing volunteer hospital work as a candy-striper, or joining a scout troop. Teenagers play at whatever behavior is prescribed by the peer group. And because there is considerable value in being just like everyone else, adolescents do not play in spheres not shared by the group.

Among young people, the peer group continues to be important. Moreover, since many young people have not gotten serious about advancing their careers just yet, and relationships with the opposite sex may be transient, having fun with classmates in college or buddies at work on weekends is an almost universally important event. Those who are not with a group on Saturday night feel very much left out.

Having a recreational activity to engage in helps a new person in town find and fit into a new social group. A new kid on the block who takes his basketball down to the park is likely to find some other youngsters to play with. A woman new to a company may find it easier to make friends if she joins the outing club or the bowling team.

Among some adults, play is the only sphere of life where feelings of friendship can be expressed easily to those who are not family members. Some

Play Bonds Adolescents Together

"You can't understand those kids unless you can get into their gangs." Systematic observation over a six-month period confirmed this and similar remarks. Persistent study revealed the vast majority of a particular boy's or girl's waking hours are spent in the comppany of a few pals. When he leaves home in the morning he generally walks or rides to school with them. In and around the high school he can be seen talking, laughing, walking, playing with them. Through the day he is with them whenever some formal demand on his time, such as classes or the job, frees him for informal activities. Before school opens in the morning, little groups of friends can be seen talking together, laughing over some joke or prank, planning future activities, or reliving past ones through talk and shared memories. Later the same little band of boys or girls can be seen going to or from lunch, and usually together; if they pack their lunch they may be grouped in a corner of the Common Room or in the Central School gymnasium.

After school two or three out of a group of five or six may go uptown to the pool hall if boys, or to the drug store or bowling alley if girls. The same two or three boys or girls may be seen early in the evening on their way to a show or a friend's home. This persistent relationship between a few boys or a few girls which carries over from one activity to another throughout the day, and day after day, is the most obvious thing about the behavior patterns of the high school pupils.

SOURCE: From Hollingshead, A. *Elmtown's youth: The impact of social classes on adolescents.* New York: John Wiley & Sons, Inc., 1949, pp. 204–205.

This turn-of-the-century photo shows a group singing in a New England church choir. Social bonding may be one type of satisfaction coming from this playful activity. Can you think of others?

work environments are so competitive or mechanized that friendly relations are impossible. "I make it a practice to avoid having friends at work," one executive says. His friends are at his country club, and his medium for relating to them is a golf game and the bar at the "nineteenth hole." The workman's friendships are not cemented on the assembly line but by playing on the softball team, catching a few beers after the game, and playing cards at the Elks Club.

Participation in ceremonies and in ceremonial games fosters a sense of social membership for all ages. The ceremony may be extraordinary — the American Bicentennial celebration or the Olympic Games. Or it may be commonplace — watching or marching in a local parade, attending confirmations, bar mitzvahs, school graduations, weddings, or the Fourth of July picnic in the park. William James saw these events as basic to human nature because of the excitement we feel in being part of a crowd of people acting together (James, 1890). Performing in ceremonial games or watching them stimulates our feeling of sharing in the collective experience with our relatives, friends, and neighbors. Generally, we leave these events in better spirits and feeling more firmly connected to one another.

Competence

Just as with work and love, play provides a reality basis for the experience of competence. If we watch children at play, it is hard not to be impressed by their joy at being a cause — having at least momentary control over their environment. A girl piles blocks higher and higher and then gleefully knocks them all down. A boy fits together the pieces of a puzzle. Both may have played the same way day after day, yet they continue to be attracted to these activities because of the opportunity they provide to express their competence.

At every stage of the life span, we learn to do things that gratify the need to express competence. Unlike the drive for arousal, the need for competence does not require that the task be new, complex, or dissonant. Making something happen that we have done many times before — putting a ball through a hoop or in a hole, playing a familiar piano piece, knitting a sweater, or planning a garden for the twentieth consecutive year — gives us a feeling of pleasure because we are making something happen. What keeps us at these playful routines is the joy of being a cause of something of our own choosing. Also, when we pursue recreational activities at which we are competent, we do not need someone to say, "How wonderful!" We can give ourselves pleasure when we watch the ball go through the hoop, hear the proper notes, or harvest the radishes.

As we grow into maturity, we build a repertoire of competencies in play, just as we do in the domains of work and love. I know I am skilled at basketball, singing, and camping. You know you are good at bridge, cooking, and carpentry. These self-perceptions form a solid basis for experiencing ourselves as independent and unique individuals, and so are a cornerstone of our identity.

Many normal playing behaviors can gratify more than one need. For example, a game of table tennis can be highly exciting, allow for considerable catharsis, foster social attachment, and provide an opportunity for an awesome display of competence.

Playing and Adjustment

In Chapter 1 we studied a summary of Vaillant's findings showing that the ability to play is associated with better adjustment. Table 1.1 on page 16 shows that his best-adjusted subjects took full vacations and still enjoyed sports after age 40. By the same token, about two-thirds of the men who were not adapting well skimped on their vacations, and three out of four played no sports at all (Vaillant, 1977).

Actually, Vaillant's findings support the earlier thinking of William James. Writing over one hundred years ago, James (1873) argued for the value of a vacation because he thought Americans were wrecking themselves by overwork. He prescribed this:

> An employer . . . should see to it that every man and woman working for him got a good solid month of holiday in the course of a year. . . . [The employer would] make money by it in the long run; for there is hardly an occupation from sawing wood to writing poetry in which the mental state of the workman does not influence the result; and wherever the mental factor exists the man will do more and better work in eleven months than in twelve.

At the time he advocated a month's vacation for employees, it was thought exceedingly generous to grant half that much — and still is by many employers.

Table 8.2   Effects of physical fitness training on emotions, personality, and self-concept

STUDY	PRIMARY FOCUS	SUBJECTS	OUTCOME
R.S. Brown et al. (1978)	Depression	High school and university athletes	Improved
de Vries (1968)	Tension	Middle-aged males	Improved
Folkins (1976)	Moods	Middle-aged males at risk of CHD	Improved (anxiety)
Folkins et al. (1972)	Personality moods, work, sleep	College males and females	Improved (females)
D.S. Hanson (1971)	Anxiety	4-year-olds	Improved
Karbe (1966)	Anxiety	College females	Improved
Kowal et al. (1978)	Moods, self-concept, personality	Male and female recruits	Mood improved (males)
Lynch et al. (1978)	Moods	Middle-aged males	Improved
McPherson et al. (1967)	Moods	Post-coronary and healthy males	Improved
Morgan et al. (1970)	Depression	Adult males	No change
Morris and Husman (1978)	Well-being	College students	Improved
Popejoy (1968)	Anxiety	Adult females	Improved
Tredway (1978)	Moods	Older adults	Improved
Young (1979)	Well-being, anxiety	Male and female adults	Improved
Buccola and Stone (1975)	Personality	Older males	Some improved
Duke et al. (1977)	Locus of control	Children	Improved
Folkins et al. (1972)	Personality (present adjustment)	College males and females	Improved (females)
Ismail and Young (1973)	Personality	Middle-aged males	Some improved
Ismail and Young (1977)	Personality	Middle-aged males	No change
Kowal et al. (1976)	Moods, self-concept, personality	Male and female recruits	Mood improved (males)
Mayo (1975)	Personality	Seventh- and eighth-grade females	No change
Naughton et al. (1968)	Clinical scales	Post-coronary males	No change
Tillman (1965)	Personality	High school males	No change
Werner and Gottheil (1966)	Personality	College males	No change
Young and Ismail (1976)	Personality	Middle-aged males	Some improved
Bruya (1977)	Self-concept	Fourth graders	No change
Collingwood (1972)	Body and self-attitudes	Adult male rehabilitation clients	Improved

Table 8.2 Continued

STUDY	PRIMARY FOCUS	SUBJECTS	OUTCOME
Collingwood and Willett (1971)	Body and self-attitudes	Obese male teenagers	Improved
J.S. Hanson and Nedde (1974)	Self-concept	Adult females	Improved
Hilyer and Mitchell (1979)	Self-concept	College males and females	Improved
Martinek et al. (1978)	Self-concept	Elementary age children	Improved
Mauser and Reynolds (1977)	Self-concept	Elementary age children	No change
McGowan et al. (1974)	Self-concept	Seventh-grade males	Improved

SOURCE: Adapted from Folkins, C. and Sime, W. Physical fitness training and mental health. *American Psychologist*, 1981, 36, 373–389. Copyright 1981 by the American Psychological Association. Reprinted by permission.

Note: CHD = Coronary Heart Disease

When Vaillant noted that men who play competitive sports are better adjusted than men who don't, he not only validated the thinking of psychologists of former times but anticipated a wave of modern scientific findings detailing the effects of regular exercise on mental and physical health.

In Chapter 3 we noted that physical activity operates as a direct control technique to relieve depression and other stress emotions. Studies of sedentary normal individuals who began regular exercise programs — for instance, jogging three times a week for half an hour — almost always find that these people feel better afterwards (Greist, Klein, Eichens, Faris, Gurman, and Morgan, 1979). A summary of the relationship between physical fitness training and mental health has been compiled by psychologist Carlyle Folkins and Wesley Sime (1981). They pulled together research showing the impact of exercise on emotions, personality traits, and self-concept. Their summary is shown in Table 8.2. Basically, Folkins and Sime's review of the studies in this area suggests that physical fitness training is associated with improved mood, lowered physical tension, better self-concept, and increased work efficiency. It also bolsters intellectual functioning during and after stress. Related research indicates that joggers and others who are in the worst physical condition to begin with benefit most from regular exercise (Folkins, Lynch, and Gardner, 1972).

Folkins and Sime caution us against too enthusiastic a view of exercise as a cure-all for emotional problems. They point out that much of the research is poorly designed. An imaginary but typical example: eighteen college sophomores claiming to be depressed were instructed to jog as a group every other day for a half-hour; ten weeks later, they said they were less depressed. Then the researchers conclude that exercise improves mood. Can you tell what might be wrong with their reasoning?

Regular exercise enhances physical as well as mental well-being. For instance, it helps us control our weight by burning calories which might otherwise be retained as fat. It is a fact that an hour of scrubbing floors uses about the same number of calories as skating, and pounding an electric typewriter all morning burns as much energy as a round of golf (Katch, McArdle and Boylan, 1979). It is far more enjoyable for most people, however, to keep fit by burning calories in leisure activities rather than in an occupation. Table 8.3 shows the number of calories expended per hour in several recreational sports.

The physical benefits of routine moderate conditioning are being documented. A Duke University medical research team studied sixty-nine healthy adults from 25 to 68 years old, before and after a ten-week period of regular exercise. They found that activity increases the body's *fibrinolytic response* — a chemical activity in the blood that dissolves clots and therefore reduces the risk of cardiovascular disease (Williams, Logne, Lewis, Barton, Stead, Wallace, and Pizzo, 1980).

How can we determine whether we are getting enough exercise to improve or maintain our physical fitness, but not put too much strain on our heart in

Table 8.3   Calories expended per hour of exercise

ACTIVITY	CALORIES PER HOUR	ACTIVITY	CALORIES PER HOUR
Archery	315	Hunting	355
Backpacking	585	Jogging (1 hour)	
Badminton	480	6 mph	720
Basketball		8 mph	935
game	705	10 mph	1175
non-game	430	12 mph	1500
Bicycling	410	Scuba diving	540
Bowling	225	Schuffle board	185
Canoeing	410	Skating (ice or roller)	480
Dancing	355	Skiing	
Fencing	585	water	435
Golf		downhill	480
Using power cart	185	cross country	675
Carrying clubs	405	Soccer	630
Handball, paddleball		Softball	335
racquetball, squash	750	Table tennis	285
		Tennis (singles)	480

SOURCE: Adapted by permission from Pollock, M., Wilmore, J., and Fox, S. *Health and fitness through physical activity.* New York: Wiley, 1978, pp. 128–129.

Note: The calories expended per hour of exercise are based upon a person of 154 pounds of body weight.

Table 8.4   Recommended pulse rates during exercise to promote fitness

AGE	MAXIMAL HEART RATE	70%	85%
20	200	140	170
30	190	133	162
40	180	126	153
50	170	119	145
60	160	112	136
70	150	105	128

the process? Doctors believe that exercise that improves cardiovascular stamina should increase the pulse rate for a prolonged period of time (Johnson and Goldfinger, 1981). Types of exercise that result in a sustained increased pulse rate are activities such as jogging, swimming, bike riding, and skipping rope.

We can estimate roughly whether we are exerting ourselves too much or not enough by taking our pulse during exercise. In general, the maximal heart rate for a healthy person is 220 minus his or her age. Exercise at less than 70 percent of the maximal heart rate loses some of its value in developing cardiovascular fitness. Exercise which drives the pulse beyond eighty-five percent of the maximal heart rate brings unnecessary stress and no further improvement in fitness. A *rough* guide to these lower and higher limits is shown in Table 8.4. The amount of exercise needed is at least twenty minutes (after a warm-up period), at least three times a week. This program should be built up gradually.

Playing Through the Life Cycle

In the following sections we will identify normal playing behaviors that are specific to or begin at each stage of the life span. Special attention will be paid to the relationship of play to work and love. We will also examine factors that interfere with pleasure from play and consider what we might do to minimize them.

Childhood and Preadolescence

Three types of play accompany growth during childhood and preadolescence: imitative play, cognitive play, and mastery and application.

Imitative Play. Do you remember dressing up in your mother's clothes or pretending you were your father? Much of the leisure time of children is spent imitating adults. At first, youngsters copy their parents' dress or behavior; then gradually they range further afield, pretending to be cops and robbers, soldiers, doctors, nurses, teachers, or astronauts.

Imitation is the way many young people imagine and begin to prepare for adult occupations. As they play at doing what they know about grown-up roles, children can start to see if they have an aptitude or interest in a field. After watching a movie about an architect, 7-year-old Walter might imitate him by building things. Before long, he might decide he likes constructing imaginary buildings from his toy blocks, is good at it, and go on to create more and more elaborate structures. His friend, who watched the same movie, may give it up after a day or so of play.

Boys and girls learn something about the codes governing the adult world by playing games organized by particular rules. They learn to try their best, be a team player, and be a good sport. They might also learn that "winners never quit and quitters never win," that "winning isn't everything — it's the only thing," and that "every time you lose you die a little." The dangers of making winning too important are readily described in popular and professional writing. The impact on most youngsters of this kind of pressure to be victorious is to drive them out of these activities into areas of play where being first or best is not as important as participating.

Another function of imitative play is to help a youngster master fear or anxiety about a troubling experience or thought by playing out the event. Often the experience is one in which the young person was made to sit passively and

This young girl's dancing is an example of imitative play; having seen others dance, she imitates their movements. Some psychologists may also see the dance as a form of recapitulative play because aspects of it resemble the traditional dances of her forebearers.

to "take it." An example Freud (1931 p. 223) used is a child who has just been to the doctor:

> Children's play, too, is made to serve this purpose of supplementing a passive experience with an active piece of behavior and . . . annulling it. When a doctor has opened a child's mouth, in spite of his resistance, to look down his throat, the same child, after the doctor has gone, will play at being the doctor himself, and will repeat the assault upon some smaller brother or sister who is helpless in his hands as he was in the doctor's.

By imitative playing at being doctor, the child masters his fear by "becoming" that which he or she fears.

Cognitive Play. Cognitive theory assumes that specific types of play accompany and enhance the natural unfolding of intellectual growth. The man who first thought this could be true was Jean Piaget. A Swiss psychologist, Piaget (1957; Inhelder and Piaget, 1964) thought that everyone passes through four eras of intellectual growth. Each of these stages is characterized by a particular type of play (Piaget, 1957).

□ *Stage 1, Sensorimotor (age 0–2):* The child understands the world through touching, sucking, pulling, and pushing. Typical play of this phase with a ball might be tasting it and then pulling it and pushing it away. As soon as the ball is out of sight, the child loses interest, because the capacity to imagine an object in its absence has not yet been developed.

□ *Stage 2, Pre-Operational (age 2–7):* The acquisition of language and the capacity to think symbolically are the new mental skills of this phase. The child is able to imagine a ball that isn't there. Typical play involves the capacity to use one object to symbolize another, yet shaping reality to fit the whim of the youngster (Flavell, 1963). For instance, a 6-year-old girl might imagine a cigar box to be a school bus and the marbles scattered around the floor to be children at the bus stop. She may spend many hours imagining herself as the driver picking the youngsters up and delivering them to school.

□ *Stage 3, Concrete Operations (age 7–11):* The ability to think logically is a primary feature of this phase. An example is mastering the concept of *conservation.* This is the recognition that substance, volume, and number of things remain constant even though they may change their appearance: when a wadded-up napkin is twisted into a long, thin shape of a snake, this is the same amount of napkin, not more; when milk is poured from a short, wide glass into a tall, narrow one the volume of the liquid does not change; when a handful of marbles is spread out on the floor, there are not more but the same number. The play of this stage is generally governed by rules that are often quite rigid and unchangeable. Ten-year-olds in a game of marbles might strictly follow the rules as though the rules were sacred.

□ *Stage 4, Formal Operations (age 11 onwards):* The growth of the ability to think more and more abstractly characterizes this final stage in Piaget's scheme. In play, young people understand that rules are no longer sacred, and they can alter them by mutual consent. A game of basketball might be altered to allow a team more than six points behind to have the ball after every basket.

Recognizing the value of play in intellectual development, some parents and other adults make the mistake of trying to subtly manipulate children's play to enhance mental growth. In doing so, they often drive the fun out of it. They surround youngsters with educational toys, but when the little girl or boy reaches for an old ball or raggedy doll, mothers and fathers pressure the youngsters to play with the new home computer instead. Kids seem to have an instinct for such coercion and back away quickly from any "playful" activity that they may feel forced to enjoy. Young people need to feel free to explore spontaneously and play with whatever seems like fun at the moment, rather than that which others may think is best for their intellectual growth.

Mastery and Application. Piaget was concerned with the role of play in learning. Vandenburg (1979) expanded his theory to encompass all human learning responses to unfamiliar objects or complicated situations. He suggested that all learning behaviors occur in an exploring – play – application sequence. Can you recall the first time you saw a hammer? What were your reactions? One scenario might have gone like this: At first you explored it to be sure it wouldn't hurt you. After deciding it wasn't dangerous, the play might have involved feeling its shape and weight, pretending it was a gun, using it to hit a ball. Gradually, you began to find its most appropriate application and before long were able to use it to pound nails into wood. After we've acquired mastery of an object, we can store this skill to be retrieved later when we need it — to hammer nails in the wall to build a birdhouse or hang posters.

An illustration of mastering a complicated task through play might be learning to work a computer or doing gymnastics. The desire to master unfamiliar or complex experiences continues much through life, though it is most evident in the child and the preadolescent.

Having a child who shows early mastery or development of a skill through play can cause parents and other adults to put a great deal of pressure on the child to develop this talent further. An example might be a 10-year-old girl with considerable potential in dramatics at school. Her parents and drama teacher applaud her and then begin to pressure her to develop her "God-given potential." The young girl might be convinced to attend a high-level pre-professional drama program on the assumption that she should develop her capability. Reluctantly she goes. Halfway through the program, she tells her parents she hates drama and wants to come home. The parents are mystified and upset. Eventually, they talk to the veteran drama coach, who points out that many youngsters seem to be pressured by well-meaning adults into high-level training programs before their interest and commitment have matured enough to sustain them through the competitive rigors of this experience. This

This impressionistic paint-ing — *The Piano Lesson* by Henri Matisse — conveys the feeling of a child when playful interest is converted by adults into work. As you look at the painting, can you sense the child's feeling of being trapped between the piano in the foreground and the figure in the background? (Collec-tion, The Museum of Modern Art, New York. Mrs. Simon Guggenheim Fund.)

can lead to disheartening disillusionment. As the coach puts it, "Whenever some grown-ups find a spark of genius in the children, they drench it with enthusiasm."

This is not to say that the talent of the young should not be developed. It's just that when adults unwittingly or by calculation convert a playful activ-ity into one that is obligatory and requiring high-quality performance, fitting the expectations of others, it is no longer play. It becomes work. When this happens, the child needs to find another area of recreation.

Adolescence and Youth

Two types of play are most often seen among adolescents and youth. They are impulse diversion and preparation. The play of the teenager also blends with work and love, supporting and augmenting the pleasures from each domain.

Impulse Diversion. In Chapter 6 we saw how working can channel energies that otherwise might be a source of frustration. In the same way, play gives individuals an opportunity to divert impulses that could be bothersome into areas where their partial expression is acceptable. Sexual and aggressive feelings are especially bothersome to adolescents and young people. Traditionally, sports have been looked upon as providing young people a way of managing the sexual drives through **sublimation,** a process in which sexual urges are transformed into competitive drives and channeled into safe areas of expression.

The usefulness of sports to sublimate feelings applies to other emotions as well. An example is a boy with strong aggressive drives. Sport gives that young man an opportunity to vent accumulated tensions and frustrations. Also, sport serves a controlling function. Commenting on the value of sport in disciplining aggressive behavior, biologist Konrad Lorenz (1966) said:

> The value of sport . . . is much greater than that of a simple outlet of aggression. . . . It educates man to a conscious and responsible control of his fighting behavior.

Might it be that the requirement in schools for all students to compete in sports or physical activity contains as a small part of its rationale the channeling of strong sexual and aggressive drives of young people? Some, including Freud (1905), thought that should be the case, and applauded the efforts of schools to help young people sublimate these urges. We should recognize, however, that sports meet many other needs as well: arousal, catharsis, social bonding, and competence.

Sport is not the only thing, however, that can divert the normal drives of young people. Consider the protests of young people in the late 1960s. It may be true that some of these actions should be considered the "work" of these young people. It was certainly motivated by honest concern for inequality, a bad war, and a superannuated bureaucracy. But the protests served other needs as well. James Simon Kunen reported his experiences in his first-person account, *The Strawberry Statement* (1968). A Columbia undergraduate at the time of the riots, Kunen reported how much fun these protests were and how much there was of a powerful sense of being close to one's fellow protestors. For him, it was the most exciting game he'd ever played.

But it is not only the violent, physical expression of play that gives release. Many find that any form of artistic creation — painting, singing, playing a musical instrument, or writing a poem — provides them a more than adequate sublimation of pent-up impulses.

Participation in activities is a beneficial counterbalance to the mental and physical passivity encouraged by television and electronic games. There is no doubt that being able to watch sports twenty-four hours a day and play hundreds of different simulated games while never leaving a chair could be amusing. But for a young person, is this more gratifying than playing a game of Frisbee in the park?

During the twentieth century, the play of young people has changed from outdoor to indoor, from makeshift toys to plastics and computer simulation. Current evidence, however, suggests that the play of children, adolescents, and young people has moved again toward the outdoors and is being based again on more ingenuity and imagination (Albert, 1980). An indoor game with nearly unlimited imagination is *Dungeons and Dragons*. It is typical, perhaps, of the ingenuity being brought to playing in the past few years. This is one of the fastest growing games in America. It appeals to both young and older persons because there is no limit to the complexity the game can encompass.

We've already considered the pressure on some children to develop unique talents, which often converts a recreational activity to work. Another example might be pressuring a young person to continue a playful activity because it serves other ends. A high-school boy with academic and social problems is encouraged to stay on the soccer team, on which he is a star, on the assumption that the self-confidence generated on the field will carry over into the classroom. Aside from the dubious logic of this assumption, the pressure may begin to erode the boy's satisfaction from soccer. The activity has ceased to be freely chosen. If parents or teachers are convinced that physical competence will lead to academic competence, fine. But if a student's fun is weighted down with worklike goals, he or she may have to find other avenues of recreation.

Preparation. In Chapter 6 we noted that young people ready themselves for the world of work by imagining themselves with increasing clarity in adult occupations. The value of projects in school or part-time work in directing adolescents toward one field or another was discussed. Playing also readies teenagers and youth for the workplace by reinforcing approved values and behaviors, as well as providing practice in activities that anticipate future careers.

It should be understood that this is still play for its own sake, however beneficial the side effects may be. The subtle misuse of play by earnest parents and teachers has "useful" ends as its only goal.

After defeating Napoleon, the Duke of Wellington said, "The Battle of Waterloo was won on the playing fields of Eton." This statement underlines the conviction of grown-ups that adolescent games prepare the next generation for adulthood by teaching commitment, teamwork, perseverance, and abiding by the rules. Indeed, adults often use games and sports as metaphor for real-life activities. A regional sales manager in Atlanta may exhort his salesmen by stressing team spirit and besting the other regions by selling more; a vicious fight for power in a top corporate echelon is called "playing hardball."

Because it is whimsical, changeable, and with no direct value except to please the person doing it, playing has a unique place for the young in preparing them for adult roles. They can vigorously pursue a number of interests and occupations through play without being committed to any of them. Because it is "not for keeps," a boy can nurture the notion of being a professional basketball player without the necessity of putting his ego on the line and risking the possibilities of not making it. A young girl might begin taking flying lessons "for fun." As her enjoyment of this activity grows, she learns more about it, and her skills develop. Gradually she begins to imagine herself as a commercial pilot. She might invest increasing energy, time, money, and commitment to this recreation. Eventually, as her facility and sense of self crystalize, she may be willing to make a commitment to a career in aviation.

Since play occurs in the world between fantasy and reality, it enables us to try on vague notions about what being a professional athlete or pilot or artist, teacher, nurse, priest, is all about. Through play, young people can flesh out their understanding of these occupations, gaining clearer feelings of whether they wish to follow a specific career line. Play also provides some protection of self-esteem. If the boy stops growing or the girl has trouble flying on instruments, the play value remains even if the career plans must be rethought.

Finally play may give people an opportunity to pursue two careers, start a second career, or even second-guess the first career choice. A woman who worked as a computer scientist until she was 29 quit to pursue her calling as a cellist. She had been playing the cello as a hobby — four hours a day all during her teens and twenties. She had never committed herself to the cello fully because she feared she might not be able to make a living at it and should work in a more secure occupation. Finally she followed her inner calling, which had been sustained through play.

Adulthood

The types of play that reach prominence in the adult years are relaxation and compensation. These forms of leisure-time activity may have begun many years before. But they are often obscured by life-long playing or recreation that is more characteristic of an earlier phase of the life cycle. In adulthood, as working and loving patterns are established, relaxation and compensation become dominant.

Relaxation. In the words of Walt Whitman (1855), **relaxation** is the ability to "loaf and invite my soul." Relaxation is the shutting down of stimulating input, enabling tensions and other stress emotions to dissipate and permitting recuperation to begin. People whose lives are active and stimulating often spend their leisure time in a setting that reduces sensory experiences. Thus, an accountant working sixty hours a week says, "On weekends, I don't *do* anything. I just like to lie around and graze." Others may engage in relaxing play that stimulates just a little: watching TV shows with predictable plots, reading Gothic novels, walking the dog, or going for Sunday afternoon drives.

Relaxation enables those whose working and family lives are stressful to take time out to recuperate. Adulthood, especially middle age, can be extremely taxing. There are pressures and threats to satisfaction from work, demands of older and younger generations to whom care must be given, and efforts to maintain loving relationships with a spouse or friends. The ability to relax and allow the emotional wounds suffered during the week to heal, while energies and spirits are renewed, is essential to a productive and satisfying life.

Writing over one hundred years ago, William James (1873) was one of the first psychologists to note that American businessmen were ruining themselves by a combination of overwork and the inability to relax:

> [There] was a time when we lived under the dispensation of the favorite American proverb — no half truth even but an invention of a Sabbathless and unvacational Satan — "Better wear out than rust out." But of those who repeated it with most faith, how many have since had enforced leisure to repent their shortsightedness. . . . [W]ho that has travelled in Europe is not familiar with the type of the broken down American businessman, sent abroad to recruit his collapsed nervous system. With his haggard, hungry mien unfitted by life-long habit for taking any pleasure in passive contemplation [he] seems to draw a ghostly comfort from a peevish and foolish criticism of everything he meets. . . . Many of us . . . have grown so used to the harness that when the hour of leisure comes we are unable to use it.

No doubt James would be an enthusiastic supporter of programs in industry that pay for longer vacations, fund sports and recreational activities, and support part-time study for personal growth.

James may also have been intrigued by modern techniques to assist individuals who have trouble letting go and relaxing. An example is progressive muscle relaxation. Essentially, this procedure works by tensing muscle groups one at a time and then relaxing them. Tightening these muscles and letting go allows them to become more relaxed than before. This technique takes about twenty-five minutes. If you want to try this relaxation technique, locate a quiet place, a recliner or a comfortable chair, or lie down. Practice this procedure twice a day. It can be quite helpful, especially during stressful times.

The urge to do something useful with leisure time works against relaxation. Businessmen speak of "working vacations." College faculty members say to each other, "I can't wait for my vacation to get some writing done." Instead of spending Memorial Day weekend in recreation, some of us have to plan to use the time "productively." Columnist Ellen Goodman put her finger on what is wrong with this notion. There is nothing wrong with mowing the lawn, opening up the cottage, getting some writing or business accomplished over a long weekend or the summer, but we should not delude ourselves that we are relaxing. We are merely working a little less vigorously.

Compensation. For many adults, play provides **compensation** for needs not met in the rest of our lives. It is a rare job that is a true calling, consuming our energies, interests, and skills. Compensatory leisure play gives fullness to our lives, providing an opportunity for counterbalancing occupational activities that are specialized, sedentary, or boring.

The doctor who specializes in noses but not knees, the plumber who fixes toilets but not sinks, can find satisfaction in making wine or building an addition to the house, whereby of necessity they are generalists; a technician whose work is with things may spend his weekends entertaining people; a worker in the same plant whose days are spent with people who talk may devote her weekends to sailing a small boat, which does not.

Progressive Muscle Relaxation

Settle back as comfortably as you can and close your eyes. Direct your attention to your left arm, your left hand in particular. Clench your left fist. Clench it tightly, and study the tension in the hand and forearm. Study those feelings of tension, and now let go. Relax the hand, and let it rest on the arm of the chair. Note the difference between the tension and the relaxation. (10-second pause.) Once again, now, close your left hand into a fist, tightly, noticing the tensions in the hand and forearm. Study those tensions, and now let go. Let your fingers spread out, relaxed, and note the difference again between the muscular tension and the muscular relaxation. (10-second pause.) Now do the same thing with the right hand. Clench the right fist. Study the tensions (10-second pause). Now relax the right fist. Note the difference between the tension and the relaxation, and enjoy the contrast. (10-second pause.) (Repeat the procedure.)

Now bend both hands back at the wrists so that you tense the muscles of the back of the hand and in the forearm, fingers pointing toward the ceiling. Study the tension and now relax. Let your hands return to their resting positions and note the difference between the tension and the relaxation. (10-second pause.) (Repeat the procedure.)

Now clench both your hands into fists, and bring them toward your shoulders so as to tighten your biceps muscles, the large muscles in the upper part of the arm. Feel the tension and now relax. Let your arms drop to your sides, noting the difference between the tension that was in your biceps and the relative relaxation you feel now. (10-second pause.) (Repeat the procedure.)

Now we can direct your attention to the shoulder area. Shrug your shoulders, bringing both shoulders up toward your ears, as if you wanted to touch your ears with your shoulders, and note the tension in your shoulders and up in your neck. Study the tension. Hold it, and now relax, letting both shoulders return to a resting position. Just keep letting go, further and further. Once again, note the contrast between the tension and the relaxation that's now spreading into your shoulder areas. (10-second pause.) (Repeat the procedure.)

You also can learn to relax the various muscles of your face. Wrinkle up your forehead and brow. Wrinkle it until you feel all your forehead very much wrinkled, the muscles tense, the skin furrowed, and now relax. Smooth out the forehead. Let the muscles become loose. (10-second pause.) (Repeat the procedure.)

Now close your eyes very tightly. Close them tightly so you can feel the tension all around your eyes in the many muscles that control the movements of your eyes. (5-second pause.) Now relax those muscles. Let them relax, noting the difference between the tension and the relaxation. (10-second pause.) (Repeat the procedure.)

Now clench your jaws, biting your teeth together. Study the tension throughout the jaw. (5-second pause). Relax your jaws now. Let your lips part slightly and note the difference between the tension and relaxation in the jaw area. (10-second pause.) (Repeat the procedure.)

Now press your lips together. Press them together very tightly and feel the tension all around the mouth. (5-second pause.) Now relax. Relax those muscles around the mouth and let your chin rest comfortably. (10-second pause.) (Repeat the procedure.)

And now turn your attention to your

As many of our lives become increasingly sedentary, play as compensation becomes more attractive. Sales of sports equipment are at an all-time high. The number of adult men and women who are taking up new sports ranging neck. Press your head back against the surface against which it is resting. Press it back so you can feel the tension primarily in the back of the neck and in the upper back. Hold it. Study it. (5-second pause.) And now let go, let your head rest comfortably now, and enjoy the contrast between the tension you created before, and the relaxation you feel now. (10-second pause.) (Repeat the procedure.)

Now I'd like you to bring your head forward and try to bury your head in your chest. Feel the tension especially in the front of the neck. (5-second pause.) And now relax, let go further and further. (10-second pause.) (Repeat the procedure.)

Now direct your attention to the muscles of the upper back. Arch your back, arch it, sticking out your chest and stomach so you feel the tension in your back, primarily in your upper back. (5-second pause.) Study that tension, now relax. (10-second pause.) (Repeat the procedure.)

Now take a deep breath, filling your lungs, and hold it. Hold it, and study the tension all through your chest and down into your stomach area. (5-second pause.) Study the tension. Now relax, let go, exhale, and continue breathing as you were. (10-second pause.) (Repeat the procedure.)

And now tighten up the muscles in your stomach. Tense those stomach muscles. Hold it, making your stomach very hard. (5-second pause.) Now relax. Let those muscles become loose. Just let go and relax. (10-second pause.) (Repeat the procedure.)

I'd like you now to stretch both legs. Stretch them so you can feel the tension in the thighs, way out. (5-second pause.) And now relax and note the difference once again between the tension in the thigh muscles and the relative relaxation you feel now. (10-second pause.) (Repeat the procedure.)

Now tense both calf muscles by pointing your toes toward your head. If you point your toes upwards toward your head, you can feel the pulling, the tension, the contraction in your calf muscles and your shins as well. Study that tension. (5-second pause.) And now relax. Let the legs relax, and note once again the difference between the tension and the relaxation. (10-second pause.) (Repeat the procedure.)

Now as you sit there in the chair, review the various muscle groups that you've covered. If you notice any tension in those muscles, send messages to them to relax and to loosen. (5-second pause.) Relax the muscles in your feet, ankles, and calves (5-second pause), shins, knees, and thighs (5-second pause), buttocks and hips (5-second pause). Loosen the muscles in the lower body. (5-second pause.) Relax your stomach and waist and lower back. (5-second pause.) Upper back, chest, and shoulders. (5-second pause.) Relax your upper arms, forearms, and hands right to the tips of your fingers. (5-second pause.) Let the muscles of your throat and neck loosen. (5-second pause.) Relax your jaw and facial muscles. (5-second pause.) Let all the muscles of your body become loose. (5-second pause.) Now sit quietly with your eyes closed. (5-second pause.) Do nothing more than that. Just sit quietly with your eyes closed for a few minutes. (2-minute pause.) Now count from 5 to 1. When you reach 1, open your eyes, stretch and be wide awake and feel very relaxed.

SOURCE: From *Clinical behavior therapy* by Marvin R. Goldfried and Gerald C. Davison. Copyright © 1976 by Holt, Rinehart and Winston. Adapted by permission of Holt, Rinehart and Winston, CBS College Publishing.

from racquetball to camping and kayaking appears to be growing at about the same rate as money spent for leisure.

A unique feature of play is that it can be tailored to advancing age so that it provides almost as much pleasure as it did when we were younger. Fishing is no less fun sitting in a boat on a lake at the age of 70 than wading through a trout stream all day with a fly rod at the age 40.

Because more older people now enjoy good health, many men and women over 40 are engaging in vigorous leisure-time sports. For instance, the number of entrants above the age of 40 in the Boston Marathon rose from about 500 in 1970 to approximately 2500 in 1980, in spite of the fact that the qualifying time was lowered.★

One of the runners during this decade was a man who worked all of his life as a machinist. In high school he never participated in athletics. At the age of 60 he decided he wanted to train for and run in the Boston Marathon. Eventually he ran in five consecutive races. In June 1973, he broke the national mile-run record for his age group (Cantu, 1980).

Experiencing a different life style is another version of compensatory play. A man who works in an office may enjoy going to a nice place for lunch or

★Personal communication from Will Cloney, Director of the Boston Marathon.

Weekends Are for . . .

Just about everyone is spending this weekend.

There are, after all, three days of it and that means 50 percent more to spend, 50 percent more to use . . . UP. So, just about everyone is spending this Memorial Day weekend.

Many of us are Going Away. We are Going Away on roads which were originally built to help us get where we used to want to go, only faster. Now we spend more time than we used to Going Away further than we used to, to places we never wanted to visit before there were highways to get us there. But . . . we do Go Away there faster.

Then again, many of us don't Go Away. We spend the weekend on the lawn, or on a new basement ceiling, or on the shutters. We spend it frugally, wisely, getting so much done. Our plants get planted, our boats get painted, our fences nailed and we are as busy as beavers, worried as White Rabbits. Not a minute wasted, no sir.

Certainly not a minute wasted on ourselves.

Others of us spend time spending. More and more stores are open all weekend long for our "convenience." We never run out of milk; we run out for milk. And we call that "handy."

There are those of us who practically spend-thrift the weekend in what are called Leisure Time Activities — and never mind the contradiction in that term. (There is even a "Leisure Industry.") Of course we dress for the occasions in Leisure suits and supply ourselves with Leisure equipment — props like golf clubs, metal tennis racquets, autographed softball mitts, 10-speed bikes, Addidas sneakers and coordinated jogging suits. We wait in long lines for a tennis court or a golf game and count the number of laps we run, left, right, left, right.

We call this relaxation, even recreation.

In one way or another we cash our weekend in, spend it all. We fill it up the way we fill the "empty" air with transistor radios and the "empty" landscape with housing developments. After all, we can't just be there and do nothing can we?

Or could we?

Is it possible that there is nothing to be done? And what would happen if we did it?

taking his brown bag into the park on a sunny day. A woman who spends her life in a conservative community, leading a highly disciplined existence, finds great pleasure traveling to Greece, staying up late, eating and drinking and dancing until dawn.

Each summer, nearly 50,000 Americans experience a different life style by becoming college students for a week. This opportunity is created by the Elder Hostel Program. For those 60 and older, over four hundred colleges in the U.S.A. and Canada provide week-long mini-courses in subjects ranging from Shakespeare to psychopathology and Greek civilization, to how to manage stress. These older students have the opportunity to choose among three or four courses to pursue for a week. They eat and sleep in the dormitories. After classes they are encouraged to use the libraries, view the cultural events, and to take advantage of the athletic facilities. Special tours and programs enrich the week. Every state has an Elder Hostel coordinator. The cost for this week-long experience is nominal. Programs are planned to start in several European countries.

Disuse and misuse of play are the primary threats to pleasure during the

---

What would happen if this Memorial Day we did not use the car, open the purse, finish the chores, "play" golf, turn on the television set? If we did not do anything that could conceivably fit on any list of Things to be done?

Would all those couples we see spending their weekends in parallel play or work, turn and face each other? Would they find out that, when they have nothing to do, the kids don't get in the way of it? Would their kids discover that when they are doing nothing, they aren't waiting for what happens next?

But, what could we do all day, you ask?

Pay attention. I mean that's what we could do. Pay attention to each other, ourselves, to letting go of the restless sense that we should be Doing Something.

Henry Thoreau, who was a superb nothing-doer once wrote, "I have traveled extensively in Concord."

He never did Go Away. He did not have a list of Shoulds in his hip pocket or Triptik on his walking stick. He traveled extensively, in Concord, and paid attention to his own "backyard" and his relationship to it.

Doing nothing is getting rid of all the agendas that stand between us and our feelings. It's lying on the grass without worrying about mowing it, being together instead of doing together.

It's real re-creation, the space to let go of the chores of life, to re-order them, to let our "feeling" cells regenerate. It's thinking, holding hands, listening, day dreaming, and making love in the afternoon. You don't have to fit it into traffic patterns and sign-up sheets.

It's spending leisurely time on ourselves and each other.

Does that sound hard? Well, it comes slowly for many of us. We have to wean ourselves from weekday purposefulness and "leisure activity."

But it can begin now. All we have to do is tell our Old Plans: "We're terribly sorry. We won't be able to be with you. You see, we are doing Nothing this weekend."

SOURCE: From Ellen Goodman, At large, *The Boston Globe*, 28 May 1976. © 1976 The Boston Globe Newspaper Company/Washington Post Writers Group, reprinted with permission.

Growing numbers of older adults are enjoying vigorous leisure-time activities.

adult years. The first perhaps is the greatest hazard. Three fallacies contribute heavily to adults' forgetting how to play. The first is the assumption that play is instinctive and therefore it is not necessary to practice. The reality is that, like work and love, there is no inner drive to play. This is especially true for hard-working, overextended adults. It is far easier than it seems to forget how to play and forsake gratification from it.

The second fallacy is that, as adults, we can play spontaneously. Most adults have far less time than they imagine for spur-of-the-moment activities. Days are filled with work, children, seeing relatives and friends, and keeping up the place. The man who waits for an uncommitted weekend to go camping, or the woman for some space in her week to play racquetball, will not find these by accident. As with most other activities in adulthood, they need to be planned and scheduled well in advance.

The third fallacy that undermines adult play is the thinking that play should wait until other responsibilities are met. There is always more to do in the course of a day than can possibly be accomplished. If we put off playing until everything that needs doing has been done, the wait will be lengthy indeed.

Pleasure from play can also be compromised by the requirement that we be good at it. Many men and women don't like to play at anything unless they perform well and see improvement. However, an alto in the church choir singing for fun needs to be sure she still enjoys singing, even though she misses notes here and there because she hasn't had enough time to practice. Or consider the overweight salesman taking up jogging for recreation. At first, he's happy to be able to run a mile without dropping. But as soon as he starts to improve and run faster, he may begin to carry a stopwatch. Unless he keeps his jogging in perspective, he may find himself driving to make monthly improvements, the same way he tries to better last quarter's sales.

Many people will take up recreation for a while and improve at it until they reach a point where further gains will cost too much effort and emotional energy. It becomes work. At that point they may choose to remain at a level that provides pleasure, or they may move to another type of play.

Addiction in play, as in love, is to be avoided if possible. A Hungarian doctor who immigrated to the United States liked to fence in his leisure time. One day he gave it up and never fenced again. A friend asked him how he could give up a sport with which he'd been involved for so many years and obviously loved. The man replied, "There's a difference between affection and addiction."

Summary

1. Currently, about one dollar in eight is spent by Americans on play.
2. A playful activity is characterized by a feeling of a lack of obligation, freedom from the necessity of high achievement, and malleability to current interests.
3. Human needs gratified by recreation in all phases of life are arousal, catharsis, social bonding, and competence.
4. Play fosters human adjustment. Routine physical exercise lifts mood, lowers tension, enhances self-esteem, and improves cardiovascular functioning.
5. Though specific playing behaviors are difficult to assign to particular stages of life, some are more prominent in one era or another. In childhood and preadolescence, the primary types of play are imitative, cognitive, and mastery and application.
6. In adolescence and youth, playing serves as impulse diversion and preparation.
7. In the adult years, play provides a reliable source of gratification when the inevitable toll of time may diminish pleasure from other spheres. Two types of recreation that dominate adulthood are relaxation and compensation.
8. Disuse of play in adulthood is caused by three fallacies: that play is instinctive, that it can be engaged in spontaneously, and that it should wait for all other responsibilities to be met first. A misuse of play can be the imperative to be good at it, or continuously improve to the point that it becomes work. Addiction is found in play just as it can in love.

A Look Ahead

This chapter ends the second section of the book. In the next section we will examine states of adaptation ranging from normal to abnormal. A chapter each will be devoted to normal adaptation, temporary overload conditions, crisis reactions, and neurotic disorders.

Key Terms

play	**sublimation**
arousal	**relaxation**
catharsis	**compensation**

Suggested Readings

Reasons for play

Ellis, M. *Why people play.* Englewood Cliffs, N.J.: Prentice-Hall, 1973.

> Encyclopedic summary of the reasons for play.

Play and development

Piaget, J. *Play, dreams and imitation in childhood.* (1951). Translation by C. Gattegno and F. Hodgson. New York: Norton, 1962.

Garvey, C. *Play.* Cambridge, Mass.: Harvard University Press, 1977.

> Cognitive, psychological and social development documented as occurring because of children's play.

Excess rationalized as play

Erikson, E. *Toys and reasons: Stages in the ritualization experience.* New York: Norton, 1975.

Maccoby, M. *The Gamesman.* New York: Simon & Schuster, 1976.

> Adults rationalizing excessive competitiveness or violent political acts by cloaking them in the vocabulary and rituals of childhood play.

Play throughout life

Dangott, L., and Kalish, R. *A time to enjoy: The pleasures of aging.* Englewood Cliffs, N.J.: Prentice-Hall, 1979.

> Types of play for all ages.

Part III
States of
Adaptation

This section portrays states of adjustment. The first state is normal adaptation, which describes the majority of us in usual times. State 2, temporary overload condition, occurs when we are under time-limited, agreeable stress. Crisis reactions, State 3, are painful responses to severe trauma or loss. Neurotic disorders — persistent, disabling behaviors, thoughts, or emotions — comprise State 4. Each chapter will consider ways of handling the different states — maintaining normal adaptation, dealing with temporary overload or crisis less painfully, and recovering from a neurotic disorder.

At some time we are likely to experience States 2 and 3, when we face greater than usual stress or must cope with a shocking loss. Just as we are not ourselves with the flu, chicken pox, or poison ivy, we are unlikely to behave normally with psychic upsets. And just as we recover from these physical ailments, we return to normal spontaneously following the end of a temporary overload or crisis-producing stress. Neurotic disorders are not common in most people's experience, but can become chronic, disabling behavior patterns.

Notice that the word *state* describes the type of adjustment — not stage or level. Stage or level implies a relationship between one mental condition and another, while the word state does not. There may be a transition from one state to the adjacent mental condition; but just as often someone may be functioning normally at one moment and in crisis or suffering from neurotic symptoms the next, without seeming to pass through any intervening states.

You, the individual, can do more for your own
health and well-being than any doctor, any
hospital, any drugs, any exotic medical device.

SOURCE: Statement by Joseph A. Califano,
Jr., in foreword to *Healthy people: The surgeon general's report on health promotion and disease prevention*,
U.S. Department of Health, Education, and Welfare.
Washington, D.C.: U.S. Government Printing
Office, 1979.

Chapter Preview

CHAPTER 9

State 1: Normal Adaptation

Questions to think about

□ What would you measure in yourself to decide if you were normal?

□ How much is the definition of normal adaptation limited by culture?

□ Why might a sense of humor be associated with normal adjustment?

□ What kinds of self-help programs can you think of to help us get the most out of life?

In this chapter we study the characteristics of normal people, the largest part of the population in this country or elsewhere. We look at normally functioning men and women, so that we can compare this state of adjustment to other types of adaptation. We begin by looking at the question of how to go about evaluating the adjustment of ourselves and others. We consider the question of cultural differences in normal adaptation and whether a general set of criteria might be applied to individuals from different backgrounds to determine whether they are behaving normally.

The primary features and secondary characteristics of normal adaptation are described. We look at the question of how adjustment at one stage of life is related to adjustment at another, and we study influences that affect emotional balance. At the chapter's end, we consider ways of maintaining normal adaptation as we each confront our daily menu of frustration, threat, conflict, and loss.

Measuring Normal Adaptation

In Chapter 1, we defined normal adaptation as the capacity to find satisfaction from a balance of work, love, and play in the presence of high-level responses to stress. The state of normal adaptation is not a fixed condition, but rather a continuing capacity for readjustment (Devereux, 1956). It is a process, a fluid condition of balance, imbalance, and rebalancing as we respond to inner and outer stresses that affect our lives.

The equilibrium we may achieve after managing a stressful event may not be the same as the balance we maintained before. As Menninger points out, a growing person is not concerned with maintaining the stability of what was, but with moving away from the status quo toward ". . . new and unsettled states in contrast with the automatic return to the comfortable and relatively tension-free previous . . . balance." (Menninger, 1967, p. 85)

After graduation, this woman will move away from her adjustment to school to a fresh environment with different challenges and pleasures — and requiring a new adaptation.

While Menninger may overstate it a bit — sometimes we are quite pleased to find a previous emotional balance restored — there are many times in life when the new equilibrium is quite different from any we knew before. Take Hillary, who was a competent, well-adjusted high-school senior. She could cope with whatever stresses her world held for her, and she enjoyed life. In November of her freshman year at college, however, she was coping with a range of problems she had never faced before and was not getting nearly the same enjoyment from work, love, and play as she had before. When she finally adapted to the changes in her life, the normal state she achieved was very different from the one that had characterized her adjustment during her high-school years.

How do we determine whether we are functioning normally? What would we assess? Would we count how many units of stress we are experiencing? Measure the height of our anxiety or depth of depression? Test for need for achievement or aggression? Calibrate the strength of our ego? These specific elements can be evaluated, but we cannot judge a person's level of adjustment by assessing them. It's a little like trying to draft the best split end for a professional football team. Coaches measure a player's height, weight, time in the forty-yard sprint, strength, flexibility, and ability to catch the ball. But why one young man becomes an all-pro while another with apparently the same assets fails to make the team always mystifies the coaches. In assessing adjustment, as in evaluating football players, the whole is far greater than the sum of the parts.

One principle in assessing adaptation is **holistic functioning**: that we behave as whole people, not as the sum of our separate elements. Robert White (1972) notes that we sometimes talk of our urges and tendencies as though they were lodgers in a boarding house, each leading a separate and distinct life apart from the others. Yet in actual practice, White points out, we don't think of ourselves as a boarding house full of independent traits:

> If I lose my temper and make a childish scene, I do not blame one of my tenants, an aggressive urge. . . . If my neighbor starts an unpromising venture and makes a success of it, I do not congratulate his need for achievement; I congratulate the man.

The self is indivisible, so when we evaluate someone's level of adjustment, we have to look at the total person.

The second principle in measuring adjustment is that people's **actions** tell us much about their overall mental condition. Philosophers, ancient and modern, say that we are what we do (Thomson, 1975; Sartre, 1956). Actions are large-scale, simple, everyday behaviors. Examples are working at a job, relating to loved ones, or having fun in the sun. Psychologists of today see the interaction between an individual and the environment as the basic unit of personality (Hettema, 1979). People's actions tell us whether they are tranquil, happy, or depressed; tense, placid, or enraged; enthusiastic or bored. Men and women who are functioning normally can report accurately how they feel, and others who know them will agree.

But, we might protest, aren't inner thoughts and feelings sometimes at odds with outside behavior? Some of us have known a troubled person who appeared pleasant and successful to everyone but who, like Edwin Robinson's Richard Cory, may put a bullet through his head at any moment. If inner thoughts and feelings substantially diverge from overt actions, then the idea of assessing normalcy by observing behavior will not work.

If we think about these smiling, suicidal people a little more carefully, however, we are likely to discover behavior that is consistent with their inner state. For example, if we observe the Richard Corys of the world, we will note that their lives are not providing them very much satisfaction. They will usually tell us this if asked. We also could observe that the balance of their life is disturbed. They may derive some satisfaction from one realm of their lives, such as being a workaholic or a playboy, but gratification in other areas is seriously diminished.

Cultural Differences in Normal Adaptation

Normal behavior in one culture can be considered deviant in another. Anthropologists have found some tribes in which it is usual for people to eat other humans, mutilate themselves, have visions, or dress like members of the opposite sex. Even in the United States, acceptable behavior varies by region, ethnic group, race, and social class. How then can anyone say that this or that behavior is normal?

A man who wrestled with this question was French psychiatrist and anthropologist George Devereux (1956). Devereux was interested in the cross-cultural aspects of normal adjustment because he wanted to provide mental health workers with a means of diagnosing and treating individuals in a culture about which they knew little or nothing. His thinking led him to two obser-

Richard Cory

Whenever Richard Cory went down town,
We people on the pavement looked at him:
He was a gentleman from sole to crown,
Clean favored, and imperially thin.

And he was always quietly arrayed,
And he was always human when he talked;
But still he fluttered pulses when he said,
"Good morning," and he glittered when he
    walked.

And he was rich — yes, richer than a king —
And admirably schooled in every grace:
In fine, we thought that he was everything
To make us wish that we were in his place.

So on we worked, and waited for the light,
And went without meat, and cursed the bread;
And Richard Cory, one calm summer night,
Went home and put a bullet through his head.

SOURCE: Robinson, E. A. Richard Cory, from *Children of the Night* (1890–1897), in *Collected Poems*. New York: Macmillan Company, 1925.

vations that address the problem. First, most people have a concept of themselves based on how they fit into their culture. Second, the way in which an individual experiences and handles the culture indicates the level of adjustment.

These ideas are consistent with much of the thinking about self-concept and self-esteem examined in Chapter 2. Our self-concept is largely based on how we see ourselves in the society in which we live. An Arab sheik, a Tibetan monk, and a millionaire owner of an American baseball team all may be extremely powerful and successful as well as being perfectly normal. But their self-concept may rest on how closely they fit their culture's view of what is appropriate to possess, to do, and to feel. Each may exhibit his possessions and power differently according to the customs of his society, and each may be content or not with himself based on how closely major areas of his life conform to cultural expectations. All three may be happy with their loving relationships for different reasons — the sheik because he has a harem of four wives, the monk because he is celibate, and the American because he is on his third marriage.

Self-esteem — how we value ourselves — is largely based on how we react to the picture we have of ourselves in the surrounding society. To some extent this rests on what others tell us: your mother tells you you are adorable and mine tells me I am amusing. And to a large degree self-esteem is rooted in the degree of similarity between how we ideally would like to see ourselves functioning in our world and how we actually see ourselves. In normal people a high degree of similarity exists.

Three primary features help us understand how successfully a person experiences and handles his or her culture: (1) the capacity to find satisfaction from a balance of work, love, and play; (2) the ability to manage stress with relatively high-level adaptive responses; and (3) the stability of personality style. What constitutes a satisfying occupation, appropriate expressions of affection, or just having fun varies greatly from culture to culture. The degree to which a society reinforces particular modes of coping with anxiety also differs hugely, and there is enormous diversity in acceptable types of personality. While each culture will shape the normal expression of these primary features, each of them is a reliable beacon of adjustment whatever the culture.

Primary Features of Normal Adaptation

Satisfaction in Work, Love, and Play

In a normally functioning person, the ability to find satisfaction from a balance of work, love, and play is unimpaired. Typical behaviors that give satisfaction (described in Chapters 6, 7, and 8) are summarized in Figure 9.1 for each stage of the life cycle.

Normal people may not find satisfaction in work, love, and play each day, but if we watch these individuals during a week or month, we would note that

Age		Working	Loving	Playing
60	Later adulthood	Continuing to feel useful Generativity Anticipation of a planning for retirement	Grandparenting Coping with life alone Accepting care of others	
55				
50	Middle adulthood	Making it Reappraisal	Finding a workable marital style Caring for two generations Maintaining friendships	Relaxation
45				Compensation
40	Early adulthood	Settling down Forming an occupational identity Getting ahead Dual careers	Sharing a dream Marriage Caring for children Alternative loving styles	
35				
30	Youth	Non-commitment to occupation or school expressed in multiple job changes or dropping out	Maximum distance from parents Widening circle of diverse friends Remaining comfortable in culture Living together Formation of primary bond	
25	Adolescence	Part-time work Acquisition of skills for personal growth and career management	Involvement with a gang Altruism Finding outlets for sexual desire First big romance	Impulse diversion Preparation for adult roles
20				
15	Preadolescence	Learning to develop habits Learning self-care Carrying out chores Performing satisfactorily in school Imagining adult work	Best friend	
10				Imitative Cognitive Mastery and application
5	Childhood		Objects of love Parallel and cooperative play Remaining connected to adult-controlled groups Close contact with parents	
0				
		Life long needs expressed through working: Preservation, Channeling of Energies, Social Bonding, Competence, Appreciation	Life-long needs expressed through loving: Preservation, Social Bonding, Competence	Life-long needs expressed through playing: Arousal, Catharsis, Social Bonding, Competence

Figure 9.1 Types of working, loving, and playing activities associated with each developmental stage

they engage in some of the activities summarized in Figure 9.1 and obtain adequate pleasure from them. For instance, the absence of displeasure may be the most that Bubba, who is a good football player but not a great student, is able to wring from studying and going from sports to class. His satisfactions come from sports, from evenings and weekends, which he lives for, when he can enjoy being with his friends, watching TV, and playing with the dog. For many of us, the pleasures from work, love, and play are interdependent. Working has more meaning for Walter when he uses his wages to support loved ones or buy a new fishing rod.

The relative percentage of gratification from the three spheres of living is a matter of age, taste, and opportunity. In fact, it is probably true that no two people obtain the same amount of pleasure from each area. The domains of life which satisfy us may change from stage to stage. A man coming back to his twenty-fifth reunion said to his classmates that he was successful in business but a total failure as a husband and father. In the next twenty-five years he said he hoped to change and be more loving to his family and de-emphasize his work, if it were not too late. Many women move in the other direction. Having spent much of the third and fourth decades of their lives nurturing others, at mid-life their desire is for achievement more than love. As Sophie put it, "I'm tired of it. I'm tired of caring for everyone. It's my turn!" At 35, Sophie found that her interest in loving was waning and her desire to achieve satisfaction in work was growing rapidly. When she entered the bank management training program, she found she looked forward to each day more than she could remember. She also discovered she found loving others far easier when this sphere was not her only source of satisfaction and she was gaining pleasure from the sphere of work as well.

High-Level Adaptive Responses

Few of us go for long without being frustrated by something on our job, upset by a loved one's actions, or feeling conflicted by competing emotions which cry for release. Being normal does not exempt us from common unhappiness, flurries of temper, or lurid fantasies. It is how we handle these events and emotions, not the stresses or feelings themselves, that determines whether we continue to function normally.

Normally behaving individuals show a larger proportion of adjustment mechanisms in dealing with day-to-day problems. We all differ in which ones we use. An exam on Shakespeare's *Julius Caesar* may bring out in you a tendency to try to anticipate what will be on the exam by looking at old tests and talking to students who took the course last term. The woman sitting next to you may do neither, because she seems to know instinctively which characters, soliloquies, and ideas the professor will think are most important. She will study those and nothing else. Generally, the ways we use to manage problems have been employed before and are congenial. You are far more comfortable dealing with exam stress by anticipation, and the woman next to you counts on her empathy to prepare for the exam.

Resources are intact and accessible in State 1, and their use helps us withstand daily stresses. Family and friends remain reliable, no serious exhaustion of physical stamina occurs, intellectual capability is undiminished, competencies in skills and hobbies continue, money is not drained away alarmingly, faith in powers greater than our own remain, and dreams are sustained. Normal women and men don't need to exploit resources constantly to benefit from them. Just knowing they are available is enough.

While adjustment mechanisms predominate in State 1, all of us employ a mix of self-protective responses when we are under considerable stress or when we do not have the energy or will power to combat an unpleasant reality. Vaillant's study of normal men (1977) revealed that half of the time they used either coping devices or ego defenses to manage stress. Indeed, those who had selective access to these lower-level self-protective responses under stress were judged to be better-adjusted than those who used them less often. Imagine you, me, and a friend in a pre-law college program, each of us with a good deal of anxiety about it. You may wonder whether you really want to be an attorney, but you not willing right now to look squarely at these doubts, so you suppress your questions, continuing to work at your studies, knowing that you'll have to face them someday — but not right now. I may practice meditation or resort to other direct control responses to quiet my nerves so I can concentrate on my academic work. This is because I want to be a lawyer more than anything, but I am at the bottom of my class and can't yet look at whether I might be better off somewhere else. Our friend, who is brighter than either of us, spends much of his time playing pool (at which he's getting very good) during his sophomore year because he hates law but his attorney father demands he follow him into the legal profession. At some point he'll have to make a decision, too.

Your suppression, my repression supported by the direct control response of meditation, and our friend's using the resource of his pool-hall skills as a direct control response are not effective in the long run. But they reduce the emotional pain we feel and allow us to find relief for a while. Later, when we are feeling stronger, we will try to resolve the problems by direct action.

Stable Personality Style

A third primary feature of normal adaptation is maintaining a stable personality style — having the same habitual responses, interests, quirks, and tastes. Usually we express the major features of our dominant personality style where it counts: at work and, to a lesser extent, in loving relationships and play. A normally functioning person is likely to act in a manner consistent with the expectations of those who know that individual well.

No one fits a particular personality type exactly. Moreover, some aspects of a person's behavior are usually at odds with the dominant temperament. For instance, Luis doesn't collect stamps as an avocation — his hobby is playing the saxophone. Darlene, even though she seems scatterbrained, is competent under pressure; it was others who panicked. For active Walter, one of his avocations is the relatively placid enterprise of fishing.

Normal people put their own unique stamp on their personality. The result is as unique as fingerprints. Far more variation occurs in the personalities of individuals in a normal condition than in other states of adaptation. This is also true among marriages. Couples who are unhappy resemble each other, whereas those in successful marriages seem to be happy in their own fashion (Rausch, Bary, Hartel, and Swain, 1974).

Among normal individuals the "fit" between temperament and environment is comfortable. We can find a way to be reasonably productive in our occupations, maintain affectionate touch with others, and have some fun. The environment is not antagonistic to the type of person we are. Our strengths are not devalued, nor are our weaknesses amplified: Luis's pessimism is an asset in his work as an engineer, and when he has periods of being "down" he can still be effective, because he doesn't have to relate closely with others.

Normally functioning people are not forced to withstand an antagonistic environment for too long without the hope of a change for the better. The change may be accommodation — altering a habit that annoys our friends. It can be an effort to alter a work environment to suit us better. Or, if all else fails, we can find another group of friends or job.

Secondary Characteristics of Normal Adaptation

Numerous other characteristics reflect normal adaptation. Significant among these are the usual degree of environmental stress, a sense of feeling pretty well physically, typical mental organization, characteristic mood, and intact relations with others. These are summarized in Table 9.1.

Usual Stress

In an average, familiar environment people can gratify needs usual to the culture and stage of life in which they live. Individuals unable to find a suitable job, who are in relationships that cause chronic misery, or even whose play environment is compromised, a man whose hobby is raising dogs in the country and who receives a promotion requiring him to move to New York City — all are dealing with unusual stress that can eventually erode normal adaptation. We differ in our ability to tolerate unpleasant events before either the magnitude of them or the length of time we must confront them causes our adjustment to deteriorate.

Average, expectable environments also refer to the inner world. In a normal state, inner needs and impulses are in keeping with what others are experiencing. A 13-year-old experiencing rapid growth, the appearance of secondary sexual characteristics, and sexual desires can more easily accommodate these changes if there is a peer group to share these experiences with.

In State 1, stress has a clear cause. People believe they know why they are angry, depressed, or tense, and they believe that the distress is only temporary. Indeed, it is frequently the assurance that things will improve that makes it possible to bear substantial hardship and continue to exhibit normal adaptation.

Table 9.1   Secondary characteristics associated with State 1: Normal adaptation

Usual Stress
   Average, expectable outer and inner
      environment
   Clear cause of common unhappiness
   Stress seen as resolvable

Feeling Well
   Sense of feeling typically well
   Disabilities with clear causes
   Stability of vital functions
   Customary grooming
   Drugs used to assist coping rather than
      compromise it

Typical Organization
   Oriented in person, place, time, and
      situation
   Openness to inner and outer experi-
      ence leading to action
   Flexibility of action within behavioral
      repertoire
   Reasonable correspondence between
      belief and action

Characteristic Mood
   Consistency according to personality
      style
   Variation with cause
   Background moods do not affect plea-
      sure from living for long
   Usual humor and enthusiasm

Intact Interpersonal Relationships
   Focus follows developmental expecta-
      tions, as modified by personality
      style
   Seeking satisfaction does not adversely
      affect others
   Irritation toward others passes

Feeling Well

In the words of American songwriters Lester Santhy and Thomas "Fats" Waller (1929) "lookin' good but feelin' bad is hard to do." If asked how they feel, most people in State 1 will say they feel well. They recognize this physical status as typical for them. When they are unwell, it is usually because they are afflicted with a short-term disease such as chicken pox or the flu. Or they have a temporary condition caused by a clear-cut event of short duration — a hangover from drinking too much, a bad rash from walking through poison ivy, or severe cramps at the beginning of a menstrual cycle.

Normally functioning individuals usually exhibit stable vital functions. Physically this usually means they are maintaining internal **homeostasis.** Homeostasis refers to the complex working of the whole organism to maintain a physical equilibrium in the face of external or internal events. Shivering when we are outside in cold weather or sweating when we have a fever are examples. Homeostasis is evidenced by stability of observable body signs. Weight does not fluctuate exceptionally; respiration and pulse are usual; eating, sleeping, and elimination patterns are experienced as typical; and skin color, condition, and texture are unchanged.

As with any human attribute, there is expectable variation. One of us may sleep better in the fall, another may gain weight in the winter, and someone else has skin problems in the spring. The key question is, "Is this variation expectable?"

Grooming is another physical quality that reflects normal adaptation. For many people, the way they take care of themselves, how they are groomed and how they dress, is a personal statement. A normally functioning individual's grooming and care remain within what is usual for that person. It may be three-piece suits during the week and sweatshirt and jeans on weekends, or it may be sweatshirt and greasy jeans all the time. But it is customary, predictable, and congenial.

People with chronic illnesses or disabilities are hard put to remain in State 1 since it is difficult to obtain satisfaction from the spheres of work, love, and play when we don't feel well or can't enjoy what we used to. Yet some people are able to manage it. Cardinal Cushing of Boston was able to function normally in the final years of his life, even as he was dying of cancer. Asked by a parishioner how he was feeling, he is reported to have said, "For how I am feeling, I am feeling pretty well."

To relieve physical or emotional distress from chronic illnesses or disabilities, some people take medication. Many others take drugs to relieve day-to-day stress stemming from unavoidable realities: young people at school develop headaches because of the pressure of studies; their teachers can feel tension building at the end of the day; and the aches and pains of older people can make them irritable. Medication which relieves the physical and emotional reactions to these stresses and lets us do our job, relate congenially to others, and enjoy life, is clearly beneficial.

There are abuses, however, that we all need to watch out for. If we are concerned about the possibility that someone we care for is abusing drugs, we might ask these questions: Is the drug use increasing? Can it be given up voluntarily? Are unwanted side effects occurring? Does drug use block direct action to alter the stressful environment? A "yes" answer to these questions suggests a high probability of drug abuse or habituation. The student who medicates his tension headaches needs to be sure he isn't moving from four pills a day to twenty of extra strength. The teacher who typically has a couple of beers at night to unwind should know she can go without alcohol without experiencing severe withdrawal symptoms. And the cost to older people of relief of their ailments must not be drug-induced apathy or fogginess. All of us who use drugs of some sort regularly should be sure that the good feeling they provide does not encourage us to stay in highly stressful situations that should be changed or abandoned.

Typical Organization

How we organize varies according to our personality style. Hillary might be neat and orderly while Darlene is messy and intuitive. The organizational style of both, however, enables them to be productive, relatively trouble-free, capable of enjoying life.

The normal individual is **oriented to a reality,** a reality that others agree exists. There are four spheres of orientation: person, place, time, and situation. The woman who works in a bank would be able to tell us that her name is Sophie, she is in the downtown office of the First National Bank of Hartford, it is 9:30 a.m. on October 12th, and she is an assistant loan officer.

Normal organization allows openness to outer and inner experience that leads to action. As we know from our study of personality styles in Chapter 4, each of us differs in what types of experience we react to most strongly. For you, it may be hard facts; for me, it may be my subjective reaction to outside events. All of these ways of perceiving experience provide useful information. The decisions we make are likely to be strengthened by paying attention to objective data as well as our responses to this information.

How facts and impressions are processed and the manner in which decisions are reached and actions planned also vary according to personality style. Some lean heavily in the direction of the rational, analytic, and logical. Others are guided by their "gut feel." Major decisions — what occupation to follow, whom to marry, whether to have children, where to live — are likely to have a significant intuitive ingredient.

Being open to experience and taking action also means learning from experience. Sophie granted a loan to someone whose credit was marginal on the basis of her feelings which had guided her correctly in the past. If the loan goes bad she'll be sure to check an applicant's credit more carefully the next time her intuition tells her the applicant is a good risk.

State 1 individuals seem to be free to act flexibly within their behavioral repertoire (Coan, 1974). The freedom and power to act intentionally is one of the most reliable indicators or normal adaptation. Simply stated, this is being *able* to do what we *choose* to do. Thus, the high-school student is able to forsake the TV and put off talking to her friends in order to sit down at her desk and do the homework because she knows it is in her best interests to complete it.

Finally, the normal state features a strong correlation between belief and action. In the ideal world, everyone would be capable of autonomous action in perfect correspondence with their beliefs. In the real world, however, two forces limit independent behavior: unconscious motives and group influence.

Normal people may be affected from time to time by unconscious urges that cause them to behave in a way that is at odds with their cherished values. For instance, a man may make fun of his 5-year-old son's inability to catch a ball. When he sees the uncomprehending tears in his boy's eyes and the fire in his spouse's, he stops abruptly. He is able to undo the damage with more loving attention. Eventually he may even remember that his own father used to humiliate him as a child because of his ineptness in sports. To his horror he discovers that he is acting out the very behavior that he both feared and despised.

Autonomous action is also influenced by others who cause people to behave differently in a group than they might on their own. Social psychologists have demonstrated that being a group member causes some people to behave

Sitting alone on the Washington seacoast, a man portrays the aloneness each of us experiences when we must make difficult decisions and prepare to take action.

in ways greatly different from their stated morals, values, and common sense. Part of the reason lies in the desire to be in agreement with one's peers. For example, subjects asked to compare the length of a line with three others — one shorter, one longer, and one the same length — would report correctly when alone. But if placed with a group of others who had been instructed to say that the shorter line was the same length, the subject was often influenced in the direction of the majority's opinion. About a third of the time, these students changed their initially correct judgment to fit the consensus (Asch, 1951).

Autonomy can also be overridden by one other person in authority. In his book *Obedience to Authority,* psychologist Stanley Milgram (1974) gives an appalling account of a group of subjects whose ethics and values were nullified by their desire to please authority.

There are enough reports of bystanders' watching others being assaulted or victimized to recognize the essential truth of the work of Milgram, Asch, and others that normal people are so influenced by the presence of others that their behavior is occasionally at odds with inner convictions. How often "occasionally" occurs is determined by personality style, experience, and reliance on our own will rather than social pressure.

Obedience to Authority

Individuals were recruited and paid to aid in what they were told was an experiment to improve learning. They were asked to deliver electric shocks to a subject when he responded incorrectly to a problem. This person was an actor and, in fact, received no shock at all. The subjects were told, however, that the severity of the shocks ranged from mild to very severe. The shocks were "administered" from a machine whose dial indicated the voltage being delivered. The maximum level was clearly labeled as dangerously severe shock.

During the project, the subjects were accompanied by an experimentor in a white coat. When the actor pretended to make an error, the subjects were instructed to administer the electric shock to enhance his "learning." At a relatively low level of shock the actor winced; as the voltage increased, he cried out; later he screamed in pain and pleaded a heart condition. As the subjects observed the actor's simulated pain, some were reluctant to continue. The experimentor in the white coat prodded them and told them finally they had "no choice" but to continue to administer the shock. Two-thirds of the subjects administered the maximal shock while watching the actor writhing in pain. The subjects included executives, teachers, and laborers.

SOURCE: Adapted from Milgram, S. *Obedience to authority*. New York: Harper and Row, 1974.

Characteristic Mood

Consistency of mood is typical of individuals in State 1. We will say that our present temper is about the way it usually is and our friends will agree. People's prevailing temperament varies widely. You may be typically optimistic, while I am consistently pessimistic. We may have a classmate whom we both think is introverted. When a change in mood persists for more than a short time, it has a clear cause. A usually quiet ninth-grade girl becomes elated when she is asked to the spring dance. Her father is suddenly irritable for the same reason. Before too long, the moods of both return to normal.

Apparently, biological variations occur in mood. Researchers have discovered subtle differences during the waking day based on daily body rhythms. Some of us are larks and are liveliest in the mornings, slowing down noticeably in the afternoon. Others are owls, becoming active only as the sun sets. Many women experience monthly changes in mood as a function of the menstrual cycle. Some data on men also show monthly rhythmic variations (Rossi and Rossi, 1977).

People in State 1 can tolerate common unhappiness and depression from time to time (Freud, 1895; Hartmann, 1939). The adolescent girl who doesn't receive an invitation to the high-school prom, because a boy she likes asked someone else, may become moody for a brief period. But she continues to go to school, gets through her homework, and spends time with friends. Though she's obviously not quite herself, her disappointment doesn't significantly compromise her other enjoyments. Gradually the mood lifts.

When normal people feel the downward pull of depression, they are able to control it by taking several steps (McLean, 1974). One characteristic pattern for the girl above might be to recognize (1) that she has a valid reason for being upset; (2) that before long she will feel better; (3) that feeling sorry for herself will only make the depression worse, so she needs to stop thinking about how hurt she is; (4) that there may be a positive side to the whole thing — if the boy didn't want to go with her, she would have had a lousy time anyway; and (5) that she will be able to do some things which will make her feel better — call a friend, go shopping, hit a softball. This approach works with other problems as well.

The presence of humor is one of the most reliable indicators of normal adaptation. A sense of humor that is not aggressive or designed to evade responsibility promotes **self-objectification,** the ability to perceive the incongruities between one's own stated values and pretensions and how one really acts (Allport, 1937). A 19-year-old boy can be amused afterwards in the retelling of his fumbling efforts to be suave and seductive with a woman who rejected him. When a person's adjustment begins to fail, the first casualty is a sense of humor about the self.

Humor is an invaluable resource. After being burned in an accident and nearly dying, Richard Pryor has been able to hasten his psychological recovery by joking about the event in nightclub and movie appearances.

By the same token, the ability to laugh at oneself as an index of the return to mental health of their patients. Just as northerners look for the first robin as evidence that spring is on its way, mental health workers watch for the expression of humor about the self as a sign that normal adaptation is returning.

The second casualty, when personal adjustment fails, is enthusiasm. Nearly every normal person has a zest for living. This too varies with personality style. Some people seem to have a lot more enthusiasm than others, but each one has a usual level of zest. A person in State 1 does not lose enthusiasm for long without cause.

Intact Interpersonal Relationships

Getting along with others is one of the hardest things we have to do. Generally, normal people are able to relate to others in a way that roughly corresponds with some of the loving behaviors for each developmental stage described in Chapter 7: the preadolescent has his best friend, and the adolescent has his gang.

Not everyone follows developmental expectations for interpersonal growth. Some delay in one stage for years beyond the time when movement to the next period of interpersonal relationships is anticipated (Vaillant and Mikofsky, 1980). One example is the boy or girl whose primary relationship in adolescence is with parents instead of with a best friend or a gang. The father is the best friend and mother is the closest confidante. This doesn't mean the child is abnormal. He or she may just be slow. Later, the child may pass through the stations of growth that were missed earlier.

Normal people usually relate to others in a manner consistent with their personality style. Some are gregarious, others shy; some lead, others follow; some have a large network of friends and acquaintances, others possess a few intimates; some retain contact with the same friends over a lifetime, others make a new batch every three or four years; and with some, relationships with parents remain primary and with others, the relationship diminishes markedly from the onset of adolescence.

State 1 individuals do not do violence to others, either emotionally or physically. This means that the person can live in harmony with loved ones, finding pleasure in the major domains of living without substantially impeding the opportunity for others to realize the same pleasures.

Harmonious State 1 relationships can be broken by discord. What discriminates normal adjustment is that the cause of hostility is easily identified, can be aired, and passes. "Your sarcastic comments about my new dress really hurt my feelings," one friend says to another. Or, "When I tried to tell you about my day at school you turned on the TV," an exasperated son tells his father. Irritations can be talked out. Grudges are not held so interpersonal wounds can heal.

Normal Adjustment Changes with Age

If we apply these primary features and secondary characteristics associated with normal adjustment to ourselves or someone we know and find we are functioning normally, can we know how long that condition will last? What are the odds of a normal child becoming a normally functioning teenager? How many State 1 adolescents grow up to be normal adults? What is likely to promote normal adaptation or disrupt it?

Longitudinal studies of children followed to adulthood provide indirect information. These long-term projects seem to support three observations about human behavior over time: (1) adult mental stability cannot be predicted from evidence of adjustment in childhood or adolescence; (2) where continuity of particular personality characteristics does occur, it is from one developmental stage to the period of life immediately following; and (3) personality is greatly affected by cultural reinforcement.

Regarding the first observation, we might remind ourselves of Vaillant's studies of Harvard undergraduates (1977). He discovered that, like acne, much of the men's adolescent maladjustment cleared up by mid-life. Others, working with youngsters from a wider spectrum of social class and ethnic backgrounds, found little carry-over of childhood disturbances into adult life (Cass and Thomas, 1979).

At the Fels Research Institute in Yellow Springs, Ohio, psychologists Jerome Kagan and Howard Moss (1962) evaluated nearly 100 men and women in their mid-20s whose personality traits had been carefully studied — first as infants, then as children and adolescents.

Many of these traits are indirect indicators of adaptive level — passivity, dependency, and aggression. Almost none of these traits exhibited by these individuals in the first six years of life carried over into adulthood. However, some characteristics found among the subjects when they were adolescents extended into their adult lives — examples of these were dependency in females, competitiveness in males, and interest in intellectual achievement for both sexes.

The second observation — that personality traits continue from one stage into the stage immediately following, but weaken beyond that period — also receives support from the research of Kagan and Moss. Most of the time when a personality trait persisted, it was in the stage immediately succeeding the one in which it first appeared. For instance, children rated as strongly dependent or aggressive were likely to score high on these same qualities as preadolescents. But if we skip a stage — if we compare ratings of dependency or aggressiveness at childhood and adolescence rather than childhood and preadolescence — we find little similarity.

Just as dawn does not unfailingly tell us what the day will bring, neither do characteristics of the child invariably predict adult personality. But more often than not, the dawn tells us what the weather will be like for the morning.

Many of our attitudes about appropriate dress and behavior are influenced by the media and other forces in the culture.

The final observation is that those few traits persisting into adulthood are many times those which are socially reinforced. An example is intellectual mastery. An interest in doing well in intellectual tasks in childhood continued into adulthood when it was steadily rewarded by parents and teachers in the environment.

Superwoman:
Can Women Have "It" All?

Can women have it all? The "it" includes the pain, pleasure, and power built into occupying the executive suite, children's room, and boudoir — a balancing act seeming to require a superwoman effort. Or are women forced into impossible choices: being exhausted by the relentless demands of work, family, and house care without time for themselves, and retiring from the rat race to live the life of the "liberated woman" at home; or being Ms. Newly Minted Professional, with shiny brief-case and degree, starting up the ladder of success with no time for a sustained relation-ship, trying to suppress those little, nagging doubts about whether she wants to spend the rest of her life married to a profession and giving birth to new ideas, while she watches her biological time clock speed by.

Researchers interviewed 200 women in groups and sixty-eight women individually to examine the unique stresses of working, married women today. The women were aged 20 to 60-plus; about forty percent were nonwhite; and over ninety percent had college or advanced degrees. They worked in institu-tions of higher education, businesses, govern-ment, or foundations, earning salaries from under $10,000 to over $75,000 per year.

All of the women were asked to define the Superwoman and then describe their roles — e.g., administrator, wife, housekeeper, single parent, lone woman in the office, counselor, or risk-taker.

Among the behaviors that were reinforced, Kagan and Moss observed considerable sex stereotyping. Boys were expected to grow up to be aggressive and girls to be dependent. A much lesser relationship between childhood and adult traits occurred when a behavior was not rewarded. An illustration is the relationship between childhood and adult aggression in females. It appeared that the culture made them pay a psychological price for their assertiveness. Unlike some passive boys who grew up to be passive men and were relatively comfortable with the outcome, these competitive women had considerable conflict about whether their assertiveness compromised their relationships with others.

A present-day example of lack of cultural reinforcement, or indeed antagonism toward normal personal growth, is the difficulty women have in advancing their careers. Imagine the problems faced by Sophie who has to somehow balance a demanding job with the needs of her children, the care of the house, and finding time for her husband, Luis. Every day, she reads about job and salary discrimination toward women, rushes home to cook for her faintly hostile family, tries to engage Luis in an interesting conversation, stops her daughter from throttling her little brother, and ignores the dust balls collecting under the bed.

Much has been made of the pressures on working women, and doubtless the adjustment of some is adversely affected. However, many women cope well in spite of the pressures. To some extent, this is because of the reinforcement that many women have received for functioning in multiple roles and building support networks.

Two major findings emerged. First, the women responded very differently in groups than they did individually. In groups, some females reacted negatively to the idea of Superwoman, because it implied having to carry heavier burdens than males. Others, especially black women, thought the question was silly because they had been playing the Superwoman role for generations. In the individual interviews, however, the women expressed far more interest in grappling with the pressures on themselves. Many of them, particularly those in their mid-30s and beyond, felt they did indeed function as Superwoman.

The second finding was that most of those interviewed individually, and many of the women in groups, said they were not suffering from too many responsibilities or stresses. They felt pleased with being able to raise a family and develop a career while other women were doing one or the other. They acknowledged stress reactions — tiredness, headaches, feelings of never-enough-time and guilt, but almost all could do something to relieve this. Those women liked the activity, the absence of boredom, having the family as a sanctuary, and learning new things. Finally, they reported being increasingly confident of their abilities, feeling that they could take on more responsibility.

SOURCE: Adapted from Wolfman, B. and Bean, J. *Superwoman, Ms. or myth: A study of role overload.* Paper presented at the annual meeting of the American Educational Research Association, Boston, Mass., September, 1980.

As Wolfman and Bean's study indicates (1980), many women seem to have been trained to deal with many activities at once. In addition, women bring another strong resource, rewarded by culture, to the working world that has been trained out of many men: the instinct to enmesh themselves in relationships at work as well as at home. This concern for involvement with people can sustain women through difficult times.

Maintaining Normal Adaptation

It is not difficult to imagine maintaining the state of normal adaptation when things are going smoothly: we are warmly embedded in a nest of loved ones, have a lot of fun playing, and work at a challenging job that gives us numerous opportunities to express our competence. Each morning we bound out of bed, knowing that the day will be sunny and warm and the wind will be at our back.

If there is one thing we have learned about the life cycle, however, it is that life is not one upward surge. From time to time, the pleasures from important dimensions of our life are shut down. Loved ones are alienated, leave, or die; we tire of needlepoint, TV, jogging, or whatever we used to enjoy in our leisure time; our grades in school slip or we are fired. We feel ourselves being savaged by events beyond our control, our adaptive capabilities break down, and we feel overwhelmed by life. Depression, anger, or anxiety become chronic companions. We notice that we are smoking dope in the morning before class, needing a six-pack at lunch to get through the day, binge-eating on weekends. Or we are beginning to behave in ways that alarm and concern our friends. What can we do to try to help ourselves? Two types of direct action responses can improve both the quality of our lives and the chances for recovering our emotional balance. One type of action helps us cope with specific stresses. The second reduces unacceptable stress reactions.

The first are actions we can take to deal with particular events in our personal lives — single parenthood, difficulty with loved ones, being a woman working in a "man's" world, being a homosexual in a straight community, being unemployed, or just not being able to get what we want out of life. In every community, resources in the form of agencies and self-help groups can assist us in maintaining or improving our adjustment in the face of considerable stress. Although the list is not encyclopedic, here are examples:

□ *Loved ones who drink or gamble.* For people whose adjustment is being threatened by loved ones who abuse alcohol or gamble heavily, *Al Anon* or *Gam Anon* can provide mutual support and advice to relatives of those who are members of Alcoholics Anonymous or Gamblers Anonymous. They are also open to loved ones of alcoholics and compulsive gamblers who will not attend Alcoholics Anonymous or Gamblers Anonymous. Openness and the sharing of mutual feelings are stressed.

□ *Women at work.* Classes, seminars, and support groups address issues that women deal with at work as well as at home and with the family. Also, there are clubs and service organizations where working women can find other individuals with similar interests and concerns. Weekend and summer seminars abound on subjects such as time management, time and salary issues, and sexual harassment.

□ *Single parenthood.* Support for single parents is found in groups such as Parents Without Partners and similar organizations. Many are specialized by interest, education, age, religion, or ethnic background. Some businesses offer day care or flexible working hours. Invaluable assistance with children can be obtained through the Big Brother/Sister organizations, Foster Grandparents, Boys' Clubs, "Y" programs, Scouts, Outward Bound, summer camp, and special tutorial/activity programs at local colleges and universities.

□ *Gay life style.* The past decade has seen an increase in open commitment to the gay life style. It is now possible to imagine someone being stable, productive, and gay. However, because of pressures that oppose a homosexual orientation, gay men and lesbians sometimes need to reach out for support. One source of help is the Boston-based *Gay Community News*, which lists resources in many large cities. Many communities have organizations comparable to these in the Boston area, which include clubs and groups to combat loneliness, places where special interests can be pursued, and clinics or professionals who can provide medical services.

□ *Unemployment.* Finding our way back to work when we are let go can be helped by a Division of Employment Security in every state. They can often make recommendations for temporary positions, operate job-seeking strategy seminars, and identify retraining opportunities. Also, they can put people in touch with volunteer organizations, which not only uncover job openings but also provide guidance as to how to find a job, teach women and men to write more effective résumés and interview more effectively, and provide support during the depressing period of finding a job. Some books, such as *What Color Is Your Parachute?* (Bolles, 1972; updated annually) can be extremely useful.

□ *Job boredom.* Having a job that has lost its vitality can be compensated for by trading with someone in a different part of the world. An example is the Job Exchange aiding psychologists (Table 9.2). For twenty-five dollars psychologists can register with this organization and negotiate an exchange for a year or two with someone working either in the same or different job somewhere else. Many professions have similar organizations where workers can relieve boredom by cross-training within an organization or through evening extension courses.

□ *Regeneration.* Individuals and couples find personal regeneration in workshops and courses expressly designed to promote openness to feeling, catharsis, communication, and the imagining of a more vital life style. Examples are encounter groups, courses in transcendental meditation, or religious retreats. These are frequently sponsored by service agencies or churches. In addition, there are dozens of books designed to assist us with a number of general or specific problems we might have.

Support for the Lesbian and Gay Life style

Boston Area (617) Information/Service/Social

(Boston Area Lesbian and Gay Schoolworkers)
P.O. Box 178, Astor St., Boston, 02123
Boston Asian Gay Men & Lesbians
c/o Glad Day Bookshop, 22 Bromfield St.
Boston, 02108   542-0114
El Comite Latino de lesbianas y homosexuals
de Boston
P.O. Box 365, Cambridge, 02139
354-1755
Gay Recreational Activities Committee
(GRAC), c/o GCN Box 8000   282-9161
Lesbian and Gay Folkdancing
c/o GCN Box Dee, 22 Bromfield St.,
Boston, MA 02108   661-7223
Older and Other Gays, c/o GCN, Box 1500,
22 Bromfield St., Boston 02108
Parents of Gays   542-5188, 426-9371

Political/Legal

Cambridge Gay Political Caucus,
P.O. Box 218, E. Cambridge
02141   491-0968

GLAD (Gay and Lesbian Advocates and
Defenders), 2 Park Sq.   426-1350
Harvard Committee on Gay Legal Issues
Roscoe Pound Hall, Cambridge, 02138
Mass Gay Political Caucus
Suite 407, 739 Boylston St.   242-3544

Student

Gay People at BU, c/o Program Resources
Office, George Sherman Union, Boston
University.   353-3646
Gay/Lesbian Concern Group of Boston College
P.O. Box L 199, Chestnut Hill, MA
02167
Gay People's Group, UMass/Boston
(Harbor Campus), Bldg 1, 4th fl, Rm
178   287-1900x2169
Harvard-Radcliffe Gay Student Assn.
876-1487
MIT Gays, Rm. 50-306   253-5440
Northeastern Gay Student Org., c/o Student
Activities Office, 255 Ell Ctr.
Tufts Gay Community, c/o Student Activities
Office, Medford 02155

□ *Aging*. Difficulties associated with aging can be lessened by associating oneself with active older men and women. One of the most vital of such organizations is the **Gray Panthers,** who promote a variety of service work as well as form a significant political lobby. Those wishing to remain active in some sort of work can continue to be productive through the Action Corps (VISTA, the Peace Corps, and SCORE), which recruits older women and men. Other participatory or action-oriented programs for elders include the Foster Grandparents, who receive an hourly stipend for spending time with children in day-care centers, infant homes, convalescent hospitals, or schools for the retarded or disturbed; homemaker/health care aides who are paid to provide personal care services for older, physically disabled, or chronically ill individuals in their home and receive wages for this work; and Friendly Visiting, a service begun in Chicago in which older people are provided to visit individuals who are home-bound (Lowry, 1980). Not everyone is interested in action programs. Those older people who are interested in continuing growth have found the Elder Hostel Program both exciting and informative.

Women

Daughters of Bilitis, 1151 Mass. Ave.,
    Cambridge 02138   661-3633
Gay Professional Women's Assn.,
    Box 308, Boston U Sta., Boston 02215
Massachusetts Feminist Federal Credit Union
    186½ Hampshire St., Cambridge   661-
    0450

Religious

Friends (Quaker) for Lesbian and Gay
    Concerns   776-6377
Lutherans Concerned for Gay People
    536-3788
Metropolitan Community Church   523-7664
Fr. Paul Shanley (Exodus Center)   964-0996
Unitarian Universalists Office of Gay Concerns
    25 Beacon St., Boston 02108   742-2100

Media

Closet Space WCAS (740 AM)   492-6450
Gay Community News   426-4469
Xanadu Graphics, 143 Albany, Camb.
    02139   661-6975

Medical/Counseling

Gender Identity Service   864-8181

Homophile Alcoholism Treatment Ser-
    vice   542-5188
Homophile Community Health Service
    542-5188
Lesbian and Gay Hotline   426-9371
    Tufts Skin Care Clinic (VD treatment)
    956-5293

Books/Bars

Red Bookstore, 136 River St., Camb.
    491-6930
The Bar (Disco Dancing, Mostly Men)
    252 Boylston St.   247-9308
Chaps (Men)
    27 Huntington Ave.   266-7778
Jacques (Mixed, Dancing)
    79 Broadway   338-9066
Paradise (Talking, Mostly Men)
    180 Mass. Ave. (Cambridge)   864-4130
Somewhere (Disco Dancing, Mostly Women)
    295 Franklin St.   423-7730
Sporter's Cafe (Men) 228 Cambridge St.
Club Boston (Gay men's baths)
    4 LaGrange St.   426-1451

SOURCE: *Gay Community News*, June 25, 1982,
Boston, MA

This is not intended to be a comprehensive list of specific stresses or recommended actions to alleviate them. But they illustrate that help is available from a variety of sources for specific difficulties which arise through life.

The second avenue of direct action responses addresses unacceptable stress reactions. Here we are concerned with means we might take to eliminate or minimize harmful ways we respond to difficulties in our lives. Examples are overeating, coronary-prone Type A behavior, or chronic disability or illness. Hospitals, clinics, and nonprofessional groups sponsor programs designed to lessen the severity of difficulties such as these.

☐ *Overeating.* Dozens of commercial weight reduction programs are advertised in the daily paper to combat this most common way of responding to stress. All have their adherents. Nearly every hospital or outpatient clinic has a weight control program. One particularly helpful program for people who are too heavy is **Overeaters Anonymous.** Patterned after Alcoholics Anonymous, Overeaters Anonymous tries to help compulsive binge eaters, but it can help people who are not seriously overweight, too. It

Table 9.2 Psychology Job Exchange

NAME/ ADDRESS	PRESENT LOCATION	JOB TYPE	LANGUAGE	SALARY	LOCATION DESIRED	ADDITIONAL LANGUAGES	DATES/ DURATION	ADDITIONAL INFORMATION
Alaska, U.S.	Sm. city	University teach. (undergrad & grad)/couns., teach. couns., psychother., adjustment	English	$40 U.S. 9 mos.	U.S., other English speaking	None	9 months	Near ocean
Queensland, Australia	Sm. city	Clin. Psycho., postgrad., qual. team leader, psychiatric ward, testing, therapy, lecture, consult., in/outpat., adult	English	$16 Aust.	Open, pref. not winter	None	3–6 months, open	Great Barrier Reef, cattle stations
Idaho, U.S.	Sm. town	Sp. Ed. Admin., Sch Psych, M.A. M.Ed., State Cert req., exp. diag & eval of learn problems.	English	$25 U.S. 11 mos	Europe, Australia, New Zealand	German	1 yr. June to June	Near Yellowstone and Grand Teton National Parks, outdoor recreation
The Netherlands	Sm. city	Assoc. Prof., Univ., Behav. mod., ment. retard., teach grads	English	$28 U.S.	Australia (prefer S.E.)	None	1 yr. 82–83	Located central Europe. Opport. Res., ther. state hospital
Lancashire, England	Sm. town	Sen. Clin. Psych., outpat. behav. psychother., adults	English	£8 U.K.	Open	None	1 yr.	—

SOURCE: Adapted from *The Job Exchange—Psychology Registry*. Edition 2. Box 1502, Kingston, Ontario, Canada K7L 5C7.

uses a combination of specific guidelines, support groups, suggestions to control eating, and the assignment of a sponsor to help discipline food intake and guide the person through the steps to recovery. They present twelve guidelines, which are associated with normal eating patterns.

□ *Type A behavior.* In Chapter 2, we noted that Type A behavior significantly raises the probability of heart attacks. It is possible to teach individuals to control their Type A behavior, which makes them prone to coronary conditions. Canadian psychologists Roskies and Avard (1982) devised a thirteen-session stress management program for middle-aged businessmen who had Type A personalities. Blending several types of therapies, they first taught the men to recognize signs of Type A behavior. Then the

---

Suggested Guides to Abstinence by Overeaters Anonymous

1. *Three measured meals a day with nothing in between but low- or no-calorie beverages.* If, because of a medical problem, you need smaller, more frequent meals, we still suggest nothing in between but no- or low-calorie beverages.

2. *Weigh and measure all your foods after cooking.* We use 8 oz. and 4 oz. measuring cups (level) and a postal or kitchen scale. This may seem hard at first, but it will prevent rationalizing double portions and help you establish an eye for the proper amount of food and drink to meet your requirements.

3. *Avoid all your individual binge foods.* Be honest with yourself. If a food is stimulating to you, or if it sets up a craving because of its consistency, smell, taste, etc., THEN DON'T EAT IT. When in doubt, leave it out!

4. *Write down your eating plan every day.* You will then make sure you have available (and defrosted, if necessary!) everything you need to eat that day.

5. *Call your food plan in to your sponsor each day for at least the first three or four weeks* (and as long as you wish thereafter). Also call at any time when you find yourself becoming preoccupied with food.

6. *Don't take second helpings at meals.* Overeating begins with one bite too much, so take all of your planned portions at one time.

7. *Eat slowly, taking small bites.*

8. *Eat your meals sitting down.* Standing up while you eat encourages licking, tasting, grabbing, and gobbling. This sloppiness in discipline can lead to sliding off your eating plan altogether, which inevitably leads to compulsive eating.

9. *Don't skip any meals.* You'll get too hungry and may find yourself overeating again.

10. *Weigh yourself only once a month.* Remember how discouraged you felt when you hadn't lost as much as you thought you should have? Remember how excited you felt when you had lost more than you had planned? And remember how confused you felt when you "went off your diet" because of either of these two reasons? Frequent weighing or refusal to weigh gives too much power to your scale. If you are eating honestly and properly, you will lose weight.

11. *A commitment to abstinence is the most important thing in your life without exception!* Each time you take a bite, you weaken yourself for the next time. Each time you don't eat when you want to, you are stronger for the next time. Many times you will be afraid you won't make it. Don't be afraid of the craving. It is this very fear that leads us to eat. The craving cannot hurt you, and it will pass!

12. *MAKE that telephone call to your sponsor before you take the first compulsive bite!*

SOURCE: Adapted from *A Commitment to Abstinence*, Overeaters Anonymous, Inc., 1976.

men learned techniques to help them relax, modulate negative emotions and unrealized expectations, and improve their communication and problem-solving skills. Finally, the men were instructed to fantasize stressful situations at work and imagine using one of the relaxation techniques they had been taught in order to reduce distress and then tackle the problem. The follow-up data indicate that many of these men have been able to modify the most lethal aspects of their Type A behavior.

☐ *Chronic disability/illness.* Sooner or later, the majority of us will have a serious physical limitation or ailment. This can come early, in the form of paralysis from combat in Vietnam or a car accident. It can come later with arthritis, a heart condition, or diabetes. All of these affect the quality, but not necessarily the quantity, of life. We are disabled or afflicted with a chronic illness; what can we do to help ourselves? Two types of assistance are possible: aid from others and self-help.

Most communities have organizations, often coordinated by hospitals or Red Cross, United Fund or public services, which provide in-home assistance. An example is the Homemaker/Health Care aides, who may do light housekeeping, shop, cook meals, and provide supervision of young children. Other services include Meals on Wheels, transportation for necessity or pleasure, friendly visitation, or telephone lifelines (Lowry, 1980). The extent of these services varies from city to city, and the demand exceeds the supply, but they help millions of disabled and ill people every month.

In times of severe stress many people find solace in religion. This resource offers the comfort and security that enables them to maintain a normal adaptation.

Self-help is always available to us because we administer it ourselves. Doctors marvel at the ability of some patients who continue to function reasonably well in spite of a crippling disease. Four differences between those who live as fully as possible and those who do not were found in one study to be (1) an optimistic outlook — discovering and enjoying those parts of life that remain available; (2) letting feelings out — angry outbursts and complaining; (3) active fantasies — finding a pleasant escape in daydream; and (4) denial — refusing to accept the long-term consequences of an illness or minimizing the effect of a disability (Felton, Hinrichson, Revenson, and Elron, 1980).

These coping strategies can assist people with severe disabilities or illnesses to ward off mental disturbance while at the same time maintaining optimum physical health.

None of us has very much control over the stresses life has in store for us. We *do* have considerable control over how we cope with them. It is greatly to our advantage to anticipate how we will cope with the problems of life and our reactions to events we all will face someday. These strategies will help us live our lives as fully as possible for as long as possible.

Summary

1. Normal adaptation is not a fixed condition but a continuing capacity for readjustment.
2. Two principles to be acknowledged when assessing an adaptive state are holistic functioning and the notion that behavior reflects mental status.
3. Three primary features that are likely to reflect how an individual is adjusting to his or her society are (1) the ability to find satisfaction from a balance of work, love, and play; (2) managing stress with relatively high-level adaptive responses; and (3) stability of personality style.
4. Secondary characteristics associated with normal adaptation are (1) usual environmental stress, (2) a sense of feeling well, (3) internal organization typical for personality style, (4) consistent mood, and (5) interpersonal relationships that follow developmental expectations.
5. Studies of human behavior over time suggest that adult mental stability cannot be predicted from childhood adjustment. Where continuity of a particular personality characteristic does occur, it is usually from one developmental stage to the following one. Personality is greatly affected by cultural reinforcement.
6. One type of direct action assists us in coping with stresses coming from specific needs or problems — loved ones who drink or gamble, single parenthood, gay relationships, unemployment, or aging.
7. A second type of direct action helps people deal with specific maladaptive reactions to stress, such as overeating or coronary-prone Type A behavior.

A Look Ahead

The next chapter will describe State 2 — temporary overload condition. Using five cases for illustration, we will examine how the balance of work, love, and play is affected in this state; note subtle changes in adaptive responses to stress; and see how particular features of personality style become accentuated. We will also examine how stress is experienced, as well as note changes in physical status, inner organization, and interpersonal relations.

Key Terms

holistic functioning   self-objectification
actions   Gray Panthers
homeostasis   Overeaters Anonymous
orientation to reality

Suggested Readings

Culture and normal adaptation

Kluckhohn, C., and Murray, H., in collaboration with D. Schneider. *Personality in nature, society, and culture.* Second Edition. New York: Knopf, 1956, chapter 46.

> Still up-to-date thinking about what is normal behavior from a cross-cultural perspective.

Varieties of normal adjustment

Goethals, G., and Klos, D. *Experiencing youth.* Second Edition. Boston: Little, Brown, 1976.

King, S. *Five lives at Harvard.* Cambridge, Mass.: Harvard University Press, 1973.

Offer, D., and Offer, J. *From teenage to young manhood.* New York: Basic Books, 1975.

> A variety of ways of normally adapting in adolescence and youth.

Mental organization

Coan, R. *The optimal personality: An empirical and theoretical analysis.* New York: Columbia University Press, 1974.

> Perceptive summation of normal mental organization that allows for openness to inner and outer experience.

Self-enrichment

Schutz, W. *Joy: Expanding human awareness.* New York: Grove, 1967.

Gaylin, W. *Feelings.* New York: Ballantine, 1979.

Brothers, J. *How to get whatever you want out of life.* New York: Random House, 1978.

Harris, T. *I'm OK — you're OK.* New York: Harper & Row, 1969.

> Useful — though oversimplified — advice about how to improve the quality of our lives.

When the alarm rang at 6:00 A.M. Karl quickly turned it off because he didn't want to wake his wife. Then he groaned, rolled to a sitting position, and put his feet on the floor.

Karl is a policeman and had been averaging fourteen hours of work per day, seven days a week, for the last two weeks. A detective was seriously wounded while on stake-out, by a man who had threatened to kill a supermarket chain owner in Chicago unless he was paid $100,000. A drop of marked bills was made, and several detectives waited for the money to be picked up. Unfortunately, the extortionist got away after seriously wounding one of the detectives. All days off and holidays were cancelled from that time on while everyone hunted for the extortionist.

As Karl shaved, he tried to recall what his wife told him about their 16-month-old daughter's first sentence yesterday. It was something about "Daddy" but Karl fell asleep as she was talking.

Karl arrived at the police station just before 8:00 A.M. and found everyone upset. The detective had died the evening before. The captain in charge of the case was angry because the commissioner assigned an additional twenty men to search for the killer and the captain had no idea what to do with them. He yelled at the sergeants who in turn yelled at the policemen.

Karl had talked to his wife during the day and they agreed that she and their daughter would meet him at a cafeteria for supper before he went back to work. They talked for nearly an hour before his partner came running in to tell him that a liquor store operator had identified the killer as a man living in a nearby boarding house. Karl and his partner were on their way.

As he was leaving the cafeteria, his daughter repeated her first sentence: "Bye, bye, Daddy."

Chapter Preview

CHAPTER 10
State 2: Temporary Overload Condition

Questions to think about

□ Have you experienced high-pressure situations in your life — such as final exams — which caused brief and expectable changes in your personality?

□ What do you like and dislike about the changes in you these situations cause?

□ How do others react to you when you are in this state?

□ How long before you are back to normal when the stress is over?

The story of Karl, with which we open this chapter, shows a man experiencing greater than usual pressure from outside sources — which he sees as short-lived — that causes a reordering of priorities, a redirection of energies, and alterations in behavior. This reorganization of personality is State 2, temporary overload condition.

People in State 2 have voluntarily freighted themselves with greater than usual stress, typically at work, for what they see as a short period. Each willingly undergoes stress, works harder and longer, and sacrifices current pleasures to obtain something which makes all the effort worthwhile. Examples are a writer trying to finish a book for a deadline, or a working mother-to-be in her last trimester. In order to finish the book or have everything ready for the new baby, they willingly put themselves on a rigorous schedule. The writer divides each day into blocks of time with specific sections of the book to be ground out during these periods. Acts that do not directly support those goals are stripped away. The pregnant woman has no time for her friends, though she continues to swim because she is told that it is good for her and the baby. Both are aware of the sacrifices they are making and say to themselves they will return to normal when they give birth to their book or baby.

A temporary overload condition is like filling the family car with pets, food, clothing, and all the rest for a drive to the summer place. The occupants are cramped, the springs have little give left, and tempers are short. So long as the trip is not too lengthy and there are no unexpected delays or detours, the journey can be completed successfully.

We begin this chapter by a look at five examples of individuals experiencing a State 2 adaptation. Then we will examine how the primary features of adjustment are reorganized: the balance of satisfaction from work, love, and play emphasizes one sphere, and satisfaction from others is put off; familiar middle-level coping devices are present; and some qualities of the personality style are accentuated. We also look at the secondary characteristics associated with this state of adjustment. At the chapter's end we follow up on the five people who experienced the temporary overload condition to see what happened afterward. Then we consider ways for assisting someone experiencing a State 2 adjustment.

Five Examples of a Temporary Overload Condition

The five examples below each portray a temporary overload condition. They will be used to illustrate the primary features and secondary characteristics associated with State 2.

Bubba's Championship Season

Big things had been expected of Bubba's football team, the Rattlers, that season, but no one expected them to go undefeated. And no one in his wildest imagination could have imagined that the Rattlers would play for the state championship.

Since early in the season, football increasingly dominated Bubba's life and encroached on other areas of living as well. It was increasingly harder to think about English and math when he was concentrating on Friday night's opponent. Homework assignments began to be missed about the end of September, and by mid-October Bubba's attendance in classes had diminished, particularly Friday and Monday mornings.

Relations with others who were not team members were somewhat strained. His girl friend found him distant and preoccupied, and his parents were bothered by his moodiness. Both sometimes thought that Bubba was better-natured last year when the Rattlers were five-and-five.

Haunted by the clock, we are late because we've had to rush to do something else first. In State 2 we feel that we barely have enough time to do all that needs doing.

Hillary's Final Exams

In the first week of December Hillary has four final exams, a lab report, and a paper to complete before the term ends on the twenty-first. Until now Hillary has been an excellent student and has begun to nourish the dream of becoming a doctor. But the competition is tough, and she is wondering if she really has the stuff to make it to medical school. Hillary is pretty sure her first term grades will give her the answer.

Because so much is riding on these finals, Hillary has been quite nervous. Her friends don't understand it. "Hillary always moans and groans about exams or papers, about how poorly she will do and always winds up getting A's or B's," they note. "Why does she always worry so much?" they comment without sympathy.

Grace's Love Affair

Grace is a single mother. She is 32 and has a boy and a girl, aged 13 and 11. Grace has been alone since Bill died in Vietnam. "We were married right after I graduated from high school," Grace said. "Bill was two years ahead of me and was *too much* in that Marine uniform of his." Grace was pregnant with their second child when Bill stepped on a land mine and was killed instantly.

Grace works as a secretary for the sales manager of an electronics firm in Raleigh, North Carolina. Her mother, also a widow, and two sisters live in the same town. "Nobody ever leaves here if they can help it," Grace says. If the kids are sick or Grace has to work late, they can turn to their grandmother or aunts. "They are my safety net," says Grace.

Grace's week is a long one. Counting commuting time, she is at work almost ten hours a day. Then there are two hours of cooking and housework every day during the week and nearly the equivalent of a full day's work on the weekend. Grace doesn't mind the long hours and hard work. What she misses most is someone like Bill to share her life with. That's why she joined Parents Without Partners where she met Tom.

Two years younger than Grace, and divorced, Tom is a computer operator. Very quickly Grace and Tom fell in love with each other. "Neither of us had felt anything for a long time until we met — and *wow* — the chemistry was sensational!" said Grace. They wanted to spend as much time together as possible. Grace had to reorganize her life to squeeze out a few more hours from a day to be with Tom.

"Having a lover is like a second job," Grace said to one of her sisters. After staying up late the night before, Grace finds it a little more difficult to get up in the morning, but then she has always been a slow starter. Otherwise, the only other change Grace notices is that she has put on ten pounds.

Walter's Partnership

Walter is responsible for coordinating a team of architects to prepare for a waterfront redevelopment along the river. This is the biggest project the firm is working on.

Walter knows he'll be considered to become a partner in the firm this year, and being assigned to supervise the project is an opportunity to show he has the stuff partners are made of. Since he was assigned this client, Walter has been working longer hours. "Though my team is first class, I've got to be certain what they do is correct," Walter says, "so I spend most of Saturday and some of Sunday afternoons going over the past week's work and laying out the schedule for the coming week."

In spite of the lengthy hours, Walter says he feels fine. "It's a long week, but the waterfront is a marvelous piece of property," he says. And Walter knows that if he does a good job his partnership is assured. "Right now my family is taking the brunt of my long hours because they hardly ever see me," Walter acknowledges. "But I tell them as soon as I make partner I'll throttle down and we'll spend a lot more time together."

Luis's Layoff

Luis had seen it coming for six months. "As soon as we didn't get the missile contract, I knew the pink slips would start coming," he said. As an electronics engineer in Hartford, Connecticut, he has been through it before when the aerospace industry lost its government support and thousands of scientists and engineers were laid off. Unfortunately, when they did not receive the new missile contract, it was necessary to cut back the company's personnel.

"Having been over this ground before, I felt better prepared," Luis said. "I got permission from my boss to use the phone to make contacts and the secretaries to type letters for me." He also read the want ads scrupulously, reworked his résumé, got in touch with friends who might know of job openings, and checked back with his university's placement service. "I think of myself as having a job," Luis stated. "It's looking for a job!" His wife said he

Being unemployed — especially when the size of the family is increasing — may trigger a temporary overload condition.

seemed to work as many hours in the job search as he put into his occupation when he was employed.

Luis avoids worrying about not finding a job. "That negative thinking is a luxury I can't afford," he says. He also avoids people who are unemployed. He doesn't like to be seen with them.

Primary Features of Adjustment in State 2

The primary features of adjustment are clearly affected in State 2, reflecting the alteration in adaptation that has occurred. One sphere of living becomes dominant and satisfactions from others are reduced or put off. Familiar middle-level coping devices are present. Finally, some characteristics of the usual personality style become accentuated.

Choosing Among Work, Love, or Play

The temporary overload condition arises from a *reorganization* of behavior in order to focus on gratifications — or absence of dissatisfaction — from one area of living. Activities are sharply focused to complete a specific task. This means less freedom of action, leftover energy, or attention for other matters. Even though we may be working hard and giving up other pleasures, we bear the hardship willingly because we perceive the choice to be our own. The stress of preparation for the game or exam, squeezing time out for a lover, driving for a partnership, or looking for work, is taken on willingly. It is not an alien goad.

Accompanying this commitment is the willingness to put off pleasure from other areas for the present. Bubba is willing to endure great physical hardship in football practice, ignore non-football-playing friends, distance himself from his family, and give up his love of fishing. He increasingly puts off his homework. "I'll worry about that later," he says. When the season is over, it will all be worth it, he tells himself, and everything will return to normal.

In this state, other spheres of life are frequently harnessed in the service of work. Walter's wife says, "I feel I'm with a front-line soldier back for a forty-eight-hour pass." Playing, too, is to help him recuperate rather than being enjoyed by itself. "I need to jog four miles a day to relax," Walter says. "If I didn't, I couldn't do my job right."

Middle-Level Coping Devices

In a temporary overload condition we use the familiar ways of coping employed with success in the past. Primarily middle-level self-protective responses, their appearance is a reliable sign of a State 2 adjustment. They are transitory, passing when the stress is resolved.

Menninger describes them this way (1967):

> They are regarded both by the subject and by those about him as "perfectly normal" or at worst as idiosyncratic characteristics. They are his way of getting along, his method of coping with life. . . . [T]hey are opportunistic and transitory and when the disintegrative threat disappears, the tension diminishes and the established life style continues virtually uninterrupted. The special coping measures employed are dropped — until the next time. (p. 147)

Using coping devices such as those mentioned in Chapter 3, we may worry about one thing at a time, rationalize away an unpleasant reality temporarily, transform our anger into competitiveness through sublimation, or vent hostility with a smile. These are techniques that have worked in the past.

The coping devices in State 2 allow us to experience a manageable amount of anxiety, which motivates us to do something to relieve the source of discomfort. Consider Hillary. The nervousness she feels before exams drives her to work very hard. Indeed, she may say afterward that the anxiety brought out maximum performance in her, even though she felt considerably upset at the time. Using their stress emotions as a prod, people in State 2 almost always can take direct action to attack the problem.

At this level of adjustment we use resources to cushion stress. Sports, hobbies, or interests are often vigorously pursued. But instead of being non-obligatory play, they are engaged in purposely to discharge tension.

Grace consciously taps her physical reserves as she makes time for Tom and she begins to average two hours' less sleep per night. During periods of time when she has to work overtime at the office, she may go with as little as eight hours' sleep over a two-day period. Grace knows she's taxing herself physically as well as emotionally by forcing her mind and body to function when the primary impulse is to rest.

When the emergency condition is over, physical and emotional reserves regenerate. But as Selye warned us (see Chapter 2), the rebuilding process seems to take longer than we anticipate. When you have crammed for exams, how long did it take you to return to normal? When Hillary finished her exams, she found that her old energy level and zest did not come back right away during vacation and felt still frazzled when the new term began.

The primary weakness of middle-level coping mechanisms is in their strictly present orientation, which can undermine future adjustments. As the undefeated season builds, Bubba has to suppress his mounting anxieties about his class attendance, which is slipping, and his homework, which he isn't doing. He compartmentalizes his worries about academic work, saying to himself he will start going to classes regularly and studying hard as soon as the season is over. He may not realize how far behind the class he is and how long it will take him to return to normal.

Accentuation of Personality Style

State 2 brings an **accentuation** of some characteristics of the usual personality style. These more pronounced personality traits are extremely functional, proven veterans of successful coping in the past. In a temporary overload condition we are likely to have less range within our personality. Just as we cut out superfluous activities in order to cope with whatever problem is at hand, so we strip away those aspects of our behavior that are least functional. The result is greater efficiency but less variety.

In a temporary overload condition some traits are intensified and altered in ways that are not particularly attractive. Table 10.1 illustrates hypothetical changes in certain characteristics of the dominant personality style as the normally adjusted person shifts into State 2.

An example of the change in personality associated with a temporary overload condition is Walter, the architect. Always an energetic, active personality, Walter is even more so in State 2. Idea after idea comes into his mind about the design: how about renovating the old factory on the wharf rather than putting up a glass and steel high-rise hotel? Maybe an area designated for parking can become a park, with a garage underneath? Walter is willing to work out the details of these new ideas himself, spending long, arduous hours at the task.

Many marvel at his enthusiasm and energy. Others wish Walter would slow down. Since active people are strong in delegation, his assistants and secretary find that every new idea of his results in three times as much work for them. Moreover, because active persons tend to be "big picture" people, they overlook small flaws in ideas, which require a great deal of effort to fix or considerably detract from the concept. The temporarily overloaded active person loses some of his ability to pick up obvious flaws in reasoning.

For most in State 2, these changes occur without awareness. Unless someone who works with Walter points out to him that he is in danger of ignoring important information, or causing significant hardship to those that work with him, he may persist in behavior that can cause long-term problems for the project or alienate others.

Table 10.1 Hypothetical alteration in selected traits within personality styles from State 1 to State 2

PERSONALITY STYLE	STATE 1: NORMAL ADAPTATION	STATE 2: TEMPORARY OVERLOAD CONDITION
Controlled	1. Keeps things regulated and predictable	1. Is upset by surprises
	2. Orderly, precise, neatness facilitates	2. Orderliness, precision, neatness retard action
	3. Detail-oriented	3. Detail-bound
	4. Temperate, wary of impulses	4. Distrusts impulses
	5. Delegates anxiously	5. Restricts freedom of subordinates
Pessimistic	1. Tragic vision	1. Moody, withdrawn
	2. Looks for flaws, the unexpected	2. Awareness of flaws and the unexpected inhibits action
	3. Examines instincts	3. Analysis of instincts slows actions
	4. Resigned risk-taker	4. Repetitive doubting of outcomes
	5. Delegates critically	5. Scrutinizes subordinates for flaws
Prickly	1. Oppositional, feisty, charming	1. Irritates
	2. Cynical, looks for flaws with zest	2. Focuses on flaws
	3. Instincts guide	3. Aggressive instincts guide
	4. Enthusiastic risk-taker	4. Exhibits poor judgment
	5. Delegates erratically	5. Becomes overloaded
Theatrical	1. Dramatic and impressionable	1. Expressive without accountability
	2. Ignores facts and flaws	2. Sticks to instincts in face of opposing facts
	3. Disorderly	3. Scattered
	4. Changeable	4. Strongly inconsistent in actions/emotions
	5. Delegates poorly	5. Shows lack of follow-through
Active	1. Energetic, busy	1. More energetic, busier
	2. Uses instincts	2. Relies on instinct
	3. Accepts flaws, missing information	3. Ignores flaws, missing information
	4. Shifts attention smoothly	4. Shifts attention rapidly
	5. Delegates easily	5. Delegates less critically

Table 10.1 Continued

PERSONALITY STYLE	STATE 1: NORMAL ADAPTATION	STATE 2: TEMPORARY OVERLOAD CONDITION
Optimistic	1. Idealistic but aware of pitfalls	1. Idealism inhibits caution
	2. Selective attention, rationalizes flaws, problems	2. Suppresses awareness of flaws, problems
	3. Is concerned with beginnings, regeneration	3. Starts new projects when old ones bog down
	4. Values social cohesion	4. Demands agreement
	5. Benign neglect	5. Lack of follow-through

Secondary Characteristics of State 2

The reorganization of the personality resulting in a temporary overload condition is reflected in changes among the secondary characteristics. These are useful in recognizing the presence of State 2 adaptation. These are summarized in Table 10.2.

Greater than Usual Stress

Temporary overload conditions develop in response to an unusually strong external demand. We perceive the stress as greater than usual. The difference may be *quantitative*, as when Walter works more hours, or it may be *qualitative*, as when Hillary faces exams on which a decision to enter the field of medicine will ride.

Not everyone who experiences greater than usual stress develops a temporary overload condition. We noted in Chapter 2 that the higher number of Life Crisis Units, the larger the proportion of men and women who exhibited physical and mental illness. While the correlation linking life stress to maladaptation may describe groups of people, it is not especially accurate for the individual. Everyone has his or her own hierarchy for ranking problems. Consider Hillary and her sister. For Hillary, who has to work hard for her grades, final exams are stressful and bring about a temporary overload condition as she faces the anxiety and doubt that will surely attend this experience. Her honor-roll sister, on the other hand, looks forward to the same event with pleasure, relishing the chance to exhibit mastery and obtain recognition.

In State 2 the stress is clearly perceived. We have no doubt what the problem is. The individual has warning and time to prepare to meet the task. Hillary knows when exams are and studies for them. This knowledge brings with it the assumption that the stress will end and life will resume its normal pace. Even though the stress is considered substantial, it is not seen as alien

Table 10.2 Secondary characteristics associated with State 2: Temporary overload condition

Greater than usual stress	Hierarchy of neglect
Clearly perceived	Highly efficient, familiar concentration
Time-limited	and choice-making process
Seen as congenial	Paper-thin time margins
Maximum effective stress tolerance	Behavior at times out of keeping with
	values to cope with stress
Heightened physical sensitivity	Superstitious behavior
Expectable fluctuation in sleeping,	
weight, digestive system, and vital	*Familiar mood under stress*
signs	Maximum focused enthusiasm
Eating indulgences or rituals	Touchy, changeable
Conscious use of familiar drugs to sup-	Humor for tension release
port coping	Losing touch with mood
Notable nonoffensive variation in self-	
care	*Strained interpersonal relations*
	Expectation of others' support during
Intense, efficient organization	stressful period
Orientation sharp, with occasional	Limited responsiveness to needs of
lapses in noncrucial spheres	others unless clear signal given

because of the assumption of long-term benefit. Hillary doesn't mind final exams too much because she knows they are the means to the end of being a doctor.

In State 2 we are at **maximum effective stress tolerance.** As with a car whose tachometer is at the red line or a ship loaded to the maximum, we can tolerate no more or else something is likely to give way. Because all attention and energy are narrowly focused on the major stress, Bubba will say "I don't want to talk about it right now," when his mother asks him how his school work is coming along. Already burdened with worry about finding a job, Luis cannot think about the weeds that are taking over his usually flawless lawn. When he finds a job he'll extirpate the crabgrass.

Heightened Physical Sensitivity

Heightened physical sensitivity is a characteristic of State 2. This is both an accentuated awareness of our physical self and also the recognition that some aspects of our body have expectable reactions to stress.

It may be that the heightened awareness of our body comes from the desire to feel as well as possible in a temporary overload condition. Players readying themselves for a big game know this, as do hard-driving executives. When former California Senator S. I. Hayakawa was president of San Francisco State during the student protests of the late 1960s, he was asked how he felt at the beginning of an academic year in which there was sure to be trouble. He replied:

> My blood pressure is down, my cholesterol level is down, my reflexes are fast. No ulcers, trimmed down waistline, I couldn't feel better! (*Newsweek*, Sept. 22, 1969, page 68)

Dr. Hayakawa was in fighting trim for what he imagined to be a State 2 year.

Just as often, we consciously indulge our body during a period of increased stress. Overeating is a common means of pampering ourselves. So are long baths, jacuzzis, whirlpools, hot tubs, and massages. An increase in masturbation for tension release is another usual physical gratification.

Occasionally we make "deals" with ourselves, postponing physical pleasure. "Tom and I are taking a long weekend at the ocean next month," Grace says, "and when we get there I'm going to do nothing but put my body in the sun like a turtle on a log." Along with the indulgences of the body there is often a ritualistic consumption of food. During exams, college students have been known to subsist on diets of mashed potatoes and Cokes or peanuts and beer — eating patterns marked by heavy consumption of protein, carbohydrates, or fat. These patterns continue beyond the school years: Grace can't wake up without her coffee in the morning, and Walter can't cope without his favorite brand of tea in the afternoon.

In State 2 we do not regard ourselves as ill but don't feel quite well either (Menninger, 1967). Almost everyone has a system that is especially sensitive to a temporary overload condition. You might expect your sleeping patterns

Pulling an "all-nighter," cramming for exams, students sometimes drive themselves to exhaustion. Recovering their normal state after finals takes some students a long period of time.

to change, I might anticipate gaining or losing weight, and a friend of ours may not be surprised when stomach pains occur. We may be afflicted by familiar headaches, back pain, skin eruptions, or frequency of urination. We take potions to relieve headaches, settle stomachs, tranquilize the nerves, or regulate the bowels. Often we are not aware that we may be using self-medication in the form of extra cups of coffee, cigarettes, alcohol, or unregulated drugs to control the impact of a temporary overload condition. If it is pointed out to us, we may acknowledge we are using slightly more of particular drugs so we can cope effectively. Often increased drug use will continue for considerable time after the stress is over. For instance, some of us began smoking during a period of stress in our lives and continued it for years after the overload condition ended.

This old-fashioned remedy was one of the many that promised relief to over-stressed men and women of earlier times. Tonics were the ancestors of today's treatments that seek to reduce symptoms of temporary overload.

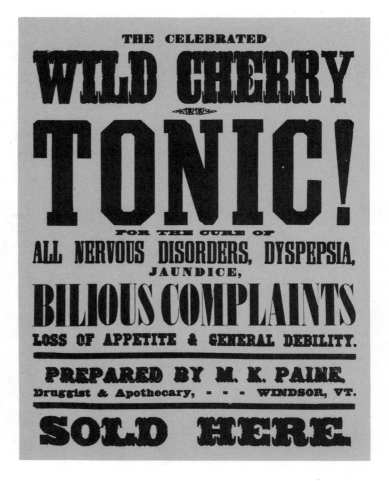

Intense, Efficient Organization

In State 2 we are oriented well in most spheres, though occasional lapses will occur in unimportant domains. The intense concentration on a task may cause us to lose track of something unessential, such as the date. Looking hard for a job, Luis may know that it is sometime after the twenty-seventh of August but not yet the first of September. If someone asks him whether it is the twenty-eighth or twenty-ninth, Luis may not know. When she receives a call from an irritated friend waiting for her to appear for a forgotten movie date, Grace becomes aware of her selective inattention.

People in State 2 usually develop a hierarchy of neglect. Grace rivets her attention to the most important matters in her life: she makes sure the kids are cared for, plans the meals and shops for the week, has clean clothes, and knows the car is in running condition. Beyond that, discretionary tasks as well as pleasures may be increasingly neglected. She doesn't have time to clean the house as well as she would like, laundry piles up, light bulbs are not replaced, and unread newspapers and magazines pile up.

In State 2 we think positively. Like a competitive athlete, we do not dwell on doubt or failure. Focused entirely on finding a job, Luis willfully shuts out intruding questions about the likelihood of finding work or why he failed to receive an offer for any of the last three positions he applied for. Like a good baseball shortstop, he doesn't think about the one that just went through his legs. Rather, he concentrates on the next opportunity.

Resistance to stress in State 2 is supported by behavior patterns that are familiar, habitual, economical, and have proven their worth in the past. Many people report that one of the more pleasing aspects of being in this state of adaptation is the feeling of thinking with unusual clarity, working efficiently, and learning rapidly and making decisions crisply. We feel as though we are guided by an internal gyroscope. We have maximum reliance on our own thoughts and feelings. We are sure of ourselves and make choices with certainty. When the opinions of others are solicited or received without asking, we make critical judgments quickly as to their usefulness.

Studying for exams, Hillary feels as though her mind is working in another gear of intensified concentration and recall. She reads and understands books in half the time it normally takes. Assignments that formerly consumed days are finished in hours. Discrimination of the essential from unessential facts is decisive. Feeling this "high" prior to exams, it is a rare student who doesn't think, "If I study half as well during the rest of the year I'll get straight A's!"

People who are overloaded temporarily often operate on paper-thin margins. All the slack time in their lives is consumed already. We function well and efficiently in State 2 as long as everything goes exactly right. But because there is no "give" anywhere, the slightest problem cuases immediate backup and serious difficulties. With a lover, a job, and kids to care for, Grace has all she can do to handle this and still function reasonably well. An overflowing toilet, a sick child, the failure of the dry cleaner to have a dress ready on Thursday, or a traffic jam can have a serious domino effect in her life, which can make it extremely difficult for her to make it through the day.

A study of 400 students in two medical schools discovered that eighty-eight percent reported cheating at least once in college and over half cheated at least once while in medical school (Sierles, Hendrikx, and Circle, 1980). Colleges and graduate and professional schools vary considerably as to the frequency of cheating on tests, pilfering copies of the examination beforehand, stealing books from the library, or copying a neighbor's answer. However, even in those institutions in which the honor code is strictly enforced, it is not unusual to find students who experience themselves in a temporary overload condition behaving counter to the prevailing ethic or their own values.

Students are not the only ones who experience an abrupt gap between what they say they believe and what they do. In her book *Lying,* Sissela Bok (1978) inventories the rationales for lies that people tell. Often it is the presence of unusual stress the sets the stage for deception: lies to avoid real or potential harm, lies in a crisis situation, lies for revenge, or lies to cushion bad news. Most of the time individuals whose behavior under stress departs from their usual code of ethics will use these or other reasons to justify it.

One of the distinguishing properties of many persons in a temporary overload condition is the presence of superstitious behavior, **rituals,** and other agreeable regressive behavior. Watching Hillary prepare for final exams, we might note the appearance of certain four letter words in her vocabulary, the donning of especially dilapidated clothing, increasingly unusual eating habits, or other qualities that clearly say, "I am under unusual pressure." This is how people in State 2 let off steam or signal those watching that they are heavily burdened and may require special handling.

When the day of final exams arrives, individuals in a temporary overload condition often go through elaborate rituals not unlike team members before a game. There is the pre-exam food, which has ceremonial significance. There are the scruffy jeans and sneakers that have helped the student avert disaster in previous final exams. There is the lucky ball-point pen, the favorite route to the building where the exams are given. These rituals are followed tenaciously. Observing a group of students shuffling into exams, bleary-eyed and worried, their raggedy clothes festooned with lucky charms, one is reminded of a sadly gallant tatterdemalion legion thrusting themselves "Once more unto the breach dear friends, once more. . . ." (Shakespeare, *Henry V,* II,i.1)

Familiar Mood Under Stress

In State 2 the normal mood shifts to the familiar prevailing disposition of a temporary overload condition. The "new" mental condition varies according to personality style, and we can recognize it when it appears. If we watch members of the Rattler football team the week before the state championship game, we can see the gradual assumption of mood characteristic of each person's behavior in State 2. We note that Bubba starts to laugh loudly at everything, or we begin to feel the cornerback's growing irritability.

If asked afterwards, the players would tell us this is their "game face," an attitude they usually assume to ready themselves mentally for the contest. Every person at this level of adaptation, whether it's getting ready for a game or a man looking for a job, prepares his or her own game face to prepare to cope with an unusual stress.

In State 2 our maximum enthusiasm is mobilized for the type of person we are. The enthusiasm is focused sharply on the task to be managed, and other stresses are put out of mind. It is a rare football player preparing for a Friday game who can generate much interest in a college interview or physics exam scheduled for the following Monday morning.

Rapid mood changes are usual (Menninger, 1967). One minute Bubba is talking and laughing and the next he is touchy and withdrawn. His brothers

Lined up for the finals in the 1981 NCAA championships, this swimmer is well acquainted with the feelings, thoughts, and behavior associated with a State 2 adjustment.

and sisters notice a marked shift in his ability to tolerate frustration as Friday night approaches. They may feel a little like they are tiptoeing around a temperamental, unpredictable child, trying to keep things as placid as possible so as not to cause an explosion. Blowups occur in a flash and pass rapidly. Though those around him may be shaken, Bubba goes on as though nothing has happened.

Most of us begin to lose track of our mood in State 2. We are less aware of our irritability, variations in disposition, or the effect we may be having on others. It may come as a surprise to us that we are moody, unpredictable, or touchier than usual. When our attention is directed to the subject, however, we can look at ourselves objectively and will agree with this outside assessment. We can even laugh about it — afterwards.

The humor of people in a temporary overload condition generally functions to relieve tension. Humor may be expressed in loud, explosive outbursts, out of keeping with how funny the triggering event is. It may be expressed in vicious, rapier-like wit. However, there is little ability to laugh at oneself. Hence, Bubba may be adept at parodying rival coaches and players, but will find it next to impossible to satirize members of his own team or himself.

Strained Interpersonal Relations

The expectation of support from others is a characteristic of a temporary overload condition. It is a stated or unstated assumption that friends, family and co-workers will recognize our needs and will gladly adjust their lives for a short time to help out. Those most intimately involved with us when we are temporarily overloaded are likely to find themselves harnessed to our service. Consider Grace. Her children may be asked to take on more of the responsibility for managing themselves and the household. Her friends and sisters may notice they are being called upon more and more to help out if small difficulties occur. Could the neighbor check her son, who has a sore throat and has to stay home from school? Will her sister mind picking up a few things from the grocery store? The plumber is coming to fix one of the toilets sometime during the morning; could she leave the key with her mother? The requests gradually mount. At work there may be the same unstated expectations that her co-workers, too, will come to her aid when she needs it.

Before long her relatives, friends, and co-workers will realize the covert assumptions being made. While they may have been glad to help out for a while, they may resent being manipulated. They may begin to find ways to say no, or a nasty confrontation may occur. While people surrounding someone in State 2 may feel they are being manipulated, it is more likely that their needs and reactions are simply being ignored. Individuals are so fixed on their own tasks at this level of adaptation that they are not perceptive about the feelings of others. That is to say, they are less spontaneously perceptive. The attention of Grace can be clearly focused on the problems she is creating for her family and friends if they mention it and she is capable of altering her behavior to accommodate them.

Follow-up

Bubba

Bubba's team went undefeated, to a large extent because he was able to block the all-star end when it mattered. After the last game in November he felt let down; he missed the feeling of being part of the team, the daily admiration of his classmates, and the organization that the Friday night football game gave to his week.

Bubba had fallen behind in most of his courses during the season. Though he had a lot more time after the season ended, Bubba had a hard time getting caught up. "I don't know why I don't have more ambition to study," Bubba said to his mother when she yelled at him because his grades continued to fall after the season ended, and he was doing almost nothing. Even though he had a lot more time he did less than during the season. Bubba also noted he felt tired all the time.

Gradually, Bubba recovered his normal energy and enthusiasm. Halfway through February he brought home a B− from a math test. Both he and his parents were pleased.

Hillary

Hillary survived her first exam period all right. She made an A and a B+ in her two science courses, a B in French, but a C+ in English because her paper was written in a rush. These grades were adequate for her to continue to think about medical school.

During Christmas vacation she stayed close to home. She ate a lot, gaining 8 pounds. Hillary also slept a lot, though her pattern of sleep had changed. She spent hours reading Gothic novels. She found herself staying up watching ancient movies on the late, late show and then sleeping until afternoon.

When her boy friend saw her, he found her quieter than usual. She had a hard time gearing up for the second term, but by February she was back in stride. What Hillary didn't know was that another problem was beginning. We'll follow her in the next chapter.

Grace

Gradually, Grace's romance with Tom lost momentum because of real life obstacles they couldn't overcome. The first problem was that her son broke his leg playing on the children's swings at the playground the day before Grace and Tom were planning to get away for their much-anticipated long weekend at the ocean. Grace was upset because he had hurt himself, and because she couldn't leave him with any of her relatives with a cast on his leg. Tom was furious with the boy for breaking his leg in such a stupid way and told Grace his feelings. Her son attacked, Grace bristled and told Tom never again to criticize *her* children.

Then, Tom started to wonder whether he wanted to be involved with a woman with children. He didn't like the fact that, for Grace, they seemed to come before him. Also, he never knew how to act around them. He wasn't their father, but he was too old to be a friend.

The final event which brought the relationship to a halt occurred the night they were together and Tom said that if they got married he wanted her to stop working. "You take care of the house and kids, and I'll take care of you," is the way Tom put it. For Grace—who hated housework, liked working, and was even thinking of taking a part-time course at North Carolina State—this was the last straw. From then on they were friends but not lovers.

Though she missed having a boy friend, Grace felt relieved. "I didn't realize how tired I was getting, trying to keep this thing with Tom going," she had told her sister. "It was almost like a second job." Her sister told her she felt relieved, too, since she was getting a little tired of picking up Grace's loose ends.

Walter

Walter's presentation was well received and the city accepted his design for the renovation of the waterfront. Shortly afterward he was offered a partnership.

Walter and his wife went to a plush resort on the Yucatán Peninsula for two weeks. But while there, Walter couldn't relax. He was obsessed by the redevelopment project. He lay on the beach making notes about changes in the design. Every afternoon he called the office to see how the project was going.

His wife noticed Walter's inability to relax but didn't say anything. She waited for him to wind down, but he didn't. With four days remaining on their vacation he suddenly said, "I've really got to get back to work. I've made reservations to leave tomorrow. Do you mind?"

We will meet Walter again in Chapter 12.

Luis

In spite of two months of concerted effort, Luis was unable to find work. Feelings of anxiety and panic began to increase and he could feel himself becoming more and more disorganized and moody. His story continues in the next chapter.

Assisting Ourselves and Others in State 2

Most of us move smoothly from State 1 to State 2 and back again with little awareness of the readjustments taking place. Although the adjustment takes time, these stages are easily reversible in most cases, as the experiences of Bubba, Hillary, and Grace illustrate.

Menninger makes the point that two other alternatives are possible in addition to the return to normal adjustment (1967). The first is a steadily worsening state of adjustment as resistance is worn down by too long an exposure to stress. Recall Selye's General Adaptation Syndrome in Chapter 2: a state of exhaustion sets in along with a definitely lowered level of functioning. Luis is an example of someone for whom the temporary overload condition will eventually be a transition into a crisis reaction.

A second alternative is a chronic overload condition that some individuals seem to seek and others are encouraged into by organizations in which they work. Some people elect to remain in an overburdened state in spite of opportunities to return to a normal existence. They enjoy the Superbowl intensity of a great deal to do in a short amount of time. They like the image of themselves as someone who is burdened by awesome responsibility, and they pride themselves on their ability to outwork their contemporaries and how little sleep they need. They lament that each day is not two hours longer. In spite of being overworked they are always available to lend a hand and almost never say no. "When you want something done always ask a busy person," these individuals will say.

Some of these men and women are prototypical Type A personalities. Many are potential burnout cases.

Some organizations subtly or not so subtly encourage employees into a chronic temporary overload condition. Walter's architectural office is an example. Many other companies have the ethic of the eighty-hour week. Professional partnerships that bill by the hour, for example public accountants and lawyers, make it plain to younger employees that their value to the firm is directly proportional to the number of hours worked. And once partnership is achieved some men and women can't seem to get out of the habit of working maximum hours.

If we are pushed into a temporary overload condition, might we help ourselves? Generally, three factors hasten a return to normal adaptation (McLean, 1976): (1) **time-limited** rather than chronic stress: we can handle a lot of pressure when we see an end to it; (2) confidence in our ability to cope with the problems; and (3) resources or other positive compensating experiences that cushion the distress we feel. Generally, we need to monitor our condition to make sure that we begin our transit back to normal when the stress is over. We want to avoid remaining under stress or deteriorating into a lower state of adaptation.

Suppose our roommate is in State 2, and we worry that his behavior may be harmful or is beginning to alienate his loved ones and others. What might we do to help? If we sit down with him and suggest that he cut down on the amount of work that is being undertaken, the response is likely to be, "Bear with me, the pressure will be off shortly and then everything will be fine!" If we suggest to him that he see a doctor because his health is being menaced or his loved ones hurt by his behavior, this suggestion may be greeted with astonishment, perhaps with the recommendation that we ourselves probably need therapy.

If we honestly believe someone we care about in a temporary overload situation is behaving in a manner harmful to the self or antagonistic to others, we must first get his or her attention. Since these individuals are intensely focused on dealing with a task they see as vital, this may be hard to do. Sometimes a direct confrontation by roommates who are tired of living with a thoughtless, touchy, self-centered State 2 person works reasonably well. Or a teacher or dean who feels that success in one area is being obtained at too great a cost in another is willing to sit down and confront the person and can get through. Once the individual's attention is directed to the negative fallout from a temporary overload condition, that person will usually recognize the problem and begin corrective action.

Summary

1. The temporary overload condition is a reorganization of personality caused by greater than usual pressure from an outside source. It causes a reordering of priorities, redirection of energies, and alteration in behavior and mood.
2. The three primary features of adjustment are reorganized in State 2: need for gratification from one sphere is strong and satisfaction from others is put off, familiar transitory middle-level coping devices appear, and some characteristics of the usual personality style are accentuated.
3. Secondary characteristics associated with a temporary overload condition include the experience of greater than usual environmental stress, heightened physical sensitivity, intense and efficient organization, familiar mood under stress, and strained interpersonal relations.
4. Three possible outcomes for individuals in a temporary overload condition are: a return to normal, a gradually worsening state of adjustment as resistance is worn down by too long exposure to stress, and a chronic overburdened condition.
5. Recovery from State 2 is to a large degree based on the extent to which the stress is seen as time-limited, confidence in the ability to cope with it, and resources or other positive compensating experiences.
6. Because their focus is upon the task at hand it is difficult to deal with friends, roommates, or others when State 2 behavior menaces their own health or antagonizes intimates. Confrontation is sometimes necessary. Once the individual's attention is directed to the negative fallout from a temporary overload condition, corrective action can be started.

A Look Ahead

In the next chapter we will look at crisis reactions. These are State 3 adjustments. Using five cases for illustration, which will include Hillary's unexpected pregnancy and Luis's continued inability to find work, we will note how the primary features and secondary characteristics associated with this level of adjustment are affected.

Key Terms

personality accentuation
maximum effective stress
    tolerance

rituals
time-limited stress

Suggested Readings

Coping behaviors in State 2

Menninger, K., with M. Mayman and P. Pruyser. *The vital balance: The life process in mental health and illness*. New York: Viking, 1967. Chapter VII.

Emotional and physical ways of dealing with temporary overload.

Overload and judgment

Janis, I., and Mann, L. *Decision making*. New York: Free Press, 1977.

How excess stress plays a role in poor decision making.

Costs of State 2

Selye, H. *Stress without distress*. New York: Signet, 1974.

A reminder that excessive stress for an extended period reduces adaptive energies.

Self-help in State 2

Greenwald, H. *Direct decision therapy*. San Diego: EDITS, 1973.

Smith, M. *When I say no I feel guilty*. New York: Dial, 1975.

Understanding why we overload ourselves, and practical approaches to overcome this tendency.

In Albert Camus's novel *The Stranger* the protagonist, Meursault, commits an absurd murder and undergoes an even more absurd trial; he sees himself being judged not for his crime alone, but also for his failure to "emote properly" on the day of his mother's funeral. This "flaw" in his character influences the outcome of the trial and seals his doom. In our own society, openly expressing sorrow, anger, or pain is sometimes seen as a good thing, and "holding things in" is seen as deviant.

Clinical evidence and cross-cultural research do not support the contention that openly showing grief is a universally healthy response to the loss of a loved one. Psychiatrist Ned Cassem says that "denial can be a constructive force, enabling people to put out of mind morbid, frightening, and depressing aspects of life."

Groups of black Americans, Japanese-Americans, Mexican-Americans, and white Americans in Los Angeles were asked if they would try very hard to control the way they show their emotions in public after losing a loved one. Japanese and black respondents said they would (82 percent, 79 percent) more often than white Americans and Mexican-Americans (74 percent, 64 percent). Japanese-Americans were the most reticent about public grief.

A survey of seventy-three societies found that the form and intensity of grieving varies greatly. While most weep at death, the Balinese laugh to avoid crying. In eighteen societies, self-injury (such as cutting off a finger at a joint) is regularly attempted.

Where is the line separating a healthy expression of grief from a pathological loss of control? The answer rests in the individual and in the culture that clearly influences the process of grieving.

SOURCE: From Klein, N. Is there a right way to die? *Psychology Today*, October 12, 1978.

Chapter Preview

CHAPTER 11

State 3: Crisis Reactions

Questions to think about
- [ ] Have you ever lost anyone or anything important to you?
- [ ] What was the effect on you?
- [ ] What helped you through this period?
- [ ] How long before you were back to normal?

Of all the states of adaptation, none is more painful or dramatic to witness than crisis reactions. As we will see, a crisis reaction is actually a series of responses. As the box opening the chapter informs us, the culture in which we are raised greatly influences the outward response to severe loss. The inner rection to crisis is more universal.

Crisis reactions develop in response to sudden and traumatic events, such as a meeting in the doctor's office in which we are told that our last X ray showed the possibility of lung cancer and we should put our affairs in order. Other occasions that precipitate us into a State 3 condition are any major loss — the death of someone close to us; the loss of a dream, as when a pre-law student is caught cheating on the LSATs; the loss of a place, as when we receive a notice in the mail that our shabby but comfortable apartment is being converted into a condominium and we know we won't be able to afford to live there anymore.

Losing everything we own in an apartment fire can trigger a crisis reaction.

Not everyone is propelled into a crisis reaction by a sudden event. Some of us seem to be gradually eroded into a State 3 adjustment by continuous stress that wears us down. The continued unemployment of Luis is an illustration, as is military combat for others.

People having a crisis reaction can exhibit a vast array of mental and physical symptoms. Menninger (1967) lists more than three dozen, from severe mood swings to heart palpitations. Signs of far more serious disorders — overpowering guilt or rage, phobias, hallucinations — may appear for short periods.

We begin this chapter with five examples of people experiencing a State 3 adaptation. Then a brief description of the crisis reaction in relation to other states of adaptation is presented. Next, we consider the impact of a crisis state on the primary features of adjustment. The secondary features associated with a crisis reaction are described at the end of the chapter. Follow-up is presented on the five cases. Finally, we consider how we might assist someone experiencing a crisis reaction.

Five Examples of Crisis Reactions

Following are five portrayals of crisis reactions. They are typical in depicting the sudden or gradual stress that calls forth a State 3 adjustment. They will be used to illustrate the primary features and secondary characteristics associated with a crisis response.

The Divorce of Phyllis's Parents

Phyllis was 7 when it happened. After several years of trying and failing to make their marriage work, her parents decided they couldn't live together any longer and agreed to divorce. One evening after supper they told Phyllis of their plan to split up. They reassured her that she should not worry because they both loved her. Though the plan was that she would live with her mother, Phyllis would see her Daddy regularly.

At first Phyllis said "Oh no!" and began to cry. Shortly afterward she announced that she didn't want to talk about it anymore and went to her room to be alone. While her younger brother was intermittently hysterical, Phyllis seemed to have no reaction after her first outburst. Calmly, she told her parents she understood the reasons for their separation and that it would be better for everyone if they didn't fight all the time. Her parents concluded that Phyllis was "taking it well."

In school, however, her teacher saw a major change. Previously bright, pleasant, and a good student, Phyllis became alternatively withdrawn and hostile. She volunteered answers less and seemed extremely sensitive to criticism. Before long her classroom work began to slide. When asked about it, there was an angry outburst at the teacher for "picking on her" and tears followed. When Phyllis was asked by her teacher why she was having trouble, Phyllis said she didn't feel as though she was the same student she was a few months ago. "I don't know how I did so well before," she said.

Hillary's Pregnancy

While she had imagined what it would be like to be pregnant, Hillary never thought it would happen to her without planning it. When the doctor told her the unexpected news in the spring following exams, she was overwhelmed and frightened. Her first response was "It can't be true. You must have my lab test confused with somebody's else's." Gradually the reality sunk in. The more she thought about it, the more upset Hillary became.

She talked to her boy friend and then her roommate about what to do. Both were sympathetic and assured her it was relatively easy to have an abortion these days. The man offered to pay for it. But this didn't seem to help much. Nor did the advice of her friends. They seemed to automatically think she should have an abortion. Should she? Would she have a post-abortion depression? Should she have the child? Then would she keep it or put it up for adoption? And what about her plans for medical school? The questions kept multiplying, going around and around in her head. No answer helped for very long.

As Hillary's anxiety mounted, it began increasingly to interfere with her academic work. She would go for periods functioning perfectly well and then would notice moments in which she felt very anxious. She had to hold a coffee cup with both hands or she shook so much the coffee spilled everywhere. She began to have trouble sleeping. Though she didn't like taking medication she began using her roommate's tranquilizers.

Finally, one of her professors called her into his office because she had missed several classes and had not handed in a term paper. As soon as he came in, Hillary broke down and told him the story. "Good grief," said the startled teacher. "What are you going to do?" "That's just it," said the sobbing Hillary, "I don't know. What do you think? Right now I'll do anything you think is right."

Angus's Reluctance to Graduate

Angus loved his years at a small upstate New York college. He had lots of friends and was on the varsity hockey team, edited the school newspaper and earned honor grades. He was an economics major and told people he was "thinking of going into the family auto parts business." The truth was that he didn't have the faintest ideas of what he wanted to do after college. As the fall of his senior year began, his parents became worried because Angus had not shown any interest in talking to them about when he would start work.

In April, a month before graduation, his parents talked to him. When his father asked why he hadn't told them when he was coming to work, Angus said that he had been "too busy." Pressed further, Angus said he didn't know why he had done nothing. Maybe it had something to do with the growing feelings that he didn't want to be in the family business. Knowing how much his parents, especially his father, wanted to pass the business on to the next generation, Angus felt he couldn't tell them about his reservations. "So I've just kind of gone numb," Angus said.

As they talked, Angus said he'd been thinking he might do something other than the auto parts business but wasn't sure what. "Maybe even something as crazy as trying to be a writer," Angus said. His dad said that was the wackiest idea he'd ever heard, and the talk ended with bad feelings on all sides. After that, when Angus thought about trying to talk to his parents, he would get a knot in his stomach. At one point in the spring, he said wistfully to a roommate, "Sometimes I think I don't want to graduate."

The Death of Maria's Mother

Just before Easter, Maria's mother, who lived in Corpus Christi, suddenly had a stroke and was not expected to live. Maria's immediate reaction when the doctor called was, "It can't be. I just talked to her yesterday." After an hour or two of alternately crying and frantically making arrangements for her own family to be cared for, Maria was on the plane for El Paso.

On the way she felt vaguely upset and a little numb. When she arrived at the hospital, it was clear that it was just a question of time before her mother died. Maria spent her time caring for her father and sitting at her mother's bedside. Ten days later her mother died. Maria arranged for the funeral, selected a casket, picked a dress for the visitation, and even called the hairdresser to do her mother's hair for the last time.

Maria experienced alternating waves of powerful emotion. One minute she was tranquil and the next her emotion ranged from intense self-pity to rage.

She intermittently was furious at the doctors, funeral directors, florists, and others. "The doctor's bill came before we put Mother in the ground," she said to an old friend. But old friends were on the receiving end of her anger, too. When a former high-school classmate said it was fortunate that her mother didn't linger on, Maria was furious.

Her husband arrived the night before the funeral. He found Maria coping well but obviously upset. She cried for several hours that evening. When they went to bed Maria found herself highly aroused and they made love passionately. Both were a little embarrassed about it the next day.

Maria handled the funeral all right. The following morning, however, she thought she saw her mother walking down the street. She ran after the woman, only to find it was someone else. During the next six months, Maria periodically thought she saw her mother. She didn't discuss these experiences with her friends because she was sure they would think she might be crazy.

Six months after her mother's death, Maria was able to get through the day without feeling too much sadness about the loss of her mother. She thought she had worked through her grief. One weekend Maria and her husband had dinner with close friends. Sitting around after dinner, she found herself washed over with the same feelings she had when she learned her mother was dying. Then Maria said, "Did I tell you how my mother died?"

Luis's Unsuccessful Job Search

After two months of looking for work, Luis realized he had been out of a job longer than ever before. It was obvious to him that his usual ways of finding work were not successful. The controlled optimism he maintained while looking for work began to erode. He started to doubt his judgment, second-guessed himself and became more self-critical. The fears and doubts he'd suppressed earlier bothered him more and more.

The preparation and organization that marked earlier efforts to find work deteriorated. He felt himself panicking. "One day I just went to the Southwest Industrial Park and went door to door," Luis stated. "I don't know why, but it made me feel better." Another day he drove into another industrial section around town and looked for a job by stopping at personnel offices of companies where the parking lots were full, on the assumption that these companies might have openings.

Luis tried to write a new résumé, but he had lots of difficulties. One time, in responding to ads in the newspapers, he wrote four different résumés which seemed to him to describe four different people.

Increasingly, Luis felt angry. He was angry with the government for breaking up the aerospace industry and angry with universities for training people for jobs that no longer existed. Sometimes these feelings of anger were turned on himself. At one point, after a very difficult week of being turned down at several places and being unable to get an interview at another, Luis looked at his shotgun and thought maybe he should kill himself. "You know, sometimes I wonder if ending it all wouldn't be better than going through this," he said to himself.

Crisis Reactions and Other States of Adjustment

At one time or another in our lives, most of us will confront events that are likely to cause us to respond with a crisis reaction. The term "crisis reaction" encompasses several conditions described in the third edition of *The Diagnostic and Statistical Manual of Mental Disorders,* commonly referred to as the DSM-III (American Psychiatric Association, 1980). These include the categories of transient adjustment disorders; bereavement; and maladjustments in reaction to family, school, job, or phase-of-life stress.

Four characteristics distinguish the crisis reaction from other states of adjustment: (1) no mental disorder was evident prior to the stress; (2) the stress is clearly perceived and experienced as alien; (3) the reactions are excessive or different in quality from usual responses to stress; and (4) the crisis reaction gradually wanes after the stress ends.

Prior to the onset of the crisis reaction, a person is functioning within what mental health workers would call "normal limits." They may be in a State 1 adjustment or in a State 2 temporary overload condition. They are functioning effectively, they are reasonably content with their lives, and their mental behavior is undisturbed.

A second characteristic separating State 3 adjustments from a temporary overload condition is the antagonistic nature of the stress and the severity of the reaction. The qualities of alien stresses that can trigger a crisis reaction were summarized in Chapter 5: the feeling of a major change occurring in a short period of time, which is seen as having an undesirable lasting future impact, and affecting large areas of life (Parkes, 1971). Sudden catastrophes are the clearest examples of these stresses: fires, earthquakes, tornadoes, tidal waves, volcanic eruptions, rape, or accidents. More universal negative experiences that bring about crisis reactions are the unexpected death of parents or other loved ones, loss of a job, physical limitations, or facing our own death.

Human beings differ greatly in what will provoke a crisis reaction. For you it may be because your girl friend leaves you. For me, it may be the realization that I have no idea what I want to do with my life. You might have considerable difficulty understanding why I'm experiencing a crisis merely because I lack a sense of identity and purpose. I, on the other hand, can't imagine falling apart if I split up with a girl friend. It is how we experience the stress that causes the State 3 adjustment.

The DSM-III makes the point that these State 3 conditions can emerge as long as three months after the stressful event. While many of us respond immediately to a severe loss or problem, not everyone does. Some of us function apparently normally for a period of time and then give way to a State 3 adjustment. Others, such as Luis, slide into a temporary overload condition to cope with being out of a job; the persistent stress will wear him down to the point that a crisis reaction appears.

This still from a 1938 movie, End of an Era, shows the face of grief. Today programs for those who have suffered the loss of a loved one — such as widow to widow counseling — help people through the bereavement process.

A third characteristic of State 3 is that people in a crisis condition exhibit a gallery of mental and physical difficulties. Anger, depression, and anxiety are most common. Other characteristics range from laughing, crying, or cursing, to withdrawal, irritability, or repetitive worrying (Menninger, 1967). Clinicians working with people following a significant trauma report hallucinations, delusions, hyperactive behavior, and hysterical episodes and phobias (Powell and Driscoll, 1973; Parkes, 1972; Lindemann, 1944).

The fourth major distinguishing characteristic of State 3 adjustment is that the most bothersome symptoms are transient, gradually vanishing as the stress recedes into the past. Sometimes flashbacks occur unexpectedly long after the event. A 40-year-old teacher attending a sex education workshop in summer school suddenly remembers all the feelings that had accompanied her own abortion at seventeen. For a day or so she is not the same, but gradually the pain passes once more.

How long might a crisis reaction be expected to last? Recent findings suggest that symptoms of crisis can exist anywhere from eight to twenty-eight weeks after the onset of the problem (Horowitz, 1980, 1976).

A crisis reaction is actually a series of responses. Elisabeth Kübler-Ross, a physician working with dying patients, identified five distinct stages which people who have been told they are going to die pass through: (1) denial; (2) anger; (3) bargaining; (4) depression; and (5) acceptance. Another sequence is suggested by the work of Horowitz (1976), who studied the reactions of individuals who suffered trauma ranging from threat-to-life to rape. His phases of the crisis reaction differ slightly from those of Kübler-Ross. His are (1) outcry, (2) denial or numbness, (3) intrusiveness/denial or numbness, and (4) working through.

Though Horowitz's model has distinct stages, it does not see a reaction to crisis as a smooth progression through a series of stages. After a period of **outcry** and then **denial or numbness** the third stage is a period of **intrusiveness**/denial or numbness. Repetitive thinking about the traumatic event and its consequences, emotional spasms of fear, guilt, rage, shame, and sorrow intrude into awareness. Denial and numbness occur to ward off these painful attacks. We may alternate between denial and numbness, and the repetitive intrusions of these painful and disorganized moments for a long period of time. Gradually the stressful events are more fully experienced, and a **working-through** process occurs. However, working through is never complete. Waves of pain, anger, and depression may intrude periodically well after the crisis has passed. When they appear, however, it is generally without the staying power and disorganizing effect of the first time.

Selye, Kübler-Ross, and Horowitz would all agree that a crisis reaction is far more complex than their own theories depict. Moreover, even though each of us has a unique pattern of responses when we manage stress, some general stages followed by most individuals can be noted.

Primary Features of Adjustment in State 3

A crisis reaction brings with it a substantial change in the primary features of behavior. At least one sphere of life is notably painful, and a marked reduction is experienced in the total satisfaction from all areas of life. New self-protective responses appear, mixed with usual ways of managing stress. And personality style shows temporary new features.

Pain in Work, Love, and Play

Someone in State 3 feels a sharp decrease in the total satisfaction from living. Moreover, there is an overall feeling that no domain of life — even areas not directly affected by the problem — gives as much pleasure as it did before the crisis. Thus, Luis finds relationships with others are not going very well.

Lovemaking and other communication with his wife increasingly are strained as both of them worry about his finding a job. His moodiness causes his children to give him a wide berth, and he may avoid his best friends because he feels the shame of not working. Even his primary hobby, playing the saxophone, is affected. He finds himself sitting with the instrument in his hand, unable to think of anything he'd like to play.

In State 3, some individuals may decide to reduce their investment or commitment to an area of life which is causing them so much pain. "I'm never going to get enthusiastic about a job anymore," Luis says. "I'm just going to do my work and take my pay." Hillary may express similar sentiments about another sphere of life, vowing never to fall in love again. These feelings will pass when the crisis is over. Old enthusiasms return, though perhaps not as intense as before. A wariness remains.

New Self-Protective Responses

Individuals in crisis have to handle distressing feelings ranging from a dull, continuous nagging ache to a sonic boom of excruciating anxiety. After the first outcry, most try to manage these feelings by the familiar coping devices seen in State 2.

But what worked for the agreeable, expectable stress is insufficient to reduce the new, often agonizing, psychic pain. Because the problem causing the emotional upset is seen as far more threatening than the agents of tension in State 2, the familiar, middle-level self-protective responses do not have the power to lower distress. New ways to handle emotional upset emerge. These are usually lower-level ego defenses. They function to shut out any unbearable anxiety for a short period. Even though her menstrual cycle was relatively regular, Hillary applied denial to hold back her anxiety. She told herself her period was "just a little" late until she missed the second one. Then Hillary thought she couldn't be pregnant, because her boy friend said he didn't ejaculate inside her. This brought relief for a while.

Individuals in State 3 often have the feeling that the resources that have been a source of support and gratification in the past are running out rapidly. They are tapped unselectively because of the feeling that if they are not used the person will not be able to continue. Thus, Maria talked to her friends at great length, often repetitively, to help her through her loss. She knew, however, that others have their own problems and would eventually tire of listening to her despair and trying to comfort her. In fact, Maria asked her best friends directly to tell her when they had enough.

The value of a storehouse of resources before a crisis is like the importance of good physical conditioning prior to a heart attack. Being in good shape may not prevent a coronary but it greatly improves the chances for recovery afterward (Fletcher and Cantwell, 1974). By the same token, having access to people or experiences that bring comfort in times of great need eases the passage back to a normal state.

New Features of Personality Style

During State 3, the major features of personality style remain intact. However, the way we normally handle stress begins to change. Familiar responses may be altered slightly, or whole new behavior patterns may be assumed. The overall effect makes someone seem very different from the one previously known.

Consider Angus, a typical prickly personality. Angus is feisty, enthusiastic, and involved in campus life. His weekly editorials are informative, amusing, or enraging, depending on an individual's point of view. A professor of his said, "Even though I often disagree with him, Angus has great enthusiasm for what he does and he often raises important issues."

In the fall of his senior year, however, not only Angus's parents but also his professors saw puzzling changes. First he seemed less energetic than before. Usually a morning person who bounced out of bed, he started having trouble getting up. He was late for his first-period classes a dozen times in the fall. In class he seemed withdrawn, whereas he used to delight in sparring with the professor. More and more he just sat there without saying much. Usually he loved to sniff out and expose dishonesty or hypocrisy at the college. In November, one of the reporters found evidence that the food service might be selling food, supposed to be served to the students, to a local restaurant. Uncharacteristically, Angus was uncertain about whether to follow up on the lead.

Secondary Characteristics of State 3

Secondary characteristics associated with crisis reactions include the feeling of a severe, alien environmental stress, questionable physical status, less effective organization, unpredictable mood changes, and intense but variable interpersonal relations. These are summarized in Table 11.1.

Severe, Alien Environmental Stress

In State 3, the stress is seen as severe and alien. We've identified three types of stressful experiences that often bring on a crisis reaction: (1) a sudden event; (2) a wearing-down process; and (3) an unwelcome but inevitable life cycle transition. An example of the first is the death of her mother, which came with unexpected suddenness to Maria. Luis's case illustrates the second type. Instead of sinking directly into the exhausted condition after a period of State 2 resistance, which Selye (1956) portrayed in Chapter 2, there is instead a period of panic along with other characteristics of a crisis reaction.

The demands for an unwelcome but inevitable and necessary transition in life is the third stress, which both Vaillant (1977) and Levinson (1978) describe as bringing about periods of instability, and which we examined in Chapter 5. Angus's crisis reaction in his senior year was caused by his having to make a choice between displeasing his father or displeasing himself as he moved into the next phase of his life.

Table 11.1   Secondary characteristics associated with crisis reactions

Severe alien environmental stress
    Can be sudden, a wearing down pro-
       cess, or an unwelcome but necessary
       developmental transition
    Unexpected or not previously experi-
       enced

Variable physical status
    Marked swings in sense of well-being
    Usual physical reactions to stress,
       along with "something new"
    Increase in intake of familiar drugs
       and/or use of new drugs to support
       coping

Markedly less effective organization
    Intermittent deterioration in one or
       more spheres of orientation

Decreasing confidence in reality testing
Inappropriate sense of agency
Inhibited openness to experience
Accumulation of problems
Urgency for decisions/actions

Unpredictable mood changes
    Severe mood variation
    Depression and anger
    Absence of humor

Intense but variable interpersonal relations
    Highly self-centered
    Uncritical soliciting of advice that
       doesn't help

Even when we have had a considerable warning, the crisis reaction may still develop. Take for example a group of Boston families who were moved out of their slum dwellings to make way for urban development. They were given plenty of notice by the Redevelopment Authority that they would be relocated a few miles away. Though they all knew well beforehand they would have to move, about one person in two showed behavior typical of a crisis reaction (Fried, 1963).

Environmental stresses having a high probability of triggering a crisis reaction are unexpected or have not been experienced previously. At one moment, Phyllis thought her parents were happily married; at the next they were splitting up. While Hillary could imagine being pregnant and having to face the question of what to do, this was not something that she had been through before.

Variable Physical Status

In Chapter 2 we noted the relationship between high levels of stress and decline in health. These changes in physical status occurred up to a year after the events precipitating the crisis. Vulnerability to injury and irreversible illness increase with greater stress. For instance, a study of three high-school football teams in New Orleans found that the risk of injury was five times greater for players whose parents had died or had been divorced in the past year (Coddington and Troxell, 1980). In his book *The Broken Heart,* Dr. James Lynch (1979) documents that sudden loss of love or of a loved one through death is a significant contributor to premature death through heart disease or other maladies.

People in State 3 are likely to experience wide swings in their sense of well-being. They may oscillate between feeling all right and definitely unwell. Maria developed pain in the lower part of her back for which the doctor couldn't find a reason. She was irritated at first when the surgeon said it was probably related to her mother's death. Gradually the pain waned and was gone a year later.

In State 2 a person's physical response to stress forms a predictable pattern. For someone with a crisis reaction, however, the physical response is likely to include the usual reactions to stress along with something new. The "something new" can be the sudden onset of a different problem. Studies of combat stress of soldiers and of grieving adults found sleep disturbances to be the most common symptom (Bartemeier, Kubie, Menninger, and Whitehorn, 1946; Parkes, 1972). Other physical disorders include shakiness, flushing, irregular heart beats, dysmenorrhea (menstrual disorders), lightheadedness, loss of appetite, diarrhea, acid stomach, excessive perspiration, and skin conditions (Menninger, 1967).

Variations in sexual behavior commonly occur in this state. Some of those who have lost a loved one through divorce, separation, or death report a sharp decrease in sexual drive. On the other hand, a minority of individuals are like Maria, experiencing a sharp increase in sexual drive following a loss. In her first-person account *Widow*, Lynn Caine (1974) describes this experience of stronger sexual urges at the time of her husband's dying.

A crisis condition may involve drugs in about the same way as did State 2: the use of various prescription and non-regulated potions to feel better. But the usual dosage of medication may not work as well any more. A greater amount is needed for the same effect. Or there may be a search for more potent drugs. It is in State 3 when solitary abuse of self-medication or prescription drugs is most likely to begin.

Markedly Less Effective Organization

The variability that characterizes every other aspect of life during a crisis response also impairs one's mental functions so that one's overall organization is markedly less effective than in State 1 or State 2. While there are long moments of functioning as usual, intermittent deterioration occurs unpredictably but with increasing frequency in one or more spheres of orientation. Shortly after her parents said they were divorcing, Phyllis started to have trouble with *time*, sometimes not even knowing what day of the week it was. Her teachers noticed she was less reliable in getting from her regular classroom to gym, art, and science, which were in different parts of the building. Phyllis's two major activities were gymnastics at the YMCA Wednesday afternoon and piano instruction on Saturday afternoon. As her crisis reaction developed, Phyllis began mixing up these appointments. Once she came into gymnastics on Thursday afternoon instead of Wednesday. Another time she rode her bike halfway to her piano teacher's house before she realized it was Wednesday and she was supposed to be headed for the Y.

Occasionally, the sense of *person* is affected. The most common example is losing someone close to us and beginning to feel our behavior resembles that of the lost individual. Maria put on weight after her mother's death and at one point felt she looked more like her mother than she ever thought before.

Self-confidence in reality testing is eroded, and we may begin to wonder whether we are seeing the world accurately. Minor transient hallucinations can be quite upsetting even though they are a usual response to a severe loss.

Another disturbance in reality testing is the inappropriate feeling of being the origin of the crisis. An illustration is the grieving teenager who feels that his poor school grades caused his father to have a heart attack. And if there is a sense of being a cause of the crisis, there is also a sense of being the source of its solution. Thus Phyllis, in what Kübler-Ross might view as the **"bargaining"** phase of her crisis reaction, promised to be a good girl if her parents remained together.

Openness to inner and outer experiences is nearly always affected. It's difficult to overestimate the tension people in State 3 feel from time to time. Even periods of numbness are pierced with racking spasms of anger, depression, and anxiety, making it difficult to focus on the acquisition of information

The Scream by Edvard Münch portrays many of the feelings of those experiencing a crisis — agitation, depression, and the terrifying sense that everything is falling apart. (Collection, The Museum of Modern Art, New York. Mathew T. Mellon Fund.)

that can help someone through a crisis. Intuitive capacity is reduced. Whereas in States 1 and 2 we will say, "I don't know what to do so I'll trust my instincts," people in crisis have lost touch with the capacity to sense the right course of action. Confronting possible job openings in Florida and the West Coast, Luis couldn't decide what to do. Should he uproot his family and move them to another part of the country, where there might be greater opportunity, or stick it out in Hartford a little while longer? Asked by friends what his plans were, Luis replied, "I don't know. I don't have a gut feel about what's right."

Judgment is adversely affected by several factors that can be lumped together under the general heading of **field dependence** (Witkin *et al.*, 1954). People who are field dependent look only to the world around them to provide clues to understand the nature of the problems they're having and what to do about them. One manifestation is obsessive worry. In State 2, individuals know where the trouble is coming from. They need to scan only certain areas looking for danger or helpful information. Not so with someone in a crisis condition. Everything is insecure, everything is subject to reevaluation. Phyllis started to wonder whether her old friends honestly liked her, whether she was really as smart as her grades showed, and whether her soccer game was going downhill. What were certainties formerly underlying her sense of self were now painfully scrutinized once more. Then there were the new problems to worry about, caused by the separation — how much money will we have, where will we live, who will help me in math, how will mother and I get along by ourselves?

Another aspect of field dependence that inhibits the acquisition of information is the tendency for people in crisis to be unduly sensitive to the very small differences in choices that need to be made. This overconcern about small gradations is called **sharpening** (Holzman and Gardner, 1959). Subtle differences in something take on inappropriately large weight. For example, Phyllis's parents once argued in her presence about visitation rights for her father. Phyllis started to worry there would be a nasty courtroom battle, and she imagined she might have to make a choice between her parents. She made an exhaustive list of characteristics of both her parents: who was the nicest, who was the best cook, which would let her watch her favorite TV programs, who was likely to keep the cleanest apartment, and who was the best at helping her with her schoolwork. She finally decided her schoolwork was most important and that math was the subject she was most troubled about. Therefore, she decided in her mind that if she had to choose between living with her father or mother, she would pick her father because he would better be able to help her with math.

Because individuals are so focused on troubles in their lives in State 3, minor problems can accumulate. This worsens an already difficult situation. While Phyllis was reacting to the separation of her parents, it was hard for her to pay too much attention to her schoolwork, friends, gymnastics, piano, and her cat, who was coughing and acting sluggish. Unless she attends to these stresses, her problems will be intensified by a poor report card, estranged friends, less satisfaction from sports and music, and a cat that has pneumonia.

The origin of the word **crisis** is a Greek word meaning "to decide." People with a crisis reaction usually have an urgent need to make a decision. A decision or plan for action seems imperative and they often communicate this urgency to others around them. They make people feel that something has to be decided *right now*.

Unfortunately, these decisions are highly unstable. The primary reason is that anxiety inhibits the acquisition and processing of information. Decisions are insufficiently rooted in reasoned judgment to resist competing ideas for very long. For example, Phyllis felt momentarily better when she decided to elect to live with her father. A half-hour later, however, her mother baked her some chocolate chip cookies, and Phyllis changed her mind.

When somebody is at the end of his or her capacity to cope with stress, that person will occasionally act in an impulsive, unrealistic, costly manner. The purpose of the physical action is to vent the mounting anxiety. So long as someone is in motion or planning it, emotional pain is reduced for the moment. Phyllis, worried about having to choose between her mother and her father, ran away from home. She packed her bag, put in her favorite books, a few clothes and her bear, and left. All the time she was planning to leave, packing, and actually leaving home, she felt better. But after Phyllis rode her bike to her second-grade teacher's house, she was miserable again.

Unpredictable Mood Changes

People in crisis are moody. Depression is a common prevailing condition, but it is unstable and variable. An outside observer does not know why a person's mood is changing so rapidly, and neither does the troubled individual. Flurries of zest and enthusiasm are followed quickly by deep pessimism and apathy. For instance, Luis's wife described him this way:

> I don't know what's wrong with him. One minute he's happy, elated, feeling on top of the world, not at all worried about finding a job. Then the next he's sullen and like a porcupine. If you say the wrong thing you'll get a barb in you. . . .

Luis knew he was up and down too. His feelings were like many others who are unemployed and starting to panic.

> It's like being on a roller coaster or a yo-yo. . . . Sometimes I feel depressed — I mean *really* depressed — and wonder if I'll ever snap out of it. After a while, I begin to feel agitated . . . you know, filled with energy. Then I'm really hyper. I spend a lot of energy but I don't seem to get much done. I race through the want ads and don't get much from them. . . . Then I go to the Unemployment Office for help . . . but I only have pieces of conversation. . . . I cut them short . . . acting as if I have somewhere important to go . . . you know, in a hurry. I know what I'm doing is not helping yet I feel better when I'm on the move (Powell and Driscoll, 1973, p. 22)

Continuing conflict between parents can cause a crisis reaction in children if they believe that their family is dissolving.

In addition to depression, anger is almost always present in a crisis reaction. Luis's fury at everyone and everything was strong enough to bring him to the point of thinking about killing himself. The anger of children whose parents are separating is very often expressed toward the remaining parent. Phyllis blames her mother for her father's moving out. The hostility common to State 3 can be triggered by a trivial event, as with Maria's lashing out at the doctor for sending the bill so soon. This anger is like a time bomb. We never know when it will explode or what will trigger it, but the intense rage will surely come.

The restorative powers of humor are not available in State 3. Though this statement may seem to underscore the obvious, it is the first state of adjustment in which humor is notably absent. No longer can we smile at adversity or be amused by the pretentions and inconsistencies underlying some patterns of human contact.

Intense but Variable Interpersonal Relations

When we are in the company of individuals experiencing crisis reactions, we will find the conversation extremely intense, but often it is a one-way street. Their troubles, their anxieties, their state of mind are paramount. Little capacity for sustained interest or being responsive to the needs of others is likely to be evident. Grappling with the problems of whether or not to have an abortion, Hillary is not able to listen to her roommate's anxieties about whether to change majors.

Individuals in crisis actively and uncritically solicit advice from those around them. Luis was offered a low-paying subsidized job at the State Employment Commission as a counselor to others out of work. Unable to decide, he spent days asking everyone he knew what he should do. Should he take a job that pays only $125 a week? Would working for the government stigmatize him and hurt his chances to get back into the private sector? What did he know about personnel work anyhow?

During this time he talked to many people, including life-long friends, his wife, engineers who were still working, secretaries, and a janitor at his old place, who knew him only slightly. The active but random nature of advice seeking is one of the hallmarks of this state of adjustment. This can be frustrating and irritating for friends and loved ones as well as experts advising people in State 3 because everyone's judgment seems to be given the same weight. However, it is not so much that people in State 3 want advice to guide them, though repetitively they appear to be doing just that; rather it seems their contact is motivated by a wish to share their plight with another human being.

People in crisis are easily influenced. In this condition they are easy prey for opportunists — the career counselors who promise the unemployed a job for a fat fee; the shady paramedical hucksters offering relief for serious illnesses; the unscrupulous funeral directors, mystics, and cultists who prey on people in crisis. Luis actually went to what was described as an executive-scientist placement agency. Luis recapped his experience this way: "For two thousand dollars they rewrote my résumé and talked to me a little. But I didn't mind too much. At least they listened."

Follow-up

Phyllis

After Phyllis ran away it was obvious to everyone that something needed to be done to help her. The teacher and her parents met with the school psychologist. As Phyllis's behavior at home and school was scrutinized, it became clear that she had lost ground since she heard of her parents' separation.

The school psychologist observed her in the classroom and noted that Phyllis seemed unsure of herself and didn't like to try things that were new. If she didn't have a monopoly on the teacher's attention, she withdrew and sulked. When Phyllis and the psychologist were alone together Phyllis talked easily. Asked about her reaction to her parents' separation, Phyllis said at first she was upset but after a short time she said she "didn't feel anything but kind of numb." Yet she noticed that sometimes at night or early in the morning — even occasionally at school — she became very sad as she thought about her mother and father getting a divorce. Phyllis said she had no idea why her schoolwork was going downhill except that maybe she wasn't as smart as others thought.

The school psychologist referred Phyllis and her parents to a community counseling service that specialized in helping families in which mothers and fathers were separating. At first the three of them met with a family therapist. Then her parents met with a group of separating adults. Phyllis participated in counseling along with several other children whose parents were splitting up. The parents were helped to mediate their differences, recognizing the effect of divorce on children, to minimize the stress around visitations with the father, and to anticipate Phyllis's reaction when both began to see other partners.

Meeting with other children was an eye-opener for Phyllis. She discovered they too thought they might have caused their parents to separate and had recurring fantasies of reuniting them and felt somehow diminished and were ashamed to tell anyone about their parents' divorce. Phyllis slowly recognized that she might not be the only one in her class whose parents were not living together. On her own she discovered three other girls whose parents were divorced or separated. She invited them to play after school and made three new friends. By the year's end her teacher said Phyllis was back to normal.

Angus

At his parents' insistence Angus finally worked in the family auto parts business over the summer and into the fall. While this cheered his mother and father, Angus didn't seem interested. His stomach problems worsened.

When he talked to his friends everyone seemed to have an opinion, but Angus still couldn't decide what to do. One moment he saw himself staying in the business and even expanding it; the next moment he was talking to the marine recruiting sergeant. At one point he thought he might just take off to think things over.

The only person he could talk to who seemed to help was the dean of his college. The dean didn't offer much advice except to say that working for a few months in the business did not commit him to it. Just before January first Angus made a decision. "I'll take a year off to think about what I want to do," Angus explained. "I've been either at home or in school all my life and never have had a chance to see much else." The spring following graduation Angus got a job with a small-town newspaper and found he loved it. The year off became a career.

Hillary

After she visited one of the abortion clinics, Hillary came back to the professor and again asked him what she should do. Since he did not believe in abortions, he told her so. But he also said it was her decision. Still Hillary couldn't decide. She felt greater and greater pressure to do something.

A crucial moment for Hillary came when the professor wondered out loud how her parents might react if she went ahead and had the baby, or an abortion, without telling them. He wondered how her mother and father had responded in the past when she was in trouble. At this point Hillary reappraised her initial conviction that her parents would be shocked by her pregnancy. In the past her difficulties had not upset them greatly. Once at ten she was caught shoplifting; they had been upset and disappointed but supportive. Moreover, she always felt she was her father's favorite of the four children. Perhaps they wouldn't be so upset after all. This assessment relieved Hillary because she realized she could call her parents for help. That day she talked with her mother. In a turbulent, emotion-packed but basically loving encounter, her mother told Hillary that she was coming over that evening. The following day Hillary told the professor she was going to have an abortion. At this point, Hillary looked haggard and disturbed, which worried him.

A week later Hillary appeared in the professor's office looking well. She was smiling and relaxed, and her usual zest had returned. The change was amazing. Still worried about her, the teacher inquired solicitously how she was feeling. Would she like to tell him about the abortion? Was she experiencing any post-abortion symptoms? Could he do anything more for her? The painful moment for them both came when Hillary responded:

> Thank you for your help and interest. Everything is fine now and I would really not like to talk about it anymore if you don't mind. I'd like to go back to being your student. Can you tell me what I have to do to get caught up . . . ?

In fact, the abortion, while painful, did not have lasting psychological effects on Hillary. From time to time she wondered whether she had made the right decision, but not for long. What she wondered mostly about was why she had allowed herself to become pregnant in the first place. Sometime in the future Hillary thought she might want to explore this.

Maria

During the year following her mother's death, Maria was overcome by moments of uncontrollable sadness. Each time she felt the anguish nearly as intense as when she had known her mother was going to die. These periods lasted a few minutes to a day or so but passed. They became less and less frequent as time went by.

About a year after her mother's death, Maria became unusually upset again. This time the grief was greater than it had been before and lasted longer. She was puzzled about it. Maria's husband wondered if it had anything to do with the fact that it was Easter again. Easters were never the same for Maria.

Luis

After about two weeks the crisis reaction abated. Luis wound down his job hunting totally. The anxiety and depression Luis felt during the crisis reaction were gradually replaced by malaise and bitterness. The impulse to die was supplanted by a cynical desire to live. "If I can't find a job then those S.O.B.s who got jobs and don't deserve them are going to support me," Luis said to another engineer in the Tuesday morning lineup to receive their unemployment compensation.

Because of imminent financial problems, his wife sought a higher-paying but more demanding banking job. She told Luis about it only after she accepted the job. His reaction was to say that he had been accepting it in the past months. Their roles had gradually shifted anyway.

Relationships with friends were increasingly a problem. Luis was certain some of his friends were avoiding him because they didn't respect a man who couldn't keep a job. "I wonder if they think what I've got is catching," Luis mused. Still his wife reported his friends were interested in seeing him but Luis seemed to be avoiding them. He began playing his saxophone again. Eventually they sold their house and moved closer to where his wife worked.

Out of the blue the phone rang and a friend in Luis's old company called. They had landed a big contract and offered him an engineering job. After hedging for a while, he accepted.

Assisting People in State 3

A considerable advantage in assisting people going through a crisis reaction is that they know they aren't functioning normally. Unlike State 2 or even lesser states of adjustment, it is obvious to individuals involved in a crisis that their adaptation is far from normal. If asked, "Do you usually react this way when you have a problem in your life?" a friend who has lost a job, a sister who has been a rape victim, or a neighbor who was recently widowed will give a resounding "No!"

This recognition makes it a good deal easier to lend assistance. People in State 3 are helped by friends, relatives, and nonprofessional volunteers as well as by those who make their living as mental health workers. Five general principles are useful in working with individuals in crisis. First, *men and women in a crisis state are generally benefited by the presence, the physical presence, of others.* Networks of people are crucial to the recovery from State 3. They prevent social isolation and withdrawal as well as provide comfort and opportunity for catharsis, reality testing, and help in bringing about appropriate adaptive responses. Those who study the relationship between losing loved ones and serious physical problems maintain that it is a *dialogue* with others which keeps us from physical and mental illness in times of crisis (Lynch, 1979). He suggests this dialogue with others not necessarily be one of love: any type of interaction will do — joy, irritation, pleasure, displeasure — just so long as the person is not cut off from interacting with others.

Being around people in a crisis state can be exhausting. Partly this is because the intensity of the feelings causes them to be able to talk for hours without stopping. As sleeping patterns are disturbed by upsetting dreams and thoughts flashing into consciousness, the need to talk at all hours of the night and day can be overpowering. These tax the stamina of those trying to help. A real danger is becoming exhausted and ineffective. Mobilizing a support system of friends, relatives, colleagues, and volunteers to assist a troubled individual is often necessary. This provides an ongoing "presence" of people who can be rotated to share the burden.

If we find ourselves alone in a crisis state, we can benefit from having the services of skilled clinicians. In the absence of such people, numerous nonprofessional groups are helpful. An example is the Samaritans, an organization begun in England that uses a telephone hot-line system to talk to individuals contemplating suicide or who are otherwise in crisis. An all-volunteer group, the Samaritans are credited with reducing the suicide rate in metropolitan London by more than a third (Fox, 1976). They now have branches in the United States. Other volunteer organizations maintain hot-lines or drop-in centers for people in crisis in nearly every city in America.

The second principle is that *information is helpful to people in crisis conditions*. A troubled friend is relieved to know that his suicidal thoughts do occur in people who are in a state of panic after losing a job. A neighbor might be relieved to find that thinking she sees a dead spouse several weeks after the funeral — which she would otherwise label "crazy" — is an experience common to recent widows. If people know that these are normal reactions of those in crisis, they don't have the added burden of worrying about whether they are losing their minds. Specific information conveyed by those who have been through a similar crisis experience, or are currently sharing it, aids the process of adjustment. Widow-to-widow programs have achieved remarkable results (Vachon, Lyall, Rogers, Freedman-Letofsky, and Freeman, 1980). Self-help groups of unemployed workers reduce the emotional consequences of being out of work and also improve job-seeking behavior (Powell, 1973).

Books can also be of value. Greatly bothered by her unusual reactions after the death of her husband, one woman told how much she was reassured by actress Helen Hayes's report of the same kind of behavior in the first two years of her widowhood (Caine, 1974). In her book about helping children cope with death, poverty, divorce, hospitalization, natural disasters, and imprisonment of a parent, Joan Fassler (1978) reviews children's books and stories about similar or analogous situations. She recommends questions and other approaches adults might use to assist youngsters in mastering the distress they feel. For example, the story *The Red Balloon* (Lamorisse, 1956) tells the story of Pascale, a lonely French boy who becomes deeply attached to a red balloon. It takes on lifelike properties, and nearly a magical relationship emerges between the boy and the balloon. Eventually, cruel boys throw rocks at the balloon and finally destroy it. Toward the end of the book the author notes that Pascale is "in tears over his dead balloon." Reading *The Red Balloon* can help initiate discussion with children about loss and death. Fassler gives an example of a young mother whose husband was killed in Vietnam. When she read the story of the red balloon to her 4-year-old son, he became fascinated by the story and even examined the photographs with great attention. When they read aloud about the balloon's destruction he commented, "Just like daddy, just like daddy." Then he began to ask questions about his father's death, a topic he previously had been reluctant to discuss.

It is useful to recognize that the presence of people can dampen the sense of urgency that individuals in crisis feel — that they have to make a decision, to do something that brings momentary relief, although it may have negative long-term consequences. Time is an ally of the troubled person. The longer someone can be supported and encouraged to bear the anxiety and deal with a painful problem, appraising and reappraising the options, the more likely that individual is to make a successful adaptation.

Because a person's judgment is likely to be impaired and such people are frequently unable to discriminate who will and will not help, an individual in crisis needs assistance in finding those people or agencies that are most likely to be helpful and those that are not. Protection is needed against the shady operators and fanatics who prey upon people in State 3.

The third guideline in working with individuals in State 3 is *recognizing our own emotions*. Though recognition of our own feelings is essential in helping people in any state of adjustment, it's particularly crucial in State 3. No one is immune to the powerful emotion evoked by these individuals. This is because they often convey to us that we are the only — the one and only — person in the world who can help. The feeling of power and responsibility for the troubled individual's welfare can be heady as well as disquieting. Those of us assisting these people are especially vulnerable to developing unrealistic fantasies about our role in their life. These fantasies have been summarized by psychiatrist Dr. Preston Munter (1977) as (1) The Rescue Fantasy, (2) The Need to Be Right Fantasy, and (3) The Omniscient Fantasy. No one can help another without the desire to rescue, to be right, and to do everything possible. Yet none of us can assist everyone, can always be right, or remake a shattered world. To be truly effective, we must appreciate our own realistic limitations.

People in State 3 can direct intense emotions toward us. These can range from extreme helplessness to raging hostility and sometimes straight sexual overtures. These strong feelings can bring out in us equally powerful, sometimes inappropriate counter-feelings. We may tell a friend to "stop feeling sorry for yourself" because of our frustration of being unable to shake him out of his despair. We may become angry at our sister when she tells us that our efforts to help her are making her feel worse. Or we may take advantage of a neighbor's sexual vulnerability. Not only are these responses likely to worsen someone's crisis reaction, they effectively eliminate us from providing further help.

The fourth guideline is to *monitor the ways of coping with the distressing event*. We may wish to advise or support various forms of direct action, such as are indicated in the list of direct action responses for recovery from rape to speed their recovery. We should recognize, however, that not every rape victim or recent widow wants to hash over the traumatic event with professional or nonprofessional experts. They may want to put the problem out of their mind for awhile and may react negatively to being thought of as a psychiatric casualty. As one woman who had been raped put it, "I just want to be alone for awhile to try to pull myself together and I don't want to talk to any doctor!"

Since most people recover from crisis reactions unaided, a reasonable course of action is to remain in close contact to observe how the person we care about is making the readjustment. To what extent is a friend using higher-level self-protective responses to cope? Is our sister taking direct actions that seem to speed her recovery?

A final guideline is to *recognize that the capacity to bear the pain of a crisis state diminishes rapidly for many who see no hope for improvement*. Maladaptive ways of coping become apparent as the person attempts to ease the pain. Imagine our neighbor, who may be now drinking too much or can't get her mind off of suicide when she is sober. To no avail we suggest cutting down on alcohol or talking to a doctor about her suicidal preoccupations. She says she is fine and doesn't want to talk to anybody. What can we do then?

Sometimes we can use our own anxiety as a lever to encourage someone we care about to obtain assistance by saying that their behavior problems trouble us and we think that a consultation with a professional might be useful. We might say something like, "This may be my problem but your behavior seems unusual to me and I would feel a lot better if you obtained an outside opinion as to how you are managing the problem. In fact, I'll go with you." Even if this confrontation doesn't succeed in propelling someone we care about into the hands of specialists, it may make it very clear to them what our concerns are and this event may initiate progress toward recovery. Specialized help is available for almost any type of problem and individuals in a crisis state might be encouraged to take advantage of these services. An example is the counseling services available to rape victims. Interestingly, this study shows that not only do many women benefit from the counseling, but also from being a counselor.

Sometimes more general medical help can benefit someone in crisis. A physical examination places someone in crisis in contact with another person—a helpful professional who might be a valuable human contact. The individual may be helped to anticipate physical problems or injury often associated with a crisis reaction. Sometimes counsel given in the context of a physical examination is heeded when the same guidance given by others is ignored.

The Japanese symbol for the word crisis is composed of two characters that translate as "danger" and "opportunity." As friends, relatives, and volunteers, there is little we can do to protect others from crisis reactions. Danger through loss and misfortune is part of everyone's biography. A period of crisis, however, also brings with it an opportunity for growth. While it may be that a significant part of the world we are used to is radically changed or obliterated, there is always a chance to strike out in a new direction, to start something fresh, to find our way, to develop new relationships, skills, or interests. A crisis also brings with it an opportunity to understand maladaptive ways in which we cope with severe stress, allowing us to make important changes. The individual, assisted by caring friends, is in a unique state of openness to learn more adaptive ways of coping with problems in the future.

Recovery from Rape

Researchers Ann Burgess and Lynda Holmstrom at Boston City Hospital followed up eighty-one rape victims to assess how their adaptive responses to this trauma influenced subsequent adjustment. Sixty of the women said they had recovered at the time of the follow-up four to six years later, and twenty-one said they did not feel recovered.

Comparing the victims in these two groups, the researchers found the recovered women used higher-level self-protective responses (SPR's) to adapt and employed a higher frequency of direct action responses.

Higher-Level Self-Protective Responses

1. *Explanation:* similar to the highest level adjustment mechanisms described in Chapter 3. This device helps the victim manage anxiety by coming up with some reason for the rape: "I hitchhiked to save twenty cents and for twenty cents I was raped."

2. *Minimization:* similar to the coping device of rationalization. This method decreases the terrifying aspects of the event, allowing the victim to think of it in tolerable portions: "All I had to do was lie there . . . I didn't have to do anything unnatural."

3. *Suppression:* as described in Chapter 3. It is putting the memory of the rape out of mind by conscious effort: "I don't dwell on things I can't change because life is too short."

4. *Dramatization:* a coping device in which the anxiety surrounding the rape is dissipated by repeatedly overemphasizing it: "I don't usually cry but when this happened I cried a lot and got it all out."

Resources

Of the women in the unrecovered group, eighteen reported either seriously abusing alcohol or drugs or making a suicide attempt. In addition, the presence of a social network was associated with recovery. Victims who had no social ties were less likely to feel better at the time of follow-up. Women who were in stable relationships with a partner recovered far faster than those who were not.

Direct Action Responses

1. *Travel or change of residence:* depending on the financial circumstances women traveled, moved to another city or neighborhood, or lived temporarily with relatives or friends.

2. *Changing or getting an unlisted telephone number:* this seemed to increase the sense of security and control over the environment.

3. *Vicarious exposure in a controlled setting:* some benefited from watching TV talk shows about rape or from reading or writing about it.

4. *Volunteer service in a rape crisis center:* of those who recovered in the shortest time, seventy percent used this type of direct action.

SOURCE: Adapted from Burgess, A. and Holmstrom, L. Adaptive Strategies in Recovery from Rape. *American Journal of Psychiatry,* 1979, *136,* 1278–1282.

The Japanese symbol for the word *crisis* consists of two characters, each with a separate meaning. The upper character means danger and the lower one stands for opportunity. This view sees the opportunity within the danger of a crisis.

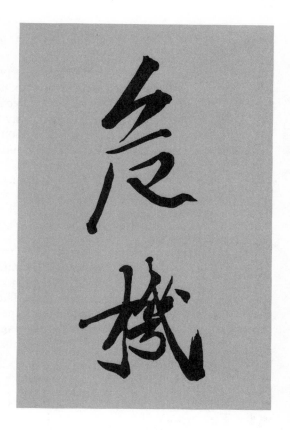

Summary

1. Four characteristics distinguish crisis reactions from other states of adjustment: (1) no mental disorder was evident beforehand; (2) the stress is clearly perceived and experienced as alien; (3) the reactions are excessive or different in quality; (4) the crisis reaction gradually wanes when the stress ends.

2. The crisis reaction is actually a series of responses. We all have our own particular sequence of reactions that signal a State 3 adjustment. Once past, phases can be subsequently revisited.

3. The primary features usually show at least one sphere of life notably painful and a marked reduction in satisfaction from all domains of living. New self-protective responses appear mixed with usual coping devices, and temporary new features are added to the usual personality style under stress.

4. Secondary characteristics associated with crisis reactions include an unexpected or not previously experienced alien environmental stress, variable

physical status, markedly less organization, unpredictable mood changes, and intense but variable interpersonal relations.

5. Five guidelines that can be helpful in assisting people with a crisis reaction are (1) being physically present and mobilizing others to assist; (2) realizing that information obtained from professional and voluntary sources, as well as books, speeds recovery; (3) recognizing that our own emotions can be triggered, which may work against our being helpful; (4) monitoring ways the troubled person is coping with stress; (5) being aware that the capacity to bear pain diminishes and maladaptive ways of coping may occur.

6. While the crisis reaction brings with it great pain, it also provides opportunities for new growth and mastering stress in the future.

A Look Ahead

The next chapter will examine the neurotic disorders. These conditions include the so-called Vietnam and burnout syndromes, though they have many less dramatic expressions. They also include continuing stress emotions in the absence of cause. Four types of neurotic disorders will be described. The effect of State 4 adaptation on the primary features of adjustment will be examined as well as the secondary characteristics associated with this condition. Guidelines for assisting those with prolonged stress reactions will be considered.

Key Terms

crisis

outcry

denial or numbness

intrusiveness

working through

bargaining

field dependence

sharpening

Suggested Readings

Stages of the crisis reaction

Kübler-Ross, E. *On death and dying.* New York: Macmillan, 1969.

Horowitz, M. *Stress response syndrome.* New York: Aronson, 1976.

Different viewpoints on the phases of the crisis response.

Stresses triggering State 3

Monat, A., and Lazarus, R. (Eds.), *Stress and coping: An anthology.* New York: Columbia Press, 1977, chapters 16, 17, 19, and 21–26.

A collection of classic articles about crisis reactions in response to stresses ranging from death to losing a home.

Helping children through crisis

Grolman, E. (Ed.), *Explaining death to children*. Boston: Beacon, 1967.

Weiss, R. *Marital separation*. New York: Basic Books, 1975. Chapter 10.

Fassler, J. *Helping children cope: Mastering stress through books and stories*. New York: Free Press, 1978.

Practical assistance for adults helping young people cope with traumatic life events.

Self-help

Ruben, H. *C.I.: Crisis intervention*. New York: Popular Library, 1976.

Kushner, H. *When bad things happen to good people*. New York: Schocken, 1981.

Recovery from crisis assisted by psychological and religious understandings.

A woman brought her husband, a 28-year-old, black manager of a fast-food drive-in and part-time student, to the Veterans Administration because of "spells of craziness." The night before, he flew into a rage, broke furniture, and ran out of the apartment, saying he was afraid he would kill somebody. At 2 A.M. he was brought home dead drunk by two fellow students and Vietnam vets.

He had been discharged from the Army two years ago. While in Vietnam, he was a platoon sergeant. His nickname was the Iceman, because he was extremely cool under the stress of battle. He was twice decorated — once for recovering wounded and dead members of his platoon from a mine field.

Six months after discharge he began to have nightmares of being in the middle of a mine field with the remains of his dead buddies all around him. Sometimes he could not stand crowds. "When I get into a crowd my heart starts beating fast, my chest gets tight, and it lasts for three or four hours," he said. Periodically the Iceman had trouble taking his two small children to the park because he became obsessed with the notion that snipers were hiding in the trees. He had to scan each tree to be sure he was safe.

Six months prior to the outburst of fury, the Iceman began drinking a quart of wine during the day. He thought it would help him sleep better, but it didn't. He was thinking of dropping out of school. His wife said he had little sexual drive: in fact, he was impotent.

His wife said he had always been happy, even tempered, and outgoing. "But," she said, "when he came back from Vietnam I didn't know him anymore."

A composite case drawn from histories reported by J. Cavenar, and J. Nash. The effects of combat on the normal personality: War neuroses in Vietnam returnees. *Comprehensive Psychiatry*, 1976, *17*, 647–653.

CHAPTER 12
State 4: Neurotic Disorders

Questions to think about

□ Have you ever known anyone who continued to behave erratically long after a serious loss or traumatic event?

□ Do you know individuals who consistently do what is wrong though they seem to know what is right?

□ What percentage of high-school seniors would you guess have used alcohol or marijuana in the last month?

□ Why do you think some people "grow out" of a maladjustment and others do not?

Described in the box is one of the most dramatic examples of the State 4 adjustment — the Post-Traumatic Stress Disorder (DSM-III, 1980), sometimes called the post-Vietnam syndrome. Many neurotic disorders are less dramatic, though just as disabling.

As the name implies, neurotic disorders are persistent, disabling behaviors, thoughts, or emotions. Typically, these conditions begin as a response to especially unpleasant events. Instead of the anger, depression, or anxiety waning when the stress passes, however, these emotional responses remain intense. A State 4 condition is not a passing phase that people grow out of quickly, nor is it part of a sequence of responses to a crisis. It is a relatively frozen state of adaptation that may last for months, years, or a lifetime.

In this chapter we focus on four types of neurotic disorders which are described in the DSM-III: symptom disorders, disorders of childhood and adolescence, eating disorders, and drug-use disorders.

Using the case examples of this chapter, we consider how neurotic disorders differ from other states of adaptation. The types of State 4 disorders described in the DSM-III are examined briefly. Then we note how the primary features of adjustment are affected and identify secondary characteristics associated with neurotic disorders. At the end of the chapter, we learn that many kinds of treatment methods are useful in helping people recover from State 4 conditions.

The stress of war. Whether or not the battle was won, something of the cost is revealed in the face of this soldier.

Five Examples of a State 4 Adjustment

Benjy: The Scapegoat

Benjy's father is an Episcopal minister. In the summer prior to Benjy's fifth-grade year, his father accepted a call to move from the small rural Virginia town they had lived in for eight years and move to a Maryland suburb of Washington, D.C.

Benjy is 10 years old, an only child, and miserable. He loved his friends and that country town. He hated the new city, the new kids, and the new school. Hardly a day went by in the fall that he didn't complain about being in Maryland and cry because he missed Virginia so much. To make matters worse, before long the other kids began to pick on him when he went to the school bus. They called him a wimp because he was so unhappy. One day they ganged up on him after school and stole his shoes so that Benjy had to walk home in his stocking feet. After a while, he began to get sick to his stomach in the morning before he was supposed to leave for the bus stop. The stomachaches miraculously disappeared after school began.

Finally, his parents were concerned enough so that they went to the elementary school to see what might be done to help him. To their surprise, they found the faculty not particularly sympathetic. "He seems to bring it on himself," the math teacher said. "We know Benjy is picked on and we've told the other kids to stop it. But pretty soon Benjy does or says something that provokes the other youngsters, and it starts all over again." The reading teacher shook his head and agreed, noting also that Benjy was inconsistent. His work in the classroom was terrific one day and poor the next.

His parents wondered why Benjy was being scapegoated. This did not happen before they moved to this town. They asked the teachers, "What should we do?"

Darlene: Thirteen Going on Twenty-one

Darlene's teenage years were stormy. "They say a woman's worse years are when she turns thirteen and when her daughter turns thirteen," Darlene's mother said. "But no one ever told me about fourteen, fifteen, and sixteen!" Darlene's mother was referring to the emotional roller coaster she'd been on since her daughter became a teenager.

During childhood, Darlene had been a model youngster — loving her parents, kind to older people, intelligent, and a student leader. She was also the best soccer player in her class. In fact, she joked about being a tomboy. Many times, boys invited her to their birthday parties, and Darlene didn't mind being the only girl there.

Then when Darlene moved from sixth grade into junior high school in the suburban Milwaukee town of Whitefish Bay, her personality changed. "Little by little Darlene went from being Miss Goody-Goody to Miss Baddy-Baddy!" her mother exclaimed. Darlene complained that her mother didn't understand her, put too much pressure on her to get good grades, didn't approve of her new friends, and restricted her freedom. Darlene's parents had reasons to be worried. She was increasingly withdrawn and moody, and the door to her room was always closed and featured a large KEEP OUT! sign. Her school grades were erratic, her friends changed, and Darlene seemed reluctant to bring them around. More and more, she didn't want to tell her parents where she was going in the afternoon or on weekends.

Increasingly nasty confrontations between Darlene and both parents ended with all of them upset: Darlene stomping off to her room, her mother crying in the bathroom, and her father pouring himself a drink.

In desperation, her parents talked to the school principal and guidance counselor. They said that Darlene was simply experiencing "an adjustment reaction," that this was a passing phase, and they should trust Darlene more. For a while her parents tried to follow this advice, but in the spring they caught her smoking. By summer Darlene began to come in hours later than she was permitted to on weekends.

In the fall of the eighth grade, Darlene spent most of her time with ninth- and tenth-graders, and was very excited when she was invited to their parties. One Saturday in March, Darlene was told she had to baby-sit her three younger sisters. When her parents arrived home unexpectedly early, they found Darlene in the embrace of a high-school boy in his car, parked in their driveway. When they opened the door, the smell of marijuana was overpowering.

In mid-May, Darlene and her parents were summoned to school by the principal. It seemed that Darlene had been caught by a teacher selling marijuana to her classmates. When confronted by her parents and the principal, Darlene didn't have much to say except that she needed the money to pay for her own daily drug use.

Chantal's Weight Problem

Chantal is 30 years old. She is of French-Canadian heritage, single, and has always lived with her mother. She works as a senior accounts receivable clerk for a trucking company in Montreal. Nearly finished with a bachelor's degree in the computer sciences after six years of night school courses at a local university, Chantal eventually plans to enter the field of data processing.

Chantal has a weight problem. She is exactly five feet tall, and weighs 218 pounds. The last four years her weight has ranged between 180 and 230. Chantal has been heavy since early adolescence. From sixth to eighth grade she gained fifty pounds. At high school graduation she weighed 170.

Off and on during the past ten years, she's gone on diets and lost considerable amounts of weight. "There's nothing I don't know about diets," she says. "I think I've lost about half a ton in my life." The lowest she ever reached was 150 pounds on two occasions, but each time her weight bounced right back up. Chantal knows she overeats but doesn't know why. "I'm so good most of the day," she says, "and then when I get home I lose all my self-control." Weekends are especially bad. Often she binges.

Chantal is an only child. Her father and mother were divorced when she was a child, so she never knew her father. Her mother is a teacher and tells Chantal she's never been the same since her divorce. She is extremely dependent upon Chantal. Whenever Chantal speaks of getting her own apartment, Mother develops chest pains.

In spite of her size, Chantal is active. She is a skier, plays squash and tennis, and backpacks. In an adult education class, Chantal found she had considerable skill in sculpting and does this for fun. In Montreal, her social life is barren. However, she recalls fondly two torrid summer romances she had while on vacation in Greece. "Those Greek men liked their women big," she says with a smile.

It was after last summer's romance that she decided to try to lose weight again. "I wonder whether I could attract a Canadian if I got this weight off," she mused. She contacted a psychiatrist who used hypnosis to help people lose weight because she hadn't tried that approach yet.

Walter's Workaholism

Walter received his partnership when the senior members of the architectural firm met at the end of the year. Walter planned to take a month off and vacation with his family at an out-of-the-way resort in the Caribbean. Ten days after he arrived, an emergency call from his office informed him that a major problem had developed with the waterfront development and he was needed back at the office. So Walter and his wife flew home with Walter promising he'd get away again as soon as he straightened things out.

In the year that followed, Walter reverted to the working habits that had characterized his rise to the top: fourteen-hour days Monday through Friday with another ten to fifteen hours' work at home or in the office on Saturday and Sunday. Asked by a friend why he put in so many hours, Walter replied it was because they were short of help; and besides, hard work "goes with the territory" of being a partner. Walter pointed with pride to the company's fee, which he had been largely responsible for negotiating.

In the five-year period following his becoming a partner, Walter's cigarette and alcohol consumption increased. In spite of his doctor's warnings, Walter remained a steady two-pack-a-day man. Though he knew he needed three or four drinks after quitting time to relax, Walter was pretty sure he did not have a problem yet because he did not drink in the morning and never missed work.

Gradually, his wife's unhappiness grew. Between them the affection, even passion, was still there, but her feelings toward him were beginning to cool. "You can't compress love between two people into occasional weekends away and two weeks in the summer," she said to herself.

Finally, Walter promised to be home one Saturday but had to work instead. He missed his son's hockey game in the morning and his daughter's afternoon birthday party. Afterwards, both children asked their mother if they were especially "good," would Daddy be home for their next special occasion.

When Walter arrived home, his wife demanded that they see a marriage counselor together. Walter agreed; he went twice but could not continue because he was too busy.

Charlie's Terror of Thunderstorms

Charlie is a 47-year-old salesman in Kansas. He had worked for the same company for twenty-five years, and had always been slightly above average, but not an outstanding salesman. The reason Charlie didn't sell more was that he was terrified of thunderstorms. Every time he heard a broadcast that a thunderstorm was likely or felt it might be in the air, he had a dramatic physical reaction. He became short of breath, dizzy, his heart pounded, and he literally shook. It didn't matter whether the thunderstorm struck or not, he was unable to control his physical sense of panic. Then he began to think, "When will it come? Where will I be? Where can I be safe? How can I cope with my panic?"

Charlie felt he went to ridiculous extremes during these possible thunderstorms. When he was on the road, he lowered the car antenna on his automobile and drove as quickly as possible to a motel. Once inside, he unplugged all of the electrical appliances and would not use the telephone. At home he demanded his entire family stay with him in the same room while the thunderstorm threatened, even though none of them was afraid.

This year Charlie returned to his small Kansas college for his twenty-fifth reunion. During the occasion, he met his former roommate, who asked him if he was still terrified of thunderstorms. Embarrassed, Charlie resolved to do something about it.

Neurotic Disorders and Other States of Adaptation

The neurotic disorders* refer to persistent, disabling behaviors, thoughts, or emotions that are not connected to a cause or are clearly excessive. They become themselves a source of distress. In other words, instead of worrying about an unpleasant event that may cause us to be depressed or nervous, or results in headaches, impotence, drug abuse, or binge-eating, we find the reactions to the stress become the major problem. Focused on these painful symptoms, we lose track of what caused them.

The crippling psychological symptoms originally were in reaction to an unpleasant event, but they have continued well beyond the time the stress ended. Unlike people in States 2 and 3, who can eventually return to normal, these individuals seem frozen in their maladjustments. Their bouts of anxiety or depression persist years after a crisis ends, they don't "grow out" of their childhood disorders easily, or they continue to use drugs though they have lost track of why.

---

*The diagnostic class of "neurosis" does not appear in the DSM-III, though it was used in earlier versions of this manual. In its place is the term "neurotic disorder," which has about the same meaning.

Often individuals with a neurotic disorder feel heavily burdened. White and Watt (1981) see this condition as similar to the girl who had polio as a child and as a result is restricted physically. Life after the illness must accommodate this handicap. Many satisfactions — playing sports, for example — will be closed off to this young woman. Some areas remain open to her to develop a sense of competence and the respect of her classmates. For instance, she can write for the newspaper or play in the orchestra. But what her classmates achieve with relative ease, she does only by expending maximum energy. This effort may tax her so that little desire remains to play or nourish relationships with others. And she is prone to moments of intense anger, helplessness, and panic.

In some cases, a clear-cut cause for a neurotic disorder is obvious: war, lengthy unemployment, burnout, or poor relationships with parents. In other cases the origin is not at all obvious, as in a tendency to overeat to the point of obesity without having any idea why.

Types of Neurotic Disorders

Looking at the array of psychological conditions catalogued in the DSM-III, four groups of mental disorders fit the criteria for neurotic disorders. The first is comprised of what is called **symptom disorders**. In these disorders the primary difficulty is with a disabling symptom — depressed mood, intense anxiety, or physical complaints with no organic cause. The second type is called by the DSM-III the disorders of childhood and adolescence. These usually begin as maladaptive responses to events — Benjy's difficulties around moving, Darlene's acting up at puberty — but go on and on rather than gradually diminishing. The third kind of State 4 condition is eating disorders. Here the primary problem is loss of control of proper food intake. The final type of neurotic disorder is the drug-use disorders.

Symptom Disorders

The major groups, subtypes, and usual symptoms of each of the symptom disorders are shown in Table 12.1.

As the name implies, the primary feature of **mood disorders** is disturbed mood. Generally this involves either depression or elation, and sometimes alternating emotions. A person with a *depressive disorder* has long periods, lasting two years or more, of feeling sad, down in the dumps, blue, or low. These depressive periods are relieved occasionally by times of normal mood, which may last from several days to a few months. When depressive states alternate regularly with unusually active behavior (e.g. high energy, optimistic, uninhibited, people-seeking, reckless) this is called a *cyclothymic disorder.*

Anxiety is present to some degree in all neurotic disorders, but as the name suggests, among the **anxiety disorders** it is the primary symptom. All

Table 12.1 Symptom disorders

GROUP	SUBTYPE	SYMPTOMS
Mood disorders: Disturbed mood is primary feature	Depressive	Persistently feeling blue or low, interrupted by periods of normal mood lasting a few days to several weeks. Loss of interest in pleasurable activities.
	Cyclothymic	Alternating periods of depression and hypomania (high energy, inflated self-esteem, restlessness, gregariousness, optimism, and reckless behavior).
Anxiety disorders: Anxiety is prominent feature	Phobia	Persistent irrational fear of a specific object, activity, or situation that results in a strong desire to avoid it. Fear is recognized as unreasonable and excessive.
	Anxiety state	Involves shakiness, inability to relax, difficulty concentrating, or insomnia.
	Post-traumatic stress disorder	Following a psychological trauma, a reexperiencing of some aspects of the event, a feeling of numbness toward or reduced involvement with the outside world and recurring hyperalertness, guilt about surviving, or overreaction to events that recall the stressful experience.
Somatoform disorders: Significant physical symptoms without organic evidence are the major feature	Somatization	A sense of being sickly for most of one's life. Recurring multiple physical complaints commonly in back, stomach, sexual organs, or chest region. Medical attention brings no diagnosis or relief.
	Conversion	Total or partial paralysis of a part of the body to avoid awareness of an underlying conflict that prevents an undesirable event from occurring.
Dissociative disorders: Sudden, temporary alteration in normal awareness, behavior patterns, or sense of self is primary feature	Psychogenic amnesia	Inability to recall important personal information after a stressful event.
	Multiple personality	Two or more distinct personalities within the same individual. Each is dominant at a particular time. The individual personalities are usually different from one another. Transition from one to the other is sudden.

Table 12.1   Continued

GROUP	SUBTYPE	SYMPTOMS
Psychosexual disorders: Sexual dysfunctions with no organic cause are the primary feature	Gender identity disorders	Persistent discomfort and sense of inappropriateness of one's own gender and continuing desire to live as a member of the opposite sex.
	Sexual perversions	Unusual thoughts or acts necessary for sexual excitement: (1) the aid of nonhuman objects for sexual arousal; (2) repetitive sexual activity with humans involving real or simulated suffering or humiliation; (3) repetitive sexual actions with nonconsenting partners.
	Psychosexual dysfunction	Disorders of sexual desire, excitement, or orgasm.

SOURCE: From American Psychiatric Association, *Diagnostic and statistical manual of mental disorders*, Third Edition, Washington, D.C., APA, 1980. Reprinted by permission.

of us have felt severe anxiety at some time in our lives: before an exam, game, or party; waiting for a grade in an important course, a doctor's report, or a judge's verdict. Signs of anxiety are all there: jumpiness, pounding heart, frequent urination, anticipation of disaster, and feeling on edge. What separates normal feelings of nervousness from an anxiety disorder is that the tension has a clear cause and diminishes when the stress is removed. In an anxiety disorder the nervousness persists without an apparent reason, causing severe distress and restricting the enjoyment of life.

Charlie's fear of thunderstorms is a classic example of a *phobia*, an anxiety disorder. He has a persistent, irrational fear of thunderstorms themselves, but also of any situation in which the weather can turn bad. He knows his fear is ridiculous but can't do anything about it.

The Iceman's symptoms are characteristic of a *post-traumatic stress disorder*. Periodically he reexperiences memories of the war — vivid dreams of being trapped in a minefield. Or he overreacts to a minor event that recollects a wartime experience, diving onto the classroom floor when a car backfires.

"Somatoform" means that the expression of the maladjustment is through the body: *soma* is the Greek word for body. The primary identifying feature of the **somatoform disorders** is the *presence* of bodily complaints suggesting an illness, in the *absence* of organic cause. In these cases, doctors' examinations and lab tests find the person in good health, so the origin of the physical problem is presumed to be psychological. This is not to say that the man with stomach pains is faking it or the difficulty swallowing of the man who believes he has throat cancer is all in his head. Their disturbances are just as real as the faintness or nausea we might experience coming upon a grisly car accident.

To a person with canine phobia, someone's mild mannered dog may appear as artist Rufino Tamayo saw dogs in his painting *Animals*. (Collection, The Museum of Modern Art, New York. Inter-American Fund.)

In these situations our emotions, rather than a physical agent, cause us to pass out or throw up.

The quality distinguishing the **dissociative disorders** is a rapid change in usual awareness or behavior, often occurring without the individual's awareness. An example is the *multiple personality*, the existence of two or more distinct, relatively fully operational personalities within the same person. Each has its own behavior patterns, social relations, and memories. Transitions from one to another are often abrupt. An interesting contemporary report of multiple personalities is the story of Sybil (Schreiber, 1973).

Nearly always the personalities are quite different from one another, as evidenced by Sybil's case. In contrast to the relatively brief dissociative reactions common to most amnesias, multiple personalities are more tenacious. Extensive therapy is frequently necessary to correct these conditions.

Psychosexual disorders feature dysfunction in the sexual area in the absence of an organic reason. *Gender identity disorders* are manifested in persistent unhappiness with one's own gender and desire to live as a member of

Sybil's Many Personalities

Sybil Isabel Dorsett grew up in a household full of "cruelty, secret rituals, punishments, and atrocities" in a small midwestern town of 1,000 persons. It was a rigidly fundamentalist town where coffee, tea, liquor, dancing, and novels were sinful. Her mother was a schizophrenic who beat, burned, and tortured her daughter, starting when Sybil was six months old, while talking of mother's love and God's wrath. Her father was engrossed in his work as a contractor-builder and did not see, or refused to see, either his wife's growing obsessions or his daughter's torment. Trapped by her mother's atrocities and her father's passive failure to protect her, oppressed by a puritanical, hypocritical religious hysteria, Sybil dissociated as a means of survival, each self a defense against an intolerable reality, yet still part of the original child.

Sybil first started experiencing periods of time lapse, with events occurring that she did not remember (although she was said to have participated in), when she was 3½ years old. She did not become consciously aware of these "blackouts" (as she called them) until she was 14. During these blackouts she was later to discover that any one of what was to become fifteen distinct personalities was in fact "taking over" and living through her body. Sybil was never conscious of these other personalities and usually did not share their memories, although they were all able to follow Sybil's life happenings. Thus, after the death of her grandmother when she was nine, Sybil lost two years to the self-named Peggy Lou. The multiplication tables that Peggy Lou learned in the third grade Sybil was not able to recall until years later. Each personality had its own speech patterns, gestures, vocabulary, handwriting, and belief systems, although all in some way did feel trapped by the church. Sybil was a gifted painter; most of the selves shared in that talent to varying degrees.

The Course of Therapy and the Emergence of the Selves

Sybil first started therapy at age twenty-two, having had to leave college because she was too "nervous." It was ten years later that she first started intense psychoanalysis to understand what was happening to her. She had no idea at that time of the existence of her other selves and still no explanation for the periodic lapses of time. That she was at least a dual personality became apparent to her analyst when Sybil appeared one day for her appointment walking, talking, and acting totally unlike "herself" and presenting herself as Peggy, who was keeping the appointment for Sybil. With long and careful probing, other selves emerged over

(Continued on p. 366)

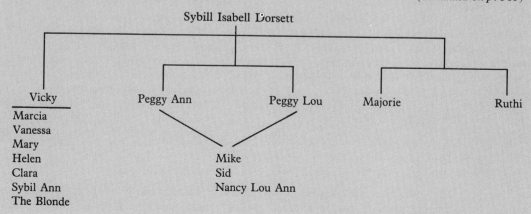

Sybill Isabell Dorsett

Vicky
Marcia
Vanessa
Mary
Helen
Clara
Sybil Ann
The Blonde

Peggy Ann

Peggy Lou

Mike
Sid
Nancy Lou Ann

Majorie

Ruthi

(Continued from p. 365)

the years, each born of new traumas Sybil had faced, each with a life and personality of its own. The time losses and memory gaps began to make sense. The years of therapy were filled with the discovery of these selves and the traumas that spurred their creation. Eventually Sybil was confronted with the fact of her multiple personalities, and the work of integration was begun, the work of forcing herself to remember the traumas and understand each self as a specific reaction to a specific trauma. Sybil's acknowledgment of the other selves, and her growing desire to once again harbor these aspects of her personality she had not consciously known since the age of 3½ years, focused on the slow integration of her selves into one self and of their memories into her now-complete memory.

The Selves and Their "Date of Birth"

Victoria Antoinette Scharleau (1926): A self-assured, attractive, knowledgeable, and sophisticated woman, with free and graceful movements, Vicky first emerged when Sybil was 3½ years old. She took over the child Sybil's poise, confidence, and capacity to negotiate with the world. She became the memory trace of all Sybil's personalities. For Vicky, there were no "blackouts" or loss of time. She felt she was the most whole of all of Sybil's selves, and became a general monitor on the others' activities, once preventing a suicide attempt by taking over and calling Sybil's psychiatrist. She acted as co-analysand with the psychiatrist and is genuinely concerned about Sybil. Like all the rest, Vicky accepted being called Sybil by the rest of the world.

Peggy Lou Baldwin (1926): Miss Baldwin was a teacher whom Sybil was fond of and trusted. Peggy Lou was assertive, mischievous, and often angry. Her voice is that of Sybil's mother, and hers is the anger that Sybil never expressed or admitted she felt. Peggy Lou contained and expressed the original child Sybil's hostility, anger, and rage. She loves the sound of broken glass, and Sybil ends up paying for the glass-breaking rampages of Peggy Lou.

Peggy Ann Baldwin (1926): A counterpart of Peggy Lou, with similar physical characteristics. Peggy Ann will become fearful over things that will make Peggy Lou angry. Both Peggys originated from Peggy Louisiana, the name Sybil's mother used for Sybil, disliking her real name. Both Peggys are assertive, theatrical, and fighters. They appeared in Sybil's life soon after the appearance of Vicky.

Mary Lucinda Saunders Dorsett (1933): Mary is thoughtful, contemplative, maternal, and homeloving. She is plumper than the other selves, and sees herself as a little old lady type. She emerged during the two years after the death of Sybil's grandmother, Mary, who died of cervical cancer when Sybil was 9. Her death seemed to be the death of all love for Sybil. Torn with religious conflict, Mary is mournful and tearful; yet as the eternal homebody and housewife, she keeps the home going for Sybil.

Marcia Lynn Dorsett (last name sometimes Baldwin) (1927): Marcia is English, a writer and a painter, who is extremely emotional and essentially a pessimist. Her feelings are Sybil's feelings intensified. When Sybil almost committed suicide, it was Marcia who was the propelling force.

Vanessa Gail Dorsett (1935): Also English, intensely dramatic, and extremely attractive,

the opposite sex. *Sexual perversions* are found among people who require bizarre mental images and/or acts for sexual pleasure. *Psychosexual dysfunctions* are disorders at one or more segment of the sexual response cycle. This

Vanessa is Marcia's best friend, with an expressive oval face and a tall willowy figure. Of the two (Vanessa and Marcia), she is the more dominant and extravagant. Both are equally dynamic; and Vanessa, especially, has a bit of detachment and a wry sense of humor.

Mike Dorsett (1928): Mike is a builder and carpenter, with olive skin and dark eyes, modeled after Sybil's paternal grandfather. Sybil's father used to call her Mike when she wore her coveralls as a child.

Sid Dorsett (1928): Sid is also a builder, whose name is taken from Sybil's initials. He is quieter and more thoughtful than Mike, modeled after Sybil's father. Both boys are eternally youths, denying that they have a female body.

Nancy Lou Ann Baldwin (?): Nancy is interested in politics as it relates to Biblical prophecy. She is afraid of Roman Catholics. She is always on the verge of terror, hearing explosions in her head, and is closer than the others to being a religious hysteric.

Sybil Ann Dorsett (1928): Sybil Ann is fragile, shrinking, and talks in whispers. Pale and timid, listless to the point of neurasthenia, she is modeled on Sybil's mother during her catatonic phase immediately following the Depression and the loss of their home. Her paintings are solitary and dreary; if there are figures, their heads are covered or turned away.

Ruthie (?): Ruthie is just an infant, who emerged while Sybil shut her eyes and ears to her parents' nightly sexual encounters in the same room with Sybil's crib. She is rebellious, indignant, full of rage and jealousy.

Clara Dorsett (?): Highly religious and highly critical, Clara is very angry at Sybil for preventing her (Clara) from doing the things she wants to do.

Helen Dorsett (1929): Helen is intensely afraid but determined, desiring fulfillment. She reenacts Sybil's terror of her mother.

Marjorie (1929): Serene, vivacious, quick to laugh and tease, Marjorie is theatrical and loves intellectual competition. She is not at all depressed, nor is she a painter, nor is she religious.

The Blonde (1946): Sybil's adolescence, alive but quiescent since Sybil was twenty, who has blond hair and a light heart. The Blonde is the girl Sybil would have liked to be. Born out of Sybil's wishes rather than her traumas, The Blonde has never been ill, does not remember Sybil's mother. She emerges to consciousness almost at the end of therapy, ready to give her as-yet untapped strength and vivacity to Sybil. Her emergence as the final personality marks a climax in the therapeutic process.

Sybil Isabel Dorsett (1965): The seventeenth personality can rightly be said to be the new integrated Sybil Dorsett, in whom have coalesced the sixteen personalities, into a person unlike the original Sybil. The new Sybil is still a painter, but her style has elements of all the other selves who painted. The different "persons" of herself have intermingled, yet she is still cognizant of the different "selves." Making a shelf might be the Mike and Sid selves, while the brightly colored new dress is bought by the part that was once Peggy Lou. As a combination and reorganization of all the other selves, the new Sybil Dorsett can indeed be said to be the seventeenth, and final, self.

SOURCE: Adapted from Schreiber, F. *Sybil.* Chicago: Regnery, 1973.

can manifest itself in inhibited desire (the inability to feel sexually "turned on"), difficulty at the point of sexual excitement (the Iceman's impotence), or with orgasm (delay or absence of climax).

Disorders of Childhood and Adolescence

The second type of problems that fit within State 4 conditions are the **disorders of childhood and adolescence.** These are emotionally based problems, noticeable prior to adulthood. They are *not* momentary developmental difficulties but rather continuing disorders that cause misery to the individual and to parents, teachers, and other adults for lengthy periods.

There are three patterns. In the first pattern, the disturbance is self-limiting, that is, it disappears totally on its own. This usually occurs as the person moves into a new developmental stage, as when a hyperactive child begins to calm down at puberty or someone with an identity disorder rebuilds a compatible sense of self as a young adult. A second pattern is the opposite: the problem goes on for years, as when a person continues to feel anxious when separated from parents and therefore can't leave home to attend college. In the third pattern, the problem disappears and reappears periodically throughout life. For example, adults who were bothered by stuttering in childhood may find it recurring at times of particular stress throughout their life.

The disorders of childhood and adolescence are divided into three major groups based on which area is affected: behavioral, emotional, or physical. The primary features of these groups, subtypes, and examples are shown in Table 12.2.

The primary symptoms of the **behavioral disorders** group are actions that are inappropriate for the young person's chronological age. The first subtype is the *attention deficit disorder*, whose major signs are a short attention span and impulsivity. A second subtype of this group are the *conduct disorders.* Essentially, these involve children and adolescents who persistently violate the rights of others or the society in which they live. Their actions are more serious than ordinary mischief.

The **emotional disorders** group is given its name because the main symptoms are excessive feelings of anxiety, anger, or general distress. The subtype *oppositional disorders* feature persistent disobedient, negativistic, and provocative behavior toward parents, teachers, and other authority figures. Like a compass that always points south, youngsters such as Darlene are continually against whatever adults are for.

Included among the **physical disorders** are frequent involuntary bodily actions which cause substantial distress. One subtype is the *tic disorders.* Tics are involuntary, purposeless rapid movements of one or more muscle groups. Benjy's persistent eye blinking is an example. Benjy also had two other subtypes of physical disorders, *stuttering* and *enuresis* (bed wetting). As with many, Benjy did not stutter when singing, reading, or talking to his dog. His bed wetting occurred involuntarily, usually at night, and happened regularly.

Eating Disorders

The three most common **eating disorders** are bulimia, bulimarexia, and anorexia nervosa. *Bulimia* is uncontrolled binge-eating to the point of discomfort. As Chantal's case shows, the food consumed is often high in calories. It is

Table 12.2 Disorders of childhood and adolescence

GROUP	SUBTYPE	SYMPTOMS
Behavioral: Inappropriate actions for age are primary feature	Attention deficit disorder	Short attention span, impulsivity with or without hyperactivity.
	Conduct disorder	Persistent behavior that violates the rights of others.
Emotional: Excessive emotional distress is primary feature	Separation anxiety disorder	Great anxiety about being apart from those to whom the child is attached.
	Overanxious disorder	Excessive but nonspecific worry about possible harm in the future.
	Oppositional disorder	A pattern of disobedient, negativistic and provocative behavior toward authority figures.
	Identity disorder	Uncertainty and conflict because of an inability to reconcile opposing interests, goals, friendship patterns, and values.
Physical: Frequent involuntary bodily actions, which cause great distress	Tic disorders	Involuntary purposeless rapid movement of several related muscle groups.
	Stuttering	Frequent repetition, prolongation of sounds or syllables or unusual hesitations which disrupt rhythmic flow of speech.
	Enuresis	Repeated involuntary bed wetting or urination during the day.
	Sleepwalking	Repeated episodes of arising from bed and walking about, unresponsive to others.

SOURCE: From American Psychiatric Association, *Diagnostic and statistical manual of mental disorders*, Third edition. Washington, D.C., APA 1980.

gobbled down rapidly, often with little or no chewing. Only when the person feels too full to ingest anything else does the eating stop.

When someone follows binge-eating by vomiting, laxatives, or suppositories, either to reduce discomfort or control undesirable weight gain, it is called *bulmarexia* (Boskind-Lodahl and White, 1978). One woman who had this problem described it wryly as "having your cake and not having your cake at the same time." This behavior becomes a problem when it is carried out involuntarily several times a day.

Of the eating disorders, the most dramatic is *anorexia nervosa*, or self-starvation. The case of Charlotte displays the primary features of anorexia nervosa: reduced food intake, no hunger, twenty to twenty-five percent weight loss, absence of menses, disturbed body image, hyperactivity, and great concern about control. For the most part, this disorder has been limited to adolescent, middle-class, white females. More and more, however, the problem is being reported in adults, in members of the lower social classes, and in men.

Drug-Use Disorders

The drug-use disorders are the fourth type of State 4 adjustments. In many countries, the use of particular drugs to improve mood, induce a sense of well-being, and lubricate social relationships is accepted and even encouraged. The beer-bust, keg or cocktail party, "coffee," or "smoker" are frequently events that bring people together. Promotion of these drugs is extensive. It is difficult to go through a day without being encouraged to get more out of life by switching to a different coffee, being enticed by an attractive, liberated woman to smoke her brand of cigarettes, or being challenged by a man's man to try his beer.

In addition, there are various pharmaceuticals available over the counter and by medical prescription designed to alleviate headaches, lower stomach

Charlotte's Anorexia Nervosa

Charlotte was always taught by her parents to be an ideal child. Sweet, loving, responsive, and helpful, Charlotte was a much-adored youngster. In elementary school her teachers said she was the best-balanced student in the class. She was frequently voted into class offices. She worked hard and obtained high grades. Something of a perfectionist, Charlotte's personal dress, room, and academic work were always neat and precise.

At age 12, Charlotte went to a summer camp she couldn't stand but stayed "because she never fought back." At camp the combination of the rapid growth characteristic of puberty and starchy food resulted in significant weight gain. Charlotte was horrified by a picture of herself in slacks taken from behind when she was bending over. Charlotte felt the only way she could win the respect of others and herself was by being thin, so she went on a starvation regime. Over the next five years she dramatically restricted her food intake. She either refused food entirely or would binge-eat and throw up. Charlotte said

losing weight wasn't hard because she completely lost her appetite. Being around food didn't bother Charlotte. In fact, she often cooked for her friends. As she lost weight Charlotte experienced a great sense of strength and independence.

Though she was becoming very thin, Charlotte seemed more energetic than ever. She worked out at least one hour daily and played on the university basketball team. She worked very hard at her schoolwork, too, maintaining honor grades.

When her periods stopped at age 16, Charlotte's parents' concern changed to alarm. They wanted to take her to a doctor for a checkup and advice about how to gain weight. "Gain weight!" Charlotte exclaimed, grabbing a piece of loose flesh above her elbow. "See that fat. I need to lose it." At the time she was five feet seven inches tall and weighed sixty-six pounds.

SOURCE: Charlotte is a composite case adapted largely from several cases in Hilde Bruch, *Eating Disorders*, New York, Harper & Row (1973).

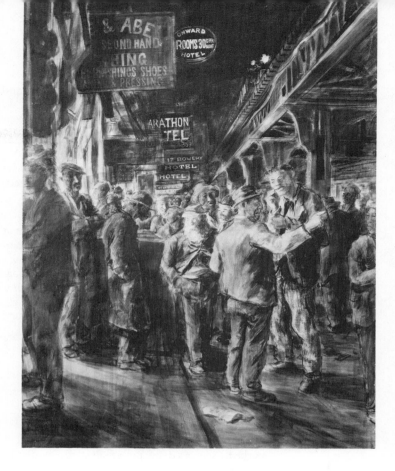

As this painting of a Bowery bar shows, alcohol abuse is not a new problem.

acidity, reduce tension, buoy sagging spirits, or deliver a sound night's sleep. Finally, numerous street drugs abound that are taken by people in an effort to feel better. These include cocaine, LSD (lysergic acid diethylamide), mescaline, PCP (phencyclidine), and hashish. None of these has any known medical value.

We know that in America enormous differences in drug use exist between specific subcultures. Many Italians don't feel a meal is complete without wine and coffee. Mormons are expected by their religion to touch neither. When does a pattern of drug use become characteristic of a State 4 maladjustment?

The DSM-III specifies two types of drug-use disorders that meet the criteria for a neurotic disorder. They are **substance abuse** and **substance dependence.** The characteristics of both are shown in Table 12.3. Both substance abuse and dependence involve impaired social and occupational functioning. A major difference between them is **tolerance** — a need for more of the drug to attain the same effect — and **withdrawal** symptoms among those dependent upon the drug.

How serious is the drug abuse and dependence problem in the United States? Evidence is relatively easily obtained about alcohol. One in six Americans report some problem associated with alcohol use (DSM-III, page 168).

Table 12.3   Characteristics of substance abuse and substance dependence

SUBSTANCE ABUSE

1. *Pattern of pathological use*
   intoxicated during the day
   repeated efforts to cut down or stop without success
   need for daily use to function adequately
   complications — e.g., blackouts

2. *Impaired social or occupational functioning because of substance use*
   social relations impaired by failure to meet obligations or erratic, impulsive, or aggressive behavior
   legal difficulties due to events associated with drug use — car accident while drunk, stealing money to obtain or purchase drugs
   deteriorated performance in school or work because of being intoxicated

3. *Duration of at least one month*
   either chronic or episodic
   sufficient to impair behavior while intoxicated

SUBSTANCE DEPENDENCE

1. *Impaired social or occupational functioning*
2. *Tolerance*
   markedly increased amount of substance required to achieve the desired effect
3. *Withdrawal*
   following the cessation or reduced intake of a substance, a range of symptoms from anxiety, irritability, insomnia, and impaired attention to due nausea, convulsions, hallucinations, and clouded consciousness

SOURCE: From American Psychiatric Association, *Diagnostic and statistical manual of mental disorders*, third edition, Washington, D.C., APA, 1980, pp. 112, 163–165.

Much less information is available about abuse of and dependence on other drugs. Figure 12.1 shows the frequency with which high-school seniors in the class of 1981 tried one of the drugs listed. This figure indicates that by their senior year in high school, seven out of ten students had used alcohol in the past month. About one in three had smoked marijuana in the past thirty days and approximately 20 percent used stimulants or sedatives at least every four weeks. How many of the class of '83 will go on to have problems with these drugs only time will tell.

Aside from the unattractive long-term effects of regular drug abuse, there are unsavory short-term consequences. There is, for example, the opportunity to contract hepatitis from dirty needles, or to be poisoned by the ingredients used to cut street drugs. Then there are the effects of malnutrition associated with drug abuse and dependency, which range from losing teeth and hair to brain damage. According to the surgeon general's report, death due to disease, traffic accidents, and murder is many times higher among alcoholics than among the population at large (1979).

Suicide

At one point or another, some people with neurotic disorders or more serious problems think of suicide. It is estimated that about five million Americans have made one or more suicide attempts, and about 10 percent of this group eventually will be successful. Suicide is the third leading cause of death among teenagers and young adults. Government studies have determined that

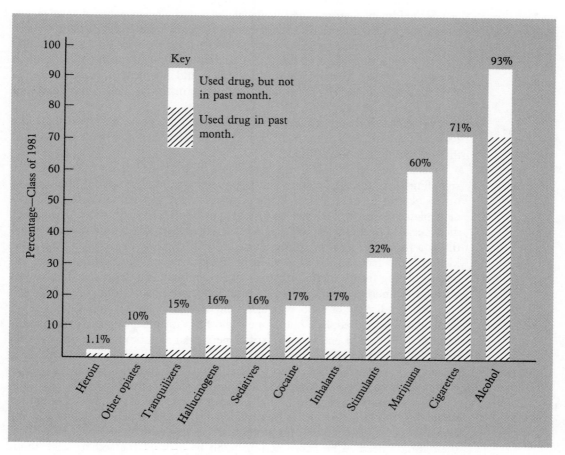

Figure 12.1 Prevalence and recentness of use of eleven types of drugs, class of 1981 (17,500 students)

about 5000 took their lives in 1977 (U.S. Department of Health, Education and Welfare, 1979).

Most people who kill themselves are — or have recently been — depressed. What is it that converts depressive feelings into a suicidal act? The answer in many cases is loss of hope and desperation (McArthur, 1972). As we have seen, hopelessness is both the cause and the result of depression. Loss of hope at some level means loss of hope of love. The suicidally depressed undergraduate is sure that because she was caught cheating on an exam she can never be worthy of her parents again and jumps out of her sixth-floor window.

Anyone who has talked to someone contemplating suicide will be aware of depression. In their minds, they can't bear the present conditions a moment longer. It is too shameful, desolate, or excruciating. Something has to be done. Full of hopelessness and desperation, a college sophomore takes poison because he can't imagine life without a girl he loves.

Schneidman distinguished suicidal acts that are intentional, sub-intentional, and contra-intentional (Schneidman, Faberow, and Litman, 1970). Those who commit *intentional* suicide are clear about what they are doing and usually carry out their purpose efficiently. Feeling another period of major depression about to overtake her and feeling that she could not bear it, writer Virginia Woolf walked to the river, placed a large rock in the pocket of her coat, and hurled herself into the water (Bell, 1972).

Sub-intentional acts are less determined and leave room for survival — like Russian roulette. A man takes all of the pills in the house, not knowing whether the amount or mixture is lethal.

Contra-intentional suicides do not expect to die, but only to make a gesture signaling their unhappiness in the hope of attracting the loving attention of others. Unfortunately, many of these acts result in accidental death. One student planning just to nick her wrists cut too deeply and bled to death. Another died because he didn't know that a hundred aspirin was a fatal dose. A third threw a rope over a rafter, put a noose around his neck, stood on a chair, and kicked it out from under him when he heard his roommate coming down the hall returning from lunch. Unhappily, his roommate suddenly decided to visit a friend in another room. When he returned the boy was dead.

The prediction of who will and who will not commit suicide is tricky, inexact business. People living alone, who harp on their hopelessness, worthlessness, and lack of energy, who suffer persistent agitation and insomnia, who drink heavily, who have experienced a recent personal crisis, who have had a parent commit suicide, and who threaten killing themselves, are at far greater risk than those who are depressed without these characteristics.

It is a mistake to conclude that a friend who talks of suicide or commits a suicidal act — whether it is intentional, sub-intentional, or contra-intentional — is merely "looking for attention." People with thoughts of suicide on their minds need to be taken seriously, to be assured that others care about them, and, if necessary, to be protected from acting on their lethal urges by the continuing presence of others or hospitalization. While there may be minor disadvantages in overreacting to someone's suicidal threat, a far greater danger is not taking that person seriously. Sometimes the indifference of friends, when confronted with an individual's desperate preoccupation with suicide, is the final proof that no one really cares and death is a reasonable alternative.

The Impact of State 4
on the Primary Features of Adjustment

The reorganization of personality resulting in a neurotic disorder affects the primary features of adjustment. The impact is not as dramatic as in the crisis reaction, but is still apparent. Life is much less enjoyable than it used to be. The cause of the maladjustment is obscured by lower-level adaptive responses. Finally, particular aspects of the personality style become overdriven and distorted.

Diminished Pleasure from Living

People in State 4 usually feel that life is a lot less enjoyable than they remember. For some, such as Benjy, the contrast is painfully and sharply apparent. For others, such as Walter, the feeling of getting less and less pleasure out of more and more effort grows gradually. Indeed, he may not even be aware of how unhappy he is unless he stops and thinks about it or an outside event forces him to take stock.

When they think about it, individuals in State 4 are aware of their unhappiness, but the pain is duller. Like a low-level backache, it may flare up from time to time, but we become used to it. It is only when the pain disappears and we are feeling good again that we know how bad we felt before.

People with a neurotic disorder lose track of what they contribute that actually maintains their maladaptive condition. They don't look objectively at their own behavior. Benjy has no idea of why others scapegoat him. Even when her sister or friends arrange for Chantal to meet eligible men, she turns down these opportunities because she thinks they won't like her.

An intriguing aspect of this state of adjustment is that the diminished pleasure from living is frequently at odds with other experience. Chantal finds romance in summers abroad. When Benjy returns to visit old friends in Virginia, no scapegoating occurs. When he told his former fourth-grade teacher how miserable he was, she couldn't believe it. Benjy was one of her most well-adjusted and finest students.

Cause of Problem Obscured

In a neurotic disorder the self-protective responses are able to quiet the distress; but in doing so, they obscure the cause of the problem. In the process of restoring inner peace, they also eliminate upsetting feelings that signal that something is wrong and needs to be changed. Without these stress emotions to trigger corrective action, the causal agent may persist for years.

Using Walter as an example, let's examine how lower-level protective responses, especially ego defenses, block awareness of his problem. An only child, Walter was raised by his mother, who passionately wanted Walter to attain the success she saw in the wealthy club members where she worked. Since they had no money, Walter had to excel in school to earn a scholarship for his education.

As soon as he began school, his mother became overconcerned about his work. In the first grade, the teacher told her that Walter was doing fine but "seemed a little lazy." She became frantic and lectured Walter about being lazy, telling him that he had to work harder than the others to get ahead. At that point, Walter realized that her love for him had a major condition: if he worked hard and produced good grades, he could count on his mother's warm affection. But no work, no good grades; no good grades, no love.

From then on, every time Walter had the urge to play with his friends or listen to the radio rather than do his homework, he became very anxious because these impulses were unacceptable. He immediately repressed any desire he might have to work less and threw himself into his studies.

Though this pattern brought him success in school, a scholarship to the University of Pennsylvania, architectural training, and entry into a prestigious firm, Walter remained unaware of why he worked so hard. His motive for hard work was *not* basically money, power, or partnership, but rather the childhood desire to retain his mother's love. Moreover, he could not look again at the early cause of his distress and reactions to it and make appropriate changes to it. For example, he didn't say to himself, "I have finally pleased my mother and now I can relax a little." Because of this use of ego defenses Walter is a prisoner of his work.

As with many aspects of life, leisure activities bring less pleasure than in the remembered past. For example, Walter recalled that he really used to like to jog in the morning with two friends. But as his State 4 condition continued, he enjoyed doing this less and less. "Running doesn't give me that afterglow that it used to," Walter said. It just seemed like a lot of work.

Overdriven and Distorted Behavior

Overall, the personality style of someone with a neurotic disorder is reduced in richness compared to earlier states of adaptation, and particular aspects are overdriven and distorted, although the basic temperament remains the same.

White and Watt (1981) point to the overdriven striving — the intensification of certain temperamental qualities in protective response to stressful feelings — of people with this type of adjustment. Consider Darlene. A girl with an outgoing theatrical personality style, she always thought she was attractive. But her development lagged behind that of the other girls in early adolescence and Darlene started to feel that she was unattractive. "When I look in the mirror," Darlene used to think to herself, "I look like a boy. If I stand sideways, I'm almost invisible." Reinforcing her own opinion of being sexually immature was the fact that her periods did not begin until October of the ninth grade.

The sense of not being as pretty as other girls bothered Darlene. She dealt with her doubts about her attractiveness in keeping with her personality style: she dressed provocatively, made outrageously flirtatious moves toward her teachers, and went places where she might meet high-school and college boys.

In Darlene's case, her normal flamboyance, coquettishness, and role-playing capacity were distorted in the service of reducing her doubts about her attractiveness. Her behavior shows three aspects of overdriven strivings: (1) *indiscriminateness:* Darlene behaves seductively around men whether she is attracted to them or not; (2) *insatiability:* she needs to prove over and over again that she is sexually attractive; and (3) great *frustration* from *blocking:* a "no" from her parents brings on a violent emotional outburst.

Secondary Characteristics of State 4

Secondary characteristics associated with neurotic disorders can include diminished alarm response, poorer physical health, less efficient mental functioning, episodic unstable moods, and weakened interpersonal relations. These are summarized in Table 12.4.

Table 12.4   Secondary characteristics associated with State 4: Neurotic disorders

Diminished alarm response
   Lower-level adaptive responses blocking awareness of cause
   Wrong focus of distress
   Intense emotion flooding capacity to resolve agent of upset

Poorer physical health
   Continuing major physical symptoms
   New small nagging problems or major physical concerns
   Increasing abuse of prescription and nonprescription drugs
   Noticeable deterioration in self-care

Less efficient mental functioning
   Trouble processing information, impaired decision making, and loss of confidence
      in capacity for taking action
   Lowered risk taking
   Reduced sense of fate control
   Some behavior consistently at odds with values
   Lowered aspirations

Episodic unstable moods
   Sudden intrusion of depression, anger, anxiety
   Background moods lowering pleasure from living
   Little zest or afterglow

Weakened interpersonal relations
   Relations with others dependent upon tolerance for and not confronting
      maladaptive behavior
   May cause maladjustments in others
   Some loved ones and friends alienated

Diminished Alarm Response

The events that provoke a neurotic disorder are the same ones that bring about a crisis reaction: (1) a sudden event; (2) being worn down by too much stress for too long; (3) an unwelcome but inevitable life cycle transition. Instead of seeing the stress clearly, however, and moving into an alarm phase of the General Adaptation Syndrome described in Figure 2.1 on page 37, an individual in State 4 has a diminished alarm reaction. Three related factors contribute to this lowered alarm response: (1) lower-level responses to emotional upset block awareness of the cause; (2) the cause of the distress is misjudged, and (3) intense emotion floods the capacity to work through the cause of the upset.

The first factor is blocked awareness of the cause of the maladjustment by lower-level adaptive reactions. The distasteful reality is pushed into the twilight zone of perception. People with a neurotic disorder can have their attention directed to the stress and will acknowledge that it is a problem and that they should so something about it. However, they don't seem to be able to sustain enough continued awareness and discomfort to act. Instead of moving from the intrusiveness described by Horowitz in Table 11.1 on page 334 to the phase of working through and completion, these individuals seem to return to the phase of denial and numbness. Periodically this phase is pierced by

Binge eating is a characteristic of both bulimia and bulimarexia. Though not hungry, individuals with this problem crave food and will continue to eat to the point of intense physical discomfort.

intruding disquieting emotion, but then numbness and denial gradually occur again.

Think about Chantal. Suppose that instead of overeating to cope with her anxiety, Chantal had explored the causes behind her anxiety. She might have discovered some of the reasons were related to her need to control her anger toward a dependent, manipulative, and alcoholic mother with whom she lived. The anxiety Chantal felt came from her conflict between the love she felt for her mother and the hostility caused by her mother's clinging. Instead of facing the conflict in her feelings about her mother, Chantal ate to relieve the tension.

The second factor diminishing the alarm response is being upset about the wrong problem. An example is Benjy, who thinks his difficulty is because other kids are mean and treat him unfairly and he can't imagine why. Instead of wondering about what he might be doing to provoke others to scapegoat him, he focuses on how bad he feels because of their behavior toward him.

The third factor perpetuating State 4 adjustment is that intense emotions flood the capacity to understand and work through the stress. Charlie is a good example. When he is in the grip of the panic he experiences when he thinks a thunderstorm is in the air, he has no interest in trying to understand the roots of the distress. All he wants is to feel safe, and when the panic passes and tranquility is restored, Charlie is not interested in dredging up the feelings again in order to find out their cause. He just wants to forget them. This is typical of individuals with problems such as this (Cavenar and Nash, 1976).

Poorer Physical Health

In State 4, health is much like that in a crisis reaction. Horowitz and his colleagues studied sixty-four men and women who had experienced a serious loss or injury and were continuing to have severe stress reactions (Horowitz, Wilner, Kaltreider, and Alvarez, 1980). Within the past seven days, more than half reported the physical signs of discomfort shown in Table 12.5. These include headaches; parts of the body that feel heavy, numb, weak, or painful; upset stomachs, faintness, and a lump in the throat.

New physical symptoms that develop can include nagging continuing problems such as skin conditions or digestive difficulties. They can be inter-mittent, such as episodic hypertension or impotence (Menninger, 1967). Or major difficulties can develop. Benjy began to manifest three continuing symptoms after the move. He reverted to bed wetting within six months after his family moved to Maryland. By Christmas he began to stutter. In the spring he developed a severe tic — periodically squeezing his eyes together rapidly in flurries of three blinks while he talked.

Prescription and nonprescription drug use increases. People acknowledge they need more medication now than in the past, but have forgotten why. They need more tranquilizers to cope with each day and greater amounts of sleeping medication or amphetamines to wake up. The increase can be in non-prescription medication: going from four to a dozen cups of coffee a day, or from a pack to two packs of cigarettes. It can be seen in the heavy use and

Table 12.5 Physical symptoms among individuals with neurotic disorders related to traumatic life events

PHYSICAL SYMPTOMS	PERCENTAGE OF INDIVIDUALS REPORTING SYMPTOM IN THE PAST 7 DAYS
Headaches	79
Feeling weak in parts of the body	77
Upset stomach	70
Soreness in muscles	66
Hot or cold spells	59
Lower back pain	58
Faintness or dizziness	56
Numbness or tingling of the body	55
Heavy feelings in arms or legs	55
Lump in throat	53
Pains in heart or chest	52

SOURCE: Adapted from Horowitz, M. J., Wilner, N., Kaltreider, N., and Alvarez, W., Signs and symptoms of post-traumatic stress disorders, *Archives of General Psychiatry*, Vol. 37, 1980, pp. 85–92. Copyright 1980, American Medical Association. By permission.

weekly abuse of alcohol and marijuana or other nonprescription agents. At one point, Walter and his wife realized they were drinking too much and read in the paper that heavy drinkers should try to be abstinent two consecutive days each week to rest their liver. Neither could think of two days a week when they would not need alcohol.

A small percentage of people who use alcohol for tension relief become alcoholics. Knowing in advance who is likely to become addicted to alcohol and who can use it safely under stress is not possible at this time. Research does indicate that individuals who abuse alcohol in order to extend its temporary pleasant effects, and in doing so increase their real-life problems, are more vulnerable to alcohol dependence (Powers and Kutash, 1980).

Self-care may show noticeable deterioration. This is not the dress and grooming of someone in State 2, but a gradual decline. A person's garments may be increasingly dirty, rumpled, or mismatched. Men may begin to shave ineffectively and women may apply their makeup carelessly or their hair may appear unkempt. All of this happens slowly, and individuals may be aware of deterioration in their physical appearance but don't feel motivated to do much about it.

Less Effective Mental Functioning

In their study of men and women who had experienced severe stress, Horowitz and his colleagues (1980) found that a large proportion reported impaired mental functioning. The symptoms noted by over half of these individuals are shown in Table 12.6. These mental difficulties divide into three types: trouble processing information (concentrating, shutting out unwanted thoughts, or remembering); impaired ability to make decisions; and loss of confidence in the capacity for taking action: feeling blocked, worrying about carelessness, working slowly, and having to check and double-check.

Perhaps because they feel they have all they can deal with and sense their diminished adaptive capabilities, people with a neurotic disorder tend to view new tasks as threatening rather than challenging (Coyne and Lazarus, 1980). This results in their being less willing to take risks in the pursuit of new opportunities for growth. Asked to give a talk on how to sell a new product at the annual sales meeting, Charlie flatly refused. He felt he would do a poor job and look bad in the eyes of his bosses. He saw this request to talk as a potential catastrophe, rather than an opportunity to demonstrate his competence.

Table 12.6 Problems in mental functioning among individuals with neurotic disorders related to traumatic life events

MENTAL DYSFUNCTION	PERCENTAGE OF INDIVIDUALS REPORTING SYMPTOM IN THE PAST 7 DAYS
Trouble concentrating	92
Unwanted thoughts, words; ideas won't leave the mind	90
Difficulty making decisions	88
Feeling blocked in getting things done	77
Trouble remembering things	75
Worried about sloppiness or carelessness	64
Mind going blank	64
Having to check and double-check	59
Having to do things slowly to insure correctness	58

SOURCE: Adapted from Horowitz, M. J., Wilner, N., Kaltreider, N. and Alvarez, W., Signs and symptoms of post-traumatic stress disorders. *Archives of General Psychiatry*, Vol. 37, 1980, pp. 85–92. Copyright 1980, American Medical Association. By permission.

A growing sense that one's destiny is being orchestrated by forces beyond comprehension is noticeable in State 4. Darlene started to think the grades she made on tests were a function of what side of the bed her teacher got out of rather than her own efforts. Increasingly, she talked about studying for exams as though these actions were not within her power. "If I can work this weekend, I'll be O.K.," or "Doing my schoolwork is not a problem as long as I'm motivated."

Many individuals with a neurotic disorder behave consistently at odds with basic values. The deviations can be relatively minor: a tendency to lie when it brings no advantage; or more serious actions, such as shoplifting, cheating, or vandalism. The Iceman regularly stole small amounts of food from the fast-food drive-in in which he worked, which he didn't need.

As a State 4 adjustment continues, the person may accept a reduced level of functioning, begin to settle for less overall pleasure from living, and lower his or her aspirations. If this happens later in the life cycle there is a reminiscence of the good old days when things were a lot better. In youth, a neurotic disorder can mean the end of a dream. As she found herself continually unable to lose weight, Chantal began to give up the idea she would ever be married and have a family.

Episodic Unstable Moods

Overall, the mood for most in State 4 is consistent with their basic personality style. However, even the most active and optimistic will have unexpected recurring bouts of despair, fury, or desperation. Most are not as dramatic as those accompanying the returning Vietnam veterans' flashbacks, but they can be as intense. Horowitz found that over half of his subjects experienced the intrusion of the emotions shown in Table 12.7 in the seven days preceding his contact with them (Horowitz *et al.*, 1980). The stress emotions of despair, anger, and anxiety come upon individuals with a neurotic disorder without warning. Unlike someone with a crisis reaction, a person in State 4 does not seem to move toward a working through of the experiences behind the intense emotion.

The background mood usually begins to compromise satisfaction from one or more areas of living. While Walter basically likes his work, he has long moments of thinking everything he does is worthless. Then he becomes bitter as he considers how hard he is working in a career that isn't fulfilling anymore. This bitterness causes his work to be less satisfying. Sometimes he becomes angry at his wife and children, who are increasingly ignoring him, because he feels they take him for granted.

Zest is an infrequent companion. For the most part, when enthusiasm appears it is associated with areas unrelated to the major sectors of living where the maladaptive behavior is most obvious. Darlene lives for weekends and Chantal for her trips abroad. But for neither of them is there an "afterglow," a positive feeling that continues into the regular work week.

Table 12.7 Upsetting moods among individuals with neurotic disorders related to traumatic life events

MOOD	PERCENTAGE OF INDIVIDUALS REPORTING SYMPTOM IN THE PAST 7 DAYS
Feeling blue	97
Blaming self for things	89
Easily annoyed or irritated	82
Feeling hopeless	75
Feeling worthless	72
Suddenly scared for no reason	56

SOURCE: Adapted from Horowitz, M. J., Wilner, N., Kaltreider, N., and Alvarez, W., Signs and symptoms of post-traumatic stress disorders, *Archives of General Psychiatry*, Vol. 37, 1980, pp. 85–92. Copyright 1980, American Medical Association. By permission.

Weakened Interpersonal Relations

Overall, interpersonal relations are notably weakened in State 4. Two-way responsiveness is possible. But smooth relationships are dependent upon the tolerance of the maladaptive behavior characteristic of State 4, and require that others do not force these individuals to confront their inappropriate actions.

For example, Darlene's relationships with adults are fine as long as they don't question her oppositional behavior. With parents of other youngsters Darlene is well-mannered, engaging, and gets along fine. The mothers and fathers of her friends can't understand why her parents are so upset with Darlene because she is so pleasant around them. This perception of Darlene is shared by many of her teachers, who have not had the experience of nasty confrontations.

When people in State 4 are directly faced with their own inappropriate actions, relations can become quickly antagonistic. This can cause others to avoid discussion of the maladaptive behavior. "We have the same arguments over and over again," Darlene's parents lament. If her parents bring up her sagging grades or poor conduct, fireworks ensue every time. "We are at the point where we don't dare bring up things we are worried about," Darlene's mother told a friend. "Can you *imagine that!* We don't *dare!*"

A neurotic disorder in one person can cause emotional problems in others. Darlene's parents are an example. "Floundering child, floundering mother," her mother said as she became increasingly frantic and upset. "She's an expert at driving a wedge between her mother and me, playing one of us against the other," Darlene's father told a friend. "If she doesn't get her way with her mother, she'll try me, being as sweet as pie. If I give in my wife kills me and if I don't Darlene makes my life miserable." During Darlene's eighth-grade year her parents started sleeping in separate bedrooms.

The strained or intensely antagonistic relationships with others take their toll. Eventually some loved ones or friends are alienated. The love Walter's wife had for him cooled and she began to think seriously of leaving him.

Follow-up

Benjy

Gradually Benjy's problems worsened. He was ridiculed by his classmates in school and pointedly left out when parties were held. In the face of these cruelties, Benjy's anger mounted and he retaliated: he made up perceptive, humorous, but vicious nicknames, which parodied ungraceful characteristics of some of the boys and girls in his class. At the YMCA he learned how to box and started to look for fights. He broke the nose of one of the bullies who had tormented him the previous year. Instead of acceptance and friendship, this fighting brought further isolation.

When the other boys' parents complained that Benjy was a bully, his father and mother were astonished. The principal told his parents that Benjy needed professional counseling. They took him to a psychiatrist in Washington. Benjy went to the first meeting with his parents under protest. He refused to go again, stoutly denying he was a "mental case." The doctor said he couldn't work with Benjy if the boy refused to recognize that he had a problem.

The junior high school years were better for Benjy. There were two reasons. The first was his size and athletic ability. Though not gifted in sports, he grew to be one of the largest boys in his class. And because he was full of aggression, he started every game in football, basketball, and lacrosse for the school teams during junior high school. Being on the team gave him a greater sense of belonging. Gradually his bed wetting abated and his tic vanished, but the stuttering continued.

The second reason junior high school was better was that he made a close friend, Kenny. Kenny moved into town in the seventh grade, and because of their mutual athletic interests, they quickly became best friends. They also both liked science. Kenny and Benjy spent long hours doing experiments with Kenny's chemistry set. It was at this point that Benjy began to imagine being a research scientist.

Darlene

Darlene was sent to a strict girls' boarding school in New England. "Maybe she'll do better in a more structured environment," her father said. "Besides, we can't cope with her anymore, and she's a bad influence on her sisters." At first grades and teacher reports were fine. Then the trouble started: grades sliding, negative attitude, and smoking in her room. She was suspended once and finally expelled when she was caught by a teacher in a bar on a Saturday night with a custodian. They were both fired from the school.

When she came home, her parents put Darlene in an alternative school within the high school. That didn't work either. She didn't study, cut classes, and failed all her courses. When one of her teachers asked her if she'd given up on college, Darlene became incensed. She still planned to attend Marquette and eventually go to dental school, she said. But then she refused to go to school anymore when the teacher wondered how her bad attitude and poor work would help her toward that goal.

Out of school, increasingly estranged from her parents and still several months short of her 16th birthday, Darlene didn't know what to do. In December she lied about her age, found a job as an orderly in a nursing home, and worked steadily thereafter. Three days before Christmas she moved into her own apartment by mutual agreement with her parents. Shortly afterward Darlene began living with a 25-year-old young man who was a college dropout working part-time as a motorcycle mechanic and full-time as a drug dealer.

During this time Darlene lost contact with her family. This was just as well, because in the next four years, Darlene was briefly addicted to heroin, had an abortion, contracted VD once, broke a leg in a motorcycle accident, and had her skull fractured when the man she lived with got drunk and beat her up.

A week before Easter Sunday, four years after she had left home, Darlene called her mother and asked if she could go to church with them. They agreed somewhat warily but were pleased at the prospect of seeing her. At church, Darlene was pleasant to everyone in the family. Afterward, Darlene said that she had separated from the young man. "Living with him was instant middle age," is how she put it. Darlene also said she was thinking of going back to school and wondered if her parents would help her.

Over the next two years, Darlene took a night course so she could take a high-school equivalency examination. When she passed, Darlene enrolled as a part-time student at a community college in Florida while keeping a thirty-five-hour a week job. Eventually she entered a full-time dental hygienist program.

Chantal

In the fall following her 30th birthday, Chantal made another attempt to lose weight. "I'd like to be 150 pounds going into my fourth decade," she told a friend. Chantal heard about a woman psychiatrist who had helped a friend of hers lose weight through hypnosis. At the first meeting, Chantal found the doctor someone she could work with, even though her skepticism remained. "I'll say this for her," Chantal commented to an acquaintance, "there was none of this Freudian nonsense about why I'm fat."

The psychiatrist used a mixture of ways of helping her lose weight. After a thorough medical evaluation, Chantal was asked to keep a precise record of what she ate every day and how many calories were consumed. Her intake of food initially averaged just over 3000 calories per day with a range of 400 to 4500. Then Chantal was treated with hypnosis. The doctor reviewed her reasons for losing weight ("to be attractive, to be in better health as I get older, to be able to ski well, to be able to wear clothes other people wear, to have people look at me normally"). She was taught to put herself in a hypnotic trance and repeat these suggestions to herself several times daily. In addition, Chantal was instructed to join a group of people who met on a weekly basis for mutual support for weight loss.

After a month her food intake was greatly reduced. A sample fourteen-day period showed her to be averaging about 800 calories per day with a range of 450 to 1800. Since this caloric intake was less than recommended by a nutritionist, she supplemented it with vitamins.

Chantal saw the psychiatrist twice monthly to monitor the controlled eating and check her emotional state. Over the first six months Chantal lost just over sixty pounds. At first she felt considerable euphoria but as she came close to the 150-pound mark something happened. She began to feel nervous again, lost control of her eating, and suddenly gained ten pounds.

In tears, Chantal made an emergency appointment with the psychiatrist. She had no idea why she felt anxious and was overeating again. Chantal and the psychiatrist reviewed the other times she had had this experience. Twice before, she had dieted, approached 150 pounds, and begun to feel tense and gained weight again. "This must be my bounce weight," Chantal smiled. "You know, that weight you hit and bounce up again."

They pursued the origins of the anxiety. After considerable struggle they discovered the cause. Since adolescence, Chantal greatly resented her mother's clinging, her heavy drinking, and her unwillingness to allow Chantal to be independent. Chantal recalled that every time she discussed moving away or going on a vacation, her mother became depressed. Sometimes she said she had chest pains and was sure she was having a heart attack. As a result, Chantal became angry but afraid to express it for fear of causing harm to her mother. Instead, she ate.

This awareness allowed Chantal to confront her fear that "something would happen" to her mother if she dared assert her independence and free herself. As she and her therapist talked, it became clear that her mother could probably cope with Chantal's desire to be on her own. She had other relatives and friends to rely on. Eventually, Chantal moved in to her own apartment. Soon afterwards, she resumed her efforts to lose weight. She was able to realize her goal of weighing 150 pounds and terminated therapy. A year later, Chantal wrote her therapist saying that she was holding at 135: "Still a little pudgy, but acceptable," and had met a man she planned to marry.

Walter

Because he dropped out of family counseling and continued to work, Walter became more and more estranged from his wife and family. He stayed late at the office because going home was too painful.

Over a five-year period Walter had put on twenty extra pounds. At his yearly physical, the family doctor said that there were some suspicious findings on the electrocardiogram that might warrant some further testing. Also, he recommended that Walter immediately begin to lose weight and cut down on smoking. Walter never did get around to taking stress tests or to losing weight. He tried a stop-smoking program, but it didn't work.

In the summer following that physical Walter noticed he felt more tired than usual. He noticed especially that he didn't seem to have much pep when he exercised. Walking up more than one flight of stairs caused him to feel pain like a toothache on the left side of his jaw. At night he occasionally awoke with what felt like indigestion and took an antacid. He chalked these symptoms up to getting older and saw no reason to talk to his doctor about them.

Then one sunny Saturday afternoon while playing doubles tennis with three friends, Walter started to feel lightheaded and definitely unwell. He noticed the pain in his jaw returned and along with it a tingling sensation in his left arm. Walter called the doctor who told him to go immediately to the emergency ward at the hospital. As soon as he arrived, the doctor ran some tests and told Walter that he was having a heart attack. Walter couldn't believe it and said that the doctor must have him confused with someone else.

Walter's doctor and family prevailed upon him to stay in the hospital in the coronary care unit. Walter's recovery was rapid. Within a few weeks he was at home and gradually building up his strength. While still in the coronary care unit, Walter and his wife met with other post-heart attack patients and their families. These meetings stressed the need for proper diet, exercise, and stopping smoking and drinking. The value of a balanced life was stressed through individual and group discussions. In these meetings, run by a social worker and a nurse-practitioner, Walter learned that he was a "Type A" personality: always busy, obsessed with making the most of every minute, finishing people's sentences for them, given to doing two things at once, and also given to angry outbursts. As such, he needed to be especially vigilant about controlling those tendencies that are associated with the high percentage of second heart attacks. He recognized also that his overworking was based on a childhood fear of not pleasing his mother.

Gradually, Walter modified his living style. He worked fewer hours, exercised regularly, gave up smoking and drinking. He renewed his relationships with his family and friends. Years later, on the eve of his 50th birthday, he remarked to his wife that he felt better than he had at 35. His wife replied, "Me, too."

Charlie

Charlie found a psychologist who specialized in treating people with phobias and other problems like his. During the first few sessions, Charlie told of his terror of thunderstorms and his fearfulness any time one threatened. He said that nothing helped much, though sometimes he found that if he could touch an old rubber sneaker he felt better. "I know it's crazy," Charlie said, "but I feel safer if I'm in contact with something made of rubber!"

During these initial sessions, he commented to his therapist, "You know,

I remember my grandmother, who lived with us until I was ten, was also scared of thunderstorms. Her farmhouse had been set on fire by lightning when she was a child. When there was a thunderstorm, she used to make me stay with her in a closet. Maybe that's why I'm afraid." The therapist replied, "That was a long time ago." And Charlie agreed that knowing part of the cause didn't seem to help.

The psychologist decided to treat the phobia using a cognitive learning approach. The treatment involved three phases. In the first part, which was an educational phase, the doctor explained to Charlie that the phobia was a learned reaction that could be unlearned. The second phase involved skills training. Charlie learned how to relax in the face of worry when a thunderstorm was imminent. He and the therapist discussed what he might do if he found himself in the middle of a thunder and lightning storm.

In the third phase, Charlie was taught to apply these techniques to relax in the face of the stress and then bring coping skills to bear. Once relaxed, he found that he had a number of options. Sometimes he could reason his way out of the fears by recognizing that his car was not likely to be hit by lightning and had rubber tires to prevent it from conducting electricity. Or he could tell himself that his home was protected with a lightning rod and that lightning almost never comes in through electrical outlets. If reason failed, he learned to find relief by seeking the company of a large number of others in a store, movie theatre, or library. As he learned to control these anxiety attacks, he began to fear them less. Eventually they shrank to a minor annoyance.

Freed of these fears, Charlie was able to make more calls. Within two years he became one of the firm's top salesmen. Just before he headed back for his thirtieth class reunion, he threw out the old rubber sneaker.

Assisting People with Neurotic Disorders

Neurotic disorders can go on for years, greatly reducing the quality of life for individuals with these problems and those close to them. As the follow-ups indicate, recovery from these conditions occurs as a function of the passage of time and—more often—with professional assistance.

Bergin and Lampert (1978) have estimated that spontaneous recovery from mental disorders such as these occurs in about forty percent of individuals. By this they mean that these recoveries were unassisted by professional counselors. One of the reasons people are able to overcome their problems is a significant shift in environment. Such changes can be gradual, sharply defined, or traumatic. A beneficial gradual alteration in surroundings gradually occurred with Benjy as he slowly developed physical skills that caused him to obtain admiration rather than scorn from his classmates.

Sharply defined environmental changes are moving to a new town or school. They can be a physical event, such as the onset of puberty; confirmation, marriage, or birth of a first child; retirement; or — as in Charlie's case — a twenty-fifth college reunion. An example of a traumatic environmental change is Walter's heart attack. It motivated him to make needed changes in the quality of his personal adjustment. Every time an environmental change is made, or a milepost is reached, we have the opportunity to reassess the quality of our lives, wipe the slate clean, and choose another way to behave.

The dedicated help of loved ones and others who are not professionals in the mental health field contributes a share to the four in ten troubled individuals who recover on their own. Among the ways they can assist are by sounding the alarm about maladaptive behavior to encourage resolving the agent of the distress, and by providing positive reinforcement of actions in the direction of normal adjustment. However, helping someone recognize and eliminate a State 4 adjustment is hard work and frustrating. It requires dedication and inspiration. Coping with the growing desire to yell, "Why don't you shape up, Darlene!" or "Stop avoiding your problems, Walter!" is a common problem for anyone trying to assist these individuals. Sometimes people without training in the mental health field working with someone in a State 4 adjustment find it useful to consult with a professional counselor for advice about how to proceed.

If a State 4 maladjustment doesn't improve with environmental change or with the help of friends or loved ones, then it is usually helpful to turn to professionals for help. Professional counselors with different training and different approaches all treat neurotic disorders with considerable success. The three most prominent counseling professions are psychiatry, psychology, and social work. The qualifications for each are shown in the box below. Individuals in each of these professions must have had two or more years of supervised clinical experience plus several more years in the field before they can be licensed by their state or obtain certification from their own professional organization.

In addition to the major counseling professions, there are two other rapidly blooming groups that carry out effective therapy. These are pastoral counselors and nurse practitioners. As their names imply, they have stepped over into counseling from adjacent professions — the ministry and nursing. To qualify, ministers and nurses must have two or more years of supervised training.

Professional counselors are not only organized by discipline, but by type of therapy: psychoanalytic, behavioral, humanistic, or cognitive. Counselors may also specialize in specific problems: vocational, marital, sex, phobias, depression, or drug or alcohol. The Yellow Pages spill over with other help for mental problems. Psychotherapist — which has no legal meaning in most states — may include individuals who are psychiatrists, psychologists, and social workers, and have considerable training and experience in fields as diverse as dance therapy or massage. The label "psychotherapist" also collects a large number of well-intentioned but not very well-trained or skilled individuals who want to "help people." It is wise to investigate unlicensed individuals carefully before entering into treatment with them.

Counseling Professions

Psychiatrists are medical doctors specializing in mental disorders. Most psychiatrists will have the following diplomas: bachelor's degree from a four-year college, M.D. from four years in medical school, internship certificates from 1 to 2 years of internship training, and a certificate showing the completion of at least three years of specialized training in psychiatry. Psychiatrists are licensed by the state as physicians and by the American Psychiatric Association as psychiatrists. Psychiatrists use many types of treatment processes. They are the only counseling profession legally entitled to prescribe drugs or administer electroconvulsive or other physical treatment. Being physicians, they can admit patients to general and psychiatric hospitals.

Psychologists (*clinical, counseling, and school*) were originally scholars interested in the study of the mind. In the past 50 years, many psychologists have become interested in the diagnosis and treatment of mental disorders. Today, these individuals are found among the ranks of clinical, counseling, and school psychologists. All share the requirement of a bachelor's degree from college, along with a doctoral degree (Ph.D., Ed.D., or Psy.D.) requiring a minimum of another four years of study. Each then has had an additional 1 to 2 years of training. In order to be licensed, psychologists in most states are required to have several more years of experience, plus being able to pass appropriate tests. Most practicing psychologists are members of their appropriate divisions of the American Psychological Association. Psychologists are trained to administer and interpret psychological tests. As the title implies, clinical psychologists are more likely to be found in mental health or community clinics dealing with more severe

Getting help is not so hard once you realize that you are not going to get better without it. The best referrals are personal — one made by someone who knows you and knows a therapist who would work compatibly with you. The match of a therapist's personality with our own is crucial for successful therapy. If you do not know someone to make a referral, usually you can locate someone through local clergy, hospitals, clinics, YMCA, or a psychology department of a local college or university. If that fails, you can approach a local medical school, multi-service center, family agency, health maintenance organization, or community guidance clinic for help. Those with training arrangements with medical or graduate schools are likely to offer the highest quality service at the lowest price.

Professional counselors from a variety of psychological persuasions treat successfully a high percentage of State 4 conditions. We will look briefly at how behavioral, humanistic, and cognitive therapists might approach Walter's drinking problem. Then we will examine the Iceman's case, which has been treated by a blend of two therapies.

One type of behavioral therapy is **aversive conditioning.** This operates by attaching a negative reaction to a specific temptation we want to resist. Many hospitals treat alcoholics in this manner. In a medical setting, Walter might be given whatever he wants to drink. But the bourbon, gin, or scotch is paired with a drug that causes prolonged vomiting. Walter's treatment would consist emotional problems. Counselors in university centers respond to adjustment, academic, and vocational concerns. School psychologists work in educational systems below the college level, helping youngsters and parents with adjustment difficulties at that level. There is considerable overlap in the work of these three disciplines.

Clinical social workers are the professional descendants of the social caseworker who previously focused on alleviating the social problems associated with physical and mental illness, poverty, social change, and family turmoil. Currently they typically work in psychiatric, medical, and family service settings, or in private practice. The roots of clinical social work are still evident in the strong interest in interpersonal interaction and family functioning, in group therapy, and in family therapy. However, psychodynamic psychology is the foundation for the individual casework or psychotherapy that comprises the bulk of what most clinical social workers do.

Clinical social workers are college graduates who have taken 2 years of graduate work leading to a Master's Degree (M.S.W.) and in some cases a doctoral degree (D.S.W.) requiring several more years of study. Only those certified by the Academy of Certified Social Workers, which requires at least 2 years of post-M.S.W. experience under supervision, or those of comparable training who are licensed by their states for independent practice, may practice privately as well as in clinics. Previously called caseworkers, clinical social workers specialize in individual, group, and family practice, focusing especially on emotional and social dysfunction and interaction. Social workers, working alongside psychiatrists and psychologists, comprise well over 50 percent of the staff of community clinics and agencies across the nation.

of taking alcohol and the emetic together about every day for a 2-week period. He would be cured when taking his favorite drink causes him to vomit without the drug. Follow-up data indicate about half the individuals with drinking problems treated this way remain abstinent (Lemere and Voegtlin, 1950).

The humanistic approach to Walter's drinking difficulties would be based on the assumption that we do not need outside conditioning to change our behavior. Each of us has within us the capacity to turn the course of our lives. The best known of the humanistic therapists is Carl Rogers, who developed **client-centered therapy.** The guiding principle of client-centered therapy is unconditional positive regard. The therapist tries to be unqualified in accepting and seeing as worthwhile and legitimate whatever the client says. Rogers calls this "unpossessive caring." A slice of client-centered therapy with Walter might go approximately this way:

WALTER: After working my tail off all day I *need* a drink.
COUNSELOR: *Need* to have a drink?
WALTER: You got it! I don't think I could cope without 12 oz. of booze every night.
COUNSELOR: About a half a bottle every night.
WALTER: Yes, sometimes more.
COUNSELOR: You need it.

The array of therapeutic techniques promising relief from emotional problems is vast, and — as this cartoon shows us — can be confusing to someone seeking help.

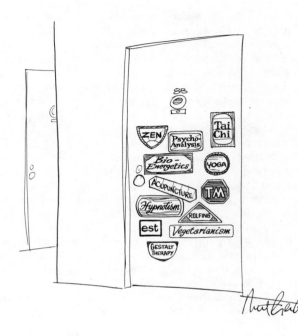

WALTER: Yeah. Without it I couldn't make it.

COUNSELOR: *Make?* What is it you want to make?

WALTER: Well, you know. . . .

COUNSELOR: I should know . . . what?

WALTER: Boy, I'd like a drink right now. You know . . . why does everyone work so hard? . . . Money, power, recognition.

COUNSELOR: Money, power recognition. . . . You don't have those now?

WALTER: Well, yes, *now* I do, but I didn't used to. And . . . I don't know.

COUNSELOR: It's hard to know, now.

WALTER: Y'know something? I don't have the faintest idea why I work so hard.

COUNSELOR: Uhh huh?

WALTER: I got everything I always wanted. . . . Along with some things I didn't want, such as a bad marriage, a heart condition, and I'm a drunk. . . . Good grief!

COUNSELOR: The problem doesn't seem to be getting ahead, anymore. . . . But taking care of those other things.

WALTER: That's right! Of course, I've known for a long time. But I just haven't done anything about it.

COUNSELOR: So far you haven't.

WALTER: Yeah. Maybe I'll start going to AA. What do you think?

COUNSELOR: You want to know what I think?

WALTER: Well, actually, I don't really care what you think. I think I know what I want to do now.

This brief glimpse of Walter working with a client-centered therapist shows the extent to which the counselor strives to be empathetic — seeing the world from Walter's perspective — and not take the lead. The role of the clinician is to accept, understand, and assist Walter in getting to the root of what is bothering him. Gradually, self-deception is washed away as Walter is able to see the reasons for his heavy drinking are no longer valid. This opens the road for Walter to work toward giving up alcohol.

A cognitive approach to the drinking problem might involve **problem-solving therapy**. This technique is rooted in the idea that much of what we call abnormal behavior is caused by not knowing how to solve certain problems (D'Zurilla and Goldfriend, 1971). This theory would see Walter's heavy drinking as the result of his not knowing what else to do. Doctors at a Veterans Administration hospital in Seattle noted that recovering alcoholics often returned to drinking when they were frustrated or were in social situations in which others were using alcohol. They designed an effective problem-solving-oriented program for patients under their care (Chaney, O'Leary, and Marlatt, 1978).

Doctors using this approach would first explain to Walter the theory of problem-solving therapy. Then in a group setting they would present a likely situation in which he would be tempted to drink — for example, having a long, frustrating day at work, or being out with a friend who says, "Let's stop by The Lounge for a drink." Through group discussion, Walter might be taught to consider alternatives to drinking. Then he would be required to develop a problem-solving strategy for coping with imagined situations that usually pressured him to drink. His approaches would be criticized by others in the group.

None of these techniques helps everyone with a drinking or other type of State 4 problem, but they do illustrate the range of specific techniques that can be employed effectively.

Frequently, more than one type of treatment is used with these emotional problems. An example is the therapy to assist the Iceman. This technique blended drugs with supportive therapy. A drug such as sodium pentothol was given to the Iceman to induce a state of light sleep, so that powerful, repressed feelings surrounding his war experiences could be felt, and then gradually relieved by venting them in a safe place with a doctor who could help him put these feelings to rest (Grinker and Spiegel, 1963). Aided by the drug treatment and supportive counseling, which enabled him to go over the horror he felt at having to recover the remains of his platoon and the anguish at losing a buddy, and the guilt he felt for the atrocities he had taken part in and at being a survivor. It was only when he could confront them in the relative sanctuary of the hospital and continuing counseling that he could free himself of these emotions and get on with the business of living.

Because just about anything in the armory of psychological treatment has been tried at some time or another with personal problems, disagreement exists among mental health workers as to what the best approach is. However, more and more professional counselors of all callings recognize that much of what helps a troubled person is common to the practice of all treatment methods (Murray and Jacobson, 1978; White and Watt, 1981). Factors central to the resolution of emotional problems are shown in the box. Recognizing that we have a problem that requires outside assistance, being taken seriously, the growth of hope, building an alliance with another person, and recognizing and correcting maladaptive beliefs all lead to positive behavior change. These are all found in effective treatment modes.

Whatever the theory about what caused the trouble, whatever the mode of therapeutic intervention, these essentials are found in each helping relationship. The troubled individual is assisted as much by the human qualities of the therapist as by whatever school of therapy is practiced. Moreover, the therapist's technical expertise is transmitted to the client through the personal qualities as viewed by the client as a *person* exerting personal influence rather than merely an expert applying a technique (Bergin and Lampert, 1978).

The Iceman's Recovery

Upon admission to the Veterans Hospital the Iceman talked freely and openly until his Vietnam experiences were approached; then he would say, "I just don't get into that area." He refused to discuss his recurrent dreams about Vietnam.

Doctors treated the Iceman with a drug that put him into a light sleep, and then they encouraged him to talk about his traumatic memories. In his first interview, he talked of losing thirty men of his platoon when a mine field was encountered and of helping to recover the casualties as well as the remains of those who had been killed. During the interview, the Iceman cried, screamed, and sobbed that he would give his life to get these men back. During the second interview, another explosion of emotion was seen as he described how a buddy had died in his arms and he had held the dead body for many hours. In the third interview, there was much crying and tremen-dous anxiety as he described the atrocities that he had taken part in. The final interview dealt with his picking seven men to accompany him on a patrol: the patient was the only survivor of that patrol. He expressed extreme guilt, saying, "I am alive and they are all dead."

After the drug-aided interviews were completed, the Iceman was treated with individual supportive counseling, during which he was able to experience and deal with some of the intense feelings again. His mood improved and he began to sleep soundly. When seen in follow-up one month after his discharge, he reported that he was "feeling good," sleeping soundly, and no longer bothered by nightmares of his Vietnam experiences. He seemed happy and was expressing optimism for the future.

SOURCE: A composite example of recovery from a post-traumatic stress disorder drawn from the case histories reported by Cavenar, J. and Nash, J. The effects of combat on the normal personality: War neuroses in vietnam returnees. *Comprehensive Psychiatry*, 1976, *17*, 647–653.

Essentials in the Therapeutic Process

Recognition that a Problem Exists

The self-definition of having a personal problem that is distressing, unresponsive to usual self-corrective efforts, and persistent results in the motivation to seek professional help.

Sense of Worthiness

An attentive therapist gives the client a sense of competence at being able to convey the inner distress, a feeling of being taken seriously, and of being worthwhile.

Expectation of Help

An awakening of hope that a help can be found to relieve suffering.

Therapeutic Relations

An alliance between the client and therapist in which bizarre feelings, thoughts, and behavior can be expressed without condemnation, and in which both are committed to relieving the distress.

Relearning

Maladaptive beliefs about the self and the world are recognized and corrected.

Behavioral Change

Recognition and correction of maladaptive beliefs lead to altered patterns of action, which leads to greater satisfaction from living.

SOURCE: Adapted from Murray, E. and Jacobson, L. Cognition and learning in traditional and behavioral psychotherapy. In S. Garfield and A. Bergin (Eds.), *Handbook of psychotherapy and behavior change.* Second edition. New York: Wiley, 1978.

Summary

1. The neurotic disorders are responses to an unpleasant event that continue well beyond it. A person in State 4 adjustment seems frozen in a maladaptive condition.

2. Neurotic disorders differ from State 3 because it is the symptoms themselves, or a group of symptoms, that are the source of distress.

3. Four types of mental disorders fit within the State 4 maladjustments: symptom disorders, disorders of childhood and adolescence, eating disorders, and drug-use disorders.

4. About five million Americans attempt suicide at one time or another, and over 25,000 succeed each year. It is possible to distinguish three types of suicide: intentional, sub-intentional, and contra-intentional.

5. The primary impact of a State 4 condition on the primary features of adjustment are diminished pleasure from living, the causes of the maladjustment being obscured by lower-level self-protective responses and direct control responses, and features of the normal personality style becoming overdriven and distorted.

6. Secondary characteristics of neurotic disorders include a diminished alarm response, poorer physical health, less efficient mental functioning, episodic unstable moods, and weakened interpersonal relationships.

7. About forty percent of individuals with State 4 disorders recover unas-

sisted by professional counselors. Two types of experiences that seem particularly helpful are environmental change and the dedicated assistance of friends and loved ones.

8. Professional counselors of all types from many different persuasions all report a high percentage of success in working with neurotic disorders.

A Look Ahead

In the final section, we discuss guidelines for living. The next chapter is called The Road Beyond. In it, we consider some of the realities that confront everyone after their college years. We also consider the extent to which our destiny is determined by gender, race, and social class background. Then we consider ways we can help ourselves maintain self-esteem in the face of inevitable stress.

Key Terms

symptom disorders	substance abuse
mood disorders	substance dependence
anxiety disorders	tolerance
somatoform disorders	withdrawal
dissociative disorders	intentional suicide
psychosexual disorders	sub-intentional suicide
disorders of childhood and adolescence	contra-intentional suicide
	psychiatrist
self-limiting	psychologist
behavioral disorders	social worker
emotional disorders	aversive conditioning
physical disorders	client-centered therapy
eating disorders	problem-solving therapy

Suggested Readings

Types of neurotic disorders

American Psychiatric Association. *Diagnostic and statistical manual of mental disorders*. Third Edition. Washington, D.C.: Author, 1980.

Comprehensive description of State 4 and other maladjustments.

Experience of State 4

Horney, K. *Neurosis and human growth: The struggle toward self-realization*. New York: Norton, 1950.

McNeil, E. *The quiet furies: Man and disorder*. Englewood Cliffs, N.J.: Prentice-Hall, 1967.

Readable accounts of the subjective experience of a neurotic disorder and of the progress toward recovery.

Drugs

Julien, R. *A primer of drug action*. Third Edition. San Francisco: Freeman, 1981.

Detailed and understandable summary of drugs and their effects.

Methods of professional help

Kanfer, R., and Goldstein, A. *Helping people change: A textbook of methods*. Second Edition. New York: Permagon Press, 1980.

Techniques used by professional counselors in treating State 4 and other disorders.

Part IV
Implications for the Life Cycle

This final section contains two chapters. Chapter 13 looks at the road beyond the college years. We will examine the influence of gender, social class background, or race on life changes for each of us, and then look at ways of maintaining self-esteem and personal effectiveness. Strategies for managing stress-related emotions are discussed, as important ingredients in the response to the demands of life events.

Chapter 14 begins by asking you to imagine yourself giving this year's commencement address to the graduating class, and to compose your own obituary. What would you say to the graduates to raise the probability that they will live their lives as fully as possible? What would you say in your obituary about how happy and successful your life has been? This last chapter lists ten guidelines for living that help in addressing these questions, distilled from the wisdom of the many learned people we have studied.

We see, overall, a better future for most youth — even a much better future — for the next two decades than the past two. There should be . . . more and better choices for youth; less segregation of youth from age, of race from race . . . or opportunities for the poor from those for the rich; less sense that youths are "outsiders" in relation to the rest of society — unwanted and often uncared for.

These developments can help to restore some of the largely lost challenge to youth that you "have the world before you."

SOURCE: Carnegie Council on Policy Studies in Higher Education. *Giving youth a better chance: Options for education, work, and service.* San Francisco: Jossey-Bass, 1979, p. 29.

Chapter Preview

CHAPTER 13
The Road Beyond

Questions to Think About
- What is your reaction to the quotation above?
- To what extent will your gender, social class background, or race influence your chances after college?
- What balance of satisfaction from work, love, and play do you want from your life?
- What can you do to maintain your self-esteem and personal effectiveness in times of severe stress?

Imagine yourself on graduation day. There you are in cap and gown, diploma in hand, posing for the picture and looking past the camera into the future. What do you see? Do you think you will have a better future than the youth of the '60s and '70s? Will society be more open to those from both sexes, all races, and all backgrounds? Does your generation of college graduates truly have the world before you? Or is this commencement address hokum?

In this chapter we address ourselves to some of the realities you may deal with in the next portion of your life. We will start by thinking about how much each of us is controlled by our sex, the social class of the family we were born into, and our skin color. We look at several of the prevailing myths about why females, individuals from the lower social classes, and minority group members have difficulty getting ahead. Then we consider several of the realities that influence the lives of men and women differently and reflect upon the importance of our family's race and socioeconomic status.

In the final section of this chapter, we consider how self-esteem and personal effectiveness can be maintained in the face of difficulties that will inevitably arise in the years ahead. We pay particular attention to the self-management of depressive reactions, and strategies for enhancing personal effectiveness.

Does Gender, Social Class Background, or Race Determine Destiny?

In Chapter 7 we learned that better educated people get better jobs and have a greater chance of remaining employed. And in spite of recession and high unemployment of the early 1980s, the opening box tells us that the overall prospects for educated youth are still good. But, does a college education really raise the probability that people who are female, poor, or black will get ahead? Or are their opportunities as limited as ever?

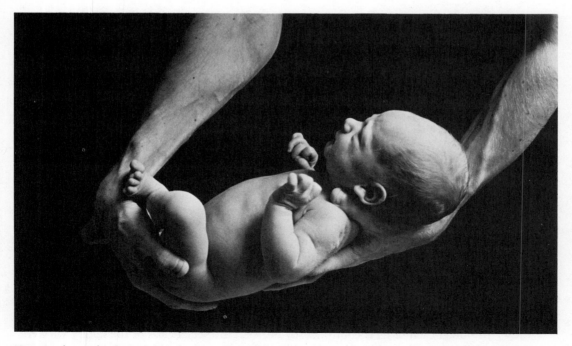

How much are this baby's life chances affected by gender, race, and socioeconomic class? Though these are powerful influences, their impact can be overcome by individual initiative.

How much of your competitiveness or desire for success is a function of whether you are male or female? Does the fact that you are born into a poor rather than well-off family raise the odds of your being maladjusted or just not caring whether you get ahead? To what extent is your family structure and intellectual aptitude related to the color of your skin?

In our society, instead of openly acknowledging that discrimination exists, legends abound about why women, the poor, and minorities don't succeed: the reason women don't get ahead is that they have an inborn tendency toward depression, fear of success, and are less "masculine"; the children of the poor are limited by parents who are psychologically maladjusted or without ambition; blacks and other minorities remain mired in poverty because of absent fathers and low intelligence. In this section we pay particular attention to the specific myths about what limits the achievements of these groups. Then we examine the evidence presently available about the impact of sex, socioeconomic status, and race on opportunities for living a satisfying and productive life.

Gender

Today, women earn only about sixty percent of the wages of men in comparable jobs, a figure that is only slightly less than in 1950 (Masnick and Bane, 1980). College teaching is a case in point. Government surveys show a larger percentage of females in lower academic ranks, who advance more slowly, and who are paid less than men for similar work (Marwell, Rosenfeld, and Spilerman, 1979). Traditionally "female" occupations, such as nursing, pay less than traditional male occupations, such as maintenance, though nursing requires more training and responsibilities.

Why might this be? Some psychologists have attempted to explain the differences in male and female success by pointing to the predominance of depression in women. Some statistics show that psychiatric hospitals treat two to six times as many women for depression as men. Female patients at the University of Washington psychiatric clinic in Seattle were twice as often as men diagnosed with a type of depression (Stangler and Printz, 1980). It might be argued that women become depressed more often because they worry about relationships with others, including competitors, rather than winning the race.

This argument leaves out two crucial points. First, emotional maladjustments of all sorts impair performance at work, not just depression. While it is true that, on the whole, females are more often diagnosed as being depressed than men, it is widely acknowledged that men do not seek help for emotional problems as readily as women, though they may be just as impaired. Second, a closer look at the data on diagnoses of depression indicates that the major differences are not in the major depressive episodes or manic-depressive psychoses, but in less serious depressive states. There is no evidence that individuals with these depressive conditions function any less effectively on a job than people with obsessive-compulsive disorders, a disorder applied to a larger proportion of men (Stangler & Printz, 1980). The crucial question is not whether women get depressed more often than men, but what the impact is on their performance at work.

It has been suggested that a reason women have a harder time succeeding is that they have an instinctive caring for others that inhibits their competitive urges. Matina Horner's research on the **fear of success** motive in women, which we looked at in Chapter 5, led to many other studies of women's feelings about getting ahead, being "masculine" as opposed to being "feminine," and competitive as opposed to being sensitive and caring. Though further studies have questioned some of Horner's notions about the fear of success, it now appears that women who have strong *"masculine" characteristics* — independence, self-confidence, and activeness — are just as ambitious as men who have the same traits. Moreover, women *and men* with stronger *"feminine" qualities* — gentleness, helpfulness, warmth, understanding — have more fear of success (Olds, 1979).

Could it be that the alleged differences between men and women are just crude stereotypes whose purpose is to "justify" discrimination against women? Relatively clear-cut evidence suggests that the standards used to evaluate normal males and females in the American culture are quite different. For instance, even mental health workers have different stereotypes in their minds when they think of a well-adjusted man and a well-adjusted woman.

Seventy-nine clinically trained psychologists, psychiatrists, and social workers (forty-six men and thirty-three women) were asked to describe a mature, socially competent man and woman. There was strong agreement on the characteristics as shown in Table 13.1.

The same clinicians were then asked to characterize a healthy adult, sex

Table 13.1 Sex role stereotypes

HEALTHY MAN	HEALTHY WOMAN
dominant	more submissive
independent	less independent
adventurous	less adventurous
not easily influenced	more easily influenced
aggressive	less aggressive
competitive	less competitive
not excitable in minor crises	more excitable in minor crises
feelings not easily hurt	more likely to have feelings easily hurt
not conceited about appearance	more conceited about appearance
objective	less objective
likes math and science very much	more likely to dislike math and science

SOURCE: From Broverman, I., Broverman, D., Clarkson, F., Rosenkranz, P. and Vogel, S. Sex-role stereotypes and clinical judgments of mental health. *Journal of Consulting and Clinical Psychology*, Vol. 34, 1970, pp. 1–7. Copyright 1970 by the American Psychological Association. Adapted by permission of the authors.

unspecified. Their concepts of the healthy adult and the healthy man were indistinguishable. However, their picture of a healthy adult differed significantly from their description of a healthy woman. A double standard for the mental health of women and men does exist in our society. Normal men are like healthy adults; normal women are not.

Are females with more "masculine" characteristics likely to be better adjusted and be more successful in their life, than those with stronger "feminine" traits? On the whole, research suggests that women with stronger "masculine" qualities are better adapted and competent than females with traditionally "feminine" characteristics. Moreover, men with high "feminine" traits were less secure, more neurotic, and had greater problems with alcohol abuse than males with more "masculine" qualities (Jones, Chernovetz, and Hansson, 1978).

Women with "masculine" characteristics expressed a strong desire to get ahead — but who still maintained their sensitivity — functioned very well. On the other hand, those women who were rated as highly competitive, but not sensitive, had a number of symptoms of emotional distress. It may be that being competitive for a woman at the cost of her sensitivity to others is still not in keeping with the role assigned to females by this culture, and the price they pay for this lack of conformity is psychological distress (Olds and Shaver, 1980).

Psychologist Sandra Bem has said that we should not identify behaviors as "masculine" or "feminine," but rather as simply "human." What sex we are should not dictate whether we "should be" ambitious or understanding, competitive or sensitive. These are traits that should be available to all of us (1981). Moreover, what sex each of us is should be no obstacle to getting what we want from life. As a college president noted, "The test of whether we have equal opportunities for women in college teaching is not whether an outstanding female is granted tenure, but whether a mediocre woman makes it along with an equally unexceptional man."

Having to function both productively and reproductively is a burden that men do not have to bear. And there is little question that the world of work is still less receptive to women than men at higher levels of responsibility and pay. These limitations are not a function of something that is inborn in women but rather the way society is organized. Things are changing gradually but many feel far too slowly. The majority of women in college today will continue to be the agents, rather than the beneficiaries, of change, supporting legislation that benefits women, directing the attention of government agencies to situations in which equal opportunity and affirmative action are not being practiced, and working for change within companies to make them more suitable for working women.

We can see encouraging signs that opportunities for women are growing. In the past few decades, efforts have been made to counter discriminatory practices toward women. Improvements are noticeable. Less role stereotyping goes on in the elementary schools, more women are being admitted into ad-

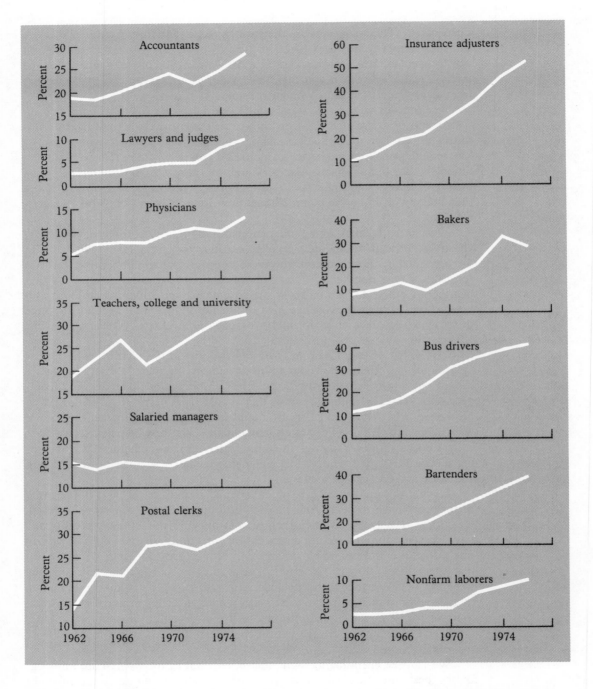

Figure 13.1   Women as a percentage of employed workers in selected traditionally male occupations: 1962–1976

vanced programs to prepare them for occupations previously dominated by men, and a greater proportion of women are currently in management and professional careers than at any time in the nation's history. Figure 13.1 shows the growing percentage of women presently in traditionally "male" occupations. Another encouraging sign is the narrowing gap between the salaries of women and men in several occupations. Table 13.2 shows the average monthly salary offers made to men and women college graduates in 1976–1977 in several fields. Generally, women were offered close to the same money as men. In two cases they actually had higher starting offers.

Social Class Background

Among the nations of the world, the United States has symbolized the land of opportunity. It remains the place where it is possible for people with talent, ambition, and the willingness to work at particular tasks (e.g. college) to be

College students on the march in Philadelphia for women's suffrage, 1915. Today's college females continue to be agents of change.

Table 13.2 Average monthly salary offers to bachelor's degree candidates by sex and occupation, 1976–1977

OCCUPATION	MEN (DOLLARS)	WOMEN (DOLLARS)
Accounting/auditing	1,065	1,060
Business administration	940	849
Communications	829	721
Community and service organizations work	747	702
EDP — programming/systems	1,115	1,090
Engineering	1,279	1,328
Farm and natural resources management	895	941
Finance and economics	936	927
Health (medical) services	937	864
Home economics and dietetics	853	685
Law enforcement services	933	798
Library and related work	742	598
Manufacturing and/or industrial operations	1,212	1,122
Marketing: Consumer product-services	931	890
Marketing: Industrial product-services	1,055	1,029
Mathematics/statistics	1,016	1,016
Merchandising/sales promotion	883	812
Personnel/employee relations	973	869
Public administration	879	762
Research — nonscientific	990	789
Research — scientific	1,119	1,062
Rotational training — technical	1,241	1,195
Rotational training — nontechnical	911	866

SOURCE: From *Work in America — The Decade Ahead*, edited by Clark Kerr and Jerome M. Rosow. Copyright © 1979 by Van Nostrand Reinhold Company. Reprinted by permission of the publisher.

upwardly mobile, rising from poverty to wealth and power. Less than in most nations of the world does the family we are born into limit our chances to achieve what we want in life (Lipsit and Bendix, 1959). Still we know of talented poor people who just can't seem to get ahead, and others from wealthy backgrounds with questionable ability and motivation who seem to advance not because of merit but because their relatives open the doors for them into proper schools and occupations. Seeing such things happen, it is difficult to avoid the conclusion that the chances for success in the United States are not the same for everyone. How much can our social class background be overcome in our generation, and how much of it is an unbreakable caste that forecloses our life chances?

Our **socioeconomic status** is measured by factors such as the occupations of our parents, their education, where we live, what the family income is, the source of the income (salary, investments, a trust fund) and, if our parents have money, how long they have had it (Kahl, 1957; Warner, Weeken, and Eels, 1949).

Numerous studies have been made comparing socioeconomic status and life chances. Usually they look at two types of information: (1) the chances for success being lessened by a larger percentage of disease, death, imprisonment, and emotional maladjustments in the lower social classes; and (2) the frequency with which individuals from lower echelons are **upwardly mobile,** that is, are able to exceed the social class rank of their parents.

If we look at men and women born into families from higher and lower socioeconomic rankings, we would find that a greater percentage of poor people have worse health and die younger, are imprisoned, or judged psychotic than members of the upper or middle classes (McKee, 1969). Here are two case illustrations. The first concerns the female passengers aboard the *Titanic* when that ship rammed an iceberg and sunk on its maiden voyage. Of the female passengers who were drowned, three percent were in the first-class cabins, sixteen percent were traveling second-class, and forty-five percent were in third-class (Lord, 1955). The reason for the differing death rates was that the order of boarding the lifeboats was determined by how much they paid for their staterooms. The first to leave the ship were the wealthiest women. The last to go were the poorest female travelers.

The second illustration comes from a series of interviews with a cross-section of Manhattan residents during the 1950s (Srole, Langer, Michael, Opler, and Rennie, 1962, Vol. I). Among the findings was a high correlation between social class and the presence of emotional distress. Table 13.3 shows the socioeconomic status of the parents of people studied and their degree of mental health. Table 13.3 tells us that those from the richest families were most often rated as being well or as having mild psychological problems. Conversely, almost two times as many of those from poorest families were rated as seriously impaired.

One of the hypotheses offered to explain such differences in mental health usually includes the idea of **downward drift** — the tendency for people with

Table 13.3 Socioeconomic class and the mental health of midtown Manhattan residents in the 1950s

SOCIAL ORIGIN OF PARENTS	PERCENTAGE OF MIDTOWN RESIDENTS WITH:		
	NO OR MILD PSYCHOLOGICAL SYMPTOMS	MODERATE PSYCHOLOGICAL SYMPTOMS	SYMPTOMS PLUS ROLE/ IMPAIRMENT
Top third	61	22	17 = 100%
Middle third	56	21	23 = 100%
Bottom third	46	23	31 = 100%

SOURCE: From Leo Srole, *Mental health in the metropolis,* revised and enlarged edition (New York University Press, 1977). Copyright © 1962, 1975, 1977 by Leo Srole. Reprinted by permission.

serious emotional problems to slide toward the bottom of the socioeconomic ladder because of their inability to obtain and hold a good job. They may produce children for whom the road to success is potholed by poor upbringing as well as a constitutional vulnerability to emotional disorders.

Another reason is that doctors are quicker to label the problems of the upper or career class as mild or moderate, while the same symptoms with lower-class people are interpreted as evidence of a psychosis. This tendency was noted many years ago by French psychiatrist Pierre Janet (cited in Page, 1975, p. 172), who wrote:

> If a patient is poor he is committed to a public hospital as a psychotic; if he can afford the luxury of a private sanitarium he is put there with the diagnosis of neurasthenia; if he is wealthy enough to be isolated in his own home under constant watch of nurses and physicians he is simply an indisposed eccentric.

How often are young people from lower social origins able to improve their status during their lives? Or is social class inherited like blue eyes? Overall, research shows a modest relationship between a family's social position and how successful their children are. For instance, in 1973, thirty-eight percent of men from the lower social classes exceeded their fathers' occupational status. This is contrasted with sixty-five percent in the highest social classes. These figures are unchanged since World War II (Featherman, 1980).

What is the difference between the individuals from lower socioeconomic classes who move upward and their neighbors who don't? Typically, they are

Ducks vs. Hard Rocks

In Brooklyn you fall into one of two categories when you start growing up. The names for the categories may be different in other cities, but the categories are the same. First, there's the minority of the minority, the "ducks," or suckers. These are the kids who go to school every day. They even want to go to college. Imagine that! School after high school! They don't smoke cheeb (marijuana) and they get zooted (intoxicated) after only one can of beer. They're wasting their lives waiting for a dream that won't come true.

The ducks are usually the ones getting beat up on by the majority group — the "hard rocks." If you're a real hard rock you have no worries, no cares. Getting high is as easy as breathing. You just rip off some duck. You don't bother going to school; it's not necessary. You just live with your mom until you get a job — that should be any time a job comes looking for you. Why should you bother to go look for it? Even your parents can't find work.

I guess the barrier between the ducks and the hard rocks is the barrier of despair. The ducks still have hope, while the hard rocks are frustrated. They're caught in the deadly, dead-end environment and can't see a way out. Life becomes the fast life — or incredibly boring — and death becomes the death that you see and get used to every day. . . .

Hard rocks do what they want to do when they want to do it. When a hard rock goes to prison it builds up his reputation. He develops a bravado that's like a long, sad joke. But it's all lies and excuses. It's a hustle to young people with an identifiable pattern of family values, friends, and interest in education. In Chapter 1, we noted that youngsters from the lower class who are successful are those whose parents themselves were dissatisfied with their place in life and wanted more for their children. Other data indicate that boys and girls who are raised to be responsible, ambitious, and self-directing; to look ahead; to put off gratification for later reward; and to exceed the accomplishments of their parents, are candidates for upward mobility (Featherman, 1980; Warner and Agegglin, 1955). Copying the middle-class value structure is one — but may not be the only — type of home environment that stimulates upward mobility in lower-class youngsters.

Who our friends are influences our ambitions. If the people we spend time with are oriented toward success in life and reinforce ambition, hard work, studying when we would rather be playing, and staying out of trouble, we are likely to get ahead. If our friends have no particular goals, live day to day, are indifferent to school, and have a tendency to get crosswise with the law, our chances for social mobility are greatly reduced. As 15-year-old Deairich Hunter tells us, however, choosing to be a "Duck" instead of a "Hard Rock" can be difficult to do.

Education is the third ingredient that can make the difference for a youngster in the lower classes. School, perhaps more than any other aspect of American society, is a place where individuals can be judged on their merits rather than on who their parents are. If poor young people are able to find their way into a college preparatory track and go on to college, they will dis-

keep ahead of the fact that he's going nowhere . . . .

I guess the best way to help the hard rocks is to help the ducks. If the hard rocks see the good guy making it, maybe they will change. If they see the ducks, the ones who try, succeed, it might bring them around. The ducks are really the only ones who might be able to change the situation.

The problem with most ducks is that after years of effort they develop a negative attitude, too. If they succeed, they know they've got it made. Each one can say he did it by himself and for himself. No one helped him and he owes nobody anything, so he says, "Let the hard rocks and the junkies stay where they are" — the old every-man-for-himself routine.

What the ducks must be made to realize is that it was this same attitude that made the hard rocks so hard. They developed a sense of kill or be killed, abuse or be abused, take it or get taken.

The hard rocks want revenge. They want revenge because they don't have any hope of changing their situation. Their teachers don't offer it, their parents have lost theirs, and their grandparents died with a heart full of hope but nothing to show for it.

Maybe the only people left with hope are the only people who can make a difference — teens like me. We, the ducks, must learn to care. As a 15-year-old, I'm not sure I can handle all that. Just growing up seems hard enough.

cover that their grades are likely to be a function of how bright they are and how much they learn, rather than their socioeconomic status (Featherman, 1980).

Race

What effect does race have on our chances to achieve a productive and satisfying life? Over the years, much has been made of the lack of upward mobility of some racial minorities — primarily blacks, but also Mexican-Americans and Native Americans and, more recently, Hispanics from the Caribbean and Central and South America — compared with other minority groups. Two reasons have been cited for a larger proportion of black people — the minority group studied in greatest detail — remaining mired in poverty, poor health, and unemployment or underemployment: instability of the family and lower intellectual ability.

In a position paper written in 1965 to justify massive federal funding for President Johnson's "War on Poverty," former professor, government advisor, and senator Daniel Patrick Moynihan put the first argument this way:

1. The instability of black families is demonstrated by the high rate of illegitimacy and marital separation, causing a large number of households to be headed by females.
2. The result is a "tangle of pathology" in the black community, leading to poorer school performance and earlier dropping out of education, failure to qualify for jobs that will produce a decent income, and higher rates of delinquency, drug problems, crime, and dependence on welfare.
3. For black men, a vicious cycle operates: denied access to opportunity because of discrimination, they have no chance of getting ahead in a job; as a result they are alienated from the workplace and eventually from their families; this leads to an absence of a strong father and a stable family structure for children to grow up in; the children cannot look forward to a stable life, and so drop out of school, therefore starting the cycle all over again (Moynihan, 1967).

This report reflected the belief in the early 1960s that the government should attempt to improve the living conditions of minority group members through expanding educational opportunities, job training, health care, and eventually enforcing laws granting equality of access to colleges and universities and managerial and professional occupations. While some of the programs failed badly because of poor planning, inept leadership, an intractable establishment, or graft, many have been successful (Moynihan, 1969).

As might be imagined, the argument justifying the war on poverty was roundly condemned by civil rights leaders and others around the country. Among the most telling rebuttals is that this argument confuses race with social class. A far larger proportion of black people and other minority individuals are poor. If we compare poor individuals from minorities with poor whites, we find a similar percentage of female-headed families, poor school achievement, illegitimacy, and delinquency among their children (Lewis, 1967). Moreover, it appears that pervasive discrimination in the schools and in the workplace, dangerous slum conditions, and limited health care have far more to do with the failure of young people from lower social classes to get ahead than the color of their skin.

How about children born into middle-class black and white families? Here the evidence has been clear for twenty-five years. A classic piece of research carried out by Chicago social scientists Allison Davis and Robert Havighurst (1956) compared the child-rearing patterns of black and white parents in middle- and lower-class families. They found that middle-class mothers from both races emphasized traditional middle-class values: good habits, taking responsibility for oneself early, and doing well in school and in life. The child-rearing practices of lower-class black and white parents resembled each other more than those of middle-class families of the same race.

The second argument offered for our destiny's being a function of skin color involves intelligence. The reasoning is deceptively simple: I.Q. is largely inherited; black people score lower on I.Q. tests than white people; I.Q. is associated with achievement in school and at work. Therefore, black individuals have less chance to climb the ladder of success in a society based largely on achievement (Herrnstein, 1977; Jensen, 1969).

The argument that I.Q. is largely inherited has been the subject of intense debate. Far from unanimous opinion exists on this subject. Present evidence suggests that small differences in measured I.Q. between large groups of blacks and other races may exist. But the amount is not enough to explain the vast disparity of attainment in school and at work among races.

If I.Q. isn't the primary ingredient in how we do in school, then what is important? As we have seen, social class background does have an impact. Also important, however, is who our classmates are. James Coleman and his colleagues discovered that black students do better in classrooms with a majority of middle-class white classmates (Coleman *et al.*, 1966). This finding has been used to justify a stormy decade of busing, something that Coleman himself has opposed.

In addition to classroom peers, black students, like white ones, profit from parents who are ambitious for their children and respect their doing well in school. However, this can be difficult for poor minority group parents, because they feel separated from the power structure. They may perceive themselves as having little ability to influence decisions made by school personnel affecting their children. They convey this sense of powerlessness to their offspring, as well as the notion that these boys and girls are likely to be victims of discrimination and no matter how hard they try they will be frustrated (Bronfenbrenner, 1979).

An illuminating case illustration is that of the Burgerside area of Stockton,

Black and white middle-class children are raised with similar values.

California. Burgerside is a poor section that is predominantly black and Mexican-American. The families send their children to Stockton public schools staffed largely by middle-class whites who do not live in Burgerside. Typically, the children from this section are inferior to the middle-class Stockton students in every way: poorer grades, higher dropout rate, and far fewer going on to college. Anthropologist J. U. Ogbu (1974) set out to find out why. He interviewed many of the Burgerside families, middle-class residents of Stockton, and teachers at school and community meetings. He isolated three possible causes of the poor school performance of the Burgerside youngsters: (1) failure to exhibit great effort to do well in school; (2) a patron-client relationship between school personnel and Burgerside families; and (3) defining educational problems as a clinical disorder.

The first explanation isn't surprising. Like many lower-class kids, these youngsters did not come to school with the voices of their parents ringing in their ears to get A's or at least "do your best." Because their parents suspect that their children may be victimized by discrimination and have their best efforts frustrated, they are not as likely to stress that attending school regularly and getting good grades are virtues.

The patron-client relationship was revealed in several ways. Communication between school personnel and Burgerside families was a one-way street. Parents had no say in how the school was being run, were not consulted about which of the faculty should be retained, and could not voice their objections to their children's having bilingual education. Also, the teachers believed that the parents were not interested in the school, and that the families were content to remain trapped in a cycle of poverty.

Finally, personnel in the school were quick to see the Burgerside boys and girls as having psychological, rather than educational, problems. Because of their "disadvantaged" home situations, instead of having their school deficiencies defined as a problem requiring tutoring or academic advising, these children were often referred for therapeutic counseling or other types of treatment.

While minority groups have it harder than their white counterparts, it is also true that some, especially blacks, have made significant progress since the years of Johnson's War on Poverty. A far higher proportion of blacks are presently enrolled in college preparatory programs, as well as college and postgraduate institutions, than at any time in history.

But school is not life. The bottom line is whether increased educational opportunities have had an effect on occupational attainment. Specifically, we might be interested in the question of whether the percentage of black children exceeding their father's occupational level has grown. A recent report compared the effect of education on occupational level and upward mobility of blacks graduating in 1962 and 1973 (Featherman, 1980). The findings are encouraging. In 1973, blacks were upwardly mobile at a rate far exceeding that of 1962. In the early 1960s, a minority group college graduate had a good chance of being a well-educated waitress or factory laborer. Today, a college degree has a greater tendency to lead to a white-collar or professional occupation.

All in all, it appears that the value of school and the opportunity for upward growth for minority group members approximates — though it is not yet equal to — that of whites.

Being female, being poor, and being a minority group member raise the odds against getting ahead for large groups of people. However, within this large population are many individuals who are successful. They do well in school and college, enter rewarding occupations, and have satisfying lives. They are neither especially gifted nor classic overachievers. For the most part they: have parents with ambitions for them; have a dream that moves them along the path of the Ducks rather than that of the Hard Rocks; find supportive friends with similar motivation to work reasonably hard and get advice about pathways that are likely to lead them to their goals. Gender, social class, and race influence only probability, not destiny.

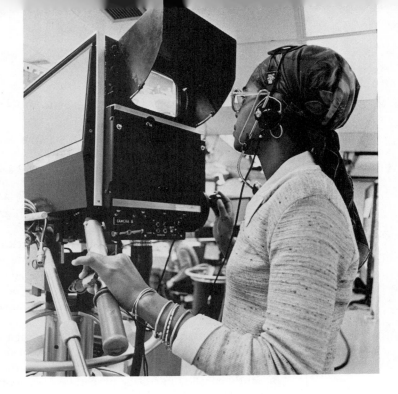

Opportunities for college-trained minority group members are greater now than at any time in history, though they are still fewer than those of their white classmates.

Maintaining Self-Esteem and Personal Effectiveness in the Years Ahead

In Chapter 2 we learned that our self-esteem is based on how we evaluate the picture we have of ourselves (see pages 59–60). If we have a positive view of ourselves, we can be said to have high **self-esteem.** But when our view of ourselves is far less than we would like it to be, then we are likely to have low self-esteem.

From what we have studied so far, what can we identify as essential building blocks of self-esteem and **personal effectiveness** that might help us on the road beyond college? From earlier chapters we can isolate three areas: 1) finding satisfaction from a personal balance of work, love, and play; 2) maintaining resources; and 3) developing effective ways of managing stress.

A Personal Balance of Satisfaction from Work, Love, and Play

By now, the phrase "finding satisfaction from a balance of work, love and play" may be wearing a little thin, because it has been repeated so often. As we have seen, however, studies of people over time, as well as clinical findings with normal individuals, consistently show this to be a primary criterion of adjustment. The relative contributions of each sphere will differ according to individual personalities.

Each of us needs to keep in mind the need to develop and maintain the capacity to obtain pleasure from the separate domains of working, loving, and playing. These are not instincts, but rather learned behaviors. Like driving a car, once the skills are learned, they require practice in order to preserve our ability to use them competently.

The spheres that provide greatest pleasure are often fragile. As Luis's example so clearly showed, our enjoyment from work can be suddenly shut down by being laid off. The same thing can happen when a career "tops out" or when we retire. Nothing is more certain than losing loved ones through death, departure, or estrangement. And, as the fisherman who has had a stroke will tell us, even certain types of play can be a temporary pleasure. What this means is that we need to be ready to make substitutions if we can — locating a decent job, making new friends, replacing one avocation with another.

For instance, when a favorite recreation is shut down it is hard to find something else to do for fun. The bass fisherman who had a stroke decided to start a fishing lure business. Eventually it became highly successful. To this day he misses the thrill of hooking a smallmouth; but he does enjoy designing and selling artificial bait, and it gives him a chance to be with his old fishing cronies.

Finding a balance of work, love, and play which fits our own personalities is essential to our self-regard and effectiveness. We need to be alert to the danger of continuing overwork: it jeopardizes satisfaction from love and play as well as threatens physical health. In the years from 30 to 45, we are all especially vulnerable to unbalancing our lives in favor of work.

In the last decade, human development specialists have begun to suspect that overwork retards psychological growth in the early and middle adult years. Haverford College psychologist Douglas Heath (1968, 1977a) for instance, reported on the emotional maturation of men at middle age. He observed that some men in occupations that encourage overdriven achievement recognize the distortion this is causing in their life balance and become increasingly dissatisfied with the overall quality of their lives. As a result, some have been able to decrease their commitment to the career and increase the amount of time for family and recreational enjoyment (Heath, 1977b).

Osherson's follow-up studies (1982) of nearly 400 normal men who were also at mid-life found that nearly half ranked the most gratifying part of their daily lives as being a husband and father. Married men with children also said they felt more successful at work than those who were childless. Interestingly, Osherson also looked at men whose wives worked and those whose spouses were at home. Men in dual-career marriages with youngsters reported that their careers fit their abilities and interests far more often than husbands who were the sole breadwinners.

Maintaining Resources

The relationship between the degree of unpleasantness in life and the amount of resources at our disposal has been demonstrated to be associated with overall adjustment. Of all the resources we can develop, the three most important are a supportive network of friends, a dream, and a belief in something greater than ourselves.

We have discussed the value of supportive relationships with others in combating stress. For example, research with students in an academically demanding California college found that those whose residence units were academically and socially competitive had a higher than usual rate of visits to the health service for medical and psychological problems than those who lived in socially supportive living groups (Moos, 1981). A year-long study of about 500 middle-aged men and women looked at the relationship between social supports and the appearance of depression and physical symptoms in reaction to stressful events. The researchers discovered, when they held the amount of stress constant, that those adults who had relationships with family members and co-workers that were characterized by mutual support, open expression of feeling, and lack of conflict exhibited fewer signs of maladjustment after twelve months (Holahan and Moos, 1981).

A dream gives our life purpose, vitality, organization, and the tolerance for frustration. Instead of a life of random activity, a dream focuses on what we do and gives it meaning. If you decide your purpose in life is to make a lot of money, that is likely to improve your energy level and determine how you spend your time. With a vision of what you want out of your working years, you may quit your secure but modest-paying job for one with a better financial future, amaze your friends by showing a vigor in pursuing the new occupation, and get rid of old habits and activities that don't further your ambition. Dreams enable us to tolerate hard work, sacrifice, and frustrating setbacks because we have a picture of ourselves doing something worthwhile. In the words of an old Lutheran hymn, dreams enable us to "trace rainbows through the rain."

As Levinson (1978) so accurately warned us earlier, dreams can become illusions. What are we left with when our visions of the purpose in our lives are shattered? While we are trying to put our existence back together at a painful time of transition, what can we draw upon while we reform our dream? An answer is something greater than ourselves. In moments of severe duress, being able to fasten onto someone or something as a basis for hope can keep us from going under. Today, more and more people, many in their teens and early 20s, are finding that a sense of being secure in the Lord's grace fulfills a need to rely on something greater than themselves. Others are sustained by a faith in the supremacy of science, in universal ethical principles, or in the essential value of the human species. And doubtless, some find solace in being a Capricorn or in knowing that their biorhythms are pointing in the right direction.

Developing Effective Ways of Managing Stress

Scattered among the years ahead will be painful moments when the gap between how we would like to be and how we realistically see ourselves is large. We may founder — feeling overwhelmed, disoriented, cut off, angry or dispirited. What causes you or me to founder differs greatly. Each of us has one or more built-in deficits that may result in our feeling blocked from getting ahead, in our being disliked, or in our being generally miserable. We are the wrong sex, have the wrong parents, or are the wrong color. We are too short, not attractive enough, are of the wrong religion, or are socially unskilled. Instead of trying to compensate for these supposed liabilities, we feel victimized by them. How we deal with these moments in our lives is the key to maintaining our self-esteem and remaining effective.

A story is told about an alcoholic's two sons — one a drunk and the other a teetotaler. Asked about their drinking habits, both gave the same answer: "With a father like that, what do you expect?" (Selye, 1980). The moral of the story is a familiar one: it is not the stress we face, but how we deal with it, that makes the difference. Our self-regard and our personal effectiveness throughout life are greatly improved by knowing what types of things upset us most, what our reactions habitually are, what the control of these feelings costs us, and considering whether we should learn new adaptive strategies.

Nothing is stressful until we make it so. I may fly into a fury when my girl friend tells me she likes someone else, but the same experience doesn't bother you at all. On the other hand, you may feel depressed because a professor gave you a mediocre grade on a test, while a low mark doesn't concern me. Each of us benefits from being clear about those things we care about, *and* respect the extent we can be upset if they are threatened.

Before we are very old, we come to know what our feelings are likely to

Maggie Kuhn, 70-year-old leader of the Gray Panthers, an advocacy group for the rights of older Americans. Much of her work consists of building support groups among the aged to help them cope with the stresses of growing older.

be when we are upset — depression, anger, anxiety, or a headache or churning stomach. And as we grow, we become familiar with how we typically control these reactions to stress. It is usually obvious to ourselves and others that something is wrong with the way we cope with adversity if we always reach for a bottle.

Sometimes, however, the maladaptive response is less obvious. If my anger always converts to explosive rage and your depression unfailingly turns into a conviction of hopelessness, then we both can be on our way to unhappy, unproductive lives with the possibilities of an emotional disorder in the bargain. What can we do to help ourselves in these situations?

A large part of the answer is in recognizing our tendency to overreact and take steps to interrupt the slide toward a maladaptive emotional state. Let's look at strategies for managing excessive anger or depressive reactions.

In Chapter 3 we studied some examples of controlling upsetting emotions by direct control responses, for example, the relaxation response for anxiety. Anger can be handled in the same way. A recent report summarized several key studies in which a combination of direct control responses was used to manage explosive rage. This was followed by using a problem-solving approach to learn alternative reactions to events that usually trigger a temper tantrum (Novaco, 1978).

After the anger-prone individuals were prepared to deal with the stress by first learning relaxation, they went through the following steps: (1) identify people and situations that trigger anger; (2) distinguish anger from explosive rage; (3) understand how initial anger leads to outbursts of rage; and (4) learn about alternative coping strategies. Then the individuals were instructed to rehearse new ways of managing anger in imaginary situations and in role playing with others. An example of managing a conflict without becoming angry is shown in Table 13.4.

If I applied this strategy to manage my anger at my girl friend, I might *prepare* to talk with her by recognizing that the situation will be rough, but I will try to stick to the issues. I anticipate the *impact and confrontation* and remind myself that I don't have to prove myself and that I don't want to make more out of this than the situation demands. I am ready to cope with the *anger that is aroused*, recognizing the signs — tenseness and rapid breathing. At that point, I try to slow things down and try to deal with the problem constructively. If our talk is unsuccessful, I try to forget about it, not take it personally, and not let it interfere with the rest of my life. If the conflict is resolved without my being angry, I feel good about this and try to apply this learning to future situations.

A depression swelling into helplessness can ruin the quality of our lives. Two types of self-initiated activities which can limit negative thoughts and begin the restoration of a normal state are self-management and personal effectiveness strategies. To see how these activities might operate to help us keep up the positive image of ourselves and continue to perform competently, imagine being Walter, who had a heart attack at 40. Recovering from a coronary

Table 13.4   Steps in conflict management

Preparing for a provocation

This could be a rough situation, but I know how to deal with it. I can work out a plan to handle this. Easy does it. Remember, stick to the issues and don't take it personally. There won't be any need for an argument. I know what to do.

Impact and confrontation

As long as I keep my cool, *I'm* in control of the situation. You don't need to prove yourself. Don't make more out of this than you have to. There is no point in getting mad. Think of what you have to do. Look for the positives and don't jump to conclusions.

Coping with arousal

Muscles are getting tight. Relax and slow things down. Time to take a deep breath. Let's take the issue point by point. My anger is a signal of what I need to do. Time for problem-solving. He probably wants me to get angry, but I'm going to deal with it constructively.

Subsequent reflection

a. Conflict unresolved

Forget about the aggravation. Thinking about it only makes you upset. Try to shake it off. Don't let it interfere with your job. Remember relaxation. It's a lot better than anger. Don't take it personally. It's probably not so serious.

b. Conflict resolved

I handled that one pretty well. That's doing a good job. I could have gotten more upset than it was worth. My pride can get me into trouble, but I'm doing better at this all the time.

I actually got through that without getting angry.

SOURCE: From Novaco, R. Anger and coping with stress: Cognitive behavioral interventions. In J. Foreyt and D. Rathjen (Eds.), *Cognitive behavior therapy: Research and applications.* New York: Plenum, 1978. Reprinted by permission.

to a full and productive life is dependent upon the ability to cope with the psychological reactions to the traumatic event. The heart heals quickly, but the psychological wounds are slower to mend. Most coronary patients are depressed and worry that any physical exertions will cause another heart attack. Rehabilitation involves helping these individuals manage their upsetting feelings and rebuild their sense of physical competence.

Self-Management Strategies

In his article, "Self-Management of Depression," Houston psychologist Lynn Rehm (1982) describes five steps in a strategy for improving this mental condition. They are self-monitoring, understanding the immediate and long-term consequences of events, overcoming distortions about the causes of events, setting realistic goals, and positive *self-reinforcement.*

Central to *self-monitoring* is the idea that mood is determined by behavior. The behavior can be actual activity or self-statements that accompany an activity. Many depressed people focus excessively on negative events and are prone to make negative self-statements. Walter, having just had a heart attack, is likely to focus on what he can't do rather than on what he will be able to do. He may make critical comments to himself: he should have taken better care of himself; his life will never be the same; he will be a burden to others. If Walter follows Rehm's self-monitoring suggestions, he will record the number of positive events that happen to him each day, as well as positive self-statements. A positive event might be having a friend drop by to chat and play cards, seeing a good mystery movie, or making progress in physical rehabilitation. A positive self-statement might be, "I'm a good card player," "I enjoyed figuring out who the murderer was," or "I am working hard at improving my stamina."

As Walter keeps track of these positive events, he is likely to be surprised and perhaps a little pleased that he has so many things that can make him feel good in the course of a day. He also may come to recognize that he has been overlooking them in favor of negative activities.

The second component of a self-management program for depression is *gaining a clearer understanding of the immediate and long-term consequences of events.* People who are depressed are more likely to be affected by immediate, rather than long-term, consequences of actions. This is why they often indulge themselves in something they later regret. Feeling down in the dumps, Walter eats three eclairs. Though he feels a little better immediately, the failure to maintain his diet has long-term depressing effects. A way to control indulgent behavior is to make a two-by-two table of the sort shown in Figure 13.2. This shows the positive and negative consequences of an activity, evaluated in immediate and long-term time periods. Figure 13.2 shows the positive and negative consequences of inviting a friend to drop by the hospital and talk, in both the immediate and long-run periods.

Overcoming distortions about why events occur is the third element. Rehabilitation from the heart attack will require that Walter walk and then jog on the

Figure 13.2
Evaluating positive and negative consequences of a desired activity: immediately and in the long run

Activity: Inviting a friend to talk.

	Immediate	Long run
Positive consequences	Enjoyed the talk	Better friendship
Negative consequences	Felt nervous about calling	Tired after talk

treadmill. Gradually, he improves. Since he is depressed, he is likely to attribute a good performance on the treadmill to just luck, as having no meaning as far as his recovery is concerned, and as unlikely to occur again. If his doctors and nurses and loved ones help him to see that his strong performance on the treadmill is something that he accomplished rather than being a fluke, that it means that he is improving physically, and that he will be able to do it again, Walter may find his depression lifting.

Setting realistic goals is the fourth ingredient. Depressed individuals often set unattainable or overly vague goals. Because they can never realize these outcomes, they remain depressed. Imagine Walter being told to lose weight. In a depressed state he might say to himself "I have to lose 40 pounds," or "I'm not exercising enough." The overly ambitious and vague nature of these two goals contributes to his depression. Proper goal setting will alleviate his depression. Proper goals have four properties: (1) they are divisible into smaller sub-goals, (2) they are defined in a positive fashion, (3) they are attainable, and (4) they are within the person's control. Walter will be less depressed if he reformulates his unattainable or overly vague goals in keeping with these properties. Instead of telling himself he has to lose 40 pounds — a discouraging task — Walter will tell himself that he wants to lose two to three pounds a week. Instead of saying that he isn't exercising enough, he might set the positive, clearly attainable goal, within his control, of jogging fifteen minutes a day.

Positive self-reinforcement is the final part of this program to improve pressed feelings. People who are depressed rarely are moved to do anything to reward themselves for their behavior. If Walter can be encouraged to reward himself for goals that he achieves, he may tend to feel less depressed. A reward or reinforcement can simply be activities that bring pleasure. If Walter is able to lose two or three pounds within a week, he might reward himself by going to a baseball game he always enjoys. This is not an indulgence, but a reward well-earned.

Personal Effectiveness Strategies

A second type of activity that can improve our depressed mood and self-regard are strategies for enhancing personal effectiveness. Stanford psychologist Alfred Bandura (1982) thinks that judgments about personal effectiveness are based on four types of information: objective performance, modeling by others, persuasion that we possess certain capabilities, and proper interpretation of certain physiological reactions to stress. Let's see how Walter can use these sources of information to restore his confidence in his physical abilities.

The most influential source of information in rebuilding confidence in physical capabilities is *objective performance* data. Success heightens self-confidence. Walter is likely to believe his heart is on the mend if he can see his stamina improving in regular treadmill or other exercises.

His opinion about recovery to a full life also can be influenced by *modeling* by others like him. We learned in Chapter 2 that modeling is an influential behavioral technique in shaping actions of children. If Walter can meet with former patients — men like himself who exemplify active, productive lives — he will see that he too has the capability for successful rehabilitation.

Verbal persuasion and allied kinds of social influence are widely used to motivate people to improve their performance. This is especially useful if the exhortation is to achieve a realistic goal. In Walter's case, the persuasion might be of two kinds. His doctor might give him objective information about how much exertion he will be able to tolerate and when he will be able to resume normal activity. Another type of persuasion might be to have Walter's wife present to watch his performance on the treadmill. Not only is her presence often good for morale — assisting Walter to keep at a boring and grueling task — but it also means there is someone with whom to share the sense of improvement.

The *proper interpretation of certain physiological reactions to stress* is the fourth important source of information. Each of us has reactions to the way our body feels under stress, and we often interpret this as evidence of capability or vulnerability. Before a basketball game, an athlete knows that a racing pulse, tightness in the chest, nausea, and overall worry is a normal response to stress and will pass as soon as the ball is put into play. From personal experience, however, Walter now knows these also can be associated with a coronary. To help him become effective again, he has to learn the differences between the physiological signals telling him he is on the road to another heart attack and normal, tolerable cardiac acceleration in physical activities, under stress at work, and in sexual relations, so that he does not misread them.

Obviously, the control of a strong temper or the improvement of depressive reactions to traumatic events is more difficult than is sketched by these examples. And, we sometimes need the help of professional counselors, doctors, or others to show us and start us on the way to recovery. Yet, most of the unpleasant events that lie ahead are not nearly as stressful as a heart attack. The work of individuals such as Rehm and Bandura point to ways in which we can help ourselves maintain self-esteem and personal effectiveness in times of future stress.

Summary

1. Present evidence is that gender, social class background, and race influence the probability of being successful for large groups of people. However, the opportunities for individuals to achieve their goals are greater now than at any time in history.

2. We can identify building blocks that are the foundation of self-esteem and personal effectiveness. The first is finding satisfaction from a personal balance of work, love, and play. These are not instincts, but learned behaviors and are fragile. There are times in which it is important to find alternative opportunities for gratification within a domain or redirect energies into other areas.

3. The second building block is maintaining resources to cushion and comfort us. Of all the resources to develop, the three most important are a supportive network of friends, a dream, and a belief in something greater than ourselves.
4. The third building block involves developing effective ways of managing stress. Our adjustment is improved by understanding what upsets us, what our usual reactions are, what the control of these feelings costs us, and considering new adaptive strategies.
5. Self-management techniques can help when we are under stress. The essentials of this strategy include self-monitoring, understanding the immediate and long-term effects of events, overcoming distortions about causes, setting realistic goals, and positive self-reinforcement.
6. The ingredients of personal effectiveness strategies are using objective performance data, modeling by others, obtaining verbal persuasion, and properly interpreting physiological reactions to stress.

A Look Ahead

We will begin the next, and last, chapter in this book by asking what you would like your obituary to say about how happy and successful your life has been. This question sets the stage for guidelines for living. We will consider ten guidelines for living, distilled from the wisdom of many of the scholars and clinicians whose work we have studied.

Key Terms

fear of success	**self-esteem**
socioeconomic status	**personal effectiveness**
upwardly mobile	**positive self-reinforcement**
downward drift	

Suggested Readings

Gender

Basow, S. *Sex-role stereotypes: Traditions and alternatives.* Monterey, Calif.: Brooks/Cole, 1980.

Nieva, V., and Gutek, B. *Women and work: A psychological perspective.* New York: Praeger, 1982.

   Alternatives to the traditional sex-role stereotypes for modern women.

Social class and race

Featherman, D., and Hauser, R. *Opportunity and change.* New York: Academic Press, 1978.

Featherman, D. Schooling and occupational careers: Constancy and change in worldly success. In O. Brim, Jr., and J. Kagan (Eds.), *Constancy and change in human development*. Cambridge, Mass.: Harvard University Press, 1980.

Examines the relationship of socio-economic background and race to life chances, noting the value of education.

The dream

Levinson, D., with Darrow, C., Klein, E., Levinson, M., and McKee, B. *Seasons of a man's life*. New York: Knopf, 1978.

Sustaining value of the dream as it forms, fades, and is reestablished through the adult years.

Self-management of stress reactions

Karoly, P., and Kanfer, F. *The psychology of self management: From theory to practice*. New York: Pergamon, 1982.

Flach, F. *The secret strength of depression*. New York: Bantam, 1975.

Ways of helping ourselves cope more effectively with distressing feelings.

To dream the impossible dream,
To fight the unbeatable foe,
To bear with unbearable sorrow,
To run where the brave dare not go.

To right the unrightable wrong,
To love, pure and chaste, from afar,
To try, when your arms are too weary,
To reach the unreachable star!

This is my quest, to follow that star,
No matter how hopeless, no matter how far;
To fight for the right without question or
    pause,
To be willing to march into hell for a heavenly
    cause!

And I know, If I'll only be true
To this glorious quest,
That my heart will lay peaceful and calm
When I'm laid to my rest.

And the world will be better for this,
That one man, scorned and covered with
    scars,
Still strove, with his last ounce of courage,
To reach the unreachable star!

Chapter Preview

CHAPTER 14
Guidelines for Living

Questions to think about

☐ Can you think of guidelines which may be useful in directing your future growth?

☐ How did you decide to pick these?

☐ How might you improve the quality of your life now?

☐ What would you like your obituary to say about how happy and successful your life has been?

Imagine you have been asked to give the address at your college's commencement this year. Suppose you decided to offer several guidelines to the graduates that might help them live more satisfying and productive lives. What would you say? Then consider the end of your life. If you could write your own obituary, how would you describe your life? Have satisfactions outweighed difficulties? Have you productively pursued your goals?

This chapter contains ten guidelines distilled from the wisdom of many of the scholars and clinicians whose thinking we already have studied. At the chapter's end, we consider how thinking about our death can help us improve the quality of our living.

Guidelines for Living

There you are at commencement, on the podium, looking into the expectant faces of this year's graduating class. What guidance might you give them to raise the probability of their going on to live as fully as possible?

Here are ten guidelines for living. They are drawn from the thinking of philosophers, doctors, psychologists, religious thinkers, and others who have devoted their lives to understanding and caring for human beings.

I. Care for the Body

Our bodies are the vessels within which our psychological adaptation occurs. Without physical health, it is difficult to imagine feeling well psychologically. It has been said that most of us are born healthy but become ill because we don't take care of ourselves (Knowles, 1977). What can we do to raise the probability of staying in good health? Here are six suggestions: (1) regulate stress, (2) take sensible safety precautions, (3) have regular physical checkups, (4) watch what we eat, (5) moderate drug use, and (6) maintain fitness (Matarazzo, 1982; Dawber, 1980; U.S. Department of Health, Education, and Welfare, 1979).

We already know the connection between stress and physical and mental disorders. None of us can tolerate too much stress for too long. If we find ourselves in a taxing situation, we should try to alter the environment to relieve the pressure. If not, perhaps we should consider changing the situation.

Avoiding physical danger by following reasonable safety precautions is the second suggestion (Matarazzo, 1982). An example is using seatbelts. One American in forty dies in automobile accidents. Death and serious injury rates would be reduced by over half if all of us remembered to wear seatbelts. Wearing helmets when riding bikes or motorcycles might save the lives of many of the more than 5,000 people who are killed each year. Following basic rules of safety on the road, at home, and at work can help avoid a sudden end to a promising life.

Regular physical checkups for younger people can result in the diagnosis of harmful conditions that do not have clear-cut symptoms (Dawber, 1980). Two of these conditions, which can be diagnosed by regular checkups, are diabetes and high blood pressure. The detection of these diseases in apparently well young people — long before physical damage occurs — can result in preventive action that can greatly improve the quality of adult life.

Watching what we eat is the fourth suggestion. Recommended **dietary goals** and proper eating patterns are shown in Table 14.1. Opinion varies about the effects on health of sugar, caffeine, and food additives. Doctors are more certain about the influences of substances such as cholesterol. Cholesterol is contained in eggs, dairy products, and fatty meats. The relation between the level of cholesterol and coronary heart disease is convincing (Dawber, 1980). Though many men and women are able to ingest large amounts of these foods and maintain a normal cholesterol level, others cannot.

Table 14.1   Proper eating patterns

U.S. DIETARY GOALS

1. To avoid overweight, consume only as much energy (calories) as is expendable; if overweight, decrease energy intake and increase energy expenditure.
2. Increase the consumption of complex carbohydrates and "naturally occurring" sugars from about 28% of energy intake to about 48%.
3. Reduce the consumption of refined and processed sugars by about 45% to account for about 10% of total energy intake.
4. Reduce overall fat consumption from approximately 40% to about 30% of energy intake.
5. Reduce unsaturated fat consumption to account for about 10% of total energy intake; and balance that with polyunsaturated and monounsaturated fats, which should account for about 10% of energy intake.
6. Reduce cholesterol consumption to about 300 mg a day.
7. Limit the intake of sodium by reducing the intake of salt to about 5 g a day.

RECOMMENDED SERVINGS FROM EACH FOOD GROUP

Milk and milk products
    Two or more servings daily; examples of one serving dishes include:

1 cup milk
2 slices cheese
1 cup cottage cheese
1 cup yogurt

Meat and meat alternatives
    Two or more 3-ounce servings daily of meat, fish, poultry, or cheese. Eggs, dry beans, peas, nuts, and peanut butter are acceptable alternates.

Fruits and vegetables
    Four or more servings daily, including a citrus fruit or tomato to provide vitamin C. One serving of dark green or yellow or orange vegetable should be eaten every other day for vitamin A.

Bread and cereals
    Four or more servings of whole grain or enriched breads and cereals daily.

SOURCE: From Everly, G. and Rosenfeld, R. *The nature and treatment of the stress response: A practical guide for clinicians.* New York: Plenum Press, 1981, pp. 72, 73, 75. By permission.

While moderate drug use can be relaxing and pleasant, few of us can take in any substance regularly — whether it's tobacco, alcohol, coffee, marijuana, or whatever — without worrying at some time that we may be abusing these substances or becoming dependent. Recognizing this potential problem may stave off serious difficulties. We know, for example, that men who smoke more than a pack a day have coronaries at more than twice the rate of ex-smokers or nonsmokers (U.S. Department of Health, Education, and Welfare, 1979). The short- and long-term effects of immoderate alcohol use range from causing a large percentage of highway fatalities to its contribution to a large number of medical conditions. The cost to the economy of chronic alcoholism is estimated in 1982 at about 42 *billion* dollars (Matarazzo, 1982a).

The final suggestion is maintaining fitness. Included in this category can be relatively simple activities, such as using dental floss regularly, to more complex operations such as proper nutrition and regular, moderate exercise (Matarazzo, 1982; Dawber, 1980). Being fit does not require that we condition ourselves to run the next marathon, but that we have enough regular exercise to remain in reasonable shape for our age and situation.

Insurance companies use many of these six suggestions to predict life expectancy. A prospective client for life insurance might be asked to fill out a questionnaire such as the one shown in Table 14.2. Though experts differ on which questions should be asked and what weight to assign to each response, they all agree that lower stress, following safety precautions, regular medical checkups, keeping weight under control, moderate drug use, and regular exercise are associated with longer life expectancy.

II. Cultivate Hope

Hope is the expectation of something desired. It is the anticipation of future pleasure along with feeling a strong possibility that we may attain it. Few ideals are we so often urged to embrace as hope.

Erikson (1976) makes hope the foundation upon which his scheme of human development proceeds. It is the origin of the adult's faith. Hope plays a role in healing. Positive expectations generate optimistic feelings, energy, and an overall sense of well-being that actually promotes recovery from both physical and mental disorders (Frank, 1974). It is the basis for the placebo effect in which people get over their illnesses after being given a sugar pill by a doctor in whom they have trust. Hope is one of the roots of the belief in God, which results in cripples' abandoning their crutches and walking away from the altar after being blessed by a priest at Lourdes or a faith healer in West Virginia.

The value of hope in stressful times is that it enables us to look difficulty squarely in the eye, bear the stressful feelings, and try to live as fully as possible in spite of them. It has been shown over and over again that people who continue to have hope are less likely to be found among the burnout victims; are more likely to be survivors of prison camps, serious illnesses, and ship wrecks; and are more often able to overcome obstacles in their lives (Pines and Aronson, 1981; Frank, 1974).

Many individuals seem to possess a large measure of hope from their early years. Some of us have experienced something that has been so upsetting as to dampen our usually positive outlook. We have to work hard at cultivating hope. Hope can be achieved by minimizing negative aspects of a stress, putting things in a more positive light, and keeping the faith that somehow we will prevail.

Some of us feel hopeful because of a faith in God. This faith might be sorely tested by tragedy: a child develops cancer, a 20-year-old sister is raped,

Table 14.2   Calculate your life expectancy

- What do you eat?
- How much do you exercise?
- How much do you weigh?
- How safety-conscious are you?
- How well do you control stress?
- How well do you get along with yourself with others?

These are the chief hazards to your personal health, and the chief avenues by which you can reach total wellness in the shortest time. By knowing where you stand in each of these areas, you can change your health practices to prevent simple bad habits from becoming major problems that can cripple your lifestyle and bring you closer to death.

But where do you stand right now? Let's look at how a life insurance company's statistical view might add up your life. We start with the number 72.

Personal data:

If you are male, *subtract 3*.
If you are female, *add 4*.
If you live in an urban area with a population over 2 million, *subtract 2*.
If you live in a town under 10,000 or on a farm, *add 2*.
If a grandparent lived to 85, *add 2*.
If all four grandparents lived to 80, *add 6*.
If either parent died of a stroke or heart attack before age 50, *subtract 4*.
If either parent, brother, or sister under 50 has (or had) cancer or a heart condition, or has had diabetes since childhood, *subtract 3*.
Do you earn over $50,000 a year? *Subtract 2*.
If you finished college, *add 1*. If you have a graduate or professional degree, *add 2* more.
If you are 65 or over and still working, *add 3*.
If you live with a spouse or friend, *add 5*. If not, *subtract 1* for every year alone since age 25.

Healthstyle facts:

If you work behind a desk, *subtract 3*.
If your work requires regular, heavy physical labor, *add 3*.

If you exercise strenuously (tennis, running, swimming, etc.) five times a week for at least a half-hour, *add 4*. Two or three times a week, *add 2*.
Do you sleep more than 10 hours each night? *Subtract 4*.
Are you intense, aggressive, easily angered? *Subtract 3*.
Are you easygoing and relaxed? *Add 3*.
Are you happy? *Add 1*. Unhappy? *Subtract 2*.
Have you had a speeding ticket in the last year? *Subtract 1*.
Do you smoke more than two packs a day? *Subtract 8*. One to two packs? *Subtract 6*. One-half to one? *Subtract 3*.
Do you drink the equivalent of a quart bottle of liquor a day? *Subtract 1*.
Are you overweight by 50 pounds or more? *Subtract 8*. By 30 to 50 pounds? *Subtract 4*. By 10 to 30 pounds? *Subtract 2*.
If you are a man over 40 and have annual checkups, *add 2*.
If you are a woman and see a gynecologist once a year, *add 2*.

Age adjustments:

If you are between 30 and 40, *add 2*.
If you are between 40 and 50, *add 3*.
If you are between 50 and 70, *add 4*.
If you are over 70, *add 5*.

Add up your score to get your life expectancy at this time. How do you compare to the national averages?

AGE NOW	MALE	FEMALE
0–10	69.8	77.2
11–19	70.3	77.5
20–29	71.2	77.8
30–39	71.3	77.9
40–49	73.5	79.4
50–59	76.1	79.0
60–69	80.2	83.6
70–79	85.9	87.7
80–90	90.0	91.1

SOURCE: Allen, R., and Linde, S., *Lifegain: The exciting new program that will change your health — and your life*. Norwalk, CT: Appleton-Century-Crofts. © 1981 by Robert F. Allen. Reprinted with permission.

An accident severely paralyzed Jill Kinmont, a champion skier; but her continuing hopeful outlook has allowed her to build a new life as a high school teacher.

our parents are robbed, a fire in our apartment burns up our uninsured worldly possessions, or we are driven into bankruptcy by a friend who cheats us. How could a God who loves us let this happen? We don't deserve it.

In his book, *When Bad Things Happen to Good People*, Rabbi Harold Kushner (1981) discusses the problem of maintaining faith in the midst of this suffering. Kushner points out that these are the acts of nature, *not* the acts of God. The laws of nature are morally blind, and they don't make exceptions for good people. In Rabbi Kushner's mind, God provides solace, not protection from tragedy. For example, the Old Testament psalmist writes, "I lift mine eyes to the hills; from where does my help come? My help comes from the Lord, maker of heaven and earth" (Psalm 121:1-2). It does *not* say, Kushner notes, "My pain and suffering come from the Lord." The psalm says "My *help* comes from the Lord."

Like hope, the value of religious faith is keeping our mind and spirits strong to endure suffering caused by random or unfair events, to accept limitations tragedy may place on us the rest of our lives, and to appreciate the good things that remain as part of our experience.

III. Take Opportunities for New Experiences

Our growth is to a large degree based on our grappling with novel experiences. From kindergarten onward, every grade in school has been filled with new things to learn. Puberty was brand new. Then there was learning how to drive. Each of these was a fresh challenge. As we master each one, we move on to a life with greater pleasure and productivity.

We know that each of us has our own level of willingness to experience new events. You may be instinctively more venturesome, liking to explore a new city or trying your hand at wilderness survival for 10 days. Your mother, age 55, is delighted at learning how to learn a new dance and is thinking about trying pot. I, on the other hand, may be made nervous by new things, preferring familiar sights and sounds.

Many stagnate because they are unwilling to alter their own status quo (Selye, 1980). The willingness to open ourselves to the unfamiliar can enrich our lives by experiencing ourselves more fully, helping us to master stress, and developing feelings of competence. In doing things that are different and challenging, we experience our life far differently. Thinking about what it might be like to tap dance is quite different than doing it. No drug-induced high can match the feelings of hurtling through space before our parachute opens, reaching the crest after hiking all day, or singing with a group that is in perfect harmony. These experiences ground our emotions in reality. Delight, terror, or joy are not something conjured up on a TV screen. We have lived them.

Each of us has a different degree of interest in pursuing new experiences. Taking these opportunities can improve our short and long term adjustment.

Studies of individuals who score high on tests of sensation-seeking discover that these men and women have a greater tolerance for negative life events and for a wider range of discomfort that those with lower scores (Zuckerman, 1979). In daring to pursue new experiences, we learn how to manage our reactions to unpleasant events, which can result in the ability to deal successfully with problems later in life (Beiser, 1971).

IV. Be in Touch with and Express Emotions

Recognizing our feelings and giving voice to them is associated with higher-level psychological functioning. By the same token, blocking out emotions for long periods can lead to emotional maladjustment. All of us differ as to how likely we are to express mental and physical discomfort and the extent to which we choose to tell someone else about them.

An unfortunate effect of withholding feelings is a lower capacity to feel joy or love. When we do not express one end of our emotional range, we tend to restrict the opposite as well (Freud, 1915). When we do not express feelings of anger, depression, or worry, we are unlikely to feel positive emotions either. In his book, *The Transparent Self,* psychologist Sidney Jourard (1971) makes the point that self-disclosure — the willingness to share what we are feeling with those we care about — is essential to the formation and maintenance of satisfying human relations.

Among older individuals, men who talked more about bothersome ail-

---

Taking Care of Ourselves

I have also learned to respect my psychological needs. Three years ago a workshop group helped me to realize how harried and driven I felt by outside demands — "nibbled to death by ducks" was the way one person put it — and it captured my feelings exactly. So I did what I have never done before; I spent 10 days absolutely alone in a beach cottage which had been offered me, and refreshed myself immensely. I found I thoroughly enjoyed being with me — I *like* me.

I have been more able to ask for help. I ask others to carry things for me, do things for me, instead of "proving" that I can do it myself. I can ask for personal help. When Helen, my wife, was very ill, and I was close to the breaking point from being on call as a twenty-four-hour nurse, a housekeeper, a professional person in much demand, and a writer, I asked for help — and got it from a therapist-friend. I explored and tried to meet my own needs. I explored the strain this period was putting on our marriage. I realized that it was necessary for my survival to live *my* life, and that this must come first, even though Helen was so ill. I am not quick to turn to others, but I am much more aware of the fact that I can't handle everything within myself. In these varied ways, I do a better job of prizing and looking after the person that is me.

SOURCE: Adapted from Rogers, C. Growing old — Or older and growing. *Journal of Humanistic Psychology*, 1980, *20*, 5–16.

ments were in better health than those who said they were fine when they were not (Lowenthal *et al.*, 1976). Finding in general that women complain more about small things than men, psychologists have wondered if one of the reasons for female longevity is that women are more aware of their feelings and express them more often.

Being able to feel distress is also the first step in taking direct action to relieve it. Humanistic psychologist Carl Rogers (1980) tells the story of something he learned in his "older and growing years." He said that he always had been better at taking care of others than of himself. But in his last few years he learned to think about himself, too. In looking after himself, it is clear that Carl Rogers is better able to reach out to those who need him.

V. Define the Not-Me

In the quote by Rogers in the box, one of the points he is conveying is that, at nearly 80, he no longer feels that he has to be responsible for a lot of things he previously managed. He was able to say no. This gave him the freedom to do what mattered most, and was most uniquely him.

From a very different perspective, Erik Erikson makes the point that successful resolution of the stages from adolescence onward depends on the definition of the **Not-Me** (Erikson and Erikson, 1981). For example, no true identity is possible without repudiating some roles — I can't be a Republican unless I am willing to decide to reject being a Democrat. Developing intimacy with one person depends on saying no to other close attachments. In order to be generative, it is necessary to focus our attention on those we care about. This may mean rebuffing others.

As Erikson so rightly observed, many adolescents who are unable to decide among values or attitudes sometimes wind up estranged from all of them. Young adults who can't decide among partners with whom to establish an intimate relationship become alienated and despairing. An older adult who can't reject anything for cause or principle can become self-rejecting. And there are people of all ages who can't seem to decide what *not* to worry about. They are obsessed with the local political scene, the energy crisis, the plight of whales, and the stability of the dollar. But in worrying about everything, they somehow don't give enough attention to those issues most central to their happiness: their work, love, and play, and how they are managing problems in their lives. There is much to be said for establishing a priority list of things about which to worry.

Rather like a black background that allows a white figure to form itself, knowing what we are against helps us decide what we believe in. As former Boston Celtics basketball player Bill Russell put it, "Show me a person with no prejudice and I'll show you a person with no taste" (Russell and Branch, 1979). While our prejudices for something must stop short of bigotry, which can infringe upon the rights of others, knowing what we don't care for permits us to focus our energies on goals in keeping with what *is* central to our identity.

VI. Practice Self-Reliance

In his essay *Self-Reliance,* Ralph Waldo Emerson (1880), a preacher and philosopher from Concord, Massachusetts, wrote that when we are in the company of others, it is easy to follow the opinion of the majority. When we are by ourselves, it is easy to follow our own conscience. It is the exceptional person, however, who is able to follow his or her own conscience in the midst of a crowd. This is **self-reliance.** Emerson went on to point out a characteristic of human nature that psychologists rediscovered over 100 years later: that society, either by pressure from peers or by the demand that we obey authority, tends to stifle individual dissenting voices.

Yet how many times, Emerson wondered, do we regret not having spoken our mind? How many times have we had an intuitive insight running counter to prevailing opinion, and dismissed the thought because it was "merely" our own? Then a few moments later, someone else has said exactly what we were thinking and was praised for the idea. Emerson felt that society advances not because of the common will but on the backs of those whose self-reliance leads

In Montgomery, Alabama, 1956, Martin Luther King, Jr., was booked by the police for leading a bus boycott protesting the company's segregation policy. The self-reliant King pursued his dream of freedom and equality for all Americans in spite of vigorous opposition.

them to discover new worlds, ideas, scientific principles, or ways in which we can live more harmoniously.

Living at about the same time in Concord was a man who practiced the self-reliance Emerson preached: Henry David Thoreau. Thoreau decided to live simply in a small hut by the shore of nearby Walden Pond, from 1845 to 1847. His book, *Walden* (1854), about these experiences, emphasizes the doctrine of simplicity and escape from the complications of urban existence. In a now-famous passage about following one's own convictions, Thoreau (1854, p. 347) stated: "If a man does not keep pace with his companions, perhaps it is because he hears a different drummer. Let him step to the music which he hears."

Marching to his own drummer, Thoreau once refused on principle to pay his poll tax. As a result he was put in jail. A story is told that Ralph Waldo Emerson visited Thoreau in jail and asked, "Henry, why are you here?" Thoreau is said to have replied, "Waldo, why are you *not* here!" (Stern, 1970). Thoreau was exceedingly upset when a relative paid his poll tax so that he remained behind bars for only one night.

Feeling robbed of the chance to put the poll tax to legal test, he wrote an article that was to have world-wide influence. It was called "Civil Disobedience" (1849). Mohandas Gandhi, the man who led the passive resistance of the Indians against the British colonial rule after World War II, was greatly influenced by Thoreau's writing. As he was leading the civil rights marches, Martin Luther King, Jr., said that he and his people were heir to the legacy of Thoreau's creative dissent (Stern, 1970). Doubtless the students protesting the Vietnam War in the late 1960s would have agreed.

One of the strongest forces acting against self-reliance is the feeling of futility. "What good will it do?" we say to ourselves. "I'm just one person. Everyone is either against me or doesn't care." In these moments we might take heart from others who have felt the same way but found that, when acted upon, the power of an individual conscience can be a considerable force in replacing reflexive submissiveness to society and compliance to authority with obedience to an inner voice.

VII. See the Future as a Series of Nows

In his short story "The Beast in the Jungle," Henry James (1903), novelist brother of William, tells the story of a young man, John Marcher, who feels something rare and wonderful, perhaps even strange and terrible will happen to him eventually.

The only other person he tells about this is a young woman, Mary Bartram, who is in love with him. Though he feels strongly for Mary, John can't marry her because he feels he must be ready to meet this fate, which he sees waiting, ready to spring at him like a beast in the jungle. You don't take a lady on a tiger hunt, is how he rationalizes not wedding Mary.

Years pass. John travels the world awaiting the awesome event, but nothing happens. Eventually both grow old and Mary dies. John feels her loss keenly and visits her grave regularly. One day he sees another man weeping at the freshly dug graveside of his wife. Suddenly John is overwhelmed with anguish as he recognizes how much he loved Mary. He also becomes aware that while waiting for the awesome future event, he had forfeited the joys he could have had sharing his life with the only person he had ever loved.

By being so focused on the future, John Marcher lived outside of his present life. Like John, many individuals overlook the potential of the here-and-now because their attention is riveted on the years to come. We see this among industrious high-school students working night and day to get into a "good college." We witness it in pre-meds who are too busy to do anything but study so they can eventually be admitted to medical school. We can observe it in the budding workaholic who is too preoccupied to spend time with family. Though there is much to be said for delaying gratification, we should not live so much for some distant time that we do not partake of enjoyment now.

It is also true that, like John Marcher, the joys we anticipate in the future may not be worth what we gave up along the way. Further, sometimes when we put off eventual happiness, we tend to think that it will all be worth it when we achieve our future goal. As soon as we get into college, are accepted into medical school, or make partner, we will experience all the joy we sacrificed — with twenty percent interest. This almost never happens. The depression or bitterness that some people feel when they finally achieve their long-sought goal is often based on the realization that what they have given up is gone.

Like a movie film, our lives are connected to the future by frames of now. Though we need to pay attention to the continuity of our life span and not seriously disrupt the flow of our lives by compromising the years ahead for current gratification, we should recognize the opportunity for joy and happiness that each dawn brings with it.

VIII. Resow the Seeds of Love

As we grow, the stability of our loving relationships is increasingly a criterion for the success of our emotional adjustment. Yet loss of loved ones through death, moving, or alienation is one hardship all of us have in common. We will do well, therefore, to heed the maxim that we must resow the seeds of love for as long as we live (Vaillant, 1977).

Three obstacles hinder making new friends: shyness, estrangement, and getting older. Shy people often have the same feelings of learned helplessness described in Chapter 2. Individuals who are shy frequently have feelings of inferiority — a deep-seated sense of deficiency. This can be because of pimples or crooked teeth, social ineptness, slowness of wit, or feelings that our morals and values are different from everyone else's (Allport, 1961). One study of college students found that about ninety percent of them reported feeling inferior at one point or another (McKee and Sherriff, 1957).

Most people who are separated from old friends are able to overcome feelings of shyness or inferiority on their own. They grit their teeth and launch

The seeds of love must be re-sown all through life.

themselves into situations where they can meet people informally. Or they make up their own program such as was described in Chapter 7, page 210. Others benefit from social skills training, which applies behavioral and cognitive learning techniques to helping people meet others. These services are a fundamental part of most comprehensive mental health facilities (Liberman and Reigen, 1979). Short courses usually are offered in community adult education programs. One course is often entitled "What Do You Say After You've Said Hello?"

Resowing the seeds of love can also include overcoming estrangement from former friends. Earlier in Chapter 7, we considered the value of forgiveness as an antidote to estrangement. There are, of course, legitimate reasons that can bring close relationships to an end. But it is sad to see old friendships wrenched apart by a momentary lapse or misunderstanding. We have so few old friends, and they mean so much to us because of the memories we share with them and no one else, that we are definitely poorer when we allow ourselves to become alienated.

As we grow older, our pool of friends shrinks because we lose people and do not replace them. Though it is difficult to make younger friends, the value of establishing affectionate bonds with the generation that succeeds us is good insurance against an old age of loneliness.

IX. Develop a Sense of Humor

The ancient Greek physician and sage Hippocrates said that the clown does more for a community than twenty asses laden with medicine. Among the qualities we welcome most in another person is a sense of **humor.** This is one of the most important adaptive aspects of human beings. A sense of humor can be a high-level self-protective response that allows us to view a stressful event clearly but relieve the pain by wittiness. Humor allows us to call a spade a spade without too much discomfort or unpleasantly affecting others (Vaillant, 1977).

Mark Twain observed that the source of humor is sorrow, not joy (Clemens, 1894). He was only partially right, however. A sense of humor also serves to promote fellowship, relieve tension, and vent anger. We've all been to parties where a large component of the enjoyment has been laughing together at the jokes, puns, or parodies of teachers and bosses, or other witty remarks made by the people there.

A humorous comment injected at the proper moment can quickly deflate growing tension or embarrassment (White, 1972). A young man with a poor academic record was being interviewed for a job after graduation. When the discussion got around to his grades, there was an unpleasant silence. At that point, the young man made everyone feel better when he remarked, "I was in that half of the class that made the top half possible!" When the Associated Press erroneously reported the death of Mark Twain, their embarrassment was greatly relieved when they received a cable saying, "The reports of my death are greatly exaggerated."

Humor is valuable in providing an acceptable outlet for hostility. Usually this involves veiling aggression in witticism. Freud (1909) gives the example of two crooked businessmen who wanted to become socially acceptable. They decided that the best way was to have their pictures painted by a famous artist and then invite the leading citizens of the community to a large party where these paintings would be displayed. Among the guests was a prominent art critic. The two men asked him what he thought of the pictures hanging side by side. The critic thought to himself, "You're both thieves but I can't say that or you'll have me thrown out of the party." The critic bent forward, focused his eyes on the space between the two pictures, and exclaimed, "And where is Jesus?" By this comment the critic suggested that they were like the two criminals who hung on crosses on each side of Jesus when he was crucified.

On a less subtle note is the story told about Winston Churchill and Lady Nancy Astor. At a meal with several others, Churchill and Lady Astor began to argue ferociously. Finally Lady Astor said to the great statesman, "Winston, if I was married to you I'd put poison in your coffee." Without missing a beat, Churchill replied, "If I was married to you, Nancy, I'd drink it" (Sykes, 1972, p. 127).

This nineteenth-century print depicts the legendary hero Don Quixote de la Mancha. His quest in the face of over-powering opposition has come to symbolize the universal struggle to realize a dream.

X. Value the Struggle

As the words of "The Impossible Dream" tell us dramatically, the richness of life comes largely from the quest, the struggle to attain our dream. You and I may differ as to how hard we are willing to fight, how many wounds we are willing to endure, or how far into hell we will go in pursuit of our star. But it is through this pursuit that we grow and become more than we have been. To struggle is to live (Dubos, 1968).

The enjoyment of life can be measured only partially by what we achieve. American humanistic psychologists believe that our uniqueness as individuals depends on the choices we make between the conflicting desires to remain in the secure status quo and the need to move forward to greater self-realization (Maslow, 1967). Within each of us, an inner struggle occurs between the impulse to preserve what has been gained by taking no risks in the quest for something beyond what we have (Weisskopf, 1959). Being willing to struggle means taking responsibility for our actions and making choices. We all have our ways of avoiding taking responsibility to act: we are too busy with other things, we let others struggle for us, we view ourselves as innocent of events we can't control, or we imagine someone who will somehow make everything all right (Yalom, 1980).

While realistic limits do exist — physical handicaps, poverty, or malevolent others — our attitude toward these limitations can determine whether we will give up and be defeated by them or continue to try to find a way to put together a life of purpose in spite of them.

To struggle also means making choices to act. We almost always have some freedom of choice to act, even in the most desperate circumstances. Psychiatrist Allen Wheelis (1973) gives an example:

> Look at the wretched people huddled in line for the gas chambers at Auschwitz. If they do anything other than move on quietly, they will be clubbed down. Where is the freedom? . . . But wait. Go back in time, enter the actual event, the very moment: they are thin and weak, and they smell; hear the weary shuffling steps, the anguished catch of breath, the clutch of hand. Enter now the head of one hunched and limping man. The line moves slowly . . . he sees the sign, someone whispers "showers," but he knows what happens here. He is struggling with a choice: to shout "Comrades! They will kill you! Run!" — or to say nothing. This option, in the few moments remaining, is his whole life. If he shouts he dies now, painfully; if he moves on silently he dies but minutes later. Looking back on him in time and memory, we find the moment poignant but the freedom negligible. It makes no difference in that situation, his election of daring or of inhibition. Both are futile, without consequence. History sees no freedom for him, notes only constraint, labels him victim. But in the consciousness of that one man it makes great differences whether or not he experiences the choice. For if . . . "Nothing is possible," then he is living his necessity; but if, perceiving the constraint, he turns from it to a choice between two possible courses of action, then — however he chooses — he is living his freedom. This commitment to freedom may extend to the last breath.

As human beings, we are never without choice. Even when we feel that we are faced with something — death, illness, divorce, age — we know we cannot change, we still have the choice of deciding our attitude toward that unchangeable "thing." With acceptance or bitterness, with courage or fear, we can choose how we will face life's inevitable stresses. In every situation and for every one of us, a realm of freedom exists for us to quest for something of value. And as we get older, many of us will find that the "something of value" has become the struggle itself.

Epilogue

Let us return now to the question with which we opened this chapter: if you were writing your obituary, what would you say about yourself to assess the quality of your life? To what would you point as evidence about whether your life had been happy and productive? This may seem like an awfully gloomy subject with which to end a book about living. Yet recognizing that none of us gets out of here alive can motivate us to ask ourselves how we want to spend the years that we have to live. Each of us has our own individual answers to these questions, but it's hard to improve on the guidance of Rabbi Hillel two thousand years ago (Herford, 1962):

If I am not for myself, who will be?
But if I am only for myself, what good am I?
And if not now, when?

Summary

1. Ten guidelines for living include
   I. Care for the body
   II. Cultivate hope
   III. Take opportunities for new experiences
   IV. Be in touch with and express emotions
   V. Define the Not-Me
   VI. Practice self-reliance
   VII. See the future as a series of nows
   VIII. Resow the seeds of love
   IX. Develop a sense of humor
   X. Value the struggle
2. Thinking about the inevitability of death can help us determine how we wish to spend the years we have to live.

Key Terms

dietary goals   self-reliance
hope   humor
not-me

Suggested Readings

Physical care

U.S. Department of Health, Education and Welfare, Public Health Service. *Healthy people: The Surgeon General's report on health promotion and disease prevention.* Washington, D.C.: U.S. Government Printing Office, 1979.

Johnson, G., and Goldfinger, S. (Eds.), *The Harvard Medical School Health Letter Book.* Cambridge, Mass.: Harvard University Press, 1981.

Practical advice for staying healthy.

Marching to your own drummer

Emerson, R. *Essays.* (1847) Boston: Houghton Mifflin, Riverside Library, 1980.

Milgram, S. *Obedience to authority.* New York: Harper & Row, 1974.

Reading these back-to-back brings out the value and the difficulty in following our own conscience.

Resowing love

Vaillant, G. *Adaptation to life*. Boston: Little, Brown, 1977. Chapters 12, 14, and 16.

Levinson, D., with Darrow, C., Klein, E., Levinson, M., and McKee, B. *Seasons of a man's life*. New York: Knopf, 1978.

> Loving relationships, essential to normal adaptation, require continuing maintenance throughout life.

Self-realization

Wheelis, A. *How people change*. New York: Harper & Row, 1973.

Fromm, E. *The revolution of hope: Toward a humanized technology*. New York: Bantam, 1971.

Rogers, C. *A way of being*. Boston: Houghton Mifflin, 1980.

> The fullness of our growth is largely a function of our willingness to struggle with difficult choices.

Glossary

A-B-C model of faulty thinking Presumed by Ellis to be responsible for continuing emotional distress. **A** is a stress in our lives; **B** is how we think about the event; and **C** is our resulting emotions and behavior.

actions Large-scale, simple, everyday behaviors that reflect overall adjustment.

active personality A personality style that is energetic, on the move, and needing something to be enthusiastic about.

adaptation A continuing process of maintaining inner harmony while fitting into an average, expectable environment without undue compromise.

adjustment mechanisms High-level, self-protective responses. They permit awareness of the stress, a fluid reappraisal of the reaction to it, are present and future oriented, and allow people to lower inner tension without significantly compromising other areas of living.

aesthetic orientation According to Spranger, attitudes possessed by people who value anything that enriches the subjective experience.

age-related events Physical and social experiences that happen to people of similar age at about the same time and in the same way, and that influence their development.

aggressive reaction An urge to attack the agent of frustration.

alarm reaction The first phase of Selye's General Adaptation Syndrome — a reaction to a sudden or unfamiliar stressful event, characterized by disrupting anxiety, fear, depression, or mental disorganization.

altruism Renouncing one's own desires and replacing them with someone else's needs or the demands of a higher calling.

ambivert A person with an exact balance of extraversion and introversion.

anal stage In psychoanalytic theory, referring to the second and third years of life when the focus is on pleasure coming from bowel control in response to parental pleasure in toilet training.

androgen The hormone that causes and maintains the development of secondary sexual features in males.

anorexia nervosa An eating disorder characterized by self-starvation.

anticipation A high-level self-protective response, this adjustment mechanism works by predicting the influence of current choices on the future.

anticipatory fear Worrying about a stress in advance.

anxiety Uneasiness, apprehension, or tension.

anxiety disorder A disorder in which anxiety is the primary symptom.

approach-approach conflict Stress caused by having to choose between two agreeable but mutually exclusive alternatives.

approach-avoidance conflict Stress caused by

having to choose between alternatives that are simultaneously attractive and unattractive.

arousal   In play, the need to seek an optimal level of excitement or interest that is not provided by loving and working.

artistic occupations   Work that attracts people who are aesthetically motivated and seeking expression of their sensitivity.

attention deficit disorder   Characterized chiefly by short attention span and impulsiveness.

aversive conditioning   A type of behavioral therapy that works by attaching a negative reaction to a specific temptation in an effort to establish resistance to the temptation.

avoidance-avoidance conflict   Stress caused by having to choose between equally undesirable options.

balance in work, love, and play   The capacity to obtain satisfaction from each of these spheres without compromising pleasure from another. Each of us develops our own personal balance.

bargaining   A stage in Kübler-Ross's theory of crisis reaction involving an offer to change one's behavior in an attempt to restore the equilibrium before a crisis. An example is a little girl who promises to be "good" if her separating parents will agree to stay together.

behavioral disorders   A maladjustment in children and adolescents featuring actions inappropriate for a young person's chronological age. An example is short attention span.

best friend   An intimate, same-sex relationship usually found among preadolescent youngsters.

biofeedback   Learning to control physical states such as hand temperature through displays of information on sensitive recording devices.

biological model   A view of the life cycle that assumes that psychological growth proceeds in the same way as physical development: stages unfold in a predictable sequence; they begin and end at approximate ages; each stage contains growth tasks essential to that era and no other; the stages are irreversible; and they apply to everyone.

bulimarexia   Binge-eating followed by vomiting, laxatives, or suppositories either to reduce discomfort or to control undesirable weight gain.

bulimia   An eating disorder characterized by un-

controlled binge-eating to the point of discomfort.

burnout   Wearing oneself out and exhausting physical and mental resources by excessive striving to fulfill unrealistic expectations imposed by oneself or by the larger society.

career   A sequence of jobs, positions, or occupations throughout a working life.

carry-over skill   Successfully coping with a stress develops the ability to manage future difficulties.

catharsis   The purging of built-up tensions and stress emotions, restoring one to a placid and relaxed state.

choleric temperament   An irascible temperament.

client-centered therapy   A humanistic form of nondirective therapy developed by Carl Rogers that is guided by the principle of unconditional positive regard.

cognitive learning theory   A theory that holds that how we interpret our immediate physical and emotional reactions to a stressor determines whether we will continue to feel the same way.

compensation   In play, leisure that provides an opportunity for counterbalancing occupational activities which may be specialized, sedentary, or boring.

competence   The pleasure in being able to make something happen.

conditioned reflex   Learning that occurs when a neutral stimulus is paired with another stimulus that elicits a response. Eventually the neutral stimulus elicits the same response. An example is a bell that is rung when a dog is about to be fed: eventually the dog will salivate at the sound of the bell even without the food.

conduct disorders   Characterized by actions of children or adolescents that violate rights of other people or of society in ways that are more serious than ordinary mischief.

conflict   Stress resulting from the presence of two competing but mutually exclusive courses of action.

conscious (awareness)   In psychoanalytic theory, those behaviors, thoughts, desires, and recollections that one is presently aware of.

contra-intentional suicide   Acts of suicide in

which a person does not intend to die but rather to signal unhappiness in the hope of attracting attention and support from others.

controlled personality A personality style mainly concerned with keeping things regulated and predictable.

conventional occupations Work that is characterized by orderliness, working within a chain of command, and dealing with specific, clear-cut problems.

coping devices Middle-level, self-protective responses. Coping devices are triggered by more than usual stress, permitting greater recognition of unsettling emotions and the events causing them. Their major problem is that they do not allow for much reappraisal, and their orientation is primarily in the present. When the stress is over, coping devices usually disappear until the next time they are needed.

counterphobic behavior Handling anxiety feelings by doing what is disliked or feared.

crisis reaction A series of responses to a sudden event, a wearing-down process, or an unwelcome but inevitable life-cycle transition. Usually the person feels that major changes occur in a short time; the changes are seen as having undesirable lasting future impact; and they negatively affect large areas of life. Crises may last from a few weeks to more than six months.

crisis symbol The Japanese symbol for crisis comprises two characters. The first symbolizes danger and the second, opportunity.

critical incidents Environmental or physical events occurring unpredictably that profoundly shape our growth. These can occur within any culture and at any time in a person's life.

cross-sectional studies Studies that look at people at one period of their lives and compare them with similar individuals at other stages.

cyclothymic disorders Depressive states alternating regularly with unusually active behavior, often characterized by high energy, extreme optimism, recklessness, or lack of inhibition.

denial A low-level self-protective response, this ego defense works by rejecting the existence of an unmistakeable threatening reality or the consequences of that reality.

depression Complex of feelings that can include helplessness, low self-esteem, and an inner sense of deserving whatever bad things happen.

depressive disorders Characterized by long periods of feeling sad, blue, or low.

dietary goals Recommended patterns of eating to maintain health.

direct action responses High-level adaptive responses involving recognition of the source of stress and taking action to change it.

direct control response Middle-level adaptive responses that reduce psychological and/or physical reactions to stress, but doing nothing to affect the cause.

disorders of childhood and adolescence Emotionally-based problems noticeable prior to adulthood that are not momentary developmental difficulties, but rather are continuing disorders. They can cause considerable, prolonged periods of unhappiness for the individual as well as for involved adults.

dissociative disorders Sudden, temporary alteration in normal awareness, behavior patterns, or sense of self.

downward drift The tendency for people with serious emotional problems to slide to the bottom of the socioeconomic ladder because of inability to obtain and hold good jobs.

dream A view of the way the world is, how people are, a sense of self, a specific goal, or a continuity of purpose.

drug use disorders Undesirable behavioral changes associated with regular use of substances that affect the central nervous system.

DSM-III The third edition of the *Diagnostic and Statistical Manual of Mental Disorders*, published by the American Psychiatric Association. It catalogs emotional disorders.

dual careers Both members in a marriage concerned with advancing in their occupations.

eating disorders Characterized by gross disturbance in eating patterns, including anorexia nervosa, bulimarexia, and bulimia.

economic orientation According to Spranger, attitudes possessed by people who are drawn to activities or ideas that contribute to self-protection and the enterprise of accumulating wealth.

ego In psychoanalytic theory, that part of the personality which organizes the personality to meet the requirements of the outer world and to mediate between the competing forces of the id and the superego.

ego defenses   Low-level self-protective responses that guard us from awareness of alien thoughts and emotions by automatically blocking them out of our awareness.

Elder Hostel   An international program for individuals 60 and older to take week-long mini-courses in a variety of subjects in colleges and secondary schools.

Elektra complex   In psychoanalytic theory, referring to the girl's erotic feelings toward the father and jealousy of the mother.

empathy   A high-level self-protective response, this adjustment mechanism works by allowing a person to sense how others feel or think without being aware of making an effort to do so.

enterprising occupations   Work that consists of tasks that involve management, sales, and adventurous activities.

enuresis   Bed wetting.

esteem needs   According to Maslow, the need to have self-respect, to feel useful, and to demonstrate competence in one's life.

estrogen   The hormone that causes and maintains the development of secondary sexual features in females.

exhaustion   The third phase of Selye's General Adaptation Syndrome, continued exposure to stress, wears down resistance until exhaustion sets in and feelings of hopelessness and apathy are evident.

extravert   An individual who is objective, positive, pragmatic, outgoing, conventional, team-oriented, and dominant.

fantasy   A middle-level self-protective response, this coping device works when the individual imagines the venting of stress emotions in imagined ways because the real ways are closed off.

fear of success   The motive to avoid success because of expected negative consequences following successful achievement.

field dependence   A condition in which a person looks to his or her environment to provide more than the usual clues to understand and deal with problems.

friendship   Two or more people who are neither lovers nor relatives, joined together in a benevolent bond that may range from casual relationship to intense intimacy.

frustration   The discomfort caused by environmental forces that prevent or delay the expression of desired behavior.

gender identity disorders   Characterized by persistent unhappiness with one's own gender, and a desire to live as a member of the opposite sex.

general adaptation syndrome   A model developed by Hans Selye intended to describe physiological and psychological reaction patterns to stress, consisting of three phases — alarm, resistance, and exhaustion.

generativity   Erikson's term for blending procreation, productivity, and creativity.

genital stage   In psychoanalytic theory, the period of life beginning with approximately the teenage years, in which the adolescent gradually learns to control inner impulses for sexual satisfaction and to love others, and begins to think about getting a job, settling down, and raising a family.

Gray Panthers   The national organization of senior citizens that coordinates service and lobbies for political support of older individuals.

habits   Automatic, repetitive behavior patterns requiring no new learning or acts of will to carry out.

historical influences   Occurrences such as a depression, epidemic, or war that affect everyone within a specific culture. They may trigger significant changes in personal development.

histrionic personality   A personality style that is dramatic and impressionable, likely to be characterized by strong reactions to events, great enthusiasm, and intuitiveness.

holistic functioning   The behavior and mental activity of a person taken as a whole and not as the sum of separate parts.

homeostasis   A condition of maintaining or restoring physical equilibrium in the face of external or internal stress.

hope   Desire combined with the expectation of its realization.

humor   The ability to be amused by frustration

or the contrast between pretense and performance in one's self and in others.

hyperventilation　A physical condition in which too much carbon dioxide is exhaled, resulting in dizziness, numbness, tingling, and feelings of faintness.

id　In psychoanalytic theory, the part of the personality that houses impulses for gratification that are the major source of emotional energy.

ideal perspective (of normality)　A positive statement about what robust mental health should be.

idealistic love　Involves altruism and a passionate concern with an abstract concept; for example, protection of all life, fervent desire to help the needy, or love of nature.

identification　A high-level self-protective response, this adjustment mechanism involves a selective process of assuming characteristics of those seen as admirable.

identity　The feeling of who one is and who one is not, the values and behaviors one embraces and those one rejects, and the sense of what one wants to do with the next portion of one's life.

intentional suicide　Suicidal acts characterized by the lack of ambivalence about killing oneself.

intimacy　The link between two people characterized by close and confidential communication through nonverbal as well as verbal channels.

introvert　A person who is subjectively oriented, has difficulty finding ideals to guide living, may be stubborn, and is inwardly oriented, unconventional, individualistic, and aloof.

intrusiveness　One of the middle stages of Horowitz's theory of crisis reactions: the penetration into consciousness of desperately painful feelings associated with the loss that precipitated the crisis reaction.

investigative occupations　Work attracting people whose interests center around science and scientific activities, who are task-oriented and not especially drawn to work with other people.

job　A task or responsibility within an organization performed by one person.

Life Change Unit　A measure of the relative amount of readjustment required to manage a stressful event on the Social Readjustment Rating Scale.

life cycle　A way of looking at a human life and breaking it up into specific periods of time, each of which is characterized by particular events associated with that stage.

Life Experience Inventory　A questionnaire for measuring stress. It asks the individual taking the test to rate the impact of a stressful event numerically on a seven-point scale ranging from positive to negative.

longitudinal studies　Studies that follow the same group of subjects for a long period of time; for example, from adolescence to the later adult years.

love　A special type of relationship with another that is characterized by a feeling of warm affection and desire for attachment.

love and belonging needs　According to Maslow, the desire to be the object of affection by others — parents, relatives, friends, and special loved ones.

maximum effective stress tolerance　The greatest amount of stress an individual can stand before performance begins to deteriorate.

maximal heart rate　The number 220, minus a person's age. Exercise at less than 70 percent of the maximal heart rate loses some of its value in developing cardiovascular fitness. Exercise driving the pulse beyond 85 percent of the maximal heart rate brings unnecessary stress and no further improvement in fitness.

melancholic temperament　A serious or gloomy temperament.

mental health perspective (of normality)　Normality defined as the absence of illness.

mentor　Levinson's term for an individual, usually an older man or woman at the workplace, who helps a younger person by serving as teacher, sponsor, host, guide, exemplar, and/or counselor.

modeling　A form of learning that involves imitating the responses of others.

mood disorder　A significant disturbance of mood, whether of depression or elation.

moral anxiety　The sense of anxious guilt that we are likely to be punished or humiliated if we act on an inner desire, even though it may be entirely appropriate at that time.

moral judgment The ethical standards we use to justify our behavior. These range from a desire to avoid punishment to the inner drive to conform to universal ethical principles.

multiple personality The existence of two or more distinct, relatively full-operational personalities within the same person.

negative reinforcement Removing an aversive stimulus when a desired response is achieved.

neurotic anxiety Arises from the apprehension that an impulse will slip its controls, resulting in undesirable consequences. It does not stem from the stress itself, but from leftover childhood remembrances.

neurotic disorders Persistent disabling behaviors, thoughts, or emotions that are not connected to a cause and are clearly excessive. They themselves become a source of stress.

normal adaptation The capacity to find satisfaction from a balance of work, love, and play, in the presence of high-level adaptive responses to stress.

normal curve A bell-shaped curve describing normal distribution.

normal distribution Test scores of a large group of individuals cluster in the middle, with a smaller number that are higher or lower. A graph of these scores is bell-shaped.

not-me The repudiation of some values, positions, and identities in order to have a firmer sense of one's self.

occupation A classification of work, usually based upon an economic or psychological perspective.

Oedipus complex In psychoanalytic theory, the boy's erotic feelings toward and jealousy of the father.

oppositional disorders Feature persistent, negative, or provocative behavior toward authority figures.

optimistic personality A personality style characterized by hopefulness.

oral stage In psychoanalytic theory, referring largely to the first year of life in which most of the infant's pleasures come from the mouth.

orgasmic dysfunction Chronic inability of a female to achieve climax during sexual relations.

orientation to reality This is assessed by determining whether someone is aware of time, place, person, and situation.

outcry The initial stage of a crisis reaction.

Overeaters Anonymous Patterned after Alcoholics Anonymous, this is a self-help group designed to enable people to control obesity.

personal effectiveness A strategy for improving ability to combat stress by obtaining objective performance data, modeling the behavior of others, seeking the persuasion of others, and interpreting certain reactions to stress accurately.

personality accentuation The intensification of certain useful and functional personality traits during a temporary overload condition.

personality style Consistency of functioning over broad areas of human behavior that remain stable for a lengthy period of time.

pessimistic personality A personality style characterized by preparation for disappointment, focusing on uncertainties and sufferings, limitations and paradoxes, and having a sense of the tragic or heroic.

phallic stage In psychoanalytic theory, covering the years from about three to five, during which the child gradually realizes pleasure coming from his or her sexual organs.

phlegmatic temperament A placid or cool temperament.

phobia Strong fear of an object or situation is the primary feature.

physical disorders A maladjustment in children and adolescents featuring frequent involuntary bodily actions causing great distress, such as stuttering.

physiological needs According to Maslow, needs that must be met to support life itself: oxygen, water, food, shelter, activity, and rest.

play An activity characterized by lack of obligation, freedom from the necessity for high achievement, and malleability.

pleasure principle According to psychoanalytic theory, the single purpose driving the id, seeking gratification for impulses such as the need for food and the release of sexual tension or anger.

pluralistic model A conception of human growth that combines biological age-related and historical events as well as critical instances, all of which can affect the course of life.

political orientation   According to Spranger, the orientation of people who seek power.

positive reinforcement   Waiting for someone to make a desirable response and then rewarding it.

POSSLQ   An acronym meaning *P*erson of the *O*pposite *S*ex *S*haring *L*iving *Q*uarters.

post-traumatic stress disorder   Following psychological trauma, a re-experiencing of some aspects of the event, a feeling of numbness and reduced involvement with the outside world, hyperalertness, guilt about surviving, or over-reaction to events that recall the stressful experience.

preconscious   In psychoanalytic theory, those behaviors, thoughts, desires, and recollections that are in the twilight of awareness and can be brought into consciousness if our attention is directed to them.

premature ejaculation   Male climax just before or shortly after penetration during sexual intercourse.

prickly personality   A personality style characterized chiefly by an inclination to irascibility and a tendency to play the devil's advocate.

primary bond   A mutual commitment of affection, support, and sharing of future plans.

primary impotence   Chronic inability for a male to achieve an erection.

problem-solving therapy   A cognitive approach to therapy oriented toward helping individuals develop systematic and effective procedures for solving their problems.

progressive muscle relaxation   A system for achieving relaxation by alternately clenching and relaxing groups of muscles in the body.

projection   A low-level self-protective response. This ego defense works by assigning unacceptable urges to others. Two types of projection are found: seeing in others those desires that cannot be faced in the self, and seeing others as being critical of alien desires that cannot be acknowledged.

psychiatrist   A medical doctor specializing in mental disorders. Training involves a medical degree and at least three years of specialized training in psychiatry. A psychiatrist uses many types of treatment; it is the only counseling

profession legally entitled to prescribe drugs or administer electroconvulsive or other physical treatment. As physicians, they can admit patients to general and psychiatric hospitals.

psychoanalytic theory   A system of theories of personality developed by Sigmund Freud. It emphasizes the idea that personality results from the interplay between the opposing forces of the id, superego, and ego. According to psychoanalytic theory, early childhood experiences and intrapsychic conflicts and processes have a large part in explaining adult behavior.

psychologists   Clinical, counseling, and school psychologists are active in the diagnosis and treatment of mental disorders. Most have a doctoral degree, following the receipt of a bachelor's degree from college. One to two additional years of training are required. To be licensed, in most states psychologists must have several more years of experience. Psychologists are trained to administer and interpret psychological tests.

psychosexual disorders   Characterized by dysfunction in the sexual area, in the absence of an organic cause.

psychosexual dysfunctions   Disorders that occur at one or more segments of the sexual response cycle, manifesting themselves either in inhibited desire, difficulty with sexual excitement, impotence, or achieving orgasm, due to delay or absence of climax.

psychosocial moratorium   Erikson's term for a period in youth in which a person takes time out from school or work to do something entirely different, while forming a clearer sense of identity.

rationalization   A middle-level self-protective response, this coping device works by avoidance of certain important distasteful truths while being aware, in part, of their existence.

reaction formation   A low-level self-protective response, this coping device operates when the person behaves in a manner directly opposite to a strong, undesirable feeling.

realistic occupations   Work that attracts people whose interests are practical and outdoors-oriented.

reality anxiety   Tension in reaction to stressful events in the real world.

reality principle Reconciling inner desires with the demands of the environment. Usually this involves the delay of gratification of needs until an appropriate time when it is not costly to the individual or others.

reinforcement Shaping behavior by responding to some actions and ignoring others.

relaxation Shutting down a stimulating input, enabling tensions and other stress emotions to dissipate, and permitting recuperation to begin.

relaxation response A direct control response for coping with stress. One technique involves sitting quietly in a comfortable position, closing the eyes, and relaxing the muscles while repeating a particular word silently with each breath.

religious orientation According to Spranger, the orientation of people who value striving for unity with an absolute immortal all-embracing God.

repression A low-level self-protective response, this ego defense operates by one's unconsciously blocking thoughts or feelings that would cause anxiety if they entered the level of awareness.

repressor A person who tends to avoid and deny feelings.

resistance The second phase of Selye's General Adaptation Syndrome — a stage of coping with a sudden or unfamiliar stressful event resulting in a higher level of functioning.

resources Anything we can call upon to cushion the effects of frustrations, bad news, loss, and/or provide compensating positive experiences.

rituals Repetitive actions that help individuals manage a temporary overload condition.

romantic love Love characterized by the blending of sexual desire with caring, attachment, and intimacy.

safety needs According to Maslow, the need to be guarded against physical harm.

sanguine temperament A cheerful temperament.

satisfaction (from work, love, and play) Reasonable pleasure or the absence of displeasure from these domains.

SCIENCE An acronym made up of the first letters of the seven steps in a cognitive learning approach to dealing with stress developed by Mahoney.

secondary impotence Chronic difficulty for a male to maintain an erection during sexual intercourse.

self-actualization needs According to Maslow, the ongoing fulfillment of potentials, capacities, talents, or mission (or a call, fate, destiny, or vocation), as a fuller knowledge of, and acceptance of, a person's own intrinsic nature and as an unceasing trend toward unity, integration, or synergy within the person.

self-concept Our view of ourselves, which generally includes the self as an object — what we think of ourselves and of the self as a doer — our activities.

self-esteem How much we value ourselves.

self-limiting Symptoms that disappear of their own accord.

self-management A strategy for coping with stress emotions. One example of the self-management of depression involves self-monitoring, understanding the immediate and long-term consequences of events, overcoming distortions about the causes of events, setting realistic goals, and positive self-reinforcement.

self-objectification The ability to perceive the incongruities between one's own stated values and intentions and how one really acts.

self-protective response One kind of adaptive response — automatic mental processes that go to work before we realize it, to reduce distress.

self-reliance The ability to follow one's own conscience in the midst of others.

sensation-seeking scale This measure combines four types of desire for sensory input: adventure seeking, experience seeking, disinhibition, and boredom susceptibility.

sensitizor A person who is relatively open to feelings.

separation anxiety A fear of leaving the mother and home and entering a new environment. A common phobia in young people.

sexual desire Intense genital drives that press increasingly for release through ejaculation and orgasm.

sexual perversions Characterized by the requirement of bizarre mental images or acts to achieve sexual pleasure.

sharpening An aspect of field dependence characterized by over-concern about small gradations of choice.

signal anxiety A small amount of anxiety that triggers ego defenses without awareness or volition.

16PF Test A paper-and-pencil personality test measuring sixteen separate personality factors.

social occupations Work attracting people who are humanistically oriented and concerned about the welfare of others.

social orientation According to Spranger, the orientation of people for whom loving others above anything else is the most important value.

Social Readjustment Rating Scale A numerical rank ordering of major sources of stress according to severity, developed by Holmes-Rahe.

social workers This designation includes psychiatric and other types of social work. Social workers are trained in behavioral sciences and in the diagnosis and treatment of mental disorders. They are college graduates who have taken additional studies leading to a master's degree, and, in some cases, a doctoral degree. Social workers specialize in individual, group, and family practice. They comprise most of the staffs of community clinics and agencies across the nation.

socioeconomic status Measured by factors such as occupation, education, where we live, the amount of family income, the source of income, and, in the case of upper social echelons, how long the family has had money and position.

somatoform disorders Characterized by bodily complaints in the absence of any organic cause.

sour grapes Rationalization of a disappointment by believing that the object not attained was overrated.

spontaneous recovery Recovery from mental disorders unassisted by professional counselors.

state anxiety A temporary condition of anxiety that diminishes once the stress is removed.

statistical perspective (of normality) Definition of normal as average; that is, those people in the middle of a normal distribution.

stress Any event that taxes emotional and physical balance enough to cause an unpleasant reaction.

stress inoculation The reduction of the psychological impact of a future stress by anticipating the realities of the event.

sub-intentional suicide Ambivalent suicidal attempts that leave room for survival.

sublimation A middle-level self-protective response, this coping device works by transforming an unwelcome feeling or thought into a more acceptable form.

substance abuse Pathological drug use for at least one month that impairs social and occupational functioning.

substance dependence Impaired social or occupational functioning caused by continuing drug use. Tolerance and withdrawal are central features of substance dependence.

superego In psychoanalytic theory, the part of the personality that sets standards and rewards good thoughts and behavior and punishes bad thoughts and behavior.

supportive network A group of others we can count on to help us combat stress.

suppression A middle-level self-protective response, this coping device works by deliberately pushing an unsettling reality or emotion out of direct awareness. The individual is aware of what has been done.

sweet lemon Rationalization of an unpleasant event by the conviction that it happened for the best.

symptom disorders Maladjustments in which the disabling symptom is the primary feature, such as depressed mood, high anxiety, psychosomatic conditions, or sexual dysfunctions.

temporary overload condition A state of adjustment reached when a person voluntarily takes on greater than usual stress, typically at work, for what is thought to be a short period of time.

theatrical personality A personality style that is dramatic and impressionistic, romantic, intuitive, changeable, disorderly, and expressive.

theoretical orientation According to Spranger, attitudes possessed by people who value reason, objectivity, and skepticism above all else.

Theory X An approach to management defined by McGregor, Theory X assumes people are inherently lazy, dislike working, and will avoid it if they have a chance. Only security motivates them. To drive Theory X people to produce, they must be coerced, threatened, and manipulated by a carrot or a stick.

Theory Y   An approach to management defined by McGregor, Theory Y assumes that working is as natural as resting; that individuals are ambitious with an inborn desire to be challenged, and seek responsibility. With encouragement, workers can be self-directed and will exercise their own initiative and creativity on the job.

threat   An expectation of the inability to manage a future situation.

tic disorders   Characterized by involuntary, purposeless rapid movements of one or more muscle groups.

time-limited stress   The perception of stress as being for a short, manageable period. This perception is characteristic of individuals in a temporary overload condition.

tolerance   The level at which an increased amount of a drug is required to achieve a desired effect.

topping out   Reaching the peak of our aspiration within a particular occupational field.

total marriage   Cuber and Haroff's term for a kind of stable marriage in which almost everything is shared.

trait   An enduring, stable personal quality.

trait anxiety   Anxiety that is an enduring, stable personality quality.

Type A behavior   A pattern of behavior consisting of insecurity, absence of self-esteem, time urgency, excessive hostility, and anxiety.

unconscious   In psychoanalytic theory, that layer of the mind consisting of mental states completely outside immediate conscious awareness, consisting of instinctive, aggressive, and sexual urges and impulses, thoughts, and memories that have been repressed.

undoing   A middle-level self-protective response, this coping device works by annulling undesirable action as the individual behaves in a manner directly opposite to it.

upwardly mobile   Exceeding the social class rank of one's parents.

vocation   A calling to an occupation.

wedge theory   The theory that responsiveness to a healing environment diminishes as a person grows older.

withdrawal   The symptoms that occur following the cessation or reduced intake of a drug, ranging from anxiety, irritability, insomnia, and impaired attention, to nausea, convulsions, hallucinations, and clouded consciousness.

work   An activity characterized by the feeling of obligation involving expenditure of energy to make something happen that is approved by society.

workaholism   A passion for satisfaction from an occupation resulting in chronic overwork and severely less gratification from other spheres of life.

working through   In Horowitz's model of stages of a crisis reaction, the final phase in which the traumatic stress is more fully experienced and accepted.

Bibliography

Abbot, G. State child legislation. In G. Abbot, ed., *The child and the state*. Vol. I. *Legal status in the family, apprenticeship and child labor: Selected documents, with introductory notes*. New York: Greenwood, 1968.

Abramson, L., Seligman, M., and Teasdale, J. Learned helplessness in humans: Critique and reformulation. *Journal of Abnormal Psychology*, 1978, *87*, 49–74.

Albert, S. Memories of play in the 21st century. *Journal of Child Clinical Psychology*, 1980, *9*, 179–181.

Allport, G. *Pattern and growth in personality*. New York: Holt, Rinehart and Winston, 1961.

Allport, G.; Vernon, P.; and Lindzey, G. *A study of values*, 3rd ed. Boston: Houghton Mifflin, 1960.

American Psychiatric Association. *Diagnostic and statistical manual of mental disorders*. 3rd ed. Washington, D.C.: American Psychiatric Association, 1980.

Asch, S. Effects of group pressure upon the modification and distortion of judgments. In H. Guetzkow, ed., *Groups, leadership and men*. Pittsburgh: Carnegie, 1951.

Azubike, U. The myth of the nuclear family. *American Psychologist*, 1979, *34*, 1095–1106.

Baltes, P. Life-span developmental psychology: Some converging observations on history and theory. In P. Baltes and O. Brim, Jr., eds., *Life-span development and behavior*. Vol. II. New York: Academic Press, 1979.

Baltes, P., Reese, H., and Lipsett, L. Life-span developmental psychology. *Annual Review of Psychology*, 1980, *31*, 65–110.

Bandura, A. Self-efficacy mechanism in human agency. *American Psychologist*, 1982, *37*, 122–147.

———. Self-efficacy: Towards a unifying theory of behavioral change. *Psychological Review*, 1977, *84*, 191–215.

———. *Social learning theory*. Englewood Cliffs, N.J.: Prentice-Hall, 1977.

Bandura, A., Blanchard, E., and Ritter, B. Relative efficacy of desensitization and modeling approaches for inducing behavioral, affective and attitudinal changes. *Journal of Personality and Social Psychology*, 1969, *13*, 173–199.

Bandura, A., Ross, D., and Ross, S. Transmission of aggression through imitation of aggressive models. *Journal of Abnormal and Social Psychology*, 1961, *63*, 757–782.

Bane, M. *Here to stay: American families in the twentieth century*. New York: Basic Books, 1975.

Baretmeier, L., Kubie, S., Menninger, W., and Whitehorn, J. Combat exhaustion. *Journal of Nervous and Mental Disease*. 1946, *104*, 374–375.

Basow, S. *Sex role stereotypes: Traditions and alternatives*. Monterey, Calif.: Brooks/Cole, 1980.

Baum, M. Love, marriage and division of labor. In H. Dreitzel, ed., *Family, marriage and the struggle of the sexes*. New York: Macmillan, 1972.

Beck, A. *Cognitive therapy and emotional disorders*. New York: International Universities Press, 1976.

Beiser, M. A study of personality assets in a rural community. *Archives of General Psychiatry*, 1971, *24*, 244–254.

Bell, A., and Weinberg, M. *Homosexualities: A study of diversity among men and women*. New York: Simon and Schuster, 1978.

Bem, S. Gender schema theory: A cognitive account of sex typing. *Psychological Review*, 1981, *88*, 354–364.

Benson, H. *The relaxation response*. New York: Morrow, 1975.

Bergin, A., and Lambert, M. The evaluation of therapeutic outcomes. In S. Garfield and A. Bergin, eds., *Handbook of psychotherapy and behavior change: An empirical analysis*. 2nd ed. New York: Wiley, 1978.

Bernard, J. *The future of marriage*. New York: World Book, 1973.

Betz, B., and Thomas, C. Individual temperament as a predictor of health and premature disease. *The Johns Hopkins Medical Journal*, 1979, *144*, 81–89.

Bok, S. *Lying: Moral choice in public and private life*. New York: Pantheon Press, 1978.

Bolles, R. *What color is your parachute?* Berkeley, Calif.: Ten Speed Press, 1972.

Brazelton, B. *On becoming a family: The growth of attachment*. New York: Delacourt Press, 1981.

Brim, O., and Kagan, J., eds., *Constancy and change in human development*. Cambridge, Mass.: Harvard University Press, 1980.

Bronfenbrenner, U. *The ecology of human development: Experiments by nature and design*. Cambridge, Mass.: Harvard University Press, 1979.

Brown, C. *Manchild in a promised land*. New York: Macmillan, 1963.

Brown, G. *The new celibacy*. New York: McGraw-Hill, 1980.

Burgess, A., and Holmstrom, L. Adaptive strategies in recovery from rape. *American Journal of Psychiatry*, 1979, *136*, 1278–1282.

Butler, E. *Traditional marriage and emerging alternatives*. New York: Harper and Row, 1979.

Butler, J., and Haigh, G. Changes in the relation between self-concepts and ideal concepts consequent upon client-centered counseling. In C. Rogers and R. Dymond, eds., *Psychotherapy and personality change: Coordinated studies in the client-centered approach*. Chicago: University of Chicago Press, 1954.

Cabot, R. *What men live by*. Boston: Houghton Mifflin, 1914.

Caine, L. *Widow*. New York: Morrow, 1974.

Cantu, R. *Toward fitness: Guided exercise for those with health problems*. New York: Human Services, 1980.

Carnegie Council on Policy Studies in Higher Education. *Giving youth a better chance: Options for education, work and service*. San Francisco: Jossey-Bass, 1979.

Cass, L., and Thomas, C. *Childhood pathology and later adjustment: The question of prediction*. New York: Wiley, 1979.

Cavenar, J., and Nash, J. The effects of combat on the normal personality: War neuroses in Vietnam returnees. *Comprehensive Psychiatry*, 1976, *17*, 647–653.

Chaney, E., O'Leary, M., and Marlatt, G. Skill training with alcoholics. *Journal of Consulting and Clinical Psychology*, 1978, *46*, 1092–1104.

Clarke, A., and Clarke, A. *Early experience: Myth and evidence*. New York: Free Press, 1976.

Clemens, S. Pudd'nhead Wilson's new calendar. In *Pudd'nhead Wilson, a tale by Mark Twain*. London: Chatto and Windus, 1894.

Cloney, Will, Director, Boston Marathon, Personal communication, 1981.

Coan, R. *The optimal personality: An empirical and theoretical analysis*. New York: Columbia University Press, 1974.

Coddington, R., and Troxell, J. The effect of emotional factors on football injury rates — A pilot study. *Journal of Human Stress*, 1980, *6*, 3–5.

Cohen, F., and Lazarus, R. Active coping processes, coping dispositions, and recovery from surgery. *Psychosomatic Medicine*, 1973, *35*, 375–389.

Cohen, S., and Gans, B. *The other generation gap: The middle-aged and their aging parents*. Chicago: Follet, 1978.

Cohler, B., and Grunebaum, H. *Mothers, grandmothers and daughters: Personality and child care in three-generational families.* New York: Wiley, 1981.

Coleman, J., ed., *Youth: Transition to adulthood.* Chicago: University of Chicago Press, 1974.

————. *The adolescent society.* New York: Free Press, 1961.

Coleman, J., et al. *Educational opportunity.* Washington, D.C.: U.S. Government Printing Office, 1966.

Coyne, J., and Lazarus, R. Cognitive style, stress perception, and coping. In I. Kutash, L. Schlesinger and Assoc., eds., *Handbook on stress and anxiety: Contemporary knowledge, theory, and treatment.* San Francisco: Jossey-Bass, 1980.

Craddock, D. *Obesity and its management.* Baltimore: Williams and Wilkins, 1973.

Craik, D. Young and Old. In Bartlett, J., ed., *Familiar Quotations.* 15th ed. Boston: Little, Brown, 1980.

Cuber, J. Adultery: Reality versus stereotype. In G. Neubeck, ed., *Extramarital relations.* Englewood Cliffs, N.J.: Prentice-Hall, 1969.

Cuber J., and Haroff, P. *Sex and the significant Americans: A study of sexual behavior among the affluent.* Baltimore: Penguin Press, 1965.

Cunningham, J., and Antill, J. Love in developing romantic relationships. In S. Duck, and R. Gilmore, eds., *Personal relationships. vol. 2: Developing personal relationships.* London: Academic Press, 1981.

Daniels, P., and Weingarten, K. *Sooner or later: The timing of parenthood in adult lives.* New York: Norton, 1982.

Dangott, L., and Kalish, R. *A time to enjoy: The pleasures of aging.* Englewood Cliffs, N.J.: Prentice-Hall, 1979.

Davis, A., and Havighurst, R. Social class and color differences in child rearing. In C. Kluckhohn, and H. Murray, eds., *Personality in nature, culture and society.* New York: Knopf, 1956.

Davison, G., and Neale, J. *Abnormal psychology: An experimental clinical approach.* 2nd ed. New York: Wiley, 1978.

Dawber, T. *The Framingham study: The epidemiology of atherosclerotic disease.* Cambridge, Mass.: Harvard University Press, 1980.

Devereux, G. *Basic problems in ethnopsychiatry* (1956). Translated by B. Gulati and G. Devereux. Chicago: University of Chicago Press, 1980.

Dickens, C. *A tale of two cities.* London: Chapman and Hall, 1859.

Dickens, W., and Perlman, D. Friendship over the life cycle. In S. Duck and R. Gilmore, eds., *Personal relationships. vol. 2: Developing personal relationships.* London: Academic Press, 1981.

Douvan, E., and Iglehart, A. *Work as a buffer in transitions in motherhood.* Presented at the annual meeting of the American Psychological Association, New York City, September, 1979.

Drucker, P. *Management: Tasks, responsibilities, practices.* New York: Harper & Row, 1973.

Dubos, R. *So human an animal.* New York: Scribner's, 1968.

D'Zurilla, T., and Goldfried, M. Problem-solving and behavioral modification. *Journal of Abnormal Psychology,* 1971, *78,* 107–126.

Eckland, B. College drop-outs who come back. *Harvard Educational Review,* 1964, *34,* 402–420.

Elder, G. Historical change in life patterns and personality. In P. Baltes, and O. Brim, Jr., eds., *Life-span development and behavior.* Vol. II. New York: Academic Press, 1979.

————. *Children of the great depression.* Chicago: University of Chicago Press, 1974.

Elder, G., and Rockwell, R. Economic depression and postwar opportunity in men's lives: A study of life patterns and health. In R. Simmons, ed., *Research in community and mental health.* Greenwich, Conn.: JAI Press, 1978.

Ellis, A. Rational-emotive therapy. In R. Corsini, ed., *Current Psychotherapies.* Itaska, Illinois: Peacock, 1973.

————. *The essence of rational psychotherapy: A comprehensive approach to treatment.* New York: Institute for Rational Living, 1970.

————. *Reason and emotion in psychotherapy.* New York: Stuart, 1962.

Ellis, M. J. *Why people play.* Englewood Cliffs, N.J.: Prentice-Hall, 1973.

Emerson, R. W. *Essays* (1847). First and second series. Boston: Houghton Mifflin, Riverside Library, 1980.

Entwhistle, D., and Doering, S. *The first birth: A family turning point.* Baltimore: Johns Hopkins Press, 1981.

Erikson, E. Reflections of Dr. Borg's life cycle. *Daedalus,* 1976, *105,* 1–28.

———. *Identity, youth and crisis.* New York: Norton, 1968.

———. *Childhood and society.* New York: Norton, 1950.

Erickson, E., and Erikson, J. On generativity and identity: From a conversation with Erik and Joan Erikson. *Harvard Educational Review,* 1981, *51,* 249–269.

Eron, L., Huesmann, L., Lefkowitz, M., and Walder, C. Does television violence cause aggression? *American Psychologist,* 1977, *27,* 253–263.

Escalona, S., and Heider, G. *Prediction and outcome.* New York: Basic Books, 1959.

Everly, G., and Rosenfeld, R. *The nature and treatment of the stress response: A practical guide for clinicians.* New York: Plenum, 1981.

Fabe, M., and Wikler, N. *Up against the clock.* New York: Random House, 1979.

Fassler, J. *Helping children cope: Mastering stress through books and stories.* New York: Free Press, 1978.

Featherman, D. Schooling and occupational careers: Constancy and change in worldly success. In O. Brim Jr., and J. Kagan, eds., *Constancy and change in human development.* Cambridge, Mass.: Harvard University Press, 1980.

Felton, B., Hinrichsen, G., Revenson, T., and Elron, R. *Coping with chronic illness: A factor analytic exploration.* Presented at the annual meeting of the American Psychological Association, Montreal, Canada, September, 1980.

Fiske, M. Changing hierarchies of commitment in adulthood. In N. Smelser and E. Erikson, eds., *Themes of work and love in adulthood.* Cambridge, Mass.: Harvard University Press, 1980.

Flavell, J. *The developmental psychology of Jean Piaget.* New York: Nostrand, 1963.

Fletcher, G., and Cantwell, J. *Exercise and cor-onary heart disease: Role in prevention, diagnosis, treatment.* Springfield, Ill.: Thomas, 1974.

Folkins, C. Effects of physical training on mood. *Journal of Clinical Psychology,* 1976, *32,* 385–388.

Folkins, C., Lynch, S., and Gardner, M. Psychological fitness as a function of physical fitness. *Archives of Physical Medical Rehabilitation,* 1972, *53,* 503–508.

Folkins, C., and Sime, W. Physical fitness and mental health. *American Psychologist,* 1981, *36,* 373–389.

Fox, R. The recent decline of suicide in Britain: The role of the Samaritan Suicide Prevention movement. In E. Schneiderman, ed., *Suicidology: Contemporary Developments.* New York: Grune and Stratton, 1976.

Fraiberg, S. *The magic years.* New York: Scribner Lyceum, 1959.

Frank, J. Can workers still feel a sense of accomplishment? *Management Review,* 1973, *62,* 56–58.

Frank, J. D. *Persuasion and healing: A comparative study of psychotherapy.* Rev. ed. New York: Schocken, 1974.

Freud, A. Adolescence as a developmental disturbance." The writings of Anna Freud, vol. VII. New York: International Universities Press, 1971.

Freud, A., and Bullitt, W. *Thomas Woodrow Wilson: A psychological study.* Boston: Houghton Mifflin, 1967.

Freud, S. An example of psychoanalytic work (1940). *The standard edition of the complete psychological works of Sigmund Freud.* Edited and translated by James Strachey, in collaboration with Anna Freud. London: Hogarth Press, 1953–1964, *23.*

———. An outline of psychoanalysis (1940). *The standard edition of the complete psychological works of Sigmund Freud.* Edited and translated by James Strachey, in collaboration with Anna Freud. London: Hogarth Press, 1953–1964, *23.*

———. Female sexuality (1931). *The standard edition of the complete psychological works of Sigmund Freud.* Edited and translated by James Strachey, in collaboration with Anna Freud. London: Hogarth Press, 1953–1964, *21.*

————. Civilization and its discontents (1930). *The standard edition of the complete psychological works of Sigmund Freud.* Edited and translated by James Strachey, in collaboration with Anna Freud. London: Hogarth Press, 1953–1964, *21.*

————. Inhibitions, symptoms, and anxieties (1926). *The standard edition of the complete psychological works of Sigmund Freud.* Edited and translated by James Strachey, in collaboration with Anna Freud. London: Hogarth Press, 1953–1964, *20.*

————. *A general introduction to psychoanalysis* (1924). New York: Doubleday Permabook Paperback, 1956.

————. Group psychology and the analysis of the ego (1921). *The standard edition of the complete psychological works of Sigmund Freud.* Edited and translated by James Strachey, in collaboration with Anna Freud. London: Hogarth Press, 1953–1964, *18.*

————. Mourning and melancholia (1917). *The standard edition of the complete psychological works of Sigmund Freud.* Edited and translated by James Strachey, in collaboration with Anna Freud. London: Hogarth Press, 1953–1964, *14.*

————. Instincts and their vicissitudes (1915). *The standard edition of the complete psychological works of Sigmund Freud.* Edited and translated by James Strachey, in collaboration with Anna Freud. London: Hogarth Press, 1953–1964, *14.*

————. Five lectures on psychoanalysis (1910). *The standard edition of the complete psychological works of Sigmund Freud.* Translated and edited by James Strachey, in collaboration with Anna Freud. London: Hogarth Press, 1953–1964, *11.*

————. Three essays on the theory of sexuality (1905). *The standard edition of the complete psychological works of Sigmund Freud.* Edited and translated by James Strachey, in collaboration with Anna Freud. London: Hogarth Press, 1953–1964, *7.*

————. The psychotherapy of hysteria (1895). *The standard edition of the complete psychological works of Sigmund Freud.* Edited and translated by James Strachey, in collaboration with

Anna Freud. London: Hogarth Press, 1953–1964, *2.*

Freudenberger, H., with Richelson, G. *Burnout: The high cost of high achievement.* Garden City, N.Y.: Anchor Doubleday, 1980.

Fried, M. Grieving for the lost home (1963). In A. Monat and R. Lazarus, eds., *Stress and coping: An anthology.* New York: Columbia University Press, 1977.

Friedman, M. Type A behavior: A progress report. *The Sciences,* February, 1980, 10.

————. The modification of Type A behavior in post-infarction patients. *American Heart Journal,* 1979, 97, 551–560.

Friedman, M., and Rosenman, R. *Type A behavior and your heart.* New York: Knopf, 1974.

Garmezy, N. DSM-III: Never mind the psychologists: Is it good for the children? *Clinical Psychologist,* 1978, *31,* 1–4.

Gesell, A. *Youth: The years from ten to sixteen.* New York: Harper & Row, 1956.

Gesell, A., and Ilg, F. *The child from five to ten.* New York: Harper & Row, 1946.

Gesell, A., Ilg, F., and Ames, L. *Infant and child in the culture today: The guidance of development in home and nursery school.* Rev. ed. New York: Harper & Row, 1974.

Gesell, A., et al. *The first five years of life: A guide to the study of the preschool child.* New York: Harper & Row, 1940.

Giapa, J. Children's friendships. In S. Duck and R. Gilmore, eds., *Personal relations. vol. 2: Developing personal relationships.* London: Academic Press, 1981.

Gilligan, C. *In a different voice: Psychological theory and women's development.* Cambridge, Mass.: Harvard University Press, 1982.

————. Woman's place in man's life cycle. *Harvard Educational Review,* 1979, *49,* 431–446.

Ginzberg, E., Ginsburg, S., Axelrad, S., and Herma, J. *Occupational choice: An approach to a general theory.* New York: Columbia University Press, 1951.

Goethals, G. Love, marriage and mutative relationships. In K. Pope, ed., *On love and loving.* San Francisco: Jossey-Bass, 1980.

———. *Stage theory and critical events: A reconsideration of critical events.* Paper presented at the Eastern Psychological Association, Boston, Massachusetts, 1978.

———. Symbiosis and the life cycle. *British Journal of Medical Psychology*, 1973, *46*, 91–96.

Goldstein, M., Baker, B., and Jamison, K. *Abnormal psychology: Experiences, origins, interventions.* Boston: Little, Brown, 1980.

Gordon, M. *The American family: Past, present and future.* New York: Random House, 1978.

Graubard, S. Preface to the issue Adulthood. *Daedalus*, 1976, 105, p. v.

Greenberger, E., Steinberg, L., and Vaux, A. Adolescents who work: Health and behavioral consequences of job stress. *Developmental Psychology*, 1981, *17*, 691–703.

Greist, J., Klein, M., Eichens, R., Faris, J., Gurman, A., and Morgan, W. Running as treatment for depression. *Comprehensive Psychiatry*, 1979, *20*, 41–54.

Grinker, R., Sr., Grinker, R., Jr., and Timberlake, J. 'Mentally healthy' young males (homoclites). *Archives of General Psychiatry*, 1962, *6*, 405–453.

Grinker, R., Sr., and Spiegel, J. *Men under stress.* New York: McGraw-Hill, 1963.

Gross, M., and Wilson, W. *Minimal brain dysfunction.* New York: Bruner/Mazel, 1974.

Guze, S. Can the practice of medicine be fun for a lifetime? *Journal of the American Medical Association*, 1979, *241*, 2021–2023.

Haan, N. *Coping and defending: Processes of self-improvement organization.* New York: Academic Press, 1977.

———. Personality development from adolescence to adulthood in the Oakland growth and guidance studies. *Seminars in Psychiatry*, 1977, *4*, 399–414.

Hall, G. *A primer of Freudian psychology.* Cleveland: World, 1954.

Hall, G. A., and Lindsay, G. *Theories of personality.* New York: Wiley, 1957.

Hartmann, H. *Essays on ego psychology: Selected problems in psychoanalytic theory* (1939). New York: International Universities Press, 1964.

———. *Ego psychology and the problem of adaptation.* New York: International Universities Press, 1958.

Heath, D. *Maturity and competence: A transcultural view.* New York: Gardner, 1977.

———. Some possible maturing effects of occupation on the maturing of professional men. *Journal of Vocational Behavior*, 1977, *11*, 263–281.

———. *Growing up in college: Liberal curriculum and maturity.* San Francisco: Jossey-Bass, 1968.

Herford, R. *Ethics of the Talmud. Sayings of the Fathers (Pirke Aboth).* Translation, with commentary. New York: Schocken, 1962.

Herrnstein, R. *I.Q. in the meritocracy.* Boston: Atlantic Monthly Press, 1973.

Hersen, M., Eisler, R., and Miller, P. An experimental analysis of generalization in assertive training. *Journal of Behavior Research and Therapy*, 1974, *12*, 295–310.

Hettema, P. *Personality and adaptation.* Amsterdam: North-Holland, 1979.

Hinsie, L., and Campbell, R. *Psychiatric dictionary.* 4th ed. New York: Oxford University Press, 1970.

Holahan, C., and Moos, R. Social support and psychological distress. *Journal of Abnormal Psychology*, 1981, *90*, 365–370.

Holland, J. *Making vocational choices: A theory of careers.* Englewood Cliffs, N.J.: Prentice-Hall, 1973.

Holmes, T., and Masuda, M. Life change and illness susceptibility. In B. S. Dohrenwend and B. P. Dohrenwend, eds., *Stressful life events: Their nature and effects.* New York: Wiley, 1974.

Holzman, P., and Gardner, R. Leveling and repression. *Journal of Abnormal and Social Psychology*, 1959, *59*, 151–155.

Horner, M. The measurement and behavioral implications of fear of success in women. In J. Atkinson, and J. Raynor, eds., *Personality, motivation and achievement.* Washington, D.C.: Hemisphere, 1978.

———. Toward an understanding of achievement-related conflicts in women. *Journal of Social Issues*, 1972, *28*, 157–174.

———. Femininity and successful achievement: A basic inconsistency. In J. Bardwick, E. Douvan, M. Horner, and D. Gutman. *Feminine personality and conflict.* Belmont, Calif.: Brooks/Cole, 1970.

Horney, K. *Feminine psychology.* New York: Norton, 1967.

———. Personality Changes in Female Adolescents. *The American Journal of Orthopsychiatry*, 1935, *5*, 19–26.

Horowitz, M. Psychoanalytic therapy. · In I. Kutash, L. Schlesinger and Assoc., eds., *Handbook on stress and anxiety: Contemporary knowledge, theory, and Treatment.* San Francisco: Jossey-Bass, 1980.

———. *Stress response syndrome.* New York: Aronson, 1976.

Horowitz, M., Wilner, N., Kaltreider, N., and Alvarez, W. Signs and symptoms of post-traumatic stress disorders. *Archives of General Psychiatry*, 1980, *37*, 85–92.

Horton, P. *Solace: The missing dimension in psychiatry.* Chicago: University of Chicago Press, 1981.

Hulin, C. Effects of community characteristics on measures of job satisfaction. *Journal of Applied Psychology*, 1966, *50*, 185–192.

Huston, T., Surra, C., Fitzgerald, N., and Cate, R. From courtship to marriage. In S. Duck, and R. Gilmore, eds., *Personal relationships, vol. 2: Developing personal relationships.* London: Academic Press, 1981.

Inhelder, B., and Piaget, J. *The early growth of logic in the child.* New York: Harper & Row, 1964.

Jacobson, B. *Young programs for older workers: Case studies in progressive personnel policies.* New York: Van Nostrand Reinhold, 1980.

Jahoda, M. *Current concepts of positive mental health.* New York: Basic Books, 1958.

James, H. The beast in the jungle. In *The better sort.* New York: Scribner's, 1903.

James, W. *Varieties of religious experience.* New York: Modern Library, 1936.

———. The gospel of relaxation (1897). In James, W. *Pragmatism and other essays.* New York: Pocket Books, 1975.

———. *The will to believe, and other essays in popular philosophy* (1896). New York: Longmans, Green, 1897.

———. *Principles of psychology* (1890). Volumes I and II. New York: Dover, 1950.

———. Vacations. *The Nation*, August 7, 1873, p. 91.

Janis, I. Adaptive personality changes. In A. Monat and R. Lazarus, eds., *Stress and coping: An anthology.* New York: Columbia University Press, 1977.

———. *Psychological stress: Psychoanalytic and behavioral studies of surgical patients.* New York: Wiley, 1958.

Jensen, A. How much can we boost I.Q. and scholastic achievement? *Harvard Educational Review*, 1969, *39*, 1–123.

Johanson, D., and Edey, M. *Lucy: The beginnings of humankind.* New York: Simon and Schuster, 1981.

Johnson, G., and Goldfinger, S., eds., *The Harvard Medical School health letter book.* Cambridge, Mass.: Harvard University Press, 1981.

Jones, M. A laboratory study of fear: The case of Peter. *Journal of Genetic Psychology*, 1924, *31*, 308–345.

Jones, W., Chernovetz, M., and Hansson, R. The enigma of androgyny: Differential implications for males and females. *Journal of Consulting and Clinical Psychology*, 1978, *46*, 298–313.

Jourard, S. *The transparent self.* Rev. ed. New York: Van Nostrand, 1971.

Jung, C. *Psychological Types* (1923). Revision by R. Hall of translation by H. Baynes. Princeton, N.J.: Princeton University Press, 1976.

Kagan, J., Kearsley, R., and Zalaso, P. *Infancy: Its place in human development.* Cambridge, Mass.: Harvard University Press, 1978.

Kagan, J., and Moss, H. *Birth to maturity: A study in psychological development.* New York: Wiley, 1962.

Kahl, J. *The American class structure.* New York: Holt, Rinehart, and Winston, 1957.

———. Educational and occupational aspirations of 'common man' boys. *Harvard Educational Review*, 1953, *23*, 188–201.

Katch, F., McArdle, W., and Boylan, B. *Getting in shape: An optimum approach to fitness and weight control.* Boston: Houghton Mifflin, 1979.

Katz, J., and Associates. *No time for youth: Growth and restraint in college students*. San Francisco: Jossey-Bass, 1968.

Keniston, K. *Youth and dissent: The rise of a new opposition*. New York: Harcourt Brace Jovanovich, 1971.

King, S. Coping mechanisms in adolescence. *Psychiatric Annals*, 1971, *1*, 10–29.

Kinsey, A., et al. *Sexual behavior in the human female*. Philadelphia: Saunders, 1953.

Kirkpatrick, M., Smith, K., and Roy, R. *Adjustment and sexual identity of children of lesbian and heterosexual single mothers*. Presented at the annual meeting of the American Psychological Association, New York City, September, 1979.

Kitto, H. *The Greeks*. New York: Pelican Paperbacks, 1951.

Kluckhohn, F. Dominant and variant value orientations. In C. Kluckhohn and H. Murray, eds., *Personality: In nature, society and culture*. 2nd ed. New York: Knopf, 1956.

Knowles, J. The responsibility of the individual. In J. Knowles, ed., *Doing better and feeling worse: Health in the United States*. New York: Norton, 1977.

Kobasa, S. *Personality and stress resistance across professional groups*. Paper presented at the annual meeting of the American Psychological Association, Montreal, Canada, September, 1980.

Kohlberg, L. *The philosophy of moral development: Moral stages and the idea of justice*. San Francisco: Harper & Row, 1981.

———. From is to ought: How to commit the naturalistic fallacy and get away with it in a study of moral development. In T. Mischel, ed., *Cognitive development and epistemology*. New York: Academic Press, 1971.

Kohlberg, L., and Gilligan, C. The adolescent as a philosopher: The discovery of the self in a post-conventional world. *Daedalus*, 1971, *100*, 1051–1086.

Kohlberg, L., and Kramer, R. Continuities and discontinuities in childhood and adult moral development. *Human Development*, 1969, *12*, 93–120.

Kohn, M. Job complexity and adult personality. In N. Smelser and E. Erikson, eds., *Themes of work and love in adulthood*. Cambridge, Mass.: Harvard University Press, 1980.

Kotelchuck, M. *The nature of the child's tie to the father*. Unpublished Ph.D. dissertation. Cambridge, Mass.: Harvard University, 1971.

Kreitler, P., and Bruns, B. *Affair prevention*. New York: Macmillan, 1981.

Kretchmer, E. *Physique and character*. Translated by W. Sprott. London: Routledge and Kegan Paul, 1925.

Kroeber, T. The coping functions of ego mechanisms. In R. White, ed., *The study of lives*. New York: Atherton, 1963.

Kübler-Ross, E. *On death and dying*. New York: Macmillen, 1969.

Kunen, J. *The strawberry statement*. New York: Random House, 1968.

Kushner, H. *When bad things happen to good people*. New York: Schocken, 1981.

Lamorisse, A. *The red balloon*. Translated by F. Mack. Garden City, New Jersey: Doubleday, 1956.

Lantos, B. Work and the instincts. *International Journal of Psychoanalysis*, 1943, *24*, 114–119.

Lawler, E., and Hackman, J. Impact of employee participation in the development of pay incentives: A field experience. *Journal of Applied Psychology*, 1969, *53*, 467–471.

Lazarus, R. *Psychological stress and coping process*. New York: McGraw-Hill, 1976.

Lazarus, R., Averill, J., and Opton, E. The psychology of coping: Issues of research and assessment. In G. Coelho, D. Hamburg, and J. Adams, eds., *Coping and adaptation*. New York: Basic Books, 1974.

Lemere, F., and Voegtlin, W. An evaluation of the aversion treatment of alcoholism. *Quarterly Journal of Studies on Alcohol*, 1950, *11*, 199–204.

Leshan, E. *The wonderful crisis of middle age*. New York: McKay, 1973.

Lever, J. Sex differences in the games children play. *Social Problems*, 1976, *23*, 478–487.

Levinson, D., with Darrow, C., Klein, E., Levinson, M., and McKee, B. *Seasons of a man's life*. New York: Alfred Knopf, 1978.

Levinson, H. *The great jackass fallacy*. Cambridge, Mass.: Division of Research, Harvard Graduate School of Business Administration, 1973.

Lewin, K. *A dynamic theory of personality.* New York: McGraw-Hill, 1935.

Lewis, C. *Four loves.* New York: Harcourt Brace Jovanovich, 1960.

Lewis, H. The family's resources for change — Planning sessions for the White House conference 'To Fulfill These Rights.' In Rainwater, L., and Yancey, W., eds., *The Moynihan report and the politics of controversy.* Cambridge, Mass.: Massachusetts Institute of Technology Press, 1967.

Lewis, M., Gottesman, D., and Gutstein, S. The course and duration of crisis. *Journal of Consulting and Clinical Psychology,* 1979, *47,* 128–134.

Liberman, R., and Reigen, J. Behavioral group therapy. In P. Sjoden, S. Bates, and W. Dockens, eds., *Trends in behavior therapy.* New York: Academic Press, 1979.

Liddell, H. *A Greek-English lexicon, compiled by Henry George Liddell and Robert Scott* (1870). Rev. and augm. by Sir Henry Stuart Jones. Oxford: Clarendon Press, 1968.

Lindemann, E. Symptomatology and management of acute grief. *American Journal of Psychiatry,* 1944, *101,* 141–148.

Lipsit, S., and Bendix, B. *Social mobility in industrial society.* Berkeley, Calif.: University of California Press, 1959.

Loevinger, J. *Ego development.* San Francisco: Jossey-Bass, 1976.

Lord, W. *A night to remember.* New York: Holt, Rinehart and Winston, 1955.

Lorenz, K. *On aggression.* New York: Harcourt Brace and World, 1966.

Lowenthal, M., Thurnher, M., Chiriboga, D. and Associates. *Four stages of life: A comparative study of women and men facing transition.* San Francisco: Jossey-Bass, 1976.

Lowry, L. Mental health services in the community. In J. Birren and R. Sloan, eds., *Handbook of mental health and aging.* Englewood Cliffs, N.J.: Prentice-Hall, 1980.

Lumsden, C., and Wilson, E. *Genes, mind and culture: The coevolutionary process.* Cambridge, Mass.: Harvard University Press, 1981.

Lynch, J. *The broken heart: The medical consequences of loneliness.* New York: Basic Books, 1979.

Maddi, S. *Personality as a resource in stress resistance: The hardy type.* Presented at the annual meeting of the American Psychological Association, Montreal, Canada, 1980.

Magarrel, J. Today's new student, especially women, more materialistic. *The Chronicle of Higher Education,* January 28, 1980, pp. 3–5.

Mahoney, M. Personal science: A cognitive learning therapy. In A. Ellis and R. Grieger, eds., *Handbook of rational psychology.* New York: Springer, 1977.

Mahoney, M., and Arnkoff, D. Cognitive self-control therapy. In S. Garfield and A. Bergin, eds., *Handbook of psychotherapy and behavior change.* 2nd ed. New York: Wiley, 1978.

Mandel, J., Hotvedt, M., Green, R., and Smith, L. *The lesbian parent: Comparison of heterosexual and homosexual mothers and their children.* Presented at the annual meeting of the American Psychological Association, New York City, September, 1979.

Marcuse, H. *Eros and civilization.* Boston: Beacon, 1966.

Marland, S. *Career education: A proposal for reform.* New York: McGraw-Hill, 1974.

Marwell, G., Rosenfeld, R., and Spilerman, S. Graphic constraints on women's careers in academia. *Science,* 1979, *205,* 1225–1231.

Maslow, A. *The farther reaches of human nature* (1967). New York: Penguin, 1971.

———. *Motivation and personality.* 2nd ed. New York: Harper & Row, 1970.

———. *Toward a psychology of being.* 2nd ed. Princeton, N.J.: Van Nostrand, 1968.

———. *Toward a psychology of being.* Princeton, N.J.: Van Nostrand, 1962.

Masnick, J., and Bane, M. *The nation's families: 1960–1990.* Boston: Auburn House, 1980.

Masters, W., and Johnson, V. *Human sexual inadequacy.* Boston: Little, Brown, 1970.

———. *Human sexual response.* Boston: Little, Brown, 1966.

Masters, J., Johnson, V., and Kolodny, R. *Human sexuality.* Boston: Little, Brown, 1982.

Matarazzo, J. Behavioral health's challenge to academic, scientific and professional psychology. *American Psychologist,* 1982, *37,* 1–14.

May, R. *Love and will.* New York: Norton, 1969.

McGregor, D. *The human side of enterprise*. New York: McGraw-Hill, 1960.

McKean, R., ed. *Introduction to Aristotle*. New York: Modern Library, 1947.

McKee, J. *Introduction to sociology*. New York: Holt, Rinehart and Winston, 1969.

McKee, J., and Sheriff, A. The differential evaluation of males and females. *Journal of Personality*, 1957, *25*, 356–371.

McLean, P. Depression as a specific response to stress. In I. Sarasan and C. Spielberger, eds., *Stress and anxiety*. New York: Wiley, 1976.

Mechanic, D. Social structure and personal adaptation: Some neglected dimensions. In G. Coelho, D. Hamburg, and J. Adams, eds., *Coping and adaptation*. New York: Basic Books, 1974.

Menninger, K., with Mayman, M., and Pruyser, P. *The vital balance*. New York: Viking, 1967.

Middleton, L., and Roarke, A. Living together is widely accepted among students today. *Chronicle of Higher Education*, July 6, 1981, pp. 2–3.

Milgram, S. *Obedience to authority*. New York: Harper & Row, 1974.

Millar, S. *The psychology of play*. New York: Aronson, 1974.

Miller, N., and Dollard, J. *Social learning and initiation*. New Haven: Yale University Press, 1941.

Moos, R. *Creating healthy human contexts: Environmental and individual strategies*. Paper presented at the annual meeting of the American Psychological Association, Los Angeles, California, August, 1981.

Morse, H., and Weiss, R. The function and meaning of work and the job. *American Sociological Review*, 1955, *20*, 191–198.

Mortimer, J. *Changing attitudes toward work*. Scarsdale, N.Y.: Work in America Institute, Inc., 1979.

Moynihan, D. *Maximum feasible misunderstanding: Community action in the War on Poverty*. New York: Free Press, 1969.

————. 1965. The Negro family: The case for national action. In Rainwater, L., and Yancy, W., eds., *The Moynihan report and the politics of controversy*. Cambridge, Mass.: MIT Press, 1967.

Munter, P. *The needs of the teacher*. Paper presented at the Northfield Counseling Institute, East Northfield, Massachusetts, June, 1977.

Murphy, L., and Moriarty, A. *Vulnerability, coping and growth: From infancy to adolescence*. New Haven: Yale University Press, 1976.

Murray, E., and Jacobson, L. Cognition and learning in traditional and behavioral therapy. In S. Garfield and A. Bergin, eds., *Handbook of psychotherapy and behavior change: An empirical analysis*. 2nd ed. New York: Wiley, 1978.

Neugarten, B. Time, age and the life cycle. *American Journal of Psychiatry*, 1979, *136*, 887–894.

Neugarten, B., and Hagestad, G. Age and the life course. In Binstock, R., and Shanas, E., eds., *Handbook of aging and the social sciences*. New York: Van Nostrand-Reinhold, 1976.

Neugarten, B., and Weinstein, K. The changing American grandparent. *Journal of Marriage and Family*, 1964, *26*, 199–204.

Newsweek. Survival Test. January 20, 1975, p. 69.

Newsweek, September 22, 1969, p. 68.

Novaco, R. Anger and coping with stress: Cognitive behavioral interventions. In J. Foreyt and D. Rathjen, eds., *Cognitive behavior therapy: Research and applications*. New York: Plenum, 1978.

Offer, D. *The psychological world of the teenager*. New York: Basic Books, 1969.

Offer, D., and Offer, J. *From teenage to young manhood*. New York: Basic Books, 1975.

Offer, N., and Sabshin, M. *Normality: Theoretical and clinical concepts of mental health*. 2nd ed. New York: Basic Books, 1974.

Ogbu, J. *The next generation: An ethnography of education in an urban neighborhood*. New York: Academic Press, 1974.

Olds, D. *Masculinity, femininity, achievement conflicts and health*. Paper presented at the annual meeting of the American Psychological Association, New York City, September, 1979.

Olds, D., and Shaver, P. Masculinity, femininity, academic performance and health: Further evidence concerning the androgyny controversy. *Journal of Personality*, 1980, *48*, 323–341.

Osherson, S. *Work-family dilemmas of professional careers*. Final report to the National Institute of Education of Project No. NIE–G–77–0049. January, 1982.

———. *Holding on or letting go: Men and career change at midlife*. New York: Free Press, 1980.

Oxford English Dictionary. *The Compact Edition of the Oxford English Dictionary*. (1971) New York: Oxford University Press, 1979.

Page, J. *Psychopathology: The science of understanding deviance*. Chicago: Aldine, 1975.

Parkes, C. *Bereavement: Studies in grief in adult life*. New York: International Universities Press, 1972.

———. Psychosocial transitions: A field for study. *Social Science in Medicine*, 1971, 5, 101–115.

Pavlov, I. *Lectures on conditioned reflexes*. Translated by G. Anrep. London: Oxford University Press, 1927.

Peck, R., and Hughes, R. *Social adjustment and achievement: A cross-national survey*. Paper presented at the annual meeting of the American Psychological Association, New York City, September, 1979.

Peele, S., and Brodsky, A. *Love and addiction*. New York: New American Library, 1975.

Perry, C., et al. *The impact of governmental manpower programs*. Philadelphia: University of Pennsylvania Press, 1975.

Piaget, J. *The moral judgment of the child* (1932). New York: Free Press, 1965.

———. *Play, dreams and imitation in childhood* (1957). New York: Norton, 1962.

Pines, A., and Aronson, E., with Kafry, D. *Burnout: From tedium to personal growth*. New York: Free Press, 1981.

Pollock, M., Wilmore, J., and Fox, S. *Health and fitness through physical activity*. New York: Wiley, 1978.

Pope, K., ed., *On love and loving*. San Francisco: Jossey-Bass, 1980.

Powell, D. The effects of job strategy seminars upon unemployed engineers and scientists. *Journal of Social Psychology*, 1973, 91, 165–166.

Powell, D., and Driscoll, P. How middle-class unemployed men feel and act: Four progressive stages. *Society* 1973 January/February, 18–26.

Powers, R., and Kutash, I. Alcohol abuse and anxiety. In I. Kutash, L. Schlesinger and Assoc., eds., *Handbook on stress and anxiety: Contemporary knowledge, theory and treatment*. San Francisco: Jossey-Bass, 1980.

Rainwater, L., and Yancey, W., eds. *The Moynihan report and the politics of controversy*. Cambridge, Mass.: Massachusetts Institute of Technology Press, 1967.

Rausch, H., Bary, W., Hartel, R., and Swain, M. *Communication, conflict, and marriage*. San Francisco: Jossey-Bass, 1974.

Rehm, L. Self-management in depression. In P. Karoly and F. Kanfer, eds., *The psychology of self-management: From theory to practice*. New York: Pergamon, 1982.

Reich, W. *Character analysis* (1933). New York: Orgone Institute Press, 1949.

Reisman, D., with Glazer, N., and Denny, R. *The lonely crowd: A study of the changing American character*. New Haven, Conn.: Yale University Press, 1950.

Reisman, J. Adult friendships. In S. Duck and R. Gilmore, eds., *Personal relationships. vol. 2: Developing personal relationships*. London: Academic Press, 1981.

Rist, R. Student social class and teacher expectations: The self-fulfilling prophecy in ghetto education. *Harvard Educational Review*, 1970, 40, 411–451.

Rogers, C. Growing old — or older and growing. *Journal of Humanistic Psychology*, 1980, 20, 5–16.

———. Client-centered therapy. In S. Arieti, ed., *American handbook of psychiatry*. Vol. III. New York: Basic Books, 1966.

Rogers, C., with Dorfman, E., Gordon, T., and Hobbs N. *Client-centered therapy: Its current practice, implications and theory*. Boston: Houghton Mifflin, 1951.

Rohrbaugh, J. *Women: Psychology's puzzle*. New York: Basic Books, 1979.

Roskies, E., and Avard, J. Teaching healthy managers to control their coronary-prone (Type A) behavior. In K. Blankstein and J. Polivy, eds., *Self-control and self-modification of emotional behaviors.* New York: Plenum, 1982.

Rosow J., and Zager, R. *The future of older workers in America: New options for an extended working life.* Scarsdale, N.Y.: Work in America Institute, Inc., 1980.

Rossi, A., and Rossi, P. Body time and social time: Mood patterns by menstrual cycle phase and day of the week. *Social Science Research*, 1977, 6, 273–308.

Royce, W., and Arkowitz, H. Multi-modal evaluation of practice interaction as treatment for social isolation. *Journal of Consulting and Clinical Psychology*, 1978, 46, 239–245.

Rubin, I. Sex over 65. In J. Wiseman, ed., *The social psychology of sex.* New York: Harper & Row, 1976.

Rubin, Z. *Liking and loving.* New York: Holt, Rinehart and Winston, 1973.

Rush, B. *Medical inquiries and observations upon the diseases of the mind* (1812). New York: Hafner, 1962.

Russell, W., and Branch, T. *Second wind: The memoirs of an opinionated man.* New York: Random House, 1979.

Saad, S., Lenauer, M., Shaver, P., and Dunivant, N. Objective measurement of fear of success and fear of failure: A factor analytic approach. *Journal of Consulting and Clinical Psychology*, 1978, 46, 405–416.

Sartre, J. *Being and nothingness: An essay on phenomenological ontology.* New York: Philosophical Library, 1956.

Sassen, G. Success anxiety in women: A constructionist interpretation of its source and significance. *Harvard Educational Review*, 1980, 50, 13–24.

Schafer, R. The psychoanalytic vision of reality. *International Journal of Psychoanalysis*, 1970, 51, 279–296.

————. *Aspects of internalization.* New York: International Universities Press, 1968.

Schrecker, P. *Work and history: An essay on the structure of civilization.* Princeton, N.J.: Princeton University Press, 1948.

Schreiber, F. *Sybil.* Chicago: Regnery, 1973.

Schwartz, M., Jenusaitis, E., and Stark, H.

Motivational factors among supervisors in the utility industry. *Personal Psychology*, 1963, 16, 45–53.

Sears, R., Maccoby, E., and Levin, H. *Patterns of child rearing.* Evanston, Ill.: Row, Peterson, 1957.

Selman, R., and Jacquette, D. Stability and oscillation in interpersonal awareness: A clinical-developmental analysis. In E. Keasey, ed., *Nebraska symposium on motivation.* Vol. 25. Lincoln, Nebraska: University of Nebraska Press, 1977.

Selye, H. The stress concept today. In I. Kutash, L. Schlesinger and Assoc., eds., *Handbook on stress and anxiety: Contemporary knowledge, theory and treatment.* San Francisco: Jossey-Bass, 1980.

————. *Stress without distress.* New York: Signet, 1974.

Shakespeare, W. *Henry V.* With notes by E.F.C. Ludowyk. Cambridge: Cambridge University Press, 1966.

Shanas, E., Townsend, P., Wedderburn, D., Friis, H., Milhoj, P., and Stehower, J. *Older people in three industrial societies.* New York: Atherton, 1968.

Shapiro, D. *Neurotic styles.* New York: Harper, 1965.

Shaw, G. *Man and superman.* London: Westminster Constable and Co., Ltd., 1903.

Sheehy, G. *Passages: Predictable crises in adult life.* New York: Dutton, 1976.

Sheldon, N., and Stevens, P. *The varieties of temperament: A psychology of constitutional differences.* New York: Harper & Row, 1942.

Sheleff, L. *Generations apart: Adult hostility toward youth.* New York: McGraw-Hill, 1981.

Shipley, R., Butt, J., Horowitz, B., and Farbry, J. Preparation for a stressful medical procedure: Effect of amount of stimulus pre-exposure and coping style. *Journal of Consulting & Clinical Psychology*, 1978, 46, 499–507.

Sierles, F., Hendrikx, I., and Circle, S. Cheating in medical school. *Journal of Medical Education*, 1980, 55(2), 124–25.

Skinner, B. *About behaviorism.* New York: Knopf, 1974.

————. *The behavior of organisms.* New York: Appleton-Crofts, 1938.

Smelser, N. Issues in the study of work and

love in adulthood. In N. Smelser and E. Erikson, eds., *Themes of work and love in adulthood.* Cambridge, Mass.: Harvard University Press, 1980.

Sorenson, D. The return of the college dropout. In C. Blaine and C. McArthur, eds., *Emotional problems of the student.* 2nd ed. New York: Appleton-Century-Crofts, 1971.

Special Task Force to the Secretary of Health, Education and Welfare. *Work in America.* Cambridge, Mass.: Massachusetts Institute of Technology Press, 1972.

Spence, J., and Helmreich, R. *Masculinity and femininity: Their psychological dimensions, correlates, and antecedents.* Austin, Texas: University of Texas Press, 1978.

Spielberger, C. *Anxiety: Current trends in theory and research.* New York: Academic Press, 1971.

———. Theory and research on anxiety. In C. Spielberger, ed., *Anxiety and behavior.* New York: Academic Press, 1966.

Spranger, E. *Types of men: The psychology and ethics of personality.* Translation of the German, 5th ed. by P. Pigors. New York: Hafner, 1928.

Srole, L., Langer, T., Michael, S., Opler, M., and Rennie, T. *Mental health in the metropolis: The midtown Manhattan study.* Vol. I. New York: McGraw-Hill, 1962.

Staines, G., and O'Connor, P. *The relationship between work and leisure.* Ann Arbor, Michigan. Survey Research Center, 1979. Paper presented at the annual meeting of the American Psychological Association, New York City, September, 1979.

Stangler, R., and Printz, A. DSM-III: Psychiatric diagnosis in a university population. *American Journal of Psychiatry*, 1980, *137*, 937–940.

Stehower, J. *Older people in three industrial societies.* New York: Atherton, 1968.

Stein, P. Singlehood: An alternative to marriage. In A. Skolnick and J. Skolnick, eds., *Family in transition.* 2nd ed. Boston: Little, Brown, 1977.

Steinberg, L., Greenberger, E., Jacobi, M., and Garduque, L. Early work experience: A partial antidote to adolescent egocentrism. *Journal of Youth and Adolescence*, 1981a, *10*, 141–157.

Steinberg, L., Greenberger, E., Vaux, A., and Ruggiero, M. Effects of early work experience on adolescent socialization. *Youth and Society*, 1981b, *12*, 403–422.

Stern, P., ed. *The annotated Walden.* New York: Bramhall House, 1970.

Stewart, R. Natural childbirth, father participation, or what-have-you. *Medical Times*, 1963, *91*, 1064–1068.

Strodtbeck, F. Family interaction, values and achievement. In D. McClelland, A. Baldwin, U. Bronfenbrenner, and F. Strodtbeck, eds., *Talent and society.* New York: Van Nostrand, 1958.

Sullivan, H. *Personal psychopathology: Early formation.* New York: Norton, 1972.

———. *The interpersonal theory of psychiatry.* New York: Norton, 1953.

Super, D., et al. *Vocational development: A framework for research.* New York: Bureau of Publications, Columbia Teachers College, 1957.

Swidler, A. Love and adulthood in American culture. In N. Smelser and E. Erikson, eds., *Themes of work and love in adulthood.* Cambridge, Mass.: Harvard University Press, 1980.

Sykes, C. *Nancy: The life of Lady Astor.* London: Collins, 1972.

Symonds, P., and Jensen, A. *From adolescent to adult.* New York: Columbia University Press, 1961.

Tanner, J. Sequence, tempo and individual variation in the growth and development of boys and girls aged twelve to thirteen. *Daedalus*, 1971, *100*, 907–930.

Terkel, S. *Working.* New York: Pantheon, 1974.

Thomson, J. *The ethics of Aristotle: The Nichomachean Ethics translated.* New York: Penguin Books, 1953.

Thoreau, H. Civil disobedience (1849). In P. Stern, ed., *The annotated Walden.* New York: Bramhall House, 1970.

———. *Walden* (1854). Introduction by B. Wiley. New York: Bramhall House, 1961.

Tresemer, D. *Fear of success.* New York: Plenum, 1977.

Troll, L. *Early and middle adulthood: The best is yet to be — maybe.* Monterey, California: Brooks/Cole, 1975.

Turin, A., and Johnson, W. Biofeedback

therapy for migraine headaches. *American Journal of Psychiatry*, 1976, *33*, 517–519.

Twain, M. *The adventures of Tom Sawyer.* New York: Nelson Doubleday, 1876.

U.S. Department of Commerce, Bureau of the Census. *Current Population Reports*, Series P-20, No. 365. Washington, D.C.: U.S. Government Printing Office, 1981.

———. *Current Population Reports.* Washington, D.C.: U.S. Government Printing Office, 1977.

U.S. Department of Health, Education and Welfare. *Healthy people: The Surgeon General's report on health problems and disease prevention.* Washington, D.C.: U.S. Government Printing Office, 1979.

U.S. Department of Health, Education and Welfare: Health Care Financing Administration, Health Standards and Quality Bureau. *Working with older people: A guide to practice.* Vol. I. *The knowledge base.* Washington, D.C.: U.S. Government Printing Office, 1978.

U.S. Department of Health and Human Services, Public Health Service, Office of Health Research, Statistics and Technology. *Monthly vital statistics report*, vol. 29, no. 13. September 17, 1981.

U.S. National Center for Health Statistics. *Vital statistics of the United States.* Washington, D.C.: U.S. Government Printing Office, 1977.

U.S. News and World Report. September 8, 1980, p. 52.

Vachon, M., Lyall, W., Rogers, J., Freedman-Letofsky, K., and Freeman, S. A controlled study of self-help intervention for widows. *American Journal of Psychiatry*, 1980, *137*, 1380–1384.

Vaillant, G. *Adaptation to life.* Boston: Little, Brown, 1977.

Vaillant, G., and Milofsky, E. Natural history of male psychological health: IX. Empirical evidence for Erikson's model of the life cycle. *American Journal of Psychiatry*, 180, *137*, 1348–1359.

Vaillant, G., and Vaillant, C. Natural history of male psychological health: Work as a prediction of positive mental health. *American Journal of Psychiatry*, 1981, *138*, 1433–1440.

Vandenburg, B. Play and development from an ethological perspective. *American Psychologist*, 1979, *33*, 724–738.

Vecchio, R. The function and meaning of work and the job: Morse and Weiss (1955) revisited. *Academy of Management Journal*, 1980, *23*, 361–367.

Veroff, J., and Feld, S. *Marriage and work in America: A study of motives and roles.* New York: Van Nostrand-Reinhold, 1970.

Visher, E., and Visher, J. *Stepfamiles: A guide to working with stepparents and stepchildren.* New York: Bruner/Mazel, 1979.

Voydanoff, P. The relationship between perceived job characteristics and job satisfaction among occupational status groups. *Sociology of Work and Occupation*, 1978, *5*, 179–192.

Wagner, C. Sexuality of American adolescents. *Journal of Adolescence*, 1980, *15*, 567–580.

Lookin' good but feelin' bad. Music by Thomas Waller, and lyrics by Lester Santly. Chappell Music, 1929.

Warner, W., and Agegglin, J. *Big business leaders in America.* New York: Harper, 1955.

Warner, W., Weeken, M., and Eels, K. *Social class in America.* Chicago: Science Research, 1949.

Weingarten, H., and Kulka, R. *Parental divorce in childhood and adult adjustment: A two-generational view.* Presented at the annual meeting of the American Psychological Association, New York City, September, 1979.

Weiss, E., and English, O. *Psychosomatic medicine.* Philadelphia: Saunders, 1957.

Weiss, R. *Going it alone: The family life and social situation of the single parent.* New York: Basic Books, 1979.

———. *Marital separation.* New York: Basic Books, 1975.

———. *Loneliness: The experience of emotional and social isolation.* Cambridge, Mass.: Massachusetts Institute of Technology Press, 1973.

Weisskopf, W. Existence and values. In A. Maslow, ed., *New knowledge in human values.* Chicago: Regnery, 1959.

Weitzman, L. To love, honor and obey? Traditional legal marriage and alternative family form. In A. Skolnick and J. Skolnick, eds.,

Family in transition. 2nd ed. Boston: Little, Brown, 1977.

Wheelis, A. *How people change.* New York: Harper & Row, 1973.

White, B. *The first three years of life.* Englewood Cliffs, N.J.: Prentice-Hall, 1975.

White, R.   Strategies of adaptation: An attempt at systematic description.   In B. Coelho; A. Hamburg; and J. Adams, eds., *Coping and adaptation.* New York: Basic Books, 1974.

———. *The enterprise of living: Growth and organization in personality.* New York: Holt, Rinehart and Winston, 1972.

White, R., and Watt, N. *The abnormal personality.* 5th ed. New York: Wiley, 1981.

Whiting, B., and Pope, C.   A cross-cultural analysis of sex differences in the behavior of children age three through eleven. *Journal of Social Psychology,* 1973, *9,* 171–188.

Whiting, B., and Whiting, J. *Children of six cultures: A psycho-cultural analysis.* Cambridge, Mass.: Harvard University Press, 1975.

Witkin, H., et al. *Personality through perception.* New York: Harper, 1954.

Whitman, W.   Song of Myself (1855).   In *Leaves of Grass.* New York: W. E. Chapin and Company, Printers, 1867.

Wilde, O. *Lady Windemere's fan,* Act III. London: S. French, Ltd., 1893.

Williams, R., Logue, E., Lewis, J., Barton, P., Stead, N., Wallace, A., and Pizzo, S.   Physical conditioning augments the fibrinolytic response to venous occlusion in healthy adults. *New England Journal of Medicine,* 1980, *302,* 987–992.

Wilson, E. *On human nature.* Cambridge, Mass.: Harvard University Press, 1978.

Wolfman, B., and Bean, J. *Superwoman, Ms. or myth: A study of role overload.* Paper presented at the annual meeting of the American Educational Research Association. Boston, Mass., September, 1980.

Wolman, B. *Mental health and mental disorders.* In B. Wolman, ed., *Handbook of clinical psychology.* New York: McGraw-Hill, 1965.

Yalom, I. *Existential psychotherapy.* New York: Basic Books, 1980.

Ziegler, E. Letter to the editor. *New York Times Magazine,* July 18, 1975.

Zuckerman, M. *Sensation seeking: Beyond the optimal level of arousal.* Hillsdale, N.J.: Erlbaum, 1979.

Zuckerman, M., Eysenck, S., and Eysenck, H. Sensation seeking in England and America. *Journal of Consulting & Clinical Psychology,* 1978, *46,* 139–149.

Acknowledgments (*continued from page iv*)

page 58, Peter Vandermark; page 60, Pablo Picasso, *Girl before a Mirror*, 1932, March 14, oil on canvas, 64″ x 51¼″, collection, The Museum of Modern Art, New York, gift of Mrs. Simon Guggenheim. Chapter 3: Page 68, Joan Liftin/Archive; page 75, drawing by Charles Addams/© *The New Yorker Magazine, Inc.*; page 79, Peter Vandermark; page 87, Peter Vandermark, courtesy of Department of Psychological Medicine, Children's Hospital, Boston; page 87, Peter Vandermark, courtesy of Blackwell Medical Associates, Inc. Chapter 4: Page 96, Owen Franken/Stock; page 97, © Shelley Rotner/Omni-Photo; page 101, Ulrike Welsch; page 114, Peter Vandermark; page 117, Arthur Grace/Stock. Part II, page 121, Cary Wolinsky/Stock Boston. Chapter 5: Page 125, Robert Eckert/EKM-Nepenthe; page 131, National Archives #210-GC-160 Dorothea Lange, WRA; page 138, © Joe Teodorescu; page 142, Bobbi Carrey/The Picture Cube; page 145, *Valley News Dispatch*, Tarentum, Pa. Chapter 6: Page 159, Richard Wood/Picture Cube; page 160, State Historical Society of Wisconsin; page 169, Sepp Seitz/Woodfin Camp; page 180, Martha Stewart/Picture Cube; page 187, George Bellerose/Stock. Chapter 7: Page 197, Philadelphia Museum of Art, The Louise and Walter Arensberg Collection; page 207, Ulrike Welsch; page 213, Ulrike Welsch © The Boston Globe; page 221, Jerry Howard/Positive Images; page 237, Department of Natural Resources, Atlanta, Georgia. Chapter 8: Page 245, George Bellerose/Stock; page 250, Library of Congress; page 256, Ulrike Welsch © The Boston Globe; page 259, Henri Matisse, *Piano Lesson* (1916), oil on canvas, 8′½″ x 6′11¾″, collection, The Museum of Modern Art, New York, Mrs. Simon Guggenheim Fund; page 268, Ulrike Welsch © The Boston Globe. Part III, page 273, Janice Fullman/The Picture Cube. Chapter 9: Page 276, Johathan Goell/Picture Cube; page 287, Read Brugger/Picture Cube; page 289, Wide World; page 292, Margaret Thompson/Picture Cube; page 300, Kirk Williamson. Chapter 10: Page 307, Timothy Eagan/Woodfin Camp; page 309, Douglas Kirkland/Contact; page 315, Arthur Tress/Woodfin Camp; page 316, New York Historical Society; page 319, Christopher Brown/Picture Group. Chapter 11: Page 328, Jack Prelutsky/Stock; page 333, Dorothea Lange Collection, The Oakland Museum; page 339, Kirk Williamson; page 342, Edvard Münch, *The Shriek* (1895, signed 1896), lithograph, printed in black, comp.: 13¹⁵/₁₆″ x 10″, collection, The Museum of Modern Art, New York, Mathew T. Mellon Fund.

Chapter 12: Page 356, Bob Thayer/Picture Group; page 364, Rufino Ramayo, *Animals*, oil on canvas, 30⅛″ x 40″, collection, The Museum of Modern Art, New York, Inter-American Fund; page 371, The Metropolitan Museum of Art, Arthur H. Hearn Fund, 1932; page 378, Joseph Kovacs/Stock, Boston; page 392, drawing by Mort Gerberg © *The New Yorker Magazine, Inc.* Part IV, page 399, Nick Smoran, Staff Photographer, Dickinson College Information Service, Dickinson College, Carlisle, Pa. 17017/Stock Boston. Chapter 13: Page 402, Cynthia & William Koechling; page 407, Culver; page 414, Allen Ruid; page 416, J. Berndt/Stock; page 419, Mark Jury. Chapter 14: Page 434, Burk Uzzle/Magnum; page 435, Timothy Eagan/Woodfin Camp; page 438, Wide World; page 441, John Fogle; page 443, EPA.

Art and text credits
Chapter 1: Figure 1.1, Reprinted from *The I.Q. Argument: Race, Intelligence, and Education* by H. J. Eysenck by permission of The Open Court Publishing Company, La Salle, Illinois. Copyright © 1971 by Hans J. Eysenck. *Chapter 2:* Figure 2.1, Adapted from *Stress of Life* by Hans Selye. Copyright © 1956 by Hans Selye. Used with permission of McGraw-Hill Book Company. Figure 2.2, From Samuel A. Stouffer et al., *The American Soldier: Combat and Its Aftermath*, Vol. II. Copyright 1949, © renewed by Princeton University Press. Chart XIII, p. 381, adapted by permission of Princeton University Press. Figure 2.3, From M. Zuckerman, S. Eysenck, and H. Eysenck, "Sensation seeking in England and America: Cross-cultural, age, and sex comparisons," *Journal of Consulting and Clinical Psychology* 46 (1978), 139–49. Copyright 1978 by the American Psychological Association. Adapted by permission of the publisher and authors. Figure 2.4, From Robert H. Shipley, James H. Butt, Bruce Horowitz, and John E. Farbry, "Preparation for a stressful medical procedure: Effect of amount of stimulus preexposure and coping style," *Journal of Consulting and Clinical Psychology* 46 (1978), 499–507. Copyright 1978 by the American Psychological Association. Adapted by permission of the publisher and authors. *Chapter 3:* Page 85, "Eliciting the relaxation response" from *The Relaxation Response* by Herbert Benson, M.D., with Miriam Z. Klipper. Copyright © 1975 by William Morrow & Company, Inc. By permission of the publisher. *Chapter 5:* Figure 5.1, Adapted by permission of Alfred A. Knopf, Inc., from *Seasons of a Man's Life*, by Daniel J. Levinson et al. Copyright © 1978 by Daniel J. Levinson. Figure 5.2, From Ann M. Clarke and A. D. B. Clark, *Early Experience: Myth and Evidence* (New York: The Free Press, 1979). © Ann M. Clarke and A. D. B.

Clarke. Reprinted by permission of Macmillan Publishing Co., Inc.

Chapter 6: Figure 6.1, From *The Chronicle of Higher Education*, 28 January 1980, p. 3. Reprinted by permission. Figure 6.2, From *The Chronicle of Higher Education*, 15 December 1975, p. 4. Reprinted by permission. Page 177, From "On the fast track to the good life," *Fortune*, 7 April 1980. © 1980 Time Inc. Reprinted by permission. Photo © Jim McHugh. Page 182, Excerpt from *Burn Out: The High Cost of High Achievement* by Dr. Herbert J. Freudenberger with Geraldine Richelson. Copyright © 1980 by Herbert J. Freudenberger, Ph.D. and Geraldine Richelson. Reprinted by permission of Doubleday & Company, Inc. Page 183, From Ellen Goodman, *Close to Home.* Copyright © 1979 by The Washington Post Company. Reprinted by permission of Simon & Schuster, a Division of Gulf & Western Corporation. Page 185, From Douglas Powell and P. Driscoll, "How middle-class unemployed men feel and act: Four progressive stages." Published by permission of Transaction, Inc., from *Society*, Vol. 10, No. 2, Copyright © 1973 by Transaction, Inc.

Chapter 7: Page 1975, Excerpted from the book *On Becoming a Family: The Growth of Attachment* by T. Berry Brazelton, M.D. Copyright © 1981 by T. Berry Brazelton. Reprinted by permission of Delacorte Press/Seymour Lawrence. A Merloyd Lawrence Book. Figure 7.1, Drawings from William H. Masters and Virginia E. Johnson, *Human Sexual Response* (Boston: Little, Brown, 1966). Copyright © 1966 by William H. Masters and Virginia E. Johnson. Text from William H. Masters, Virginia E. Johnson, and Robert C. Kolodny, *Human Sexuality* (Boston: Little, Brown, 1982). Copyright © 1982 by William H. Masters, Virginia E. Johnson, and Robert C. Kolodny. Reprinted by permission.

Page 219, From Gabrielle Brown, *The New Celibacy: Why More Men and Women Are Abstaining from Sex — and Enjoying It.* Copyright © 1980 by Gabrielle Brown. Reprinted by permission of McGraw-Hill Book Company. Figure 7.2, Adapted with permission from T. Huston, C. Surra, N. Fitzgerald, and R. Cate, "From courtship to marriage," in S. Duck and R. Gilmore, eds., *Personal Relationships, 2: Developing Personal Relationships*, p. 77. Copyright: 1981 Academic Press Inc. (London) Ltd. Page 224, Excerpted from Judith Viorst, "Sometimes I hate my husband," *Redbook*, November 1976, pp. 73–74. Copyright © 1976 by Judith Viorst. Reprinted by permission.

Chapter 8: Figure 8.1, Reprinted from *U.S. News & World Report*, 30 September 1980, p. 52. Copyright 1980, U.S. News & World Report, Inc. Page 264, From *Clinical Behavior Therapy* by Marvin R. Goldfried and Gerald C. Davison. Copyright © 1976 by Holt, Rinehart and Winston. Adapted by permission of Holt, Rinehart and Winston, CBS College Publishing. Page 266, From Ellen Goodman, "At large," *The Boston Globe*, 28 May 1976. © 1976 The Boston Globe Newspaper Company/Washington Post Writers Group, reprinted with permission.

Chapter 13: Figure 13.1, From *Work in America — The Decade Ahead*, edited by Clark Kerr and Jerome M. Rosow. Copyright © 1979 by Van Nostrand Reinhold Company. Reprinted by permission of the Publisher. Page 410, From D. Hunter, "Ducks vs. Hard Rocks," in "My turn," *Newsweek* 18 August 1980. Copyright 1980, by Newsweek, Inc. All rights reserved. Reprinted by permission. Figure 13.2, Reprinted with permission from "Self-management in depression," by L. Rehm in P. Karolny and F. Kanfer, *Self-Management and Behavior Change*, copyright 1982, Pergamon Press.

Name Index

Subject Index